W9-CLP-482

THE INTERNSHIP, PRACTICUM, AND FIELD PLACEMENT HANDBOOK

A GUIDE FOR THE HELPING PROFESSIONS

Fifth Edition

BRIAN N. BAIRD

PEARSON

Prentice
Hall

Upper Saddle River, New Jersey 07458

Library of Congress Cataloging-in-Publication Data

Baird, Brian N.,
  The internship, practicum, and field placement handbook: a guide for the helping
professions / Brian N. Baird.—5th ed.
    p. cm.
  ISBN–13: 978-0-13-223880-9
  ISBN–10: 0-13-223880-2
    1. Counseling—Study and teaching.   2. Social work education.   3. Counselors—Training of.
4. Human services personnel—Training of.   5. Internship programs.   I. Title.

BF637.C6B26   2007
158'.307155—dc22   2007000559

Editorial Director: Leah Jewell
Executive Editor: Jeff Marshall
Project Manager: LeeAnn Doherty
Editorial Assistant: Jennifer Puma
Senior Marketing Manager: Jeanette Moyer
Marketing Assistant: Laura Kennedy
Assistant Managing Editor: Maureen Richardson
Production Liaison: Joanne Hakim
Manufacturing Buyer: Sherry Lewis
Cover Art Director: Jayne Conte
Full-Service Project Management: Bruce Hobart/Pine Tree Composition, Inc.
Composition: Laserwords Private Limited
Printer/Binder: Bind Rite Graphics
Cover Printer: The Lehigh Press, Inc.

**Copyright © 2008, 2005, 2002, 1999, 1996 by Pearson Education, Inc., Upper Saddle
River, New Jersey 07458.** Pearson Prentice Hall. All rights reserved. Printed in the United
States of America. This publication is protected by Copyright and permission should be
obtained from the publisher prior to any prohibited reproduction, storage in a retrieval
system, or transmission in any form or by any means, electronic, mechanical, photocopying,
recording, or likewise. For information regarding permission(s), write to: Rights and
Permissions Department.

Pearson Prentice Hall™ is a trademark of Pearson Education, Inc.
Pearson® is a registered trademark of Pearson plc
Prentice Hall® is a registered trademark of Pearson Education, Inc.

Pearson Education LTD., London
Pearson Education Singapore, Pte. Ltd
Pearson Education, Canada, Ltd
Pearson Education—Japan
Pearson Education Australia PTY, Limited
Pearson Education North Asia Ltd
Pearson Educación de Mexico, S.A. de C.V.
Pearson Education Malaysia, Pte. Ltd
Pearson Education, Upper Saddle River, New Jersey

10 9 8 7 6 5 4 3 2 1
ISBN-13: 978-0-13-223880-9
ISBN-10: 0-13-223880-2

To my parents

William N. Baird (1927–2001)

Edith S. Baird (1930–1987)

Contents

Preface

Professionals and students in the helping professions consider internships, practicums, and field placements among the most influential experiences of their careers. At the same time, however, students also report that their normal coursework typically provides only indirect, and in many cases insufficient, preparation for their first "real world" exposure. This book is designed to bridge the gap between academic coursework and the knowledge, skills, and emotional challenges that are found beyond the classroom.

In writing this book, I sought to draw upon the best and most current information available from psychology, social work, counseling, psychiatry, and other helping professions. Toward that end, every chapter of this fifth edition has been updated to reflect a thorough and comprehensive review of the latest research and clinical literature across all of the major helping professions. This edition also addresses the most recent ethical codes of the leading professions along with the latest legal and regulatory developments at federal and state levels. I have also continued to consult with numerous faculty and supervisors in each discipline and in various types of academic institutions and internship settings. Equally important, I have sought and received feedback from interns themselves about how to make the text the most meaningful and helpful to the most important people of all, those who are actually using the text.

Based on this research and having hundreds of students and trainees in beginning and advanced placements, my goal with every edition has been to write a book that will be valuable at many levels. Students in their first or second field experience will likely get the greatest benefit from this text, but even advanced graduate students and their instructors consistently tell me they find the book covers key areas and material that might otherwise not be addressed in their training.

OVERVIEW OF THE CONTENTS

A glance at the table of contents reveals that the book is organized along both chronological and thematic lines. The chapters have been organized sequentially to anticipate the stages interns pass through and the understandings or skills that will be required in those stages. Initial chapters deal with such things as selecting placements and supervisors, meeting staff and clients, and key ethical and legal issues. Middle chapters deal with supervision, working with individuals of diverse cultural and ethnic backgrounds, clinical writing, and self-care. Discussions of termination, finishing the internship, and lessons learned conclude the book. Finally, appendices provide examples of forms useful for establishing learning plans, supervision agreements, ethical guidelines, evaluations, and other procedures.

Because internship training and clinical work involve a constant process of self-exploration and change, the textual material of each chapter is accompanied by self-exploration and experiential learning exercises. I encourage you to use these exercises and be open to the experiences. The more one works in this field the more acutely one realizes the importance of self-examination and understanding.

Since the initial publication of this book, the response from students, instructors, and supervisors has been tremendously gratifying. Students are finding many of their questions answered here, and the practical suggestions help them deal more effectively with both the challenges and the opportunities of internships. Instructors have found that students who have read the chapters are better informed and have a greater awareness of issues and information they need to know. Supervisors have reported to me that the interns who are using this book are much better prepared and more knowledgeable than others. Indeed, a number of on-site supervisors have told me they will not supervise any interns unless the intern has read this book.

This fifth edition builds on the base established already and incorporates the most recent research and clinical literature in the field. Of particular importance in this new edition is discussion of personal and clinical issues stemming from the military conflicts in Iraq and Afghanistan and from the terrorist attacks of September 11. Given the numbers of people impacted either directly or indirectly by those events, interns need an awareness of relevant clinical issues and need also to deal effectively with the potential for vicarious traumatization. Also important to this edition is the expanded discussion of recent developments in the Health Insurance Portability and Accountability Act (HIPAA), particularly the security provisions. Related to this is the continued and extended discussion of relevant ethical and clinical issues pertaining to computerized record keeping, electronic communications, and even remote supervision and delivery of clinical services. Other topics that have been expanded or added include the influence of managed care on practice and ethics, the movement toward "evidence based practice," multimodal and research-based approaches to self-care, evolving issues in the ethics of informed consent, and new forms for use in tracking clinical and supervisory experience.

Those who are familiar with previous editions of this book will recognize that there have been some organizational changes as chapters pertaining to clinical writing and record keeping have been merged, as have chapters dealing with stresses of clinical work and self care. In addition, material on internship classes has now been integrated into Chapter 2, and, as relevant, in later chapters on supervision and ethics. As a result, there is now no separate chapter on internship classes as there had been in prior versions of the text. Finally, as in previous editions, I have also incorporated many of the valuable suggestions offered by students, faculty, and supervisors.

I first wrote this book when I was teaching and chair of the Department of Psychology at Pacific Lutheran University, in Tacoma Washington. Since then, I have been honored to be elected to serve in the United States Congress as the Representative from Washington State's Third District. I am currently beginning my fifth term in Congress. While my duties in Congress have necessitated, at least for now, that I leave the classroom and clinical supervision, I remain as committed as ever to the mission of human service and to the importance and value of training students in field settings. Perhaps not surprisingly, I am also more convinced than ever that those who work and teach in the helping professions have a responsibility to also be involved as citizens in the political process. Our professions are uniquely qualified and positioned to offer critical insights into some of the most vexing issues facing our nation today. Juvenile violence, drug abuse, early childhood education, healthcare funding, environmental protection, and even conflict resolution in international affairs have all been the topic of both study and direct intervention by human service professionals. Thus, it is my hope that while students, faculty, and supervisors use this book to help enhance the quality of their internship experiences, they will also use their own talents in some way in the public arena to expand their contributions to the public good.

ACKNOWLEDGMENTS

This book reflects the influence and contributions of many people, and it would not be possible to list everyone to whom I owe a debt of thanks. My many colleagues, friends, and students in recent years, as well as my instructors, supervisors, and mentors during undergraduate, graduate, and post-graduate training have all shaped this book and its author. I am grateful for all the positive, and even some of what at the time seemed to be negative, experiences they have given me.

Among the individuals who I want to thank directly, I begin with Andy Carey, who was instrumental in helping formulate the initial plan for this book and provided insightful comments and information throughout its development. Andy's understanding of how students learn and the challenges they face as beginning counselors has been extremely valuable. I have great respect for his skills as a counselor and educator and am fortunate to consider him both a friend and colleague.

I am grateful for the support of Pacific Lutheran University, which granted me the sabbatical leave during which much of the writing of the book was completed. The input and support of my colleagues in the PLU psychology department, especially that of Dana Anderson, Mike Brown, Jerry LeJeune, and Christine Moon, has been and is much appreciated. My secretaries, Karen Fleischman and Sharon Raddatz, and several student workers also provided great support typing, transcribing my garbled dictation, and helping with countless other details along the way.

In addition to the individuals acknowledged in prior editions, this fifth edition benefited significantly from the insightful reviews and many helpful suggestions provided by Amy Barnett, Southwestern OK State University; Judith Burnett, Stetson University; Amy Ginsberg, Long Island University; Pat Moretti, Santa Clara University; and Bath Potter, Anne Arundel Community College. I wish to thank the editorial staff of Prentice Hall: Jeff Marshall, Executive Editor; Leah Jewell, Editorial Director; and Bruce Hobart, Production Editor. I want to thank each of them for their time, professionalism, and abilities to be direct with criticism and constructive in their suggestions.

Thanks also to some of the many professors and mentors who helped me get into the field and learn some things along the way: Thomas Schenkenberg, Raymond Kesner, Don Strassberg, Dick Hemrick, Randy Linnel, B. J. Fitzgerald, Wilson Walthall, Richard Pasewark, Judith Olson, Max Rardin, Karen Nicholas, Helen Crawford, Leo Sprinkle, Steve Bieber, Geoff Bartol, Lance Harris, Marvin Brown, Mark Seeley, Jarret Kaplan, Vic Ganzer, Katherine Mateer, and Tedd Judd; to peers, who shared the challenges and fun: Mike Hawkins, Rita Valentine, Rick Jensen, Walthall's Warriors, Doreen Daly, Dick Shepherd, Mike Whitley, Warner Karshner, Deborah Frank, and Kirk Strosahl; for friendship and support during dissertation work: Dave Droge and Ray Preiss. Finally, I want to thank Bruce Bennett for his many constructive comments and suggestions and for writing the Foreword to the book.

And most important of all, I want to thank my wife, Rachel Nugent, for her support, advice, friendship, and love through this project and so much more. I also thank our two young sons, William and Walter, for periodically running into the room and lighting up my spirit with their smiles and laughter.

Brian N. Baird

CHAPTER 1

PREPARATION

I've learned more in this experience than I have in any of my classes. Every student should have the opportunity to do a practicum.

Every day there was something new that I realized I didn't know. If for no other reason than that, I'm glad I did an internship.

Comments from student evaluations of their
practicum and internship experiences

THEORY INTO PRACTICE

A friend of mine who was working overseas in the Peace Corps decided it would be fun to teach the children of his village how to play baseball. The children were enthusiastic and eager to learn, so he rounded up some equipment, drew pictures of the playing field, explained the rules of the game, and had everyone practice throwing, catching, and hitting the ball. He even gave them a test that included questions about the number of balls and strikes allowed, how many outs per inning, the distance between bases, and famous players of the past. With the basics mastered, the class improvised a field in a nearby pasture, divided up into two teams, and prepared to play ball.

As the villagers looked on, the excited children took their places on the field. The teacher asked the children if they were ready, and all assured him that they understood what to do. The leadoff batter, a wiry young boy of 13, looked nervous but determined. My friend surveyed the field and aligned his players. Then, taking an exaggerated windup, he delivered the first baseball pitch the village had ever witnessed.

To everyone's astonishment, the batter smacked the ball into deep left field. The batter was so shocked by this that he just stood watching as the teacher shouted for him to "Run, Run, Run!" Turning to see how his team fared as fielders, my friend found that all of his players had left their positions and were running as fast as they could around the bases, tagging each one, screaming, laughing, and heading for home plate. The ball, meanwhile, rolled to a stop far out in the field with no one making any effort to chase it.

When the commotion subsided, my friend was the only player left on the field. All of his team, even the batter, had raced from the field to home, thrilled with how many runs they believed they had just scored. "Somewhere," my friend declared to himself, "we've got a gap between theory and practice." With that, he ran for first base and raced around the diamond just as his players had. When he crossed home plate, he made baseball history by scoring the tenth run from a single hit. His students loved it, and the village still talks about the game today.

Students beginning their first practicum or field placement can identify with my friend's players. Enthusiasm, nervousness, determination, and uncertainty will be familiar feelings (Gelman, 2004). Regardless of all the coursework and study one may have, there is no substitute for real experience. Only by getting out there and trying things can we discover what we do or do not know.

That is why field placements are so valuable. They give you the chance to experience firsthand what you have been studying in your readings and classes. You will quickly discover that reading in a textbook about schizophrenia, alcoholism, child abuse, or other issues is not the same as meeting and interacting with real people who experience the situations or conditions you have studied. So too, reading about, or role playing, therapy and counseling techniques in a classroom differ greatly from actually participating in therapy sessions.

You will also discover that many things you need to know in the "real world," such as ethical and legal issues, how to write case notes, how to deal with supervision, and a host of other topics, probably have not been addressed sufficiently in your academic classes. Even when subjects have been studied in class, as my friend learned from his base-running fielders, instructors too often assume that students will be able to transfer what they learn in the classroom directly to the field. Students recognize this error the moment they enter their internship and say to themselves, "Now what do I do?" My goal in writing this book is to help you answer that question.

TERMINOLOGY

FIELD PLACEMENTS, PRACTICUMS, OR INTERNSHIPS?

Because this text deals with issues that are common across multiple disciplines and for students at various levels of study and training, a brief word is in order about terminology. It is helpful to understand that different disciplines use different terminologies to describe field learning experiences, and the terms that are used depend on the level of the student's training. For example, social work programs often refer to learning opportunities beyond the classroom as "field placements" or "field experiences" (Gelman, 2004; CSWE, 2001). Psychology and counseling use "practicum" to describe field experiences early in one's career, and "internship" for more advanced field training (APA, 2005; CACREP, 2001; Lewis, Hatcher, & Pate, 2005). While recognizing and respecting the terminology differences across disciplines and levels of training, for simplicity in this book we will use the word *internship*, primarily because it happens to also carry the convenient pronoun *intern*, which describes the individuals receiving training. Thus, throughout the text, except where direct quotations are cited, all field experiences, regardless of discipline or level of training, will be called internships, and all those receiving training will be referred to as interns.

SUPERVISORS AND INSTRUCTORS

With the exception of the final internship training for advanced graduate students, in most internship experiences students will be under the guidance of persons in two different roles. To clarify the terminology regarding these individuals, I will use the word *instructors* in reference to faculty from the student's educational institution who monitor the student's progress and interface with those employed by the field placement site. Those who directly monitor and direct the student's work at the placement site will be referred to as *supervisors*.

In all fieldwork, students should be aware that field placements are part of their overall academic training (Wayne, 2004) and should work closely with both their academic instructor and their field supervisor. Although the amount of direct contact students have with instructors or supervisors will vary from program to program and across placements, throughout this book I will emphasize repeatedly that both instructors and supervisors should be kept closely informed of the intern's activities and should be notified of any questions, concerns, or problems that develop.

MEETING WITH YOUR INSTRUCTOR

Your first task as an intern is to meet with the academic instructor who will work with you during your internship. Some academic programs offer structured classes to go along with internships. Other programs leave internship support or supervision for students and instructors to arrange individually. In either case, initial contact with an instructor is vital for a number of reasons.

The most important reason to work with your instructor from the outset is to ensure that you receive the best possible educational experience from your internship. Instructors can help you select placements or supervisors that are best suited to your needs, and they may assist in making contact with placement

sites or individual supervisors. If your department has established procedures governing internships, meeting with your instructor from the beginning will ensure that you follow those procedures. Necessary paperwork may be required before you begin an internship, and there may be certain requirements for you to receive credit or a grade for your internship.

An additional concern that many interns do not take into account is the liability risks that instructors and supervisors face when their students work in the field (NASW Insurance Trust, 2004; Pollack & Marsh, 2004; Zakutansky & Sirles, 1993). Given this shared liability, the faculty in your department must be involved in all aspects of your internship, from the very beginning until the conclusion.

Students should also be aware that it can take a great deal of effort on the part of instructors and supervisors to establish a relationship with various internship sites (Cornish, Smith-Acuña, & Nadkarni, 2005). So too, the decision to accept an intern or establish an intern program within an agency is not one that is taken lightly by the agency or the supervisors and staff. For this reason, many programs have a fixed set of placement sites and have long-established relationships with supervisors for their students. Such arrangements ensure that the academic program will have placements for students and, simultaneously, that the treatment agencies can rely on interns to help carry the work load. Students who might wish for greater autonomy or flexibility in placement settings sometimes find this frustrating, but it should be remembered that having well-established placement sites with experienced supervisors is certainly preferable to situations in which adequate placement sites or supervisors cannot be arranged at all.

FINDING AND SELECTING A PLACEMENT

Considering the importance of field experiences, it is surprising how little has been written about how placements are selected and how interns should be matched to specific placement sites. Holtzman and Raskin (1989) studied the process of field placement selection across different social work programs and concluded that the procedures used vary widely. At one end of the spectrum are academic programs that leave almost everything up to the student. In such programs, students are tasked with locating potential internship sites, contacting staff, arranging for permission to participate, finding a supervisor, and coordinating with an academic instructor. By comparison, other schools exercise control over every element of the internship experience. These schools have identified certain internship sites and supervisors with whom they work every year. Students seeking internships are required to work with one of these placement sites, and all students are expected to perform specific learning activities. Sometimes students are allowed to select among the various prearranged internships, but in other programs the choice is made for the student based on the department's assessment of the student's abilities and learning needs.

Within clinical psychology graduate programs, a nationwide matching system, comparable to that employed by medical schools, is now utilized for the final year-long predoctoral internship selection. Under this system, students rank, in order of preference, the sites to which they have applied. Simultaneously, the internship sites rank the applicants seeking acceptance. This system also allows students to apply to sites or areas as couples. Rankings by the interns and the internship sites are then submitted to National Matching Services (NMS) Inc., which generates a computerized list assigning interns to programs. For further details about this process and discussion of how this system has functioned, see Keilin (2000). Additional information is available from the Association of Psychology Postdoctoral and Internship Centers (APPIC) Web site (http://www.appic.org) and the NMS Web site (http://www.natmatch.com/psychint). For suggestions and tips about selecting and applying to internship sites, see Williams-Nickelson & Prinstein (2004).

Just as the process of field placement selection varies across levels and types of programs, academic institutions and field placements also use various models to conduct and coordinate field learning experiences (Bogo & Globerman, 1995). In some programs, the educational institution continues to have primary control over the student's education in the field. In others, educational responsibility is largely left to the field setting and supervisor.

Because there is such variability in approaches to selecting or assigning internships, some of the material that follows regarding internship selection may not be equally relevant to all readers. If your academic program makes all the internship arrangements for students, the sections on finding internship sites and supervisors may be of less interest to you than they will be for those who are given relatively little structure in their internship studies. If you find that some of this initial material is not pertinent to your situation, you may wish to skim it and move on to the discussion of internship agreements later in the chapter. On the other hand, if your program provides little structure or support for its interns, the material that follows should be helpful.

PEERS AND CAMPUS RESOURCES FOR LOCATING INTERNSHIPS

Your academic instructors will generally be your primary source for internship recommendations, but it also can be helpful to collaborate with other students who are going through the internship selection process or who recently have completed it. Students who have completed internships often can recommend potential internship sites and offer valuable insights into the selection process. Albin, Adams, Walker, and Elwood (2000) describe their personal experiences with internship applications and suggest specific recommendations, including the development of a shared community of peer applicants to help foster respect, community, and authenticity in the application process. Working together with fellow students also offers opportunities

for mutual review of resumes, practice interviews, and, importantly, emotional support.

Along with identifying placements to pursue, your peers may be able to suggest places to avoid. Such information can be valuable, but keep in mind that another student's experiences will not necessarily match yours. Still, if a student advises that a certain internship amounted to little more than typing data into a computer or watching television on the midnight shift, you can predict that the placement may present limited learning opportunities.

In addition to instructors and students who can serve as resources, many campuses have offices dedicated to coordinating field learning experiences. These often go by such names as "Cooperative Education" or "Community Learning" programs. Agencies with available internship positions typically send position announcements to these offices, which then post them for students. Even though you may not have heard of a program of this sort on your campus, check around to see if one is available. The program at my university was outstanding, but I was continually surprised at how many students did not take advantage of its services or even know that it existed.

While on the subject of campus resources, one other resource to check is your campus career services or job placement center. You may be less likely to find internship openings there, but you should become familiar with the services available through these offices. Internships provide an excellent opportunity to begin developing your job application file and honing the interview skills that you will need when you eventually apply for employment (Pitts, 1992). Career service offices can help you develop those skills. They can also help you write a curriculum vitae or resume, and many offices will help you establish a complete job application file, including letters of reference and other material commonly requested by employers. These offices also receive regular announcements of position openings, so stop by periodically to see if they have received word of any openings in your area.

COMMUNITY RESOURCES

Interns who look to faculty or campus resources sometimes overlook the many community resources for information. If there is a community mental health center in your area, you can call and ask whether it has lists of local agencies that you might contact. Many communities also have volunteer coordinating programs to help match programs with volunteers. United Way sometimes supports such programs. United Way has also been involved with efforts to establish 211 call centers that connect people in need with resouces and people seeking to volunteer with community opportunities. More information about 211 resources in general and in your local area can be obtained at http://www.211.org/. Another resource that may be available locally is a telephone crisis line. This may sound surprising, but because crisis lines make referrals to programs of all kinds, many of them have books listing different agencies.

Two other sources that all communities have are newspapers and phone books. In the newspaper, classified advertisements sometimes list position openings in agencies that also offer internships. Try looking in the Employment Offerings or Help Wanted section under the headings of "Counselor," "Mental Health," "Therapist," or under your specific discipline's title. These may be listed alphabetically in the general section or in special sections for "Health Care" positions. With the growth of Internet technology, online job banks or online newspaper classified ads are also efficient means of searching for placements. The added benefit of finding positions this way is the possibility of locating a paid position for an internship. The disadvantage is that such positions may require more job experience than beginning interns have. Also, in some paid positions it may be more difficult to find suitable supervision. That should not discourage one from calling to discuss a position. Interns often start a position as a student in an unpaid status but are later hired in a paid capacity as openings become available. If you inquire about a position that requires more experience than you have at present, do not be afraid to suggest working as an unpaid intern to gain the requisite experience.

Because advertisements in newspapers will only identify agencies with current position openings, your phone book is a more reliable source of placements. The yellow pages listings under "Counseling," "Mental Health," and "Social Service Organizations" will have numbers for many agencies. Some phone books include special pages listing numbers for community services and agencies. Depending on your area of interest and the requirements of your program, helpful listings may include "Schools," "Clergy," "Child Care," and "Hospitals," as well as any other directory headings for your specific discipline.

National, state, and local professional associations also can be useful resources. Most organizations have membership directories that you can use to locate individuals working in settings or areas that interest you. Many professions maintain national catalogs listing available field training opportunities. These catalogs tend to be directed toward graduate training, but there are often opportunities for undergraduates as well.

CHOOSING A PLACEMENT

Finding potential placements is the first step. The next step is to select an internship from among the possibilities. I encourage interns to approach this process thoughtfully, because it is important that your first clinical experience be positive. As an intern, you may feel that you cannot afford to be too critical when choosing an internship, because, after all, you are the one seeking the position. Nevertheless, you will be giving substantial amounts of your own time and resources to the internship, so you should consider carefully where you are likely to get the most benefit.

One way to evaluate what features to look for is to consider what other interns have found important in their selection process. The features that will be most important to you will depend on your program and your level of training, but surveys of interns have shown several key variables that influence decisions: the match of interests between the training site and the intern, the reputation of the training site, special training opportunities, the breadth of clinical populations available, location, quality of supervision, and the intern's gut feeling about the site (Stedman, Neff, Donahoe, Kopel, & Hays, 1995). In addition to the variables just mentioned, you should also consider unique personal circumstances. For example, many graduate students are somewhat older, have families, and may be taking their coursework or internship on a part-time basis or in addition to other employment (Fox, 2004; Hopkins, Bloom, & Deal, 2005). For this group of students scheduling flexibility may be especially important. There may also be unique considerations pertaining to the supervisory relationship, the openness of the setting to older students, and the willingness of the placement to work with existing employment roles.

EXERCISE

To help you select an internship that best matches your needs, skills, and interests, take a moment to list key factors that will be important to you. Then rate each possible internship on each of these key factors. For example, you might list such things as type of setting, clients served, treatment approaches, and supervisor qualities. You might also list pragmatic considerations, such as location, compensation, hours, and flexibility. Once you have done this for yourself, I suggest that you share your assessment with a peer and with your instructor to get their feedback about what you have included or what you might want to add.

After you have given some thought to the features that are most important to your own interests, the next step involves matching those interests with the internships available. Several approaches have been suggested to make the process of matching students and placements more efficient and successful. In a useful article describing multiple aspects of the internship selection and application process, Stewart and Stewart (1996) referred to a paired comparison technique that ranks internship features on a grid along with personal selection criteria. Brownstein (1981) described a comparable, but somewhat less complicated, process for organizing data on placement opportunities and student characteristics.

Building on Brownstein's model, I have developed information forms for placement sites and for student interns. These forms are provided in Appendixes A and B. On one form, interns list their interests, experience, available times, and other information relevant to internship selection. The parallel form presents agency information, such as location, types of clients, treatment approaches, supervision, and available days and times. Comparing information from the intern and agency allows instructors, students, and the agency to make informed decisions about the suitability of a given placement for a specific intern. Such information may also reduce the likelihood of placements that do not work out (Holtzman & Raskin, 1989).

To supplement the information provided in Appendices A and B, I have also provided a form, Appendix K, with which interns can evaluate their placements when they have concluded their experience. Some programs make these evaluations available to other students (typically with individual identifying information removed or in edited form) so that students seeking placements can read what their predecessors have reported about their opportunities and experiences at a particular site. You may want to ask if this is possible in your program, and if it is, you might want to peruse the reports of others from various internships before making a selection for yourself.

Another approach to selecting internship sites was described by Brill, Wolkin, and McKeel (1987), who noted that students seeking predoctoral internships in clinical psychology must choose from several hundred possibilities. Brill et al. suggested that prospective interns can narrow this field by using a visualization exercise to imagine ideal short- and long-term training goals and opportunities. The intern and instructor then consider insights gained from that process as they review information and materials collected by previous interns. Brill et al. placed special emphasis on seeking acceptance to programs that have provided positive experiences for other interns from the same university. Applicants were also advised to apply to a limited number of sites rather than dissipating their resources on many different locations. This allows them to focus greater attention on the sites they choose and tends to improve the quality of applications to those locations.

While applying to a limited number of sites and focusing your efforts may be a good strategy for some students, other authors (Mellott, Arden, & Cho, 1997) have suggested that as competition for a limited number of internship sites increases, particularly for graduate internships (Gaw, 1997), graduate interns may consider applying to as many as 15 to 20 sites to increase the probability of being accepted. Multiple applications, however, can substantially increase the costs involved in time, transportation, and application fees (Oehlert, Lopez, & Sumerall, 1997).

SUPERVISION

Although many interns select placements based on clients served, location, treatment approach, or other considerations, perhaps the most important factor to consider involves the professionals who will work with you and provide supervision. Particularly in more advanced internships, the quality of the internship experience is closely related to the quality of the supervision received (Stoltenberg, 2005). This observation has also been made by Munson (1989), who commented, "Increasingly, I have come to appreciate that supervision is the most important educational experience any clinical practitioner undergoes" (p. 2).

Munson went on to list 15 things that supervisees have a "right to expect that a supervisor will be." The list includes such qualities as being a master teacher, having confidence in knowledge but openness to questioning, being able to accept criticism without defensiveness, orienting the student to the internship setting, and knowing, and adhering to, ethical standards. Not every supervisor will possess all of Munson's desired qualities, but his list can help interns and supervisors identify some of the characteristics that lead to positive supervisory experiences.

In a more recent discussion of supervision in social work, Globerman and Bogo (2003) describe the varying motivations that individuals cite as reasons they supervise students and interns. Among the factors they identify are the intrinsic value of teaching others, supporting the growth of the profession, and organizational culture. I raise these issues here because knowing something about the reasons a person serves as a supervisor can tell a lot about how he or she will approach the responsibility and relationship.

Interns who are selecting placements need to ask this basic question about a supervisor: "Is this someone I think I can work with and who would be interested in helping me learn?" In answering this question, consider the supervisor's personality, qualifications, and areas of interest, as well as the likelihood that this person will give you sufficient supervision time and instruction. You also should take into account your level of development in your field. Stoltenberg (2005), Heppner and Roehlke (1984), and Friedman and Kaslow (1986) all described the developmental stages of supervision and suggested that the needs of supervisees change with experience. Other authors (Gandolfo & Brown, 1987; Gray, Ladany, Walker, & Ancis, 2001; Kaiser, 1992; Ladany, Walker, & Melincoff, 2001; Rabinowitz, Heppner, & Roehlke, 1986) emphasize that at all levels of training, supervisees need supervisors who are encouraging and supportive.

Apart from your competence and experience, you should also consider your personality and learning needs. You may be naturally suited to a nurturing environment and a supervisor who provides a great deal of direction. Or you may be a person who benefits more with less direction and greater autonomy. The most important point is to find a supervisor who will work with you as an individual in the way that best suits your personality and style of learning.

In selecting a supervisor, also consider compatibility of clinical philosophy or approach. Many interns broaden their views and become more confident when working with supervisors from different theoretical orientations than their own, but others have experienced significant conflicts. While placement with a supervisor of different orientation can be stimulating, if either the supervisor or intern is dogmatic and intolerant of differing views, it can leave both feeling frustrated and discouraged. Thus, while you should not limit yourself to working with supervisors who share your therapeutic philosophy, it is important for you to be open to new ideas and to select a supervisor who is willing to consider different approaches.

The best way to get to know potential supervisors is to schedule a meeting or phone interview with them. Remember that in this meeting both of you will be trying to evaluate how well an internship together would work. Supervisors will want to know about your academic training and practical experiences. They will also be interested in your personality. Can they rely on you? Are you diligent in your work? Will you take suggestions or instructions well? And, will it be in some way worth the supervisor's time to supervise you?

For your part, you will be asking some of the same questions the supervisor asks about you (Pitts, 1992). You will be interested in this person's professional experience and in any specific training or experience as a supervisor. You will also want to know if the supervisor will be a good teacher, someone who lets you take some risks and make mistakes in the process of learning but who also is there with guidance and support when you need it. I recommend that students ask specific questions about a potential supervisor's education, training, and experience in supervision. Questions about the supervisor's philosophy and approach to the role can also be helpful.

Finally, ask how much time the supervisor has to spend with you. Knight (1996) found that supervisor availability was the single best predictor of satisfaction among master of social work (MSW) and bachelor of social work (BSW) students in field placements. More will be said about this in regard to internship agreements, but before you reach the stage of formalizing your arrangement, you should be certain the supervisor can devote sufficient time to working with you. It is also wise to read Chapter 4 before finalizing an internship and supervisory arrangement. That chapter addresses theories, models, and practical issues relating to supervision.

LEARNING OPPORTUNITIES

Along with identifying a supervisor with whom you would like to do an internship, you should also consider the kinds of learning opportunities that will be available to you and clarify your role before starting an internship. The lack of sufficiently interesting or challenging learning opportunities is one of the most common causes of complaints and frustration for interns. It is not infrequent for interns to select what appear to be ideal placements only to discover that all they are allowed to do is code data for research, help with reorganizing files, or "baby-sit" students while teachers or counselors are out of the room. If you know from the outset what opportunities you desire, and what the internship can and will make available, you can avoid such disappointments. If you know other students who have been at the same internship site, you may want to ask what their experiences were.

In your first internship, most of the focus will be on learning by observing. This means you should have the opportunity to observe many different elements of the activities at your placement. Ideally, interns should have at least some opportunity to observe everything that goes on, from staff meetings and paperwork to direct treatment and other service delivery. This gives interns the broadest exposure to all elements of the placement. It is important for interns to know both the rewarding and the mundane aspects of the profession, and, if it is your first field experience, you should remember that for your benefit and that of clients you will likely be given only very limited responsibilities to begin with.

As their abilities and training allow, interns will gradually go beyond observational learning and begin to accept responsibility in clinical activities. This must be closely coordinated with the supervisor, but your goal should be to take new challenges in stages, pushing yourself slightly each time but never extending beyond your level of competence. For example, if you have been a participant observer in a group for several months, your supervisor might encourage you to become more involved in facilitating the group. Or, if you have read a number of reports about clients, you might want to try your hand at writing a report. The exact nature and extent of your involvement should evolve as you gain experience in your internship and your supervisor develops more knowledge of, and confidence in, your abilities. Again, if you hope to have a certain kind of experience on your internship, you should check with potential placements and supervisors to determine whether that experience will be available to you.

TREATMENT APPROACHES

Internships provide your best opportunity to experience firsthand what a therapy or technique that appeals to you in theory is like in actual practice. If you have a particular interest in a treatment approach, you may want to seek a placement where you can receive supervision and experience in that approach.

If you already have experience in one intervention approach, consider seeking training in a completely different approach. This does not mean you must become a convert to the other approach. It merely suggests that you should be open to different methods and give them a try to see what there is to learn from another perspective. When they actually experience a different approach in practice, interns who may have once been quite critical come to recognize that each method has something useful to offer.

CLIENTS

The next factor to consider in selecting a placement is the client base served by the program. Just as it is advisable for interns to be exposed to a variety of treatment approaches, experience with diverse client groups is also desirable. In your first internship, the exact makeup of the client population is less important than that you are out in the real world working with people. Still, there is nothing wrong with seeking a placement based on the types of client served. If you want to eventually work with a specific client group, it might be ideal to find a placement with a program for that group.

Even if you cannot find a program involving precisely the client group that most interests you, there are likely to be many other placements in which you can still receive valuable experiences. For most students, a generalized background of experience is probably more beneficial than premature specialization. You can specialize in your final years of graduate training or after you receive your degree, but in the beginning it is a good idea to be flexible and open to varied training experiences and different client groups.

In my own training, I sought opportunities to work with clients of virtually all ages and diagnostic groups. By selecting a series of internship and practicum placements, I was eventually able to work with clients ranging from small children to elderly adults and with diagnostic groups ranging from college students in a counseling center to patients in a unit for mentally ill criminal offenders. In each placement, I learned something new and expanded both my awareness and skills. This diversity of experience also helped me gain a clearer sense of the kinds of therapy and clients I was most interested in and for which my skills were best suited.

PROGRAMS AND SETTINGS

Theoretical approaches and client types are frequently foremost on interns' minds when they select internships, but you should also consider the different kinds of internship settings available. For example, although the ages of the clients may be similar, an internship in a school setting is likely to differ in many ways from an internship in a home for runaway adolescents. Similarly, although many of the clients served, and treatment techniques found, in mental health clinics may be similar to those of inpatient facilities, there will be important characteristics that are specific to each setting. Thus, apart from the clients served and the treatment approaches used, if you have experience in only one kind of setting, a placement in a completely different setting could be very educational.

RESEARCH OPPORTUNITIES

Because so much of the focus of practicums and internships is on the clinical experience, it is easy to overlook the opportunities field training can provide for hands-on research experience. Especially for students in master's- or doctoral-level programs who must complete theses or dissertations, and for pre-graduate-level students seeking to go on in their studies, it is a good idea to explore how supportive of research activities a placement may be and what opportunities it offers to be involved in research. Phillips, Szymanski, Ozegovic, and Briggs-Phillips (2004) reported substantial variability in research support across internships, but they noted that in their findings the overall quality of the institutional research training environment correlated positively with greater scholarly productivity. Among the factors that contribute to research support are modeling of research commitment by the staff and supervisors, active discussion of research as it relates to the clinical work, the opportunity for interns to work closely with a research mentor, and the provision of time and resources dedicated to the research endeavor. As you gather information about a potential internship, you may want to ask specifically about these factors and express directly any research interests you may have. As Phillips et al. point out, insofar as the various helping professions seek to produce practitioners who understand, apply, and conduct research themselves, making research a stronger, more integrated aspect of internships should receive greater attention and commitment. In addition, as the workplace changes, and evidence-based practice and empirically supported treatment (APA Presidential Task Force, 2006; King, 2006; Mccabe, 2004; Norcross, 2005;

Wampold & Bhati, 2004) become more dominant, knowledge of research and experience in conducting research can be an important asset to one's professional career.

CAREER PLANS

Most interns should avoid premature specialization, but this does not mean you should completely ignore your career plans when you choose an internship. This is particularly important if you hope to seek employment or further education in the field soon after you complete your internship. Interns who are about to enter the job market or go on to further studies often desire placement sites that make them more marketable to potential employers or graduate schools. This is a reasonable strategy, because the experience gained in an internship, and the letters of recommendation from internship supervisors, can be very helpful. If you are planning to seek employment, you may want to check the job market to identify the skills and experience that employers are looking for.

This point was made well by Steadman, Hatch, Schoenfeld, and Keilin (2004), who asked rhetorically, "At a time when the economic future of clinical providers is in question, is it not important for all internships to make major training efforts with the patient populations, therapy modalities, and speciality areas most likely to equip the new clinical with marketable skills?" (p. 5). These authors went on to advise interns to avoid early specialization and seek instead placements with the "most comprehensive offerings possible."

If your career or academic plans are not yet clear, you may want to discuss any career or educational questions with your instructor before you choose an internship. You could also review any current publications about careers in your chosen field. These are often published by and are available through your professional organization. By getting a sense of your interests and the feasible options, you can better select an internship that gives you the experience to help make decisions about future career directions.

Before pursuing training experiences, interns may also find it helpful to develop mentoring relationships. Having a mentor available for consultation throughout your training can enhance clinical skills and assist with career decisions (Ragins & Cotton, 1999). There may be particular benefits to mentor relationships for women and minority students (Foxhall, 2001; Waters, 2001).

PRACTICAL ISSUES: LOCATION AND TIMES

The issues addressed thus far have primarily been concerned with the nature and quality of the clinical experience and training you will receive. More mundane, but not to be overlooked, are such practical considerations as where the placement is located and how your available days and times match those of the placement site. Particularly for students who are trying to juggle obligations of parenting, work, and academic classes with an internship, it will be important to match the internship placement expectations with other scheduling needs.

If you can, try to pick readily accessible placement sites. This will allow you to spend more time at the placement site and less time in transit. In some areas, you should also consider safety factors associated with getting to and from a placement. Wherever you find an internship, it is a good idea to ask your supervisor and other staff members about any safety issues associated with the location. Sometimes, areas assumed to be "terribly dangerous" are really not such a problem if you take a few precautions. Do not be embarrassed to express any concerns or to ask your coworkers for their suggestions.

It is important for interns to be on their placement site at regularly scheduled times. Ideally, interns should be at the placement a minimum of two to three hours a day for at least three days per week. Interns who are on site at irregular or infrequent times do not fully integrate into the routine of the placement. Unless interns are present on a regular basis, staff and clients are unlikely to be sufficiently comfortable or confident with them to really involve them in activities. Keep in mind, too, that insofar as the internship serves as preparation for employment, dependable attendance is a key way to demonstrate employment readiness.

As you consider your schedule and make arrangements with an internship placement, be as realistic as possible about the times at which you will be available. Many interns do not heed this advice and overextend themselves because they have a great desire to learn and will try to do whatever their placement sites ask. The motivation to learn is admirable, but if you extend yourself too far you may end up disappointing yourself and the agency.

When you schedule times with your internship, consider the other factors in your life, including family, friends, and other coursework. Try to take into account predictable "crunch" times that you can anticipate in your academic or personal schedule. If you know that midterms and finals will demand additional time for study, or if you will be working on a thesis or dissertation, talk about that with your supervisor and make arrangements well in advance. Similarly, if you are involved in extracurricular activities, take these into consideration as you schedule your internship. If academic and other time demands will severely limit the time available for an internship, or if your schedule is so variable that you cannot set aside consistent times for the internship, consider doing the internship at some other time or perhaps changing other elements of your schedule to better accommodate the internship. It is better to forgo an internship than to try to force one into an overcrowded schedule and have a bad experience.

Although I have emphasized the importance of keeping consistent schedules, the activities of many agencies vary from day to day and at different times of the day. To get a feel for the rhythms of your placement, try to be at the internship at other times in addition to your regularly scheduled times. This can be particularly valuable in institutional placements or other residential settings where clients are present around the clock. In such placements, the activities and atmosphere on evenings or weekends can differ remarkably from the 8-to-5 weekday hours. Interns who can come in during the evening or join staff and clients on weekend outings often will see a much different side of the clients and the institution. Such occasions can also provide excellent opportunities to interact with and get to know clients or staff on a more personal level.

COMPETENCE AND SAFETY

The final consideration here is by no means the least important. When you select an internship, you should carefully consider your level of ability and training in relation to the tasks you will be expected to perform. An internship should stretch your knowledge and skills, but you must not extend your responsibilities to a point that would be dangerous for yourself or your clients. If you are concerned about personal safety at an internship, you may want to read Chapter 8 now and discuss any safety concerns with your instructor and supervisor. So too, if the kinds of clients served, or the technical demands of treatment, assessment, or other services are beyond your current abilities, you should recognize this and discuss any limitations fully with your instructor and supervisor before you begin a placement.

Not only does this principle apply in selecting an internship, it also holds throughout whatever internship you eventually select. If at any time you are asked to do something that exceeds your skill and knowledge and might therefore be hazardous, you should express this to your supervisor or instructor and be sure that you have the necessary support or assistance before proceeding. This issue is discussed in Chapter 3, which deals with ethical issues.

PREPARING YOUR INTERNSHIP APPLICATION

As you consider which internship sites best match your interests, keep in mind that the people at those sites are also looking for specific qualities in applicants. Surveys of internship site directors have identified factors that are used in selection and rejection of applicants (Mellott et al., 1997; Rodolfa et al., 1999). Among the most commonly cited determinants of selection are fit between applicants' goals and site opportunities, letters of recommendation, supervised clinical experience, personal interview, applicants' personal statements, academic coursework, graduate grade point average, professional publications and presentations, and congruence of specialty training area. Lopez, Oehlert, and Moberly (1996) also described common deficits in unsuccessful intern applicants, including lack of clinical experience, lack of experience with special populations, poor writing skills, and poor special skills.

There are several steps you can take to prepare in advance and improve your chances of being accepted wherever you decide to apply. Two key elements are the preparation of letters of application and recommendation and practice for the interview. Given the importance assigned to clinical writing and the frequency with which supervisors express concerns about deficiencies in their interns' writing skills, you may also want to review Chapter 7, which addresses clinical writing and case notes. Another good source of suggestions for writing applications and interview preparation is the workbook produced by the American Psychological Association of Graduate Students (Silverman, 2004; Williams-Nickelson & Prinstein, 2004). Though written for graduate-level psychology students, the suggestions about letters, interviews and other application procedures apply well across disciplines.

LETTERS OF APPLICATION AND RECOMMENDATION

Your application letter and supportive letters of recommendation are two key areas where you can strengthen your application. Mitchel (1996) offered several simple but important suggestions regarding your application letter and ways to help ensure that the letters others write on your behalf are as effective as possible.

In your own letter of application, Mitchel emphasizes, it is important to tell something about yourself that is not simply a reiteration of your vitae and will help you stand out in some way for the reader. This might be a noteworthy personal experience or achievement of some kind. Based on my own experience reviewing applications, I concur with Mitchel's advice and find that such personal elements often serve as important mnemonics that help selection committees recall and distinguish individuals. For example, a member of a committee discussing applicants might say something like "Isn't that the person who played in the band?" or "I liked the one who had volunteered in Guatemala." As you write your own application, think about what might help you stand out in addition to your academic achievements, research, and clinical and other experiences.

In describing yourself, it is also a good idea to be honest about not only what you consider to be your strengths but also about areas you hope to develop further. I find that a mix of accurate self-confidence with sincere humility and a desire to learn are desirable qualities in letters and in interns themselves. Letters that are too self-aggrandizing or self-deprecating tend to raise red flags.

Along with describing you, your letter should also be sure to address your specific reasons for seeking the particular internship you are addressing, and you should mention specific goals you hope to achieve while there. Showing that a particular site matters to you in some specific way demonstrates that you have done your homework about where you are applying, and that you have a personal interest and commitment to that location. This goes a long way to help a site select between students who are just looking for any placement versus those who are seeking the selection committee's placement.

Just as you give attention to writing your own letters, I suggest you also give some time to helping others write letters of recommendation on your behalf. When asking someone to serve as a reference, be sure to give plenty of advance notice and make his or her task as easy and convenient as possible. Always ask permission in person before giving a name as a reference, and when you provide written material, such as recommendation

forms, it is a courtesy to complete as much of the form as you can, leaving only the evaluative sections for the reference source to complete. You should also provide preaddressed, stamped envelopes along with notes indicating how and when the letter should be sent (e.g., some programs request that the outside of the envelope be signed over the seal). Follow-up inquiries a week before the due date are usually welcomed and are considered a courtesy. After someone has written a letter on your behalf, be sure to send a note of thanks and let the person know how things went in your application process.

INTERVIEWS

Most people do not realize it, but the key to an effective interview is what you do before the interview, not simply what happens during the interview. The reason for this is that careful preparation beforehand will substantially increase the likelihood of things going well; if you are well prepared, the actual interview will usually take care of itself.

As you prepare for an interview, begin by studying information about the prospective internship site. You should know about the history of the site, something about the clients served, and something about the staff, especially the person with whom you will have the interview. You should also make an effort to speak with other interns or staff to learn about the day-to-day operations of the site, what is expected of interns, and what opportunities are available. In addition to learning about the site, review your own qualifications so that you can confidently describe your experiences and what you have to offer the internship. It is also extremely helpful to practice responding to questions the interviewer may ask you. This practice should not just be mental; have another person fill the role of the interviewer and ask you questions directly. You might even want to videotape the process so that afterward you can review the practice session and get feedback about both the content and the style of your responses (Lopez & Draper, 1997). As you practice for an interview, be sure you have your portfolio ready and use it to illustrate your experiences and work products.

Here are some questions you are likely to be asked during an interview (Hersh & Poey, 1987; Mellott et al., 1997): Why are you applying to this particular internship site? What are your primary learning and training goals? What supervisory experiences are you seeking? What specific skills or abilities do you bring that make you well suited to the internship? What areas or skills do you feel you need to improve? What are your long-term career goals?

In addition to answering specific questions, you may also need to respond to hypothetical case situations. A good strategy in such situations is to approach the task systematically. Begin by reviewing out loud the information you have just been given. Then, proceed through a step-by-step process of identifying what you would consider and why. In most cases, the goal in responding to such questions should not be to quickly arrive at the "right answer." Rather, it is to demonstrate that you are capable of careful, systematic, and informed reasoning. The key is not so much to demonstrate what you would do, but to demonstrate how and why you reach that decision. Remember that it is perfectly acceptable to indicate an awareness of the need for consultation or assistance if a case is beyond your experience or knowledge.

A final element of interviews that applicants frequently overlook is sending a thank-you note a day or so after the interview. Interviewers will notice and appreciate this simple courtesy, and it is too often neglected.

EXERCISE

Get together with a fellow student and prepare for an internship interview by asking one another the questions identified earlier. Each of you should role-play both the interviewer and the applicant. Try to videotape the interactions so that you can watch them later. If feasible, have a third person watch both of you to give constructive feedback. You may also want to meet with someone from your university's career service center and ask for help in preparing for a job interview. As with any skill, repeated practice will lead to further improvements, so practice the interview several times and with different people who ask slightly different questions each time.

THE RIGHTS OF APPLICANTS AND CHARACTER REQUIREMENTS FOR INTERNS

Before concluding our discussion of the application process, a few words should be offered concerning the rights of job or internship applicants and the importance of character requirements in selecting interns. Juni (1997) points out that the rights of applicants are often neglected in the internship selection process. For example, intrusive questions about family or health matters are generally prohibited by law in application interviews but are sometimes asked of internship applicants. In some instances, applicants have also been asked to waive their right to see letters of recommendation. As important as an internship is, you should not feel that you have to answer overly intrusive questions or abandon your rights to be selected for a job or an internship.

While being mindful of your own rights in the application process, you should also have an appreciation of the responsibilities of the internship site to protect its clients and institution (Buseri, Tyler, & King, 2005). Johnson and Campbell (2004) suggested that training programs often pay too little attention to pre-screening to identify significant character flaws, unethical behaviors, or instability that could adversely impact performance. Part of the reason for this is a lack of empirically proven mechanisms for gathering and evaluating this information in the context of clinical training and screening. At the same time, however, there is broad agreement among training directors that such issues are very important and should be identified (Fuentes, Wilmuth, & Yarrow, 2005).

Johnson and Campbell recommended some possible approaches to this problem, including requiring formal legal background checks of all applicants (Erwin & Toomey, 2005), conducting in-person behaviorally based interviewing of applicants as well as checking their references, and making greater use of psychological tests as part of the application process, Johnson and Campbell also emphasize that evaluation of character and stability do not end with the application process but must be an ongoing element of training, with regular procedures for providing feedback to interns and directly addressing any concerns that may arise. Finally, there needs to be greater coordination about these issues between training programs and state licensing boards, with licensing boards also looking more closely at legal background as well as academic history to identify any concerns about fitness or character (Johnson, Porter, Campbell, & Kupko, 2005).

INTERNSHIP AGREEMENTS

Once you have found a placement, supervisor, and learning opportunities that suit your needs, and after the internship has offered to accept you for training, the next step is to establish an agreement about what the internship will entail. Two types of agreements should be formalized before you begin an internship. First, there should be a written agreement between your academic institution and the internship site. Next, together with your instructor and supervisor, you should formulate an agreement that describes the specific features of your individual internship experience. Establishing such agreements in writing at the outset will help avoid later misunderstandings or confusion about what the internship site and supervisor expect of you and what you expect of them.

INSTITUTIONAL AGREEMENTS

There was a time when internship arrangements were rather informal. Agencies in the field and academic institutions alike recognized the need to train students, so instructors and fieldwork supervisors made collaborative arrangements with relative ease. A simple word-of-mouth agreement on the telephone was often sufficient to make the arrangements for an internship. In other cases, the interested parties drafted a friendly letter to make things official.

As society and health care have become increasingly litigious, the need for more formal and detailed internship agreements has grown. Wayne emphasizes that for certain legal purposes, particularly for performance evaluations or disciplinary actions, field placements are treated by the courts like academic courses, thereby making it essential that programs have "clearly defined learning objectives and evaluation criteria that are known to the student, the field instructor and the faculty liaison at the start of the course" (Wayne, 2004, p. 409). In spite of this admonition, it is interesting to note that Lewis, Hatcher, and Pate (2005) found that many of the practicum settings they studied did not describe having "very clear" agreements detailing the expectations of the academic institutions from which practicum students came.

I encourage internship and practicum placements to correct this situation. I further suggest that interns ask their instructor and supervisor about what sorts of agreements have been reached between their academic program and the field placement. Of course the intern cannot be responsible for drafting the agreement, but asking the questions may help spur action if explicit accords are lacking. If there are extant agreements, it is a good idea for the intern to be aware of them and, if possible, read them.

Because no two internship sites or academic programs are identical, there is no single model for such agreements. There are, however, a number of common ingredients that should be addressed (Gelman, Pollack, and Auerbach, 1996; Thibadeau and Christian, 1985). In a study of the elements included in social work field-training agreements, Gelman and Wardell (1988) analyzed survey responses from 271 social work programs, including both graduate and undergraduate programs. In addition to questionnaire responses, the same survey collected actual training agreements from 92 of the responding schools (Gelman, 1990). Based on this information, Gelman identified four types of training agreements. These ranged from what he described as "friendly," essentially the sort of cordial, nonlegalistic letter arrangements described earlier, to a much more technical document dealing primarily with liability avoidance. Gelman labeled another type the "disclaimer" agreement. Gelman's data suggested that about half of the agreements he analyzed could be classified in the friendly category, while only a handful fit the disclaimer model. The bulk of the remaining agreements were described as "cooperative/joint" agreements, which Gelman finds preferable for most programs.

Cooperative/joint agreements typically begin by recognizing the importance, mutual benefits, and shared responsibilities of field learning opportunities for the academic institutions, students, and field placements. This initial recognition is then followed by a description of the agreed-on expectations for each of the parties involved. The expectations for the field setting include allowing the student to observe or participate in specified activities, providing certain kinds of learning activities, providing supervision by persons with specific qualifications and at specified intervals, and maintaining contact with the academic institution and instructor. For its part, the academic institution affirms that the student is in good standing and has sufficient preparation to participate in the specified internship activities. The academic institution also agrees to provide a liaison instructor to work with the field setting. The agreement may also clarify the role of the instructor and address the evaluation process to be used. The student's responsibilities as described in such agreements include adhering to the professional code of ethics, attending the internship as scheduled, carrying out any agreed-on responsibilities, and informing the supervisor and instructor of any problems or concerns. Guidelines for dress and conduct and, again, a description of evaluation procedures are sometimes included in the description of the student's responsibilities.

To update the results from Gelman and Wardell's 1988 study, Gelman and coworkers (1996) surveyed more than 268 graduate and undergraduate institutions offering social work training. This study revealed that over 95% of programs have written agreements with fieldwork agencies. Consistent with the original study and with the previous discussion, the social work programs responding reported that their agreements address such matters as responsibilities of students and supervisors, ethical issues, performance evaluation, and legal issues.

Two of the most common areas of legal concerns covered in agreements are (1) the possibility that the intern might be involved in activities that injure or otherwise harm a client or other person at the internship site, and (2) the possibility that the intern might be injured or otherwise harmed while at the internship site. Portions of the agreement that deal with these issues specify how responsibilities will be shared in the event of such incidents. This includes clarification of liability insurance.

Many field agencies provide both liability and injury coverage for interns under their existing insurance for volunteers or employees. If this is the case, it is essential for the intern and the school to complete any necessary paperwork officially designating the intern as a member of the class of individuals covered by the policy. The fact and extent of such coverage should also be specified in the field learning agreement.

Apart from, or in addition to, any agency liability protection, Gelman (1990) found that 60% of the schools with cooperative/joint agreements provide liability protection for their students. In addition to this institutional policy, some schools also expect individual students to obtain their own insurance. Other programs leave the matter of insurance for students entirely up to the students. Considering that in the 1996 study by Gelman et al., 2.3% of programs reported that one of their students, and in five of six cases the supervising faculty member as well, had been named in liability cases, it would certainly seem advisable for more institutions to provide insurance for students and supervisors alike. In any case, the field learning agreement should clearly specify who holds what insurance and the extent and limitations of coverage. The same applies to insurance for the field placement supervisor and for the academic internship instructor.

Depending on the academic program and internship, field learning agreements may include additional information or address other issues, but as a minimum they should cover the matters discussed above. The agreement should then be signed by the academic instructor, the field supervisor, and responsible administrators for the university and field agency. In many instances, students sign the documents as well.

Given the concerns about liability and other legal matters, it is advisable for attorneys and risk-management officers from both the academic institution and the field agency to be involved in drafting and reviewing the field learning agreement.

At the same time, however, Gelman (1990) has expressed concern that if the attorneys who draft or review the documents are unfamiliar with the importance and function of field learning, the agreements may become so detailed or restrictive that field learning will no longer be possible. The academic institution and the agency need to recognize the value of field learning and then work collaboratively to ensure that this experience is safe for clients, students, supervisors, instructors, and others. Well-crafted field learning agreements are an important part of the process, but they cannot substitute for responsible professional practice by the participants.

Whether or not your academic program or internship currently operates under a formal agreement, it is in your best interest as an intern to clarify the issues that such agreements address. If a written agreement exists between your school and agency, be sure to obtain a copy, read it, and understand how it affects your role, responsibilities, and risks. The best person to ask about this is your academic instructor. If a written field agreement does not exist, you may want to raise your concerns tactfully and ask your instructor for written clarification of at least the issues relating to liability. Liability and other legal and ethical issues are discussed in Chapter 3, and you should read that chapter carefully before beginning an internship.

INDIVIDUAL INTERNSHIP AGREEMENTS

A sample individual internship agreement form is provided in Appendix C. As illustrated by that form, internship agreements should record the days and hours you will be expected to work, what your responsibilities will be, and the nature and extent of supervision to be provided. The internship agreement should also provide space to identify your goals and how you hope to achieve them during the internship.

A formal agreement encourages people to be clear about their expectations and commitments from the outset. As Costa (1994) and Freeman (1993) pointed out, this structure can reduce the anxiety that trainees often feel as they start an internship. As they write the agreement, the intern, instructor, and supervisor can work out the details of exactly when the intern will be expected at the placement, when supervision will be provided, what activities the intern can observe and participate in, and how the intern's performance will be evaluated.

EVALUATION

Because each internship offers different experiences and sets different expectations, and because interns differ in their personal goals, it is a good idea to be involved in the evaluation process from the beginning. To help ensure the most effective and constructive learning experiences, and to avoid future misunderstandings when evaluations are due, interns, instructors, and supervisors should agree on the evaluation and grading criteria and process before the internship begins (Wayne, 2004). Everyone can then work together to ensure that the evaluation

process is predictable, productive, and contributes to the overall learning experience of the intern (Bogo, Regehr, Hughes, Power, and Globerman, 2002; Regehr, Regehr, Leeson, and Fusco, 2002).

As you think about the evaluation process, it is important for you to understand going into the internship that you are not doing yourself a service if you only seek, expect, or accept positive feedback when you receive evaluations. I say this for several reasons. First, it is unrealistic to believe that you will excel in everything you do from the very outset. Therefore, you should expect that in some areas your performance may be exemplary and in others it may need some work to improve. That is what learning is all about. It is also true that if you are only receiving positive feedback, you will not be very able to identify or work to advance areas in which you are not as strong or as skilled. Kadushin and Harkness (2002) emphasize that in many instances student evaluations of supervisors reflect a desire for more, not less, critical feedback and for more specific constructive comments rather than general impressions.

Hoffman, Hill, Homes, and Feitas (2005) made a similar observation and report that supervisee attitudes toward feedback can influence the willingness of supervisors to address challenging issues. Furthermore, Hoffman et al. (2005) found that supervisors who avoid giving difficult or critical feedback often wish later that they had offered the feedback or critical evaluation for the sake of the student, their clients, and ultimately the profession.

In my experience, the students who eventually go on to be most successful are not only open to constructive criticism, but they actually seek it out so that they can learn more about themselves and their work. Smith and Agate (2004) described a method of addressing overconfidence among counselor trainees as a way of encouraging interns to reflect more critically on their own inferential and assessment processes.

Along the same lines, students should also keep in mind that one of the most difficult but important roles faculty and supervisors fill is that of "gatekeeper" for the profession (Busseri, Tyler, and King, 2005; Gibbs and Blakely, 2000; Johnson and Campbell, 2004; Morrow, 2000; Vacha-Haase, Davenport, and Kerwsky, 2004; Wayne, 2004; Wilkerson, 2006). Not everyone who seeks to work in these professions is up to the task and, like it or not, your faculty and supervisors have the difficult but essential responsibility of identifying those who do not make the grade and should not continue with their studies or training.

Given the concerns just mentioned, there is no single evaluation approach that works best. Regehr et al. (2002) reviewed a variety of approaches to evaluation in field placements and emphasize the importance of obtaining a baseline of student competence at the beginning of an internship. Having an accurate baseline assessment as a starting point helps to identify what learning needs and opportunities should be addressed during the internship and serves as a foundation for subsequent evaluation. Regehr and colleagues then recommend identifying specific learning goals that meet the needs of the student and the agency and the expectations of the school and the supervisor.

If your instructor or supervisor has an established format for evaluation, review it carefully to be sure you understand it. If your instructor or supervisor does not have a fixed format, you may want to consider the sample evaluation forms provided in Appendixes D and E. More will be said about the evaluation aspect of supervision in Chapter 4.

USING THIS BOOK

Just as internships are different from ordinary classes, this book is not a typical textbook. Here are a couple of tips for how to use the book most effectively.

"FRONTLOADING"

One of the differences between this text and others is that the material in this book is heavily "frontloaded." By this I mean that in comparison to courses and texts in which you may read a chapter each week or so during a quarter or semester, in this book you may want to read much or all of the book during the first few weeks of your placement, then refer to specific chapters again as you proceed through the internship.

The reason for this is that due to the nature of internships you may find that you need to draw upon knowledge from later chapters early on in your experience. For example, many students find it helpful to review the chapters dealing with clinical writing and case notes from the very start of an internship. So, too, it is a good idea to give some consideration to personal safety issues and self-care chapters right from the outset of your experience rather than waiting until after something arises.

Of course some chapters, such as termination and ending the internship, can wait till later, but even these topics are good to consider, because understanding how to close cases and conclude a placement successfully can help you better prepare for these events ahead of time.

RESOURCES AND REFERENCES

A second difference between this book and other texts is the emphasis on practical skills and knowledge. In writing this book I have tried to present information that will be immediately relevant to your internship and will be of practical use to you in the field. All the chapters have been designed to address the skills or issues that are most likely to emerge during your internship and are certain to be part of your eventual work as a professional. I hope you will use the book as a reference source to help prepare yourself for the internship and to answer questions that arise along the way. I recognize, however, that entire books have been written about the topics of each of the chapters. If you are interested in more detail about a topic, I have provided references throughout the text, and I hope you will refer to these as you read. The practice of going beyond a textbook and pursuing additional resources is a good habit

to develop because it is part of how professionals pursue topics of interest. Throughout your internship and your future study and training, make it a practice to not simply accept a single source of information but to pursue different sources and learn from different perspectives.

READING AS ACTIVE INTERACTION

It is a cliché, but nevertheless true, that you get out of things what you put into them. If you read this book like any other textbook and primarily look to highlight things that may come up on a test, you will be wasting your time. This book is not meant to be read that way. As you read, you should ask questions, make connections, and consider the implications for your own work. You should seek clarification of things you do not understand and challenge my ideas if you disagree with them. Feel free to write in the margins, highlight key ideas because they interest you, take notes, and discuss your reading with peers and supervisors.

The process should not be just "I wrote the book—now you read it." Rather, it should be "Here are some of my ideas and information, now what do you think?" Whatever your reaction, what matters most is that you have some reaction. That will get things started, and learning can proceed from there.

DOING THE EXERCISES

Part of the reason I enjoy working with interns is that I believe strongly in the value of experiential and discovery-based learning. In helping interns make the most of their experiences, I see the task as both to provide information and stimulate thinking in new ways. In this book, one of the ways I try to stimulate thinking is by providing exercises related to the topics of each chapter.

If your goal is simply to get through the book, or if you are pressed for time, you may be tempted to skim over an exercise or suggested activity. I hope you will resist that temptation and devote some time to the exercises. A given exercise may be unnecessary for you, but you will not really know unless you test your knowledge. It is one thing to tell yourself that you already know something, but it is another matter to really explore and reflect on an issue in a structured, systematic way. In my experience as an instructor and supervisor, and in my own work as a practicing clinician, I am constantly surprised by how often I think I know something but then discover a completely new insight or understanding.

KEEP THIS BOOK

Some students indiscriminately sell their textbooks back the minute a class is over. That is a mistake. If you plan to go on to work or further study in the field, this book as well as your other basic textbooks should begin to make up the core of your professional library; you should have them handy as references for future classes and as you work in the field. The marginal return you might gain from a resale is far outweighed by the value of having your own resources to draw on and refer back to in the future. Developing a personal library is part of the process of becoming a professional, and you might as well begin that process with this book. If you do go on to work in the field or to future internships, you will have many occasions to refer back to the chapters on ethics, writing, supervision, diversity, stress, and other topics. Keep this book when the class is over and read it again in the future.

REFERENCES

Albin, D., Adams, M., Walker, S., & Elwood, B. (2000). The quest for an internship: Four students' perspective. *Professional Psychology: Research and Practice, 31*(3), 295–299.

American Psychological Association Committee on Accreditation (2005). Guidelines and principles for accreditation of programs in professional Psychology. http://www.apa.org/ed/gp2000.html

American Psychological Association Presidential Task Force (2006). Evidence-based practice in psychology. *American Psychologist, 61,* 271–285.

Bogo, M., & Globerman, J. (1995). Creating effective university-field partnerships: An analysis of two inter-organization models for field education. *Journal of Teaching in Social Work, 11,* 177–192.

Bogo, M., Regehr, C., Hughes, J., Power, R., & Globerman, J. (2002). Evaluating a measure of student field performance in direct service: Testing reliability and validity of explicit criteria. *Journal of Social Work Education, 38,* 385–399.

Brill, R., Wolkin, J., & McKeel, N. (1987). Strategies for selecting and securing the predoctoral clinical internship of choice. In R. H. Dana & W. T. May (Eds.), *Internship training in professional psychology* (pp. 220–226). Washington, DC: Hemisphere.

Brownstein, C. (1981). Practicum issues: A placement planning model. *Journal of Education for Social Work, 17*(3), 25–28.

Busseri, M. A., Tyler, J. D., & King, A. R. (2005). An exploratory examination of student dismissals and prompted resignatios from clinical psychology PhD training programs. *Professional Psychology: Research and Practice, 36,* 441–445.

Council for Accreditation of Counseling and Related Educational Programs. (2001). 2001 Standards. http://www.cacrep.org/2001Standards.html

Council on Social Work Education, (2004). Educational Policy and Acreditation Standards. http://www.cswe.org/.

Cornish, J. A. E., Smith-Acuña, S., & Nadkarni, L. (2005). Developing an exclusively affiliated psychology internship consortium: A novel approach to internship training. *Professional Psychology: Research and Practice, 36,* 9–15.

Costa, L. (1994). Reducing anxiety in live supervision. *Counselor Education and Supervision, 34,* 30–40.

Erwin, W. J., & Toomey, M. E. (2005). Use of criminal background checks in counselor education. *Counselor Education and Supervision, 44,* 305–318.

Fox, R. (2004). Field instruction and the mature student. *Journal of Teaching in Social Work, 24,* 113–129.

Foxhall, K. (2001). Mentoring giant almost didn't find his own way. *Monitor on Psychology,* 60–63.

Freeman, S. C. (1993). Structure in counseling supervision. *Clinical Supervisor, 11,* 245–252.

Friedman, D., & Kaslow, N. J. (1986). The development of professional identity in psychotherapists: Six stages in the supervision process.

In F. W. Kaslow (Ed.), *Supervision and training: Models, dilemmas and challenges,* 29–50. New York: Haworth Press.

Fuentes, C. de las, Wilmuth M. E., & Yarrow, C. (2005). Competency training in ethics education and practice. *Professional Psychology: Research and Practice, 36,* 362–366.

Gandolfo, R. L., & Brown, R. (1987). Psychology intern ratings of actual and ideal supervision of psychotherapy. *Journal of Training and Practice in Professional Psychology, 1,* 15–28.

Gaw, K. F. (1997). The demand for APA internships: A challenge for us all. *Psychotherapy, 32*(3), 23–25.

Gelman, C. R. (2004). Anxiety experienced by foundation-year MSW students entering field placement: Implications for admissions, curriculum, and field education. *Journal of Social Work Education, 40,* 39–54.

Gelman, S. R. (1990). The crafting of fieldwork training agreements. *Journal of Social Work Education, 26,* 65–75.

Gelman, S. R., Pollack, D., & Auerbach, C. (1996). Liability issues in social work education. *Journal of Social Work Education, 32,* 351–361.

Gelman, S. R., & Wardell, P. J. (1988). Who's responsible? The field liability dilemma. *Journal of Social Work Education, 24,* 70–78.

Gibbs, P., & Blakely, E. H. (Eds.) (2000). *Gatekeeping in BSW programs.* New York: Columbia University Press.

Globerman, J., & Bogo, M. (2003). Changing times: Understanding social workers' motivation to be field instructors. *Social Work, 48,* 65–73.

Gray, L. A., Ladany, N., Walker, J. A., & Ancis, J. R. (2001). Psychotherapy trainees' experience of counterproductive events in supervision. *Journal of Counseling Psychology, 48,* 371–383.

Heppner, P. P., & Roehlke, H. J. (1984). Differences among supervisees at different levels of training: Implications for a developmental model of supervision. *Journal of Counseling Psychology, 31,* 76–90.

Hersh, J. B., & Poey, K. (1987). A proposed interviewing guide for intern applicants. In R. H. Dana & W. T. May (Eds.), *Internship training in professional psychology* (pp. 217–220). Washington, DC: Hemisphere.

Hevern, V. W. (1994). *Faculty supervision of undergraduate field experience coursework.* Paper presented at the annual meeting of the American Psychological Association, Los Angeles.

Hoffman, M. A., Hill, C. E., Holmes,. S. E., & Freitas, G. F. (2005). Supervisor perspective on the process and outcome of giving easy, difficult, or no feedback to supervisees. *Journal of Counseling Psychology, 52,* 3–13.

Holtzman, R. F., & Raskin, M. S. (1989). Why placements fail: Study results. *Clinical Supervisor, 6,* 123–136.

Hopkins, K. M., Bloom, J. D., & Deal, K. H. (2005). Moving away from tradition: Exploring the field experiences of part-time, older, and employment-based students. *Journal of Social Work Education, 41,* 573–585.

Johnson, W. B., & Campbell, C. D. (2004). Character and fitness requirements for professional psychologists: Training directors' perspectives. *Professional Psychology: Research and Practice, 35,* 405–411.

Johnson, W. B., Porter, K., Campbell, C. D. & Kupko, E. N. (2005). Character and fitness requirements for professional psychologists: An examination of state licensing application forms. *Professional Psychology: Research and Practice, 36,* 654–662.

Juni, S. (1997). Where have students' rights gone? *American Psychologist, 52*(12), 1386–1387.

Kagle, J. D. (1993). Record keeping: Directions for the 1990s. *Social Work, 38,* 190–196.

Kaiser, T. L. (1992). The supervisory relationship: An identification of the primary relationship and an application of two theories of ethical relationships. *Journal of Marital and Family Therapy, 18,* 283–296.

Kaslow, N. J., Pate, W.E. II., & Thorn, B. (2005). Academic and internship directors' perspectives on practicum experiences: Implications for training. *Professional Psychology: Research and Practice, 36,* 307–317.

Keilin, G. (2000). Internship selection in 1999: Was the Association of Psychology postdoctoral and internship centers' match a success? *Professional Psychology: Research and Practice, 31*(3), 281–287.

King, M. C. (2006). Preparing psychology and psychologists for new health care markets. *Canadian Psychology, 47,* 51–56.

Knight, C. (1996). A study of MSW and BSW students' perceptions of their field instructors. *Journal of Social Work Education, 32,* 399–414.

Ladany, N., Walker, J. A., & Melincoff, D. S. (2001). Supervisory style: Its relation to the supervisory working alliance and supervisor self-disclosure. *Counselor Education and Supervision, 40,* 263–275.

Lewis, B. L., Hatcher, R. L., & Pate, W. E. II. (2005). The practicum expderience: A survey of practicum site coordinators. *Professional Psychology: Research and Practice, 36,* 291–298.

Lopez, S. J., & Draper, K. (1997). Recent developments and more internship tips: A comment on Mellott, Arden, and Cho (1997). *Professional Psychology: Research and Practice, 28,* 496–498.

Lopez, S. J., Oehlert, M. E., & Moberly, R. L. (1996). Selection criteria for American Psychological Association–accredited internship programs: A survey of training directors. *Professional Psychology: Research and Practice, 27,* 518–520.

McCabe, O. L. (2004). Crossing the quality chasm in behavioral health care: The role of evidence-based practice. *Professional Psychology: Research and Practice, 35,* 571–577.

Mellott, R. N., Arden, I. A., & Cho, M. E. (1997). Preparing for internship: Tips for the prospective applicant. *Professional Psychology: Research and Practice, 28,* 190–196.

Mitchel, S. L. (1996). Getting a foot in the door: The written internship application. *Professional Psychology: Research and Practice, 27,* 90–92.

Morrow, D. F., (2000). Gatekeeping for small baccalaureate social work programs. *Journal of Baccalaureate Social Work, 5(2),* 67–80.

Munson, C. E. (1989). Editorial. *Clinical Supervisor, 7*(1), 1–4.

National Association of Social Work Insurance Trust (2004). Supervisor beware: Reducing your exposure to vicarious liability. http://www.naswinsurancetrust.org/understanding_risk_manage ment/pointers/PP%20Vicarious%20Liability.pdf

Oehlert, M. E., Lopez, S. L., & Sumerall, S. W. (1997). Internship application: Increased cost accompanies increased competitiveness. *Professional Psychology: Research and Practice, 28,* 595–596.

Phillips, J.C., Szymanski, D. M., Ozegovic, J. J., & Briggs-Phillips, M., (2004). Preliminary examination and measurement of the internship research training environment. *Journal of Counseling Psychology, 51,* 240–248.

Pitts, J. H. (1992). Organizing a practicum and internship program in counselor education. *Counselor Education and Supervision, 31,* 196–207.

Pollack, D., & Marsh, J. (2004). Social work misconduct may lead to liability. *Social Work, 49(4),* 609–612.

Rabinowitz, F. E., Heppner, P. P., & Roehlke, H. J. (1986). Descriptive study of process and outcome variables of supervision over time. *Journal of Counseling Psychology, 33,* 292–300.

Ragins, B., & Cotton, J. (1999). Mentor functions and outcomes: A comparison of men and women in formal and informal mentoring relationship. *Journal of Applied Psychology, 84*(4), 529–550.

Regehr, C., Regehr, G., Leeson, J., & Fusco, L. (2002). Setting priorities for learning in the field practicum: A comparative study of students and field instruction. *Journal of Social Work Education, 38,* 55–65.

Rodolfa, E., Vieille, R., Russell, P., Nijjer, S., Nguyen, D., Mendoza, M., & Perrin, L. (1999). Internship selection inclusion and exclusion criteria. *Professional Psychology: Research and Practice, 30*(4), 415–419.

Silverman, H. L. (2004). *Internship in psychology: The APAGS workbook for writing successful applications and finding the right match.* Washington, DC: American Psychological Association.

Stedman, J. M., Hatch, J. P., Schoenfeld, L. S., & Keilin, W. G. (2005). The structure of internship training: Current patterns and implications for the future of clinical and counseling psychologists. *Professional Psychology: Research and Practice, 36,* 3–8.

Stedman, J. M. (1997). What we know about predoctoral internship training: A review. *Professional Psychology: Research and Practice, 28,* 475–485.

Stedman, J. M., Neff, J. A., Donahoe, C. P., Kopel, K., & Hays, J. R. (1995). Applicant characterization of the most desirable internship training program. *Professional Psychology: Research and Practice, 26,* 396–400.

Stewart, A. E., & Stewart, E. A. (1996). Personal and practical considerations in selecting a psychology internship. *Professional Psychology: Research and Practice, 27,* 295–303.

Stoltenberg, C. D. (2005). Developing professional competence through developmental approaches to supervision. *American Psychologist, 60,* 855–864.

Thibadeau, S. F., & Christian, W. P. (1985). Developing an effective practicum program at the human service agency. *Behavior Therapist, 8,* 31–34.

Vacha-Haase, T., Davenport, D. S., & Kerewsky, S. D. (2004). Problematic students: Gatekeeping practices of academic professional psychology programs. *Professional Psychology: Research and Practice, 35,* 115–122.

Wampold, B. W., & Bhati, K. S. (2004). Attending to the omissions: A historical examination of evidence-based practice movements. *Professional Psychology: Research and Practice, 35,* 563–570.

Waters, M. (2001). So many hats, so little time. *Monitor on Psychology, 32*(1), 56–59.

Wayne, R. H. (2004). Legal guidelines for dismissing students because of poor performance in the field. *Journal of Social Work Education, 40,* 403–414.

Wilkerson, K. (2006). Impaired students: Applying the therapeutic process model to graduate training programs. *Counselor Education and Supervision, 45,* 207–217.

Williams-Nickelson, C., & Prinstein, M. J. (2004). *Internship in psychology: The APAGS workbook for writing successful applications and finding the right match.* Washington, DC: American Psychological Association.

Zakutansky, T. J., & Sirles, E. A. (1993). Ethical and legal issues in field education: Shared responsibility and risk. *Journal of Social Work Education, 29,* 338–347.

CHAPTER 2
GETTING STARTED

ANXIETY AND EXCITEMENT

Now that you've made arrangements for your internship and are set to go, let's start by acknowledging again that when we first undertake any new venture it is normal to feel a combination of anxiety and excitement. Anxiety comes because we are not sure what lies ahead and may not be certain we can meet all the challenges. At the same time, we are excited because this, after all, is what we have trained for, and we're now getting a chance to try out in the "real world" what we've learned from coursework. The key to dealing with these emotions is, first, to recognize that you are not alone, and second, to understand that with experience, time, and support you will get more comfortable more quickly than you might imagine.

In a study of MSW students entering their foundation-year practicum, Gelman (2004) found that prior experience, age, and specific coursework all contributed to lower anxiety scores than those reported by younger, less experienced students with less prior coursework. When asked to identify specific concerns, Gelman's respondents identified worries about lack of skill or knowledge, logistical details like commuting, safety issues, questions about the workload and expectations, and concern over the kind of relationship and support that would be provided by the supervisor.

To help students explore the strengths they would bring to their practica, Gellman asked her respondents to list the knowledge and skills they already felt they possessed. The most commonly identified strengths in this group included prior experience, knowledge, and basic listening and empathy skills. Students also identified strategies for managing anxiety, including relaxation, positive thinking, social support, and personal therapy. A number of students also suggested that schools and practicum settings could do more to help students adjust at the very beginning of their placements. What follows in this chapter is designed to do just that, to help make your entry into the internship a positive and successful experience.

This chapter addresses common questions and concerns that arise in the first few days of an internship. It also discusses the role of the intern, some of the opportunities you can expect, and the limitations inherent in internships. Typical areas of concern include working with other staff, meeting clients, fees for service, managing paperwork, and coping with other tasks that are part of professional life but will probably be new to most interns. This chapter also gives suggestions for using two tools that are particularly well suited to internships, journaling and portfolios. Finally, while there is much you can and should learn on internship sites, there may also be lessons that are best left unlearned. Recognizing these can be just as important as discovering the positive things you want to retain from your experience.

FIRST IMPRESSIONS

One of the great things about aphorisms is that for every famous saying there is an equal and opposite saying. Two mutually contradictory sayings relate particularly well to internships. The first is, "You never get a second chance to make a first impression." The counterpoint advice is, "Don't judge a book by its cover." As you begin your internship, keep in mind the importance of the first impressions you make on others. Remember also not to judge an internship setting or the people there based solely on your first impressions.

When you begin an internship, first impressions will go both ways. On the one hand, as you are introduced to the staff, clients, and internship facility, you will begin to form your impressions of them. At the same time, the staff and clients with whom you work will begin to form impressions of you. Because first impressions can leave lasting effects, you should think about what kind of first impression you want to give others.

It would be foolish for anyone to tell interns exactly what they should wear or precisely how they should act their first days on the job. Fortunately, power ties are not an expected part of the helping professional's wardrobe. Nevertheless, interns would be well advised to consider the nature of their internship setting, the kinds of activities they will be involved in, and what the institutional norms are for attire and conduct. Most people have had the awkward experience of arriving at an event for which they were either dressed more formally or informally than everyone else. One way to avoid this experience at internships is to ask your supervisor beforehand what the norms for clothing are and what activities will be happening on the first day.

The value of this simple advice was demonstrated by the experience of an intern who, keen on making the best first impression he could, arrived at his internship the first day dressed in a suit and tie. The intern could not have looked finer, but it happened that his first day was "games" day at the internship site. Everyone else on staff was wearing shorts or jeans because, among other things, the games day activities included softball, egg tossing, and a tug-of-war through a mud pit. Dressed as he was, the intern did not participate in any of the events. What could have been a wonderful way to get to know people resulted in a rather uncomfortable experience of feeling out of place.

Experiences in the opposite direction have also befallen interns. Some students, accustomed to dressing, talking, and acting any way they want on the college campus, may insist on their right to "be themselves" at the internship. I know this argument rather well, not only because I have heard it from students on occasion but, more personally, because I made it myself when I arrived at a rural internship placement with my very long hair, long beard, and dressed casually in levis and a flannel shirt. My supervisor was not at all happy with how I presented myself on the first day of work, so he summarily sent me home with advice to return looking more professional. Very reluctantly, and with a degree of righteous indignation, I trimmed my beard and hair, traded in my jeans for khakis, and put on the only sport jacket I owned. In turn, the supervisor, also reluctantly, allowed me to continue the placement and, though this rough introduction took some time to work through, I ended up learning a great deal and somehow managed to demonstrate that even long-haired, bearded guys can have something to offer. I also came to realize that lost in the defense of an intern's own individuality is the more important principle that in clinical work our focus needs to be on caring for clients in the most effective way possible, not simply "being ourselves." Just as therapists or counselors must understand the needs of clients and adapt their interventions accordingly, interns should be sensitive to the institutional needs of their placement site. If that includes dressing, acting, or talking in a way that is different than one would outside the internship, so be it. In a very real sense, you are a guest at the internship and should dress and conduct yourself in a way that respects the internship's customs and needs.

While interns should carefully consider the first impressions they will make on others, many people at the internship will not be as concerned about the first impressions they make on the interns. This is only to be expected, because the experience and perspectives of staff are substantially different from those of interns.

Recently, one of our promising young interns returned from the first day at her internship site terribly distraught and convinced that the next three months were sure to be awful. When she went to visit her supervisor, he was at first too busy to meet with her. When they finally met late in the day, he asked a lot of questions about her approach to treatment, her

experience, and what she was doing there. During the conversation, he corrected some of the things she said, used "rough" language, and never asked about who she was as a person. Almost in tears, she said to her instructor, "I'm sure there's no way we'll ever get along. I'm sure he hates me already, and I just can't work with someone like that."

As it turned out, the instructor knew the supervisor and was aware that his style was often perceived to be gruff. The instructor also knew that the supervisor was extremely dedicated to his clients and to the interns he trained. The gruffness was in part his natural style, in part because he was overworked, and in part his way of getting past the surface talk to see how interns performed in response to stress. The supervisor had worked with many different interns and had come to believe that, given the clients and the nature of the work at that internship site, interns had to be able to cope with confrontation.

In response to a request from the intern, the instructor called the supervisor, who reported that, contrary to the intern's first impressions, he was quite impressed by her and thought she would work out just fine. The next day he apologized for any misunderstandings, complimented the intern on how she had responded, then set to work providing her with the best training and supervision received by any student that semester. Not all supervisory relationships work out as well as this one did, but it demonstrated the importance of not making decisions based solely on first impressions.

ENTHUSIASM MEETS EXPERIENCE

Supervisors and staff who work with interns consistently say that the greatest thing interns bring to placements is a sense of enthusiasm and optimism. Fresh from their studies and eager to try out their knowledge and skills, some interns practically radiate energy. Other interns, perhaps less sure of themselves, may radiate insecurity. All interns have in common that they bring something new to the institution. This is one of the reasons why institutions and supervisors agree to accept interns. For the most part, they appreciate the interns' new perspectives, and they value the opportunity to be part of training future professionals (Globerman & Bogo, 2003).

Interns should be aware, however, that their own perspective and experience differ markedly from those of the staff and clients who are already at a placement. Caught up as they are in their own feelings and in all there is to do and learn, interns often do not pause to think about this difference. For the intern, each placement is a new and potentially exciting experience, but each placement is also transitory. Throughout their time in the placement, interns will be on the steep upward slope of the learning curve, and every day can bring new discoveries and opportunities. By comparison, many of the staff at placement sites will have worked there for years and have a different perspective. They already know the people, system, and clients. They may also have seen many interns come and go. As a result, although each intern's experience is unique, having interns at the site may be a frequent occurrence for the staff, and they may not share in the intern's sense of novelty or enthusiasm.

This does not mean the staff are any less invested than the interns in the treatment of clients. It simply means that their perspective will differ from that of the interns. One long-time staff member explained it to an intern by comparing the experience to "falling in love versus marriage. The initial sense of wonder is fantastic, but it can't last forever. That doesn't mean the love is gone, it's just taken a different form that might not be so easy to see from the outside."

The same staff member went on to point out another factor that differs for staff and interns. For interns, the experience is limited in time. At the completion of the internship, the intern will go back to school, move on to another internship, or do something else, but seldom will the intern stay on at the site. Staff, on the other hand, were there before the intern came and will be there after the intern leaves. This is part of the reason interns may feel that some staff members do not reach out to form the close contacts the interns might desire. The staff may have become accustomed to interns coming and going; it is not realistic to expect them to form repeated close contacts that will almost certainly be temporary. Many interns do form valuable and lasting relationships with supervisors and others at internships, but it is helpful for interns to understand the situation so that they will not be disappointed if such relationships do not develop.

EXERCISE

Take a moment to think about the role of intern as viewed from several different perspectives. For example, how do each of the following view interns: Supervisors? Other professional staff? Staff with less formal education? Administrators? Clients? The interns themselves? As you think about these perspectives, ask what positive ideas each group might hold about interns and what negative ideas they might have. Giving some thought to this beforehand will better prepare you for the different relationships and reactions you will encounter during your internship.

THE ROLE OF THE INTERN

The role of intern occupies a gray area somewhere between student and professional. As an intern, you will still have many things to learn, but you may also be counted on to possess certain knowledge and skills. Depending on your experience and training, you may be given gradually increasing responsibilities, but your position will probably not be equal to that of full staff. This ambiguity is compounded because others at the internship, including staff and clients, may also be unclear about what interns are and what the purpose of the internship is.

Your role as intern may be further complicated by precedents set by previous interns. Many placement sites have had many interns over the years, and your predecessors have created certain expectations, positive or negative, with which you are likely to be compared. If a terrific intern preceded you, staff at the placement are likely to welcome you but may hold you to high standards. If the former intern did not do well, a negative attitude toward interns may carry over to you. Although you cannot do anything about what happened before you arrived, being aware of these possibilities can help you understand that the ways in which people relate to you are often influenced by experiences that have nothing to do with you as an individual.

Two principles can help interns deal with role ambiguity and any precedents that other interns may have set: (1) Be honest with yourself and with others; (2) do your best. Although these rules may sound simplistic, many interns have reported that remembering these basic principles helped them keep it together when things became confusing at placements.

Being honest with yourself means you accept that your role is ambiguous, not only for you but for others. It also means that you are open about your relative strengths and limitations. If you have no experience doing something, let people know and be open to learning. If you have some experience or knowledge, do not be afraid to share it. If situations arise in which you need clarification about your role or the expectations others have, do not try to read people's minds. Ask for clarification and be willing to share your own thoughts and feelings about the matter.

Doing your best means that as someone in training you do not already have to be the world's greatest therapist, social worker, psychologist, or counselor, and it is not your sole responsibility to save all of the clients or do everything anyone asks of you. As an intern, you should set the highest possible standards for yourself, but do not set or try to meet unrealistic expectations. You are at your internship to learn, not to prove you already know. If people around you seem much more experienced than you, do not be intimidated. They probably do have more experience, and that gives you the opportunity to learn. Enjoy the opportunity and make the most of it.

There may be times when you feel pressured by time or other constraints to do less than your best work. People tend to remember the quality of your work, not the circumstances under which it was done. For this and other reasons, it is generally advisable to concentrate on providing a high quality of service rather than emphasizing quantity. There may be situations when you feel you have to compromise; but whenever possible, do your best work and try to avoid pressured situations that might compromise quality. If you feel that time or other demands are causing you to compromise quality, discuss this with your instructor and supervisor so that adaptations can be made.

THE ROLE OF THE PROFESSIONAL

Because interns are exploring and beginning to establish their professional identity, it is important to consider how the role of professional differs from that of student (Elman, Illfelder-Kaye,

& Robiner, 2005). The easiest way to understand this difference is to think in terms of standards. I use this word often because, for me, being a professional means setting the highest possible standards for what I do in my professional life. As an intern, I hope you will aspire to this as well. Because our work as professionals impacts the lives of others, this means we must always conduct ourselves ethically and must do our utmost to stay current with research literature, clinical practices, organizational standards, legal issues, and other matters that may affect our practice, the people we serve, or our profession.

For students, there tends to be an implicit assumption that learning about a subject has a start and an end-point at the conclusion of class. For students, the goal is often to get the best possible grade or, perhaps, simply to do the minimum needed to pass a course. For a professional, learning is ongoing, never stops, and the standard cannot be the minimum needed to pass a course. If there is something you need to know to better serve a client or perform some other function, then you must do what it takes to fully and solidly acquire the necessary skill or knowledge. There is no room for "just good enough to pass," and there is no room for kidding ourselves into thinking we know or can do something when in fact this is not so. The demand for meeting high standards will be ongoing throughout your professional work, and it can be very challenging, but it is also rewarding and is part of what you sign up for when you enter a profession.

To appreciate why this is so, ask yourself what you expect from other treatment professionals when you put your life in their hands in some way. Do you expect anything less than their full commitment to adhere to the highest standards of ethics and quality care? Do you expect them to pay full attention to your concerns and do whatever it takes to study and learn about your condition and treatment? Of course you do, which is why you must set the same high standards for yourself.

Another important difference between students and professionals is that students are viewed as individuals and their conduct can vary accordingly. Professionals, on the other hand, are expected to meet certain standards of conduct because they are members of and represent a larger, identified group. Earlier I described the student who was sent home from an internship because he was not dressed suitably. In addition to dress, there are standards for the kind of language that is acceptable, the way one relates to others on the job, and the quality of work one produces. Professional and student standards are also different for more mundane but nevertheless extremely important details, such as coming to work on time and keeping appointments. Students typically have a great deal of freedom in each of these areas, but the professional must be prompt, reliable, and act in ways that maintain an image of respectability.

For most students, this will not be a problem; but if you find it difficult to balance your personal habits or identity with your professional role, you might want to reexamine your own conduct or select another internship that more closely matches your style. I also encourage you to understand that meeting standards does not mean abandoning your individuality. If all professionals were clones, they would not be able to meet the needs of diverse clients. There is room and need for individuality among therapists, but it is also your responsibility to find ways to remain an individual while still serving your internship and clients (Pipes, Holstein, & Aguirre, 2005).

When I work with students who choose to dress or act differently than the norm, I almost never tell them they must change in order to work as interns. That is not my role; and, frankly, I enjoy the diversity. In fact, I have certainly not met "the norm" myself at various times in my life, and I would have resented greatly having someone tell me how I had to dress or act. What I do tell interns is that they owe it to themselves and to their placement and clients to think seriously about the effects of their appearance and actions. Interns must also realize that there may be certain placements, supervisors, or clients who will have narrower limits of tolerance than the intern might be comfortable with. Some interns may not be able to work within those limits, so they will have to either make adjustments or forgo that particular training opportunity in favor of something else. Although part of becoming a professional is finding ways to balance your individuality with your professional role, there are countless ways to do this, and the internship is a perfect time to experiment and discover what does or does not work.

JOINING YOUR PROFESSIONAL ASSOCIATION

If you have not already done so, let me strongly encourage you to join your professional association. Membership in your association provides a host of benefits and helps advance your entry into the role of a professional. Among the many benefits are the chance to get to know, work with, and learn from others in your profession from your own area and from across the nation and globe; access to journals, newsletters, and other communications that help you stay current with your field; access to selected insurance programs—including professional liability insurance; opportunities for continuing education programs that are valuable today and will be essential to continuing licensure when the time comes; participation in policy and advocacy efforts on behalf of your profession and the people you serve; and helping to advance the profession itself both for your own interest and the interest of the next generation of professionals. For many associations, membership may also include somewhat more quotidian but nevertheless useful things like rental car discounts or special rates on magazine subscriptions.

Though most students and interns do not fully appreciate it, you are able to study and practice today because people who came before you worked and sacrificed to help build the profession you are entering and created the educational and training opportunities you now enjoy. By joining your professional association, you can take up the torch and make your own contributions before passing it on to the next generation.

The easiest way to sign up for membership is to access the Web site for your profession. As a student in training, you will likely be eligible for discounted membership rates and for discounts at conferences, workshops, and similar events. All of the major organizations can be easily accessed through any Internet search engine, but for convenience the sites for the largest organizations are listed below. Keep in mind too that each of these organizations comprises specialty groups that you may also want to join. These groups focus on specific areas of practice or service and can provide focused information and contacts relevant to these focus areas.

American Association of Marriage and Family Therapy: http://www.aamft.org/index_nm.asp

American Counseling Association: http://www.counseling.org/

American Psychiatric Association: http://www.psych.org/

American Psychological Association: http://www.apa.org/

National Association of Social Workers: http://www.socialworkers.org/

National Staff Development and Training Association: http://nsdta.aphsa.org/

MAKING THE MOST OF YOUR INTERNSHIP

ACADEMIA MEETS THE "REAL WORLD"

One thing all interns discover is that internships require a different set of skills and knowledge than academic classes. Formal academic classes emphasize knowledge of facts. The focus of most academic exams is on what you know, and the "what" that you must know has been explicitly taught in the class. By the time you are in college, most students know this system pretty well. If you pay attention in class, study hard, and memorize the material, you are likely to pass the exam. Contrast this situation with the internship world.

In the internship, the focus is not on what you know, but what you do. Being able to identify the founders of every major therapy technique or to describe in detail five theories of personality is fine if you are in a class, but such abilities may be of limited use at your internship. At your internship, usefulness of information depends on what you do with what you know and how you relate your knowledge to the situations you encounter. Lewis, Hatcher, and Pate (2005) described this difference from the perspective of academic training directors compared to practicum site coordinators, noting that the willingness of the latter to accept interns into their facilities depends on weighing the benefits of the service provided by the trainee against the costs of providing training and supervision.

Ronnestad and Skovholt (1993) referred to the challenge of applying knowledge in a practical way as the *theory–practice gulf.* If you experience this gulf when you begin your internship, you are not alone. Indeed, the issue of translating academic knowledge to practical applications was at the core of the

first internships in psychology (Routh, 2000; Thorp, O'Donohue, & Gregg, 2005). After nearly a century of field education and training, Raskin (1994) reported that experts in the study of field education in social work agree there is still a "lack of fit" between classroom courses and field instruction.

The other difference between internships and classroom study is that it is never clear beforehand just what you will have to know. One of the truest statements I know about life applies well to internships: "Life gives the test first, then the lesson." At an internship, at any given moment you may be called on to use any knowledge or skills you have and possibly some you do not have. Therefore, your study approach must prepare you with the skills of understanding people and interactions in general. It must also teach you to be flexible, think on your feet, expect the unexpected, and understand that the grades are not at all what you are accustomed to.

If you expect the internship to be just like class but taking place in the community, you surely will be surprised and almost certainly will be confused, and you may not do very well. On the other hand, if you appreciate that the experience is related to, yet markedly different from, academic coursework, you are more likely to benefit from and succeed at your internship.

REMEMBER YOU ARE A STUDENT

Internships are not the same as class, but your role at the internship will still primarily be to learn. This is helpful to remember because it frees you from feeling you must already know everything. Friedman and Kaslow (1986) described how supervisees in the early stage of training are "frequently plagued by the self-doubts and ambivalent feelings which reflect both the inchoate nature of their professional identities and the minimal degree of skill they as yet have amassed with which to perform their work" (p. 36). Similar observations were made by Kaslow and Rice (1987) and by Stoltenberg (2005) in their discussions of the developmental phases interns experience during their placements.

One way to reduce the pressure that comes with this phase of training is to be honest about your limited skill or knowledge. If there is something you do not know, you can simply say "I don't know." If you see or hear something you do not understand, you can ask your supervisor or instructor for an explanation. Your goal at an internship is not to impress everyone with how smart or skilled you are. Because trainees sometimes try to disguise what they do for fear of looking foolish or ignorant, I encourage students to be open about how much they need to learn. If you can do this and admit that there are things you do not know but want to learn, your internship will be much more beneficial.

MAKE THE MOST OF IGNORANCE

Many students are afraid that being open about their own ignorance will leave them feeling vulnerable. To an extent this is true, but valuable learning and growth can take place when we are vulnerable. Moreover, it is a mistake to assume that vulnerability is synonymous with helplessness or incompetence. It is helpful to remember that ignorance can be an advantage.

Precisely because interns are not expected to know everything, they can ask questions that others might be afraid to raise. Similarly, interns who are new to settings may see things in ways that people working in that setting for years have never noticed. By acknowledging what you do not yet know, you not only enhance your potential to learn, you also gain a unique kind of permission and influence not always accorded to professionals. You should appreciate this opportunity while you still have it. When you obtain your degree and are in the role of professional, it may not be so easy to admit that you do not know everything.

WORK NEAR YOUR "LEARNING EDGE"

If acknowledging what you do not know is a first step toward learning, being willing to take some risks and extend yourself is a key second step. Internships allow you to try new skills that you may have only read about before. To develop these skills, you have to test them and learn from both your successes and your mistakes. A concept that is useful to interns, and will later be useful in treatment, is the idea of a "learning edge." This term refers to the point just beyond one's present level of knowledge or skill. It is not so far ahead that we are in danger of making mistakes that could be calamitous for ourselves or others, but it is beyond our habitual level of functioning and comfort.

In your internship, you will often be right at your learning edge. This is comparable to Vygotsky's concept of the "zone of proximal development," namely, functioning in the skill area between your actual development and your potential development (Van Geert, 1998). If you find yourself feeling too comfortable, you should probably talk with your supervisor about extending your activities in some way. If you recognize that there is an area of knowledge or skill that you need to develop, you can expect that it will be a bit uncomfortable, but you must also realize that you need to accept this discomfort and push yourself in order to advance. Apart from specific skills you might develop or information you might acquire, becoming familiar and comfortable with your own learning edge is one of the most important lessons you can learn from internships.

TAKE RESPONSIBILITY FOR LEARNING

In all aspects of learning, students need to take personal ownership for what and how they learn. Merely accepting passively what an instructor tells you to read or do is not a recipe for success as a student, and it is certainly not a recipe for success as a professional. Taking responsibility for learning is particularly important in the context of internships, because the nature of the learning setting and opportunity is so different than a typical classroom. Internships do not usually provide structured syllabi, reading assignments, exams, or any of the other methods that tend to direct students. At the same time, it is very possible that your supervisor will be quite busy and not able to give the time you might need or want unless you assert yourself in some way.

An especially useful resource for all students is the book *On Course* by Skip Downing (2006). This text was recommended to me by one of the reviewers of this edition, and I want to pass the recommendation on to you. Now in its fourth edition, this book, and the accompanying Web site (http://www.oncourseworkshop.com/), helps students take control of their own learning by first assessing how they learn today, then offering a host of tips and exercises to develop key principles of success, including accepting self-responsibility, discovering self-motivation, and mastering self-management. Students report that they find the text and the exercises tremendously helpful and institutions which have adopted the program report substantial gains in student performance.

Whether you use this program or some other strategy, the key point is to take charge and be proactive in your education and training. Ultimately, your education is your responsibility, and it is in your own best interest to be as assertive and focused as you can be.

REMEMBER THAT YOU DO KNOW SOME THINGS

Along with developing and trying out your skills, the internship should also give you a chance to bring together information learned during your academic program. Internships are not the same as academic courses, but they can provide valuable opportunities to review what you have studied. Courses in human development, culture, gender issues, community systems, theories of personality, assessment, abnormal psychology, and other subjects are all relevant to your internship.

Integrating your knowledge is important. Students who have studied a subject in class often seem to forget what they have learned when they begin their internship. Try to avoid that mistake. If you have had a course in human development, consider what you learned as you work with people of different ages. If you have taken a theories of personality class, ask yourself how different theorists might view the people in your clinical setting. If you are working in a community agency, give some thought to ways in which knowledge from a community systems course helps you understand the agency and its clients. Such opportunities will strengthen your understanding and give you the chance to compare theory with reality. The emphasis is not just on what you know. It is on what you can do with that knowledge in the context of your internship.

EXERCISE

To boost both your confidence and your humility, take a few moments to list the courses or learning experiences you have had that you think will help you on your internship site. For each course, try to identify specific concepts, theories, findings, or applications that you can put into practice to help you understand the setting and the people you will work with as clients.

For example, a course in human development might help you understand the challenges adolescent clients are facing. Similarly, a course in systems theory might give you insights into the family dynamics of your patients. When you have listed the things you feel you know that will help you, then give some thought to identifying the areas in which you do not know something and wish you had further training. This list can alert you to areas you should be cautious about approaching and may help you plan your studies to fill in any noticeable deficits.

GET HELP WHEN YOU NEED IT

The final suggestion for making the most of an internship will be offered repeatedly in this text: If you have any problems or questions, be sure to get assistance. During your internship, it is essential that you recognize when situations or assignments are beyond your ability and you need help to deal with them. You may need help with anything from questions about ethics to how to write a certain kind of case note. It might also happen that you are working with a particularly challenging client, or perhaps you are not getting along well with a staff member or supervisor. Whatever the difficulty, when problems develop, get help and do so early.

People you can use as resources include your faculty instructor, placement supervisor, peers, and other faculty or staff. If none of these persons are available, other professionals outside the setting or university may also be helpful. The main point is that you are not alone and are not expected to be able to do everything yourself. This is not a precept you must practice only in your internship—it is a fundamental principle of responsible professional conduct. You will be off to a good start if you follow it in your first placement.

Because it is absolutely essential that interns be willing to seek help and know where to get help if they need it in an emergency, it is a good idea to complete the Emergency Contact and Procedures Information form provided in Appendix F. The form lists the names, phone numbers, and other information needed to contact site supervisors, faculty instructors, or other individuals as backup if the immediate supervisors or instructors are not available. The form also lists step-by-step procedures and specific people to contact for dealing with crises and situations involving possible hospital commitment.

Completing this crisis contact form may not seem necessary at present, but if a crisis occurs in the middle of the night and you cannot locate your primary supervisor or instructor for help, you will be very glad to have the numbers of other contacts readily available. Having needed just such support when I was an intern, and having provided it to students in my roles as supervisor and instructor, I cannot emphasize this too strongly. Complete the form when you start your internship, keep a copy at work and home, and use it whenever you need help. Any supervisors or faculty members worth their salt would much rather be called unnecessarily than to find out later that they were not consulted about something important.

MEETING CLIENTS

When they first begin placements, one of the most common concerns of interns is how they will be received by clients.

EXERCISE

Before reading further, write down some of your hopes and concerns about meeting clients. Talk about these with your peers and, if possible, with students who have recently completed internship experiences. Also schedule some time to discuss these issues with your supervisor and instructor. They will undoubtedly be familiar with these problems already, but it can be useful for you to express any concerns openly.

In most cases, the anxieties of interns about meeting clients are often quite different from the realities. In spite of the common fears of interns, most clients readily accept interns and relate to them as they do to other staff members. Clients generally understand the need to train future professionals. Some are even solicitous, wanting to help ensure that the interns have a good experience. Other clients may be overly accepting of interns, and some will be extremely trusting of the intern's skills. Friedman and Kaslow (1986) contrasted the supervisee's anxieties with the patient's trust by noting that patient reactions "attest to the fact that at least one member of the trainee-patient dyad believes that the former is actually a therapist" (p. 34).

This does not mean that all clients will welcome all interns. There will be clients who reject working with interns and want to work with a "real therapist." Clients who resist working with the intern can be intimidating and remarkably able to make interns feel unwelcome or incompetent.

As you prepare for your first interactions with clients, you should understand that whether clients are extremely trusting, instantly hostile, or react in some other way, your task is to understand these reactions in the clinical context. This means you should not necessarily be overly flattered by clients who are immediately trusting, nor should you be deeply hurt or intimidated by clients who are initially distant or hostile. Instead, your primary task is to understand the client's reaction from the client's perspective and be aware that each interaction is part of the overall clinical process. It also helps to beware of first impressions, both positive and negative, because first impressions can often be misleading.

Along with concerns about how clients will respond to them, interns also ask questions about how they should introduce themselves to clients. As recommended earlier, the best practice is to be honest. When asked, interns should say they are interns, tell their field of study, and, if it is relevant, explain a bit about why they are at the internship. For example, "Hi, I'm Alyson Jones. I'm an intern in counseling, and I'll be working here for the next three months." That is usually sufficient. If more information is requested, such as what experience you have, you should also be honest about that. If you have experience working with a certain treatment approach or setting, it is fine to say so. If you have no such experience, you might say, "I haven't had any experience working in a setting of this kind. That's why I'm here. I'll be working closely with my supervisor and hope to learn some things."

Zakutansky and Sirles (1993) assert that whenever interns will be working directly with clients, the intern's field supervisor should make it a point to meet directly with the clients at the start of treatment. In addition to ensuring that clients are aware that the intern is being supervised, meeting with the supervisor allows clients to know that there is someone they can speak with if they have concerns about their treatment. These issues are discussed further in Chapter 3 in the context of the ethical obligation to provide informed consent. Before working directly with clients, all interns should read that chapter carefully and be well versed in their ethical obligations.

AGE AND EXPERIENCE ISSUES WITH CLIENTS AND SUPERVISORS

The age and experience of interns are issues that sometimes arise when interns meet clients or with supervisors. These issues are particularly likely with undergraduate students, many of whom will be in their early 20s or perhaps even in their late teens. On the other hand, it can also happen, especially with adult returning students, that the intern will be older than the supervisor and perhaps even than the instructor (Fox, 2004; Hopkins, Bloom, & Deal, 2005).

Considering first the situation of interns who are younger than clients, two types of problems are most likely to arise. If you are young and working with clients very near your age, clients may expect you to relate to them as a friend rather than as an intern. They may also test your limits and your role and authority, or they may ask you to let them do things that other staff would not. If this happens, you will need to be clear with yourself and with the clients that you are indeed part of the staff and have the same responsibilities and authorities of staff.

A different sort of problem can arise if you are working with older clients, who may ask, "So how can somebody your age have anything to tell me?"

In response, interns should first try to understand what the question might mean to the client. Does it mean, for example, that the client is sincerely interested in the treatment program and wants to know whether he or she can rely on the intern for help? Or does it mean that the client is interested in taking a position of power over the intern because that is how the client relates to most people? What else might a question of this type mean to clients?

How one understands the meaning of the client's question should help in forming a response. As a general guideline, interns need not be defensive about age, experience, or, for that matter, any other issues on which clients might challenge them.

Instead, the intern might wish to acknowledge the importance of the question. Then, without being defensive, the intern may explore any specific concerns or issues with the client. This displays genuine concern for the client's needs and shows that the intern is honest. The following example shows one way this might occur in practice.

A male client has been court-ordered to seek counseling because he has abused his wife and children. The following dialogue takes place when the client meets a new intern who will be working with his primary therapist. The intern will also be observing interactions between the client and his family members:

Client (rather gruffly): So you're an intern from the college, huh? How old are you?

Intern: I'm 21. And you?

Client: Forty-two. Old enough to be your father. (Pauses for a moment looking over the intern. Then, with some hostility, asks) What the hell are you supposed to tell me that I don't already know?

Intern (calmly, but assertively and without being confrontational): I'm not here to "tell" you anything. I'm here to observe and learn.

Client: Well, I don't need any know-it-all kid telling me how to raise my family. I've got enough of those already.

Intern (still calmly): I don't think it's my job to tell you how to raise your family. But I might be able to listen to how things are going and maybe help you folks get things back together.

Client: Yeah. We'll see.

In this example, the client appears to want to diminish the intern's credibility or provoke a conflict. This reaction may be based on legitimate concerns about the intern's qualifications, or it may be an attempt to shift the focus from the client's reason for being in treatment to questions about why the intern is there. The intern's response is thoroughly professional. She does not attempt to elicit the client's approval on the spot, nor does she become defensive, counterattack, or apologize. Instead, she stays right with the client and with the interaction process. She acknowledges the presence and legitimacy of the client's concerns and offers to do what she can to be of help. That is all that can reasonably be expected.

An interaction such as this would probably not be very pleasant for the intern or the client, but not all clinical work is pleasant. It may also happen that, despite the intern's best efforts, a client will continue to be hostile and challenging. This can make things even more unpleasant, but it provides important clinical information that can help the intern understand the client. The intern should keep in mind that it is perfectly legitimate for clients to have questions about the intern's age and experience. At the same time, however, the real issue of importance is the issue the client brings, not the intern's age. By remaining professional and receiving what the client is saying without becoming defensive, the intern can help keep the focus where it needs to be.

In contrast to scenarios that arise when interns are much younger than clients, a host of different, but not entirely unrelated, issues arise when an intern is older than supervisors or instructors. This situation is becoming more common as increasing numbers of adults return to college or take on new careers later in life. Two rather paradoxical challenges can be present in these situations.

Many older students describe feeling some anxiety as they interact with much younger peers and feel self-conscious or worry that they can't keep up with the seemingly hypersonic speed of the younger students. On the other hand, older students may also become frustrated with what they perceive as naive or "wet behind the ears" younger classmates. So too, it can sometimes be very difficult for interns who are older than their instructors or clinical supervisors to really trust and respect the guidance of someone who is younger and, presumably, less experienced in life.

A couple of practical suggestions may be helpful in these circumstances. First, in internship settings one is not in competition with other students, regardless of age differences. Rather, the task at hand is to develop one's own skills to the greatest extent possible. To achieve that goal, openness to learning will be a much more beneficial perspective than a sense of competition or anxiety. An attitude of openness can also help make it easier for older students to take instruction or guidance from younger faculty or supervisors. The mere fact that one person has logged more time on the planet than another does not mean he or she knows more about everything than the other person. Before concluding that younger faculty or supervisors haven't got all that much to offer, older students may wish to give some thought to how much time and experience their instructors and supervisors have, not simply on the planet, but doing what it is they are trying to learn to do. For their part, instructors can also benefit by recognizing that older or nontraditional students bring valuable experiences and knowledge that can be assets to the class as a whole and from which the instructor can help build new learning opportunities.

TIME LIMITS

Although some clients may not want to work with interns, others often form close connections with interns, perhaps because many clients are in great need and interns are usually approachable, interested, and eager to work with them. While relationships between interns and clients can be highly beneficial to both, they also raise unique clinical issues that must be carefully considered in selecting clients to work with interns and in developing treatment approaches.

One of the real strengths of interns is that their enthusiasm and openness often make it possible to form contacts with difficult clients. Indeed, some experienced supervisors make a habit of assigning the most hopeless cases to interns because they have learned that where others may have failed, the enthusiasm and effort of an intern can sometimes break through.

Interns know from the first day, however, that their placement is time-limited and that termination may be inevitable within just a few months. Under such circumstances, is it therapeutic, or even fair, to encourage interns and clients to build strong relationships that must end in a very short time?

This question has no easy answer, but it must be addressed. First, interns must be very clear about the time limits of their placements when dealing with staff, clients, and, most important, themselves. This means that when they begin working with individual clients, in groups, on projects, or whatever else they may participate in, interns must inform those involved of the time constraints. This is part of the informed-consent process.

Interns must also remember their own time constraints; they should not create unrealistic fantasies about what they can accomplish or should attempt within the time available. It is dishonest, for example, to tell clients that you will always be there for them if you know that in another two months you will be gone. Similarly, taking on a project that will require a year to complete is unwise if the internship only lasts six months. It may be difficult to limit a relationship with a client or to decline involvement in an interesting project, but it is better to be realistic than to create false hopes that will inevitably lead to disappointment.

When interns hear this advice, they sometimes wonder if they should avoid working with any clients or projects at all. That would be going too far. Rather than avoiding all involvement or contact, the wise response is to be selective about one's involvement. This is the second element of working within limited time. Not all cases or projects will require extended time periods. Many clients can be helped within a few weeks or months, and many projects can also be completed in a short time. One of the intern's responsibilities is to select cases and activities wisely. Supervisors should play a role in these choices and should be aware of time constraints when they assign interns to clients or duties. An intern who is assigned a case or project for which time limitations will pose a problem should discuss this with the supervisor.

A third element to working within time constraints is to consider the approaches used. It is not necessary to limit involvement to short-term cases or activities as long as the treatment selected takes the time factor into account and includes provisions for continuing the treatment or other work after the intern leaves. An intern can also deal with time constraints by working with clients in the presence of another professional who will continue the case when the intern leaves. Arrangements of this type often involve interns seeing clients jointly with their supervisor. The supervisor can then maintain the case after the internship concludes. A comparable situation also holds when the intern is involved in treatment groups. Because the group provides the continuity for clients, there is a less dramatic change when an intern leaves.

However limits are addressed, interns need to consider termination issues even before they accept a case. By thinking about termination as part of selecting cases and choosing intervention techniques, interns can prevent many potential difficulties of termination from the outset (Penn, 1990). More is said about concluding treatment in Chapter 9, but for the reasons described here, interns should keep time limits in mind at all stages of their internship and work with clients.

FEES FOR SERVICE

Most interns who are just starting out do not have to deal with charging for their individual services, but the agencies where you work will very likely have at least some fees. As you gain experience and training, you may begin to see clients on a fee-for-service basis yourself. Whether or not this is part of your internship, the idea of charging for helping people is an awkward issue for many interns, so it is useful to discuss this matter early on in your training. It is also important to be aware that important ethical and legal issues are associated with fees. These issues will be discussed in more detail in Chapter 3. For very useful discussions of all aspects of fees in therapy, see the NASW handbook, *2005 Third-Party Reimbursement in Clinical Social Work Services, 13th Edition (NASW,* 2005). This concise resource, which is relevant to all related professions, reviews and provides contact information pertaining to a host of reimbursement sources, including managed care and government insurance providers. In addition, ethical and legal issues are discussed along with HIPAA rules as they pertain to reimbursement. Another useful resource, which focuses more on clinical issues and fees, is Herron and Welt (1992), *Money Matters: The Fee in Psychotherapy and Psychoanalysis.* For insights into setting fees in the current professional climate, see Sears (2005), and for results of a study of gender differences in fee structures, see Newlin, Adolph, and Kreber, (2004).

There are several reasons why interns find it difficult to charge for services. One reason is simply that it is a new experience. Most interns will have worked for pay before, but the work was probably at a different type of job that did not require them to directly collect fees. If a previous job did require them to collect fees, the service provided probably seemed more tangible than therapy or other social services. For example, tutoring, teaching, waiting tables, sales, construction, and other jobs may all require asking customers for payment, but in these situations it seems relatively clear what the payment is for.

ALTRUISM VERSUS MONEY

Fees can also pose a challenge because of an apparent conflicts many interns experience with the altruistic motives that initially brought them to the helping professions. If a person goes into a profession out of a desire to help people but then charges those

people money, the conflict between the motives of altruism and profit is likely to create dissonance (Wolfson, 1999). Resolving this dissonance is not easy, because one runs the risk of compromising the altruism or simply rationalizing away one's sense of guilt.

I must confess that I am not always comfortable with the matter of charging for what I do, but I can share a few thoughts that have been useful to my own understanding. To begin with, it may help to recognize that what human service professionals are really billing for is our time. We are not necessarily promising to cure clients or solve their problems. We are, however, agreeing to spend time with clients and do the best we can to help them in some way. Psychologists, counselors, and social workers are not the only professionals who bill for services in this way. Attorneys, physicians, and many others bill in similar ways. The common element to these professions is that billing is based on the professional's time. Attorneys do not always win their cases, doctors do not always cure their patients, and even plumbers cannot always fix your sink.

Professional services are offered to and paid for by clients who believe that the knowledge and training the professionals have received are valuable. The central principle is that the professional's time is of value. Thus, when you charge clients, what you are really charging for is your time and the skills and knowledge you apply during that time. In addition to time spent directly with clients, as Callahan (1994) reminded clinicians, direct contact with a client is not the only time the therapist or counselor will spend on the client's case. Taking notes, dealing with correspondence, scoring and writing test reports, and so on, all take time and must be considered when professionals determine their fees and how much they actually receive for their services.

One of the reasons professional services are valued is that the professional has dedicated a great deal of time and money to receiving education and training. The training alone does not guarantee that a person is competent, but it is hoped that certain skills and knowledge have been acquired during training and will be of use as the professional works with clients. Because admission to professional training is selective and is usually followed by further screening for licensing, it is also assumed that professionals possess intelligence and knowledge that will be useful in their work. Finally, possession of a professional degree and license implies that the individual is bound to act within certain established ethical constraints designed to protect the client.

Are interns sufficiently skilled to justify charging for services? By their nature, internships involve a trainee working in a clinical setting under the guidance and instruction of a supervisor. This means that the intern is not working independently. Interns work closely with supervisors who help them review cases and who review the interns' treatment with clients. Thus, when clients are billed for services provided by interns, they are not being charged solely for the intern's time. The bill must also include the time of the supervisor and the resources of their internship site. What is more, although interns may not yet be ready for independent practice, this does not mean that their time is without value. Many interns, particularly those completing graduate degrees, are in fact quite skilled, and in conjunction with the aid of their supervisor and the support and resources of their internship site, it is thoroughly appropriate that they bill and be compensated for their services. For a more extensive discussion of when trainees are ready to practice independently, see Rodolfa, Ko, and Petersen (2004).

Speaking personally again and returning to the matter of altruism versus fees, I did not enter this field because I wanted to get rich. If that was my goal, I could have pursued any number of other occupations. My primary motive was the desire to help people and society in the best way I could. In selecting a profession, I tried to identify one in which I could contribute to society and to others while at the same time putting food on the table for myself and my family. In other words, I set out to find a way to reconcile altruistic motives with the legitimate need to earn an income. For me, it was not altruism versus income, it was altruism and income. The helping professions seemed to fit that aim well. I have found that many of the same motives that led me to this field are shared by my students and interns. Similar motives were described by Berger (1995), who noted that very few of the senior therapists he interviewed even mentioned financial rewards as a factor sustaining their commitment and enthusiasm for the profession. More important than monetary compensation, such things as personal experience, mental attitude, and interpretation of the work that we do may be bigger determinants of the happiness or satisfaction we glean in our careers (Csikszentmihalyi, 1999).

Many agencies and professionals work on a sliding scale in which clients are charged according to their ability to pay. Consistent with such values and the professional codes of ethics of our professions, a portion of clinical services are also provided free as a direct service to the community. The key point is that whether I am charging full fee, reduced fees, or am providing services gratis, my time and skills are valuable and merit fair compensation. As long as I am doing my best and my fees are reasonable, I am balancing altruistic motives with financial needs.

CLINICAL AND ETHICAL ISSUES PERTAINING TO FEES

Although this discussion has pointed out the similarities between fees in the helping professions and other fields, there is also an important difference that must be understood. In psychotherapy, how clients and therapists deal with fees is not just a business arrangement, it is also part of the material and process of therapy. For example, Rabkin (1994) described how clients with such diagnoses as dependent personality or obsessive-compulsive personality may react in unique ways to fees, and this reaction can become part of the therapeutically useful material therapists address in treatment.

There has also been discussion and research evidence suggesting that charging fees may enhance the effectiveness of therapy (Conolley & Bonner, 1991; Wong, 1994). There is a matter of pride involved for many clients who sincerely need help but do not want to accept "charity." For these clients, it is important to respect both their need and their pride and allow them to pay for services to the best of their ability. For a review of other research on this topic, see Herron and Sitkowski (1986), Wolfson (1999), and Waehler, Hardin, and Rogers (1994).

Along with clinical considerations, interns need to be aware of certain ethical issues pertaining to fees. As an intern, you are unlikely to deal with the matter directly, but you should realize that collecting fees when clients fail to pay can raise delicate and ambiguous ethical issues (Goodman, 1994). For example, in some agencies unpaid client bills will be given to a collection agency, thus raising questions about confidentiality. Some experts on legal issues have advised against the practice, arguing that the fees that might be obtained through such means are probably not sufficient to justify the risks (E. Harris, personal communication, February 3, 1995).

Again, all of these issues will be more relevant to you when you have completed your training, but even in your role as intern you need to know your agency's policy concerning fees, and you need to know very clearly how to address this matter with clients. As always, if you are unsure about these matters, be sure to discuss them with your supervisor.

IS TREATMENT EFFECTIVE?

Along with the other issues just addressed in regard to fees, interns may also ask a more fundamental question that should be addressed early on in training. This questions is: Does what we do really work? Does it make a difference, and is it really worth anything?

For the mental health or human service professional, this is a core existential matter. Because the services we provide and the outcomes we seek are largely intangible, it is not always as clear what those services are or how much they are worth. Personally, I believe it is actually desirable for interns to question the effectiveness of treatment. As Friedman and Kaslow (1986) pointed out:

> It is highly unusual for a trainee to enter the field with a firmly entrenched belief in the efficacy of psychotherapy. It is therefore very much the task of supervisors and teachers to nurture the growth of the trainee's faith in the power of the healing process. (p. 37)

An example of this situation happened just as I was writing this chapter. During a recent internship class, I noticed that one of the students seemed to be considerably more relaxed and comfortable than he had previously appeared. It turned out that the student, who was involved in a research internship involving biofeedback, had decided to experience the biofeedback himself as part of his training. When I commented on the apparent change in his level of comfort, the student said with genuine surprise and pleasure, "You're right. I've been doing the biofeedback myself, and it's working great. Really great. I can't believe it. I thought it was all a bunch of baloney, but some of this stuff really works!"

Such personal experience of therapy efficacy is tremendously valuable. It can help students understand the client's experience in treatment, and it can help build confidence in the potential for treatment to be helpful (Norcross, 2005).

Apart from personal experience, concerns about treatment efficacy can also be addressed by reviewing the research literature. Here one finds that the answer to whether therapy and counseling are really helpful is a qualified but confident yes. Although a number of methodological issues complicate research in this area, numerous reviews (Boisvert & Faust, 2003; Bovasso, Eaton, & Armenian, 1999; Crits-Christoph, 1992; Jacobson & Addis, 1993; Kazdin, 1991; Lambert, Weber, & Sykes, 1993; Lee, Picard, & Blain, 1994; Lipsey & Wilson, 1993; Roth & Fonagy, 1996; Seligman, 1995; Shadish et al., 1993; Whiston & Sexton, 1993) have concluded that for most clients, including adults, children, couples, and families, psychotherapy has positive effects and produces results superior to what would be expected if the client had not been in therapy or had received placebo treatment (for additional information, see also the special issues of *American Psychologist,* October 1996, and *Psychotherapy,* Summer 1996, which presents a superb collection of articles pertaining to treatment outcomes and research).

Summarizing the findings of numerous outcomes studies, Strupp and Binder (1992) noted, "Improvements from psychotherapy are surprisingly durable" (p. 123). Strupp and Binder went on to acknowledge that relapse will affect a percentage of patients, but said that this should not necessarily be considered a treatment failure: "It is now considered entirely reasonable for patients to seek further therapy when stresses and associated problems recur" (p. 123).

That is the good news. Now for some qualification and a few words of caution. Although research suggests that, overall, therapy has positive effects compared with control and placebo groups, it has been difficult, with the exception of certain behavioral treatments for specific anxiety disorders, to demonstrate that different therapy approaches produce markedly different outcomes (Luborsky, Singer, & Luborsky, 1975). There has also been substantial discussion about how to define and measure outcomes and how they should be compared across studies (Ankuta & Abeles, 1993; Speer, 1992).

Some years ago, Paul (1967) pointed out that we should not simply ask whether therapy in general is effective. Instead, we should ask, "What treatment, by whom, is most effective for this individual with that specific problem, and under which set of circumstances?" (p. 111).

The goal of answering these questions is certainly appealing, but as Beutler (1991) explained, the many variables involved and the research techniques and designs used thus far have made it impossible to identify the optimal combination of patient characteristics and psychotherapy approaches. As a result, to date about all that can be stated with confidence regarding therapy differences is what Whiston and Sexton (1993) concluded: "On the whole, the research indicates that no one theory is any more effective than any other. Similarly, adherence to any one theory or approach does not guarantee successful outcome" (p. 48).

Given the previously mentioned evidence that therapy, broadly defined, is generally effective, the lack of conclusive evidence that one therapy approach is necessarily superior to another need not be disheartening. It does, however, suggest that the heated arguments that sometimes arise between therapists of different schools are in most cases based on philosophical differences rather than empirical evidence.

Of greater concern than arguments over theoretical superiority is evidence that between 6% (Orlinsky & Howard, 1980) and 11% (Shapiro & Shapiro, 1982) may get worse rather than better in therapy. Strupp (1989) identified some of the factors, notably "communications that are experienced by patients as pejorative" (p. 717), that may contribute to negative outcomes. Strupp argued that therapists need to be more attentive to such factors in their practice and in training of students. This means that we must be mindful of our potential to do harm as well as good and that the effectives of our interventions will not always be in positive directions.

EVIDENCE-BASED PRACTICE AND EMPIRICALLY SUPPORTED TREATMENTS

The question of treatment efficacy has gained attention well beyond the professional community of practitioners and researchers. As health care costs have risen, there are growing and legitimate calls to constrain costs and improve the quality and outcomes of care by insisting that only empirically, evidence-based diagnoses and treatments are paid for by insurance. This increased scrutiny is coming from private insurers as well as from government entities that administer Medicare, Medicaid, and other programs.

In theory, one might assume that health care practice and social service have always been driven by research. In practice, however, there are numerous examples in which this has not been the case, and in some instances, treatments have not merely been costly and ineffective, they have been iatrogenic. On the one hand, it too often happens that treatments, diagnostic procedures, or social services are applied without sufficient empirical or clinical evidence to support their use, and in some instances in spite of evidence that would contraindicate their use. On the other hand, it also happens that treatments, diagnostic approaches, and services that have demonstrated efficacy and positive cost/benefit returns are going unused or underused either because of lack of awareness by practitioners, the inertia of existing practices and biases, or social or economic forces.

Two terms are commonly used to describe the movement to counter these problems. In the field of medicine, the term "evidence-based practice" (EBP) is predominant, while in the social sciences one also finds reference to "empirically supported treatments" (EST) (McNeil, 2006; Norcross, Beutler, & Levant, 2006; Wampold & Bhati, 2004). There are subtle differences between these terms, but whichever term is used, what is most important here is that treatment, assessment, and services in all areas of health care and social services should be driven by sound research and clinical evidence and by rigorous cost/benefit analyses.

I am introducing this concept to you early in this text and in your training because, as an intern and throughout your practice, you need to be aware of EBP and EST for a number of reasons. First, insofar as you should desire to ensure that your own treatment or assessment activities are well founded and effective, you will need to appreciate and be able to put into practice the underlying principles, terminology, research methods, and findings. Second, it is very likely that the internship setting in which you work will be coming under increasing pressure to implement and demonstrate that its interventions are evidence based and cost effective. Third, for legal reasons one is well advised to know and practice the most empirically sound methods, because, if challenged in court, one's ability to demonstrate both knowledge of and adherence to such methods affords a strong defense against liability claims. Fourth, professional associations are weighing in heavily on this matter and establishing official policies and guidelines. For example, the CACREP 2008 draft guidelines for accreditation of counseling programs incorporate evidence-based standards throughout their practice-training guidelines (CACREP, http://www.cacrep.org/StandardsRevisionText.html). So too, the APA Presidential Task Force (2006) has issued an official paper on issues relating to evidence-based practice. Finally, as someone who pays taxes and insurance premiums yourself, you should know how these issues may impact the costs of your own insurance or care and the kinds of treatments you receive.

The key concepts and possible limitations of EBP in the context of social work are described well by Edmond et al. (2006), McNeill (2006), and Gilgun (2005), who identified four "cornerstones" of EBP: knowledge from research and theory; "practice wisdom" including knowledge gained from clients and experience; the personal experience of the provider; and the knowledge, information, and experience clients bring to the situation. Gilgun emphasized that in addition to considering research findings, it is important in the human service professions to incorporate unique patient values and provider qualities, elements not so easily incorporated into empirical research. McNeill (2006), in particular, also stressed the role of clinical judgment, while Nelson and Steele (2006) emphasized the importance of looking at factors other than just treatment outcome, including economic considerations as well as patient and provider preferences.

McCabe (2004) approached the same issues from the perspective of psychology and offered an especially informative discussion that includes, in addition to a comprehensive Internet reference list and useful appendix of key terms and concepts, practical suggestions for incorporating EBPs into clinical practice and settings. McCabe also discussed some of the limitations of the EST/EBP approach as applied to mental health and social services. Similar concerns about the unique applications of EST/EBP approaches to mental health care were identified by the APA task force on evidence-based practice (2006), and were discussed by Norcross, Beutler, and Levant (2006).

For an informative resource on EBP in counseling, see the Web site of the Evidence-Based Practice Panel at the Center for School Counseling Outcome Research (http://www.umass.edu/schoolcounseling/EvidenceBasedPanel.htm). Further evidence of the increasing importance of the EBP/EST movement is seen in the growing number of professional journals and online resources dedicated to the topic. Examples include "Evidence-Based Medicine" (http://ebm.bmjjournals.com/), and the *Journal of Evidence-Based Social Work*.

Just as professional associations and practitioners are giving increasing attention to evidence-based practice, so too are government agencies. For example, the National Institute of Mental Health (NIMH) http://www.nimh.nih.gov/, along with the Substance Abuse and Mental Health Services Administration (SAMHSA) http://www.samhsa.gov/, have established programs and grants to help implement evidence-based practices within state mental health and substance abuse treatment programs (http://grants2.nih.gov/grants/guide/rfa-files/RFA-MH-03-007.html). Elsewhere in the government, the federal Agency for Healthcare Research and Quality (AHRQ) of the United States Department of Health and Human Services has developed a network of "Evidence-based Practice Centers" (http://www.ahrq.gov/clinic/epc/) in health care centers across the nation. The mission of these centers is to "develop evidence reports and technology assessments on topics relevant to clinical, social science/behavioral, economic, and other health care organization and delivery issues—specifically those that are common, expensive, and/or significant for the Medicare and Medicaid populations." (ibid.). Examples of the work of one such center, located at the Oregon Health Science University, can be found at (http://www.ohsu.edu/epc/usptf/index.htm).

Perhaps the most important lesson for you to understand as an intern is that, across all disciplines in mental health and social services, there is growing attention to basing practice on research and paying close attention to issues of costs and benefits in everything we do. In your training now and later in your professional work, I strongly encourage you to at all times have certain questions somewhere in your mind: What is the clinical and research evidence behind doing what we are doing in the way we are doing it with this particular patient in this particular situation? What other options are we not using, and have we considered them carefully? How can we evaluate, either through formal empirical studies or careful, critical clinical examination, the efficacy of what we are doing? What are the total costs of this treatment relative to the likely benefits, and how do the costs and benefits compare to other options? Finally, as will be discussed in the next section, it is always worth asking, What are the risks and possible harm of doing what we are doing with this particular patient in this situation? Have we carefully and critically evaluated the possibility that we may be doing more harm than good?

All of the questions just described are not simply things you should ask yourself, they are also legitimate topics for discussion with your internship supervisor and instructor. If you ask these questions, be aware that in many instances there may not be fully satisfactory answers. In part, this is inherent in the nature of the work we do, and in part it is simply a reflection of the limitations of human knowledge in all fields, It may also happen that you will ask these kinds of questions of individuals or in settings where an empirical, evidence-based approach to practice is not a core value. Sometimes the answer you will be given to a question may simply be, "Because that's how we've always done it." Other times there may be references to personal clinical experience, a particular theoretical orientation, or "expert knowledge" without other substantiation or empirical evidence.

Should this happen, it does not mean that the questions are not legitimate or that you cannot learn from the setting or individuals. It may, however, mean that you will want to explore answers yourself beyond the responses you are given by others. Do not be disappointed or discouraged by this. In fact, it is the reality of how one learns as a professional. There often is no one right answer, but by asking questions, gathering information and ideas from multiple sources, carefully reviewing the literature, and keeping a critical, questioning attitude not only about what others do and say but about what you do and say yourself, you will gradually grow in your understanding and skill and will be less likely to make errors of either commission or omission.

INOCULATION: WHAT NOT TO LEARN

While evidence-based practice may represent the kinds of knowledge and skills you hope to acquire during your internship, you may also be exposed to some things you should not learn. Throughout this book, you will be encouraged to be open to learning, but that does not mean you must uncritically model everything you observe or accept everything you are told as truth. I raise this point now because interns sometimes begin to model behaviors that are not necessarily worthy of emulating. Modeling and listening are wonderful ways to learn, but it behooves you to be aware and thoughtful about the behaviors you observe or the information you receive.

For example, in some placement sites staff members constantly express negative attitudes toward clients. They may display this through a hostile tone of voice, derogatory statements, mean-spirited jokes, or in other overt or subtle ways. Interns who observe this attitude may not feel comfortable with it at first; but if the atmosphere of a setting and the behavior of the staff set an example of negativity, it is easy for the intern to adopt similar attitudes and behaviors, often without even realizing what is happening. I have observed interns who began with positive, idealistic feelings begin to shift toward negativity and hostility within just a few weeks at a placement. When I point this out, the interns are often surprised and somewhat ashamed of themselves, but most are glad to have the feedback and to understand what they have modeled and why.

Similar issues were voiced by Gross (2005), who solicited student perceptions of their practicum experiences and, in addition to many positive reports, also discovered a number of concerns. These included the presence of negative attitudes of staff toward patients, poor treatment quality, unmotivated staff, cultural insensitivity, inefficient procedures, dysfunctional organizational culture, and violations of ethical strictures on confidentiality and boundaries. Unfortunately, Gross reported, many of the students who had these concerns did not share them with their placement site or their supervisor or academic instructor because there was no established mechanism to do so or because they did not feel safe in doing so. Gross believes these issues must be better addressed and recommends that field training sites and academic institutions review their own mechanisms that allow or discourage critical and constructive feedback from interns. It is easy for faculty or supervisors to become accustomed to certain conditions or overlook legitimate concerns, but interns can bring fresh eyes to a setting, and the feedback they can offer needs to be received.

In addition to actions or conditions that might be easily recognized as negative or ineffective, interns may also be exposed to, and tempted to model, more subtle but nevertheless counterproductive behaviors. In most institutions, for example, it is common for staff to use jargon—"stock" words or phrases—when speaking to or about clients. A pet peeve of mine is the word *inappropriate*. This is probably the most overused word in all the helping professions: In response to a client's statement or action, a staff member might say, "Tim, that is inappropriate," or a therapist might write a note that says, "Tim acted very inappropriately in group today." I recently attended a conference in which a speaker used the words *appropriate* or *inappropriate* more than 20 times in a five-minute presentation. Interns observe this usage and quickly incorporate it into their own vocabulary. Unfortunately, more often than not the word *inappropriate* is used in counter-therapeutic ways (i.e., the term blocks rather than enhances intern and client understanding and growth). As a result, interns who model the use of the word *inappropriate* are learning a behavior that will inhibit rather than enhance their therapeutic development.

When I introduce this example into discussions with interns (and sometimes supervisors) who are already working in the field, many protest that they and the rest of the staff use the word *inappropriate* all the time, and they do not perceive anything wrong with it. Others argue that it is just a word, and I am making too much out of it. In response, I offer two observations. First, the fact that interns have so quickly adopted this jargon and, perhaps more important, accepted the term is evidence of just what I have been saying about how people model unconsciously and why it is important to be careful with what one models. Second, as for the word *inappropriate* per se, I find it useful to ask interns what they mean when they say "inappropriate." Most interns initially have great difficulty defining their meaning without resorting to the tautology of using the term to define itself. When they begin to work toward a definition, it becomes apparent that the meaning depends on the situation. It is also evident that, in general, the word is used broadly to express generic staff displeasure or disapproval of a client's behavior.

In place of saying "inappropriate," I suggest that professionals and clients can benefit by confronting more specifically the real issues in a given situation. For example, suppose a client told a staff member that he thought the staff member was ugly. Instead of saying, "Tim, that is inappropriate," the staff member might respond by saying, "It hurts my feelings when you say that," or "You sound angry today. Shall we talk about what is going on?" The first response, "That's inappropriate," does not tell the client what is inappropriate, why it is inappropriate, or what *inappropriate* means. By comparison, the alternatives give specific information about the effects of the statement or about possible motives behind the statement. "That's inappropriate" might "shut the client up," but it is much less likely to promote a genuinely therapeutic interaction. Formulating an alternative response requires more effort and insight from the staff, but compared with a meaningless reflex response it is much more likely to be therapeutic.

Misuse of the term *inappropriate* is but one example of how interns model behaviors without thinking about their purpose or why they are modeling them. Other terms or phrases that are used excessively and imprecisely include *manipulative, denial, acting out, resistant, doing it to get attention,* and certain diagnostic categories that come in or out of vogue. If you are attentive, you will no doubt encounter others along the way.

This is not to say that these words should never be used or that their mere utterance will be damaging to clients. Words, however, are among the primary tools of treatment and are how we communicate our assessment results. Therefore, it is vital that interns learn to use them thoughtfully. My goal here is to inoculate interns against uncritical acceptance of words, behaviors, or attitudes that would inhibit their development. The thing that is most crucial to avoid is not some specific word or action; it is the tendency of all of us to imitate behavior, accept information, or adopt attitudes without thinking for ourselves about what we are doing. Beginning with your internship and throughout your career, you should think about everything you do and observe. You should ask questions and seek explanations. If done politely, this can be a valuable learning experience not only for you but also for staff, many of whom may not have thought carefully about the issues themselves. Thus, as you begin your internship and for the remainder of yor professional career, strive to think carefully about what you observe, avoid

preconceptions, and be open to learning. In the end, the ability to think critically and wisely is the most important thing you can gain from any internship experience.

INTERNSHIP CLASSES AND PEER GROUPS

Internships can be tremendous learning opportunities, but they can also feel pretty lonely if you are not connected to others having similar experiences. If an internship class or peer group is part of your program, you have the chance to learn from the experiences of your peers as well as from your own internship. Classes and peer groups provide a place for you to try out skills during the normal course of discussion and through activities such as role-plays and self-exploration (Sklare, Thomas, Williams, & Powers, 1996). Internship classes and groups also give peers a chance to share in the excitement of discovery and success or offer a much-needed emotional support when the internship experience feels uncomfortable or confusing (Hayes, 1990).

This section describes some common activities and necessary ingredients for successful internship classes and peer groups. If you are part of an established class or group for interns, your instructor may address many of the topics discussed in this chapter. If classes or groups are not established at your internship, you may want to consider organizing peer study groups on your own.

FORMING INTERNSHIP PEER GROUPS

A distinction should first be made between peer study or support groups and the friendly gatherings that take place apart from work or school. For example, interns might get together informally as a group to go canoeing or bicycling after work or classes. Others might see films together every weekend or perhaps someone might organize monthly potlucks. Although these get-togethers are important, they differ from peer learning groups. To focus on peer learning and support, you need a structure and setting that are conducive to that work.

In settings where there are many interns from the same discipline and perhaps even from the same school, it is usually simple to form a peer group. You just talk with your peers, see if they are interested in getting together, and find a convenient time and place to meet. Because peer groups are so important, I encourage interns to ask their supervisor to allow time and a location where interns can meet during the regular working hours as part of their training. Most internships are happy to support such requests.

If you are at an internship site where there are few or no other interns, or where there are no other interns from your discipline, forming a peer group may be more difficult. Under such circumstances, you may need to expand your horizons and speak with students from other disciplines or who are doing internships at other placements. Although this requires more effort, meeting with interns from other disciplines or settings has advantages. These students will bring perspectives and information that you may not have been exposed to in your own training. Similarly, interns working in other placements may have experience working with completely different clients or treatment approaches than are found at your placement. Interacting with one another can expand everyone's awareness and bring valuable insights that might not come from a more homogeneous peer group.

MODELS OF PEER GROUP LEARNING

Several models have been proposed for peer group learning and peer supervision (Sklare et al., 1996). Benshoff (1993) developed an approach to peer supervision that combines goal setting, journal article discussion, reviews of taped therapy sessions, case presentations, and evaluation and termination discussion. In studies of the effectiveness of this approach, Benshoff found that the vast majority of students rated the experience of peer supervision positively and felt that they had gained useful input and information from the process. Subjects reported that the peer supervision felt more relaxed than more traditional supervision, and they appreciated the feeling of being free from grading or other evaluation by supervisors.

In a somewhat similar model described by Borders (1991), individual interns or counselors take turns receiving assistance from their peer group. In this peer learning approach, the interns seeking assistance first specify questions they would like addressed and the kinds of feedback they are seeking. They then present a taped therapy session or a description of a case. As they listen to the case, peers in the group take different roles or focus on specific aspects of the interaction. For example, one person might focus on the nonverbal behavior of the therapist or client. Another might listen for the sequence of the content addressed. Group members might also be invited to view the session from different roles. These roles might include the client, therapist, or significant people in the client's life. Another approach to the case would be for members to listen from different theoretical perspectives. Some members might approach the case from a behavioral perspective, others from a psychodynamic model, and still others from a cognitive framework.

Borders pointed out that the focus, roles, or theoretical perspectives assigned to or chosen for group members provide instructional experiences for the group as well as for the person receiving the supervision. Interns who need to develop greater nonverbal awareness can be assigned to focus on this element of the interaction, while those who are learning about a certain theoretical model can apply that model as they view the case. Borders also noted that because the role of observer relieves the stress experienced as a therapist, trainees are often able to notice things or display skills as observers that they have not yet manifested when they are in the therapy role themselves.

When the tape or description of the case concludes, peers give feedback based on the initial questions posed and the roles or perspective each individual assumed while the case was presented. As peers give feedback, the supervisor or another group member monitors the feedback to note any patterns that emerge and to observe the process of the group. The individual receiving the feedback can ask questions of the observers and is invited to reflect on how the feedback has or has not helped address the questions raised at the outset of the session.

Many of the elements described by Benshoff and Borders are also found in a model developed by Wilbur, Roberts-Wilbur, Morris, Betz, and Hart (1991). Their Structured Group Supervision (SGS) model includes five phases: the Request-for-Assistance Statement, the Questioning Period and Identification of Focus, the Feedback Statements, a Pause Period, the Supervisee Response, and finally an Optional Discussion Period. Wilbur and colleagues noted that during the request for assistance, the supervisee may seek assistance with technical skills, personal growth, or integrating aspects of the therapy process. During the questioning period, group members use a round-robin technique, taking turns, with each member asking one question of the supervisee. Depending on the nature and focus of the initial request for assistance, the group members ask questions that tend to focus on what Wilbur and coworkers described as "skill-development and task-process," "personal growth and psycho-process," or "socio-process." These different foci are also referred to as "extra-, intra-, or interpersonal," respectively.

Following the questioning, group members offer feedback relating to the initial request for assistance. The supervisee can take notes during this feedback but is asked to remain silent and not respond to the feedback. Wilbur et al. pointed out that this reduces the common "Yes, but . . ." or "I have tried that already" types of responses that supervisees often give to feedback. Group members are encouraged to offer feedback in the form of statements such as "If this were my client . . . ," or, "If I were in your situation . . ."

Perhaps the most unique feature of the SGS model is the "pause period" that follows the feedback statements. It was noted that during the feedback the supervisee can take notes but is not allowed to respond verbally. Following the feedback, there is a period of 10 to 15 minutes during which the supervisee is invited to think about the feedback but is not allowed to discuss the case further with group members. Group members may take a brief break to have coffee or interact with one another, but the supervisee's task is to reflect on the feedback.

In my experience, the concept of structuring a time for reflection is particularly valuable. The overriding U.S. and Canadian cultures, and academia in particular, place a premium on quick responses and give relatively little value to thoughtful reflection. Yet instantaneous responses make it difficult for recipients of feedback to fully explore what they have heard or how they are reacting to the feedback. Quick responses also tend to go hand in hand with defensiveness rather than open receiving of feedback. By structuring time for thought, supervisees are encouraged to give deeper attention and consideration to the feedback they have received. This is likely to lead to more effective learning, and it models the importance of careful thought and time in the therapy process.

When sufficient time has elapsed for a period of reflection, the group gets back together, and the supervisee responds to the feedback he or she has received. This may include sharing of new insights, identification of what feedback seemed particularly helpful and why, or any other comments the supervisee wants to make. If time allows, the supervisee's response can be followed by open discussion.

ELEMENTS OF SUCCESSFUL CLASSES AND GROUPS

To be most effective, classes or peer groups need to include many of the same elements that are essential to effective therapy or counseling. Trust, support, openness, honest feedback, safety, and willingness to explore and experiment are all ingredients of successful groups. Peer support is also vital and is often cited by our interns as the single most important element of internship classes.

Internship classes are enhanced when students and instructors remember to intentionally address and promote a positive, supportive atmosphere within the group. One way to do this is by talking about the topic directly within the class. Interns are asked to share how they think the class is going and how they feel about working together and to express any desires or concerns they might have for the class. As you work with your internship class or peer group, you may find it helpful to ask yourself and your group some of the same questions. The following exercise is designed to assist in that process.

EXERCISE

As a beginning toward developing a caring class or peer group, each intern should explore several questions:

1. Am I willing to take some risks myself, ask for help, and be open about my questions, areas of competence, and feelings of inadequacy?
2. Am I willing and able to empathize with and support my peers as they deal with difficulties in their internship and in the class?
3. Am I willing and able to empathize with and support my peers as they deal with success and accomplishments in their internship and in the class?
4. As I imagine it and as I demonstrate it in my behavior, what is my goal in this class? Am I seeking to learn and help others learn, or am I (a) just trying to get the grade or (b) trying to improve my status by showing what a good clinician I am? What is my real goal in this class?
5. Do I realize that it often seems easier to understand what is happening from the outside looking in? This means that we must be gentle with ourselves when someone else points

out something we have overlooked. We must also be gentle with our peers if we recognize something in their work that they have been overlooking.
6. When I have something to ask or say to another student, do I act on it, or am I passive and quiet? If I do act, is it in a way that conveys respect and empathy? If I do not speak up, is it because of my own characteristics or because I have determined in this instance that my input or questions are not necessary at this time?

OFFERING FEEDBACK TO PEERS

As part of an internship class or study group, you will be involved in a give-and-take of ideas, observations, and suggestions. For this process to be most effective, it is helpful to keep in mind certain guidelines for giving and receiving feedback. Kadushin and Harkness (2002) offered guidelines for supervisors to use in giving feedback to supervisees. These guidelines are just as valid for peer-to-peer feedback and include such principles as the importance of offering feedback soon after an action, giving specific rather than vague feedback, focusing on concrete, objective behaviors, keeping feedback descriptive rather than judgmental, focusing on behaviors rather than personal qualities of the person receiving the feedback, and offering feedback in the form of tentative statements instead of authoritative conclusions or directions. Kadushin and Harkness also stressed the importance of positive feedback and of considering feedback as part of an idea-sharing rather than advice-giving, process. Finally, Kadushin and Harkness remind us that feedback must be selective and not overwhelm the recipient by its amount or nature. Similar recommendations were offered by Woit and Brownlee (1995) in their description of "reflecting teams" as a clinical tool and as a classroom learning activity.

Emerson (1995) concurs with these suggestions but advises against giving what she calls "yearbook feedback" to peers. General, vague, and uncritically positive comments may feel good to give and receive, but they provide little educational or learning benefit. Emerson notes that although specific and sometimes critical feedback may be more challenging, in the long run it can lead to increased learning and deeper group cohesiveness if delivered and received well.

Whenever one offers feedback about a case, and particularly when students offer suggestions for peers, it is important to remember that the role of outside observer is much easier than the role of therapist. Observations that might seem obvious to an outsider may be difficult to recognize or accept when one is directly involved in the complex role of treatment provider (Borders, 1991). Thus, peers should not let themselves become overly confident or feel superior to one another if it happens that one person recognizes something about a case that others did not.

While it may be easier to be in the role of observer than therapist, peers should keep in mind that whatever impressions they might draw from a case description or tape, there will always be many things they do not know about the history of the case or the interaction between the therapist and client. This suggests another reason to avoid becoming overly confident as an observer. It is entirely possible that overconfidence is based not on an accurate impression but on misunderstanding the case.

Consistent with the principles of the two preceding paragraphs and with the suggestions of Kadushin and Harkness, it is a good idea for interns to offer feedback to one another with a degree of "intentional tentativeness" rather than as conclusive statements. Instead of saying "This client is clearly manipulating you!" or "At that point you should have asked him to . . . ," peers might try, "As I watched the tape I got a feeling the client was trying to get your approval or permission. Did you have that feeling too, or is something else happening?" or, "I wonder what might have happened if you had asked the client to . . ."

Phrasing feedback in this way respects the difference between observer and therapist and does not imply that the observer has all the answers. Not only is this practice useful in peer feedback, it is also a valuable technique in therapy. Just as observers of therapy can mistakenly think they have the answers for their peers, therapists sometimes think they have the answers for their clients. Tentative phrasing can help reduce resistance and encourage clients to explore possibilities.

THE IMPORTANCE OF EMPATHY

In many instances, the most helpful response interns can give one another is empathic understanding. On numerous occasions, I have observed interns being overwhelmed by suggestions from instructor and peers. Often, what the intern needed most was for a peer to acknowledge how tough the case was and how frustrated, sad, or angry the intern must have felt. This is so important that, before offering suggestions or feedback about a case, interns are well advised to ask themselves if they really understand how their peer is feeling and what he or she needs most at the moment.

Empathy and support are also important because as we go through internships or other learning experiences, the rest of our lives are going on as well. This means that you and your peers, in addition to the responsibilities of school and your internship, may also be dealing with everything from the illness or death of loved ones to sorting out romantic relationships. Depending on how they are dealt with, these personal life events can interact positively or negatively with your academic and internship training experiences. This was pointed out by Furr and Carroll (2003), who studied "critical incidents" in the development of student counselors and found that students often cited events occurring outside the training program as having the most impact on their personal growth. Furr and Carroll also noted an intriguing synergy in which insights and knowledge gained as part of internship training impacted the personal lives of interns, and, in turn, events in personal lives influenced the internship training. Again, if handled well, this synergy can be tremendously productive and helpful in both spheres of life.

When an intern needs empathy and support, the relief that comes when a peer provides them is almost palpable. It is sometimes as if a great weight has been removed from the intern, and he or she is at last able to breathe again. By comparison, until the empathic connection has been made in a group, all the well-intentioned technical suggestions, no matter how valid, are likely to be of little benefit. Interns are in a unique position to provide empathic understanding and support to one another because they are most closely in a position to feel what their peers are experiencing both within the internship training and in life outside. Instructors and supervisors easily get caught up in the theoretical or technical aspects of a case and may forget to attend to the intern's affective needs. By remembering to attend to empathy, peers can meet an essential need for one another and in the process can both practice and directly observe the effects of this key therapy skill. More will be said about dealing constructively with the stresses of training and life in Chapter 7.

RECEIVING FEEDBACK

Along with considering ways to give feedback, it is equally important to think about how one receives feedback. The first thing to understand is that receiving feedback is not easy. This awareness will help you better understand your own experience at receiving feedback from supervisors or peers. It can also help you appreciate some of what clients experience in therapy.

Whenever you expose yourself to feedback from others, you make yourself vulnerable. You run the risk of revealing weaknesses, errors, or personal qualities that you might wish others were unaware of or at least would not comment on. As an intern in the helping professions, the stakes are even higher because you have been charged with the responsibility for helping others. This makes it easy to feel that perceived mistakes, failures, or shortcomings mean you have somehow let down or perhaps even harmed the clients who have come to you for help.

The matter is complicated still further because therapy involves using the therapist's self, or at least the presentation of self, as part of the healing process. As a result, even the most well-intentioned suggestions or feedback can easily be experienced as intimations or outright assertions that there is something amiss with one's presentation of self. That is seldom easy to cope with, but it is part of the learning process. It is also part of what clients experience whenever they come to therapy and must explore who they are.

ACKNOWLEDGING IMPERFECTION

To help interns accept feedback from peers and supervisors, it is useful to remind and give permission to be something other than perfect and flawless. Although interns should do their best, that does not mean they can never make mistakes. Therapists and interns are only human, and part of learning is that there will be some things you do not know.

If you do not feel you have to be or appear perfect, it is easier to accept the possibility that others can offer suggestions or observations that will help you improve. I encourage interns to experiment with an attitude that says: "I hope others will recognize some things I do well, but I also hope they will recognize some things I am not doing as well as I could. If people identify my mistakes, that will help me learn, and I am grateful to them." If interns approach learning with this attitude, they are much more likely to be open to suggestions from others. They are also more likely to receive helpful suggestions, because people will recognize that suggestions are welcome.

Most students have not been taught to hope that others will recognize their weaknesses. The alternative, however, is actually absurd. Being in school or internship training includes the assumption that one has not yet mastered a body of knowledge or skill. Therefore, the best way to learn is to identify areas of deficiency and seek to remediate them. If one seeks to hide those areas, how can growth and learning in those areas occur?

The best thing that can happen to you as an intern or student is to discover what you do not know or what you think you know or understand but in fact do not. If this sounds strange, ask yourself whether you would rather go on to practice without knowing that you lack certain information or misunderstand key concepts.

One way to put this attitude into practice is to develop the habit of thanking people whenever they offer suggestions, corrections, or constructive criticism. I know a person who travels around the world and speaks several languages with fluency that most people would envy. Despite his proficiency, he makes a point of asking people who speak the language as their native tongue to correct him whenever he makes a mistake. My friend explains his approach this way:

> I know it might seem impolite to correct me, and of course I appreciate compliments, but for me the sign of true friendship is when someone cares enough to correct my mistakes. That is the only way I can learn, and I'd rather be corrected than go around thinking I'm speaking properly when I'm really making some glaring mistake.

My friend is quite sincere about this, and he always makes a point of acknowledging his appreciation and thanking people when they offer corrections. That attitude is probably why he speaks so many languages so well. By acknowledging mistakes and being open to feedback, he lets everyone become a teacher, and he is able to learn much more rapidly than people who fear mistakes and do not accept suggestions.

VIDEO OR AUDIO RECORDINGS OF SESSIONS

In the models described earlier by Borders and by Wilbur and colleagues, group case discussions often center around audio- or videotapes of therapy sessions. Because these media enable the supervisor and class to observe the actual clients and treatment interactions, they can be extremely valuable tools for clin-

ical training (Romans, Boswell, Carlozzi, & Ferguson, 1995). If you can incorporate taped sessions in your training, several suggestions may be helpful.

A question that often arises is which part of the session to review in class or supervision. Because time limitations generally prohibit reviews of entire treatment sessions, it is necessary to select portions of the session for presentation. This poses an interesting paradox. Most interns want to present a positive impression of their clinical skills and work, so there is a temptation to choose only those points in a session where one feels particularly confident in one's work. Friedman and Kaslow (1986) noted that beginning therapists may not fully share their work with supervisors or others because they fear looking silly or incompetent.

Though understandable, this is not necessarily the best way to learn. As an alternative, interns might choose to pick a few sections where they feel they were doing their best work (it is perfectly valid and important to want and receive some positive strokes) and a few other sections where they felt lost, confused, overwhelmed, on the spot, tense, or frightened. One intern took this suggestion to heart and had the courage to bring in a tape in which the client actually fell asleep during a session. For several minutes, the tape consisted only of the client's snoring. Sharing this with the internship class and supervisor took courage on the part of the intern, but it took even more to then play another portion of the tape and reveal that for a few minutes there were two people, the client and the intern, snoring. (This really happened.) In your own work, you will probably not have an experience exactly like this, but you will feel sleepy at times, and you will undoubtedly say and do things that you will immediately wish you could take back or try again. Do not be ashamed to acknowledge such mistakes or to share them with your peers so that you and they can learn from the experience.

As you listen to tapes of your sessions or those of peers, you may find it interesting to attend to the tapes in various ways. When most beginning interns observe or listen to therapy sessions, they focus primarily on the words people say to each other. This focus is consistent with how people interact during ordinary conversations, but one of the lessons of therapy is that the content (the words) of an interaction often carries far less information than the process (the way the words are said, the position of the speakers, the sequence of the overall interaction, and a host of other nonverbal elements). When you participate, listen to tapes of sessions, and as you work in actual therapy interactions, learn to receive other elements than the words alone.

EXERCISE

I learned this exercise during a supervision workshop presented by Jesse Geller. The exercise involves listening several times to a brief taped portion of a therapy session. The first time through, simply play the tape and listen to it with no specific instructions. Then play the tape again, but focus very carefully on the words the participants use as they interact. Next, listen to the tape a third time, but this time focus on receiving not the words but the affect—the emotional messages and experiences of the participants. What do you experience as you receive with your attention focused on different elements of the interaction? Most people report that they get something different out of the interaction each time through. Moreover, in the third listening, in which the focus is on affect rather than words, people usually feel they begin to understand the client in a different way than before.

The preceding exercise introduced you to the experience of receiving elements of an interaction other than words. In this case, the focus was on affect, but it would also have been possible to emphasize such things as rate of speech, length of pauses, or tone of voice. A similar process was described by Latz (1996), who separated the video and audio portions of therapy sessions as a way of teaching family therapists to focus on subtle verbal and nonverbal communications in therapy.

ROLE-PLAYS

An alternative to working with recorded therapy sessions is to enact therapy sessions within the group (Akamatsu, 1980). Because role-plays may be a new experience, it may help to have a brief introduction about their purpose and function and how to make the most of them. Students who are interested in learning more about role-plays as part of the therapy process may wish to consult writings on the subject of psychodrama or Gestalt therapy techniques.

Role-plays involve class members taking the roles of clients, trainees, or other staff members and acting these roles as they portray a situation or interaction of interest. Role-plays can be particularly helpful in developing basic helping skills and in learning to deal with difficult clients or staff. Role-plays can also help interns become more aware of their therapeutic style and, in some instances, of significant issues in their own lives. Field instructors can also use role-plays to learn about issues and techniques of supervision. Cohen and Ruff (1995) described five role-play scenarios and offered suggestions for accompanying discussion.

Role-plays are most productive when participants are aware of several principles. First, the goal of the role-play is not necessarily to provide an exact replication of the real situation or people. While realism may be useful, role-plays also exist as experiences in themselves and need not be perfectly accurate for learning to occur. Indeed, there are times when the deviation from reality provides important clinical insights about what is happening and how things might change. Thus, although several of the following suggestions offer hints about how to enhance the realism of role-plays, keep in mind that realism is not the primary goal; experiencing, understanding, and learning are the goals that matter.

A second key to successful role-plays is for the people involved to not just imagine or act their role, but temporarily to "become" the person they are portraying. Role-players should not just talk about what they are doing. They should try to get out of their own mind, feeling, and behavioral set and into that of the person they portray. Feel what that person feels, hold or move your body as that person might, use the tone and volume of voice that person might use. Experience what life has been like for the person you are playing. Experience what this moment and interaction mean for that person and how his or her body feels.

"Becoming someone else" not only facilitates role-plays; it is also an excellent way to develop or enhance empathy. By trying to get inside someone else's skin, we gain understanding at a much deeper level than if we merely discuss the person as some abstract object of clinical interest. This was brought home to me when I worked with a man in his late 30s who had lost both arms and hands below the elbow. To increase my awareness of what life was like for this man, my supervisor induced a light hypnotic trance, suggested that I too had lost my arms and hands, then created images of otherwise mundane activities, such as opening doors, dressing, shaking hands, and going to the bathroom. The images progressed from these activities to the more profound awareness of wanting to hug a child, caress a lover, wipe away a tear. The point of the exercise was not to evoke pity for the client. Rather, it was to help me get some sense of an important aspect of the client's life that I had never experienced myself.

In some form, this kind of learning experience applies to all our interactions with clients. We have never experienced exactly what another person has, yet we must try to get a sense of what it is like to be that person. In your role-plays, do your best to make this happen. As you do your best to portray an individual in a role-play, it is also important to be open to suggestions about how to adjust your actions to more closely approximate the person you are representing. If you are unsure of how to play a role, ask for suggestions. Similarly, if you are directing a role-play, you may need to give feedback to your players about how they need to act, move, and speak. For example, if two students who are good friends are trying to role-play a relationship between people who despise each other, it may help to suggest that the friends not think about each other as friends but instead try to imagine someone else whom they detest. I once observed an instructor deal with a similar situation by asking the students in the role-play to think of a time when they had been sick to their stomach and at the point of vomiting. When this image was so real, the students were almost sick themselves, the instructor said, "Okay, now imagine that you feel that way whenever you are around this other person."

Suggestions for images and deep involvement in characters can enhance the accuracy and benefits of role-plays, but there will probably be times when you find it almost impossible to portray certain clients or situations. During role-plays, it sometimes happens that interns who normally do very well in such exercises suddenly find they are blocked and cannot act like the person or cannot play a certain kind of behavior.

This may be experienced as an inability to understand the character intellectually or as feeling a strong emotional reaction to the role.

Such experiences can lead to valuable insights for the participants. When a person who is otherwise skilled at role-plays is suddenly unable to portray a role or situation, this may be a clue that some unresolved issues are being touched. The exact issues may be unclear from the immediate experience, but it is a good sign that something important has been evoked and is worth exploring further. If you experience this kind of reaction, ask yourself if one of the characters, the situation, or the setting of the role-play is somehow reminiscent of an experience or person in your own life. Is it difficult for you now to portray anything about a person, or are there only certain qualities that you are blocking on or feeling troubled about?

Through awareness of your own experiences in role-plays, and by pursuing and trying to understand your reactions, you may learn more about yourself than about the specific situation or client that stimulated the role-play. This can be very beneficial. If there was something in your own life that needed to be dealt with and that was related to the client's issues, your own issues might block not only the role-play but also the work with the client. Experienced psychodramatists have observed that as people deal more effectively with underlying issues, their ability to portray the related roles also improves. Thus, just as the initial difficulty may be an index of underlying issues, changes in your role-playing can be an indication of progress in your self-awareness. As you become more aware of and able to deal with your own issues, your ability to interact therapeutically with clients is also likely to improve.

A final suggestion about role-plays is that, as a general rule, role-plays are more useful when not interrupted by frequent discussions or commentary. If you are involved in a role-play, it will probably work best if you get into the role, stay with it, and see what happens. Try not to stop and ask for guidance or talk about the role. If you find yourself frequently interrupting the role, that could be a sign, as was just discussed, of some issues in your own life. On the other hand, many interns interrupt role-plays because they are most accustomed to learning by talking "about" a subject, not by trying to experience something. After the role-play, it is useful to discuss what you experienced or observed, but during the role-play be very careful not to substitute intellectualization for experience.

INTRODUCTION TO JOURNAL WORK

To conclude this chapter, let me encourage you to begin using two tools that can be tremendously beneficial pedagogically and for personal and professional development. The first tool is a personal journal, the second is a professional portfolio.

Consistent with the emphasis in this book on active learning and self-reflection, personal journal work can be an exceptionally valuable part of your internship experience. Effective journal use takes time, but journals that are done well provide a unique and valuable form of learning.

Many students and instructors who use journals do not make the most of the process because they are not clear about what should go into a journal or why. To make the most of journal work you should use a journal to (1) record experiences at your internship, (2) reflect on your experiences to better understand your emotional reactions, thoughts about clients, impressions of treatment, and so on, (3) make notes about questions, ideas, or discoveries that you wish to discuss or study further, and (4) complete exercises presented throughout this text.

A RECORD OF EXPERIENCES, REACTIONS, AND THOUGHTS

I recommend that you make a journal entry for every day at your internship. Begin by listing the day, the date, and the hours you were at the internship. The entry should then list and briefly describe your major activities at the internship that day. A chronological format is convenient: note the activities, clients, and staff you worked with and any other salient information for the day. Remember confidentiality issues as you write in your journal. As discussed in Chapter 3, it is good practice to use generic terms or single-letter abbreviations, rather than names, to signify clients. Here is an example of a journal entry of this type:

Thursday, April 21, 2001, 10:00 A.M.–2:00 P.M.

10:00–10:30. Met with Rachel (Supervisor) and followed up on yesterday's group. Agreed that J. and R. had dominated group. B. was distracted by something, but we do not know what. We will discuss these observations in tomorrow's group. Also spoke with Rachel about plans to be at conference next Friday. She approved of my absence. In staff meeting the following Wednesday, I will report back to staff about the conference.

10:30–12:00. Participated in recreation activities with clients under supervision of Robert Jones, Rec Therapist. Played softball at Jefferson Park. Close game; clients seemed to enjoy it.

12:00–1:00. Lunch in dining room. Ate with two clients I had not met before, A. and N. Today was A.'s first day, and she was nervous but seemed to be coping. N. has been here three weeks. He is looking forward to visit from his family this weekend.

1:00–2:00. Administered and scored the Beck Depression Inventory for F. Discussed results with supervisor and with F. Wrote brief summary for patient records.

In addition to journal entries describing events of the day, you should also establish a record in which you keep a running total of the number of hours spent in different activities, such as milieu observation, assessment, therapy, and case conferences.

If you conduct intake interviews, write case reports, or perform psychological assessments, maintain a count of these, including specific information about which tests were given, interpreted, and/or scored by you.

Recording your experiences in the internship serves several purposes. This documentation of your activities can keep your supervisor or instructor apprised of what you are doing. Your journal record also will be useful later on when you seek employment and need to indicate your experience in various clinical activities. The record in which you document numbers of interviews, therapy sessions, and assessments, and so on, will be especially useful for this purpose. Such information is often requested for graduate-level internships, and in many states it is required as part of the professional licensing process.

Along with serving as a record of what you have done, the process of keeping regular journal entries helps to establish a habit of record keeping. Accurate and current records are essential to responsible clinical practice, but record keeping is often neglected (Kagle, 1993). By getting into the habit of keeping records each day, you are less likely to develop poor record-keeping practices later on. To serve this function and maintain accuracy, you must avoid the common intern strategy of neglecting the journal until the end of the term and then trying to fill it in by memory. Instead, as part of the time allotted for your internship, include a few minutes at the end of each working day for writing in your journal.

REFLECTION AND EXPLORATION

The record-keeping function of journals is important in itself, but their real value emerges when interns go beyond record keeping and use their journal as a place for deeper reflection on their experiences. By using their journals as opportunities to explore and process their experiences, interns can gain a deeper understanding of clients, the internship setting, the clinical process, and, most important, themselves. Journaling then becomes a form of self-supervision and can markedly enhance the benefits of the journal and the internship.

To illustrate this approach to journal work, suppose an intern noticed that a client who usually was quite talkative seemed extremely quiet. This observation might lead the intern to think and write about what might be associated with the change in the client's behavior. The intern might consider recent events at the internship or in the client's life. The general mood of the placement could also be taken into account, as could topics and stages of therapy, anticipated events on the unit, and a host of other pertinent factors. It is not necessary for the intern to arrive at the right explanation in the journal. What really matters is that the intern is observing things carefully and trying to understand them.

Of course, it is not possible to engage in detailed exploration of every event that happens every day at the internship. This means you will have to be selective about what you write about in your journal. One approach is to focus on two or three main ideas or concerns and write about them in detail. You might attend to the progress of a specific client, changes in the setting, supervision experiences, or other topics of interest.

Whatever external events your journal addresses, for maximum benefit it is essential to include internal observations in your journal. Interns should use their journals to reflect on their emotional reactions, thoughts, and behaviors. The goal of this reflection should not be to "evaluate" or reach conclusions about whether you did things well or poorly. Rather, the goal is to increase self-awareness and understanding by reflecting on what you experienced or did. A journal entry from one of my students illustrates this process:

> One of the students at the school really blew up at me today. T. has kind of been a favorite for me, and we usually get along great. Today he was causing all kinds of trouble, so I asked him what was up. He totally lost it. He called me all kinds of names and acted like he wanted to hit me. I was blown away. I didn't understand what caused him to act like that, and I was really hurt by what he said. I felt as though maybe it was my fault that he was so upset and that I should have been able to do something to help calm him down. It was especially hard because some of the other kids saw it all, and so did a couple of the staff. The staff were nice afterward, but still I felt like I'd screwed up. I'm supposed to be here to help these kids, and sometimes it seems like there's nothing I can do to really reach them. Sometimes I wonder if I need everyone to like me too much.

This process of self-reflection can go a long way toward helping you work through, and learn from, your experiences as an intern. It also provides a useful basis for discussions with instructors or supervisors. The key to making the process worthwhile is to be as open and honest as you can about what you thought, felt, or did and what your impressions are after you have time to reflect.

NOTING QUESTIONS, IDEAS, AND DISCOVERIES

Because ideas that arise during an internship might be forgotten before you have a chance to discuss them, you can also use your journal to record any questions, exciting insights, or discoveries you want to remember. Questions about treatment approaches, agency procedures, or specific client diagnoses or behaviors would be examples of the kinds of things an intern might want to note in a journal and later address with a supervisor. Discoveries could include themes that appear to be crucial for certain clients, newly acquired skills to emphasize in the future, or perhaps some ideas for possible research.

EXERCISES FROM THE TEXT

Journals are also an excellent place to write about and keep your responses to the exercises in this book. By keeping your work in the journal, you will be able to refer to it later in class discussions or supervision sessions. In the future, when you have been practicing for a few years, you can look back in your journal and remember where you started.

PORTFOLIOS

Whether or not your academic program or internship site explicitly incorporates portfolios into the curriculum or training, I strongly encourage you to begin and maintain a portfolio throughout your internship. I hope you will pass this suggestion on to your peers and beginning students. In essence, portfolios are collections of material from courses and other experiences during your academic coursework and field learning opportunities (Mellott et al., 1997). A common practice is to organize a portfolio into sections based either on classes (with a different section for each class) or by type of material (e.g., course syllabi, books or other readings, exams, papers you have written, evaluations, honors or awards, extracurricular activities, letters of recommendation).

A somewhat different portfolio structure was offered by Alvarez and Moxley (2004), who suggested that portfolios serve several functions for students who are developing as professionals. These functions include the collection of tangible products that substantiate the intern's claims of competencies or achievements, the explanation of the relevance of these claims in regard to current practice, and a case for how the achievements, as manifested through the portfolio material, distinguish the individual as a practitioner. Consistent with these functions, Alvarez and Moxley recommended that each portfolio include a lengthy narrative describing, and supplementing with material evidence, the individual's philosophical orientation, domain of practice, learning experiences, practice competencies, and professional development plan. This material is then discussed with faculty and supervisors, and can be used to evaluate what the student has accomplished to date and what ongoing or future academic, personal, and professional needs might be addressed.

Portfolios are especially valuable as you accumulate clinical experience and want to keep track of such things as the number of hours spent in various settings, types of and hours spent in clinical activities, numbers and kinds of clients seen, intervention techniques used, and hours and nature of supervision (Bartle and Rodolfa, 1999). If you have written any interview, assessment, or other reports, keeping copies of them as examples (with names and other identifying information deleted to protect confidentiality) will be helpful when you apply for further studies, internships or, eventually, professional licensing or employment (Mellott et al., 1997). Some programs in counseling are now also using portfolio development as the central part of their overall doctoral examination practices (Cobia et al., 2005). As an aid to facilitate your own record keeping and documentation of your internship experiences, you may want to use the form I have provided in Appendix J.

By starting a portfolio early in your studies and training, you will accumulate a ready and organized record throughout your career. Unlike students, who can only report a grade point average and courses taken, you will have real, tangible evidence of your work product. This is a tremendous advantage to you and will help your internship supervisor and academic instructor have a much fuller and more accurate appreciation of your qualifications. As an additional benefit, the kinds of information you store in your academic portfolio will also be useful when you eventually apply for licensure, because many licensing bodies request detailed information about the types of clients you have seen, reports written, supervision hours, and so on.

REFERENCES

Alvarez, A. R., & Moxley, D. P., (2004) The student portfolio in social work education. *Journal of Teaching in Social Work, 24,* 87–103.

American Psychological Association Presidential Task Force (2006). Evidence-based practice in psychology. *American Psychologist, 61,* 271–285.

Ankuta, G. Y., & Abeles, N. (1993). Client satisfaction, clinical significance, and meaningful change in psychotherapy. *Professional Psychology: Research and Practice, 24,* 70–74.

Bartle, D., & Rodolfa, E. (1999). Internship hours proposing a national standard. *Professional Psychology: Research and Practice, 30*(4), 420–422.

Benshoff, J. M. (1993). Peer supervision in counselor training. *Clinical Supervisor, 11,* 89–102.

Berger, M. (1995). Sustaining the professional self: Conversations with senior psychotherapists. In M. B. Sussman (Ed.), *A perilous calling: The hazards of psychotherapy practice* (pp. 302–321). New York: Wiley.

Beutler, L. E. (1991). Have all won and must all have prizes? Revisiting Luborsky et al.'s verdict. *Journal of Consulting and Clinical Psychology, 59,* 226–232.

Boisvert, C. B., & Faust, D. (2003). Leading researchers' consensus on psychotherapy research findings: Implications for the teaching and conduct of psychotherapy. *Professional Psychology, Research and Practice, 34*(5), 508–513.

Borders, L. D. (1991). A systematic approach to peer group supervision. *Journal of Counseling and Development, 19,* 248–252.

Bovasso, G., Eaton, W., & Armenian, H. (1999). The long-term outcomes of mental health treatment in a population-based study. *Journal of Consulting and Clinical Psychology, 67*(4), 529–538.

CACREP (2006). http://www.cacrep.org/StandardsRevisionText.html.

Callahan, T. R. (1994). Being paid for what you do. *The Independent Practitioner* (Bulletin of the Division of Independent Practice, Division 42 of the American Psychological Association), *14*(1), 25–26.

Cobia, D. C., Carney, J. S., Buckhalt, J. A., Middleton, R. A., Shannon, D. M., Trippany, R., & Kunkel, E., (2005). The doctoral portfolio: Centerpiece of a comprehensive system of evaluation. *Counselor Education and Supervision, 44,* 242–254.

Cohen, M. B., & Ruff, E. (1995). The use of role play in field instructor training. *Journal of Teaching in Social Work, 11,* 85–100.

Conolley, J. C., & Bonner, M. (1991). The effects of counselor fee and title on perceptions of counselor behavior. *Journal of Counseling and Development, 69,* 356–358.

Crits-Christoph, P. (1992). The efficacy of brief dynamic-psychotherapy: A meta-analysis. *American Journal of Psychiatry, 149,* 151–158.

Csikszentmihalyi, M. (1999). If we are so rich, why aren't we happy? *American Psychologist, 54*(10), 821–827.

Downing, S. (2006). *On course: Strategies for creating success in college and in life* (4th ed.). Boston: Houghton Mifflin.

Edmond, T., Megivern, D., Williams, C., Rochman, E., & Howard, M., (2006) Integrating evidence-based practice and social work field education. *Journal of Social Work Education, 377–396 42.*

Elman, N. S., Illfelder-Kaye, J. & Robiner, W. N. (2005). Professional development: training for professionalism as a foundation for competent practice in psychology. *Professional Psychology: Research and Practice, 36,* 367–375.

Emerson, S. (1995). A counseling group for counselors. *Journal for Specialists in Group Work, 20,* 221–231.

Fox, R. (2004). Field instruction and the mature student. *Journal of Teaching in Social Work, 24,* 113–129.

Friedman, D., & Kaslow, N. J. (1986). The development of professional identity in psychotherapists: Six stages in the supervision process. In F. W. Kaslow (Ed.), *Supervision and training: Models, dilemmas and challenges.* New York: Haworth Press.

Furr, S. R., & Carroll, J. J. (2003). Critical incidents in student counselor development. *Journal of Counseling and Development, 81,* 483–489.

Gelman, C. R., (2004). Anxiety experienced by foundation-year MSW students entering field placement: Implications for admissions curriculum, and field education. *Journal of Social Work Education, 40,* 39–54.

Gilgun, J. F. (2005). The four cornerstones of evidence-based practice in social work. *Research on Social Work Practice, 15,* 52–61.

Globerman, J., & Bogo, M. (2003). Changing times: Understanding social workers' motivation to be field instructors. *Social Work, 48,* 65–73.

Goodman, K. J. (1994). When patients don't pay: Practical aspects of fee collection. *Independent Practitioner* (Bulletin of the Division of Independent Practice, Division 42 of the American Psychological Association), *14*(1), 24–25.

Gross, S. M. (2005). Student perspectives on clinical and counseling psychology practica. *Professional Psychology: Research and Practice, 36,* 299–306.

Hayes, R. L. (1990). Developmental group supervision. *Journal for Specialists in Group Work, 15,* 225–238.

Herron, W. G., & Sitkowski, S. (1986). Effect of fees on psychotherapy: What is the evidence? *Professional Psychology: Research and Practice, 17,* 347–351.

Herron, W. G., & Welt, S. R. (1992). *Money matters: The fee in psychotherapy and psychoanalysis.* New York: Guilford Press.

Hopkins, K. M., Bloom, J. D., & Deal, K. H. (2005). Moving away from tradition: Exploring the field experiences of part-time, older, and employment-based students. *Journal of Social Work Education, 41,* 573–585.

Jacobson, N. S., & Addis, M. E. (1993). Research on couples and couple therapy: What do we know? Where are we going? *Journal of Consulting and Clinical Psychology, 61,* 85–93.

Kadushin, A., & Harkness, D. (2002). *Supervision in social work* (4th ed.). New York: Columbia University Press.

Kaslow, N. J., & Rice, D. G. (1987). Developmental stresses of psychology internship training: What training staff can do to help. In R. H. Dana & W. T. May (Eds.), *Internship training in professional psychology* (pp. 443–453). Washington, DC: Hemisphere.

Kazdin, A. E. (1991). Effectiveness of psychotherapy with children and adolescents. *Journal of Consulting and Clinical Psychology, 59,* 785–798.

Lambert, M. J., Weber, F. D., & Sykes, J. D. (1993). *Psychotherapy versus placebo therapies: A review of the meta-analytic literature.* Poster session presented at the annual meeting of the Western Psychological Association, Phoenix, AZ.

Latz, M. (1996). Brief report: On an exercise for training beginning marital and family therapists in language skills. *Journal of Marital and Family Therapy, 22,* 121–126.

Lee, C. M., Picard, M., & Blain, M. D. (1994). A methodological and substantive review of intervention outcome studies for families undergoing divorce. *Journal of Family Psychology, 8,* 3–15.

Lewis, B. L, Hatcher, R. L., & Pate, W. E. II. (2005). The practicum experience: A survey of practicum site coordinators. *Professional Psychology: Research and Practice, 36,* 291–298.

Lipsey, M. W., & Wilson, D. B. (1993). The efficacy of psychological, educational, and behavioral treatment: Confirmation from meta-analysis. *American Psychologist, 48,* 1181–1209.

Luborsky, L., Singer, B., & Luborsky, L. (1975). Comparative studies of psychotherapy: Is it true that "everyone has won and all must have prizes"? *Archives of General Psychiatry, 32,* 995–1008.

McNeill, T. (2006). Evidence-based practice in an age of relativism: Toward a model for practice. *Social Work, 51,* 157–156.

Mellott, R. N., Arden, I. A., & Cho, M. E. (1997). Preparing for internship: Tips for the prospective applicant. *Professional Psychology: Research and Practice, 28,* 190–196.

National Association of Social Workers. (2005). *Third-party reimbursement for clinical social work services.* Washington, DC: Author.

Newlin, C. M., Adolph, J. L., & Kreber, L. A. (2004). Factors that influence fee setting by male and female psychologists. *Professional Psychology: Research and Practice, 35,* 548–552.

Norcross, J. C. (2005). The psychotherapist's own psychotherapy: Educating and developing psychologists. *American Psychologist, 60,* 840–850.

Norcross, J. C., Beutler, L. E., & Levant, R. F. (2006). *Evidence-based practices in mental health: Debate and dialogue on the fundamental questions.* Washington: APA.

Orlinsky, D. E., & Howard, K. I. (1980). Gender and psychotherapeutic outcome. In A. M. Brodsky & R. Hare-Mustin (Eds.), *Handbook of psychotherapy and behavior change* (pp. 3–34). New York: Guilford Press.

Paul, G. (1967). Strategy in outcome research in psychotherapy. *Journal of Counseling Psychology, 29,* 268–282.

Penn, L. S. (1990). When the therapist must leave: Forced termination of psychodynamic therapy. *Professional Psychology: Research and Practice, 21,* 379–384.

Pipes, R. B., Holstein, J. E., & Aguirre, M. G. (2005). Examining the personal-professional distinction: Ethics codes and the difficulty of drawing a boundary. *American Psychologist, 60,* 325–334.

Rabkin, L. Y. (1994). On some character styles and fees in psychotherapy. *Independent Practitioner* (Bulletin of the Division of Independent Practice, Division 42 of the American Psychological Association), *14*(1), 26–28.

Raskin, M. S. (1994). The Delphi study in field instruction revisited: Expert consensus on issues and research priorities. *Journal of Social Work Education, 30,* 75–89.

Rodolfa, E., Ko, S. F., & Petersen, L. (2004). Psychology training directors' views of trainees' readiness to practice independently. *Professional Psychology: Research and Practice, 35,* 397–404.

Romans, J. S. C., Boswell, D. L., Carlozzi, A. F., & Ferguson, D. B. (1995). Training and supervision practices in clinical, counseling and school psychology programs. *Professional Psychology: Research and Practice, 26,* 407–412.

Ronnestad, M. H., & Skovholt, T. M. (1993). Supervision of beginning and advanced graduate students of counseling and psychotherapy. *Journal of Counseling and Development, 71,* 396–405.

Roth, A., & Fonagy, P. (1996). *What works for whom? A critical review of psychotherapy research.* New York: Guilford Press.

Routh, D. K. (2000). Clinical psychology training: A history of ideas and practices prior to 1946. *American Psychologist, 55,* 236–241.

Sears, M. (2005). How to decide what fees to charge. *National Psychologist, 14(5),* 21.

Seligman, M. E. P. (1995). The effectiveness of psychotherapy: The *Consumer Reports* study. *American Psychologist, 50,* 965–974.

Shadish, W. R., Montgomery, L. M., Wilson, P., Wilson, M. R., Bright, I., & Okwumabua, T. (1993). Effects of family and marital psychotherapies: A meta-analysis. *Journal of Consulting and Clinical Psychology, 61,* 992–1002.

Shapiro, D. A., & Shapiro, D. (1982). Meta-analysis of comparative therapy outcome studies: A replication and refinement. *Psychological Bulletin, 92,* 581–604.

Sklare, G., Thomas, D. V., Williams, E. C., & Powers, K. A. (1996). Ethics and an experiential "Here and Now" group: A blend that works. *Journal for Specialists in Group Work, 21,* 263–273.

Speer, D. C. (1992). Clinically significant change: Jacobson and Truax (1991) revisited. *Journal of Consulting and Clinical Psychology, 60,* 402–408.

Stoltenberg, C. D. (2005) Developing professional competence through developmental approaches to supervision. *American Psychologist, 60,* 855–864.

Strupp, H. H. (1989). Psychotherapy: Can the practitioner learn from the researcher? *American Psychologist, 44,* 717–724.

Strupp, H. H., & Binder, J. L. (1992). Current developments in psychotherapy. *Independent Practitioner* (Bulletin of the Division of Independent Practice, Division 42 of the American Psychological Association), *12(3),* 119–124.

Thorp, S. R., O'Donohue, W. T., & Gregg, J. (2005). The predoctoral internship: Is current training anachronistic? *Professional Psychology: Research and Practice, 36,* 16–24.

Van Geert, P. (1998). A dynamic systems model of basic developmental mechanisms: Piaget, Vygotsky, and beyond. *Psychological Review, 105,* 634–677.

Waehler, C. A., Hardin, S. I., & Rogers, J. R. (1994). College students' perceptions of the relationship between fee and counseling. *Journal of Counseling and Development, 73,* 88–93.

Whiston, S. C., & Sexton, T. L. (1993). An overview of psychotherapy outcome research: Implications for practice. *Professional Psychology: Research and Practice, 24,* 43–52.

Wilbur, M. P., Roberts-Wilbur, J., Morris, J. R., Betz, R. L., & Hart, G. M. (1991). Structured group supervision: Theory into practice. *Journal for Specialists in Group Work, 16,* 91–100.

Woit, J., & Brownlee, K. (1995). Reflecting teams in the classroom: An effective educational tool? *Journal of Teaching in Social Work, 11,* 67–84.

Wolfson, E. R. (1999). The fee in social work: Ethical dilemmas for practitioners. *Social Work, 44,* 269–273.

Wong, J. L. (1994). Lay theories of psychotherapy and perceptions of therapists: A replication and extension of Furnham and Wardley. *Journal of Clinical Psychology, 50,* 624–632.

Zakutansky, T. J., & Sirles, E. A. (1993). Ethical and legal issues in field education: Shared responsibility and risk. *Journal of Social Work Education, 29,* 338–347.

CHAPTER 3
ETHICAL AND LEGAL ISSUES

The first rule of all health care and helping professions is "Do no harm." As simple as that rule is to state, the implications and applications in practice are by no means always self-evident. One of the ways professions have sought to ensure quality treatment and reduce the potential for harm to clients is through the establishment of professional codes of ethics. Because internships represent a key step in the process of becoming a professional, as an intern it is vital that you understand and adhere to established standards of professional ethics.

Each of the major helping professions has its own code of ethics, but the essential elements and functions of the codes are consistent across professions. These functions include promoting the welfare of the people you serve, avoiding harm, maintaining your professional competence, protecting confidentiality and privacy, avoiding exploitation or conflict of interest, and upholding the integrity of your profession (Koocher & Keith-Spiegel, 1998).

Along with understanding ethics, you must also understand and follow the laws and regulations pertaining to your profession and your activities as a professional. Just as professional organizations have established ethical codes to protect consumers and the profession, the federal government and the states have worked to protect the well-being of consumers by enacting regulations and laws governing the licensing and practice of various professions. This chapter discusses key ethical and legal issues relating to clinical practice and internships. The importance of this chapter to your work as an intern and to your development as a professional cannot be overstated. Read it carefully, discuss it with your instructor and supervisor, and study your professional organization's code and any applicable laws and regulations. Review these often and in detail, and keep up to date with changes.

ETHICAL GUIDELINES OF THE HELPING PROFESSIONS

Membership in professional organizations carries with it a commitment on the part of each member to know and adhere to the ethical guidelines of the organization. Ethics codes are not handed down as final truths from above, and being a moral or ethical person is not the same as being and practicing as an ethical professional (Behnke, 2005). Professional ethics codes are arrived at through extended discussion and review among the organization's members. As conditions change, ethics codes are updated; and even before a code has been officially published, debate may have begun on how the code may need to be modified and improved (Keith-Spiegel, 1994; Knapp & Vande-Creek, 2003; Kocet & Freeman, 2005; Walden, Herlihy, & Ashton, 2003). Once ethics codes have been established, professionals within the organization continue to discuss the strengths, applications, and shortcomings of the code, and this discussion will provide the basis for future revisions (Fisher & Younggren, 1997; Kocet, 2006). While ethics codes evolve over time, during the period an ethics code is in effect, members are expected to abide by it. Lack of awareness or misunderstanding of ethical principles is not a defense to charges of ethical misconduct; and in many states, licensing and practice laws incorporate the professional ethics codes into law (APA, 2002, 2003).

Not all ethical standards or state laws are identical for all professions, but most professional ethics codes share certain basic principles (Kitchener, 1984). Ethical guidelines for several of the leading professional organizations can be found in the sources listed below. I encourage you not only to consult the ethical code for your own profession, but to also review the standards of related fields so that you can see how different associations have dealt with similar problems. As you review the different codes, keep in mind that different professions may be treated differently in the laws of different states (Glosoff, Herlihy, & Spence, 2000):

American Association for Marriage and Family Therapy (2001). *AAMFT Code of Ethics.* http://www.aamft.org/resources/LRMPlan/Ethics/ethicscode2001.asp

American Counseling Association (2005). *American Counseling Association Code of Ethics and Standards of Practice.* Alexandria, VA: Author. http://www.counseling.org/Resources/CodeOfEthics/TP/Home/CT2.aspx

American Psychological Association (2002). Ethical principles of psychologists and code of conduct. *American Psychologist, 57,* 1060–1073. www.apa.org/ethics/code2002.html

American Psychiatric Association (2006). *The principles of medical ethics: With annotations especially applicable to psychiatry.* Washington, DC: Author. http://www. psych. org/psych_pract/ethics/ppaethics.pdf

National Association of Social Workers (2000). *NASW code of ethics.* Silver Spring, MD: Author. www.social workers. org/pubs/code/code.asp

National Staff Development and Training Association (2004). The NSDTA code of ethics for training and development professionals in human services: Case scenarios and training implications. http://nsdta.aphsa.org/PDF/Code_Ethics.pdf

Along with each discipline's code of ethics, you may also want to review accompanying books that have been written to expand upon the codes and give practical examples of their applications in clinical work. Examples include:

Dolgoff, R., Loewenberg, F. M., & Harrington, D. (2005). *Ethical decisions for social work practice* (7th ed.). Belmont, CA: Thomson/Brooks/Cole.

Herlihy, B., & Corey, G. (eds.) (2006). ACA *ethical standards casebook* (6th ed.). Washington, DC: ACA.

Knapp, S. J., & Vandecreek, L. (2006). *Practical ethics for psychologists: A positive approach.* Washington, DC: APA.

Nagy, T. F. (2005). *Ethics in plain English: An illustrative casebook for psychologists.* Washington, DC: APA.

Reamer, F. G. (2006). *Ethical standards in social work: A review of the NASW code of ethics* (2nd ed.). Washington, DC: NASW.

SPECIFIC ETHICAL PRACTICE AND TREATMENT GUIDELINES

In addition to general ethical standards, some organizations have developed more specific guidelines that apply to clinical practitioners working in specified areas of practice or with certain client populations. Examples of such guidelines include the APA's Guidelines on Multicultural Education, Training, Research, Practice and Organizational Change for Psychologists (APA, 2003a) and the NASW's Standards for Cultural Competencies in Social Work Practice (2001). Similar standards have been proposed for counselors (Ibrahim & Arredondo, 1992).

Still more specific than guidelines for ethical practice are specific treatment or clinical practice guidelines. Closely related to the concepts of evidence-based practice and empirically supported treatment that were discussed in the last chapter, practice guidelines are designed to help professionals and clients make better decisions about the most appropriate interventions for specific clinical circumstances. Guidelines may also inform legal decisions and public policies (APA, 2005). A clearinghouse of guidelines has been established, the National Guidelines Clearinghouse, which is sponsored by the Agency for Healthcare Quality and Research (www.guideline.gov). Close to 100 guidelines relating to behavioral health are now listed.

Even though you are just beginning your work as a professional, there are several reasons you should know about and refer to practice and treatment guidelines. The most important of these is that treatment guidelines are intended to represent the generally agreed upon professional experience and scientific findings that can guide both practioners and patients to make the most effective diagnostic and treatment decisions. You should also be aware that some treatment agencies and many insurance providers have expectations that professionals will adhere to specific guidelines in working with specific illnesses. Some insurers go so far as to specify that they will provide financial compensation only if specific treatment interventions are offered in specific ways by professionals who have received specified training in a designated treatment modality (Messer, 2003). Finally, treatment guidelines are also important to know about because they may be used as evidence in litigation if there are allegations of professional negligence or malpractice.

As you consider treatment guidelines, be aware that they are not without controversy. There are legitimate professional differences and conflicting empirical data about varying treatment approaches. What is more, parochial differences between professions may be reflected in the treatment standards proposed by one profession as compared to another (Messer, 2003). Thus, while it is good to be aware of the guidelines that may exist for your particular areas of practice or for specific client groups with whom you work, guidelines, just like any other source of information, should be considered critically and in the context of other information.

ENFORCEMENT OF ETHICAL STANDARDS

Ethical guidelines are established by professional organizations to govern the conduct of their members. Organizations have established procedures for investigating ethics complaints and disciplining members who are found to have violated ethical standards (APA Ethics Committee, 2006; Kocet & Freeman, 2005). Within the governing organization, the consequences of ethical violations can range from warnings and required educational efforts to dismissal from the organization.

Because ethical guidelines are established by organizations to govern member conduct, they do not formally apply to practitioners who are not members of the organization. Thus, social workers who do not belong to the NASW, counselors not in the ACA, and psychologists who are not members of the APA cannot be sanctioned by these organizations for violating their ethics codes. The same is true for members of other professions and organizations. This does not mean there will be no consequences for unethical conduct. Students, in particular, should know that violations of ethical standards for their profession can be considered grounds for academic discipline and possibly dismissal from a training program (Busseri, Tyler, & King, 2005; Cobb, 1994). Furthermore, legal sanctions, both civil and criminal, apply regardless of organizational membership.

ETHICS, LAWS, AND REGULATIONS

It is important to be aware that ethical standards exist, and ethical practice must take place, within a broader social and legal context that is constantly evolving. Ethical principles of leading professional organizations are often incorporated into the licensing and practice laws of individual states, and ethical standards of practice must also be followed in the context of various state and federal laws. To the extent that state laws incorporate or parallel professional ethical standards, practitioners who violate those laws face possible loss of license as well as possible criminal prosecution and even jail time for certain violations (Swenson, 1997). Civil actions for monetary damages may also result from unethical actions or from actions that are not considered unethical but nevertheless result in harm to a patient or the patient's family (Bennett, Bryant, VandenBos, & Greenwood, 1990). Also, remember that laws vary from state to state and are continually evolving as new cases arise.

A practical and useful source for information about state-specific laws is the "Law & Mental Health Professionals" series, published by the American Psychological Association, which provides individual volumes addressing specific legal standards and issues relating to mental health professionals for each of more than two dozen states. You can also check with your state professional association for state-specific information and to find workshops and other educational material pertaining to your state laws. A more general reference source for legal issues affecting all mental health professions is the book by Sales, Miller, and Hall (2005). Finally, an excellent and concise primer on legal terms and concepts, plus an accompanying reference list, is provided by the APA Committee on Professional Practice and Standards (2003).

THE HEALTH INSURANCE PORTABILITY AND ACCOUNTABILITY ACT (HIPPA)

Without doubt, the most consequential and far-reaching law relating to ethical practice is the federal Health Insurance Portability and Accountability Act, or HIPAA (commonly pronounced like *hippo,* but with an *a*). Congress passed this law in 1996 as part of a broad effort to make sure that people can maintain their health insurance coverage even if they change jobs or move and in response to growing concerns about the confidentiality of electronically stored and communicated information (Benefield, Ashkanazi, & Rozensky, 2006). Specific details of this act were subsequently reviewed both in the Congress and by the U.S. Department of Health and Human Services (HHS), with final modifications published in August of 2002 and the standards taking effect in April of 2003. Subsequent provisions for the security of records were published in February of 2003,

with compliance required by April of 2005. For the full text of HIPAA, plus answers to frequently asked questions, go to the official HHS Web site at http://www.hhs.gov/ocr/hipaa/.

It is fair to say that HIPAA will have a more significant impact on issues of confidentiality and record keeping than any previous federal or state legislation. Indeed, a number of authors have advised that although HIPAA confidentiality and record-communication standards technically only apply to health care providers who directly participate in, or are part of an agency that participates in, the electronic storage and exchange of information, HIPAA will soon be a standard that everyone must follow because it is likely to affect state laws as well, and because virtually all health care providers will in some way be associated with electronic data storage and communication (Zur, 2003).

It is highly likely that the vast majority of internship sites will be subject to HIPAA rules, so it behooves you as an intern to have at least a basic familiarity with HIPAA requirements and your obligations for meeting them. What is more, as will be discussed throughout this chapter, most elements of professional ethics code are at least in some way affected by HIPAA rules.

Like many federal regulations, HIPAA rules are not impossibly complex, but neither are they simple. As a result, a whole new industry of sorts sprang up to teach practitioners and health care agencies how to comply with the rules. In this chapter I highlight some of the areas in which HIPAA interacts with ethical principles and will have an impact on your internship, but the discussion is far from complete for such a far-reaching piece of legislation. For further information, you may wish to consider a training program designed specifically to teach HIPAA concepts for mental health professionals. A good place to start is by contacting your professional association. Most associations, including the APA, NASW, and ACA, have put together special training programs for their members. These can be accessed or ordered through the respective Web sites. At the very least, you should review the HIPAA guidelines provided by your internship placement, and, as mentioned earlier, the HHS Web site also has extensive information to assist with HIPAA compliance.

ETHICAL AGREEMENT FORMS FOR INTERNS

Because it is so important for interns to adhere to ethical standards and follow the relevant laws and regulations, I require each intern I supervise to read and sign the Ethical Guidelines form presented in Appendix G. I keep this form in my class records for future information purposes. The form covers some of the essential guidelines that all professionals must know and follow. It also provides space for the intern, the field supervisor, and the instructor to sign indicating that the material has been addressed, along with any local or placement-specific ethical concerns. Since certain work settings (such as those involving children) and specific treatment modalities may present unique ethical issues, I also advise students that they must be aware of these issues and adhere to any relevant standards, including HIPAA (Montgomery, Cupit, & Wimberly, 1999).

Ethical Decision-Making and Ongoing Ethics Study and Training

Reading and signing the ethics form should not be considered the last word on ethics. Rather, it is a fundamental starting point from which further discussion and ongoing evaluation should proceed. As Welfel and Lipsitz (1984) observed in their review of ethics training, mere knowledge of ethical codes does not guarantee ethical behavior. This was clearly evident in the findings of Fly, van Bark, Weinman, Kitchener, and Lang (1997), who found that over half of the interns who were reported to have made ethical violations had previously completed a course in ethics.

To promote a deeper understanding of the concepts underlying codes of ethics, Kitchener (1984) distinguished between ethical principles, and codes of ethics, noting that codes of ethics derive from underlying ethical principles, and understanding the underlying principles can help guide ethical decision-making. A similar observation was made by Knapp and Vandecreek (2004), who asserted that an awareness and understanding of underlying principles is particularly helpful when ethical standards must be applied in ambiguous situations.

Included among the principles shared by virtually all helping professions are respect for autonomy, avoiding harm, and promoting good, truthfulness, and justice. This recognition of the importance of underlying values is reflected in each of the major professional codes and is expressed explicitly in the preamble or general principles that begin the codes. For example, the NASW code of ethics begins by articulating core values, including service, social justice, dignity and worth of the person, the importance of human relationships, integrity, and competence (NASW, 2000). Similarly, the "General Principles" that begin the American Psychological Association code of ethics identify five key principles to guide ethical conduct: beneficence and nonmaleficence, fidelity and responsibility, integrity, justice, and respect for people's rights and dignity (APA, 2002). Within the ACA code (ACA, 2005), core principles and values are articulated in the introduction to each major section of the code. For example Section A of the ACA code describes promoting client growth in ways that "foster the interest and welfare of clients." Section B emphasizes the importance of trust, boundaries, and confidentiality, and Section C addresses professional responsibility.

Understanding and appreciating these underlying principles is fundamental to ethical practice because, as Kitchener (1984) asserted, when ethical dilemmas or conflicts are faced, awareness of such principles provides the basis for decisions to be reached through a process of critical thought and evaluation. Kitchener's premise was supported by Cottone and Claus (2000), who emphasized the importance of helping students not simply memorize an ethics code but truly understand the values and principles that underly each code and establish a personal process for making real-world decisions consistent with the underlying principles. Handelsman, Gottlieb, and Knapp (2005) take this notion a step further and describe an "acculturation model" that helps students understand the origins of their personal moral codes and how these may differ, and occasionally conflict with, ethics codes and practical situations. These authors also point out that there is a need to go beyond the ethical training of individuals to encompass the ethos of entire organizations or programs in which interns train.

During your internship, you will discover that different stages and elements of your experience will involve different aspects of ethics codes and ethical decision-making. Zakutansky and Sirles (1993) identified six intern and supervisor relationships and discussed the ethical and legal issues relevant to each. The relationships are "(1) student-client; (2) student–field instructor; (3) field instructor–client; (4) field instructor–field liaison (representing the social work program's field staff); (5) student–field liaison; and (6) field liaison–client" (p. 338). As you deal with each of these relationships and the ethical challenges they may present, you will discover firsthand that ethical conduct requires a continuous process of self-monitoring, reference to the ethics code, reflection on underlying principles, and consultation with your supervisor, instructor, colleagues, and experts in the field. By understanding this and establishing a systematic process of approaching ethical decision-making early in your career, you are less likely to make ethical errors and more likely to be helpful to your clients.

Exercise

Before reading the discussion that follows, consider the case example below and identify any ethical concerns or violations you find. Remember to consider both the written code of ethics and the underlying principles that were just discussed. Keep in mind too that real situations often present conflicts between different values, both of which may be good in themselves, and that sometimes conflicts will also arise between different aspects of the same ethics code. When you have finished reading the chapter, review this case again and discuss it with your peers and instructor:

A therapist who specializes in work with geriatric patients also serves as head of a charitable organization. After a meeting of the organization, the therapist is approached by a woman who is both a personal friend and serves as vice chair of the charity's executive board. The woman is having problems with her 15-year-old daughter, who has been skipping school and has been moody and depressed around the house. Because she trusts her, the woman asks the therapist to see the girl for therapy. The therapist agrees to do so without charge and suggests it would be less threatening to the girl if she stopped by the therapist's house and they talked. The girl comes to visit at the appointed time, but her mother has not told her the visit is for therapy. The therapist simply says that it has been a long time since she has seen the girl and explains that she just wants to talk. While talking, the girl tearfully and rather abruptly confides that she is having "problems" with an uncle who lives with the family and has been sexually abusing her. The girl says she has tried to tell her mother, but because the uncle is the mother's brother, she fears that her mother would not believe her. The girl is so upset about the experience that she has talked with a friend about wanting to kill the uncle by poisoning him. The therapist listens; then, after the girl has left, she calls the mother to tell her what happened in therapy.

COMPETENCE

One of the most important principles of ethical practice is to operate within one's level of competence. Consistent with the principle of "Do no harm," knowing our limits means that no matter how much we may want to help others, we must recognize the extent and limitations of our abilities and seek assistance or supervision when we need it.

The importance of knowing one's abilities and limits should make intuitive sense; but in the desire to help, it is easy for us to imagine that we are more capable than we actually are. We often learn this lesson the hard way, as we start something with the best of intentions only to wind up in a mess when the situation exceeds our abilities. A personal experience in a non-clinical setting may help to demonstrate both how easy it is to overestimate abilities and the possible consequences of making that mistake.

As a break from clinical work and teaching, I sometimes go white-water kayaking. In kayaking, especially when one is learning, there are frequent occasions when one must exit the boat and swim for safety. There are also times when other boaters are swimming and need to be rescued. In these situations, the power and speed of rivers can be overwhelming, and one quickly learns that rivers are no place for the unprepared.

In river rescue situations, the first priority, even before trying to help a victim, is to not endanger yourself. As one river rescue expert explained it, "If you go jumping into a river to help someone, and you don't know what you're doing, the odds of you effecting a rescue are very, very small. Instead, the odds are high that you will become a second victim, and you may actually cause the victim and yourself to drown. Bravado and heroic intentions do not impress the river."

I observed this firsthand when an inexperienced kayaker tried to help a swimming boater by getting the swimmer to the apparent safety of a fallen tree that lay on the water surface. What neither the kayaker nor the swimmer realized was that trees in rivers, although they look safe, are actually among the most deadly hazards. The river pushes against the tree with incredible force, and even a relatively gentle current can easily entrap kayakers or swimmers. In this case, that is exactly what happened. When they reached the downed tree, the kayaker's boat overturned, trapping the would-be rescuer and the victim underwater, where they were unable to extricate themselves.

Both would almost certainly have drowned had it not been for a more experienced boater who saw what was happening and managed to free them. If not for the skill of the more highly trained boater, the swimmer and the rescuer would have died.

The purpose of this analogy is not to scare you away from your field placement (or from kayaking). Rather, it is to encourage you to be well aware of your limitations and not get in over your head. Just as beginners cannot fully appreciate the expertise required to run swift rivers or rescue swimmers, casual observers of clinical work often believe it consists of little more than listening to other people talk. The idea that anyone can do human service work without any training is not only wrong, it is dangerous. Beginning trainees who try to provide treatment, assessment, or other services on their own without supervision are surely going beyond their limits. They might get lucky and do some good, but they might also get unlucky and do a great deal of harm to their clients and themselves.

Good intentions are no substitute for competence. One of the purposes of ethics is to remind us that we are not always the best judges of our own abilities and conduct. Simply because you want to believe you can help someone does not mean you are justified in proceeding. In all your clinical work, make it a practice to ask yourself as objectively and honestly as possible if you have any real training or experience in the skills required to work with a given individual or situation. Then go a step further and ask yourself how you would provide objective evidence of your competence if required to do so by an ethics review board or a court of law.

As you consider the matter of competence, keep in mind that in the helping professions, competence is more than mere knowledge or technical skill (Rodolfa et al., 2005). Pope and Brown (1996) pointed out that the work you will be doing requires both intellectual and emotional competence. Intellectual competence refers to knowledge and skill, but emotional competence refers to one's internal emotional stability and ability to manage the emotional challenges of working with different clients. Not all therapists are equally emotionally competent to work with all types of clients or issues, and it is incumbent on therapists to recognize this. You must also recognize that competency in one domain of practice does not necessarily mean one is competent to practice in a different domain (Rodolfa et al., 2005). What is more, burnout, stress, personal issues, or other matters can all have an adverse impact on your emotional competence and your performance, regardless of your intellectual or technical skill. For suggestions on managing stress and burnout, see Chapter 7.

The principle of competence is so important that if students learn nothing else in their internship, they must at least learn how much they do not know. The fact is that no matter how much you study, there will never be a time when your knowledge is not vastly exceeded by your ignorance. From your first internship experience to the end of your career, you must continually strive to recognize when you need help and never be afraid or embarrassed to seek it. Until you have at least several years of experience, supervision should be an essential part of all your work and training (Rodolfa, Ko, & Petersen, 2004). Further, throughout your career, you should always seek supervision when you work with particularly difficult cases or if your own performance may be adversely affected by personal issues.

At no point in your career will you know everything you need to know. There is always room to learn more, and in most states some form of continuing-education credit is required for licensing. In my own practice, I read multiple professional journals, attend far more than the required number of hours of continuing education each year, and regularly consult with other professionals about challenging cases. Even with these measures, there are still many times when I recognize that I am not adequately trained to deal with certain clients or issues. In such cases, one should not hesitate to seek supervision or to refer to other professionals with greater skills in the needed areas.

A final note about competence: Students sometimes believe that because they are students or interns they will not be held accountable for their actions as they would if they were professionals. This is not the case. Students who are at advanced levels of training and have primary responsibility for a client's care "are acting in a professional role, and with this status comes the responsibility to uphold the same legal, professional, and ethical standards" (Zakutansky & Sirles, 1993, p. 339). Students who are found to have acted unethically in a training setting may be dismissed from their program (Fly et al., 1997). Students can be sued personally for malpractice, and supervisors and instructors may also be held accountable for a student's actions (Gelman, Pollack, & Auerbach, 1996). Thus, in considering your actions, recognize that part of accepting the role of intern means accepting the responsibility that goes with it.

EXERCISE

A good way to appreciate the importance of ethics and the principle of competence is to consider the matter from a client's perspective. Imagine that you are seeking a psychotherapist. What qualifications would you like the therapist to have for you to consider the person competent to help you with your particular situation? As you answer this, give some thought to such things as academic degrees, professional licenses, years of experience in general, experience working with clients with your concern, amount of supervised experience, specialized training in the areas of your concern, and continuing education. Most interns who do this exercise honestly find they have a greater sense of humility as they evaluate their qualifications and competencies for working directly with clients.

INFORMED CONSENT

The ethical principle of informed consent means that clients have a right to be informed about the treatment, assessment, or other services they will receive before they agree to participate

in or receive those services. When applied in practice, this principle dictates that in order to ensure informed consent, clients must be given certain information in a manner and language they can understand. Burkemper (2004) helped social work students understand this principle by using an informed-consent template and inviting students to develop their own informed-consent forms specific to their practice areas. Pomerantz and Handelsman (2006) and Harris and Bennet (2000) provided excellent examples of model informed-consent contracts for psychotherapists. Harris (1995) also offered suggestions for what should be included in such documents, and Kennedy, Vandehey, Norman, and Diekhoff (2003) provided similar suggestions as part of a broader 10-point strategy for day-to-day risk management. Before using any form of this type, it is a good idea to consult an attorney who specializes in legal issues regarding clinical work.

At a minimum, clients should be informed about each of the following subjects:

1. They should know the qualifications of the person providing treatment. This includes the degrees, clinical experience, specialized training, and licenses the person has received.
2. In the case of interns, clients should know that the treatment provider is an intern and will be supervised. The intern's educational and training background should also be explained.
3. Clients should be given the name and qualifications of the intern's supervisor and should have an opportunity to meet with the supervisor if they desire to do so. Clients should also know how they can contact the supervisor if they have any questions or concerns in the future.
4. Clients should know the nature of supervision, including the frequency of supervision and the activities it will entail (e.g., reviewing case notes, listening to tapes of sessions).
5. Clients should be informed about the nature of the treatment or assessment to be provided. This includes a brief description of the approach to treatment or the purpose of an assessment and the instruments that will be used. Clients should also be informed about the empirical basis of treatment, and alternative approaches should also be described.
6. The frequency and duration of treatment sessions should be explained, as well as a reasonable estimate of the typical number of sessions to treat the given concern.
7. The client's responsibilities for participating in treatment must be made clear. For example, the client should be expected to attend scheduled appointments, notify the therapist in advance if appointments must be canceled or changed, and follow through with any assignments.
8. Medication issues should be addressed, including how the therapist works with medications and prescribing professionals.
9. Fees must be explained in detail, including the costs per session or per assessment and whether or not there are

charges for missed sessions. How and when payments are to be made and the procedures that will be followed if payment is not made have to be explained. This discussion should also cover how insurance coverage will be handled, how provider contacts are made with the insurer, and how this impacts confidentiality.

10. If a client's insurance policy limits the number of sessions the insurance company will pay for, an agreement must be reached about how to proceed if more sessions are needed and the client is unable to pay without the assistance of the insurance.

11. Confidentiality must be spelled out clearly, including a specific discussion of any and all limitations to confidentiality of what is said in treatment, as well as what is contained in the client's records. This explanation should include how records are stored, how releases of information will be managed, and how government regulations (e.g., HIPAA) impact confidentiality.

12. Clients should know and agree upon procedures for getting help in a crisis situation, including emergency phone numbers and contacts. This discussion may also include mention of how phone or Internet communication is handled and what sorts of billing or fees may be associated with such communications.

13. Termination policies should be described, specifying conditions under which either the patient or the therapist may initiate termination.

14. When working with a patient who is part of a managed-care arrangement, the therapist should review with the patient any information that will be provided to the insurance company for purposes of utilization review or quality assurance.

15. What options are available if complaints arise that cannot be resolved in the therapy process.

16. How records will be handled in the event the therapist becomes incapacitated or dies.

17. Finally, there should be an opportunity to ask any questions before therapy begins or at any time during the treatment, and the client should indicate that he or she has been given that opportunity and understands the issues described above.

Although case law and ethical standards are still evolving on this issue, at least one recent article and several court cases suggest that therapists should also disclose any financial or other conflicts of interest relating to treatment. There has also been discussion of the need to disclose any personal issues, such as substance abuse, on the part of the therapist that might have an impact on the patient's treatment (Hafemeister, 2000). I should explain that I recently added item 16 to this list because it seems to me an important matter to attend to up front. To date, I have yet to encounter extensive discussion of this topic in the literature, but that may soon change following a recent event involving the death of a therapist. In that case, a client was suspected in the killing of the therapist, but the authorities were unable to explore this possibility because of confidentiality provisions. (Bradshaw, 2006) Whether or not something so dramatic occurs, responsible practice and the realities of existence suggest that we should provide for continued care and the responsible management of our records if something happens to us during the course of work with clients.

While informing patients of the preceding issues, you should document that the information has been provided and understood. A sample form that addresses informed-consent issues is presented in Appendix H. This form covers each of the critical topics and provides a place for clients to sign indicating that they have read and understood the form, and have asked any questions they have about the treatment they will be receiving. You may also want to review information provided by professional organizations, such as the American Counseling Association (www.counseling.org/consumers/ethics.htm), which offers clients and others a guide to counselor ethics, explains what clients can expect in treatment, and tells clients what options are available if they believe a counselor has acted unethically.

Beyond the ethical requirements of informed consent, you should also be aware that the Health Insurance Portability and Accountability Act (HIPAA) establishes extensive and detailed confidentiality requirements that must be scrupulously followed by health care agencies and practitioners (Knapp & Vande-Creek, 2003; HHS, www.hhs.gov). HIPAA also requires that patients be given written HIPAA Privacy Notices (separate from your other notice of confidentiality) that are written in "plain language" (the HHS Web site provides an 18-page guide to writing notices in plain language) and include the following specific elements:

- A mandatory header explaining the purpose of the notice.
- Descriptions of the uses and disclosures of information that are permitted under HIPAA for the purpose of treatment, payment, and health care operations, and an explanation of other uses of information for which the patient's written authorization will be required.
- Separate statements to explain certain uses of information (e.g., contacting the patient to remind about appointments, a statement of the individual's rights under HIPAA, including the right to inspect his or her own health information and the right to receive accounting of any disclosures of information).
- A description of the duties of the "covered entities" (i.e., you and your agency) under the law.
- Procedures the patient can follow if he or she wishes to complain or feels that privacy rights may have been violated.
- Contact information identifying a person or office the patient can contact for further information.
- The effective date of the notice.
- Optional elements that the entity may wish to include, providing they are consistent with the rest of the HIPAA requirements.
- Revisions to the notice.

In most instances your internship placement will have procedures in place for HIPAA informed-consent compliance, but you should be aware of these requirements and follow them carefully, because both fines and criminal penalties can result from violations (Zur, 2003).

Documentation of informed consent serves several functions. By scrupulously documenting that patients have been informed, therapists ensure that they are adhering to this ethical principle and are providing what is considered to be a key element of care. If questions arise later about treatment, fees, confidentiality, termination, or other matters, documenting that the client was informed about such things can be extraordinarily helpful. This is especially important if legal issues, such as malpractice proceedings, arise. In many states, such documentation is required by state ethical guidelines and/or laws. Thus, developing the habit of completing informed-consent forms is a wise, and in some cases legally mandated, practice for interns and professionals alike.

One final note about informed consent is that interns and their supervisors may want to consider establishing an informed-consent agreement for the supervisory relationship. Barnet (2005) recommended that a supervisory informed-consent agreement should include many of the elements of agreements with clients, but should also address such matters as evaluation procedures, arrangements for emergency contacts and any confidentiality issues that may arise between the internship site and the academic setting.

EXERCISE

Because informed consent is an ethical and legal obligation, this exercise is particularly important. If you are in an advanced setting and are seeing clients, informed consent may be legally mandated. If you are a beginner in your first placement, you should still complete this exercise because it will help you clarify your own qualifications and approach to therapy and your expectations for clients, and it will strengthen your knowledge of critical ethical principles. Tear out the treatment agreement and informed-consent form from Appendix H and use it to prepare a form tailored to your own circumstances. Then exchange your form with your peers and review it with your instructor. You will probably need to go through several revisions before achieving a draft that is satisfactory. In the future, as you gain additional experience or your approach to treatment changes, or as ethical or legal developments arise, you will need to adapt and revise your form.

CONFIDENTIALITY

Insofar as openness and honesty are essential ingredients of treatment, confidentiality is considered a necessary condition for effective therapy, and many patients insist that confidentiality is essential to their participation in treatment (Swenson, 1997). All of the leading professional organizations recognize and share this value and have given it prominence in their ethical codes.

It was in large part due to the recognition of the importance of confidentiality, and in response to concerns about possible breaches in confidentiality, that the Privacy Rule of the Health Insurance Portability and Accountability Act (http://www.hhs.gov/ocr/privacysummary.pdf) was established. The HIPAA Security Rule, which will be discussed shortly, was also implemented to address confidentiality issues, particularly as they apply to electronic information technologies (http://www.cms.hhs.gov/SecurityStandard/Downloads/securi tyfinalrule.pdf).

The essence of confidentiality is the principle that clients have the right to determine who will have access to information about them and their treatment. In clinical settings, clients need to feel that the information they share will stay with the professional and not be released without their permission. Without this assurance, clients are less likely to explore and express their thoughts and feelings freely. This, in turn, is likely to inhibit the client's willingness to share certain information and may distort the treatment process (Nowell & Spruill, 1993). At the same time, however, clients must be aware of the limits to confidentiality so that they can make informed choices.

Survey research suggests that clients and the general public share the belief that confidentiality is important (Claiborn, Berberoglu, Nerison, & Somberg, 1994; Kremer, & Gesten, 2003). On the other hand, Rubanowitz (1987) reported that many of those surveyed believe there are instances—for example, if crimes have been or are likely to be committed—in which the therapist should inform the necessary authorities even though it means violating the client's confidentiality.

Despite, or perhaps because of, its importance, confidentiality is the issue most frequently identified as a source of ethical dilemmas for clinicians and educators (Hayman & Covert, 1986; Pope & Vetter, 1992; Stadler & Paul, 1986). Violations of confidentiality are among the most common sources of malpractice claims against practitioners (Reamer, 1995) and the most commonly identified ethical breaches among students (Fly et al., 1997). Considering the high value placed on confidentiality, and the ethical dilemmas it frequently poses, interns must fully understand the principle of confidentiality, know how to avoid violating confidentiality through carelessness, and appreciate the consequences of such violations. Interns also need to know that confidentiality is not fully guaranteed by their role or the clinical setting in which they work. What is more, laws concerning confidentiality and patient-therapist privilege vary from state to state (Glosoff, Herlihy, Herlihy, & Spence, 1997; Glosoff, Herlihy, & Spence, 2000) and have recently been profoundly affected by the federal HIPAA laws.

There are exceptions in which you may, sometimes must, divulge information about clients. You need to know what such situations are, how to deal with them, and how to inform clients of these limitations to confidentiality.

The following discussion addresses general issues of confidentiality that apply to most settings. While these guidelines should be helpful, certain therapy approaches pose unique problems, and some settings may follow very specific approaches to protect confidentiality. For example, placements serving minors (Mannheim et al., 2002; Small, Lyons, & Guy, 2002; Sullivan, Ramirez, Rae, Peña Razo, & George, 2002; Swenson, 1997), persons who are HIV positive (Anderson & Barret, 2001; Chenneville, 2000; McGuire, Niere, Abbott, Sheridan, & Fisher, 1995; Schlossberger & Hecker, 1996), persons who have been involuntarily committed (Connor, 1996), persons in correctional institutions (Weinberger & Sreenivasan, 1994; White, 2003b), clients who are court-mandated to treatment (Regehr & Antle, 1997), persons in drug and alcohol treatment programs (Andrews & Patterson, 1995), patients and service personnel in military settings (Murphy, 2005: Stall & King, 2000), seniors (Bergeron & Gray, 2003), rural settings (Helbok, Marineli, & Walls, 2006; Johnson et. al., 2006; Schank & Skovholt, 2006), and other clients or settings may all call for special precautions and procedures. Group therapy and family therapy also pose certain unique ethical and legal issues with regard to confidentiality (Paradise & Kirby, 1990; Vesper & Brock, 1991). In addition, HIPAA has special rules that apply to alcohol/substance-abuse programs and to certain other clinical and research activities. Finally, new developments in computer communication and remote therapy also raise special ethical concerns, many of which are discussed later in this chapter and have also been addressed in the new HIPAA security directives (Heinlen, Welfel, Richmond, & Rak, 2003; Ritterband et al., 2003). In all settings, at the beginning of the field experience, the intern should ask specifically about confidentiality policy and any unique issues that apply to the particular setting, patient group, or other activity. If at any time questions arise pertaining to confidentiality, you should consult your supervisor and/or instructor.

RELEASE OF INFORMATION

To protect confidentiality, certain standards and guidelines must be followed scrupulously. First, the general principle to follow is that no one other than the client should be given any information—written, verbal, or otherwise—about the client without explicit written and signed permission from the client. Be aware, however, that within a treatment setting you are able to discuss the client with members of the treatment team. This is recognized in the HIPAA standards if the purpose is to provide quality of care (Benefeld, Ashkanazi, & Rozensky, 2006). Still, it is good practice to be careful about all communications, even within a setting. To help you deal with this issue, a suggested decision process will be offered later in the chapter.

In contrast to information that is exchanged within a treatment team, there are standard "Release of Information" forms that can be used if a client wishes to authorize the release of information to someone outside the team or setting. These forms typically provide space to identify the person(s) who will receive the information, the purpose of the release, the specific information to be released, the form in which the information will be communicated, the date of the release, the time period for which the release is to be valid, the name of the person authorized to release the information, the name of the client, and the signature of the client and the primary therapist or other professional (Bennett et al., 1990).

In practice, the requirement for written permission means that if someone calls or comes into an office claiming to have the client's permission to see records or discuss the case, one must not acquiesce to this request or even acknowledge that the person is a client unless there is written permission authorizing such disclosure to the individual asking for the information. This may seem like a nuisance, but it is necessary.

If problems arise, you can cope with insistent or demanding people by saying something like "I'm sorry, but I cannot share any information unless I have a signed release-of-information form. I'm sure you understand how important confidentiality is, and I'll be glad to provide you with whatever information I can as soon as a signed release of information is available." Note that this statement does not acknowledge that the individual in question is a client. It merely says that a release is necessary for any information to be shared. If the individual requesting the information does not accept this explanation or insists on being given information, you can refer the person to a supervisor. Under no circumstances should you let urgency, pressure, or inconvenience lead to laxity or carelessness about obtaining written releases.

SAFEGUARDING RECORDS AND THE HIPAA SECURITY STANDARDS

An important element of protecting confidentiality is the safeguarding of patient records. In considering how records are to be safeguarded, you should be aware that, as mentioned earlier, in addition to the HIPAA Privacy Rule, which mandates what health care information can and cannot be communicated, HIPAA also establishes a Security Rule, which outlines specific procedures for protecting the security of electronic information against inadvertent or unapproved access. Legally, the HIPAA security rule only applies to patient information that is electronically stored, generated, communicated, or received. In practice, because so much of what is done today involves computers and information technology, and because the HIPAA security principles are generally well founded, it is a good idea to know and follow these procedures even if you do not technically fall under the HIPAA mandates (APA Practice Organization, 2006). You should also be aware that for those who fall under HIPAA rules, one of the security rules requires that individuals and organizations conduct a formal risk assessment to evaluate and document measures taken to identify and minimize security risks.

The HIPAA Security Standard delineates a matrix of security standards that address Administrative Safeguards, Physical Safeguards, and Technical Safeguards. Briefly, Administrative Standards encompass such matters as staff selection and training, access-authorization procedures, contingency planning, and business contracts. Physical safeguards pertain to controlling access to records, workstation use and security, control of media devices, and methods for reuse or disposal of electronic devices or media. Finally, the Technical Safeguards involve such matters as user identification and authentication, encryption, and security of data transmission.

Again, whether or not you fall under the HIPAA requirements, common sense and sound practices suggest a number of measures that will help you stay in compliance with HIPAA. For example, all case notes, records, and other written or recorded information about the client should be kept in locked rooms and locked file cabinets. You should not leave notes, files, or other material with client names out in the open where others might see them inadvertently. As a further precaution, the words "Confidential Records" can be printed or stamped on all records.

Interns who keep class notebooks or journals should take care not to lose or misplace them. As an added precaution, interns should mark clearly on the outside of their notebooks that the material is confidential and should be returned unopened to the owner. I have all of our interns who keep journals write in bold letters on the front: "Confidential Personal Journal—If Found, Please Return to (intern's name and address)." In your writing for journals or classes, disguise the identity of clients via pseudonyms or false initials, such as Mr. X or Ms. B. Avoid the use of real initials or first names only, as these can easily be connected to the actual individual. These same guidelines apply to the use of computers, personal data assistants, and other means of data storage.

If case notes or any other clinical information is kept on computers, access to the files should be restricted through passwords and firewalls, automatic log-off procedures should be operative, and you should have installed effective anti-virus, and anti-spyware programs which are regularly updated and run. Other electronic security measures are explicitly spelled out in the HIPAA standards. Most internship sites will have on staff people who are expert in these matters, but I encourage you to at least familiarize yourself with the HIPAA standards and try to become conversant, if not personally proficient, with key elements of computer and Internet security.

SHARING INFORMATION WITH COLLEAGUES

Guidelines for sharing information with outside sources are relatively clear, and, with the few exceptions to be discussed later, the rule can be summarized succinctly as "Not without written permission from the client." Questions about sharing information with colleagues and other professionals concerned with a case are not as easily answered (Behnke, 2005). As each setting and situation is different, it may be helpful to offer a general framework you can use to help make your decisions. The framework revolves around the question words: what, who, why, where, when, and how. Before sharing information about a client with anyone, you should ask yourself:

1. *What is the client's privilege, and what are the client's assumptions?* What has the client been told about confidentiality and its limitations, and what does the client know about how information will or will not be shared? What documentation is there that the client has been told these things?

2. *Who is receiving the information?* Has the client given permission for them to have the information? What is their role or authority within the clinical setting? What professional training do they have? What is their relationship to the client? What do you think of their clinical skills and ethical knowledge? Also ask yourself if they know about and respect the principle of confidentiality.

3. *Why do they want the information?* Are they involved in the client's treatment in some way? Are they just curious? Are they seeking information to help them understand the client, or are they likely to use it in some counterproductive way?

4. *What information is being requested?* Are these persons asking for data such as address, phone, and so on, or are they asking for clinical information about the nature of the client's concerns or background? Are they asking for general impressions from tests or interviews, or do they want specific scores or answers to specific questions? Remember that merely because someone is asking for a certain type of information does not mean you should provide the information requested. Depending on the circumstances, you may choose to offer summaries or general impressions rather than specific test results or interview responses. You may also choose to offer no information at all if there is a probability that it will not be used responsibly and professionally.

5. *Where are you?* Is the setting private, or are you in a public place where others could easily overhear your discussion? Are the office doors closed? Could people in the waiting room hear you? Are other clients nearby?

6. *When should you discuss the information?* Is now the best time to share information? Will you have adequate time to discuss and explain things, or will you be rushed and not do an adequate job? Would it be better to schedule a specific time and place rather than sharing things in passing?

7. *How will you share the information?* Is it best to discuss information directly one on one, or can you accomplish the task over the phone? Should you formalize the exchange of information in writing, either by providing the information itself in written form or by keeping notes of the conversation? What are the relative pros and cons of direct verbal versus written exchange?

8. *What are the laws and regulations, and have I complied with them?* Most important of all, you must be sure that you are in compliance with HIPAA regulations and any other state and local laws or regulations regarding what is shared, how, with whom, and under what conditions.

ELECTRONIC HEALTH RECORDS

Issues of sharing information with colleagues, the use of electronic information technology, and the HIPAAA privacy and security standards all come together in the expanding application that is broadly referred to as health information technology (HIT). A central component of HIT is the use of electronic health records (EHR) or electronic medical records (EMR) systems. In an effort to increase efficiency, reduce medical errors, and improve communication and quality of care, a nationwide effort is underway to promote the use of electronic medical records systems. A study by the RAND Corporation (Bower, 2005; RAND 2005) estimated annual savings of $77 billion if health information technologies were fully implemented across the nation.

This initiative, promoted by government and the private sector, is intended to replace paper-based records systems with totally computerized formats. Thanks to congressional and administration actions, a national coordinator of health information technology has been tasked with establishing standards and promoting the use and interoperability of health information technologies across the health care spectrum, beginning with all federally funded programs. Ideally, the use of EHRs will speed information entry, reduce errors caused by unrecognizable handwriting, allow instant access to records from across the country or even across the globe, enhance coordination with insurance providers, and facilitate quality-assurance measures. Electronic records also allow artificial intelligence systems to check for potential complications of treatments, for example from unrecognized medication interactions. Intriguing ideas have also been put forward for ways in which EHRs can be used for both research and clinical efforts to enhance evidence-based practice initiatives (Drake, Teague, & Gersing, 2005).

While acknowledging the potential benefits of EHRs, there are also significant confidentiality issues, especially with regard to mental health treatment. Based on practical experience from a comprehensive health system using EMRs, Steinfeld, Ekorenrud, Gillett, Quirk, and Eytan (2006) offered very helpful suggestions for how such systems can be implemented and how mental health information can be incorporated. Central to this discussion is the interface between confidentiality issues, informed consent, and the technological capabilities of the EMR system. Within large, integrated health systems, there is a legitimate desire for other treatment professionals (e.g., primary physicians) to have some insight into any mental health or drug/alcohol issues that may be affecting their patients. On the other hand, patients may want to keep some of these issues absolutely private, particularly if there is the possibility that a medical records system could be accessed by someone other than their immediate mental health care professional or their primary physician. Beyond patient desires, there are also legal guidelines for how such records must be treated. Steinfeld et al. pointed out that federal law explicitly prohibits sharing information about chemical-dependency treatment with anyone outside the specific treatment program except in cases of emergency.

From a technological perspective, this raises important issues about how records can be separated and how access can be controlled to information that should not be accessed except by specified individuals for certain reasons and with specific permissions. Steinfeld et al. described a "split-note" structure in which portions of progress notes (e.g., those addressing medications or specific behavioral interventions) may be shared with other providers, but other sections (e.g., those describing personal issues or specific psychotherapy matters) are not accessible. This approach has merit, but personally I still have concerns about putting psychotherapy notes in any centralized electronic format that would be accessible to anyone other than myself. More will be said about this in Chapter 6, but I strongly recommend that, if possible, you put into an EMR only what other professionals must know in order to provide continuity of care. Furthermore, as Steinfeld et al. pointed out, informed consent is absolutely essential, and patients have a right to know how their information will be stored and managed and what will be included or excluded from any EMR.

If your placement is using an EHR or EMR system, take the time to learn not only how to enter or retrieve data from the system, but also to understand fully how access is granted or restricted, what informed-consent procedures are in place, and what your options are in regard to entering notes about clients with whom you are working.

INADVERTENT CONFIDENTIALITY VIOLATIONS

To appreciate why so much attention is paid to protecting confidentiality, take a moment to consider the possible impact of a breach of confidentiality. Consider also how, even when scrupulous procedures are implemented within systems and institutions, breaches can nevertheless occur due to lapses in judgment by professionals.

For example, I once observed a psychologist with 25 years of experience who was invited to a large introductory psychology class to discuss clinical issues. During his talk, he described a case study in which he mentioned that the patient was a 50-year-old man, divorced, with two daughters. At this point, confidentiality was still protected. However, the speaker went on to name the town the client lived in, then said that the client owned a local car dealership, was a past president of a well-known social organization, and had been struggling with a serious drinking problem for several years. The psychologist never actually divulged the client's name, but in the mid-size community where this occurred, it was easy enough for several people in the class to realize who the client was.

As a second example, over lunch in a local restaurant, an intern and his social work supervisor were discussing a family the intern was seeing. At the end of the lunch, they arose to find that the same family had been sitting one booth away. Thinking about the discussion later, the intern realized he had criticized certain family members, and he was extremely troubled about how to deal with this in the next session.

While the violations of confidentiality in the examples just cited are rather obvious, Gavey and Braun (1997) pointed out that despite the frequent usage of anonymous clinical material in teaching settings and publications, the ethical guidelines concerning such usage are still rather ambiguous. Of particular concern in this regard is the possibility that clients will read the work their therapists have published or presented about their case.

EFFECTS OF CONFIDENTIALITY VIOLATIONS

To appreciate the significance of breaks in confidentiality, imagine yourself as the client in the situations just described. How would you react to hearing your personal case discussed before a class in such a way that people would know your identity? What would be your reaction to the next therapy session if you overheard your therapist discussing your case over lunch? Would you even go to therapy, or would you simply terminate with no explanation?

Also ask how you might feel as a current or potential therapy client if you heard a therapist discussing some other client. Even for those other than the clients themselves, merely knowing that therapists speak in such ways about clients could cause people to avoid the therapy process entirely. Among the reactions from clients who have unknowingly been written about by therapists, Gavey and Braun (1997) described feelings of betrayal, powerlessness, and anger. Such problems have led some authors (Stoller, 1988) to conclude that clients should not be written about without their informed consent. Others have pointed out that the process of seeking consent for publishing case information after a case has concluded could evoke past issues (Clifft, 1986). To date, these ethical and clinical issues concerning the use of case studies have yet to be fully resolved. Gavey and Braun called for further discussion in the professional community. Their advice is well taken; but in the meantime, interns and professionals should use the utmost caution and respect for clients when discussing clients and cases in a public setting.

The clinical implications of confidentiality violations should be sufficient to promote caution, but there are also legal issues to consider. Violation of HIPAA confidentiality rules carries the possibilities of both monetary penalties and criminal prosecution for willful and serious offenses. In addition to the possibility of criminal prosecution, a client who is harmed in some way by a therapist's breach of confidentiality may well sue for damages (Conte & Karasu, 1990; Reamer, 1995; Schwartz, 1989; Swenson, 1997). Because confidentiality is such a fundamental condition of therapy, a judge or jury would not be likely to look positively on an intern's or professional's carelessness in such matters.

EXCEPTIONS TO CONFIDENTIALITY

The matter of confidentiality is complicated by the requirement that certain information about clients may or must be shared with others (Glosoff et al., 1997; Schwartz, 1989). This is further complicated by legal uncertainties and differences in interpretation and statutes for different states. HIPAA rules also describe permissible exceptions to confidentiality which, in general, are consistent with established ethical standards and existing state and case law. Only a brief review of this topic is provided here, but the information should be sufficient to help you appreciate both the importance and the complexities of this issue. You are strongly encouraged to study this matter in more detail in the references cited at the beginning and end of the chapter and in consultation with your supervisor and instructors. You should also familiarize yourself with the pertinent state and HIPAA regulations.

Without attempting to provide specific guidance for each situation, five instances will be identified in which absolute confidentiality may not hold and information may need to be revealed. The main message in this discussion is that under no circumstances should you give a client the often-heard but erroneous assurance that "nothing you say or do will be shared with anyone else without your permission." That simply is not always true, and clients have a right to know the exceptions.

Swenson referred to therapists giving clients a "psychological Miranda warning" about limits to confidentiality (Swenson, 1993, p. 70). This reference to the Miranda ruling means that therapists should tell clients beforehand how information from clinical interactions might be used in court. This allows clients to use their own discretion about what they will or will not discuss in therapy.

Findings of Miller and Thelen (1986) supported this principle, showing that most subjects want to be informed of confidentiality limits beforehand. Despite this finding and the clearly stated ethical principle, Nicolai and Scott (1994) reported that almost 20% of the respondents to their survey regarding informed-consent procedures and child-abuse reporting "indicated that they sometimes, rarely, or never provide this information to clients and more than 5 percent misleadingly tell clients that everything disclosed in therapy is confidential" (p. 159). Nicolai and Scott expressed their concern about this finding, stating:

> Without explicit presentation of information regarding confidentiality limits, the novice client may well assume that all disclosures, regardless of content, will be kept confidential. Moreover, clinicians who tell clients that everything they say will be held in confidence are clearly putting clients, as well as themselves, at risk. (p. 158)

Briefly, the five main exceptions to confidentiality occur in (1) cases of abuse, (2) cases in which clients are considered dangerous to themselves, (3) cases in which a client intends to harm others, (4) certain legal proceedings in which the case notes and other records can be subpoenaed, and (5) requests by insurance providers for case notes to assess the necessity for and benefits of services.

PRIVILEGED COMMUNICATION

Before discussing the exceptions to confidentiality, it will be helpful to introduce and explain the concept of privileged communications (Koocher & Keith-Spiegel, 1998). *Privilege* is a legal term referring to the right of individuals to withhold information requested by a court. Such privileges are established by law and pertain to professions and relationships, such as the relationships between attorney and client and between physician and patient, communications with members of the clergy, and, in most states, communications between clients and officially recognized mental health practitioners, including psychologists, social workers, counselors, and others recognized by the states. As Swenson (1993) explained the rationale for such protections, "These are relationships in which the legislatures consider the benefits of confidentiality more important than a court's need for evidence" (p. 135).

It is important to understand that the legal right of privilege resides with the client, also referred to as the "holder" of the privilege. This means that it is the client's prerogative, not the therapist's, to decide to waive privilege and allow information to be disclosed. Except in certain circumstances to be discussed in a moment, the therapist's obligation is to protect the client's privilege whenever it is applicable. If therapists refuse to release information, they are doing so on behalf of the client's privilege, not because the therapist holds the privilege. Similarly, therapists must realize that, apart from situations explicitly allowing or requiring confidentiality to be broken, the therapist cannot unilaterally waive a client's privilege. Unless the client has voluntarily waived privileges or the courts have specifically ordered otherwise, the therapist has a duty to assert the client's privilege and not release information.

The limits and protections of client-therapist privilege were clarified in an important U.S. Supreme Court decision, *Jaffee* v. *Redmond* (1996), in which the majority of the court found that privileged communication between a patient and a social worker was protected. This case was of particular significance because it specifically included social workers in the category of therapists who enjoy privileged communications and because it established a ruling at the federal level that may guide subsequent decisions by lower courts (Alexander, 1997; DeBell & Jones, 1997).

In essence, the court found in *Jaffee* v. *Redmond* that a therapist, a clinical social worker, could not be compelled to reveal the private records of a client as part of a civil suit against the client by a third party. Specifically, the court held:

> Because effective psychotherapy depends upon an atmosphere of confidence and trust in which the patient is willing to make a frank and complete disclosure. . . . For this reason the mere possibility of disclosure may impede development of the confidential relationship necessary for successful treatment. (p. 1928)

Thorough reviews of *Jaffee* v. *Redmond* and the broader concept of privilege can be found in Alexander (1997), DeBell and Jones (1997), and Knapp and VandeCreek (1997). While noting that the court's decision marked important progress toward defining privilege clients in therapeutic relationships, it is also

important to emphasize again that certain legal exceptions apply (Glosoff et al., 1997). Just as courts have ruled that clients have a privilege to not disclose information shared with therapists, the courts have also determined that in certain circumstances therapists must release information, whether or not the client would concur. Swenson explains that under normal circumstances, "a therapist is not liable for violating a client's privacy rights if the therapist discloses information covered by an exception or because a law mandates disclosure" (p. 135). Examples of such conditions are described in the following sections.

Again, I emphasize that the following material is intended to help you understand the issues you should consider in dealing with confidential material. Laws vary from state to state and change with time. Therefore, this discussion should not be taken as legal advice. You are responsible for understanding and abiding by the laws of your state and the practices of your agency. If you have any questions or specific concerns arise, consult your instructor, supervisor, state organization, professional insurance provider, or attorney. Throughout your training, it is also a good idea to attend periodic risk-management workshops. In addition to providing updates and discussion of emerging trends in ethics and risk management, attendance at such workshops may also qualify practitioners for discounts on liability insurance with certain carriers.

ABUSE

In most states, specific laws require those in the helping and teaching professions to report instances of known or suspected abuse (Kalichman, 1999; Mannheim et al., 2002; Small, Lyons, & Guy, 2002; Swenson, 1993). This principle, which primarily applies to instances of child abuse but may also apply to abuse of disabled or elderly adults (Bergeron & Gray, 2003), is designed to protect vulnerable individuals from harm. For a brief but informative and thought-provoking history and analysis of the effects of mandatory reporting laws, see Hutchinson (1993). For an important discussion of other liability issues pertaining to cases of abuse, see Pollack and Marsh (2004).

Under abuse reporting laws, if a child tells a therapist that he or she is being physically or sexually abused, or if the child has bruises or other injuries that suggest abuse, or if the therapist has other clear grounds to believe physical, sexual, or emotional abuse is occurring, the therapist is obligated to notify agencies that will intervene to investigate the matter and protect the child. These agencies are generally referred to as Child Protective Services, Children's Services Division, or, more commonly in practice, by acronyms such as CPS, CSD, and so on.

In most states that require professionals to report abuse, the laws protect those who report from civil liability, providing the reports are filed in good faith and without malice, and, importantly, providing that the professional followed the statutory requirements (Small, Lyons, & Guy, 2002). Failure to report abuse may result in criminal penalties or in civil actions (Howing & Wodarski, 1992), and this can apply even if you fail to report because you believe someone else has already filed a report. In a number of states, there are criminal penalties for knowingly making false reports of abuse.

One other issue that has developed relatively recently centers around therapists' responsibilities to the alleged perpetrators of childhood abuse. In a comprehensive review of this issue, Knapp and VanDeCreek (2001) concluded that there is no "bright line" to guide therapists in dealing with this area, but a number of challenging ethical and legal questions are raised and therapists should be sensitive to and consider them carefully in any abuse case.

From a clinical perspective, abuse situations are further complicated by concerns about how clients or families will react if a therapist files a report with a protective services agency. In this context, Howing and Wodarski (1992) reiterated the advice to inform clients in advance of limitations to confidentiality. They also suggested that treatment is not always harmed and can sometimes be enhanced if a therapist discusses such concerns and responsibilities with clients and incorporates the abuse reporting, investigation, and response into the overall context of treatment.

In your own work as an intern, you should speak with your supervisor and instructor to be sure you are informed about the abuse reporting laws in your state. You should also know the procedures to follow if you have reason to believe a client is being abused or is abusing someone else. Such procedures must always include notification of confidentiality limits at the outset of therapy, careful documentation of information, and consultation with supervisors and instructors. The charge of abuse is very serious, and professionals must not be hasty in reporting cases. On the other hand, if there are sound reasons to believe that abuse is occurring, professionals or interns may be responsible to report the abuse, and they must know what their legal responsibility is. In all such situations, interns must inform and consult with their placement supervisor and faculty instructor whenever such questions arise.

Suicide and Dangerousness to Self

When clients are considered to be at risk of harming themselves, therapists are obligated to take measures to protect the client. Given the nature of the work and the clients served by helping professionals, this is not an uncommon situation. Indeed, surveys have shown that as many as one-quarter to one-half of therapists sampled reported that at some point in their careers they lost a client through suicide (Brown, 1987; Chemtob, Bauer, Hamada, Pelowski, & Muraoka, 1989).

Assessing for suicide risk is a particularly nuanced art and contains significant litigation risk for helping professionals (Baerger, 2001; Mishna, Antle, & Regehr, 2002; NASW Insurance Trust, 2003; Paulson & Worth, 2002). As an intern, your first obligation if confronted with a potentially suicidal client is to respect the ethical principle of competence and seek assistance. It would be unusual and unwise for someone still in training to have sole or primary responsibility for working with

a client who presents a risk of suicide, and even highly experienced therapists often seek consultation when working with suicidal clients. McGlothlin, Rainey, and Kindsvatter (2005) provide helpful suggestions for how supervisors can assist interns who are working with potentially suicidal clients.

While you should not attempt to manage a suicidal case alone, it is nevertheless important for you to have some framework from which to evaluate suicide risk in order to recognize when you may need assistance and when it may be necessary to inform others of the client's condition. A number of articles and books identify suicide-risk factors and offer suggestions for working with potentially suicidal patients both from a clinical and an ethical/legal perspective (Baerger, 2001; Berman, Jobes & Silverman, 2006; Bongar, 2002; Joiner, Walker, Rudd, & Jobes, 1999; Mishna, Antle, & Regehr, 2002; Oordt et al., 2005; Sanchez, 2001; Westefeld et al., 2000; White, 2003). Sanchez (2001), Bongar, (2002), and Oordt et al. (2005) provided particularly useful reviews of both risk factors and protective factors along with practical guidelines and a checklist to record key elements considered in a risk assessment. Berman, Jobes, and Silverman (2006) focus on the challenges of understanding, predicting, and preventing adolescent suicide. Westefeld et al. (2000) review theoretical models of suicide, and Joiner et al. (1999) developed a suicidality rating scale with levels ranging from nonexistent to extreme. Another suicide assessment scale, the SAD PERSONS Scale (SPS), was developed by Patterson, Dohn, Bird, and Patterson (1983) and was reviewed by Juhnke (1994). This scale utilizes Patterson's suicide-risk-assessment acronym SAD PERSONS to create a mnemonic for 10 literature-identified suicide-risk factors. These major risk factors are sex, age, depression, previous attempt, ethanol abuse, rational thinking loss, social supports lacking, organized plan, no spouse, and sickness. One point is scored for each risk factor present, and total scores can range from 0 (suggesting very low immediate risk of suicide) to 10 (suggesting very high risk of suicide). In addition, Patterson emphasized that certain combinations of factors and situations may be more dangerous. Other factors to consider in weighing suicide potential include family history of suicide attempts, lethality of previous attempts, preoccupation with or scheduling of a plan, and evidence of rehearsal or experimentation for carrying out a plan (Clark, 1998; Peruzzi & Bongar, 1999).

If a therapist identifies a risk of suicide and the client is willing to go along with protective measures for his or her own benefit, confidentiality is not usually a problem. Oordt et al. (2005) described the use of "crisis response plan cards" developed between patient and therapist that define specific coping strategies and actions the patient will take instead of using suicide behaviors. As part of such plans, patients may be asked to complete release of information forms in the event that a therapist or the patient needs to contact a crisis treatment program or hospital. One caveat about such plans, and about alternative "no-suicide contracts," is that they may provide therapists with a false sense of security and should never be considered a guarantee that patients will not violate the agreement and actually harm themselves in spite of the agreement (Bongar, 2002).

Matters are more complicated when the therapist has reason to believe the client is at serious risk of self-harm but is not willing to comply with treatment recommendations. In these situations, the therapist may have to take steps to seek involuntary commitment to a hospital unit or pursue some other treatment option to ensure the client's safety. Koocher and Keith-Spiegel (1998) advise that you should be thoroughly versed in the laws and procedures for commitment. Before a crisis arises, you should have information readily available about the relevant phone numbers and contact persons. If you are in a setting or role where this possibility might arise, I strongly encourage you to obtain the necessary information now and complete the form provided in Appendix F. Having the knowledge and information readily available beforehand can save you a frantic and frightening search for information should a crisis arise. It could also save your client's life.

Procedures for obtaining involuntary treatment vary, but a common scenario is for the therapist to contact specifically designated mental health specialists who then evaluate the client and determine the need for commitment or other treatment. In general, as long as the therapist is acting in good faith and using sound professional judgment, pursuing such measures is protected by law, even though it means releasing information about the client to certain agencies or officials without the client's permission. This is a general rule, however, and one should check carefully about the procedures to be followed in each case and location. One should also be sure to carefully document the information on which decisions were made and the steps taken in response.

Two final points should be made before concluding this discussion of suicide risk and confidentiality. First, as in all of your clinical work, it is absolutely essential to adhere to the highest standards of care and document your actions carefully, particularly when working with high-risk patients. Berman, Jobes, and Silverman (2006), Baerger (2001), and White (2003a) all emphasized that clinicians need not live in fear of patient suicide or of being sued if a patient commits suicide if the level of care provided was sound and is well documented. It should be emphasized, however, that if legal proceedings do result from a patient's suicide, you will be expected to demonstrate through your written records that you acted responsibly and demonstrated reasonable care in the diagnosis and treatment of the individual. This means you must record both what you did to assess and treat the patient and, if risk is present, the reasons for making certain treatment decisions given the information available to you and the client's needs at the time. Baerger offers a useful review of actual case law pertaining to patient suicide, then provides practical recommendations that derive from those cases.

The second issue to keep in mind concerning suicide is the impact a patient's death can have on you personally and emotionally. This will be discussed in more detail in a later chapter

dealing with self-care for providers, but it is worth mentioning here because, as Knox and colleagues (2006) and DeAngelis (2001) pointed out, too little attention is given supporting and caring for therapists after they lose a patient to suicide.

EXERCISE

As noted a moment ago in the text, being prepared by having the necessary information available and understanding the procedures to follow in the event of a crisis should be a part of your training and practice. Whether or not you work in a setting where this issue might arise, it will be a valuable learning experience to review the process with your instructor or site supervisor. On the back of the Emergency Contact and Procedures form in Appendix F, you will find a place to complete a step-by-step procedure to follow should it be necessary to consider commitment of a patient. Review the procedures now, and complete the form now. Think of this as you would a life jacket on a boat. Chances are you may not need it; but if you do, you will be extremely grateful that you have it handy.

INTENT TO HARM OTHERS AND THE "DUTY TO PROTECT"

A second situation in which clinicians may be required to divulge information relating to danger arises when a client makes explicit threats or statements of intent to harm another person. This situation is now commonly known in the professions as a Tarasoff case, based on an incident in which a client told a therapist he wanted to harm a specific individual. The therapist believed the client was serious and took steps to pursue involuntary commitment, but the therapist did not manage to directly warn the intended victim. Several months later, the client, who had since dropped out of therapy, killed the young woman he had earlier threatened to harm. The therapist and the university he worked for were then sued for damages for not having warned the victim. Reviews of the Tarasoff case was reviewed by VandeCreek et al. (1994), Fulero (1988), and Slovenko (1988), all of whom discuss in detail the initial case and subsequent implications. Special Tarasoff-related considerations and implications for HIV patients were reviewed by Chenneville (2000), Schlossberger and Hecker (1996), McGuire et al. (1995), and Stanard and Hazler (1995).

The Tarasoff case, from which the principle known as the "duty to warn" evolved, subsequently went through a series of appeals, and the definition of the duty to warn has continued to evolve, with later rulings leading to the concept of a "duty to protect." Most recently, this concept has evolved still further as the result of a California case (*Ewing* v. *Goldstein,* http://fs news.findlaw.com/cases/ca/caapp4th/slip/2004/b163112.html) in which a therapist was apparently told by a client's family member, but not by the client, that the client intended to harm another individual. Unfortunately, the client did in fact kill the person and then himself. The therapist was sued, and an appeals court ruled that the therapist's duty to protect applied, and thus therapists must take measures to prevent possible harm, even if the information about a threat comes from someone other than a family member (Berger & Berger, 2005).

This recent ruling may go through further appeals, but the key point is that if you have good reason to believe someone seriously intends to harm another person, you may be required to take every reasonable step necessary to protect the intended victim, and this may include breaking confidentiality by warning the potential victim and advising responsible authorities such as the police. Since this will sometimes mean divulging information about a client without the client's permission, therapists are in a difficult bind, especially if, as Leong, Eth, and Silva (1992) reported, the records of therapists who warn of potentially dangerous clients may later be used in criminal prosecutions of the clients.

Strategies for dealing with potentially dangerous clients have been described by Monahan (1993), Tishler, Gordon, and Landry-Meyer (2000), and others. Critical steps recommended by Monahan include training and knowledge of risk assessment, examination of the client's past and current clinical record, direct inquiries of the patient, and estimation of the risk and development of a responsible plan. Further discussion of this topic is provided in Chapter 8, which offers suggestions for how interns can reduce risks to themselves and others when dealing with potentially violent patients.

It is beyond the scope of the present chapter to go into more detail on this topic, but you are strongly encouraged to consult the references cited here; if you encounter such situations, you should immediately seek assistance from supervisors and instructors, from your professional organization, and, if necessary, from legal counsel. Also, you should be careful to document fully the steps you take and the information on which you base your decisions. This will help ensure that you follow sound clinical practice. If something unfortunate happens despite your best efforts, accurate documentation and sound consultation can help reduce your personal risks of liability.

LEGAL PROCEEDINGS AND COURT ORDERS

A fourth situation in which you may be forced to reveal information about a client is if you are ordered to do so by a court. This may come about through a variety of processes, but one of the more common reasons involves civil suits for damages (Glossoff, Herlihy, & Spence, 2000; Schwartz, 1989). For example, if a therapist is seeing a client who sues someone else claiming the other person's actions caused psychological harm to the client, the attorney for the defendant may have the right to subpoena the plaintiff's psychological and medical records. When a client of a therapist is the plaintiff in a suit claiming mental or emotional damages, the client's records no longer fall under the protections of privilege discussed earlier. In these cases, the therapy records are considered to be evidence that is necessary and legitimate to help establish the nature and extent of the alleged damages. Here again, however, the interpretation of this principle may vary from state to state (Glosoff et al., 1997), and it is your responsibility to protect the client's privilege unless explicitly ordered by a court to release records.

In cases such as these, if someone other than the client requests your records, it is advisable to consult an attorney and do everything you can to avoid releasing information unless the client grants a release of information. Attorneys usually advise plaintiffs that their records may be requested in such proceedings, and therefore to consider the possible review of clinical information in deciding whether to pursue a lawsuit. Nevertheless, there may be instances in which a client will not sign a release to share information with the opposition's attorney. In that event, the treatment professional may be ordered to comply with a court order to release the information.

Whether or not the client has signed such a release, if a court order requires it and state or federal law does not protect the client's privilege under the circumstances, the records must be released. Be sure, however, that before you release any records without the client's permission, a court has, in fact, ordered you to do so. Merely receiving a letter from an attorney indicating that your records have been requested does not constitute a court order, and you are not, therefore, required to comply. You should also know that a subpoena to appear before a court is not the same as a court order demanding records. If you receive a subpoena to appear without a specific order to produce your records, you should preserve the client's privilege and not release records unless specifically ordered to do so, in writing, by the court. Further, you should never give information of any sort directly to a person who is serving you with a subpoena, no matter how insistent or aggressive he or she may be (Zur, 2006), Instead, you should accept the subpoena and send the person who served it away without even acknowledging that the individual is a client or that you have any involvement with the case. Then you should immediately contact an attorney and, of course, your instructor and supervisor. For a thorough review of dealing with subpoenas or court-compelled testimony, see the report by the APA Committee on Legal Issues (2006).

In light of the possibility for release of information through court order, three pieces of advice emerge. First, clients should be informed of this possibility at the start of therapy. This reduces the risk of a later lawsuit if the clinician makes an inaccurate comment, such as "There is no way anyone can have access to your records without your permission." Second, clinicians need to be selective in what they put in their case notes. This matter is discussed in more detail in Chapter 6. Third, again, before releasing any information without a client's permission, consult with an attorney to be sure that the court order or other request has legal authority and cannot be refused, and always consult immediately with your instructor and supervisor.

INSURANCE COMPANY INQUIRIES, MANAGED CARE, AND ETHICAL PRACTICE

To understand issues of confidentiality in relation to health insurance, it is helpful to know a little about the concept of managed care. The term *managed care* broadly refers to efforts to contain the rising costs of health care by "managing" the health care services that are provided and the ways they are paid for. In a traditional "fee-for-service" model, patients seek care from largely independent health care practitioners who provide treatment and bill patients and insurers for services based on the practitioner's professional judgment of what is needed. By comparison, under managed-care arrangements, patients must receive care from a selected list or panel of professionals, and the services that will be provided are tightly specified and controlled by the managed-care insurance company.

Some managed-care organizations are essentially not-for-profit cooperatives, in which members participate voluntarily and share in the benefits of lowered insurance premiums as the result of the cost-saving measures. On the other hand, there are also very large for-profit managed-care companies that provide health insurance to companies and individuals as well as through government-funded insurance plans. These managed-care insurance companies are in business to make a profit and to return those profits to their stockholders or corporate owners.

The ostensible purpose of the managed-care approach is to control rising health care costs by limiting unnecessary or ineffective treatments or services. That effort, however, has also resulted in limitations on patient choices (Kremer & Gesten, 2003), a loss of professional autonomy, and, many argue, health care decisions that are driven by economic concerns and profit motives rather than patient care needs (Cooper & Gottlieb, 2000; Rupert & Baird, 2004). In addition, as managed-care insurers have set increasingly tight restrictions on what services they will pay for and which providers they will compensate for treatment, health care professionals have been forced to provide certain types of treatments, while other therapies have not been approved of by the managed-care companies (Braun & Cox, 2005). Further, in an effort to ensure that only the covered illnesses or treatments are being paid for, managed-care companies have increasingly forced therapists to divulge previously confidential information about their clients and their treatment methods (Acuff et al., 1999). Some insurers had even gone so far as to insist that therapists allow them to review the records of other patients who are not covered by the insurer in order to compare the kinds of treatment the insurance company's clients are receiving with that of other patients.

Regrettably, the intrusiveness of insurance companies has led to increasing reports of clients who choose not to seek needed treatment because they so resent or are embarrassed by the intrusive questions of insurers. Some insurers have also begun to prescreen clients before authorizing therapy. In my judgment, this is unacceptable. For a suicidal patient, victim of sexual abuse, or anyone facing serious distress to have to discuss such issues with an anonymous insurance representative before meeting with a qualified therapist of the client's choosing is extraordinarily countertherapeutic and potentially dangerous. Professional organizations are working at the political level to pass legislation that would prevent or contain such intrusions (Sleek, 1998). I encourage professionals and interns to support those efforts.

These intrusions into the decision-making autonomy of practitioners and the confidential records of clients have raised numerous ethical concerns (Acuff et al., 1999; Braun & Cox, 2005; Cooper & Gottlieb, 2000; Kremer & Gesten, 2003; Rock & Congress, 1999). They have also spawned legislative responses in the form of the much-debated "Patient's Bill of Rights," which has been proposed in the U.S. Congress and passed in varying forms in several states (Rabasca, 1999).

While it is unlikely that you will be billing for services personally in a managed-care setting during your internship, it is highly likely that you will interact with managed care at some point in your future, either as a health care patient yourself or as a provider (Daniels, Alva, & Olivares, 2002). To get a better sense of the ethical implications of managed care, consider the following exercise.

EXERCISE

Refer back to the basic ethical values and principles discussed early in this chapter—for example, the values of service, social justice, dignity and worth of the person, and the importance of human relationships, integrity, competence, beneficence, and the like. With these values in mind, consider the ethical dilemmas that could be created by the following scenarios that can occur under a managed-care insurance arrangement. Then consider a second set of scenarios that could occur under a fee-for-service model and think about the ethical issues these raise. Finally, consult the code of ethics for your profession and others, and discuss these examples with your instructor or supervisor to determine how these matters are to be addressed in an ethical manner.

ETHICAL DILEMMAS THAT ARISE IN MANAGED-CARE ARRANGEMENTS

1. Research has shown that the relationship between therapist and client is often critical to effective therapy, but a managed-care company does not allow patients to select their own therapists, instead requiring the patient to accept a therapist who is on the panel of approved providers. If you believe a patient will have difficulty forming a therapeutic relationship with the providers on a panel, what should you recommend to the patient?
2. A patient's insurance company will pay for therapy for a certain type of diagnosis but not for a different diagnosis. You are seeing a patient who cannot afford to pay for therapy without the help of insurance. While the client demonstrates some of the symptoms that are typical of a diagnosis that is covered for treatment, the most accurate diagnosis would be for a disorder that is not included in the client's insurance coverage. Which diagnosis should you give and why?
3. In your best judgment and from your knowledge of the research literature, a patient would benefit most from a treatment approach that is not included on the list of approved

treatments covered under the insurance policy. If you treat the patient with the approach you believe is most appropriate, you will not receive payment for the treatment from the insurance company. How should you proceed?

4. A patient who is a prominent member of your community is seeing you for therapy regarding a very delicate personal matter that could be detrimental to the patient's reputation if it became public. In an effort to ensure that you are providing only approved treatments for approved disorders, the patient's managed-care company demands to see your treatment records. The patient has not given permission for you to release the records to the insurance company, but the company is threatening to withhold payments unless they are released.

FEE-FOR-SERVICE DILEMMAS

1. You know of a colleague who practices a form of therapy that has not been shown by research to be effective and is highly expensive. The colleague's patients like the treatment approach and, as long as their insurance company is willing to pay for the costs, they are happy to continue receiving the treatment for as long as they can. What are your ethical obligations, given what you know about the treatment, the costs, and the alternatives? How do broader social concerns (e.g., the overall costs of health care) relate to your decision and your ethical considerations?

2. A therapist believes that each session with a client should be considered as a unique interaction in the moment and that keeping an ongoing record of psychotherapy notes tends to interfere with the ability to focus on the present moment of each session. As a result, this therapist keeps no ongoing notes other than a simple record of visits. When the patient's insurance company asks the therapist to explain and document exactly what is being done in therapy to help the patient, the therapist refuses to divulge any information, even though the patient is willing to sign a release-of-information form.

3. A state agency contracts with a group of mental health therapists to provide services to children and adolescents in need. Because of budget constraints, the agency eventually determines that it needs to audit the treatment and outcomes to determine whether the money that has been spent has been effective in helping the children. The therapists maintain that their treatment has helped the children and they resent any intrusion or oversight into their practice. Do you believe state or federal agencies have a right or responsibility to review treatment practices and possibly limit services that will be paid for unless effective outcomes can be demonstrated?

Fortunately, thanks in part to advocacy the various professional associations, some of the ethical dilemmas raised by

managed care have been addressed and clarified by HIPAA guidelines. Now, under the HIPAA guidelines, virtually every health care agency and provider will be required to give patients very clear and specific information about precisely what information will or will not be made available to an insurance company and how the company must handle the information.

What is more, in one of the more positive changes brought about by HIPAA, the confidentiality of psychotherapy notes is now explicitly protected by law providing the notes are kept separate from the rest of the patient's record. As described in HIPAA, psychotherapy notes, which historically have been referred to as "process notes" (Kagle, 1993), are used by therapists to record ongoing therapeutic interactions, conversations, and observations of the client's dynamics. Not only are such notes protected, but under HIPAA rules, insurers cannot refuse to reimburse providers for services if the patient does not agree to the release of psychotherapy notes (Holloway, 2003). Keep in mind, however, that while psychotherapy notes may now have greater protection from disclosure to insurance companies, any writing or records regarding a client, including personal notes or process notes, may still be subpoenaed in a court proceeding.

CONFIDENTIALITY WITH MINORS

The discussion of confidentiality concludes with a topic that is frequently raised by interns but has no simple answers. Confidentiality issues with minors can be especially complex because they involve the rights and responsibilities of at least two people, the minor and at least one adult, and because there are competing values, such as protecting the privacy rights of the minor and respecting the rights and responsibilities of parents or guardians (Behnke & Warner, 2002; Isaacs & Stone, 2001; Mannheim et al., 2002). In addition, as with other aspects of ethics and the law, standards vary across states, depend on the particular issues involved (e.g., alcohol and drug treatment, as well as sexual or reproductive concerns, may be treated differently than other health matters) and have changed over time (Maradiegue, 2003; Reamer, 2005). For recent reviews of state laws pertaining to health care with minors, see Boonstra and Nash (2000) and the monograph from the Center for Adolescent Health and the Law (2003). For a comprehensive and insightful discussion of research ethics and issues, including informed consent and confidentiality with families and minors, see Margolin et al. (2005).

From a clinical perspective, research suggests, not surprisingly, that the promise of confidentiality increases the willingness of adolescents to reveal personal information and seek health care from a physician. Ford, Milstein, Halpern-Felsher, and Irwin (1997) compared the responses of adolescents exposed to three different levels of confidentiality instructions. Their results showed that subjects who were assured of confidentiality were significantly more likely to express a willingness to visit their provider again. This research also showed that 17% of all subjects said that concerns about confidentiality had caused them to avoid health care at some point in the past.

With regard to the cognitive ability of minors to make decisions on their own behalf, Gustafson and McNamara (1987) reviewed both legal and developmental considerations relating to confidentiality with minors. They noted that in empirical studies (Belter & Grisso, 1984), 15-year-olds performed as well as 21-year-olds in assessments of their understanding of clients' rights. Other studies (Kaser-Boyd, Adelman, & Taylor, 1985) showed that therapy risks and benefits can be identified by minors, including minors with learning and behavioral problems. In general, it appears that children above the age of about 12 years have a better understanding of confidentiality and related issues than younger children.

The major professional organizations and their corresponding ethical codes recognize the complexity of confidentiality issues with minors and families, but, perhaps because of that very complexity and the diversity of state laws, the codes tend not to be as specific or directive as one might wish when faced with real-world challenges. In general, the ethics codes urge professionals to address such issues by providing informed consent at the outset of treatment, clarifying who the client is, seeking specific releases of information where appropriate, and adhering to relevant laws. For example, section 1.07(f) of the NASW code advises that in work with families, social workers should "seek agreement among the parties involved concerning each individual's right to confidentiality." The ACA code of ethics, section B.5.a, advises that when counseling minor clients or adults lacking the capacity to give voluntary informed consent, counselors should "protect the confidentiality of information received in the counseling relationship as specified by federal and state laws, written policies, and applicable ethical standards." The APA code of ethics is less specific about work with minor clients. For example, Standard 4.03 of the APA code of ethics states that in working with families, psychologists should "attempt to clarify at the outset, (1) which of the individuals are patients or clients and (2) the relationship the psychologist will have to each person."

In addition to the guidance of ethical codes, HIPAA privacy standards also address the confidentiality of health records with minors (http://www.ihs.gov/AdminMngrResources/HIPAA/documents/UnemanicipatedMinorsPP31JAN03.pdf). The HIPAA standards make important distinctions regarding when and how parents or guardians can access the records of minors. For example, disclosure requirements may differ depending on whether or not a parent or guardian initially authorized the relevant treatment. HIPAA also spells out specific conditions under which state laws protecting minors rights must take precedence. As noted elsewhere, HIPAA standards also provide special provisions and protections for records from alcohol/drug abuse treatment.

Given the ethical and legal complexities of these issues, I find it helpful to follow the advice of Gustafson and McNamara (1987), who recommended that therapists working with minors

or families should establish a written professional-service agreement that explicitly states the conditions of confidentiality within which therapy will be provided. This should be reviewed with each person involved, then signed and made part of the client's permanent record. Reviewing conditions and signing an agreement beforehand reduces the possibility of later misunderstanding or conflict. This process also gives clients and therapists the right to decide whether they will participate in therapy under the established conditions. I would add that such contracts should be established for all clients, not just minors, and the contracts should reflect local, state, and federal laws.

Finally, let me add a special precaution for interns working with minors. In addition to the legal and ethical matters just discussed, interns should be aware that they may find themselves in particularly difficult situations with working with minors, especially with adolescents. Because interns may be relatively younger than other professionals, there is often a desire to befriend young clients. In turn, the younger clients may confide personal information to the intern and insist that the intern not share it with anyone, including other members of the treatment team. I am familiar with instances in which trainees got themselves and their agencies into potentially very serious legal, and, indeed, possibly life- or career-threatening, trouble by offering advice to minors contrary to the instructions of their supervisor and contrary to the wishes and legal rights of parents. The trainees were well intentioned but misguided, and their efforts wound up creating more problems than they were attempting to solve. By consulting carefully with supervisors and instructors, these students could have avoided the problems for themselves, their placement, and the clients and their families.

DUAL RELATIONSHIPS AND BOUNDARY ISSUES

The therapeutic relationship is unique. To protect the integrity of therapy, professional ethics prohibit the formation of dual relationships. Dual relationships encompass a wide spectrum of interactions, but the underlying principle is that the therapist must avoid becoming involved in relationships or roles that could compromise the therapeutic process for the client (Boryrs & Pope, 1989; Kagle & Giebelhausen, 1994; Kitchener, 1988; Kocet, 2006; Moleski & Kiselica, 2005; Reamer, 2003). Dual relationships can include such things as serving as a counselor for a student who lives in the same dormitory as you, agreeing to treat a coworker, or seeing your landlord's family member in exchange for rent reduction. In more malignant and destructive forms, dual relationships can take the form of romantic or sexual contacts between therapist and client.

The danger of dual relationships lies in the possibility that therapists will in some way, consciously or unconsciously, let one aspect of their nonprofessional relationship with the client interfere with the treatment relationship. Kagle and Giebel-hausen (1994) explain:

> Dual relationships involve boundary violations. They cross the line between the therapeutic relationship and a second relationship, undermining the distinctive nature of the therapeutic relationship, blurring the roles of practitioner and client, and permitting the abuse of power. (p. 217)

The concept and examples of boundary violations were also addressed by Johnston and Farber (1996), Younggren & Gottlieb (2004), and Gutheil and Gabbard (1993), who delineated some of the most common areas in which boundaries may get crossed in therapy. These include issues relating to the roles of therapist and patients, the timing of therapy sessions, location of interactions, payment, attire, gifts, language, therapist self-disclosure, and physical contact.

In addition to considering the effects of boundary violations on the patient's treatment, Gutheil and Gabbard emphasize that what appear to be minor initial deviations from standard practice may lead to more consequential violations. They also pointed out that in relation to legal actions, particularly those concerning physical intimacy between clients and therapists, evidence of certain nonsexual boundary violations may be interpreted as evidence that sexual violations also took place.

It is important to understand that the interference generated by dual relationships can come from the client, the therapist, or both, but it is always the therapist's responsibility to deal responsibly and ethically with the situation. If, for example, a therapist were to accept a neighbor as a client, such small matters as the neighbor's anger about the therapist's barking dog could easily block more important therapeutic issues. Similarly, if interns are involved with an on-campus clinic as part of their training, they should probably not accept as clients other students with whom they are likely to share classes. The danger would be that things said in therapy could have an impact on classroom interactions or that classroom discussions could influence therapy. The best way to avoid conflicting roles is not to accept as clients persons with whom one already has another relationship.

Essential to the strictures against dual relationships is the realization that as therapists we are also humans, and as such we are not necessarily the best judges of when our own actions might be swayed by conflicting roles. This means that the safest course of action is to scrupulously avoid any such relationships. Although this might on occasion be unnecessary and may even be counter to the perceived needs of certain clients, in the vast majority of cases avoidance of dual relationships will be in the best interests of therapist and client alike.

Having stated my position on this principle as it pertains to your internship training, I should acknowledge that others, such as Younggren and Gottlieb (2004), have described instances in which multiple relationships might be entertained. Knapp and Slattery (2004) commented on how changes in service delivery, including the practice of providing service in the homes of certain clients, may raise new and challenging boundary and relationship issues. To help manage such situations, Knapp and Slattery, and Younggren and Gottlieb offered valuable suggestions for questions one should ask and risk-management steps one should undertake if contemplating such an approach. One area, however, in which there is universal agreement across all ethical codes, and for which serious legal strictures also apply, is the strict prohibition against sexual or romantic involvement with clients.

Sexual Relationships with Clients

The most destructive and legally consequential forms of dual relationships are those involving romantic or sexual contacts with clients or with persons closely associated with clients. The prohibition against dual relationships is designed to take certain options away from therapists. In the case of sexual relationships, this is particularly important and valid (Reamer, 2003). The ethical codes of every major professional organization in the helping professions specifically prohibit sexual relationships with clients (Kagle & Giebelhausen, 1994). Failure to heed this principle has led many otherwise fine clinicians into deep trouble and has caused lasting and serious harm to their clients (Schoener, 1995). In spite of ethical proscriptions and clinical concerns, Lamb and Catanzaro (1998) found that 50 of 596 individuals surveyed (8%) reported at least one sexual boundary violation (SBV) as a professional psychologist. Of those 50 individuals, 38 (6% of the total sample) reported an SBV with a client. In a later study, the same authors (Lamb, Catanzaro & Moorman, 2003) reported that 3.5% of respondents reported engaging in a prohibited relationship with either clients, supervisees, or students.

Lest any therapist believe that having sex with clients is somehow beneficial to the client, or that clients and therapists are just like any other adults and can freely engage in whatever relationship develops, the research and clinical evidence is clearly to the contrary. Although some (Williams, 1992) have raised questions about the difficulty of conducting empirical studies of this subject, the studies that have been done (e.g., Bouhoutsos, Holroyd, Lerman, Forer, & Greenberg, 1983) have concluded that among those sampled in their research, the vast majority of cases involving therapist-patient sex produced negative consequences for the patient. At the very least, when sexual contacts develop, the therapy process is almost certain to be diverted from its original and legitimate goal, and becomes obscured or lost entirely in the sexual relationship. Therapists are also profoundly affected, with the majority of respondents to the Lamb, Catanzaro, and Moorman survey saying that their professional work was significantly impacted by the relationship, and 90% indicating that they would not do it again if given the opportunity.

Survey data are further supported by the clinical experience of therapists who have treated patients whose former therapists engaged in sexual overtures or contact (Brown, 1997).

Sloan, Edmond, Rubin, and Doughty (1998) reported that in a survey of social workers, 17% had at some point in their careers worked with at least one client who had been sexually exploited by a therapist. Pope and Bouhoutsos (1986) indicated that many clients who have formed sexual relationships with therapists find it extremely difficult ever again to trust a supposed "helping" professional. Such clients are described as suffering from what Pope and Bouhoutsos identified as "therapist-patient sex syndrome." Along with the feelings of mistrust and guilt, many of the symptoms of this syndrome are similar to those of post-traumatic stress disorder. Pope and Bouhoutsos also noted that there is an increased risk of suicide among clients who have been sexually abused by their therapist. This means that therapists who engage in such relationships with their clients are putting the clients at risk not only of psychological damage but also of death.

Brown (1997) emphasized that in addition to the clients who are directly harmed, sexual relationships with patients also harm other clients of the therapist, family members of the client, family members of the therapist, colleagues of the therapist, and the profession as a whole. Brown asserted that discussions of remediation efforts with therapists too often neglect the importance of helping to heal and make amends to everyone the therapists have harmed.

If the damage to clients and others is not sufficient to promote responsible behavior on the part of clinicians, legal and professional sanctions provide added weight (Pope, 1993). It bears repeating that every professional organization explicitly forbids sexual contact with clients. Violation of this rule leads to almost certain sanction or dismissal from the professional organization. It can also lead to loss of license. It should also be underscored that just as sexual intimacies with clients are expressly forbidden by ethical codes, such relationships are also prohibited with the relatives or significant others of clients. Furthermore, it is unethical for therapists to accept as clients individuals with whom they have previously been sexually involved.

Because managed-care companies and other health insurance companies are becoming increasingly selective about the providers whose services they endorse, professionals who have been sanctioned for sexual misconduct are unlikely to be approved for third-party reimbursement. Together, these consequences may effectively terminate one's professional career. For interns and students in the helping professions, sexual misconduct will almost surely lead to dismissal from training, thereby ending one's career before it has begun (Cobb, 1994).

In addition to ethical standards and sanctions by professional organizations, many states also have laws against such contact (Appelbaum, 1990; Strasburger, Jorgenson, & Randles, 1991). This makes therapist-patient sex not only an ethical but also a criminal matter. The reason for such laws is that practitioners who are not members of professional organizations cannot be sanctioned by such organizations. Therefore, states have acted to make all practitioners responsible for ethical conduct,

regardless of their membership status. Appelbaum reviewed existing laws and concluded, "In almost all circumstances, the crime is considered a felony, and both prison sentences and fines may be imposed."

Along with criminal laws, in all states the possibility of civil suits for damages exists (Jorgenson, Randles, & Strasburger, 1991), and the protection against such suits is often limited. From a financial perspective alone, this is perfectly understandable. Indeed, Reamer (1995) reported that 18% of the malpractice claims filed against social workers during the past two decades related to charges of sexual impropriety. These suits constituted more than 41% of the total dollars paid by the NASW Insurance Trust. Similar costs have been reported by other professional insurers. Largely due to such expenses, professional liability insurance premiums for therapists and counselors have increased markedly. To contain these costs, insurers are beginning to limit the amount of damages the insurance company will pay for such claims. In many policies, the liability insurance company agrees to defend such cases but will not pay for any damages. Thus, the costs of any damages would come directly from the therapist's financial or material assets. An additional and increasingly consequential result of sexual misconduct is that subsequent applications for malpractice insurance are likely to be denied. These measures are designed to place more of the burden on the clinician who violated the ethics to begin with, but some authors have argued that the result may instead be limiting the damages victims can collect (Pope, 1990).

Finally, the statute of limitations for sexual misconduct may offer therapists little protection. Unlike crimes such as theft or burglary, for which one cannot be prosecuted beyond a fixed period of time, in the case of sexual abuse some states do not "start the clock" on the statute of limitations until the victim becomes aware of the damage. This might be several years or longer after the actual events took place. It is also worth mentioning that there may be no statute of limitations in regard to disciplinary actions by licensing boards and professional organizations. There have been cases in which clients filed complaints with review boards for actions alleged to have occured more than a decade earlier (E. Harris, February 3, 1995, personal communication).

The situation as described here, and as it exists in law and professional standards, must be clearly understood: Helping professionals who have sexual relationships with clients or those closely related to clients are likely to be expelled from training or from the profession, lose their license, be excluded from further practice, lose large sums of money, face the possibility of a prison sentence, and be the target of complaints for an indefinite time after the misconduct occurs.

MAINTAINING PROFESSIONAL BOUNDARIES AND DEALING WITH FEELINGS OF ATTRACTION

It should be clear from the discussion thus far that therapist-client sex is almost certain to have lasting and severe negative effects on the client, the therapist, and others, including family, friends, and professional colleagues, not to mention the profession itself.

These facts highlight the strictures against and consequences of therapist-patient sex, but there is also a need to consider how to prevent sexual contact between therapist and patients and how to train interns to deal with sexual issues in therapy more effectively (Clark, Rompf, & Walker, 2001; Reamer, 2003). In an effort to educate patients about this subject, the American Psychological Association's Committee on Women in Psychology (1989) published a brochure to inform patients about the ethical and clinical implications of therapist-patient sex. Hotelling (1988) described other approaches to educating clients about both their rights and the availability of victim advocacy and self-help groups.

Along with efforts to educate patients, the issue is receiving increasing attention as part of academic and internship training (Berkman et al., 2000; Housman & Stake, 1999; Rodolfa, Kitzrow, Vohra, & Wilson, 1990; Samuel & Gorton, 1998; Vasquez, 1988). Rodolfa et al. (1994) found that of 389 survey respondents identified as working in university counseling centers, only 12% stated that they had never been attracted to a client. Pope, Keith-Spiegel, and Tabachnick (1986) reported survey results indicating that 95% of male and 76% of female therapists surveyed reported having been sexually attracted to clients at least on occasion, and 63% expressed feeling guilty, anxious, or confused by their attraction.

Despite the frequency of therapist attraction and the feelings evoked as a consequence, a later survey by Pope and Tabachnick (1993), which also addressed feelings of fear and anger toward clients, revealed that half of those surveyed said they had received either poor or no training in how to deal with sexual attraction. On a more positive note, the same survey indicated that 25% of the sample considered their training to have been good to excellent. Another encouraging finding comes from Pope et al.'s 1986 results, which indicated that 57% of the psychologists sought supervision or consultation when they were attracted to clients. More recently, Samuel and Gorton (1998) found that 98% of internship directors responding to their survey indicated that interns receive at least some education on this issue, but the extent, approach, and content of this education vary substantially across programs. To ensure that all interns receive adequate training in this area, Samuel and Gorton called for including mandatory training as part of the internship and academic accreditation requirements.

Pope et al. (1986) emphasized several points that are particularly relevant to interns. Because it evidently is common for therapists to experience attraction to clients, it is essential to address this matter openly in training programs. In this process, there is a need to recognize the fundamental distinction between experiencing feelings of attraction and acting on those feelings. Students need to feel that it is safe to discuss feelings of attraction without fear that their instructors or supervisors will condemn, ridicule, or intrusively question them. In helping students

understand and explore issues of attraction, instructors and supervisors must model the kind of professionalism they expect students to develop and exhibit as therapists.

Unfortunately, recent research suggests that in spite of such recommendations, a great deal of work still is needed in this area of training for supervisors and interns. This need was demonstrated by Housman and Stake (1999), who found that among students who had discussed a client attraction with their supervisor, many did not develop an appropriate understanding of the ethical boundaries regarding the attraction. A small but troublesome number, 7%, apparently believed that sex with current clients could be ethical and therapeutic. On the other hand, 47% thought that any sexual feelings for clients were unacceptable. While the former group may run into trouble because they fail to understand ethical and clinical proscriptions on sexual relationships, the latter may have difficulty because they will be unlikely to deal therapeutically with any feelings or attraction that may arise.

Several authors have offered advice on how therapists can deal constructively if feelings of attraction emerge in therapy. In the discussion of boundary violations alluded to earlier, Gutheil and Gabbard (1993) noted that role boundaries are fundamental to issues relating to boundary violations. They proposed a key question to help therapists understand and judge this issue. In evaluating their behavior in relation to boundaries, therapists should ask themselves, "Is this what a therapist does?" (p. 190).

Lamb, Catanzary, and Moorman (2003), Gutheil and Gabbard (1993), Simon (1989), and Gabbard (1989), all point out that in most instances a common sequence of events leads to physical intimacy with patients. This sequence typically begins with apparently innocuous actions, then progresses to problematic levels. Referring to what they call the "slippery-slope" scenario, Gutheil and Gabbard described a

> transition from a last-name to first-name basis; then personal conversation intruding on the clinical work; then some body contact (e.g., pats on the shoulder, massages, progressing to hugs); then trips outside the office; then sessions during lunch, sometimes with alcoholic beverages; then dinner; then movies or other social events; and finally sexual intercourse. (p. 188)

Recognizing this sequence can provide an early-warning system for interns and therapists. If you find yourself dressing differently because you will see a certain client that day, if you are scheduling appointments later or allowing sessions to run longer for some clients, if you are revealing more about your personal life than is typical, if you think about a client more than is normal for you when you are away from your office, if you are suggesting or accepting opportunities to meet outside therapy, or if other behaviors are beyond your usual conduct, you should recognize that something unusual is happening and should explore it in supervision.

Somer and Saadon (1999) offered further advice to help practitioners avoid actions that may lead by small, seemingly insignificant increments toward physical intimacy. Their suggestions include selecting office space in locations shared by other professionals, exercising special care in working with clients who are survivors of sexual abuse, limiting or avoiding physical consolation in times of crisis, maintaining careful records, and, again, seeking consultation and supervision.

This issue is so important to the well-being of clients, therapists, and the integrity of our professions that it is incumbent on interns and professionals to deal with it responsibly and ethically. If during your internship, or at any time in your career, you find yourself crossing therapeutic boundaries and feeling sexually attracted to a client, or if a client is attracted to you, seek supervision. You will not be the first or the last person to find yourself in this situation, but it is essential that you deal with it professionally. Two excellent additional resources on this subject are Pope, Sonne, and Holroyd's (1993) *Sexual Feelings in Psychotherapy* and the APA video training guides, *Therapist/client Boundary Challenges* and *Responding Therapeutically to Patient Expression of Sexual Attracion: A Stimulus Training Tape.* The video format of these programs can be very helpful because it presents portrayals of ways in which patients might demonstrate sexual attraction to therapists and then offers responsible methods for dealing with such situations.

NONSEXUAL DUAL RELATIONSHIPS

Because sexual relationships between therapists and clients can be so damaging, they have received the bulk of attention in discussions about the ethics of dual relationships. Less destructive, but still problematic, are dual relationships that do not involve sexual or romantic contact. Examples of such relationships were alluded to earlier; they include clients who are neighbors, fellow students, or coworkers (Reamer, 2003). Complex relationship issues can also develop when new clients are referred to a therapist by existing clients or by close friends or acquaintances of the therapist. It is not necessarily unethical to accept such referrals, but it is important to be aware of the ethical and clinical issues that can arise for both the patient and the therapist (Moleski & Kiselica 2005; Shapiro & Ginzberg, 2003; Younggren & Gotlieb, 2004).

In most instances, you can deal with ethically or clinically ambiguous situations by simply referring the individuals to other professionals. There are, however, conditions under which referral may not be practical. Barnett and Yutrzenka (1994), Campbell and Gordon (2003), Hargrove (1986), Helbok, Marineli, and Walls (2006), Schank and Skovholt (1997), and Sobel (1992) have all pointed out that few practitioners may be available in certain rural settings. In these circumstances, practitioners sooner or later are likely to have clients with whom they maintain some relationship apart from therapy. In rural settings, it is also likely that practitioners who may not have known a client prior to beginning treatment will later encounter that person in some other role after treatment has begun. For example, a therapist might discover that a former or present client is a member of a service or social organization or is the coach of the opposing Little League or youth soccer team.

In a survey of ethical dilemmas encountered by psychologists, Pope and Vetter (1992) found that circumstances such as those just described are by no means infrequent in rural settings. Based on their findings, Pope and Vetter recommended that future ethical codes take geographic concerns into account and should more clearly distinguish between situations in which dual relationships may or may not be therapeutically acceptable.

The most important issue for practitioners is keeping the well-being and best interests of the client foremost. The difficult challenge is to know when and how different roles or relationships may conflict with the treatment process. No ethical code can successfully identify every possible contingency or specify exactly what professionals must do in all circumstances. Therefore, in ambiguous conditions the professional must use discretion and judgment. However, as noted earlier, our own judgment can sometimes betray us, which makes supervision a good forum for any situations where you have such concerns.

Barnett and Yutrzenka (1994) offered useful advice to professionals who, for reasons of geography or other factors, may treat persons with whom they have other relationships. Among other things, Barnett and Yutrzenka recommended that professionals directly acknowledge their different relationships and seek to "compartmentalize roles, not relationships." In other words, professionals in rural communities must have their own identity and relate amicably to other community members, clients and nonclients alike. Compartmentalizing roles means that therapy issues should not be raised with clients outside the context of the therapy interaction, but issues outside therapy that might have an impact on the treatment process may need to be dealt with directly in therapy. This possibility should be addressed with clients at the beginning of treatment. Similar recommendations were offered by Schank and Skovholt (1997), who also addressed how overlapping relationships in small communities may affect members of the psychologist's family. For suggestions about incidental encounters with clients, a common experience in small communities, you may want to read the article by Pulakos (1994). For an insightful discussion of multiple relationship issues in military settings, and a systematic process for managing such relationships, see Stall and King (2000).

Being cognizant of confidentiality is particularly important in small communities, as is scrupulous documentation of your actions and the rationale behind them. Other precautions recommended by Barnett and Yutrzenka (1994) include trying to know yourself as well as you can but also consulting with other professionals who can help recognize any signs that you are denying or minimizing potentially problematic issues. If no other professionals are available in your local community, try to establish regular phone contact or consultation with other professionals in your region who are sensitive to these issues and would be honest and supportive with you. Finally, even though local referral options may be limited in some settings, Barnett and Yutrzenka advised that professionals should make contact with any other possible resources in the community or area and should be willing to refer whenever a dual-relationship conflict does or might occur.

POST-THERAPY RELATIONSHIPS

A final area regarding dual relationships with clients concerns the nature of relationships allowed following therapy. With regard to romantic or sexual relationships after therapy has concluded, the ethical proscriptions vary somewhat across professions and are not as clearly stated as they are for such relationships during therapy. After much debate, the 2002 American Psychological Association's ethics code set a minimum time limit of 2 years, as did the American Association for Marriage and Family Therapy (1991), before a therapist could become romantically involved with a client. The ACA ethics code (2005) sets a 5-year prohibition on intimate relationships with former clients. Each of these codes also emphasizes that such relationships, although not prohibited under the codes, often have harmful effects, and even after the specified time period they should only be considered ethical in extremely unusual circumstances and after careful consideration in which the onus falls on the professional to identify and prevent any potential harm. A similar approach is described by the NASW code of ethics, which states that social workers should not engage in sexual activities with former clients, but then adds that if they do so and claim extraordinary circumstances, the burden of demonstrating that the client has not been harmed or exploited either intentionally or unintentionally falls fully on the social worker, not the client (NASW, 2000).

Given the ambiguity across ethical codes, considering the risks of harming a client, and in light of the very real possibility of litigation, the current and safest advice is to follow the same principles used with clients in therapy: There must not be a romantic relationship with a client ever—not before, during, or after the therapeutic relationship is established (for an extended and informative discussion, see Koocher and Keith-Spiegel, 1998). This principle was stated explicitly by the American Psychiatric Association, which voted in 1992 to declare sexual relationships with clients following therapy always unethical for psychiatrists (American Psychiatric Association, 1992). I concur with this position and believe it is the safest and most ethical position to take. Ruling out any sexual relationship with clients permanently will help the therapist as well as the client avoid role or goal confusions during or after therapy and will help therapists recognize that their professional responsibility does not end when the formal therapy arrangement concludes.

Compared with sexual contacts, nonsexual and nonromantic relationships following therapy are less emotionally charged, but they nevertheless can pose important ethical and personal challenges for therapists and interns. Ethical codes provide less specific guidance regarding such contacts, but useful principles and decision-making criteria were offered by Anderson and Kitchener (1998). They suggested considering four components in evaluating the ethics of a post-therapy relationship. These include the nature and parameters of the therapeutic contract, the dynamics of the therapeutic bond, social roles, and therapist motivation. Within each component, specific questions are presented to help the practitioner determine the issues involved and the proper course of action. If you find yourself in a situation that involves interactions with a former client, you may want to consult this article for further guidance. In addition, Chapter 9 of the present text describes issues pertaining to closing cases and dealing with clients' desires to maintain contact after the intern leaves a placement.

RELATIONSHIPS BETWEEN EDUCATORS, SUPERVISORS, AND TRAINEES

The ethical guidelines for dual relationships identified in this chapter also apply to relationships among supervisors, instructors, and students (Aponte, 1994; Bowman, Hatley, & Bowman, 1995; Congress, 2001; Harrar, VandeCreek, & Knapp, 1990; Kolbert, Morgan, & Brendel, 2002; Larrabee & Miller, 1993; Miller & Larrabee, 1995). Much of the attention in this area has focused on sexual relationships between supervisors or instructors and students, but a number of other possible dual relationship issues can arise as well (Biaggio, Paget, & Chenoweth, 1997; Kolbert et al., 2002; Slimp & Burian, 1994).

Just as sexual contact between therapists and clients breaks down the therapy process, sexual relationships between supervisors and interns are likely to interfere with the supervision process (Jacobs, 1991). Recognizing this fact, the NASW code of ethics (2000), section 2.07, explicitly states that social workers who "function as supervisors or educators should not engage in sexual activities or contact with supervisees, students, trainees, or other colleagues over whom they exercise professional authority." The 2002 APA code of ethics is also clear, stating in section 7.07 that "Psychologists do not engage in sexual relationships with students or supervisees who are in their department, agency, or training center or over whom psychologists are likely to have evaluative authority." Similarly, the 2005 ACA code, section F.3.b, states, "Sexual or romantic interactions or relationships with current supervisees are prohibited."

In addition to impairing the direct supervisory relationship, the potential for sexual relationships between supervisor and trainee can also make open discussion about therapist-client attraction particularly difficult. At the conclusion of their 1986 article, Pope and colleagues stressed that in discussing issues of attraction, students must be safe from educators who might use such issues as openings to establish intimate relationships with the students themselves.

In spite of these clear proscriptions, research data suggest that sexual contacts between therapists and clients and between instructors and students are not uncommon. Pope, Levenson, and Schover (1979) reported that 16.5% of women respondents and 3% of male respondents reported that during their graduate training they had sexual contact with psychology educators.

Among educators, 8% of women and 19% of men reported having engaged in sexual relations with someone whom they supervised. This survey also suggested that those who are involved in such interactions as students may be more likely to violate the comparable ethical standard as professionals. Comparable, though slightly lower, percentages were reported by Thoreson, Shaughnessy, Heppner, and Cook (1993) and by Miller and Larrabee (1995).

Results similar to those of Pope and colleagues were reported by Robinson and Reid (1985), who found that 13% of women respondents indicated that they had experienced sexual contact with their educators during their graduate education. This research also indicated that 48% of the respondents had experienced some form of sexual harassment as graduate students. Consistent with studies suggesting that therapist-patient sex is harmful to clients, 95% of those who had experienced sexual contact or harassment felt it was detrimental. In reviewing these and other studies of sexual contact or harassment, Bartell and Rubin (1990) noted that many respondents did not feel sexual contact with instructors was coercive at the time it occurred. In retrospect, however, the majority see some degree of coercion and consider it to be an ethical problem (Glaser & Thorpe, 1986). A similar change in attitude over time was reported by Miller and Larrabee's respondents (1995).

Just as sexual contact between supervisors or instructors and students is prohibited by codes of ethics, sexual harassment is also considered unethical. Although such harassment is contrary to the ethical standards of the professions, the problems of educator-student sexual contact and harassment are real and ongoing. If you are placed in an uncomfortable position due to the unwanted comments or actions of an instructor, supervisor, coworker, or peer, you have the right to file a grievance and demand that the behavior be stopped. I suggest that students who are harassed file formal complaints both with their academic institution and with any professional organizations or licensing bodies with which the harasser might be affiliated. For harassment to stop, everyone in the helping professions must understand the problem, adhere to the principles, seek supervision when necessary, and report violations whenever they occur. Then the consequences of violations must be certain, meaningful, and effective.

Though perhaps less volatile than sexual involvement or harassment, other forms of dual relationships can be problematic as well. Kolbert et al. (2002), Congress (2001), and Slimp and Burian (1994) described issues pertaining to social, business, and therapeutic relationships between supervisors and students. Similarly, Biaggio et al. (1997) discussed issues pertaining to joint research activities and other relationships. These authors also offered a framework for evaluating ethical issues that might arise when faculty and students are involved in relationships beyond simple teacher-student interactions. This framework tests relationships against three criteria: "(a) educational standards are maintained, (b) educational experiences are provided for the student, and (c) exploitative practices

are absent" (p. 187). Biaggio et al. suggested that if faculty and students keep these considerations in mind and follow other ethical principles, the dangers inherent in multiple roles and relationships can, in most cases, be managed effectively. At the same time, however, Kolbert et al. cautioned that faculty perceptions of what multiple roles are ethical may differ considerably from student's perceptions, with students expressing much greater concern about potential conflicts than faculty. For example, students expressed concern that friendships of some students with faculty or supervisors could lead to biased evaluations or jealousy among peers. There was also concern by students that in some instances the friendship might meet the instructor's needs rather than the student's. Students also feared that performance in nonacademic tasks, such as paid work for a faculty member, child care, and the like, could affect the faculty evaluation of the student's performance in an internship or in the classroom.

The key lesson from these findings should be that even though a faculty member or supervisor earnestly considers the ethical implications of involvement in nonsexual dual roles with students, the students themselves may experience those roles very differently, but may be unlikely to express their concerns to the faculty or supervisor (Strom-Gottfried, 2000). Therefore, it is good practice to be aware of this possibility and to discuss it openly before any such relationships are entered into or at any point when they develop.

ETHICS IN CLASSES AND GROUPS

The preceding chapter described the potential benefits of internship classes or peer groups. Because internship classes and groups often include case discussions, reviews of tapes, and role-plays, and because internship classes and groups deal with personal and sensitive issues, including those of the interns themselves, care must be taken to follow all of the ethical principles and practices that have been discussed thus far.

Prieto (1997) expressed concern about the dual relationship and "captive therapy" implications for students involved in group supervision that follows a group therapy model. Similar concerns were also addressed by Sklare et al. (1996) and in the responses reported by Bogo, Globerman, and Sussman (2004). The essence of these concerns is that group supervision and learning can easily cross the line and become much like group therapy, with students feeling compelled to explore personal issues in front of their peers and instructor. Complications arising from this may include dual relationships as instructors function as both teacher and therapist. In addition, students legitimately fear that disclosing personal information might affect their grade. Sklare and colleagues recommended keeping a "here-and-now" focus in the group as a way of reducing these concerns. Prieto went a step further and advocated following a pedagogical, didactic construct as opposed to a therapeutic construct to guide group instruction and supervision. Whichever approach is chosen, it is important for instructors and students to be clear about the purpose of the activities and about their respective boundaries, roles, rights, and responsibilities.

Protecting client confidentiality is another area of concern that arises in class discussions. In most internship classes, it is standard practice for interns to review clients and clinical experiences as part of the class. Sensitive to issues of ethics, interns rightly ask if bringing case material to class is a violation of their client's or placement's confidentiality.

This is admittedly a somewhat gray area, without a definitive answer. Measures, however, can and should be taken to lessen the possibility of confidentiality breaches. The first step is for each member of the internship class to know about the principle of confidentiality and agree to keep whatever occurs during the internship class strictly confidential. This means that students do not discuss class material with anyone beyond the confines of the class. Confidentiality is important because, in addition to reviewing their cases, students and trainees must feel safe to acknowledge their own concerns, weaknesses, fears, and personal issues relating to their training. They must also be able to discuss cases and clients without fear that confidential information will go beyond the confines of the internship class or group.

Many institutional agreements with internship sites include a clause explaining that interns will be expected to discuss clients and clinical experiences with their instructor and during the class as part of their educational process. Interns are also instructed to tell clients from the outset that they may discuss the case with their instructor or supervisor and in the internship class. Interns are advised to tell clients that the client's identity will be protected in such discussions and that the discussion will be strictly for educational purposes.

Before recording therapy sessions or using audio- or videotapes in class, you must obtain permission from the client. The ethical principles of informed consent and confidentiality require that if a clinical session is to be taped, everyone involved in the session must give permission. Written permission-to-record forms should specify precisely the purpose of the taping, how the tapes will be used, the time period for which this use will be authorized, and what will happen to the tapes at the end of the time period. Clients must have the right to refuse recording clearly explained to them, and they must not be coerced into giving permission. Clients must also be given information about the purpose of the taping and the confidentiality of the information on the tapes. Clients should also be informed that the tape will be shared only with the supervisor and class, that information will be kept strictly confidential, and that the tapes will be erased by a specified date or immediately after the class use.

Another step to preserve confidentiality is to advise interns that when they discuss cases in class or write about them in a journal, they must protect the identity of clients. As discussed in previous chapters, interns may use a standard identification of simply Mr. or Ms. X to describe all clients. Interns are also instructed that if speaking about the details of a case might reveal the identity of the individual, even without explicitly saying his or her name, the intern should discuss the case with the instructor before raising it in class. This is particularly important if interns are working in a college counseling center or other setting where the identity of student clients might easily be discernible by other interns who also know the client. In such instances, caution is required, and on occasion it is better not to discuss a case in class if confidentiality cannot be preserved. For an example, an intern might be working with a student body officer whose identity would necessarily be compromised in class simply due to the concerns being addressed in the case discussion. A similar situation might exist if tape-recorded therapy sessions would reveal a client's distinctive voice and the identity of the person might be known to others in the class. Under such circumstances, the need to protect the client's confidentiality outweighs the educational benefit to the class.

Case material and information about clients is not all that must be protected by confidentiality. During internship classes, interns themselves often bring up highly personal material that must be accorded the same respect and protection. Because clinical work is so demanding and often touches on issues from the intern's own life, it is vital that interns feel they can trust their classmates enough to explore whatever arises. In other classes, it might be acceptable for a student to tell a roommate something like "You'll never believe what another student said in class today," but that is absolutely unacceptable for students in an internship class. Confidentiality is essential to your role as a professional, and the internship is the place to establish ethical standards that you will practice throughout your career.

LIABILITY AND INSURANCE

Just as you need to understand the principles of ethics and laws pertaining to your profession, you should also know about professional liability and liability insurance. Although interns are less likely than practicing professionals to be the target of malpractice lawsuits, they are by no means immune (Gelman et al., 1996). For this reason, VauPitts (1992) urged counseling programs to require liability insurance for all practicum and internship students. In addition to providing financial protection, VauPitts pointed out that obtaining such insurance acquaints students with "this reality of professional life" (p. 207).

Because many students will not be familiar with liability claims and the purpose of liability insurance, a brief review may be helpful. For more extensive discussion, see the article by Conte and Karasu (1990) or the books by Bennett et al. (1990) and Swenson (1993). For a discussion of several types of liability issues relating to social work education, see Gelman et al. (1996).

ELEMENTS OF MALPRACTICE

Bennett et al. (1990) introduced their discussion of malpractice by explaining:

> When a practitioner undertakes to treat, diagnose, assess, or in any way advise or provide psychological services to a client, that practitioner is obliged to exercise a certain standard of care and service delivery. For the practitioner to be found negligent, it must be shown that he or she did not exercise the standard and, by failing to do so, injured the client (the plaintiff in the suit). (p. 34)

Malpractice suits are special cases within the broader category of negligence. By virtue of their professional status and their relationship with clients, those in the helping professions have a responsibility to provide care that meets the standards of their profession. If a professional is sued for malpractice, plaintiffs must successfully prove each of four critical elements: (1) the existence of a professional relationship between therapist and client, (2) the existence of a standard of care and the failure of the practitioner to meet that standard in the care of the client, (3) that the client suffered some form of harm or injury, (4) that the client's harm or injury was caused by the practitioner's failure to meet the standard of care (Bennett et al., 1990; Conte & Karasu, 1990).

The best way to deal with lawsuits is to prevent them from happening by practicing within the standards of care of one's profession, scrupulously adhering to ethical codes, and thoroughly documenting what you do and why. To help reduce the risk of liability claims, leading association insurance programs have instituted risk-management practices (Reamer, 2005) and published guidelines and books with useful suggestions, checklists, and other resources. See, for example, the books by Bennett et al. (1990), and Houston-Vega, Nuehring, & Daguio (1996). See also, the four-module CD-ROM APAIT training program "Ethics and Risk Management: A Practical instructional Series" (http://www.apait.org/products/modules/), and the Web-based program "Understanding Malpractice Risk: What Social Workers Can Do." (http://www.naswwebed.org/).

LIABILITY INSURANCE

Conte and Karasu (1990) pointed out that lawsuits against psychotherapists are relatively rare, and that proving all four elements of malpractice suits is not easy. As a result, only about 20% of cases result in judgments against the psychotherapist, and the "average cost of claims is under $22,000" (Bennett et al., 1990, p. 31).

These figures notwithstanding, Bennett et al. (1990) emphasized that practitioners should have insurance for several reasons. Even if one's practice is perfectly within standards, there is no guarantee that a lawsuit will not be filed or that one would emerge unscathed from such a suit. A practitioner who is successfully sued could be required to pay damages as high or higher than hundreds of thousands of dollars. Furthermore, regardless of outcome, the process of defending against the suit can be financially and emotionally expensive. An added benefit of such insurance is that some providers, including each of the insurers listed below, have begun to provide toll-free legal consultation. The goal of this service is to prevent problems from developing or to catch them as early as possible.

The cost of liability insurance for psychologists, counselors, social workers, and others remains low relative to certain medical professions. Nevertheless, the frequency and size of claims has increased (Conte & Karasu, 1990), as has the cost of insurance. Fortunately, liability insurance is available to interns for much lower rates than for fully licensed professionals. Interns can obtain more information about such insurance by contacting their national organizations or by contacting the insurance providers. Sources of information for key associations can be obtained at:

http://www.acait.com/

http://www.apait.org/

http://www.naswinsurancetrust.org/

When you look into liability insurance, you will discover that there are two types of policies: claims-based and occurrence-based (for more detailed information, consult Bennett et al., 1990, or your professional organization's insurance provider). Understanding the differences between policies is important because the type of policy you choose will influence how much you pay and how you are covered.

Claims-based insurance provides coverage for acts that occur during the time you are insured as long as you hold the policy, but the coverage stops when you no longer carry the policy. This means that if you let a policy expire or choose to retire and no longer carry the policy, your insurer would no longer provide coverage even if you are sued for something that occurred when you did practice and did have the policy. In other words, when you discontinue the policy, your protection is also discontinued, regardless of when the event for which you are being sued occurred. On the other hand, as long as you hold a claims-based policy, you will be covered for any events that happen while you are insured under that policy, providing that you are still insured under the policy.

The advantage of claims-based policies is that they are usually less expensive than occurrence-based policies during the first years they are held. The cost increases with each subsequent year because the insurer is then providing protection for the year in which the policy is now held, as well as for events that may have occurred in previous years. If you wish to discontinue a claims-based policy, you must realize that doing so discontinues your protection against suits even if the suit concerns something that happened when you were insured. You can, however, purchase special coverage called a *tail* or *rider,* which will insure you for a period of time following termination of your regular policy. Some policies also carry a clause that if one has held claims-based insurance for a number of years and then retires from practice, the tail coverage is applied free of charge.

An occurrence-based policy provides protection for events that occurred during the time you held the policy, regardless of whether or not you are still carrying the insurance at the time you are sued. This type of policy is typically more expensive to begin with, but once you purchase an occurrence policy you are covered essentially forever for the period in which you held the insurance. If someone sues you for an event that happened five years earlier, you will be covered as long as you held an occurrence-based policy at that time, even though you may not hold the policy at the time you are actually sued.

As you evaluate different types of liability insurance policies, be sure to examine matters other than simply price and the surface differences between claims- or occurrence-based policies. Among the other factors you should consider are: What types of activities, situations, or expenses are not covered under the policy? Does the coverage include defense costs along with damages in the payment limits, or are these figured separately? What is the financial security and history of the company providing the insurance? (If your insurance provider goes bankrupt, you effectively become uninsured.)

This discussion has been intended to provide an introductory overview and should not be taken as constituting legal or financial advice. As with all insurance, it is essential to read the conditions of the terms carefully and to compare policies offered by different providers. This is particularly important in the case of malpractice insurance for interns. Such coverage may not apply to all internship placements or all activities of interns. You may also find that your internship site carries its own insurance for interns, and it may not be necessary for you to purchase your own. However, before deciding that you do not need your own coverage, it is advisable to have written assurance that you are covered under the agency policy and that such coverage includes both defense and damage costs. Be sure that you understand the nature and limitations of any coverage your internship provides or you purchase for yourself, and consider these factors carefully in light of your own activities as a student, an intern, or an employee.

TECHNOLOGY AND ETHICS

Before concluding this chapter's discussion of clinical ethics, a word is in order about the increasing use of technology and the ethical implications for interns and practitioners. Clinically, technological advances have introduced whole new categories of presenting concerns, including such issues as Internet gambling, addiction to online pornography, identity theft, and failed Internet relationships (Mitchell, Becker-Blease, & Finkelhor, 2005). At the same time, technology has also become part of the treatment repertoire, with applications ranging from telephone-based interventions to automated computerized treatment protocols. The scope of this impact is reflected in proposals for entirely new specializations, such as the call by Parker-Oliver and Demiris (2006) for the establishment of "Social Work Informatics" as a speciality area within the field of social work.

From an ethical perspective, two broad areas are the most relevant to our discussion of ethical issues. We have already discussed some of the issues relating to electronic storage and communication of information, particularly as related to confidentiality, EMRs, and HIPAA rules. In addition to these issues, new ethical issues are raised by the increasing use of electronic media to provide clinical services either through the telephone, the Internet, or specialized computer interventions (Barnett, & Scheetz, 2003; Ragusea & Vandecreek, 2003). Unique ethical and clinical issues are also associated with supervision provided remotely via the internet (Clingerman & Bernard, 2004; Kanz, 2001; Wood, Miller & Hargrove; 2005).

Nickelson (1998) defined *telehealth* "as the use of telecommunications and information technology to provide access to health assessment, diagnosis, intervention, consultation, supervision, education and information across distance" (p. 527). VandenBos and Williams (2000) found that use of the telephone in some form in the delivery of clinical services was nearly universal, while Reese, Conoly, and Brossart (2002) reported the results of an empirical study of the effectiveness of telephone counseling.

Less universal, but growing rapidly, is the use of what Budman (2000) referred to as computer mediated communications (CMC) in clinical work. This entails everything from e-mail communication with clients to online delivery of individual assessment and treatment methodologies. A slightly different term, *eHealth,* or, more specifically, *Behavioral eHealth,* was used by Maheu and Gordon (2000) to describe similar services. Other researchers have used the term *Web-Based Treatment Interventions* (WBTIs) to identify treatment approaches offered over the Internet (Ritterband et al., 2003).

Perhaps the most basic level of computer use is the posting of an informational Web site by clinicians. Palmiter and Renjilian (2003) offer useful suggestions for what clients look for on a clinician's Web site. In many ways, these suggestions mirror the content of a good informed-consent form and include such information as the clinician's personal background and professional approach, fee and payment information, licensing information and professional affiliations. Web sites can also include graphic information, such as photos of the clinician and maps to the office, plus links to self-help sites or articles. In light of these recommendations, Palmiter and Renjilian studied the actual Web sites of clinicians and found that many lacked key information sought by patients. They recommended that clinicians attend to such gaps because potential clients are increasingly looking to the Web for information and will be more likely to seek assistance from those with the most informative and user-friendly sites.

For clinicians who are considering expanding their practice to include some form of telehealth or other technological intervention, Glueckauf et al. (2003) offer a framework of issues to be considered. Using the acronym STEPS, their framework addresses state regulatory and licensure issues, technology, ethics, personal relationship issues, and specific training requirements, all considered as they pertain to the unique issues associated with technology. From the perspective of outcomes and efficacy, Among the issues such services raise, confidentiality, quality assurance, risk management, professional licensing, and regulatory oversight all have been identified (Barnett & Scheetz, 2003; Budman, 2000; Jeffords, 1999; Koocher & Morray, 2000; Maheu & Gordon, 2000; Ragusea & Vandecreek, 2003; Stamm, 1998).

Ritterband et al. (2003) discussed the need for studies of treatment efficacy and, along with reviewing some of the extant WBTIs, offered a framework for developing and validating Internet-based interventions. Group work on the Internet also presents novel ethical and clinical issues (Humphreys, Winzelberg, & Klaw, 2000) as does family therapy and the training and supervision of therapists (Baltimore, 2000). Woody (1999) pointed out that technologies may also open some surprising and easily overlooked avenues for confidentiality breaches within families. For example, telephone or voice mail messages may be retrieved by family members other than the patient, and e-mail or other computer communications may be accessed by members using the family computer.

In response to these and other ethical concerns, the American Counseling Association (1999), the Association for Counselor Education and Supervision (1999), and the National Board of Certified Counselors (NBCC) (1998) all have developed ethical guidelines or standards related to on-line counseling. The latest ACA code of ethics (2005) also includes a section (A.12) specifically detailing ethical issues associated with technology. Similarly, the NASW code of ethics contains specific references to electronic media, as in section 1.03(e), which advises that social workers providing services through electronic media must "inform recipients of the limitations and risks associated with such services." The introduction to the APA Ethics Code indicates that the code applies to activities including "telephone, internet, and other electronic transmissions," but apart from this statement the APA ethics committee has not yet incorporated technology issues directly into the APA code. The APA ethics committee, has, however, issued a statement (http://www.apa.org/ethics/stmnt01.html) referencing key parts of the existing code as they pertain to technology and services. For a more thorough discussion of the APA code in relation to technology, see Fisher and Fried (2003).

In an interesting and troubling empirical study of how well some of these ethical standards, notably those of the NBCC, are being met by online "WebCounseling" services, Heinlen, Welfel, Richmond, and Rak (2003) reported a host of shortcomings and generally low levels of compliance with ethical standards among the Web sites and services they surveyed. Of special concern from both an ethical and clinical perspective was their finding that more than a third of the sites they studied were no longer in operation just eight months later.

Similar results were obtained by Shaw and Shaw (2006), who evaluated counseling Web sites based on a 16-item checklist reflecting the ACA ethical standards for online counseling (1999). Their results showed that fewer than half of the Web sites studied were adhering to recommended practices on 8 of 16 items.

If you happen to become involved in some form of technological service delivery as part of your internship or in later practice, you can avoid some of these ethical pitfalls by following sound general ethical practices and by incorporating certain measures specifically geared toward technology. A good place to start would be to review the specific technology related ethical guidelines mentioned above. You might also want to evaluate your activities in comparison to the checklist developed by Shaw and Shaw (2006). In addition, Maheu (2003) describes a comprehensive clinical practice model that includes seven stages, beginning with training, and including such matters as referrals, client education, consent, assessment, direct care, and reimbursement. Under the rubric of training, Maheu addresses choices of technologies, emergency clinical backups, risk-management strategies, and supervision. Comparable suggestions were also offered by Koocher and Morray (2000) and by Ragusea and VandeCreek (2003).

In many ways, the guidelines offered by these authors reflect the key principles addressed throughout this chapter, with the additional application to technology. For example, Koocher and Morray (2000) began with the principle of competence but pointed out that unique technical as well as clinical competencies are required for remote delivery of services. They also emphasized that to date there is no consensus on standards of care, and that data concerning treatment efficacy may be limited. In order to ensure that liability insurance will protect a practitioner providing remote services, consultation with liability insurance carriers is recommended. Guidelines must also be established for crisis care or emergency situations, given that the location of the patient might be far from the therapist. Confidentiality limitations must also be discussed with patients and documented, with particular attention to the limited confidentiality of online communications, computerized records, and cellular or other wireless phone conversations. Ragusea and VandeCreek (2003) give particular attention to Web site designs, with an emphasis on the unique demands of informed consent with technology, and on such matters as establishing and verifying client identities and locations. Finally, Koocher and Morray (2000) observed that third-party (i.e., insurance) payments may not be available for remote services. Thus it is essential to ascertain precisely what types of services will or will not be covered by the patient's policy.

There can be little doubt that the interaction between clinical services and technology is still, if not in its infancy, in the toddler stages, and there are exciting opportunities ahead. Ensuring that the highest of ethical and clinical standards govern those opportunities will be the responsibility of all professionals. As an intern, you will likely be part of the first generation of professionals who make this happen.

RESEARCH ETHICS

This chapter has primarily focused on ethical and legal issues pertaining to clinical practice, but interns who are involved with research activities, either as part of their thesis or dissertation or in some other capacity, must also be aware of the ethical principles and guidelines concerning experimental and clinical research. Extensive discussion of these guidelines is beyond the scope of this text, but many of the same principles that apply to clinical practice (e.g., informed consent, confidentiality) also apply to research. You will also find that each of the major ethical codes includes sections specifically dedicated to research ethics.

If you participate in any way in research as part of your internship, you should carefully study the ethical principles for research of your profession as well as any relevant laws or regulations. Perhaps not surprisingly, HIPAA also includes specific research guidelines and requirements that you should know and follow. You should also be aware that most academic and clinical settings conducting research have established review boards, often called human participant review boards, that carefully study the ethical qualities of any research performed under their aegis or by their personnel. Before initiating any study, you should consult the research board of both your academic institution and your placement agency, and, of course, you should work closely with both your instructor and your supervisor.

ETHICAL AND PROFESSIONAL CONCERNS ABOUT COLLEAGUES

To conclude our discussion of ethics, I want to raise a difficult and often overlooked topic that is part of all of our responsibilities as professionals but is too often neglected in training and in practice. I am referring to the matter of how one deals with clinical or ethical lapses by fellow interns or professionals (Forrest, Elman, Gizara, & Vacha-Haase, 1999).

This issue is important for multiple reasons. First, colleagues who are acting unethically or not using sound judgment and clinical techniques are endangering the well-being of clients. Second, when one member of a profession violates the rules or performs inadequately, the profession as a whole suffers in reputation, and that, in turn, harms not only the members of the profession but other clients who might benefit from proper treatment but do not participate due to the effects of irresponsible practitioners. Professionals, clients, and society as a whole suffer in another way through increased liability insurance premiums resulting from malpractice claims against the few bad practitioners. These costs ultimately contribute to the overall increases in the costs of health care.

Later, in Chapter 7 of this text, we discuss the stresses facing interns and professionals and review literature examining the incidence of impairment or problematic students as well as mechanisms for self-care. For present purposes, it is sufficient to note, as many studies have indicated, that the factors impairing the ability of interns to perform adequately, whether academically or clinically, are by no means uncommon. Indeed, estimates of the incidence of impaired or problematic trainees range somewhere between 45% and 12%, depending on the study. What is more, interns generally feel that such issues are not dealt with well by training programs, and most interns apparently do not act affirmatively to notify training directors of their concerns. (Boxley, Drew & Rangle, 1986; Olkin & Gaughen, 1991; Oliver et al., 2004; and Rosenberg, Getzelman, Arcinue, & Oren, 2005).

These findings are troubling in many ways. In the context of our present discussion of ethics, all of the major ethical codes contain language explicitly addressing the importance of being alert to signs that we ourselves might not be functioning optimally. Interestingly, and to their credit, respondents in the Rosenberg et al. (2005) study indicated that if they were the subject of concerns by their peers or colleagues, they would want others to let them know of the concerns so that they could address them directly.

The ethics codes also contain language indicating that professionals have a responsibility to deal with colleagues who may be acting unethically or untherapeutically. Unfortunately, in the studies by Oliver et al. (2004), and Rosenberg et al. (2005), this was apparently the exception rather than the rule. Behnke (2006) points out that while it may be difficult to confront the shortcomings or transgressions of a colleague, each of us accepts this responsibility, and accepts that others may also hold us accountable, by virtue of having willingly signed up for the profession to begin with. Behnke emphasizes that central principles of ethics, such as beneficence, dictate that we must not knowingly allow clients, our own or others', to be harmed. At the same time, however, Behnke identifies a number of potential obstacles, such as uncertainty, fear of retaliation, the personal and time commitment required to see a complaint through, empathy or personal loyalty to the individual in question, and other factors that may inhibit our willingness to take the necessary steps to address a problem.

What then should you do if you have concerns about a colleague? Wilkerson (2006) and Forrest et al. (1999) offered a series of suggestions for how faculty and supervisors can respond more effectively to the issue of problematic interns. How you proceed personally will depend on a number of factors, including the nature and severity of your concerns, your relationship with the individual in question, and the resources available to you. For simplicity, two broad categories of response are available, informal and formal. As always, you should consult with your supervisor and instructor before taking any action, unless, of course, your concerns happen to be with one of those same individuals. In such instances, consider consulting with another member of your academic department or another staff member at your training site.

Informal responses to ethical or professional concerns generally entail working either directly or indirectly with the individuals involved to address the matter. This route is usually most appropriate when there is some ambiguity about the concerns, and when there is a basic level of trust and respect that allows for direct communication. Informal resolutions are also only appropriate when the concerns do not represent severe breaches of fundamental ethics or gross violations of professional standards or performance that could endanger clients. Personally, I believe that if serious ethical transgressions have occurred (e.g., sexual relations with clients), it is irresponsible to seek informal resolution because the alleged perpetrator can too easily pass the situation off with an apology and may well go on to repeat the offense in the future.

Severe matters call for more formal responses. Two primary elements of such responses would be the filing of formal complaints with the relevant professional association and with the state licensing board. One may also chose to make a formal complaint to the personnel office or board of directors of the placement site. Obviously, taking this step is a very consequential matter that could impact the career of the person involved. As such, it should not be entered into lightly. On the other hand, if a perceived violation or lapse is severe, neither should one lightly avoid filing formal complaints. Remember that while we have an obligation to our colleagues, we also have an obligation to clients and to the profession. This point was emphasized by Van Horne (2004) and by Kirkland, Kirkland, & Reaves (2004), who reviewed data from state and provincial disciplinary boards and described how formal complaints are filed, investigated, and resolved.

I have rarely met a fellow professional who has not, at some time in his or her career, encountered a peer who seemed to be either incompetent or unethical. Behnke (2006) offered a similar observation. What is troubling is that when asked if these concerns were followed up on in any meaningful way, the answer, more often than not, is no, followed by some form of rationalization.

If we are truly committed to helping others, and if we are truly committed to our profession and the responsibility that entails, I believe more professionals need to step forward and make the tough decision to report and follow through when violations of ethics or practice are observed. If we fail to do this, we are letting down our clients, the rest of our colleagues, our interns and students, and, ultimately ourselves. We are also, I should emphasize, violating our respective codes of ethics.

SUMMARY

Ethical guidelines exist to protect the well-being of clients, practitioners, and the profession. As a trainee, it is incumbent upon you to be well versed in the ethical principles established by your profession, by state and federal laws, and within your work settings. This chapter has reviewed the key ethical issues that are most relevant to interns, but you are strongly advised to review the ethical standards of your profession as well as all relevant state and federal laws. Get to know these issues well, and discuss them with your peers, instructors, and supervisors. I suggest that you make it a personal habit to conduct a regular "ethics audit," as described by Reamer (2000). As noted throughout this chapter,

ethical and legal standards evolve and change over time, and I fully expect that some of the issues addressed in this chapter will have evolved between this edition and the next one. Keeping up with such changes is part of the responsibility you are accepting in seeking to become a professional.

REFERENCES

Acuff, C., Bennett, B., Bricklin, P., Canter, M., Knapp, S., Moldawsky, S., & Phelps, R. (1999). Considerations for ethical practice in managed care. *Professional Psychology: Research and Practice, 30*(6), 563–575.

Alexander, R., Jr. (1993). The legal liability of social workers after DeShaney. *Social Work, 38,* 64–68.

Alexander, R., Jr. (1997). Social workers and privileged communication in the federal legal system. *Social Work, 42,* 387–391.

American Association for Marriage and Family Therapy. (1991). *AAMFT code of ethics.* Washington, DC: Author.

American Counseling Association. (1999). *Ethical standards for Internet on-line counseling.* Alexandria, VA: Author.

American Psychiatric Association. (1979). Task force on confidentiality in children's and adolescent's records. *American Journal of Psychiatry, 136,* 138–144.

American Psychiatric Association. (1992). Assembly takes strong stance on patient-doctor sex. *Psychiatric News, 1,* 20.

American Psychological Association (2003). Legal issues in the professional practice of psychology. *Professional Psychology: Research and Practice, 34,* 595–600.

American Psychological Association. (2002). Ethical principles of psychologists and code of conduct. *American Psychologist, 57,* 1060–1073. www.apa.org/ethics/code2002.html

American Psychological Association. (2003a). Guidelines on multicultural education, training, research, practice and organizational change for psychologists. *American Psychologist, 58,* 377–402.

American Psychological Association. (2000b). Responding therapeutically to patient expression of sexual attraction: A stimulus training tape. Washington, DC: American Psychological Association.

American Psychological Association (2005). Determination and documentation of the need for practice guidelines. *American Psychologist, 60,* 976–978.

American Psychological Association Committee on Legal Issues (2006). Strategies for private practitioners coping with subpoenas or compelled testimony for client records or test data. *Professional Psychology: Research and Practice, 37,* 215–222.

American Psychological Association Committee on Professional Standards and Practice. (2003). Legal issues in the professional practice of psychology. *Professional Psychology: Research and Practice, 34,* 595–600.

American Psychological Association Committee on Women in Psychology. (1989). If sex enters into the psychotherapy relationship. *Professional Psychology: Research and Practice, 20,* 112–115.

American Psychological Association Ethics Committee (2006). Report of the Ethics Committee, 2005. *American Psychologist, 61,* 522–529.

American Psychological Association Practice Organization (2006). Privacy compliance is not enough: Three things you should know about the HIPAA security rule. *Good Practice, 1,* 9–10.

Anderson, J. R., & Barret, B. (2001). *Ethics in HIV-related psychotherapy: Clinical decision making in complex cases.* Washington, DC: APA.

Anderson, S. K., & Kitchner, K. S. (1998). Nonsexual post therapy relationships: A conceptual framework to assess ethical risk. *Professional Psychology: Research and Practice, 29,* 91–99.

Andrews, A. B., & Patterson, E. G. (1995). Searching for solutions to alcohol and other drug abuse during pregnancy: Ethics, values, and constitutional principles. *Social Work, 40,* 55–63.

Aponte, H. J. (1994). How personal can training get? *Journal of Marital and Family Therapy, 20,* 3–15.

Appelbaum, P. S. (1990). Statutes regulating patient-therapist sex. *Hospital and Community Psychiatry, 41,* 15–16.

Association for Counselor Education and Supervision. (1999). ACES guidelines for on-line instruction in counselor education. Technology Interest Network, http://www.chre.vt.edu/thohen/competencies.htm.

Baerger, D. R. (2001). Risk management with the suicidal patient: Lessons from case law. *Professional Psychology: Research and Practice, 32,* 359–366.

Baltimore, M. (2000). Ethical consideration in the use of technology for marriage and family counselors. *Family Journal, 8*(4), 390–394.

Barnett, J. E. (2005). Important ethical, legal issues surround supervision role. *National Psychologist, 14*(3), 16.

Barnett, J. E., & Yutrzenka, B. A. (1994). Nonsexual dual relationships in professional practice, with special applications to rural and military communities. *Independent Practitioner: Bulletin of the Division of Independent Practice, American Psychological Association, 14*(5), 243–248.

Barnett, J. E., & Scheetz, K., (2003). Technological advances and telehealth: Ethics, law, and the practice of psychotherapy. *Psychotherapy: Theory, Research, Practice, Training. 40,* 86–93.

Bartell, P. A., & Rubin, L. J. (1990). Dangerous liaisons: Sexual intimacies in supervision. *Professional Psychology: Research and Practice, 21,* 442–450.

Behnke, S. (2005). Thinking ethically as psychologists: reflections on ethical standards 2.01, 3.07, 9.08 & 10.04. *Monitor on Psychology, 36*(6), 86–87.

Behnke, S. (2005). Cooperating with other professionals: Reflections on ethical standard 3.09, *Monitor on Psychology, 36*(3), 70–71.

Behnke, S. H., & Warner, E. (2002). Confidentiality in the treatment of adolescents. *Monitor on Psychology, 33*(3) (http://www.apa.org/monitor/mar02/confidentiality.html).

Behnke, S. (2006). Responding to a colleague's ethical transgressions. *Monitor on Psychology, 37,* 72–73.

Belter, R. W., & Grisso, T. (1984). Children's recognition of rights violations in counseling. *Professional Psychology: Research and Practice, 15,* 899–910.

Benefield, H., Ashkanazi, G., & Rozensky, R. H. (2006). Communication and records: HIPPA [sic] issues when working in health care settings. *Professional Psychology: Research and Practice, 37,* 273–277.

Bennett, B. E., Bryant, B. K., VandenBos, G. R., & Greenwood, A. (1990). *Professional liability and risk management.* Washington, DC: American Psychological Association.

Berger, S. E., & Berger, M. A., (2005) Duty to warn expanded by California Court. *AAP Advance, Winter,* 4. (http://www.aapnet.org/aap_winter_2005.pdf)

Bergeron, R. L., & Gray, B. (2003). Ethical dilemmas of reporting suspected elder abuse. *Social Work, 48,* 96–105.

Berkman, C., Turner, S., Cooper, M., Polnerow, D., & Swartz, M. (2000). Sexual contact with clients: Assessment of social workers' attitudes and educational preparation. *Social Work, 45*(3), 223–236.

Berman, A. L., Jobes, D. A., & Silverman, M. M. (2006). *Adolescent suicide* (2nd ed.) Washington, DC: American Psychological Association.

Biaggio, M., Paget, T. L., & Chenoweth, M. S. (1997). A model for ethical management of faculty student dual relationships. *Professional Psychology: Research and Practice, 28,* 184–189.

Bogo, M., Globerman, J., & Sussman, T. (2004). Field instructor competence in group supervision: Students' views. *Journal of Teaching in Social Work, 24,* 199–215.

Bongar, B. (2002). *The suicidal patient: Clinical and legal standards of care* (2nd ed.) Washington, DC: APA.

Boonstra, H., & Nash, E. (2000). Minors and the right to consent in health care. *The Guttmacher report on public policy* (http://www.guttmacher.org/pubs/tgr/03/4/gr030404.pdf).

Boryrs, D. S., & Pope, K. S. (1989). Dual relationships between therapist and client: A national study of psychologists, psychiatrists and social workers. *Professional Psychology: Research and Practice, 20,* 283–293.

Bouhoutsos, J., Holroyd, J., Lerman, H., Forer, B. R., & Greenberg, M. (1983). Sexual intimacy between psychotherapists and patients. *Professional Psychology, 14,* 185–196.

Bowman, V. E., Hatley, L. D., & Bowman, R. L. (1995). Faculty-student relationships: The dual role controversy. *Counselor Education and Supervision, 34,* 232–242.

Bower, A. G. (2005). *The diffusion and value of healthcare information technology,* RAND (available online at http://www.rand.org/pubs/monographs/2006/RAND_MG272-1.pdf).

Boxley, R., Drew, C., & Rangle, D. (1986). Clinical trainee impairment in APA approved internship programs. *Clinical Psychologist, 39*(2), 49–52.

Bradshaw, J. (2006). Crimes raise confidentiality questions. *National Psychologist, 15*(2), 1–2.

Braun, S. A., & Cox, J. A., (2005). Managed mental health care: Intentional misdiagnosis of mental disorders. *Journal of Counseling and Development, 83,* 425–432,

Brown, H. N. (1987). Patient suicide during residency training: Incidence, implications, and program response. *Journal of Psychiatric Education, 11,* 201–216.

Brown, L. S. (1997). Remediation, amends or denial? *Professional Psychology: Research and Practice, 28,* 297–299.

Budman, S. H. (2000). Behavioral health care dot-com and beyond: Computer-mediated communications in mental health and substance abuse treatment. *American Psychologist, 55,* 1290–1300.

Burkemper, E. M. (2004). Informed consent in social work ethics education: Guiding student education with an informed consent template. *Journal of Teaching in Social Work, 24,* 141–160.

Busseri, M. A., Tyler, J. D., & King, A. R. (2005). An exploratory examination of student dismissals and prompted resignations from clinical psychology PhD training programs. *Professional Psychology: Research and Practice, 36,* 441–445.

Campbell, C. D., & Gordon, M. C. (2003). Acknowledging the inevitable: Understanding multiple relationships in rural practice. *Professional Psychology: Research and Practice, 34,* 430–434.

Center for Adolescent Health and the Law (2003). *State minor consent laws: A summary* (2nd ed.) (2003). http://www.guttmacher.org/pubs/tgr/03/4/gr030404.pdf.

Chemtob, C. M., Bauer, G. B., Hamada, R. S., Pelowski, S. R., & Muraoka, M. Y. (1989). Patient suicide: Occupational hazard for psychologists and psychiatrists. *Professional Psychology: Research and Practice, 20,* 416–420.

Chenneville, T. (2000). HIV, confidentiality, and duty to protect: A decision-making model. *Professional Psychology: Research and Practice, 31,* 661–670.

Claiborn, C. D., Berberoglu, L. S., Nerison, R. M., & Somberg, D. R. (1994). The client's perspective: Ethical judgments and perceptions of therapist practices. *Professional Psychology: Research and Practice, 25,* 268–274.

Clark, D. (1998). The evaluation and management of the suicidal patient. In P. M. Kleespies et al. (Eds.), *Emergencies in mental health practice: Evaluation and management* (pp. 75–94). New York: Guilford Press.

Clark, J. J., Rompf, E. L., & Walker, R. (2001). Practicum instruction: Warning signs of boundary problems and what to do about them. *Journal of Teaching in Social Work, 21*(12), 3–18.

Clifft, M. A. (1986). Writing about psychiatric patients: Guidelines for disguising material. *Bulletin of the Meninger Clinic, 50,* 511–524.

Clingermen, T. L., & Bernard, J. M., (2004. An investigation of the use of e-mail as a supplemental modality for clinical supervision. *Counselor Education and Supervision, 44,* 82–95.

Cobb, N. H. (1994). Court-recommended guidelines for managing unethical students and working with university lawyers. *Journal of Social Work Education, 30,* 18–31.

Congress, E. (2001). Dual relationships in social work education: Report on a national survey. *Journal of Social Work Education, 37,* 255–267.

Connor, T. A. (1996). Ethical and clinical issues in involuntary psychotherapy. *Psychotherapy, 33,* 587–592.

Conte, H. R., & Karasu, T. B. (1990). Malpractice in psychotherapy: An overview. *American Journal of Psychotherapy, 44,* 232–246.

Cooper, C. C., & Gottlieb, M. C. (2000). Ethical issues with managed care: Challenges facing counseling psychology. *Counseling Psychologist, 29,* 179–236.

Cottone, R. R., & Claus, R. E. (2000). Ethical decision-making models: A review of the literature. *Journal of Counseling and Development, 78,* 275–283.

DeAngelis, T. (2001). Surviving a patient's suicide. *Monitor on Psychology, December,* 70–73.

Daniels, J. A., Alva, L. A., & Olivares, S. (2002). Graduate training for managed care: A national survey of psychology and social work programs. *Professional Psychology: Research and Practice, 33,* 587–590.

DeBell, C., & Jones, R. D. (1997). Privileged communication at last? An overview of *Jaffee v. Redmond. Professional Psychology: Research and Practice, 28,* 559–566.

Drake, R. E., Teague, G., & Gersing, K. (2005). State mental health authorities and informatics. *Community Mental Health Journal, 41*(3), 365–370.

Fisher, C. B., & Younggren, J. N. (1997). The value and utility of the 1992 Ethics Code. *Professional Psychology: Research and Practice, 28,* 582–592.

Fisher, C. B., & Fried, A. L., (2003). Internet-mediated psychological services and the American psychological association ethics code. *Psychotherapy: Theory, Research, Practice Training. 40,* 103–111.

Fly, B. J., van Bark, W. P., Weinman, L., Kitchener, K. S., & Lang, P. R. (1997). Ethical transgressions of psychology graduate students: Critical incidents with implications for training. *Professional Psychology: Research and Practice, 28,* 492–495.

Ford, C. A., Milstein, S. G., Halpern-Felsher, B. L., & Irwin, C. E., Jr. (1997). Influence of physician confidentiality assurances on adolescents' willingness to discuss information and seek future health care: A randomized controlled trial. *Journal of the American Medical Association, 278*(12), 1029–1034.

Forrest, L., Elman, N., Gizara, S., & Vacha-Haase, T., (199). Trainee impairment: A review of identification, remediation, dismissal, and legal issues. *Counseling Psychologist, 27,* 627–686.

Fulero, S. M. (1988). Tarasoff: 10 years later. *Professional Psychology, Research and Practice, 19,* 184–190.

Gabbard, G. O. (Ed.). (1989). *Sexual exploitation in professional relationships.* Washington, DC: American Psychiatric Press.

Gavey, N., & Braun, V. (1997). Ethics and the publication of clinical case material. *Professional Psychology: Research and Practice, 28,* 399–404.

Gelman, S. R., Pollack, D., & Auerbach, C. (1996). Liability issues in social work education. *Journal of Social Work Education, 32,* 351–361.

Glaser, R. D., & Thorpe, J. S. (1986). Unethical intimacy: A survey of sexual contact and advances between psychology educators and female graduate students. *American Psychologist, 41,* 43–51.

Glosoff, H. L., Herlihy, B., & Spence, E. B. (2000). Privileged communication in the counselor-client relationship. *Journal of Counseling and Development, 78,* 454–462.

Glosoff, H. L., Herlihy, S. B., Herlihy, B., & Spence, E. B. (1997). Privileged communication in the psychologist-client relationship. *Professional Psychology: Research and Practice, 28,* 573–581.

Glueckauff, R. L., Pickett, T. C., Ketterson, T. U., Loomis, J. S., & Rozensky, R. H. (2003). Preparation for the delivery of telehealth services: A self-study framework for expansion of practice. *Professional Psychology: Research and Practice, 34,* 159–163.

Gustafson, K. E., & McNamara, J. R. (1987). Confidentiality with minor clients: Issues and guidelines for therapists. *Professional Psychology: Research and Practice, 18,* 503–508.

Gutheil, T. G., & Gabbard, G. O. (1993). The concept of boundaries in clinical practice: Theoretical and risk management dimensions. *American Journal of Psychiatry, 150,* 188–196.

Hafemeister, T. L. (2000). Informed consent: Must a clinician disclose personal information? *Monitor on Psychology, 31*(8), 76.

Handelman, M. M., Gottlieb, M. C., & Knapp, S. (2005). Training ethical psychologists: An acculturation model. *Professional Psychology: Research and Practice, 36,* 59–65.

Hargrove, D. S. (1986). Ethical issues in rural mental health practice. *Professional Psychology: Research and Practice, 17,* 20–23.

Harrar, W. R., VandeCreek, L., & Knapp, S. (1990). Ethical and legal aspects of clinical supervision. *Professional Psychology: Research and Practice, 21,* 37–41.

Harris, E. A. (1995). The importance of risk management in a managed care environment. In M. B. Sussman (Ed.), *A perilous calling: The hazards of psychotherapy practice* (pp. 247–258). New York: Wiley.

Harris, E. A., & Bennett, B. E. (2000). Psychotherapist-patient contract. In L. Vandecreek & T. L. Jackson (Eds.), *Innovations in* clinical practice: A source book (p. 18). Sarasota, FL: Professional Resource Press.

Hayman, P. M., & Covert, J. A. (1986). Ethical dilemmas in college counseling centers [Special issue: Professional Ethics]. *Journal of Counseling and Development, 64,* 318–321.

Helbok, C. M., Marineli, R. P., & Walls, R. T. (2006). National survey of ethical practices across rural and urban communities. *Professional Psychology: Research and Practice, 37,* 36–44.

Heinlen, K. T., Welfel, E. R., Richmond, E. N., & Rak, C. F. (2003). The scope of WebCounseling: A survey of services and compliance with NBCC standards for the ethical practice of WebCounseling. *Journal of Counseling and Development, 81,* 61–69.

Holloway, J. D. (2003). More protections for patients and psychologists under HIPAA. *Monitor on Psychology, 34*(2), 22.

Hotelling, K. (1988). Ethical, legal, and administrative options to address sexual relationships between counselor and client. *Journal of Counseling and Development, 67,* 233–237.

Housman, L., & Stake, J. (1999). The current state of sexual ethics training in clinical psychology: Issues of quantity, quality, and effectiveness. *Professional Psychology: Research and Practice, 30*(3), 302–311.

Houston-Vega, M. K., Nuehring, E. M., & Daguio, E. R., (1996). *Prudent practice: A guide for managing malpractice risk.* Washington, DC: NASW.

Howing, P. T., & Wodarski, J. S. (1992). Legal requisites for social workers in child abuse and neglect situations. *Social Work, 37,* 330–335.

Humphreys, K., Winzelberg, A., & Klaw, E. (2000). Psychologists' ethical responsibilities in Internet groups: Issues, strategies, and a call for dialogue. *Professional Psychology: Research and Practice, 31,* 493–496.

Hutchinson, E. D. (1993). Mandatory reporting laws: Child protective case finding gone awry. *Social Work, 38,* 56–63.

Isaacs, M. L., & Stone, C., (2001). Confidentiality with minors: Mental health counselors' attitudes toward breaching or preserving confidentiality. *Journal of Mental Health Counseling, 23,* 342–356.

Jacobs, C. (1991). Violations of the supervisory relationship: An ethical and educational blind spot. *Social Work, 36,* 130–135.

Jaffee v. *Redmond,* 116 S. Ct. 95–266, 64L.W. 4490 (U.S. Ill., June 13, 1996).

Jeffords, J. (1999). Confidentiality of medical information: Protecting privacy in an electronic age. *Professional Psychology: Research and Practice, 30*(2), 115–116.

Jobes, D. A., & Berman, A. L. (1993). Suicide and malpractice liability: Assessing and revising policies, procedures, and practice in outpatient settings. *Professional Psychology: Research and Practice, 24,* 91–99.

Johnson, M. E., Brems, C., Warner, T. D., & Roberts, L. W., (2006). The need for continuing education in ethics as reported by rural and urban mental health care providers. *Professional Psychology: Research and Practice. 37,* 183–189.

Johnston, S. H., & Farber, B. A. (1996). The maintenance of boundaries in psychotherapeutic practice. *Psychotherapy, 33,* 391–402.

Joiner, T., Walker, R., Rudd, M., & Jobes, D. (1999). Scientizing and routinizing the assessment of suicidality in outpatient practice. *Professional Psychology: Research and Practice, 30*(5), 447–453.

Jorgenson, L., Randles, R., & Strasburger, L. (1991). The furor over psychotherapist-patient sexual contact: New solutions to an old problem. *William and Mary Law Review, 32,* 643–729.

Juhnke, G. (1994). SAD PERSONS scale review. *Measurement and Evaluation in Counseling and Development, 29*(1), 325–328.

Kagle, J. D. (1993). Record keeping: Directions for the 1990s. *Social Work, 38,* 190–196.

Kagle, J. D., & Giebelhausen, P. N. (1994). Dual relationships and professional boundaries. *Social Work, 39,* 213–220.

Kalichman, S. C. (1999). *Mandated reporting of suspected child abuse: Ethics, law, and policy* (2nd ed.). Washington, DC: American Psychological Association.

Kanz, J. E. (2001). Clinical-Supervision.com: Issues in the provision of online supervision. *Professional Psychology: Research and Practice, 32,* 415–420.

Kaser-Boyd, N., Adelman, H., & Taylor, L. (1985). Minors' ability to identify risks and benefits of therapy. *Professional Psychology: Research and Practice, 16,* 411–417.

Keith-Spiegel, P. (1994). The 1992 ethics code: Boon or bane. *Professional Psychology: Research and Practice, 25,* 315–317.

Kennedy, P. F., Vandehey, M., Norman, W. B., & Diehoff, G. M. (2003). Recommendations for risk-management practices. *Professional Psychology: Research and Practice, 34,* 309–311.

Kirkland, K., Kirkland K. L., & Reaves, R. P. (2004). On the professional use of disciplinary data. *Professional Psychology: Research and Practice, 35,* 179–184.

Kitchener, K. S. (1984). Intuition, critical evaluation and ethical principles: The foundation for ethical decisions in counseling psychology. *Counseling Psychologist, 12*(3), 43–56.

Kitchener, K. S. (1988). Dual relationships: What makes them so problematic? *Journal of Counseling and Development, 67,* 217–221.

Knapp, S., & Slattery, J. M. (2004). Professional boundaries in nontraditional settings. *Professional Psychology: Research and Practice. 35,* 553–558.

Knapp, S., & VandeCreek, L. (1997). *Jaffee* v. *Redman:* The Supreme Court recognizes a psychotherapist-patient privilege in federal courts. *Professional Psychology: Research and Practice, 28,* 567–572.

Knapp, S., & VandeCreek, L. (2001). Psychotherapist's legal responsibilities to third parties: Does it extend to alleged perpetrators of childhood abuse? *Professional Psychology: Research and Practice, 32,* 479–483.

Knapp, S., & VandeCreek, L. (2003). An overview of the major changes in the 2002 APA Ethics Code. *Professional Psychology: Research and Practice, 34,* 301–308.

Kocet, M. M. (2006). Ethical challenges in a complex world: Highlights of the 2005 ACA code of ethics. *Journal of Counseling and Development, 84,* 228–234.

Kocet, M. M., & Freeman, L. T. (2005) Report of the ACA ethics committee: 2003–2004. *Journal of Counseling and Development, 83,* 249–252.

Kolbert, J., Brendel, J., & Morgan, B. (2002). Faculty and student perceptions of dual relationships within counselor education: A qualitiative analysis. *Counselor Education and Supervision, 41*(2), 193–2006.

Koocher, G., & Morray, E. (2000). Regulation of telepsychology: A survey of state attorneys general. *Professional Psychology: Research and Practice, 31*(5), 503–508.

Koocher, G. P., & Keith-Spiegel, P. (1998). *Ethics in psychology: Professional standards and cases* (2nd ed.). New York: Oxford University Press.

Kremer, T. G., & Gesten, E. L., (2003). Managed mental health care: The client's perspective. *Professional psychology: Research and Practice, 34*(2), 187–196.

Lamb, D., & Catanzaro, S. (1998). Sexual and nonsexual boundary violations involving psychologists, clients, supervisees, and students: Implications for professional practice. *Professional Psychology: Research and Practice, 29*(5), 498–503.

Lamb, D. H., Catanzaro, S. J., & Moorman, A. S. (2003). Psychologists reflect on their sexual relationships with clients, supervisees, and students: Occurrence, impact, rationales and collegial intervention. *Professional Psychology: Research and Practice.* 102–107.

Larrabee, M. J., & Miller, G. M. (1993). An examination of sexual intimacy in supervision. *Clinical Supervisor, 11,* 103–126.

Leong, G. B., Eth, S., & Silva, J. A. (1992). The psychotherapist as witness for the prosecution: The criminalization of Tarasoff. *American Journal of Psychiatry, 149,* 1011–1015.

McGlothlin, J. M., Rainey, S., & Kindsvatter, A. (2005). Suicidal clients and supervisees: A model for considering supervisor roles. *Counselor Education and Supervision, 45,* 135–146.

McGuire, J., Niere, D., Abbott, D., Sheridan, K., & Fisher, R. (1995). Do Tarasoff principles apply in AIDS-related psychotherapy? Ethical decision making and the role of therapist homophobia and perceived client dangerousness. *Professional Psychology: Research and Practice, 26,* 608–611.

Maheu, M. (2003). The online clinical practice management model. *Psychotherapy: Theory, Research, Practice, Training, 40,* 20–32.

Maheu, M., & Gordon, B. (2000). Counseling and therapy on the Internet. *Professional Psychology: Research and Practice, 31*(5), 484–489.

Mannheim, C. I., Sancilio, M., Phipps-Yonas, S., Brunnquell, D., Somers, P., Farseth, G., & Ninonuevo, F. (2002). Ethical ambituities in the practice of child clinical psychology. *Professional Psychology: Research and Practice, 33,* 24–29.

Maradiegue, A. (2003). Minor's rights versus parental rights: review of legal issues in adolescent health care. *Journal of Midwifery & Women's Health, 48(3),* 170–177.

Margolin, G., Chien, D., Duman, S. E., Fauchier, A., Gordis, E. B., Oliver, P. H., Ramos, M. C., & Vickerman, K. A., (2005). Ethical issues in couple and family research. *Journal of Family Psychology, 19,* 157–167.

Marsh, J. C., (2003). To thine own ethics code be true. *Social Work, 48,* 5–7.

Messer, S. (2003). The controversy over empirically supported treatments. *National Psychologist, September/October,* 12–13.

Miller, D. J., & Thelen, M. H. (1986). Knowledge and beliefs about confidentiality in psychotherapy. *Professional Psychology: Research and Practice, 17,* 15–19.

Miller, G. M., & Larrabee, M. J. (1995). Sexual intimacy in counselor education and supervision: A national survey. *Counselor Education and Supervision, 34,* 332–343.

Mishna, F., Antle, B. J., & Regehr, C. (2002). Social work with clients contemplating suicide: Complexity and ambiguity in the clinical, ethical and legal considerations. *Clinical Social Work Journal, 30,* 265–279.

Mitchell, K. J., Becker-Blease, K. A., & Finkelhor, D. (2005). Inventory of problematic internet experiences encountered in clinical practice. *Professional Psychology: Research and Practice, 36,* 498–509.

Moleski, S. M., & Kiselica, M. S. (2005). Dual relationships: A contiuuum ranging from the destructive to the therapeutic. *Journal of Counseling and Development. 83,* 3–11.

Monahan, J. (1993). Limiting therapist exposure to Tarasoff liability: Guidelines for risk containment. *American Psychologist, 48,* 242–250.

Montgomery, L. M., Cupit, B. E., & Wimberley, T. K. (1999). Complaints, malpractice, and risk management: Professional issues and personal experiences. *Professional Psychology: Research and Practice, 30,* 402–410.

Murphy, W. J. (2005), Military proceedings threaten therapy confidentiality. *National Psychologist,14 (5),* 8–9.

NASW. (2001). NASW standards for cultural competence in social work practice (www.socialworkers.org).

National Association of Social Workers. (1996). *Code of ethics.* Silver Spring, MD: Author.

National Board of Certified Counselors. (1998). A set of standards for on-line counseling [On-line], http://www.nbcc.org/ ethics/wc-standards.htm.

Nickelson, D. W. (1998). Telehealth and the evolving health care system: Strategic opportunities for professional psychology. *Professional Psychology: Research and Practice, 29,* 527–535.

Nicolai, K. M., & Scott, N. A. (1994). Provision of confidentiality information and its relation to child abuse reporting. *Professional Psychology: Research and Practice, 25,* 154–160.

Nowell, D., & Spruill, J. (1993). If it's not absolutely confidential, will information be disclosed? *Professional Psychology: Research and Practice, 24,* 367–369.

Oliver, M. N. I, Bernstein, J. H., Anderson, K. G., Blashfield, R. K., & Roberts, M. C. (2004). An exploratory examination of student attitudes toward "impaired" peers in clinical psychology training programs. *Professional Psychology: Research and Practice, 35,* 141–147.

Olkin, R., & Gaughen, S. (1991). Evaluation and dismissal of students in masters level clinical programs: Legal parameters and survey results. *Counselor Education and Supervision, 30,* 276–288.

Oordt, M. S., Jobes, D. A., Rudd, M. D., Fonesca, V. P., Runyan, C. N., Stea, J. B., Campise, R. L., & Talcott, G. W. (2005). Development of a clinical guide to enhance care for suicidal patients. *Professional Psychology: Research and Practice, 36,* 208–218.

Paradise, L. V., & Kirby, P. C. (1990). Some perspectives on the legal liability of group counseling in private practice. *Journal for Specialists in Group Work, 2,* 114–118.

Parker-Oliver, D., & Demiris, G. (2006). Social work informatics: A new specialty. *Social Work, 51,* 127–134.

Patterson, W., Dohn, H., Bird, J., & Patterson, G. (1983). Evaluation of suicidal patients. *Psychosomatics, 24*(4), 343–349.

Paulson, B. L. & Worth, M. (2002). Counseling for suicide: Client perspectives. *Journal of counseling and development, 80,* 86–93,

Peruzzi, N., & Bongar, B. (1999). Assessing risk for completed suicide in patients with major depression: Psychologists' views of critical factors. *Professional Psychology: Research and Practice, 30*(6), 576–580.

Pollack, D., & Marsh, J. (2004). Social work misconduct may lead to liability. *Social Work, 49,* 609–612.

Pope, K. S. (1990). Therapist–patient sex as sex abuse: Six scientific, professional and practical dilemmas in addressing victimization and rehabilitation. *Professional Psychology: Research and Practice, 21,* 227–239.

Pope, K. S. (1993). Licensing disciplinary actions for psychologists who have been sexually involved with a client: Some information about offenders. *Professional Psychology: Research and Practice, 24,* 374–377.

Pope, K. S., & Bouhoutsos, J. C. (1986). *Sexual intimacy between therapists and patients.* New York: Praeger.

Pope, K. S., & Brown, L. S. (1996). *Recovered memories of abuse: Assessment, therapy, forensics.* Washington, DC: American Psychological Association.

Pope, K. S., Keith-Spiegel, P., & Tabachnick, B. G. (1986). Sexual attraction to clients: The human therapist and the (sometimes) inhuman training system. *American Psychologist, 41,* 147–158.

Pope, K. S., Levenson, H., & Schover, L. (1979). Sexual intimacy in psychology training: Results and implications of a national survey. *American Psychologist, 34,* 682–689.

Pope, K. S., Sonne, J. L., & Holroyd, J. (1993). *Sexual feelings in psychotherapy.* Washington, DC: American Psychological Association.

Pope, K. S., & Tabachnick, B. G. (1993). Therapists' anger, hate, fear, and sexual feelings: National survey of therapist responses, client characteristics, critical events, formal complaints, and training. *Professional Psychology: Research and Practice, 24,* 142–152.

Pope, K. S., & Vasquez, M. J. T. (1998). *Ethics in psychotherapy and counseling: A practical guide for psychologists* (2nd ed.). San Francisco: Jossey-Bass.

Pope, K. S., & Vetter, V. V. (1992). Ethical dilemmas encountered by members of the American Psychological Association: A national survey. *American Psychologist, 47,* 397–411.

Prieto, L. R. (1997). Separating group supervision from group therapy: Avoiding epistemological confusion. *Professional Psychology: Research and Practice, 28,* 405.

Pulakos, J. (1994). Incidental encounters between therapists and clients: The client's perspective. *Professional Psychology: Research and Practice, 25,* 300–303.

Rabasca, L. (1999, March). States' crop of reform bills presses Congress. *APA Monitor, 30,* 4.

Ragusea, A. S., & Vandecreek, L. (2003). Suggestions for the ethical practice of online psychotherapy. *Psychotherapy: Theory, Research, Practice, Training. 40,* 94–102.

RAND Corporation (2005). Health information technology: Can HIT lower costs and improve quality? http://www.rand.org/pubs/research_briefs/RB9136/index1.html

Reamer, F. G. (1995). Malpractice claims against social workers: First facts. *Social Work, 40,* 595–601.

Reamer, F. G. (2000). The social work ethics audit: A risk management strategy. *Social Work, 45*(4), 355–366.

Reamer, F. G. (2003) Boundary issues in social work: Managing dual relationships. *Social Work, 48*(1), 121–134.

Reamer, F. G. (2005b). Update on confidentiality issues in practice with children: Ethics risk management. *Children and Schools, 27*(2), 117–120.

Reamer, F. G. (2005a). Documentation in social work: Evolving ethical and risk-management standards. *Social Work, 50,* 325–334.

Reese, R., Conoley, C., & Brossart, D. (2002). Effectiveness of telephone counseling: A field based investigation. *Journal of Counseling Psychology, 49,* 233–242.

Regehr, C., & Antle, B. (1997). Coercive influences: Informed consent in court-mandated social work practice. *Social Work, 42,* 300–306.

Ritterband, L. M., Gonder-Frederick, L. A., Cox, D. J., Clifton, A. D., West, R. W., & Borowitz, S. M. (2003). Internet interventions: In review, in use, and into the future. *Professional Psychology: Research and Practice, 34,* 527–534.

Robinson, W. L., & Reid, P. T. (1985). Sexual intimacies in psychology revisited. *Professional Psychology: Research and Practice, 16,* 512–520.

Rodolfa, E., Bent, R., Eisman, E., Nelson, P., Rehm, L., & Ritchie, P. (2005). A cube model for competency development: Implicatios for psychology educators and regulators. *Professional Psychology: Research and Practice, 36,* 347–354.

Rodolfa, E., Ko, S. F., & Petersen, L., (2004). Psychology training directors' views of trainee's readiness to practice independently. *Professional Psychology: Research and Practice, 35,* 397–404.

Rodolfa, E. R., Hall, T., Holms, V., Davena, A., Komatz, D., Antunez, M., & Hall, A. (1994). The management of sexual feelings in therapy. *Professional Psychology: Research and Practice, 25,* 168–172.

Rodolfa, E. R., Kitzrow, M., Vohra, S., & Wilson, B. (1990). Training interns to respond to sexual dilemmas. *Professional Psychology: Research and Practice, 21,* 313–315.

Rosenberg, J. I., Getzelman, M. A., Arcinue, F., & Oren, C. Z., (2005). An exploratory look at students' experiences of problematic peers in academic professional psychology programs. *Professional Psychology: Research and Practice, 36,* 665–673.

Rubanowitz, D. E. (1987). Public attitudes toward psychotherapist-client confidentiality. *Professional Psychology: Research and Practice, 18,* 613–618.

Rupert, P. A., & Baird, K. A., (2004). Managed care and the independent practice of psychology. *Professional Psychology: Research and Practice, 35,* 185–193.

Sales, B. D., Miller, M. O., & Hall, S. R., (2005). *Laws affecting clinical practice.* Washington, DC: APA.

Samuel, S. E., & Gorton, G. E. (1998). National survey of psychology internship directors regarding education for prevention of psychologist–patient sexual exploitation. *Professional Psychology: Research and Practice, 29,* 86–90.

Sanchez, H. G. (2001). Risk factor model for suicide assessment and intervention. *Professional Psychology: Research and Practice, 32,* 351–358.

Schank, J. A., & Skovholt, T. M. (2006) *Ethical practice in small communities.* Washington: APA.

Schank, J. A., & Skovholt, T. M. (1997). Dual-relationship dilemmas of rural and small-community psychologists. *Professional Psychology: Research and Practice, 28,* 44–49.

Schlossberger, E., & Hecker, L. (1996). HIV and family therapist's duty to warn: A legal and ethical analysis. *Journal of Marital and Family Therapy, 22,* 27–40.

Schoener, G. R. (1995). Assessment of professionals who have engaged in boundary violations. *Psychiatric Annals, 25*(2), 95–99.

Schwartz, G. (1989). Confidentiality revisited. *Social Work, 34,* 223–226.

Shapiro, E. L., & Ginzberg, R. (2003). To accept or not to accept: Referrals and the maintenance of boundaries. *Professional Psychology: Research and Practice, 34,* 256–263.

Simon, R. I. (1989). Sexual exploitation of patients: How it begins before it happens. *Psychiatry Annals, 19,* 104–122.

Sleek, S. (1998). Managed-care battle waged on capitol hill. *APA Monitor, 29*(2), 24–25.

Slimp, P. A. O., & Burian, B. K. (1994). Multiple role relationships during internship: Consequences and recommendations. *Professional Psychology: Research and Practice, 25,* 39–45.

Sloan, L., Edmond, T., Rubin, A., & Doughty, M. (1998). Social workers' knowledge of and experience with sexual exploitation by psychotherapists. *Social Work, 43,* 43–53.

Slovenko, R. (1988). The therapist's duty to warn or protect third persons. *Journal of Psychiatry and Law, Spring,* 139–192.

Small, M. A., Lyons, P. M., & Guy, L. S. (2002). Liability issues in child abuse and neglect reporting statutes. *Professional Psychology: Research and Practice, 33,* 13–18.

Sobel, S. B. (1992). Small town practice of psychotherapy: Ethical and personal dilemmas. *Psychotherapy and Private Practice, 10,* 61–69.

Somer, E., & Saadon, M. (1999). Therapist-client sex: Clients' retrospective reports. *Professional Psychology: Research and Practice, 30*(5), 504–509.

Sommers-Flanagan, J., & Sommers-Flanagan, R. (1995). Intake interviewing with suicidal patients: A systematic approach. *Professional Psychology: Research and Practice, 26,* 41–47.

Stadler, H., & Paul, R. D. (1986). Counselor educators' preparation in ethics. *Journal of Counseling and Development, 64,* 328–330.

Stall, M. A., & King, R. E. (2000). Managing a multiple relationship environment: The ethics of military psychology. *Professional Psychology: Research and Practice, 31,* 698–705.

Stamm, H. (1998). Clinical applications of telehealth in mental health care. *Professional Psychology: Research and Practice, 29*(6), 536–542.

Stanard, R., & Hazler, R. (1995). Legal and ethical implications of HIV and duty to warn for counselors: Does Tarasoff apply? *Journal of Counseling and Development, 73,* 397–400.

Steinfeld, B., Ekorenrud, B., Gillett, C., Quirk, M., & Eytan, T., (2006). EMRs bring all of healthcare together. *Behavioral Healthcare, 26*(1), 12–17.

Stoller, R. J. (1988). Patients responses to their own case reports. *Journal of the American Psychoanalytic Association, 36,* 371–391.

Strasburger, L. H., Jorgenson, L., & Randles, R. (1991). Criminalization of psychotherapist–patient sex. *American Journal of Psychiatry, 148,* 859–863.

Strom-Gottfried, K. (2000). Ethical vulnerability in social work education: An analysis of NASW complaints. *Journal of Social Work Education, 36,* 241–251.

Sue, D. W., Arredondo, P., & McDavis, R. J. (2992). Multicultural Counseling Competencies and Standards: A call to the Profession. *Journal of Counseling and Development, 70,* 477–486.

Sullivan, J. R., Ramirez, E., Rae, W. A., Peña Razo, N., & George, C. A. (2002) Factors contributing to breaking confidentiality with adolescent clients: A survey of pediatric psychologists. *Professional Psychology: Research and Practice, 33,* 396–401.

Swenson, L. C. (1993). *Psychology and law for the helping professions.* Pacific Grove, CA: Brooks/Cole.

Swenson, L. C. (1997). *Psychology and law for the helping professions.* (2nd ed.). Pacific Grove, CA: Brooks/Cole.

Thoreson, R. W., Shaughnessy, P., Heppner, P. P., & Cook, S. W. (1993). Sexual contact during and after the professional relationship: Attitudes and practices of male counselors. *Journal of Counseling and Development, 71,* 429–434.

Tishler, C. L., Gordon, L. B., & Landry-Meyer, L. (2000). Managing the violent patient: A guide for psychologists and other mental health professionals. *Professional Psychology: Research and Practice, 31,* 34–41.

Van Horne, B. A. (2004). Psychology licensing board disciplinary actions: The realities. *Professional Psychology: Research and Practice, 35,* 170–178.

VandeCreek, L., Bennett, B. E., & Bricklin, P. M. (1994). *Risk management with potentially dangerous patients.* Washington, DC: American Psychological Association Insurance Trust.

VandenBos, G., & Williams, S. (2000). The Internet versus the telephone: What is telehealth, anyway? *Professional Psychology: Research and Practice, 31*(5), 490–492.

Vasquez, M. J. T. (1988). Counselor-client sexual contact: Implications for ethics training. *Journal of Counseling and Development, 67,* 238–241.

VauPitts, J. H. (1992). Organizing a practicum and internship program in counselor education. *Counselor Education and Supervision, 31,* 196–207.

Vesper, J. H., & Brock, G. W. (1991). *Ethics, legalities, and professional practice issues in marriage and family therapy.* Boston: Allyn & Bacon.

Walden, S. L., Herlihy, B., & Ashton, L. (2003) The evolution of ethics: Personal perspectives of ACA Ethics Committee Chairs. *Journal of Counseling and Development, 81*(1), 106–112.

Weinberger, L. E., & Sreenivasan, S. (1994). Ethical and professional conflicts in correctional psychology. *Professional Psychology: Research and Practice, 25,* 161–167.

Welfel, E. R., & Lipsitz, N. E. (1984). The ethical behavior of professional psychologists: A critical analysis of the research. *Counseling Psychologist, 12*(3), 31–42.

Westefeld, J. S., Range, L. M., Rogers, J. R., Maples, M. R., Bromley, J. L., & Alcom, J. (2000). Suicide: An overview. *Counseling Psychologist, 28,* 445–510.

White, T. W. (2003a). Legal issues and suicide risk management. *National Psychologist, March/April,* 12.

White, T. W. (2003b). Managing dual relationships in correctional settings. *National Psychologist, September/October,* 14–15.

Williams, M. H. (1992). Exploitation and inference: Mapping the damage from therapist-patient sexual involvement. *American Psychologist, 47,* 412–421.

Wilkerson, K. (2006) Impaired students: Applying the therapeutic process model to graduate training programs. *Counselor Education and Supervision, 45,* 207–217.

Wood, J. A. V., Miller, T. W., & Hargrove, D. S. (2005). Clinical supervision in rural settings: A telehealth model. *Professional Psychology: Research and Practice, 36,* 173–179.

Woody, R. (1999). Domestic violations of confidentiality. *Professional Psychology: Research and Practice, 30*(6), 607–610.

Younggren, J. N., & Gottlieb, M. C. (2004). Managing risk when contemplating multiple relationships. *Professional Psychology: Research and Practice, 35,* 255–260.

Zakutansky, T. J., & Sirles, E. A. (1993). Ethical and legal issues in field education: Shared responsibility and risk. *Journal of Social Work Education, 29,* 338–347.

Zur, O. (2003). HIPAA WANTS YOU! Eleven reasons to become compliant; Eleven simple ways to achieve compliance. *Independent Practitioner, 23*(5).

Zur, O. (2006) How to respond to the dreaded subpoena. *National Psychologist, March/April* 9.

CHAPTER 4

SUPERVISION

When asked to name the best part of professional training, a colleague said without hesitation, "Supervision. From one of my supervisors in graduate school, I learned more about therapy and working with people than I had learned in three years."

As such comments suggest, supervision can be a tremendous learning opportunity if it is managed well. The goal of this chapter is to familiarize you with some of the activities that are most commonly part of supervision so you understand their purpose and can make the most effective use of the opportunity. The chapter also considers how personalities and theoretical orientation play a role in the supervisory experience, and how interns and supervisors can manage differences or difficulties that may arise in supervision.

WHAT IS SUPERVISION?

Unlike academic coursework, in which the primary focus is on mastery of an established body of knowledge or skills, supervision involves ongoing work as it takes place in real time in a real-world setting. That is why supervision is so important and so valuable. Your field supervisor is the first person you will turn to if you have questions about what is happening at your placement. Your supervisor also bears direct responsibility for your actions and your training while at the internship. Supervisors will help arrange for various learning opportunities, will review your work with you, may work directly beside you as you interact with clients, and will be involved in evaluating your professional development and performance.

HOPES AND FEARS OF INTERNS

Berger and Buchholz (1993) observed that, despite the importance of the supervisory experience, supervisees rarely receive instruction in the supervisory process or in what is expected of them. Such oversight appears to be particularly unfortunate in light of findings by Knight (1996) suggesting that BSW and MSW students report greater satisfaction with supervisors who clarify roles and expectations and give students opportunities to

discuss their concerns. These authors suggest that giving supervisees an opportunity to voice their wishes and fears is one of the first steps in preparing for supervision.

When I ask interns what their hopes are for supervision, they often speak about the qualities they would prefer to find in their supervisor. Most interns want supervisors to be a combination of teacher, role model, and mentor. Interns seek supervisors who will help them learn about theories and techniques of therapy, assessment, and other clinical functions. Interns tend to prefer supervisors who give enough freedom to try new things but are careful to select activities that are not beyond the intern's abilities. Interns also want supervisors who are supportive and to whom they can turn for advice and encouragement. Finally, many interns want to get to know their supervisors as people outside the internship setting.

These impressions are supported by research in which interns have been asked to identify preferred characteristics of supervisors and supervision (Baker & Smith, 1987; Fernando & Hulse-Killacky, 2005; Fortune, McCarthy, & Abramson, 2001; Gandolfo & Brown, 1987; Knight, 1996). Results from these studies indicate that the desired supervisor qualities vary somewhat depending on experience, but across experience levels there is a consistent desire for supervisors who are available and open to discussion and who are perceived as supportive and understanding (Falender & Shafranske, 2004). Within a supportive environment, many interns feel it is valuable for their supervisor to help interns understand themselves and explore the interpersonal dynamics between interns and clients and between the intern and supervisor. Interns also express a need for direct observation and meaningful feedback and instruction about their work. Making connections between field activities and classroom work, help with problem solving regarding their own cases, feedback on process recordings, and opportunities to observe the supervisor in therapy are also rated highly.

Along with their hopes for supervision, interns also bring fears. Perhaps the two most common fears are "I am afraid I don't have a clue what I'm supposed to do or how to do it" and "I am even more afraid someone will find out I don't know what to do." Similar observations have been expressed by other authors (Gelman, 2004; Neufeldt, 1999). Charny (1986) described a number of common fears of practitioners and emphasized the value of supervision that allows interns to voice their fears. Among the most frequent worries, Charny identified fears that patients will "flake out," fears that a supervisor will discover a trainee does not like a patient or that a trainee is feeling attracted to a patient, fears of being responsible for what happens to the patient, and fears of "not really helping." Charny contended that voicing and exploring these inner fears is much more conducive to learning than supervision that stays at the "I said, then they said" level of discourse. Costa (1995) offered a similar recommendation and spoke of the value of "normalizing" the supervisee's anxiety.

Awareness of the needs and concerns of supervisees has also been stressed by those who take a developmental approach to supervision (Deal & Clements, 2006). Stoltenberg (2005) has been a leader in modeling and research studies of the development of interns and how supervisors can effectively match the developmental stage of interns. Stoltenberg emphasizes that beginning trainees are often so focused on concerns about their own knowledge and performance that it is difficult for them to give full attention to the client's concerns. Recognizing this anxiety, supervision with beginning interns may need to provide more structure and more emotional support until the trainees can get their feet on the ground and feel more comfortable.

Comparable observations were offered by Friedman and Kaslow (1986), who suggested that a key question of beginning interns is, "What exactly is my job with these patients?" (p. 35). Friedman and Kaslow also recognized interns' concerns about competence and proposed that interns who are just beginning may be plagued by self-doubts and anxieties. Quoting Barnat (1974, p. 190), Friedman and Kaslow spoke of the interns' "affirmation hunger" and suggested that it is very important for beginners to have affirming, accepting supervisors.

I find it helpful to acknowledge from the outset that fears are perfectly understandable, not only for beginning interns but for experienced therapists as well. Any time we learn something new, there are usually elements of both excitement and fear. Instead of disguising fears, interns are encouraged to acknowledge them so that the supervisor and the intern can work through the fear together. For this to succeed, interns must feel safe when they take the risk to speak about fears. In other words, interns must know that they will not be punished with poor evaluations or low grades if they are honest enough to speak about their insecurities.

HOPES AND FEARS OF SUPERVISORS

Interns are not the only ones who have hopes and fears in supervision. Supervisors have their own sets of wishes and trepidations when they accept interns. Phrases to describe the ideal intern would probably include "follows ethical principles," "well-informed and eager to learn," "gets along well with staff and clients," "shows initiative," "follows through reliably," and "attentive to detail." An intern should also be dependable, receptive to supervision, able to seek help when necessary but also willing to accept challenges, intelligent, creative, sensitive, and insightful.

The most common fear of supervisors is that an intern will do something that jeopardizes patients, the interns themselves, or the supervisor. In the clinical realm, supervisors get frightened when interns are not frightened. The supervisor's two worst nightmares are well-intentioned but overconfident or careless interns (Smith & Agate, 2004) and the occasional pathological intern who acts irresponsibly or is manipulative without concern for patients or the institutions.

Concerns of supervisors about intern actions are not without foundation. Pollack and Marsh (2004) and Harrar, VandeCreek, and Knapp (1990) described the concepts of "direct liability" and "vicarious liability" (p. 39). These authors indicate that supervisors can be and have been sued for the actions of supervisees. They also note that trainees are generally held accountable for the same standards of care as licensed professionals (see NASW Insurance Trust, 2004; Zakutansky & Sirles, 1993). Because the supervisor is responsible for ensuring that interns meet professional standards of care, it should not be surprising that supervisors are intensely concerned about the quality of work interns perform. For similar reasons, interns should not become defensive if supervisors insist on high standards of professionalism or are occasionally critical of an intern's performance. It is not the primary job of the supervisor to make every intern feel happy and comfortable. Rather, the supervisor's main task is to ensure that all interns are competent and apply themselves diligently and reliably to their responsibilities.

Along with fears that interns will make harmful mistakes or are somehow unstable, supervisors also have many of the same fears as interns (i.e., "Do I know what to do in my own clinical work or in my role as supervisor?" and "What if someone finds out or suggests that I don't know what to do?").

The supervisory role is at least as complex as the role of therapist, and it is by no means easy. A professional who agrees to serve as a supervisor is accepting a position that will undoubtedly present a unique set of demands and vulnerabilities. Although some professionals have received specific training in supervision, many have not (Deal & Clements, 2006; McMahon & Simons, 2004). In recent years, training in supervision has increased, but the nature and extent of such training varies widely. Progress toward more structured training has included development of a comprehensive curriculum guide for training counseling supervisors (Borders et al., 1991), and establishment of standards for counseling supervisors (Dye & Borders, 1990; Supervision Interest Network, Association for Counselor Education and Supervision, 1990). More recently, McMahon and Simons (2004) described a focused training program to enhance supervision skills, and they reported significant and lasting positive effects. Deal and Clements (2006) also report positive effects from a developmentally based supervision training program for field instructors.

The combination of a complex task and relatively little training places supervisors in a position that is not greatly unlike the intern's. Each is expected to be competent in a role for which he or she is not necessarily fully prepared. Just as interns must learn to deal effectively with anxieties about their role, supervisors must deal with similar anxieties about their role and responsibilities. Although the lack of specific training in supervision is likely to be a hindrance for supervisors, this does not mean supervisors have nothing to teach. In many cases, however, it does mean that both the supervisor and the intern will be in learning roles.

A final challenge that interns may not fully appreciate but supervisors struggle with is simply time. Globerman and Bogo (2003) reported that in many field placements no workload credit is given for those who engage in supervision or student education. Schindler and Talen (1994) observed that as interns have begun to appreciate the value of supervision and seek additional supervision opportunities, supervisors have found themselves pressed for time and struggling to manage complex and sometimes contradictory roles. To help supervisors deal with this situation, Schindler and Talen described an approach involving "general" and "focused" supervision, in which one supervisor handles the administrative, evaluative, and broad goals of clinical supervision, while another supervisor is available to assist interns in working with specific, more narrowly defined clinical approaches or client groups. In addition to helping supervisors deal with differing roles, this method also gives interns more time in supervision and provides exposure to different models of intervention and supervision.

EXERCISE

From the outset, interns and supervisors should be open with one another about their mutual and individual needs, fears, and concerns. Just by acknowledging these factors up front, they can reduce a great deal of anxiety, crossed communication, and frustration. To start this process, I have listed some of the common needs of supervisors and interns. Interns and supervisors can check this list, modify or add to it, and then discuss individual and joint needs together.

- *What supervisors need from interns.* Honesty and integrity, ethical conduct, openness to suggestion, respect for the supervisor's experience, careful work, deep thought, hard work, and willingness to listen even if there is disagreement.

  Others: _____

- *What interns need from supervisors.* Support, patience, knowledge of the field, guidance, accessibility, modeling, direct teaching of information, involvement, some autonomy, trust, openness, and willingness to listen.

  Others: _____

CLARIFYING EXPECTATIONS

Clarifying from the outset the expectations of interns and supervisors will prevent later confusion and help achieve the most beneficial learning experience (Freeman, 1993; McCarthy et al., 1995). McCarthy et al. along with Barnet (2005) described the use of an informed-consent procedure comparable to the informed-consent forms described in Chapter 3 for use with clients. Among the expectations that should be delineated as clearly as possible between supervisors and interns are

1. The frequency and timing of supervisor sessions.
2. The content of supervisory sessions (e.g., whether they will consist of case reviews via notes or tapes, didactic instruction in topic areas, informal personal exchanges, or some combination of techniques).
3. The theoretical orientation or techniques the intern is expected to learn and how specifically this learning will be demonstrated and assessed.
4. The extent to which personal issues of the intern or supervisor will be addressed as part of supervision.
5. Procedures for evaluation, feedback, and grading.

Appendix C offers a form that can be completed by the intern and supervisor to address many of these issues and to establish specific learning goals and evaluation procedures. I encourage you to sit down with your supervisor early on to go over this form together and agree on each of the items.

FREQUENCY AND TIMING OF SUPERVISION

As noted in Chapter 2, supervisors and interns should establish formal agreements stating how often and when they will hold supervision sessions. Once they arrive at an agreement, interns and supervisors must make their best efforts to set aside as much time as necessary for supervision and hold to that time. When schedules get busy, people begin to sacrifice supervision time for seemingly more urgent tasks. Avoid this temptation. Except for rare crises or absolute emergencies, nothing should be thought of as more urgent than supervision. Interns and supervisors should schedule other events, projects, and meetings around supervision, not vice versa. If supervisors or interns begin to allow other things to take precedence over supervision, someone may need to gently call it to their attention, emphasize the importance of supervision, and explore ways of meeting reliably.

Exactly how frequently one should receive supervision depends on several factors, including the intern's activities, the level of the intern's experience or training, and the expectations of the instructor, the placement site, or, in some cases, the guidelines established within a profession (Jarvis, 1989). In the field of counseling, the Council for Accreditation of Counseling and Related Educational Programs (CACREP) has set a standard of a minimum of 1 hour per week of individual supervision and $1^1/_2$ hours of group supervision per week (CACREP, 2001, sec. III, G). Internship policies for approved graduate programs in clinical psychology require a minimum of 1 hour of individual supervision for every 20 internship hours (APPIC, 2006). Comparable requirements have been described for social work field placements.

As a general principle, where specific professional standards are lacking or do not apply, the more interns are involved in direct services with clients, such as therapy or assessment, the more supervision they will need. Some programs suggest an initial ratio of 1 of supervision to every 4 to 6 hours of direct patient contact. This is ideal, but experience indicates that in practice it is relatively unusual for supervisors of beginning interns to have sufficient time to meet this often. More common ratios are one hour of supervision for every 8 to 10 hours of clinical contact. In settings where interns are involved in three or four cases per day, this would amount to about 1 hour of supervision every two or three days. If supervision is less frequent than this, the time span between clinical interactions and supervision is too long, and important details or impressions are likely to be forgotten.

To the extent that interns have greater clinical experience or, at the other end of the spectrum, are less involved in direct clinical services, the frequency of supervision may be lessened. However, this does not mean supervision is unnecessary. Even therapists with many years of experience recognize the value of supervision and schedule it for themselves as part of responsible practice.

CONTENT OF SUPERVISION

Most supervision involves a combination of activities, including didactic instruction, case discussions, role-plays, direct observation of sessions, joint therapy, review of audio- or videotapes, and opportunities to observe the supervisor in therapy (Fortune, McCarthy, & Abramson, 2001; Hess & Hess, 1983; Kadushin & Harkness, 2002; Romans, Boswell, Carlozzi, & Ferguson, 1995). I encourage interns to take an active role in discussing what kinds of learning experiences would be most helpful in supervision. Thus, you might want your instructor to teach you about a specific topic that you have not studied before. Or, if you feel a need for something other than didactic approaches or discussion, you might suggest to your supervisor that you role-play a case. You might also want to request the opportunity to observe your supervisor in therapy. Your supervisor will have the final say in what happens during supervision, but you should be involved in the process and make your needs and interests known.

HOW SUPERVISORS DETERMINE WHAT TO DO

Before describing specific approaches to supervision, it may be helpful to provide some insights into how supervisors determine

what should happen in supervision. For a variety of reasons, including limited training in supervision, the lack of clear consensus on what the content of supervision should be, and because people tend to do what they know best, the content and approach to supervision are likely to reflect and be closely related to the supervisor's own approach to treatment or assessment (Falender & Shafranske, 2004). This was demonstrated empirically by Friedlander and Ward (1984), who found, for example, that Gestalt therapists and psychodynamically oriented therapists differed in their supervision approaches and tended to use techniques of supervision that were similar to the therapy techniques of their orientation.

Supervisors also choose supervisory approaches that mirror their therapy approach because they believe this is a useful way to teach trainees their therapeutic orientation. Frances and Clarkin (1981) described how techniques of supervision often parallel the techniques of therapy. In a review of therapy and supervision approaches for schools of therapy including psychoanalysis, behavior therapy, brief psychotherapy, and family therapy, these authors noted that what goes on in supervision provides a model of what happens in therapy. Similar observations have been made by other authors. Martin and McBride (1987) asserted that congruence between the supervisor's therapeutic orientation and approach to supervision is a desirable training technique. In their model of supervision, trainees learn the theory and techniques of an approach by experiencing them directly during the supervisory interaction. Thus, an intern studying under a cognitive therapist would be asked to explore cognitions related to a client. Similarly, an intern studying psychodrama might be asked to participate in a psychodrama relating to one of the intern's cases.

In addition to working from their own theoretical orientation, supervisors are also encouraged to study the broad literature on supervision. Four excellent texts are Bradley and Ladany, (2001), Falender and Shafranske (2004), Kadushin and Harkness (2002), and Neufeldt (1999). The work by Neufeldt is especially geared toward supervision of students in their first practicum and contains lessons designed to enhance case conceptualization and to address ethics and evaluation issues. For a comprehensive reference list of other articles and books relating to supervision, see Peake Nussbaum, and Tindell (2002) and Robiner and Schofield (1990). For a review of cross-cultural supervision issues and research, see Leong and Wagner (1994). Supervisors should also understand the personal and developmental needs of their interns (Finkelstein & Tuckman, 1997; Friedman & Kaslow, 1986; Stoltenberg, 2005; Stoltenberg & Delworth, 1987; Tracey, Ellickson, & Sherry, 1989), and consider the process of the intern's therapy work and the supervision itself (McNeil & Worthen, 1989).

Edwards and Chen (1999) recommended a supervisory focus on therapist strengths as opposed to deficits. One suggestion for incorporating this into supervision sessions includes suggesting that the intern brainstorm options for working through problems from therapy sessions. Another way to focus on the development of interns' strengths is to have them share what they feel has been successful in therapy and encourage them to repeat those behaviors in similar situations. These approaches may help build intern confidence. Even when the intervention may not appear successful, the supervisor can emphasize the intern's good intentions. Focusing on intern strengths in supervision can also remind interns to identify strengths and assets of their clients during supervision. This may increase the respect that interns have for client strengths.

In contrast to discussing what may constitute good supervision, Falender and Shafranske (2004), Kadushin and Harkness (2002), and Magnuson, Wilcoxon, and Norem (2000) discussed problems that may interfere with effective supervision. They identified elements commonly found to hinder supervision, including not recognizing the intern's developmental needs, inflexibility in supervision sessions, supervisors using the relationship to meet personal needs rather than needs of the intern, untrained or immature supervisors, too much focus on the technical or cognitive aspects of therapy, unethical behaviors, and general examples of inhumane and inappropriate events from their supervision experiences.

Based on these considerations of both positive and negative models, supervisors can then choose among many different techniques to best match the needs of specific interns with specific clients. This may include direct modeling of the supervisor's therapy approach, but it might also involve other activities that are not included in the supervisor's normal treatment approach. The key point is that whatever activities are chosen for supervision, they should be based on an understanding of the supervisee, client, and situation, and on the research literature in supervision, not simply on habitual and familiar approaches of the supervisor. For an insightful and comprehensive discussion of supervisory approaches and therapy outcomes, see Holloway and Neufeldt (1995). For a review of the frequency of various supervisory practices and techniques, see Romans et al. (1995).

DIDACTIC SUPERVISION

One approach to supervision is similar to the process instructors and students use in academic classes. Didactic, or teaching, supervision is best chosen when an intern wants to learn, or a supervisor wants to teach, specific information about a theory, technique, diagnosis, or some other topic relevant to the intern's activities (Hess, 1980). The goal of a didactic approach is to get information across as efficiently as possible so the interns can learn and apply the information directly to their work. Didactic approaches tend to be particularly appealing to beginning interns because they feel a need for concrete, practical information to help them cope with the anxiety and ambiguity of starting something new (Ronnestad & Skovholt, 1993).

An example of didactic instruction would be a supervisor defining terminology from a certain school of therapy. Another example would be an intern asking a supervisor for instruction about the characteristics of a specific disorder. To supplement material taught directly by the supervisor, selected reading assignments or recommendations can also be given to interns. Beyond the relevance of the readings to the intern's immediate activities, this practice also establishes a model that should be followed throughout one's career. Whenever a professional is working with an individual or group, it is the therapist's responsibility to always be as informed as possible about the problems, the options available for treatment, and, where available, outcome data to help determine the most effective treatment.

If your supervisor does not initiate suggestions or assignments for readings, you may want to ask for recommendations of useful books or articles. Supervisors sometimes take it for granted that the information they have studied is known by everyone and forget that interns might not yet have studied it. A sincere request for references will typically produce resources that will help you to understand your clients better and to appreciate where the supervisor may have acquired his or her knowledge or approach.

Perhaps the main drawback to didactic methods is that over-reliance on them can cause supervision to become merely another venue for lecture-based instruction. The temptations to rely on lecture in supervision are many. Lecture-based teaching and learning are familiar to both the intern and supervisor. Lectures allow supervisors to feel they have useful knowledge to pass on and that they are benefiting their interns by conveying that knowledge. Lectures are also safe for both the supervisor and the intern. The trouble is that keeping supervision at the didactic level allows the participants to avoid more challenging issues, such as how interns feel about themselves or clients, how the supervisor and intern are interacting, and how one deals with ethical dilemmas. Although such avoidance may be tempting, it can inhibit the benefits of dealing with ambiguous material and discourages self-exploration (Ronnestad & Skovholt, 1993).

CASE NOTES AND DISCUSSIONS

Case discussions can take a variety of formats depending on the goals and preferences of the intern and supervisor. Prieto and Scheel (2002) described the use of case notes as a useful basis for case discussion, but they noted that interns are often given relatively little instruction on how to write or use case notes in a format that is helpful clinically or for supervision. Systematically integrating case notes into supervision, according to Prieto and Scheel, has the dual benefit of helping interns learn to record and use case notes more effectively and affording a source of information from which supervisors can glimpse what occurred in sessions and how the intern processed that information. By using a specialized case note format, supervisors can help students better observe client behaviors, record and monitor what takes place in therapy, understand the significance of those interactions, formulate effective treatment plans, and identify any special issues of concern.

One of the more common approaches to using case notes in supervision is through "process notes," which include not only descriptions of the observable events in therapy but also the therapist's internal thoughts and observations about what is happening and why. Fox and Gutheil (2000) offered suggestions for how process notes can be incorporated into supervision with students. They recommended that notes reflect background baseline information about the client and treatment, observations about what is happening in a session and what may have changed since a previous session, the student's integration of their own knowledge into their understanding of the case, reflections about what went well or was difficult for the student in the session, and identification of specific skills the student used at different points of the session. Finally, they suggest that the notes include planning for the next session or next steps in treatment and any questions or issues the student wishes to raise in supervision. Case notes are discussed in substantially more detail in Chapter 6.

While written case notes can provide a useful basis for case discussions, other forms of information can also serve that function. Comparing the merits of live versus videotaped supervision, McCollum and Wetchler (1995) suggested that four specific tasks can be most effectively addressed in case discussions. These are (1) helping the trainee understand "the architecture" (i.e., the integrated, strategic, developmental, and process considerations of therapy), (2) helping trainees build theoretical models of change, (3) helping trainees understand clients in broader contexts, such as social, familial, cultural, and other perspectives, and (4) helping the trainees understand their own contextual position as students functioning within certain cultural, social, ethnic, class, and other frameworks. Within each of the four areas, McCollum and Wetchler offered useful suggestions for questions to be explored jointly by the supervisor and trainee.

THE SOCRATIC METHOD

A somewhat more formalized questioning approach to case consultations was described by Overholser (1991), who proposed Socratic questioning as a technique for supervision. As Overholser described the technique, it involves three elements: "systematic questioning," "inductive reasoning," and "universal definitions." Overholser emphasized that Socratic questions are not actually requests for information but are designed to encourage the supervisee's thinking. Four content areas are targeted by systematic questions: defining the problem, generating response alternatives, thinking critically about the case, and, finally, evaluating the success of responses once they have been implemented.

The second element in Overholser's model, inductive reasoning, is designed to help interns generate general inferences about a case from specific details or events of the case. Universal definitions, the third element, refers to questioning designed to develop broader concepts about therapy in general. This can help interns understand such concepts as resistance, transference, and other important ideas of therapy.

Whether a supervisor intentionally uses Socratic questions or takes a less structured approach to case discussions, interns need to understand that these questions, suggestions, or instructions do not necessarily mean the interns are supposed to have a specific answer or have done something wrong. In supervision, questions are not synonymous with tests. Their purpose is not to elicit correct answers but to stimulate thought and understanding.

As an intern, if you are asked a factual question that you cannot answer, it is fine to acknowledge that you do not know and ask someone to explain the answer to you. If you are asked a question designed to stimulate your thinking, don't feel under pressure to have a quick response. Instead, take your time, think about the question and what you have been discussing, then explore your ideas with the other person. These questions, which encourage you to think in new ways, are part of developing your clinical knowledge and understanding. They are also an implicit element of professional work, because it is not your task as a professional to know the answers beforehand. Rather, your task is to ask yourself the same kinds of questions your supervisor would ask so you can develop an understanding of your clients and make well-reasoned treatment decisions.

EMPATHY AND EXPERIENTIAL CONSIDERATIONS IN CASE DISCUSSIONS

When using case discussions or questions, supervisors should give careful thought to their focus. As noted, Falender and Shafranske (2004), Charny (1986), and others (Bogo, 1993; Kaiser, 1992) believe it is extremely important not to focus solely on the external events of therapy but also to consider the internal experience, concerns, and feelings of the intern, and the relationship of the intern to the supervisor. A questioning approach that emphasizes the overt content of a therapy session may neglect the internal experience of the intern in the session.

Consistent with this attention to internal experience, interns need supportive, affirming, and empathic supervisors. A supervisor who focuses exclusively on Socratic or other forms of questioning might not readily communicate the support and understanding interns need. The role of empathy in supervision was studied empirically by Shanfield, Mohl, Matthews, and Hetherly (1992), who used a structured inventory to evaluate supervisor performance during videotaped supervisory sessions. Results of this research showed that the factors most closely related to ratings of supervisor excellence were the supervisor's empathy and attention to the immediate concerns and experience of the interns. By comparison, supervisors who intellectualized and offered general elaboration with little attention to intern concerns were rated as "low" in their facilitation of trainee learning. Shanfield et al. noted that their study was based on observational ratings and did not include assessment by the supervisors or interns themselves. Nevertheless, the strong relationships between empathy and excellence shown in these ratings by observers who were all highly experienced supervisors attest to the importance of supervisor empathy. This finding is wholly consistent with the previously discussed results of surveys of supervisee preferences for supervisors and with studies of the processes supervisees find most important at different stages of training (Rabinowitz, Heppner, & Roehlke, 1986).

In light of research on the role of empathy in supervision, an intern who is working with a supervisor who does not provide adequate support might consider telling this to the supervisor. The intern might also want to express this to the instructor or internship class. In many cases, supervisors may not be aware that they are not offering the needed support and will welcome feedback. As with any presentation of constructive feedback, the intern should offer suggestions about supervisory style in a positive rather than critical manner.

Just as it can be a mistake for questions to predominate in a supervisory interaction, it is generally advisable to use questions sparingly in treatment interactions. Beginning interns are often prone to ask too many questions of clients in an effort to "solve" problems. When supervisors establish a model of supervision through questioning, interns may be inclined to emulate that approach in their therapy. This is inadvisable because, much as interns need support and affirmation, clients also need more than just questions to experience therapeutic gains. This principle might not be modeled well in questioning-based supervision. As Lambert and Beier (1974) reported, when supervisors are acting as counselors, they tend to offer more empathic statements than when they are interacting with interns. Interns and supervisors should keep this in mind and recognize that the supervisory process is not necessarily an ideal model for therapy, but certain therapeutic principles definitely have a place in supervision.

TAPES AND ROLE-PLAYS

Audio- and video reviews have become some of the most commonly used learning activities of supervision (Romans et al., 1995). Ways of using video effectively were discussed in Chapter 2, and, if you have not read that chapter yet, you may find it helpful to do so now. Because most of what was said in Chapter 2 also applies to supervision, only a few key suggestions are reviewed here. For an interesting review of how tape-recording came to be used in therapy research and supervision, see Hill and Corbett (1993).

Perhaps the most important suggestion for using recordings is to select sessions in which you felt good about your work and sessions in which you felt confused or ineffective (Ronnestad & Skovholt, 1993). The successful sessions can help build your confidence and can also provide opportunities to identify what went well and why. On the other hand, you should also review less successful sessions in supervision so that you can learn from your mistakes and expand your skills. If you do not feel comfortable revealing sessions in which your performance was not ideal, that feeling itself is worth exploring. You may want to consider the comments later in this chapter regarding how to deal with conflicts in supervision. If something can be done to increase your comfort in exploring weaknesses with your supervisor, I encourage you to do it. For optimal learning and development, you must feel free, encouraged, and safe about revealing both strengths and weaknesses.

A safe, supportive relationship is also essential for effective use of role-plays in supervision. As discussed in Chapter 2, it is important to become deeply involved in the imagined role and situation when doing role-plays. Interns may find this difficult in the context of supervision, because the evaluative element of interacting with a supervisor can interfere with the ability to be open and involved. Much as you are encouraged to deal with issues concerning sharing of taped sessions, if your supervisor uses role-play techniques in supervision and you feel restricted by the evaluative component, talk about your experience with the supervisor. This may help bring out underlying issues relating to your dual role of supervisor-evaluator and intern-student. Understanding your own difficulties in role-playing with a supervisor may also help you understand your clients in new ways. Students or supervisors who are interested in research on role-plays in supervision may wish to consult Akamatsu's (1980) review of the subject.

LIVE SUPERVISION

As useful as case notes, recorded sessions, and role-plays can be, there is no substitute for directly observing therapy sessions. Interestingly, Romans et al. (1995) found that although training directors rated co-therapy and live supervision as the strongest learning activities for interns, these modalities were also among the least commonly used. Presumably, this is due to the difficulty of scheduling simultaneous times for the supervisor to directly observe or join the intern in therapy. This is certainly understandable; but, given the strength of this approach, if it is at all possible, you and your supervisor should include at least some live supervision or co-therapy in your schedules.

Several arrangements can be used for directly observing treatment (Bubenzer, West, & Gold, 1991). One way is for the supervisor to be physically present in the room with the trainee. Another possibility is to use a special observation room equipped with one-way mirrors. These allow the supervisor to remain unseen behind the glass during the therapy session.

By observing sessions as they occur, supervisors get a better sense of the process. They can listen to what is said, watch the nonverbal behaviors of the trainee and client, note key moments in the session, and get a deeper awareness of the overall "feel" of the interactions. In some arrangements, supervisors can also instruct the trainee during the interaction. Using a technique known as the "bug in the ear," supervisors observe the session from behind a mirror and can speak to trainees through a microphone connected to tiny earplug-type speakers (Gallant

& Thyer, 1989; Gallant, Thyer, & Bailey, 1991). This enables the supervisor to call the trainee's attention to certain behaviors or statements of the client. The supervisor might also point out the trainee's own behaviors or suggest specific things the trainee should say or do.

Although direct observation is an excellent way to learn therapy, it has some drawbacks. The most obvious is the intrusiveness into the therapeutic interaction. Another potential problem is that many interns, who already feel anxious about the role of therapist, are now placed simultaneously in the role of therapist and student (Costa, 1995). Friedlander, Keller, Peca-Baker, and Olk (1986) commented on the role conflict that can result for interns who are at the same time in the "subordinate" role of trainee and the "superordinate" role of therapist. This conflict can become acute when the intern receives instructions from a supervisor that contradict the intern's own sense of what should happen in therapy. One can imagine how this can play out with the bug-in-the-ear technique. If an intern is thinking about responding in a certain way but then is told through the bug to do something different, the intern must deal with the internal conflict while outwardly maintaining a composed demeanor for the client.

Because direct observation poses such problems, it is helpful for supervisors and interns to establish an agreement about how to proceed during these sessions. This agreement should clarify the expectations and goals for the therapy session, when or if a supervisor will intervene, whether the intern is expected to follow unconditionally the supervisor's lead or is allowed some discretion, and what the debriefing after the session will entail.

My own preference is to give interns a great deal of leeway and freedom to follow their own instincts. It is especially important, as Gallant and Thyer (1989) emphasized, for supervisors to keep in mind that they are teaching the interns, not doing the therapy itself. Thus, although I occasionally offer suggestions, interns are generally free to choose what to do. It is essential, however, to establish an agreed-on signal that tells interns if I have identified something important and they must follow my lead. I use this only rarely, but I make certain that the interns understand and respect the importance of this option. If the supervisor detects an issue of particular sensitivity, or if there is a possibility of significant risk, the intern must trust the supervisor's judgment and save explanations for later. The supervisor is ultimately responsible for the treatment, and interns must respect that responsibility. It is simply unacceptable for the intern and supervisor to get into a conflict during the session.

One additional comment applies not only to direct observation but to all forms of observing therapy. It is always easier for the observer to pick things up than it is for the therapist. This means the supervisor must be patient and not overly critical with an intern if the supervisor detects something in therapy that the intern may have missed. Calling things to the intern's attention is certainly useful, but the purpose must be to help educate the trainee, not to make the supervisor look good. The same principle applies when interns observe the work or are reviewing tapes of other interns.

OBSERVING THE SUPERVISOR IN THERAPY

Studies in which interns have been asked what their supervisors might have done differently have revealed that many interns desire more opportunities to observe their supervisor in clinical work (Gandolfo & Brown, 1987). Interns recognize that discussion about their own work can only take them so far. They also feel they learn a great deal when they can watch their supervisor in group or individual sessions, read reports written by the supervisor, and observe the supervisor in other actions such as staff meetings and conferences (Kaplan, Rothrock, & Culkin, 1999). Levenson and Evans (2000) suggested that many training programs tend to underutilize videotapes for teaching and supervision. They also suggested that students can benefit from greater exposure to watching teachers and supervisors doing therapy on tape. They noted, however, that this can raise touchy issues for some supervisors. "If you think students are resistant to being taped, try asking a licensed professional to tape one of his/her sessions for teaching purposes." Students wishing to observe their supervisors either in person or on tape may wish to make this desire known, but in doing so they should be sensitive to the issues raised by Levenson and Evans.

If opportunities are provided for interns to observe supervisors at work, the experience will be more effective if the intern has some guidance and structure to work from. Kaplan, Rothrock, and Culkin (1999) suggested a series of questions addressing such things as the theoretical orientation being demonstrated, the stages of the counseling process being observed, key events that take place in the session, and the like. These authors also emphasize the ethical considerations of any observed therapy session, and they provide a helpful informed consent template that can be given to confirm client approval for the the session to be observed either directly or on tape.

Another way for interns to observe supervisors in practice is for the supervisor and intern to work together as co-therapists with clients. This is most commonly practiced in group or couples therapy, but it can also be used with individual clients.

If co-therapy is arranged, the same caveats described for observation techniques must be addressed. The supervisor and intern should agree on who will be the primary therapist and how to signal the intern if the supervisor needs to take the lead. It is also important to discuss the sessions afterward to explore what happened and share impressions of the interaction.

Although most supervisors are open to co-therapy if it meets with the needs of clients, many are not aware that interns would like such an opportunity. As a result, interns may need to ask whether they can observe the supervisors in different settings. If this sounds obvious, it is, but often we neglect to do the obvious because no one thinks to ask.

EXERCISE

Many interns do not realize they can take the initiative by suggesting useful learning opportunities. Take a few moments to think of what opportunities your internship is providing and what additional experiences you might find interesting. If you had the opportunity to observe your supervisor in different aspects of clinical work, what would benefit you the most to observe? In order to better understand your supervisor's perspective, now ask yourself what concerns you might have if you were a supervisor being observed by an intern? Having considered these issues, you may want to speak with your supervisor directly about the kinds of learning experiences or opportunities for observation that you would find most helpful.

REMOTE SUPERVISION: INTERNET, TELEPHONE, AND OTHER TECHNOLOGIES

In most instances, your supervisor will be working in the same setting as you are, but it occasionally happens, particularly in rural settings, that your supervisor may not be physically present at all times or, in some instances, at all. In lieu of direct face-to-face supervision, telecommunication and computer technology can enable remote supervisory interactions. This type of supervision can be economical, and in some instance it is the only feasible way of providing any supervision to interns in remote locations. At the same time, however, remote supervision raises a number of practical, clinical, and ethical questions that need to be addressed.

Wood, Miller, and Hargrove (2003) and Kanz (2001) reviewed some of the modalities possible with remote supervision, ranging from e-mails, to mailed videotapes of therapy, to two-way (or more) video conferencing and observing actual sessions. Whichever modality is chosen, there are trade-offs from direct supervision. For example, in remote as contrasted with face-to-face supervision, a supervisor may not be as able to pick up on subtle nonverbal clues from the intern, such as anxiety or frustration. On the positive side, however, Wood and colleagues pointed out that electronic communication can also reduce some of the hierarchical tensions that exist between supervisor and trainees in face to face interactions.

Another potential limitation arises if urgent situations occur. In remote supervision, it may be more difficult for the intern to get immediate help from a supervisor who is physically distant. Another limitation of remote supervision is that the supervisor may not be acquainted with the other staff or even the basic physical location and layout of the placement site. This can be a significant shortcoming, as one of the ways a supervisor can assist interns is by helping them understand and appreciate some of the intrastaff interactions that occur in all settings and can either enhance or detract from treatment and the intern's learning experience. If a supervisor has not been to a placement personally and has not gotten to know the people there and developed a feel for the place, it will be more difficult for the supervisor to fully understand what the intern is experiencing and needs to work within that setting.

Several interesting ethical and legal issues are also raised by remote supervision. Confidentiality is an obvious and important concern if sensitive clinical material is being sent through the mail or via the Internet. Less obvious, but nevertheless very important, are issues concerning such things as what licensing laws and other requirements apply if a supervisor is located in a different state than the intern's placement. Because other legal issues (e.g., abuse reporting procedures, commitment laws) can also vary from state to state, it is important for both the supervisor and the intern to know that the laws the supervisor may be most familiar with from his or her own state may not apply in the same way in another jurisdiction. Finally, as with all supervision, clients should be fully informed about the nature of a remote supervisor relationship, and they should be given some means of contacting the supervisor if necessary.

These clinical and ethical issues notwithstanding, remote supervision has a great deal of potential to help students who otherwise might be in placements with relatively little or no direction from someone in their own field of study. If remote supervision is part of your internship experience, I strongly encourage you and your instructors and supervisors to consult the articles by Wood et al. (2003) and by Kanz (2001) for their suggestions and caveats. The key is to understand that remote supervision is different in important ways from face-to-face interactions, then take the necessary steps to address these differences responsibly for the benefit of the intern, the placement, the supervisor, and, most important, the clients.

GROUP SUPERVISON

Much of the discussion thus far has focused on activities conducted during individual supervision, but it is also likely that at least some of your supervisory experiences will take place in a group format with other interns or coworkers. Group supervision presents a number of possible advantages as well as potential disadvantages relative to individual supervision.

Reviewing the literature on group supervision Bogo, Globerman, and Sussman (2004) noted that one of the chief benefits may simply be efficiency and economics, with group work allowing a supervisor to meet with several interns at the same time and convey common concepts once instead of in each separate meeting. Group supervision also affords certain pedagogical opportunities as students learn from the examples of their peers and from peer feedback. Peers can also provide emotional support to one another and, particularly when interns are involved in group therapy as part of their clinical duties, group supervision can involve "parallel process" observations in which the supervisory group mirrors processes that might be observed by interns in their own therapy group work.

Kadushin and Harkness (2002) add to this list and point out that group supervision also affords an opportunity for the supervisor to observe interns in different interactions, and vice-versa. In addition, there may be instances in which it is easier for a supervisor to communicate a point to an intern if group members are there to share, and perhaps reinforce, the concept or skill. Finally, group work provides a forum in which interns, through the process of observing peers and offering feedback, have an introduction to the tasks of supervision themselves. Kadushin and Harkness offer a number of suggestions for how to establish, prepare, and conduct supervision groups and how to deal with any problems that might emerge.

While recognizing the potential benefits of group work, disadvantages should also be acknowledged. Kadushin and Harkness (2002) point out that it can be harder to individualize an instruction or intervention in a group setting, especially if a sensitive personal issue of the intern is involved. Groups can also pose problems if between-member conflicts emerge or group dynamics interfere with the learning opportunities. Of special importance in group work is how vulnerabilities, deficits, or "clinical errors" are dealt with. It is one thing to acknowledge a weakness or have a shortcoming pointed out in a one-on-one exchange with a supervisor. It is quite another to have such issues emerge in front of one's peers. Perhaps in recognition of this difficulty, group members may be reluctant to reveal potential weaknesses or to give honest, critical feedback to their peers. Group cohesion in supervisory groups can also create challenges, especially if the group begins in some way to work against a supervisor or if the group norms begin to reject a supervisor's input or theoretical approach.

Many of the issues identified by Kadushin and Harkness (2002) were also described by Enyedy et al. (2003), who studied what they describe as "hindering phenomena" in group supervision as reported by counseling graduate students. Responses in this study addressed a number of potential problems which Enyedy et al. sorted into five clusters: (1) between-member problems, (2) problems with supervisors, (3) supervisee anxiety, (4) logistical constraints, and (5) Group time management. For each of these areas of concern, suggested strategies were offered to reduce problems before they develop and more effectively manage those that do occur.

Central to the findings of Enyedy et al., and to much of the literature in this area, is the primary importance of a supervisor who is skilled in group work. Bogo, Globerman, and Sussman (2004) examined the role of group supervisor by conducting systematic interviews with recent social work graduates to elicit their observations about their experiences in group supervision. Respondents in this study emphasized the fundamental requirement that supervisors be available and supportive. These qualities alone, however, are not sufficient to make for a quality group supervision experience. In addition, the supervisor needs to keep an educational focus, be able to maintain structure, manage group dynamics, and must be skilled in dealing with "personal and shared experiences in a public space" (p. 204). This latter issue is of particular importance because the nature of clinical work so often and readily evokes personal issues that may be difficult to deal with and may be especially so in a group format with peers.

One final note about group supervision is that the supervisor is by no means the only key to success; the participants are at least as important. Chapter 2 of this text offered suggestions for making peer groups effective as well as more general suggestions for active participation and personal responsibilities as a learner. Those suggestions apply equally well to group supervision. The most important elements, in my experience, are for interns to be open to giving and receiving feedback, that they do so in a positive, supportive manner, and that they maintain a constructive attitude that is focused on learning and professional development. Last, but by no means least, ethical strictures about confidentiality and other matters must be rigorously adhered to in group supervision as in all of your activities.

THEORETICAL ORIENTATION

Whatever the content or style of supervision, several major themes have the potential to create conflicts in supervision. One of the most common sources of confusion and conflict between interns and supervisors has to do with differences in theoretical orientation. Theoretical issues can be dealt with in many ways, but three of the most common approaches are:

1. The supervisor believes that a certain theoretical and technical approach to therapy or assessment is best, so the intern must learn, practice, and demonstrate knowledge and skill in that approach. Often, there is an accompanying expectation that the intern must also demonstrate a personal commitment to the approach and the philosophy or research that underlies it.
2. The supervisor has studied or developed an approach to therapy or assessment that works for him or her, and the intern is welcome to learn from what the supervisor has to offer. The intern is free to choose whether or not to adopt the supervisor's techniques or theoretical perspectives.
3. The supervisor believes that no one knows what is best, so the intern is free to try any approach to see how it works. The supervisor is available to help out if needed.

The advantage of the first approach (i.e., training under a supervisor who adheres strictly to a single orientation and expects interns to do the same) derives from the clarity of focus such training provides. Faced with many different schools and techniques of therapy or assessment, interns sometimes feel at a loss to know how to proceed. By choosing a single orientation and associated techniques, the intern can gain a sense of security in that approach. This basis can then give the intern enough confidence to pursue the chosen approach further or to explore other approaches.

Focusing on a single approach also has advantages for supervisors. No one can be expert in all things, and many supervisors feel the best they can offer is to teach the approach the supervisor knows best. If interns have opportunities to train under different supervisors, and if each supervisor focuses on a single approach, the interns will be able to sample different approaches from supervisors who specialize in them. This is likely to give a much clearer impression of the different approaches than if each supervisor tries to teach from many different perspectives.

There are two main drawbacks to focusing on a single approach to treatment or assessment. The first is that if the supervisor's approach does not match well with the intern's outlook, there is a potential for conflict that will interfere with the learning experience. This potential is likely to be heightened if the supervisor demands not only knowledge and technical proficiency but "faith" in the theory. It is one thing to ask an intern to understand and be skilled in an approach. It is quite another to expect the intern to uncritically share the supervisor's commitment. I have encountered supervisors who judge interns more by their belief in the supervisor's model than on the intern's knowledge and skill. The reasoning in such instances has apparently been that the supervisor is certain his or her approach is superior, so any astute intern will also recognize the worth of the supervisor's chosen model. For interns who are not sold on the model or who want also to gain experience in other approaches, this supervisory attitude can be quite detrimental.

The second problem with this model of supervision is that emphasizing a single approach encourages interns to believe that this approach is superior to all others or works for all clients and all problems. Endorsing one approach to the exclusion of others may be part of an intern's struggle to develop professional identity, but it is preferable to find an identity that remains open to new learning and does not depend on denigrating others or exaggerating claims for one's own preferences.

Teaching a single therapy or assessment approach to the exclusion of others is not simply a matter of personal preference. Kurpius, Gibson, Lewis, and Corbett (1991) pointed to empirical evidence (Allen, Szollos, & Williams, 1986) suggesting that good supervisors respect differences in values and experience and encourage experimentation with novel strategies.

An alternative to emphasizing a single therapy approach is for the supervisor to present interns with one or more models but allow the interns to experiment and choose what works best for them. The principal advantage of this approach is that it reduces the problem of ideological conflicts and allows the supervisor and intern to focus more on skills and less on adherence to a fixed philosophy. This approach also tends to facilitate more discussion of the relative pros and cons of different interventions. The intern who does not feel pressured to adopt a specific perspective is more free to question, experiment, and learn through experience. The supervisor's responsibility in this approach is to be present for the interns as they explore and experiment and to reassure interns that one can do effective work in a variety of ways.

For the intern seeking more direction, the lack of clearly defined models can be frustrating. This is most likely if the intern has had relatively little prior training or experience and thus does not have a personal basis from which to begin to try things out independently. This approach also poses problems for interns who are intentionally seeking training in a specific theory or technique of therapy or assessment.

If this situation arises in supervision, the supervisor and intern should discuss it together. Fruitful topics of such discussion might include the intern's legitimate need for guidance or a wish to gain focused supervision from a committed role model. Other useful subjects might be why people, including interns and supervisors, need structure, and the consequences of imposing artificial structures on inherently ambiguous processes.

The third model, in which the supervisor takes a laissez-faire approach to training, is generally the least preferred of the three. With the exception of interns who have a great deal of experience and training, most interns need more structure and direction than a laissez-faire supervisor provides. In contrast to the problems posed by the potential for excessive dogmatism in the first approach described, the completely open supervision model suffers from the reverse difficulty. It is an exceptionally rare intern who will receive optimum benefit without working from at least some structure and model. Whether the intern and supervisor agree or disagree on theory or technique, interns are usually helped by having supervisors who can articulate and demonstrate a coherent approach to treatment or assessment.

Whichever approach your supervisor adapts, you should consider the pros and cons of that approach as it relates to your own needs, the supervisor, and the setting. As noted, every intern has different needs, and a supervisor who is ideal for one intern may not match at all with another. Do your best to understand the reasons for a supervisor's theoretical and supervisory approach and be willing to try new approaches. At various times in my own training, I believed certain therapy models were complete bunk until I had the opportunity to observe them and discovered that they offered valuable lessons.

SUPERVISION AND THERAPY: DIFFERENCES AND SIMILARITIES

Because clinical work and the internship experience can evoke deeply personal and often difficult material for interns, clinical supervisors must not only help interns acquire specific skills, they must also help them manage the emotional and intellectual challenges and the personal issues that emerge in their training (Aponte, 1994). This responsibility may place supervisors in a role that is very much like that of therapist for the trainee. This similarity of roles and processes is sometimes referred to as "parallel process" (Ekstein & Wallerstein, 1972; Searles, 1955) and was described by Burns and Holloway (1989), Hebert

(1992), Kadushin and Harkness, (2002), Rubinstein (1992), Schneider (1992), and others.

While recognizing the similarities between therapy and supervision, many of the authors just cited also acknowledge that interns do not sign up for their internship as clients, and they have a right to work out personal issues on their own. Thus, for both supervisor and intern there is a dilemma about how to deal with the intern's personal issues. This dilemma becomes quite acute if an intern's personal issues begin to interfere with his or her clinical work or development (Bradley & Post, 1991; Lamb et al., 1987; Stadler, Willing, Eberhage, & Ward, 1988).

DIFFERENCES BETWEEN THERAPY AND SUPERVISION

Among the more important differences between therapy and supervision are the degree of choice involved in receiving therapy or supervision, the purpose and goals of therapy versus supervision, the role of the trainee compared with client, the role of supervisor compared with therapist, and the evaluative function of supervisors (Prieto, 1997; Sklare, Thomas, Williams, & Powers, 1996).

In therapy, clients have made a conscious decision to seek assistance with personal issues. They also have freedom in choosing who will be their therapist and under what conditions the therapy will take place. By comparison, interns are often required to receive supervision as part of their education and training. They may or may not have a say in who their supervisor will be, but they are very likely not to have any say in whether or not they will receive supervision.

Thus, from the outset, consent and choice are two fundamental differences distinguishing the therapy process from supervision. One is voluntary and can be terminated at any time at the client's discretion. The other is essentially involuntary (unless a trainee wants to risk expulsion from the training program) and generally cannot be terminated without the risk of substantial consequences.

Another key difference between therapy and supervision is found in the purpose of the activity. Clients seek therapy primarily because they want to be helped personally in some way by the therapy. By comparison, as Wise, Lowery, and Silverglade (1989) noted, training programs mandate supervision of therapists not so much to help the therapist as to "protect the welfare of the client." Wise et al. went on to say, "This purpose precludes making the counselor's personal growth a primary focus" (p. 327). Such conclusions do not mean that trainees cannot grow as individuals through the process of supervision. They do, however, suggest that the supervisee's personal growth is not the primary goal of many supervision arrangements, particularly those that are required as part of training programs.

Closely related to the issues of choice and the purpose of therapy and supervision is the matter of dual roles for supervisors who would also engage in therapy with trainees. Because supervisors must perform many different functions with trainees, including instruction, mentoring, support, and, of critical importance here, evaluation, their position in relation to the trainee differs markedly from that of the therapist in relation to a client. Interestingly, several researchers have noted that although students are well aware of power differentials between themselves and their supervisors, supervisors may be relatively unaware of this issue (Doehrman, 1976; Kadushin, 1974).

A therapist may form positive or critical opinions about clients, but apart from certain institutional settings or extreme circumstances, the therapist is not in a position to take actions that would have substantial impact on the client's future outside therapy. This is not the case for supervisees. Supervisors may well hold the key to the supervisee's professional future. The "key" metaphor was underscored by Rubinstein (1992), who stressed the importance of considering the context of supervision and the power of supervisors to influence the intern's future. Citing Berman (1988), Rubinstein drew a comparison between supervision and "total institutions," and suggested that supervisors who neglect the evaluative context run the risk of replicating "the tendency of therapists working in total institutions to interpret the fears and suspicions of clients regarding intervention in their lives as transference feelings" (Rubinstein, 1992, p. 114).

The point of this comparison is that the evaluative power of a supervisor is comparable to that of a therapist who determines whether patients or inmates are ready to be released from an institution. In the face of this power, interns may have good reason to choose information carefully and not be fully honest with their supervisors. Because the dual nature of supervisory and therapy relationships would create such dilemmas, Burns and Holloway (1989) stated directly, "Although supervisors provide facilitative instructional environments, in their role as evaluators, they ethically cannot undertake counseling relationships with their trainees" (p. 48).

Similar ethical concerns were voiced by Wise et al. (1989) and by Kurpius et al. (1991), who advised

> To be sensitive to the dual relationship issue, the promotion of the supervisee's self-exploration during supervision sessions would focus primarily on his or her interaction with the client and should not extend beyond raising awareness about the supervisee's helpfulness to the client. (p. 52)

However well intentioned a supervisor might be, the inherent power differential between supervisor and trainee can cause trainees to be, as Rubinstein phrased it, in "permanent distress concerning the selection of contents through which they are to communicate with their supervisor" (Rubinstein, 1992, p. 110). One manifestation of this distress was a student-drafted "bill of rights" described by Haley (1992), which stated that teachers were not to investigate students' personal lives unless the teacher could demonstrate the relevance of the exploration to the therapy task and could show how the personal exploration would help change the therapist's behavior in a positive direction.

As this discussion has demonstrated, there are a number of critical differences between therapy and supervision, and it is essential for both supervisors and interns to be cognizant of these differences. Along with this list of differences, Rubinstein (1992) also emphasized that most discussions of therapy and supervision similarities emphasize concepts from psychodynamic theories. Those concepts do not necessarily apply as well to supervision in behavioral and other less dynamically based approaches.

Keeping in mind the differences between supervision and therapy and the differences across different approaches to therapy, certain conditions are common to virtually all supervision and have important similarities to the therapy process. Because these intrinsic conditions cannot be avoided, interns and supervisors need to be familiar with them and learn to recognize and understand how they influence the supervisory relationship and process.

EXPLORING THE NEEDS AND PERSONAL QUALITIES OF INTERNS

In a paper describing the importance of intern self-awareness, Hebert (1992) wrote:

> Becoming an effective counselor revolves around the need for interns to understand their presentation of self. An understanding of their needs, defenses, their favorite coping devices, and their psychological predispositions is crucial for providing effective professional services. (p. 124)

Of the many reasons for interns to be aware of their own needs, two stand out most prominently. First, insofar as the therapist's self is "a therapeutic instrument" (Hebert, 1992, p. 131) it is necessary for the therapist to understand and be able to adapt the instrument (i.e., the self) as needed to assist the client (Falender & Shafranske, 2004). Second, if therapists are not aware of their own needs, they are more likely to use the therapy session to satisfy those needs, sometimes at the expense of the client. Two common needs that Hebert saw as affecting most interns are "the need to please and the need to allay self doubt" (p. 125).

If self-awareness is so important to therapists, and if lack of self-awareness can lead to trainees using therapy to satisfy their needs, how is a supervisor to promote self-awareness without serving as a therapist for the trainee? Hebert (1992) advocates self-examination on the part of interns. The goal of this self-examination is to increase the interns' awareness of such things as sources of their anxieties, the struggle between wanting to change and wanting to stay the same, stimuli that trigger tendencies toward self-blame, authoritarian posturing, and other characteristics that could influence therapy.

Although Hebert (1992) stressed self-examination, he maintains that this examination should also involve the supervisor. Describing the responsibility of the supervisor, he emphasized the importance of supervisors showing confidence in the ability of interns to learn and change. Hebert's description of the supervisor's role sounds not unlike descriptions of the therapist's role and the necessary ingredients for helping relationships (cf. Rogers, 1961, pp. 50–57). Thus, although Hebert was keenly aware of the vulnerable position of trainees vis-à-vis their supervisors, he saw the task of self-awareness as primary to the development of therapists. He concluded by saying:

> It is the intern's self that all ingredients are filtered through. To avoid that filter is to risk the training of a counselor who is oblivious to his/her own exploitative tendencies. (Hebert, 1992, p. 131)

EXERCISE

This exercise has two parts. The first part asks you to explore your reactions to the ideas just presented regarding supervision and therapy. Do you think it is important to explore the needs and self of the therapist? Do you have any hesitations or concerns about this process for yourself? What would your reaction be to addressing these issues in supervision, and how would you like your supervisor to deal with this issue?

The second part of the exercise involves trying to identify any personal needs you are aware of that, if not managed well, could impede your functioning as a therapist. For example, you might consider your own needs for affection, approval, or power, and ways in which these needs could influence your actions as a therapist. After thinking about these issues for yourself, you may want to discuss them with a peer or perhaps with your instructor or supervisor.

RESISTANCE TO SELF-AWARENESS AND CHANGE

Because self-awareness is so important in therapy training and supervision, it should not be surprising that some of the same processes that accompany self-awareness and change in therapy also emerge in the supervisory process. At least three types of resistance stand out in supervision. The first, resistance to awareness, relates closely to the preceding discussion of interns' needs. Resistance to awareness refers to the challenges associated with becoming aware of personal qualities or needs that are not easily acknowledged or owned:

> In learning about human behavior we are learning about ourselves, about our defenses, our motives, our unflattering impulses. In dispassionately examining the sources of our most cherished attitudes and illusions, we are throwing open to question the way in which we order our lives. (Kadushin, 1985, pp. 237; 2002, p. 228)

Resistance to this process is perfectly understandable and is probably to be expected of most trainees. Hebert (1992) described this process well by acknowledging:

> This is a predictable and altogether acceptable defensive response. All human beings make efforts to perpetuate some fiction about themselves and others. (p. 129)

Despite the apparent inevitability of self-awareness stress and accompanying resistance, supervisors and training programs often devote relatively little attention to helping trainees cope with the process effectively. This was documented by May and Kilpatrick (1989) who surveyed social work programs and concluded, "A large majority of schools agreed that preparation of MSW students for this stress is the schools' responsibility, but little is being done about it in a formal way" (p. 316). Although these authors focused on social work programs, a similar conclusion would almost certainly emerge if one surveyed psychology, counseling, or other similar programs.

A second source of resistance has to do with the reality that to learn one must confess ignorance of what is to be learned. This is not easy for anyone, and it can be especially difficult for students who feel their competence is being tested at every turn. Kadushin (2002) described this dilemma particularly well:

> The learning situation demands an admission of ignorance, however limited. In admitting ignorance, supervisees expose their vulnerability. They risk the possibility of criticism, of shame and perhaps rejection because of an admitted inadequacy.
>
> Supervisees have the choice of being anxious because they do not know how to do their work or being anxious about confessing ignorance and obtaining help. (p. 229)

Because this paradoxical situation is inherent in the learning process, it can be very difficult for interns to resolve on their own. As such, it is extremely important for supervisors to be sensitive to it and make every effort to allow interns to acknowledge their limitations in order to make learning possible. At the same time, interns should resolve that it is better to risk acknowledging their limitations than to feign knowledge at the possible risk of harming clients or the agency.

A third source of resistance in supervision is resistance to change. In a review of this and other topics in supervision, Rubinstein (1992) paraphrased similar comments by Kadushin (1985) and Rothman (1973) and explained:

> Change requires giving up old behavior patterns, which have helped the supervisee keep homeostasis in his or her personal life. Hence, a change of this kind evokes anxiety in supervisees, who are not sure they wish to change what has taken them so much time to learn. (Rubinstein, 1992, p. 99)

Interns may resist trying, learning, or sometimes even considering certain issues or techniques of therapy because they feel that their established ways of being and doing things as people are being threatened. Although the overt content of the verbal defense may be couched in language about what is good for the client, the source of the resistance is often found in the intern's need to defend what has worked well for him or her as an individual or as a therapist.

An example of this process comes from my own experience in the early stages of training. At that time I was very resistant to reflective techniques in therapy. Although I wanted to develop the skills of therapy, I was intent on not "sounding like a therapist." This desire gained support in my first practicum placement, in which the clinical staff followed a treatment model that was not at all consistent with the reflective approach. That same semester, during a classroom role-play exercise in which students were to practice reflective techniques, I offered verbal protest but went along with the exercise at the insistence of the instructor. After the exercise, I remained unimpressed with the technique, but the instructor patiently suggested that we review a tape of the role-play to identify the statements that had elicited the most response from the client. Much to my surprise, the tape revealed that the reflective statements, which I had been so critical of before, turned out to have produced the most extensive and useful exploration for the client. Along with demonstrating the potential of reflective techniques, this experience showed how resistance to a technique can sometimes reflect our own desires to meet personal beliefs or needs more than actual knowledge about what does or does not help clients.

A somewhat different, though undoubtedly related, interpretation of resistance was described by Kadushin (2002). In a thought-provoking discussion, Kadushin suggested that change can create a sense of betrayal because the supervisee is being asked to give up behaviors or ways of thinking that were learned from parents and other significant people in the supervisee's past. Changing, therefore, implies disloyalty or infidelity to parents or other role models.

In these circumstances, resistance may take the form of arguing that a given concept or technique will or will not help clients, but the underlying issue is that accepting the new idea or approach implies that one's parents or other role models were somehow wrong. The intern resists that possibility because accepting it would introduce a host of other issues and anxieties with which most trainees are ill equipped to cope.

As this discussion demonstrates, resistance is a fact of life in supervision. How, then, can supervisors and supervisees deal with it most effectively?

Several principles have been very helpful to me. First, resistance to awareness and change should not be confused with legitimate self-protection deriving from the situational context of supervision. Students who appear to resist self-exploration may be seeking to avoid self-awareness, or they may be protecting their privacy against an unwanted and potentially damaging intrusion by their supervisor. As Rubinstein (1992) pointed out, one must be careful not to assign attributions without carefully considering the situation in which the behavior occurs. Before assigning a student's behaviors to resistance, supervisors would be well advised to consider how their own behaviors as supervisors might be contributing to the student's apparent resistance. Supervisors should also realize that, just as interns may resist self-awareness, supervisors are not always the best judges of their own behavior. Seeking an outside consult can sometimes help supervisors become more aware of their actions. Asking the supervisees themselves can also be helpful, but in extreme situations the very factors that led to apparent resistance may inhibit genuine feedback about the supervisor's behaviors.

Supervisors should realize not only how their actions might induce resistance in students but also how they can help students work through their resistance to achieve greater self-awareness and growth. The first step in this process is to help students understand the concept of resistance, its effects, and some of the possible manifestations. It may help to tell students directly that if they are to develop their skills, they will have to develop self-awareness and change certain behaviors and this process is not always easy. It follows, therefore, that students will have to deal with resistance. Supervisors can facilitate this process by acknowledging both its importance and the difficulty involved. Supervisors should also create safe and supportive environments that allow and encourage students to consciously express, identify, and explore their own resistance.

A final and extremely important point about resistance in supervision is that it provides a wonderful learning opportunity for interns to understand something of what the process of change is like for clients. Studying concepts in the abstract is never as meaningful as experiencing them firsthand. If interns can become aware of their own resistance during supervision, that awareness may help them appreciate and honor the resistance clients display in therapy. Lacking such firsthand experience, interns tend to respond to client resistance as something that "interferes with therapy" or that shows clients to be "unmotivated." By comparison, after displaying and acknowledging resistance themselves, interns are more likely to go beyond the simplistic interpretation and appreciate resistance not as an obstacle to therapy but as a normal and important part of the process.

EXERCISE

Considering the three types of resistance (i.e., resistance to awareness, to revealing ignorance, and to change), think about your education and training up to this point and try to identify instances in which you may have responded with each type of resistance. Next, try to imagine future situations that could evoke such reactions. Finally, because all of us are likely to show resistance in some areas, what matters most is that we learn to recognize and cope with the resistance productively. As you think of what might evoke resistance and how you would recognize resistance in yourself, consider how you could learn to understand your resistance and be able to work with that resistance to allow yourself to change.

TRANSFERENCE AND COUNTERTRANSFERENCE

In much the same way as resistance in supervision parallels resistance in therapy, transference and countertransference are also part of both therapy and supervision. These terms, which have

their origins in psychoanalytic approaches, have been defined in various ways by different authors (Schneider, 1992). For our purposes, it is enough to understand transference as a process in which clients, or in the case of supervision, supervisees, "replace" some other, typically earlier, person in their lives with the person of the therapist or supervisor, relating to the latter individual in ways that are similar to their relationship with the original person. For example, students may relate to supervisors much as they related to parents or other authority figures in their lives. If students happen to be older than their supervisors, it can also happen that the students will relate to the supervisors as they may to one of their own children.

Countertransference is somewhat the reverse of transference. In transference clients relate to their therapists as if they were someone else. In the case of countertransference, therapists (supervisors) relate to the clients (supervisees) as if they were someone else. For example, a supervisor may relate to a trainee as if the trainee were one of the supervisor's children or clients.

According to psychoanalytic explanations, both transference and countertransference take place unconsciously and are expressed behaviorally and emotionally. Schneider (1992) explained that in supervision, "The supervisor, just by virtue of his/her serving as an authority figure, allows a transference relationship to develop and grow" (p. 73). Kadushin (2002) points out that the supervisor-supervisee relationship tends to evoke the parent-child relationship and may, therefore, "reactivate anxiety associated with this earlier relationship" (p. 230).

As explained in regard to resistance, understanding transference and countertransference in supervision can help interns make the most of supervision, learn more about themselves, and gain greater awareness of processes they are likely to observe and experience in therapy. Recognizing and exploring transference reactions in supervision can also help interns develop greater self-understanding, which is critical to the therapist's development.

EXERCISE

Although transference is conceived to be largely an unconscious process, each of us has certain individuals in our lives who have represented authority figures in the past. Parents are perhaps the most likely to have filled this role, but others, such as older siblings, relatives, friends, or teachers could also provide such figures. The point of this exercise is not to circumvent the transference by trying to deal with it before it arises. Rather, it is to introduce a process of reflection and an understanding of transference that may be useful if or when transference occurs in supervision or therapy. To help you understand how transference might affect your own experiences with supervisors, consider this question: If you were to anticipate a transference reaction toward a supervisor based on someone from your own past, who would the most likely person be? Why?

SUGGESTED GUIDELINES FOR THERAPY AND SUPERVISION

Because of the similarities and differences between therapy and supervision, it is not easy to provide absolute demarcation between the two activities. On the one hand, as part of the training process, trainees need to explore personal needs and dynamics that may influence their work with clients. On the other hand, trainees are in a vulnerable position relative to supervisors and should have a right to choose how much personal information they wish to disclose.

Without resolving this issue completely, a number of authors refer to criteria that can help determine when or if the fine line between therapy and supervision has been crossed. The core criterion is the purpose of the activity in question. Burns and Holloway (1989) concluded their review of the topic by stating:

> It might be entirely appropriate to use counseling skills (such as facilitative conditions) when the intent is to enhance trainees' understanding of their own reactions, behaviors and attitudes toward the client. However, it may not be appropriate to use such techniques with the intent to solely affect counselor change outside of the counseling role. (p. 56)

In his discussion of the importance of interns' personal needs, Hebert (1992) established a comparable criterion by asserting:

> Psychotherapeutic efforts may coexist as long as the focus is upon the relevance that various intern personal characteristics have for their work with clients. As long as the emphasis is continuously placed upon the impact of an intern's presentation of self upon therapeutic efforts, that in itself should serve to mitigate its moving into the realm of psychotherapy. (p. 124)

The common theme in these statements is that the focus of supervision must remain on the interns' actions in therapy. As long as their actions do not violate ethical standards, what trainees do outside therapy is not the concern of supervisors and should be left for the trainees to address on their own. According to Kadushin, (2002), most supervisors report that they understand and respect these boundaries.

In my work with interns, I find that personal issues relating to an intern's clinical work can and sometimes should be identified by supervisors, but the process of working through those issues should best be left for therapy with someone other than the supervisor. I encourage interns to consider personal therapy as a valuable experience in itself and as an important, perhaps essential, step toward professional development. The benefits of individual therapy are very likely to carry over to the intern's clinical work and to supervision, but the supervisory work will not be confounded by the dual roles of supervisor/therapist or intern/client.

If an intern has access to a therapist, issues that arise in the intern's clinical work or supervisory relationship can be addressed in therapy. However, the goal of therapy should be to facilitate the intern's personal growth, not to vent frustrations or second-guess supervisors. For useful suggestions regarding personal counseling for interns as it relates to supervision issues and level of training, see Wise et al. (1989). The stresses of clinical work and benefits of personal therapy are addressed in Chapter 7 of this book.

EXERCISE

What are your personal attitudes toward seeking therapy or counseling for yourself? If you or your supervisor detect personal issues that are affecting your clinical work or training, would you be amenable to seeking therapy? If not, what are your concerns? What would the relative risks and benefits be if your supervisor began also to function as a therapist for you? How could you respond if you felt a supervisor was in some way stepping into the role of therapist and you were not comfortable with that?

CONFLICT IN SUPERVISION

FREQUENCY AND RESOLUTION OF CONFLICTS

Although most trainees have positive supervisory experiences, conflicts that interfere with learning are not uncommon (Gray, Ladany, Walker, & Ancis, 2001; Nelson & Friedlander, 2001). Moskowitz and Rupert (1983) surveyed 158 graduate students in clinical psychology and found that 38% reported major conflicts that made it difficult to learn from supervision. The three areas of conflict most identified by students were theoretical orientation and therapy approach, style of supervision, and personality issues. Each of these issues has been addressed already in this chapter, but the results of these studies provide useful information about different ways and results of dealing with conflict.

One of the most interesting findings of this research was that all the trainees who responded indicated that when conflict was present, they wanted the supervisor to identify it openly. Despite this desire, in the Moskowitz and Rupert sample, 83.8% of those who had experienced conflicts reported that the trainees, not their supervisors, had initiated discussion about the conflict. Gray et al. (2001) reported a similar finding, with most trainees wishing supervisors would recognize conflicts and bring them up to be resolved. At the same time, however, most interns indicated that they did not chose to bring the conflict up themselves, largely due to concerns about adverse reactions and even retribution from their supervisors. This finding suggests that if you experience a conflict in supervision and think it should be dealt with, you, the trainee, may have to be the one who raises the issue. Unfortunately, this also suggests that you may want to proceed with some caution should you chose to pursue this approach.

One other observation that is noteworthy from these studies is that interns rarely describe conflicts resulting from supervisors who are not sufficiently critical in their assessment or grading of the intern's performance (Veach, 2001). I mention this here because it is easy to become upset if you feel that a supervisor has unfairly given you a low grade or is overly critical of your performance, but an intern may actually have more reason to be concerned if a supervisor is not sufficiently attentive to areas in which the intern needs to improve. Remember that the purpose of your internship experience is to better your skills, not to have a supervisor simply tell you that everything you do is just fine. Keep in mind too that your supervisor is more likely to give you critical feedback, which may well be the most useful at times, if you are perceived to be open to such feedback and willing to learn from it (Hoffman, Hill, Holmes, & Freitas, 2005).

With regard to resolution of conflicts, Moskowitz and Rupert's (1983) findings reveal that outcomes relate significantly to the nature of the conflict. Overall, more than half of those who experienced conflict and discussed it with their supervisors reported that the discussion led to at least some improvement. However, 37% of the students who discussed conflicts indicated that there was no improvement or that the situation became worse. The most successfully resolved conflicts were those relating to supervisory style. In 90% of these cases, discussion led to improvement; in none of the reported cases did conditions worsen following discussion. Conflicts relating to theoretical orientation also showed improvement with discussion, but the effect, 55% improvement, was less than with supervisory style. The most difficult conflicts to resolve related to personality, with only 36% of these showing improvement and 37% indicating that the situation became worse or led to a change in supervisors.

In addition to describing the outcomes of cases in which conflicts were discussed, Moskowitz and Rupert (1983) also note that, although most students chose to discuss conflicts directly, 23% opted not to discuss the conflict. Students who did not discuss conflicts explained that they feared discussion might worsen the problem or lead to the student being blamed or negatively evaluated by the supervisor. In lieu of dealing directly with supervisors, this group of students indicated that they sought support from peers or from other staff members.

Two positive findings emerge from this research and should be emphasized. First, most interns do not report significant conflicts with supervisors. Second, most conflicts relating to supervisory style or theoretical orientation can be successfully resolved through discussion. At the same time, however, conflicts between supervisor and trainee are by no means infrequent, and discussion of the conflicts does not always lead to improvement. If your training program has an accompanying internship class or instructor, this may be an appropriate place to discuss site-related supervision conflicts. Sharing concerns or troubles encountered in accompanying classes gives interns the opportunity to learn from each other's challenges and experiences.

GUIDELINES FOR DEALING WITH CONFLICT

Because conflicts in supervision are not uncommon, several principles and useful tools may help interns and supervisors deal with conflict more effectively. Veach (2001) and Nelson and colleagues (2001) focus on the responsibilities of supervisors to deal more constructively with conflicts. They emphasize the need for improved training in supervision, mechanisms for supervisors to themselves receive supervision, the benefits of clarifying expectations from the outset, and the central importance of supervisors forming a constructive relationship and strong working alliance with trainees. These authors also suggest that conflicts can be reduced through better preparation of interns for working in supervision.

For interns who are involved in conflict with a supervisor, I believe the first principle is to approach conflicts as opportunities for learning rather than as situations that interfere with learning. In managing a supervisory conflict, you may be able to discover how you react to conflict, what kinds of issues or interactions tend to promote conflict, and how you can more effectively cope with conflicts. In raising these possibilities, my intent is not to offer the simplistic aphorism that "everything is a learning experience," nor do I want to suggest, as one supervisor was fond of telling interns, that "conflict builds character." I do, however, suggest that one of the biggest blocks to resolving conflicts is the underlying idea that "conflicts should not happen, and I should not have to deal with this." If you take an attitude of learning from a conflict, rather than an attitude of anger, fear, or avoidance, you are more likely to deal effectively with the situation.

A second general principle is to identify what a conflict is really about before raising it with your supervisor. Are you at odds over issues of theory or technique? Do you feel that the supervisor is not giving you sufficient support? What sorts of transference or countertransference issues might be present? Are logistics, such as timing of supervision, a problem? In thinking about the key subject of a conflict, recognize that often the surface content of a conflict does not reflect the real difficulty. For example, people who work together might get into a conflict over who should have the bigger office. In reality, the conflict is probably not about office size but about who wants or deserves more rewards or prestige and why.

After identifying the conflict, next ask yourself as honestly as you can what role you are playing in it. This does not mean that you should engage in self-blame, but it does suggest that you should explore your own actions and reactions to better understand your part in what is happening. If self-exploration is difficult, or if you find that it is hard to really recognize your role, you may want to get an outside perspective, perhaps from a peer or other faculty member. If you decide to get another perspective, do not approach the interaction by expecting the other person to reassure you that the conflict is all the other person's fault. There is a crucial difference between support and uncritical agreement. When you discuss a supervisory conflict with a third party, ask the other person to support you emotionally and to appreciate the difficulty of the conflict, but ask the listener also to evaluate the situation objectively and try to help you understand things you may not be aware of on your own.

For example, you might go into a discussion convinced that a supervisor places too many demands on your time. In listening to your description, someone else might hear that perhaps the supervisor is paying you a compliment by relying on you. It is also possible that you have a role in the conflict because you do not tell the supervisor when you are overbooked. The purpose of getting another opinion is to understand what is happening, not to prove you are right.

Trying to see the situation from the supervisor's perspective is another valuable step toward resolving a conflict. Is your supervisor doing or saying things for reasons that might not be immediately evident to you but that might make perfect sense from his or her position? Is your supervisor aware that a conflict exists? If so, would he or she define the conflict differently than you? Asking yourself these questions may help you resolve a conflict without speaking directly to your supervisor about it. If you do discuss the matter, this forethought will serve as preparation that should make the discussion more productive.

A more important element in dealing with a conflict is to ask yourself what it is you want to be different and what you would like to have happen to be satisfied. This might be a change in the way you and your supervisor interact, or it might be a modification of some arrangement, such as the hours you work, your caseload, or a similar matter. By thinking about your own desires, you will be more able to articulate both the present situation and your wishes for change. This clarity can help both you and your supervisor identify specific steps for dealing with and resolving the conflict.

Keeping in mind the principles just described, it can also be helpful to have structured tools to help identify and resolve potential conflicts. Two very useful instruments for this purpose are presented by Falender and Shafranske (2004). The first instrument, the Working Alliance Inventory, was developed by Audrey Bahrick. This inventory provides forms on which supervisees and supervisors can rate their impressions in response to statements indicating the level of understanding between the two, feelings and attitudes toward one another, clarity of goals and purpose, the value of activities in supervision, and similar matters. If the supervisor and supervisee both complete their respective forms and then discuss their mutual impressions, areas of commonality as well as difference can be identified and then worked on together. An alternative but similar instrument was described by Efstation, Patton, and Kardash (1990). Like Bahrick's inventory, their Supervisor Working Alliance Inventory (SWAI) includes forms for both the supervisor and the supervisee to complete and addresses several factors, including the emphasis on promoting understanding of clients, rapport

between the supervisor and client, and identification with the supervisor.

A second instrument offered by Falender and Shafranske (2004) is the Role Conflict and Role Ambiguity Inventory, developed initially by Olk and Friedlander (1992). Role ambiguity refers to an intern's uncertainty about the supervisor's expectations and evaluations. Role conflict involves situations in which the role of student conflicts in some way with that of counselor or colleague. An example of items from the Role Ambiguity Scale is "I was not sure if I should discuss my professional weaknesses in supervision because I was not sure how I would be evaluated" (Falender and Shafranske, 2004, p. 266). A Role Conflict item example is "I disagreed with my supervisor about how to introduce a specific issue to a client, but I also wanted to do what the supervisor recommended" (ibid., p. 267). For all items interns are asked to respond on a five-point scale indicating the degree to which they have experienced these difficulties. As with the Working Alliance Inventory, completing this tool can provide a basis for discussion about how things are going in supervision. Because items in both inventories can raise issues that are difficult and may be perceived as criticism, it is important for there to be an understanding that the purpose of using these or other such tools is to improve the quality of the supervisory experience for both the supervisor and intern and, as such, that criticism should be offered, received, and responded to constructively.

Finally, while offering suggestions for identifying and resolving conflicts constructively, it must also be acknowledged that for a variety of reasons, this is not always possible. Under such circumstances, the best solution may be to invite in another person, perhaps one's instructor or another supervisor or other professional, to help work through differences. If this is unfeasible or unsuccessful, it may be desirable in some instances to negotiate a change in supervisors or placements. If handled sensitively and professionally, this does not have to be a negative experience for the people involved, and it may well be more constructive than simply staying with a relationship that is clearly not constructive or conducive to learning.

EVALUATION

Lazar and Mosek (1993) observed that students who receive grades in field placements often feel they have little clear understanding of why they received a specific grade. To remedy this situation, interns, instructors, and supervisors should discuss grading and evaluation from the outset and should agree on and understand the rationale and methods to be used (Nelson et al., 2001).

One of the things that should be understood is the relationship between evaluations performed by supervisors and the grades assigned by instructors. In most placements, supervisors will conduct some form of evaluation designed to identify the intern's relative strengths and weaknesses. Ideally, evaluations provide useful feedback that can help interns learn where they are doing well and identify areas in which they need improvement.

When interns will also be receiving academic grades, they should know the relationship between the evaluations from site supervisors and the academic grades that will be assigned by the academic instructor. If the evaluation from supervisors will play a role in the instructor's grading system, interns should know how that will occur and what other factors may contribute to their grade.

Some students in internships present as being "grade motivated," which means they focus on how they think they will be graded rather than on what they are learning or how they are performing. It is essential for interns to understand that the internship experience is fundamentally different from the rest of their academic work. In a typical class, lacking knowledge or skill may lower one's grade, but otherwise little of any real consequence happens. By comparison, at internships, an intern's lack of knowledge or skill has real consequences that apply not only to the intern but to the clients, supervisor, and the agency. Because interns need to go beyond the grade mentality and focus instead on learning, they must embrace evaluation (i.e., the process of giving and receiving feedback about the quality of their performance). When they accept evaluation as an essential part of learning, mistakes, successes, and feedback can be understood for what they really should be—learning opportunities—rather than points added or subtracted from an ultimately meaningless grade book. As noted earlier, interns who communicate that they are open to feedback, even if it is critical, are more likely to receive important input that might otherwise be avoided. Difficult though such feedback may be, it is far better to receive it and deal with it than to have either the supervisor or the intern avoid something that might be important to training and performance (Hoffman et al., 2005).

PRINCIPLES OF EVALUATIONS

Kadushin (2002) has offered a series of principles that can be extremely helpful for evaluations. He emphasizes, for example, that evaluations should be a continuous part of supervision and should be agreed on in advance. Evaluations should occur in a positive, supportive environment and should be part of a mutual process that emphasizes both strengths and weaknesses, areas of recognized growth, and areas of further growth. Kadushin suggests that evaluations recognize the learning process and should be viewed as progress reports, not "final scores." To keep the role of supervision separate from therapy, Kadushin also cautions that evaluation should focus on the supervisees' professional work, not personal issues.

Consistent with Kadushin's suggestions, the responsibility for evaluating an intern's performance should fall to both the intern and the supervisor. Both should be committed to thorough, honest, accurate, critical, and constructive examination of the intern's strengths and weaknesses. One way to promote this goal is for supervisors and interns to complete evaluations of the intern separately, then bring the evaluations together and compare their impressions.

As part of the evaluation process, reviewing performance should address multiple aspects of the intern's performance, and the evaluation should be based on several observations and data sources. Thus, a single event or observation should not form the basis of an entire evaluation, and wherever possible, several forms or sources of information should be used. Multiple sources might include written material, direct observations, and impressions of more than one individual.

Based on a review of job analyses and other research relating to the tasks of counseling psychologists, Hahn and Molnar (1991) suggested that intern-evaluation systems should address the following domains:

> (a) Individual therapy, (b) couples therapy, (c) group therapy, (d) assessment (vocational and psychological), (e) crisis intervention, (f) case conceptualization, (g) teaching or structured group and workshop presentations, (h) use of supervision, (i) professionalism, (j) consultation, and (k) supervision (e.g., doctoral practicum students). Written communication skills are an important aspect of professional training that can be evaluated within several of these domains. (p. 422)

Because the guidelines proposed by Hahn and Molnar (1991) are specifically directed toward graduate-level programs in counseling psychology, evaluations for other disciplines or levels of training will undoubtedly differ. Whatever elements are chosen when evaluating separate elements of an intern's performance, efforts should be made to avoid carryover or halo effects that might influence an evaluation in one area positively or negatively based on performance in some other activity.

Avoiding halo effects in evaluations is not always easily accomplished. This was demonstrated empirically by Borders and Fong (1992), who found low correlations between supervisors' global ratings of their supervisees' counseling and external judges' ratings of supervisee behaviors in actual counseling sessions. Based on their results, Borders and Fong suggested that the evaluations of supervisors may have been influenced not only by supervisee performance in counseling but also by how the supervisees responded during supervision sessions. Borders and Fong further suggested that supervisors may adjust their expectations and evaluation criteria depending on the experience and developmental levels of their supervisees.

Comparable findings were reported by Lazar and Mosek (1993), who found that grades were affected both by the quality of the intern's performance and by the intern's relationship with the supervisor. Based on this finding, Lazar and Mosek recommended that using a pass-fail grading system would be a preferred approach for field placements and supervisors.

Along with considering the specific areas to be evaluated and the sources of information for evaluations, the form of evaluation and the "reference" by which interns will be evaluated are also important considerations. Common models for evaluation forms reference performance according to such criteria as expected levels, average, or standard. Individuals are then evaluated as either falling below, meeting, or exceeding these reference points to varying degrees. Such scales have the advantage of offering succinct and convenient feedback in several areas of performance. However, whenever they are used, there should be clarification about what the reference terms mean (Hahn & Molnar, 1991). Do "expected" or "average" levels refer to expectations or averages for interns at similar levels of experience, or do they speak to levels expected of professionals employed by the agency?

Appendix D of this book contains an evaluation form that I ask supervisors to complete for our interns. Sections of the evaluation form address such areas as basic work behaviors (punctual, reliable, etc.), knowledge of clients and treatment issues, response to supervision, interactions with clients, and interactions with coworkers. Space is also provided for more specific comments, and supervisors are encouraged to offer constructive criticism. The evaluation form contains some of the issues that can be addressed in an evaluation process. Depending on the nature of the internship and the goals of the intern, instructor, or supervisor, other areas will undoubtedly need to be addressed, and some areas currently mentioned may be deleted.

In addition to rating scales, it is also helpful for supervisors to give more specific behavioral feedback to interns. Being told one is below or above expectations can offer a general sense of how one is evaluated, but it does not provide information about what is being done well or how to improve performance. Insofar as evaluations are meant not only to rate past performance but also to guide future development, evaluations should be part of a process of developing goals and action plans for the intern. This means that areas of relative weakness are not simply acknowledged and forgotten. Once identified, areas needing improvement should be addressed with specific strategies for making the necessary changes or acquiring the needed skill or knowledge. Thus, supervisors should offer, and interns should request, specific suggestions for continued growth. An example of such feedback would be, "Tom demonstrates very good listening behaviors and develops rapport quickly with clients. He is less skilled at determining when and how to offer effective confrontations when clients have violated program rules." Another example might be, "Tom needs to work on writing more succinct reports with less jargon and more specific recommendations for the treatment team." Compared with rating-scale approaches, comments such as these focus on the individual's strengths and weaknesses without reference to an external standard of performance.

EVALUATION OF SUPERVISORS

Just as evaluation is an essential part of internship training for interns, evaluation should also provide useful feedback to supervisors. As with intern evaluation, this process should not be limited to a single event at the end of the experience but should be part of an ongoing communication process. Throughout this

chapter, it has been suggested that interns communicate with their supervisors about any concerns they may have or ideas for improving supervision. If trainees follow that advice, much of the work of evaluation will be incorporated as a natural part of the supervisory process. Nevertheless, it can still be helpful for interns to give more structured feedback at the end of an internship.

Sleight (1990) observed that compared with the availability of models for supervisee evaluation, relatively few examples have been published pertaining to supervisor evaluation. Kadushin (2002) made a similar observation and suggested that although well-intentioned supervisors often engage in self-evaluation, self-evaluation alone may not be sufficient to produce substantial changes in supervisor behavior. A further drawback of self-evaluation is that supervisor self-ratings are not necessarily consistent with the ratings that would be assigned by their interns. Gandolfo and Brown (1987) noted that supervisors and supervisees may have different ideas about the elements of good supervision, and these may vary across levels of training. In a study of supervisee ratings of actual versus ideal supervisory experiences, Gandolfo and Brown found differences in the focus of supervision, the format of supervision, the roles of supervisor and supervisee, the "evaluation and atmosphere" elements of supervision, and supervisor characteristics. Comparable findings were reported by Baker and Smith (1987), who examined differences between student ratings of supervision compared with social work field-faculty ratings.

The evidence of different perceptions of supervision suggests that supervisors and interns alike stand to benefit from increasing the use of formal evaluation procedures. Kadushin (2002) offers a brief model of items from instruments for this purpose. Falender and Shafranske (2004) also provide useful forms for evaluating the process of supervision, assessing the qualities and performance of the supervisor, and providing feedback to supervisors at the conclusion of placements.

Based on a review of the literature and comments of students, I have developed an evaluation tool that has been useful for interns and supervisors. The form is presented in Appendix I. As with the form for evaluation of interns, this supervisor evaluation tool primarily serves as an example, but it is also printed on a perforated page so it can be easily removed for use. Modifications may be needed to better fit specific needs of the supervisor or interns. What matters most is not the precise detail of any form but the process of the evaluation and the spirit in which it is performed. Interns who will be involved in evaluating the performance of their supervisors would do well to revisit the guidelines offered by Kadushin (2002) and presented at the start of this discussion of evaluation.

PLANNING FOR FUTURE SUPERVISION

Supervision is an important part of internships, but the value of supervision does not end when your internship concludes. In closing this chapter, I encourage you to think of supervision as an essential part of a therapist's work throughout your professional career. Clinical work can be extraordinarily complex, and there will be many times when you are not able to understand a client or situation on your own. At such times, you need to seek supervision and be open to the ideas and insights of a colleague. If you have positive experiences in supervision as an intern, the benefits will probably be evident, and continuing supervision as a professional will simply be a matter of remembering its value and making arrangements with a fellow professional. If your supervisory experience as an intern was not as positive, it might take some time for you to be willing to try supervision again. That is understandable, but do not let one or two unpleasant experiences dissuade you from something that has the potential to be among the most valuable learning opportunities.

In a real sense, the decision to enter a helping profession is also a decision to accept and seek supervision. The challenge is to find the right supervisor to meet your personal and professional needs, then work with that person to ensure that you both make the most of the experience.

REFERENCES

Akamatsu, T. J. (1980). The use of role-play and simulation technique in the training of psychotherapy. In A. K. Hess (Ed.), *Psychotherapy supervision: Theory, research and practice.* New York: Wiley.

Allen, G., Szollos, S., & Williams, B. (1986). Doctoral students' comparative evaluations of the best and worst psychotherapy supervision. *Professional Psychology: Research and Practice, 17*, 91–99.

Aponte, H. J. (1994). How personal can training get. *Journal of Marital and Family Therapy, 20*(1), 3–15.

Association of Psychology Postdoctoral Internship Centers (APPIC) 2006. APPIC Membership criteria: Doctoral psychology internship programs. http://www.appic.org/about/2_3_1_about_policies_and_procedures_internship.html

Baker, D. R., & Smith, S. L. (1987). A comparison of field faculty and field student perceptions of selected aspects of supervision. *Clinical Supervisor, 5*(4), 31–42.

Barnat, M. (1974). Some characteristics of supervisory identification in psychotherapy. *Psychotherapy: Theory, Research and Practice, 11*, 189–192.

Barnett, J. E. (2005). Important ethical, legal issues surround supervision role. *National Psychologist, 14*(3), 16.

Berger, S. S., & Buchholz, E. S. (1993). On becoming a supervisee: Preparation for learning in a supervisory relationship. *Psychotherapy, 30*, 86–92.

Berman, E. (1988). Ha'libun ha'meshutaf shel yechasey madrich-mudrach ke'heibet shel hadracha dinamit [The joint exploration of the supervisory relationship as an aspect of dynamic supervision]. *Sihot-Israel Journal of Psychotherapy, 3,* 13–20.

Bogo, M. (1993). The student/field instructor relationship: The critical factor in field education. *Clinical Supervisor, 11,* 23–36.

Borders, L. D., Bernard, J. M., Dye, A. H., Fong, M. L., Henderson, P., & Nance, D. W. (1991). Curriculum guide for training counseling supervisors: Rationale, development, and implementation. *Counselor Education and Supervision, 31,* 58–80.

Borders, L. D., & Fong, M. L. (1992). Evaluations of supervisees: Brief commentary and research report. *Clinical Supervisor, 9*(2), 43–51.

Bradley, J., & Post, P. (1991). Impaired students: Do we eliminate them from counselor education programs? *Counselor Education and Supervision, 31,* 100–108.

Bradley, L., & Ladany, N (Eds.). (2001). *Counselor supervision: Principles, processes and practice.* Philadelphia: Brunner-Routledge.

Bubenzer, D. L., West, J. D., & Gold, J. M. (1991). Use of live supervision in counselor preparation. *Counselor Education and Supervision, 30,* 301–306.

Burns, C. I., & Holloway, E. L. (1989). Therapy in supervision: An unresolved issue. *Clinical Supervisor, 7*(4), 47–60.

Charny, I. W. (1986). What do therapists worry about: A tool for experiential supervision. *Clinical Supervisor, 4,* 17–28.

Costa, L. (1995). Reducing anxiety in live supervision. *Counselor Education and Supervision, 34,* 30–40.

Council for Accreditation of Counseling and Related Educatioal Programs. (2001) 2001 Standards. http://www.cacrep.org/2001Standards.html

Deal, K. H., & Clements, J. A., (2006). Supervising students developmentally: Evaluating a seminar for field instructors. *Journal of Social Work Education, 42(2),* 291–306.

Doehrman, M. J. G. (1976). Parallel processes in supervision and psychotherapy. *Bulletin of the Menninger Clinic, 40,* 3–104.

Dye, H. A., & Borders, L. D. (1990). Counseling supervisors: Standards for preparation and practice. *Journal of Counseling and Development, 69,* 27–29.

Edwards, M., & Chen, J. (1999). Strength-based supervision: Frameworks, current practice, and future directions. *Family Journal, 7*(4), 349–358.

Efstation, J. F., Patton, M. J., & Kardash, C. M. (1990). Measuring the working alliance in counselor supervision. *Journal of Counseling Psychology, 37,* 332–339.

Ekstein, E., & Wallerstein, R. (1972). *The teaching and learning of psychotherapy.* New York: International Universities Press.

Enyedy, K. C., Arcinue, F., Puri, N. N., Carter, J. W., Goodyear, R. K., & Getzelman, M. A., (2003). Hindering phenomena in group supervision: Implications for practice. *Professional Psychology: Research and Practice, 34,* 312–317.

Falender C. A., & Shafranske, E. P. (2004). *Clinical supervision: A competency based approach,* Washington, DC: APA.

Fernando, D. M., & Hulse-Killacky, D. (2005). The relationship of supervisory styles to satisfaction with supervision and the perceived self-efficacy of masters-level counseling students. *Counselor Education and Supervision, 44,* 293–304.

Finkelstein, H., & Tuckman, A. (1997). Supervision of psychological assessment: A development model. *Professional Psychology: Research and Practice, 28,* 92–95.

Fortune, A. E., McCarthy, M., & Abramson, J. S. (2001). Student learning processes in field education: Relationship of learning activites to quality of field instruction, satisfaction, and performance among MSW students. *Journal of Social Work Education, 37,* 111–125.

Fox, R., & Gutheil, I. A. (2000). Process recording: A means for conceptualizing and evaluating practice. *Journal of Teaching in Social Work, 20,* 39–57.

Frances, A., & Clarkin, J. (1981). Parallel techniques in supervision and treatment. *Psychiatric Quarterly, 53*(4), 242–248.

Freeman, S. C. (1993). Structure in counseling supervision. *Clinical Supervisor, 11,* 245–252.

Friedlander, M. L., Keller, K., Peca-Baker, T. A., & Olk, M. E. (1986). Effects of role conflict on counselor trainees' self-statements, anxiety level, and performance. *Journal of Counseling Psychology, 33*(1), 73–77.

Friedlander, M. L., & Ward, L. G. (1984). Development and validation of the Supervisory Styles Inventory. *Journal of Counseling Psychology, 31,* 541–557.

Friedman, D., & Kaslow, N. J. (1986). The development of professional identity in psychotherapists: Six stages in the supervision process. In F. W. Kaslow (Ed.), *Supervision and training: Models, dilemmas, and challenges.* New York: Haworth Press.

Gallant, J. P., & Thyer, B. A. (1989). The "bug in the ear" in clinical supervision: A review. *Clinical Supervisor, 7*(2/3), 43–58.

Gallant, J. P., Thyer, B. A., & Bailey, J. S. (1991). Using bug-in-the-ear-feedback in clinical supervision: Preliminary evaluations. *Research on Social Work Practice, 1,* 175–187.

Gandolfo, R. L., & Brown, R. (1987). Psychology intern ratings of actual and ideal supervision of psychotherapy. *Journal of Training and Practice in Professional Psychology, 1,* 15–28.

Gelman, C. R., (2004). Anxiety experienced by foundation-year MSW students entering field placement: Implications for admissions, curriculum, and field education. *Journal of Social Work Education, 40,* 39–54.

Globerman, J., & Bogo, M. (2003). Changing times: Understanding social workers' motivation to be field instructors. *Social Work, 48,* 65–73.

Gray, L. A., Ladany, N., Walker, J. A., & Ancis, J. R. (2001). Psychotherapy trainee's experience of counterproductive events in supervision. *Journal of Counseling Psychology, 48,* 371–383.

Hahn, W. K., & Molnar, S. (1991). Intern evaluation in university counseling centers: Process, problems and recommendations. *Counseling Psychologist, 19,* 414–430.

Haley, J. (1992). *Problem solving therapy* (2nd ed.). San Francisco: Jossey-Bass.

Harrar, W. R., VandeCreek, L., & Knapp, S. (1990). Ethical and legal aspects of clinical supervision. *Professional Psychology: Research and Practice, 21,* 37–41.

Hebert, D. J. (1992). Exploitative need-fulfillment and the counseling intern. *Clinical Supervisor, 10*(1), 123–132.

Hess, A. K. (1980). Training models and the nature of psychotherapy supervision. In A. K. Hess (Ed.), *Psychotherapy supervision: Theory, research, and practice.* New York: Wiley.

Hess, A. K., & Hess, K. A. (1983). Psychotherapy supervision: A survey of internship training practices. *Professional Psychology: Research, and Practice, 14,* 504–513.

Hill, C. E., & Corbett, M. M. (1993). A perspective on the history of process and outcome research in counseling psychology. *Journal of Counseling Psychology, 40,* 3–24.

Hoffman, M. A., Hill, C. E., Holmes, S. E., & Freitas, G. F., (2005). Supervisor perspective on the process and outcome of giving easy, difficult, or no feedback to supervisees. *Journal of Counseling Psychology, 52,* 3–13.

Holloway, E. L., & Neufeldt, S. A. (1995). Supervision: Its contributions to treatment efficacy. *Journal of Consulting and Clinical Psychology, 63,* 207–213.

Jarvis, P. E. (1989). Standardization versus individualization in the clinical internship. *Professional Psychology: Research and Practice, 20,* 185–186.

Kadushin, A. (1974). Supervisor-supervisees: A survey. *Social Work, 19,* 288–298.

Kadushin, A. (1985). *Supervision in social work.* New York: Columbia University Press.

Kadushin, A., & Harkness, D. (2002). *Supervision in social work* (4th ed.). New York: Columbia University Press.

Kaiser, T. L. (1992). The supervisory relationship: An identification of the primary elements in the relationship and an application of two theories of ethical relationships. *Journal of Marital and Family Therapy, 18,* 283–296.

Kanz, J. E. (2001). Clinical-supervision.com: Issues in the provision of online supervision. *Professional Psychology: Research and Practice, 32*(4), 415–420.

Kaplan, D. M., Rothrock, D., & Culkin, M. (1999). The infusion of counseling observations into a graduate counseling program. *Counselor Education and Supervision, 39,* 66–75.

Knight, C. (1996). A study of MSW and BSW students' perceptions of their field instructors. *Journal of Social Work Education and Supervision, 32,* 399–414.

Kurpius, D., Gibson, G., Lewis, J., & Corbett, M. (1991). Ethical issues in supervising counseling practitioners. *Counselor Education and Supervision, 31,* 48–57.

Lamb, D. J., Presser, N. R., Pfost, K. S., Baum, M. C., Jackson, V. R., & Jarvis, P. A. (1987). Confronting professional impairment during the internship: Identification, due process, and remediation. *Professional Psychology: Research and Practice, 18,* 597–603.

Lambert, M. J., & Beier, E. G. (1974). Supervisory and counseling process: A comparative study. *Counselor Education and Supervision, 14,* 54–60.

Lazar, A., & Mosek, A. (1993). The influence of the field instructor–student relationship on evaluation of students' practice. *Clinical Supervisor, 11,* 111–120.

Leong, F. T., & Wagner, N. S. (1994). Cross-cultural counseling supervision: What do we know? What do we need to know? *Counselor Education and Supervision, 34,* 117–131.

Levenson, H., & Evans, S. (2000). The current state of brief therapy training in American Psychological Association–accredited graduate and internship programs. *Professional Psychology: Research and Practice, 31*(4), 446–452.

Magnuson, S., Wilcoxon, S. A., & Norem, K. (2000). A profile of lousy supervision: Experienced counselors' perspectives. *Counselor Education and Supervision, 39*(3), 189–203.

Martin, G. E., & McBride, M. C. (1987). The results of implementation of a professional supervision model on counselor trainee behavior. *Counselor Education and Supervision, 27,* 155–167.

May, L. I., & Kilpatrick, A. C. (1989). Stress of self-awareness in clinical practice: Are students prepared? *Clinical Supervisor, 7,* 303–309.

McCarthy, P., Sugden, S., Koker, M., Lamendola, F., Maurer, S., & Renninger, S. (1995). A practical guide to informed consient in clinical supervision. *Counselor Education and Supervision, 35,* 130–138.

McCollum, E. E., & Wetchler, J. L. (1995). In defense of case consultation: Maybe "dead" supervision isn't dead after all. *Journal of Marital and Family Therapy, 21,* 155–166.

McMahon, M., & Simons, R. (2004). Supervision training for professional counselors: An exploratory study. *Counselor Education and Supervision, 43,* 301–307.

McNeil, B. W., & Worthen, V. (1989). The parallel process in psychotherapy supervision. *Professional Psychology: Research and Practice, 20,* 329–333.

Moskowitz, S. A., & Rupert, P. A. (1983). Conflict resolution within the supervisory relationship. *Professional Psychology: Research and Practice, 14,* 632–641.

National Association of Social Work Insurance Trust. (2004). Supervisor beware: Reducing your exposure to vicarious liability. http://www.naswinsurancetrust.org/understanding_risk_management/pointers/pp%20Vicarious%20Liability.pdf

Nelson, M. L., & Friedlander, M. L. (2001). A close look at conflictual supervisory relationships: The trainee perspective. *Journal of Counseling Psychology, 48,* 384–395.

Nelson, M. L., Gray, L. A., Friedlander, M. L., Ladany, N., & Walker, J. A. (2001). Toward relationship-centered supervision: Reply to Veach (2001) and Ellis (2001). *Journal of Counseling Psychology, 48,* 407–409.

Neufeldt, S. A., (1999). *Supervision strategies for the first practicum,* Washington, DC: ACA.

Olk, M., & Friedlander, M. L., (1992). Trainees' experience of role conflict and role ambiguity in supervisory relationships. *Journal of Counseling Psychology, 39,* 389–397.

Overholser, J. C. (1991). The Socratic method as a technique in psychotherapy supervision. *Professional Psychology: Research and Practice, 22,* 68–74.

Peake, T. H., Nussbaum, B. D., & Tindell, S. D. (2002). Clinical and counseling supervision references trends and needs. *Psychotherapy: Theory/Research/Practice/Training, 39,* 114–125.

Pollack, D., & Marsh, J. (2004). Social work misconduct may lead to liability. *Social Work, 49*(4), 609–612.

Prieto, L. R. (1997). Separating group supervision from group therapy: Avoiding epistemological confusion. *Professional Psychology: Research and Practice, 28,* 405.

Prieto, L. R., & Scheel, K. R. (2002). Using case documentation to strengthen counselor trainee's case conceptualization skills. *Journal of Counseling and Development, 80,* 11–21.

Rabinowitz, F. E., Heppner, P. P., & Roehlke, H. J. (1986). Descriptive study of process and outcome variables of supervision over time. *Journal of Counseling Psychology, 33,* 292–300.

Robiner, W. N., & Schofield, W. (1990). References on supervision in clinical and counseling psychology. *Professional Psychology: Research and Practice, 21,* 297–312.

Rogers, C. R. (1961). *On becoming a person.* Boston: Houghton Mifflin.

Romans, J. S. C., Boswell, D. L., Carlozzi, A. F., & Ferguson, D. B. (1995). Training and supervision practices in clinical, counseling and school psychology programs. *Professional Psychology: Research and Practice, 26,* 407–412.

Ronnestad, M. H., & Skovholt, T. M. (1993). Supervision of beginning and advanced graduate students of counseling and psychotherapy. *Journal of Counseling and Development, 71,* 396–405.

Rothman, B. (1973). Perspectives on learning and teaching in continuing education. *Journal of Education for Social Work, 9,* 39–52.

Rubinstein, G. (1992). Supervision and psychotherapy: Toward redefining the differences. *Clinical Supervisor, 10*(2), 97–116.

Schindler, N. J., & Talen, M. R. (1994). Focus supervision: Management format for supervision practices. *Professional Psychology: Research and Practice, 25,* 304–306.

Schneider, S. (1992). Transference, counter-transference, projective identification and role responsiveness in the supervisory process. *Clinical Supervisor, 10*(2), 71–84.

Searles, H. F. (1955). The informational value of the supervisor's emotional experiences. *Psychiatry, 18,* 135–146.

Shanfield, S. B., Mohl, P. C., Matthews, K. L., & Hetherly, V. (1992). Quantitative assessment of the behavior of psychotherapy supervisors. *American Journal of Psychiatry, 149*(3), 352–357.

Sklare, G., Thomas, D. V., Williams, E. C., & Powers, K. A. (1996). Ethics and an experiential "here and now" group: A blend that works. *Journal for Specialists in Group Work, 21,* 263–273.

Sleight, C. C. (1990). Off-campus supervisor self-evaluation. *Clinical Supervisor, 8*(1), 163–171.

Smith, J. D., & Agate, J. (2004). Solutions for overconfidence: Evaluation of an instructional model for counselor trainees. *Counselor Education and Supervision, 44,* 31-43.

Stadler, H. A., Willing, K. L., Eberhage, M. G., & Ward, W. H. (1988). Impairment: Implications for the counseling profession. *Journal of Counseling and Development, 66,* 258–260.

Stoltenberg, C. (1981). Approaching supervision from a developmental perspective: The counselor complexity model. *Journal of Counseling Psychology, 31,* 63–75.

Stoltenberg, C. D. (2005). Enhancing professional competence through developmental approaches to supervision. *American Psychologist, 60,* 855–864.

Stoltenberg, C., & Delworth, U. (1987). *Supervising counselors and therapists: A developmental approach.* San Francisco: Jossey-Bass.

Supervision Interest Network, Association for Counselor Education and Supervision. (1990). Standards for counseling supervisors. *Journal of Counseling and Development, 69,* 30–32.

Tracey, T. J., Ellickson, J. L., & Sherry, P. (1989). Reactance in relation to different supervisory environments and counselor development. *Journal of Counseling Psychology, 36,* 336–344.

Veach, P. M. (2001). Conflict and counterproductiveity in supervision—When relationships are less than ideal: Comment on Nelson and Friedlander (2001) and Gray et al. (2001). *Journal of Counseling Psychology, 48,* 396–400.

Wise, P. S., Lowery, S., & Silverglade, L. (1989). Personal counseling for counselors in training: Guidelines for supervisors. *Counselor Education and Supervision, 28,* 326–337.

Wood, J. A. V., Miller, T. W., & Hargrove, D. S. (2005). Clinical supervision in rural settings: A telehealth model. *Professional Psychology: Research and Practice, 36,* 173–179.

Zakutansky, T. J., & Sirles, E. A. (1993). Ethical and legal issues in field education: Shared responsibility and risk. *Journal of Social Work Education, 29,* 338–347.

CHAPTER 5
WORKING WITH DIVERSITY

"The people I work with at the clinic are all so different than me. We listen to different music, we live in different neighborhoods, we talk differently. It's hard. It's kind of intimidating. Things I just take for granted don't connect somehow."

One of the great opportunities and challenges of internships is that you will encounter people who are different from you. Learning to understand and respond to those differences will be one of the central keys to your internship success and to your development as a professional.

BACKGROUND

Until relatively recently, helping professions and techniques developed from, and were largely directed by, a predominantly Western European/white American, male, college-educated, financially well-to-do perspective. With a few exceptions, this perspective was taken for granted and was applied in research, training, and treatment (Smedley & Smedley, 2005; Sue, Arredondo & McDavis, 1992). As a result, great numbers of people were left unserved or in many cases were disserved by our professions (Hall, 1997). For example, research by Bernal and Castro (1994) revealed that 46% of the training programs surveyed had no minority faculty, and 39% of accredited clinical psychology programs had no minority-related classes. Similar results were reported from a 1990 survey of doctoral-level clinical psychology training programs (Bernal & Castro, 1994). Further evidence of a scarcity of minority-related courses was offered by a 1995 survey by Mintz, Bartels, and Rideout (1995), who found that the numbers of institutions requiring such studies had still not increased substantially. What is more, the majority of students who had received training in minority counseling rated their training as mediocre (Mintz et al., 1995).

This limited training may help explain the general inadequacy of service deliveries to minorities (Rosado & Elias, 1993). Lack of multicultural training may also help account for results from studies described by Sue and Sue (1990), which showed that more than 50% of minority clients terminated therapy after just one contact with the therapist. Among clients who terminated early, lack of cultural competence on the part of counselors was shown by Constantine (2002) to be related to client dissatisfaction with their counseling.

Fortunately, in recent years the various professions have come to recognize the importance of multicultural competence. Arredondo & Perez (2006) offer an informative and insightful review of the history of this movement, while Smith et al. (2006) report on a meta-analytic study of multicultural education, reporting that overall the results of such efforts have been positive. All of the major helping professions now explicitly address issues of cultural awareness and sensitivity in their ethical codes. What is more, professional associations have also published specific guidelines for multicultural competencies and practice. Examples include the APA Guidelines on Multicultural Education, Training, Research, Practice and Organizational Change for Psychologists (APA, 2003), the NASW Standards for Cultural Competencies in Social Work Practice (2001), and the Multicultural Counseling Competencies and Standards (Sue, Arredondo, & McDavis, 1992). In addition, a host of books, specialty journals, and training programs have now developed to help promote research and training in cultural issues and practices.

REASONS FOR DIVERSITY TRAINING

Proctor and Davis (1994) cited three critical reasons for addressing issues of diversity in clinical practice: traditional segregation that limits the knowledge of different ethnic groups by persons outside that group, the growing percentages of non-white persons in the population, and the historical and present negative tensions that exist between groups.

Pedersen (1987) observed that, speaking strictly numerically, the Western view of the world is actually the minority perspective, but:

Despite that numerical reality, many social scientists, including psychologists, depend on textbooks, research findings, and implicit psychological theory based almost entirely on assumptions specific to European and American culture. These assumptions are usually so implicit and so taken for granted that they are not challenged even by broad-minded and insightful psychologists. (p. 16)

Sue and Sue (1990) argued that the negative effects of this self-centeredness are exacerbated by failure to appreciate the historical context of discrimination, injustice, and socioeconomic inequities that have been perpetrated against people from minority cultures or orientations.

The most recent census data (2001) indicate that traditionally underrepresented groups now comprise 25% of the U.S. population. Given this fact, professionals and interns who are not sensitive to cultural issues may be ill prepared to deal with clients of cultural backgrounds or ethnicity different from their own. Hall (1997) made a similar observation, noting that in many metropolitan areas 50% of the population already comprises persons of color, and that percentage may become the norm throughout the nation by the middle of this century. Hall went so far as to suggest that psychology is in danger of becoming "obsolescent" and may be guilty of what she referred to as "cultural malpractice."

Although the literature just described focused primarily on ethnic differences, the same principles apply to working with persons of differing economic means, religious beliefs, genders, sexual orientations, physical abilities, and geographic regions of the country (Delucia-Waack, 1996; La Roche & Maxie, 2003). To the extent that our personal experience has not afforded contact with people who differ in significant ways from ourselves and those we grew up with, and in the context of past and ongoing social tensions and prejudices, we may have difficulty understanding the experiences, strengths, needs, and perspectives of others.

During an internship, this reality was brought home to a student whose initial response to a discussion of diversity was to say:

> I think too much is made about race and all the other differences. We are all just people and if we all just treat everyone alike there wouldn't be all these problems. I'm not prejudiced myself and I try to treat everyone the same.

This student's comments were made in all sincerity; from her perspective, she believed she had achieved an understanding of how best to deal with differences. Several weeks into her internship, a journal entry revealed that she was beginning to gain deeper awareness of herself and others:

> I always thought that everyone was just the same and that I was not prejudiced at all. Working here I've started to understand that just because I think everyone is the same doesn't mean everyone else thinks that or everyone has had the same chances I have. I wonder what my life would be like if my family was as poor as the people I am working with. I always thought that people who were poor just didn't want to work hard. I think I was prejudiced and just didn't know it. Now I see this family working so hard and still not being able to afford the things I just take for granted. They

can't even take the kids to the doctor. I'm beginning to understand why they seem angry. I'm getting angry myself. It isn't fair but these people have to live with that every day and I get to go home to my comfortable dormitory. I'm starting to realize how sheltered I've been. This is opening my eyes and it isn't easy.

This student was coming to understand that one cannot simply dismiss diversity issues by saying they are unimportant or by "treating everyone alike." A much deeper awareness of ourselves and others is required, and the internship is a good place to start developing that awareness.

As professional organizations have come to recognize the importance of diversity, ethical and, in some cases, legal mandates for multicultural training have developed. In an extensive review of models and issues associated with multicultural training in the helping professions, Ridley, Mendoza, and Kanitz (1994) concluded that

> the issue of whether or not to include some form of MCT (multicultural counseling) is no longer open for debate. Graduate training programs must provide MCT. . . . With this proviso, concern is now focused on deciding what kind of MCT to offer. (p. 227)

While calling for such training, these authors cautioned that if the motivations for pursuing training in multicultural counseling are not carefully considered, the results may be counterproductive. Reluctant conformity to organizational standards can lead to half-hearted, symbolic gestures that lack substance or sincerity. Ridley, et al. (1994) also raised cautions about the potential for "paternalistic attitudes" affecting training. They warn against implying that nondominant cultural groups are weak or that white counselors in multicultural settings are somehow charitable benefactors who deserve the gratitude of the minority clients.

RESISTANCE TO DIVERSITY TRAINING

Despite the evidence and arguments that have been offered for studying multicultural differences, resistance to such training is quite common. Deal and Hyde (2004) offer an especially thoughtful discussion of this topic and view both anxiety and resistance to multicultural training in the context of broader developmental challenges facing trainees. Deal and Hyde identify three worries that emerge when students are faced with multicultural learning. The first worry pertains to the content of what students are learning, particularly as they are required to study the history and ongoing dynamics of oppression. A second fear is of self-revelation making the students feel "stupid" or "racist" or possibly discovering aspects of themselves that they were unaware of previously and would not be comfortable knowing. The third concern centers around how other students may react. In this context Deal and Hyde recognize that many students, particularly those who are new to these topics, are afraid they will "make a mistake" in what they say or that they will be subject to criticism or censorship by peers or faculty.

Perhaps in response to such worries, some students and, even more vehemently, certain faculty may protest the inclusion of multicultural issues by arguing that there is enough to learn about "basic" clinical skills without throwing additional variables into the equation. The argument is often made that we should focus on teaching basic skills first. Then, "if there is time at the end," we can consider how those skills apply to different groups.

A variation of this theme is the suggestion that the core therapy skills and theories should be taught in a required class, while issues of differences should be offered as an elective for those who are interested. Dobbins and Skillings (1991) described similar arguments from their students and note that "there are often institutional influences that foster the impression that multiculturality is somehow an ancillary specialty area" (p. 38).

Although such responses are presented as a logical rationale for why diversity issues should not or cannot be central to training, the arguments themselves illustrate the very problems that diversity training seeks to address. Indeed, such arguments sound remarkably like the "avoidant" identity described by Rowe, Bennet, and Atkinson (1994). In defining this type, which is discussed in more detail later in the chapter, Rowe et al. stated:

> Whereas members of visible racial/ethnic minority groups have little choice concerning their awareness of racial identity, White Americans have the option of minimizing the impact of racial awareness by dismissing the issue in various ways. . . . Whether these individuals find these issues merely inconvenient or actually anxiety arousing, their preferred method of responding is to ignore, minimize, or deny the existence of importance of the problematic issue. (p. 136)

Another manifestation of the avoidance of racial issues can be found in what has been called the "color-blind" approach to treatment and training. Proctor and Davis (1994) noted that this approach was once advocated as a way to account for therapist-client differences and treat people with equal regard as people. This is essentially the model that was initially advocated by the student described earlier, who believed "if we all just treat everyone alike there wouldn't be all these problems."

Although good intentions may underlie such statements, the color-blind approach tends to ignore a major part of people's lives and contributes to "unrealistic, abstract views of clients and their problems" (Proctor & Davis, 1994, p. 316). In an empirical study of the effects of a color-blind perspective, Burkard & Knox (2004) demonstrated that therapists who were less sensitive to racial and cultural differences in clients lives also scored lower on measures of empathy and offered differing causal attributions for the challenges faced by their clients. Pretending not to see differences may make the person who does

the pretending feel better, but it does not make the differences go away or solve the problem of how to deal with related issues in therapy or in society as a whole. Further, avoiding differences allows the person in power, in this case the helping professional or intern, to avoid the social issues that people of differing backgrounds must contend with on a daily basis.

Perhaps the greatest difficulty with approaches that minimize diversity stems from the implicit assumption that ideas and techniques developed primarily by one group of people would or should be helpful for people with vastly different gender, ethnic, cultural, class, and educational experiences. There is a certain irony to the fact that a field that emphasizes introspection and empiricism has managed for so long to neglect the biases inherent in its own theories and techniques.

Recognizing the anxiety and resistance that can be evoked by multicultural issues and training, Deal and Hyde (2004) emphasize the fundamental importance of creating a supporting and safe environment in which these issues can be discussed. Deal and Hyde suggest that instructors need to assess the developmental level of students (e.g., Stoltenberg, 2005), then help students understand that discomfort and risk-taking are inherent elements of clinical education. Whatever the source of discomfort, we must learn to deal with the topic and the discomfort effectively rather than through avoidance. Building on a developmental formulation, Deal and Hyde offer a matrix that lists developmental stages across affective, behavioral, and cognitive components, identifying how multicultural issues and training experiences relate to each level and component. If you find yourself encountering some unexpected difficulties or reactions to multicultural issues, it may be helpful to step back for a second and consider your own developmental level in general and as it pertains to multicultural issues specifically. To the degree that educational activities match with the developmental level of students on each of the three components, resistance is likely to be reduced and your learning will be more effective.

A REFORMULATION OF DIVERSITY

In a review of papers presented at a national conference on multiculturalism, Sue, Bingham, Porch-Burke, and Vasquez (1999) asserted that *multiculturalism* must include the broad range of significant differences (race, gender, sexual orientation, ability and disability, religion, class, etc.) that often hinder communication and understanding among people. Sue and colleagues believed this more expanded notion of multiculturalism might diminish the tendency of groups to feel excluded from the multicultural debate, find themselves in opposition to one another, and engage in a "who's more oppressed" game.

Pedersen (1991) offered a similar definition and argued that multiculturalism is not peripheral to counseling but should in fact occupy a central role:

> By defining culture broadly—to include demographic variables (e.g., age, sex, place of residence), status variables (e.g., social, educational, economic) and affiliations (formal and informal), as

well as ethnographic variables such as nationality, ethnicity, language, and religion—the construct "multicultural" becomes generic to all counseling relationships. (p. 7)

From this understanding, Pedersen (1991) observed that rather than being a barrier to counseling, as they have often been viewed, cultural issues can instead become central to the facilitation of effective clinical interventions.

I concur with Pedersen's (1991) ideas and with the expanded definition offered by Sue et al. (1999). This expanded view was also advocated by Hays (2001), who explored the many cultural influences that impact each of us, including clinicians and clients. By emphasizing diversity in teaching interaction skills we are not creating additional variables. Instead, we are raising fundamental issues that have until now been artificially subtracted from the picture. Rather than protesting the apparent addition of information, instructors, supervisors, and students should be studying how and why a topic so fundamental to education and clinical work was ignored or demeaned in the past. Understanding diversity is not a luxury, it is an essential:

> If a counselor is unable to work with those she or he is different from, with whom will that counselor be able to work? (Speight, Myers, Cox, & Highlen, 1991, p. 30)

STEPS TOWARD WORKING WITH DIFFERENCES

As we have seen, even the acknowledgment of diversity can be challenging and evoke anxiety and resistance. Still more difficult and exciting is the task of finding ways to work effectively with people from many different backgrounds. The best summary I have seen of the challenge before us as clinicians is provided by Wang and Sue (2005), who note that:

> On the one hand, some clinicians may be prone to overgeneralizations, racial mythology, and stereotyping because they overemphasize cultural influences at the expense of within-group heterogeneity. . . . On the other hand, other clinicians may decontextualize their clients by deemphasizing race and culture as relevant by treating them as generic humans or individuals in diagnostics and treatment planning. (p. 43)

The goal of multicultural counseling, and the goal of this chapter, is to help you avoid these two kinds of errors. Guidelines to help achieve those goals are provided in an influential paper by Sue, Arredondo & McDavis (1992). These authors began their analysis of multicultural competency in counseling with a three-characteristic by three-dimension matrix. The three characteristics they identified are counselors' awareness of their own assumptions and biases, understanding the worldview of the client, and developing culturally appropriate techniques and intervention strategies. For each of these characteristics the

three dimensions identified include beliefs and attitudes, knowledge, and skills (p. 481). The nine competency areas are each then elaborated upon in more detail, yielding a final total of 31 specific competencies.

The core principles elucidated by Sue, Arredondo, and McDavis are reflected in the previously mentioned counseling guidelines of the key associations. Although the specifics of the guidelines vary somewhat, they all share several elements in common. These common elements include self-awareness on the part of the therapist, knowledge and appreciation of the cultures of our clients, including within-cultural as across-cultural variations, an appreciation of historical issues and power dynamics that have accompanied issues of race and culture, development of specific culturally sensitive and relevant assessment and intervention skills, and finally, a commitment to organizational and social change. Let us consider each of these elements in more detail.

SELF-AWARENESS: KNOWING THE DIVERSITY WITHIN US

A number of authors (Locke, 1998; Sue & Sue, 1990; Toporek & Reza, 2001; Wintrob & Harvey, 1981) have recognized that awareness of self is a vital first element for therapists learning to work with clients whose backgrounds differ from their own. Consistent with these ideas, as a step toward developing your ability to work with differences, it can be extremely beneficial to think at length about your personal experience and perspective. Unless you have given careful thought to who you are, it is difficult to be sensitive to differences or similarities with clients.

Atkinson, Morten, and Sue (1993) pointed out that most discussions of counseling with "minority" clients assume that the counselor is from the majority group while the client is from a minority group. This assumption overlooks the increasingly common reality that it may well be the counselor who is from a minority group and the client from the majority. Another problem with the majority-minority distinction is that it overlooks cultural differences within these groups.

As an alternative to majority-minority distinctions, Atkinson et al. preferred the phrase "cross-cultural counseling," which, they suggested, "refers to any relationship in which two or more of the participants are culturally different" (p. 9). Similar to Pedersen's broad definition of multiculturalism, this terminology encompasses situations in which the counselor is from a minority group and the client from the majority. Cross-cultural counseling also includes counseling that crosses groupings based on economic factors, geography, religion, sexual orientation, and the like.

Anyone who has moved from one region of the country to another or from an urban to a rural community knows firsthand that great differences in cultural experience exist among people of apparently common ethnicity. Similar differences are encountered among people of different religions, educational backgrounds, sexual orientations, and positions of socioeconomic advantage. Failure to appreciate and adapt one's approach in response to such differences can only decrease the chances of successful interactions taking place.

Coleman (1997) took this a step further and pointed out that one must not only appreciate and understand ethnic and cultural differences per se, one must also appreciate differences in the ways individuals cope with those differences. Coleman hypothesized that conflicts in multicultural counseling relationships may develop either out of cultural differences or out of differences in how the therapist and client approach their differences. Thus, a counselor who believes it is important to deal directly and explicitly with cultural differences may unwittingly clash with a client who deals with differences by choosing to overlook them and believes that all people are alike.

The title of the present chapter, "Working with Diversity," reflects a belief that the issue of cross-cultural counseling is part of the broader matter of dealing with differences in counseling. In a way, the goal is to work through resistance to cross-cultural counseling by pointing out the undeniable reality that counselors must learn to work with people who are different from themselves. If this premise is accepted, then it follows that working with differences includes working with cultural differences. It also follows that counselors and interns must come to grips with such issues as racism, sexism, economic and social class, and other realities that cannot be ignored if they want to fully understand diversity and the experience of people from different backgrounds.

Echoing Pedersen's discussion of multiculturalism and emphasizing the importance of "internalized culture," Ho (1995) stated the matter well. "Those who do not know the culture of others do not really know their own" (p. 21).

EXERCISE: KNOWING YOURSELF IN RELATION TO DIVERSITY

This exercise is designed to help you become more aware of your own cultural and personal background and characteristics. Because this understanding is a first step toward understanding how you will interact with others, it is perhaps more important than anything else in this chapter. I encourage you to spend substantial time on the exercise and, if you feel comfortable and safe doing so, to discuss it with your peers and instructor.

The following list identifies certain personal and cultural characteristics that have a profound influence on how people understand the world and interact with others. For each characteristic, begin by describing yourself, then take some time to seriously consider how each aspect of yourself taken separately, and how all the aspects taken together, affect your understanding of yourself and others. Also give some thought to how these characteristics shape the assumptions you bring to your training as an intern. One way to enhance this understanding is to imagine how things you may have taken for granted about yourself are due at least in part to your ethnic or cultural background. For example,

you might ask yourself, "Because I have [pink/brown/black/red/yellow] skin, I have experienced . . ." Or, "Because my family's economic status was . . . I have experienced . . ." Another approach to enhance your understanding is to imagine how your life might be different if you had other characteristics. For example, you might consider, "If I were of a different culture . . ." "If my parents were very (poor/rich) I might . . ." "If I were a new immigrant I might experience . . ." As a final response to this exercise, you may want to discuss your own responses with a peer or other person. You may also find it helpful to discuss this with people who are much different from you in certain of the key areas identified.

1. My gender is _____, and this is how it influences my experiences and how I understand and relate to others.
2. My age is _____, and this is how it influences my experiences and how I understand and relate to others.
3. My physical appearance includes the following qualities (describe these as accurately as you can, and try to avoid oversimplifying or using racial terms):

   Skin:
   Hair:
   Facial features:
   Build:
   Other features:

   This is how those features influence my experiences and how I understand and relate to others:
4. The nationality and cultural background of my parents and grandparents are:

   My father's mother:
   My father's father:
   My mother's mother:
   My mother's father:
   My father:
   My mother:

   This is how the culture of my family influences my experiences and how I understand and relate to others.
5. With regard to economic resources, the family I was raised in was _____.
   This is how that background influences my experiences and how I understand and relate to others.
6. The religious orientation of my mother is _____.
   The religious orientation of my father is _____.
   This is how that background influences my experiences and how I understand and relate to others.
7. My mother's educational background is _____.
   My father's educational background is _____.
   This is how that background influences my experiences and how I understand and relate to others.
8. My own educational background is _____.
   This is how that background influences my experiences and how I understand and relate to others.
9. My physical health and abilities are _____.

This is how that background influences my experiences and how I understand and relate to others.

10. My sexual orientation is _____.
    This is how that background influences my experiences and how I understand and relate to others.
11. Other characteristics that have influenced my experiences and understanding of others are _____.

CONFRONTING OUR BIASES AND ACKNOWLEDGING OUR IGNORANCE

In the second edition of their book on counseling with people from different cultures, Sue and Sue (1990) wrote:

> As mental health professionals, we have a personal and professional responsibility to (a) confront, become aware of, and take actions in dealing with our biases, stereotypes, values, and assumptions about human behavior, (b) become aware of the culturally different client's world view, values, biases, and assumptions about human behavior, and (c) develop appropriate help-giving practices, intervention strategies, and structures that take into account the historical, cultural, and environmental experiences of the culturally different client. (p. 6)

Some interns come to training believing they have everything it takes to treat almost any client who comes to them. Others are not so confident, but very few are really aware of just how limited their own experiences or theories are. Carrillo, Holzhalb, and Thyer (1993) underscored this point by observing that even though students may believe themselves to be without prejudice, many are often unaware of certain beliefs and biases that will limit their empathy and effectiveness with people of different ethnic, cultural, economic, or other backgrounds.

Corvin and Wiggins (1989) stressed the importance of going beyond intellectual understanding to confront one's own intrinsic racism. This message was echoed with particular relevance to interns by Kiselica (1991), who described his own experiences in a multicultural internship:

> Questioning my ethnocentrism provoked me to recognize and confront my own racist behaviors, and this was a painful but necessary experience for me to grow even more as a person and professional. . . .
>
> By confronting my Eurocentrism, racist behaviors, and stereotypical thinking, I had a better sense of myself and how my foibles might impede the counseling process. By remaining cognizant of these imperfections during actual counseling sessions, I was able to prevent them from becoming barriers in my efforts to establish rapport with culturally different clients. (p. 29)

As Kiselica's (1991) description and the reports of other interns reveal, confronting one's own prejudice and racism is not an easy or pleasant task. Nevertheless, if one is to work with diverse clients, it is essential to be aware of personal biases and work to understand and overcome them.

EXERCISE

This intriguing, informative, and thought-provoking exercise was suggested to me by one of the reviewers for this edition. To complete the exercise, access the Web site for the "Implicit Association Test" at https://implicit.harvard.edu/implicit/. Once there, you will be given options to participate in a series of research-validated associations between specific items or words and images of people in different ethnic or other groups. I encourage you to select several of these tests and complete them, then read what your personal results suggest as well as what the experimental design and underlying theory are based on. I also encourage you, after taking these tests, to discuss them with your peers, especially, if you can, with peers from different groups to see how your responses compare. I would normally give you a bit more information about these tests here, but I am purposefully refraining from that in order to make the tests more interesting to you and the results more valid.

In recognition of the importance of cultural awareness, a number of instruments have been developed to assess the beliefs, knowledge, and skills of therapists and counselors in relation to working with persons of different ethnicities and cultures (e.g., Allison, Echemendia, Crawford, & Robinson, 1996; Sodowsky, Taffe, Gutkin, & Wise, 1994). Reviews of such instruments have been offered by Kocarek, Talbot, Batka, and Anderson (2001), Ponterotto, Rieger, Barrett, and Sparks (1994), and Carrillo et al. (1993). Zayas, Torres, Malcolm, and DesRosiers (1996) took a slightly different approach by surveying nonminority therapists to assess their definitions of ethnically sensitive therapy. Survey responses suggested that four overlapping dimensions could be identified. These were awareness of differences, knowledge of the client's culture, distinguishing between culture and pathology in assessment, and taking culture into account in therapy.

Based on principles incorporated in the instruments alluded to above, the exercise that follows is designed to encourage self-exploration of your preparedness to work with others from different backgrounds. In this exercise, you are invited to consider carefully and honestly the kinds of clients with whom you feel you have sufficient experience, knowledge, or understanding to interact in a way that will be genuinely helpful.

If you are like many of our interns, you may find that after completing the exercise you are unsure whether you should try to interact with anyone other than yourself. If that feeling emerges, do not despair. The first step toward learning is acknowledging ignorance. Following the exercise, there are concepts and suggestions to help build your awareness and abilities to work with differences.

The following list includes some of the many characteristics that distinguish individuals and groups from one another. Consider these and try to identify where your knowledge, understanding, or experience would enable you to understand accurately and relate to their experiences, concerns, thoughts, emotions, or needs in a helpful way. For each group you feel you know well enough to work with, give the reasons why. For example, what experiences, training, or personal knowledge do you have relating to this group?

Age groups:

Genders:

Appearance (e.g., skin color, facial features):

Ethnic or cultural background:

Generations lived in this country:

Economic status:

Education level:

Religion:

Sexual orientation:

Physical abilities or disabilities:
_____.

KNOWLEDGE AND APPRECIATION OF THE CLIENT'S PERSPECTIVE

The challenge of knowing one's self arise because we tend to take ourselves for granted and assume that we "just are who we are" and, further, that most other people are pretty much like us. The challenge of understanding others arises because we have not lived the lives of others. We do not know what they have experienced and why, we have not "walked a mile" in their shoes or their skin, we have not lived in their neighborhood or country, worshipped in their religion, been treated as they have been within the dominant culture. Given these realities, how can anyone hope to understand someone who is different?

THE HISTORICAL CONTEXT MUST BE ACKNOWLEDGED

A good starting point for beginning to understand groups or individuals who are different than you is acknowledging your knowledge or ignorance of their history. However tolerant, open, understanding, or empathic therapists or interns might believe themselves to be toward others, those qualities cannot erase long histories of racial, class, gender, and other discrimination or oppression. If a client, an intern, or both are from a group that has experienced historical or ongoing discrimination or oppression, that fact will unavoidably influence the clinical interaction. Similarly, clients and interns from the dominant group in society will hold certain stereotypes, prejudices, and misconceptions that will influence their actions and interactions. These realities simply cannot be avoided, and they must not be denied (Comas-Diaz, 2000).

Another way to think of this issue is to consider that it would be irresponsible to treat a patient without some knowledge of his or her individual history. That is why one of the first tasks on intake of a new patient is to take a comprehensive medical, psychological, and social history. Taking this concept one step higher helps us understand that the individual's personal history takes place within a larger context which itself has a history. While each individual's experience will be unique, that uniqueness nevertheless stands as part of the overall context of society, and having a sense of the overall context can help one interpret how the individual's experiences developed and what they may mean.

During discussions of this subject, one often hears such statements as "What happened to those people in the past is not my fault, and I can't change it. We need to get on with what is happening today." The problem with such statements is their suggestion that it is possible to somehow erase all that has gone before and all that is in fact still going on, without dealing with the cognitive, emotional, economic, social, and other effects the past and present realities have created.

A colleague who teaches multicultural education suggests, in regard to history, that "we do not have to feel guilty for the past, but we must accept responsibility for the present" (R. Hardiman, personal communication, 1994). Her point is that those who feel overwhelmed with sorrow and guilt for what their ancestors did to others, as well as those who would prefer to ignore the past completely, need to find a realistic, constructive, and, importantly, a personal way to deal with the reality of the past within the context of the present. Others (Comas-Diaz, 2000) argue that it is incumbent on helping professionals to take an active role in the political process to help overcome existing racism and to correct the lingering effects of historical racism and prejudice.

Having advised that one must be aware of the historical context in working with difference, it is unfortunate but true that very few interns or professionals are well informed about the historical treatment of persons from minority groups. Most students know little about the history of struggles for civil rights, women's rights, economic justice, or other long-fought battles to achieve fairness and respect for all peoples. If you are interested in learning more about these topics (and I believe that as part of your training you should be interested), I encourage you to immerse yourself in works describing the history of the various groups with whom you work and the history of the struggles for equality and respect. In addition to nonfiction works, I also strongly recommend studying poetry and fiction as well as other cultural works, including art, film, music, dance, and religion. This recommendation was offered by Garcia and Bregoli (2000), who give particularly useful suggestions for incorporating literary sources to help prepare counselors for multicultural practice.

TERMINOLOGY MATTERS

As you seek to better understand people of diverse backgrounds, be especially mindful of terminology and the implicit meanings that certain words can carry. For better or worse, the words we use shape how we view and understand people and the world, and this shaping often occurs without our conscious awareness.

You may not have noticed it, but up to now in our discussion of diversity, I have not referred to the "race" of clients or therapists except in direct quotations or in the concept of discussion of racism as a social phenomenon. There is a good reason for this. In a special edition of the *American Psychologist,* Smedley and Smedley (2005), along with Helms, Jernigan, and Mascher (2005), reviewed the use of the term *race* as it evolved in general usage and in psychological treatment and research specifically. Earlier reviews by Johnson (1990) and by Dobbins and Skillins (1991) addressed many of the same issues, with all of these authors emphasizing that the terms *race, culture,* and *ethnicity* are often used interchangeably and without appreciation of their different meanings. These authors explain that *culture* refers to the externally acquired, as opposed to innate, set of beliefs, laws, customs, art, and other aspects of a society. *Ethnicity* is closely related to culture in that it describes external factors, including such things as geographic location, language, and other factors that may distinguish one group from another, sometimes within a common overall culture or nationality. For example, within the same nation there may be clusters of people of different religious beliefs, countries of origin, linguistic patterns, food, dress, and so on.

In comparison to these concepts, *race* has commonly been used to imply innate biologically based factors that distinguish people from others on such variables as skin, hair or eye color, and body type. These observed characteristics are then assumed to be associated with underlying abilities, tendencies, and personality traits. See, for example, Sternberg, Grigorenko, and Kidd (2005) for a discussion of the long-standing debate about race and intelligence.

Although the word race has been used widely in society and in research, it simply does not have scientific validity. As Smedley and Smedly (2005) explain the matter, racial distinctions fail on three counts: "they are not genetically discrete, are not reliably measured, and are not scientifically meaningful" (p. 16). Similarly, Helms et al. assert "Race has no consensual theoretical or scientific meaning in psychology, although it is frequently used in psychological theory, research and practice as if it has obvious meaning" (p. 27). Why is this important? It is important because, as Smedley and Smedley stated in the title of their article, "Race

as biology is fiction, racism as a social problem is real." Attention to terminology is not a matter of being "politically correct." Rather, it is a matter of precision and accuracy in our thinking and our approach to research and treatment.

When people speak of the "race" of an individual, there is an implicit assumption that (a) they have accurately identified some salient physical feature of the individual that (b) tells them something about that person's innate abilities, weaknesses, and tendencies, and may also tell something about the individual's acquired cultural or ethnic qualities. Dobbins and Skillings note that "There is an erroneous presumption of biopsychosocial precision" (p. 39) when people describe the race of an individual. Such erroneous understandings of race are accompanied by equally inaccurate assumptions that specific sets of cultural norms and values are associated with all members of a given race. Recognizing the lack of biological meaning and the tendency to confuse culture with race, Johnson (1990) noted, "Racial classifications draw attention to group factors, ignore the individual, and contribute to the maintenance of destructive racial stereotypes" (p. 43). Dobbins and Skilling (1991) drew the same conclusions regarding racial distinctions:

> For professional purposes, confusion of biological features and cultural predispositions draws attention away from more salient determiners of behavior such as values of the neighborhood, spirituality, the extended family and one's economic situation, which have very little to do with gene pools. (p. 39)

As a professional, one learns to understand the world differently and more precisely than one may have before. In the case of discussions about race, it is important for you to understand the imprecision of the term *race,* and to appreciate how its social applications in the past influenced people's lives, and, for that matter, professional practice. To avoid repeating the conceptual and practical mistakes and the social consequences that have accompanied the uncritical use of the term *race,* let me encourage you to follow the example of this text. Except in discussions that relate specifically to racial terms in the context of racism, or when referring to writings in which other authors have referred to race, I will avoid racial distinctions and will refer instead to differences in ethnicity, culture, or background, with culture defined broadly, as discussed before by Pedersen. This does not mean that one does not talk about physical features, such as skin color, and the impact they have on individuals within our society. It does mean that those features are not used as if they described a "racial" difference that has some specific innate significance or scientific meaning.

THE CURRENT CONTEXT MUST BE ACKNOWLEDGED

Although I have just emphasized problems with the concept of race this does not mean that society as a whole recognizes these problems or that racism (i.e., social differences relating to social perceptions of race) is not a very real problem. Awareness of the historical background of different people should be accompanied by equal awareness of the current social context relating to perceived racial, gender, cultural, and other differences that racism, sexism, homophobia, and economic injustice are not things of the past. They are ongoing, daily, and destructive realities in the lives of millions of people. Those who have not experienced this reality for themselves may not understand how it affects clinical interactions. As a result, they may be unaware that clinical interactions occur in a context that is far more complex than simply "two people talking together." Sue and Sue (1990) framed the matter in strong terms:

> Thus, the world view of the culturally different client who comes to counseling boils down to one important question: "What makes you, a counselor/therapist, any different from all the others out there who have oppressed and discriminated against me?" (p. 6)

A counselor or intern who is unaware that clients may harbor such questions is likely to experience frustration, failure, and hostility without understanding the underlying causes. Furthermore, interns who are unaware of the cultural context may misinterpret the meaning of a client's actions and may ascribe erroneous diagnoses or causal explanations. In other words, professionals or interns who do not appreciate the history and daily experience of clients from different cultures are not simply not part of the solution—they may unintentionally be part of the problem.

Exercise: Observing Yourself Dealing with Diversity at Your Internship

This is a challenging exercise because it asks you to go beyond the theoretical, intellectual understanding of diversity issues and look for subtle ways you might be adjusting, or failing to adjust, your behavior on a daily basis at your internship. During the next few days at your placement, take a mental inventory of the people who are there, including not only patients but staff at all levels. Then ask yourself honestly how your approach, behavior, impressions, cognitions, and emotional reactions to some of these people may be impacted by differences between yourself and them in terms of the issues we have been discussing. For example, are you more frightened, friendly, open, or intimidated with some patients or staff than with others? Do you have certain cognitions or formulate attributions about some people's behavior because of their skin color, language, or education? Now ask yourself the reverse questions. Do you think patients, other interns, or staff may be reacting to you differently because of diversity issues? Finally, and perhaps most difficult of all, take time to speak with some of the aforementioned people (e.g., selected patients, staff, or peers) and ask them the same questions, requesting that they be as open and honest as possible.

STRENGTHS MUST BE RECOGNIZED ALONG WITH PROBLEMS

Much of the literature on multicultural counseling has focused largely on issues of injustice and inequality between different groups. As emphasized, it is essential for interns to understand these issues, consider them in their clinical work, and work to influence them in society. At the same time, however, it is important to recognize that stereotypical images may prevent us from seeing beyond repression to understand and appreciate the cultural richness and heritage of different groups.

It is not uncommon for interns to have at least some sense of the disadvantages faced by other groups but little or no awareness of the personal and cultural strengths of others. The role of family, religion, school, art, and music may be very different for members of different groups. These and other institutions and traditions are essential to understand because they can help us to appreciate the client's experience and can provide invaluable resources to help clients deal with their presenting difficulties.

Some of the most profound experiences interns describe have occurred when they have been invited into the cultures of their clients. One young intern was working in a center serving refugees from Southeast Asia. After working with a client in a vocational training program for about a year, the intern was invited to attend a traditional celebration. The intern's journal reflected his reactions:

> I had the most amazing experience tonight. Until now I've really only seen one side of my clients. They have always been poor and struggling, and I've been the one helping them try to get work. Tonight I was the only person like me in the room, and everyone else was Vietnamese. I was the minority. I felt out of place and as though I was the one who was dressed funny. But everyone treated me with so much warmth and caring. There was all kinds of wonderful food (and a little not-so-wonderful to me), and music and entertainment and everyone was laughing and having a great time. I couldn't help but think how different the images from tonight were from the things I have always thought up 'til now.

Appreciating the richness of a client's ethnic and cultural experience is essential for many reasons. Seeing only the negative side or disadvantages of a person's background is likely to arouse pity, guilt, or other such emotions. But if that is all the therapist feels, it will be difficult to accord the client genuine respect as an individual. It will also be difficult to identify personal and cultural resources the client can draw from to help deal with problems.

This does not mean that we must return to the color-blind or people-are-all-alike approach. Rather, it means we must understand, to the greatest extent possible, the challenges and resources of clients and how these stem from and relate to the client's ethnic and cultural background and the larger social context in which they occur.

ETHNIC-IDENTITY DEVELOPMENT

While many authors have addressed how established cultural differences can conflict with therapy expectations, others have addressed the challenges that individuals from nondominant cultures face when they attempt to embrace their own ethnicity or cultural background. In recent years, increasing numbers of writers have argued for the importance of reclaiming one's ethnic heritage. Parham (1989), for example, expanding on concepts introduced by Cross (1971, 1978), described a theory of "psychological nigrescence," which sought to identify how the racial identity and awareness of black persons can change through their life cycle.

Parham's (1989) model details a progression through stages he identifies as "pre-encounter," "encounter," "immersion/ emersion," and "internalization." Parham stressed the importance of understanding

> how individuals' racial identity attitudes influence their mental health as well as how racial identity attitudes influence the dynamics (i.e., relationship) of the therapeutic process itself. (p. 215)

Parham (1989) cited research suggesting that

> development of pro-Black attitudes may be indicative of healthy psychological adjustment, whereas attitudes that denigrate oneself as a Black person and simultaneously promote wishes to be White may be psychologically maladaptive. (p. 215)

According to Parham (1989), counseling and therapeutic relationship issues will vary depending on where individuals are along the stages of identity awareness. For an extensive review and new perspectives on this theory, see Vandiver (2001).

Models similar to Parham's (1989) have been developed to describe Chicano identity development (Ruiz, 1990). They have also been developed within a more broadly applicable framework proposed by Sue and Sue (2003). The Racial/Cultural Identity Development Model (R/CID) of Sue and Sue is "a conceptual framework to aid counselors in understanding their culturally different client's attitudes and behaviors" (p. 95). This model views people as trying to "understand themselves in terms of their *own culture,* the *dominant culture,* and the *oppressive relationship* between the two cultures" (p. 96; italics in the original). Much like the models described by Parham (1989) and Ruiz (1990), the R/CID model of Sue and Sue (1990) identifies five stages of identity development. The first stage represents a denial of one's own culture, and the final stage reflects full awareness of one's own culture and its relation to the dominant culture. Sue and Sue labeled these stages "conformity, dissonance, resistance and immersion, introspection, and integrative awareness." They suggested that each stage is characterized by certain beliefs or attitudes, and understanding the stages and their attitudinal correlates can help counselors better understand and communicate with their minority

clients. Sue and Sue organized these key attitudes in terms of how individuals from minority groups view themselves, others of their same minority, others of other minorities, and individuals from the majority group. Toporek and Reza (2001) expanded on this model to add a personal, professional, and institutional context and by emphasizing that change in cultural awareness must include affective, cognitive, and behavioral learning and competence.

Each of the theories I have described takes a somewhat different approach to understanding ethnic-identity development, but they share the message that therapy interventions must take into consideration the individual's cultural background and identity development in relation to that background. Depending on where individuals are in their development and the specific attitudes and beliefs that correspond with that development, different issues will need to be addressed in the counseling relationship. Sue and Sue (1990) gave particular attention to this and stressed that understanding identity development is critical because the way minority individuals relate to counseling and counselors is likely to be influenced not simply by minority-group membership but by where the clients are in their own development in relation to that membership.

A MODEL OF WHITE IDENTITY DEVELOPMENT

In addition to addressing identity development among members of minority ethnic groups, we must consider identity development among the dominant group, because members of dominant groups tend to take their own position as a given and compare all other groups or perspectives with themselves.

Building on a model developed by Hardiman (1982), Corvin and Wiggins (1989) described an "antiracism" training model that focuses primarily on stages of white identity development. Corvin and Wiggins asserted that most whites tend, largely unconsciously, to accept their own background as inherently superior to others and view diversity as inherently inferior. To understand and go beyond this position, Corvin and Wiggins proposed a four-stage model of white identity development. The first stage, labeled "acceptance," typifies people who do not consider themselves racist but nevertheless have an implicit "assumption of Whiteness as 'the norm' " (p. 108). People at this stage make overt statements, such as "people are people," without realizing that this denies cultural differences and in the process reinforces unexamined assumption of white norms. As awareness of white cultural racism begins to grow, the second stage, "resistance," is entered. In this stage, the individual acknowledges racism as a problem, but does not fully acknowledge or recognize his or her personal racism.

In my work with students, an example of this second stage of development was provided by a young woman whose family owned an orchard and depended heavily on migrant labor to harvest the crop. Describing the migrant workers, the woman said:

> I'm not a racist, but I have to say the Mexicans who work for us really are a problem. You just can't rely on them. They're dishonest, they're drunk half the time, and they don't even take care of basic things like bathing. You should see the way they live.

As she continued, it was evident that this student believed she was simply making observations of fact, not prejudicial statements. However, when I began to ask pointed questions about the treatment of workers, the limited wages the workers are paid, exposure to pesticides, the historical failure of owners to provide adequate sanitation facilities, and the racist treatment the workers often receive in the region, she became rather defensive. At one point, when asked if she thought the workers wanted to live in the conditions she had described, the student said with a critical tone:

> A lot of them could afford to live better if they wanted, but they send most of their money back to their families in Mexico.

When it was suggested that she was now criticizing people for making sacrifices for their families, something that might otherwise be considered courageous and admirable, the student became quiet for a moment, then said hesitantly:

> That's true, isn't it. I never thought of it like that before. Maybe . . . maybe I am a little prejudiced. I'll have to think about this more.

The third stage in the model of Corvin and Wiggins, labeled "redefinition," involves the individual's discovery of his or her own identity, including greater awareness of personal values, some of which are racist. This stage also includes understanding the relative luxuries and advantages that have come from being white and reflecting on how those advantages relate to membership in the white system. Through reflection about their own role and values, individuals become better able to direct energies both toward personal change and toward working to change systems. An awareness of systemic and personal racism and a commitment to change that racism signify the final stage, "internalization." In this stage, individuals are aware of the complexity of their own "racial identity," have internalized a multicultural perspective, and have made a commitment to work with others to bring about change and influence racist systems.

Corvin and Wiggins (1989) viewed their stage model as a "diagnostic tool for assessing where one is in White identity development and where one has yet to go in combating racist behavior" (p. 113). From this premise, they recommended specific training goals and learning activities designed to meet individuals at each stage of identity development.

Other writers have also offered developmental models of white racial identity, most notably Helms (1984, 1990). Such models have also been criticized. Rowe et al. (1994) pointed out that most developmental models of white racial identity tend to

parallel models of identity development for minorities, but it is likely that the identity of majority culture members may differ greatly from that of minorities.

These authors also asserted that the developmental sequence and directionality of white identity models are "imposed" movements from a racist to nonracist identity that are assumed in developmental models but are by no means a biological or social given. As an alternative to the developmental model, Rowe et al. (1994) proposed that white identity can better be described according to "types," defined according to the kinds of racial attitudes that tend to go together. One example is the avoidant type, which characterizes people who prefer to avoid ethnic issues, including the ethnicity of others as well as their own. Other types include dominative, which is characterized by a "strong ethnocentric perspective, which justifies the dominance of racial/ethnic minority peoples by the majority culture" (p. 137), and conflictive, which opposes overt discrimination but would also be likely to oppose programs designed to reduce covert discrimination.

According to this model, racial attitudes and identities do not change because of a developmental process, but "as a result of experiences that cause dissonance in the person's cognitive structures or schemas" (p. 135).

Whether one agrees with a developmental pattern or finds the model of Rowe et al. (1994) more appealing, both approaches provide useful perspectives from which to view ethnic awareness and identity among members of the majority culture. Further, because it is important to be aware of both one's own personal cultural identity and that of clients, interns are encouraged to reflect on models of majority and minority identity. The following exercise invites you to explore your own ethnic and cultural identity and your reactions to where others might be in their identity development or type.

EXERCISE: PERSONAL CULTURAL IDENTITY

The preceding discussion described models of identity for individuals from majority and minority cultures. To make this more real, this exercise explores two issues. First, in relation to these models, where would you place yourself along the stages of development, or how would you describe your identity type? Second, if you were interacting with a person from a culture or ethnicity different from your own, which stages of his or her development or which identity type might be easiest and which most difficult for you to deal with, and why? This exercise will be most effective if you discuss your reactions with peers whose ethnicity or cultural experiences are different from your own.

DEVELOPING CULTURALLY SENSITIVE AND RELEVANT SKILLS

As if it were not enough to challenge students to better understand their own backgrounds and those of others, we must now confront another difficult reality: Many fundamental principles that underlie the leading techniques of treatment and assessment are antithetical to the values and practices of people from different cultures.

We need not look far for an example. The structure of the typical therapy interaction is, if one thinks about it, a rather strange arrangement. Two or more individuals who have not formerly known one another get together and talk about the most intimate details of one of the individual's lives. The strangeness is compounded by the assumption that part of the purpose of the interaction is to help one of the people become aware of, understand, and modify things that are not even accessible to that person's own consciousness. Strangeness can be transformed into harmfulness when the assumptions of a therapy model imply that an oppressed person's problems are the sole result of intrapsychic processes, with no attention to the social pressures and challenges the person faces (Priest, 1991).

Even for people from the dominant culture and social classes, the structure and theories of psychotherapy are often a difficult adjustment. For those from other cultures, therapy may seem inherently foolish, crazy, or perhaps even harmful. If an intern who takes the dominant models and theories of treatment for granted sits down with someone from another culture and expects the client to find the interaction perfectly normal, the intern and the client are probably headed for an impasse.

Various authors have described how Western models of therapy conflict with the values and traditions of other cultures. For example, Pedersen (1987) listed ten common assumptions reflecting cultural bias in counseling. Included among these were assumptions about what constitutes normal behavior, the emphasis on individualism and independence, neglect of support systems, linear thinking, neglect of history, and a focus on changing individuals rather than systems.

Sue and Sue (1990) identified comparable issues, noting that even fundamental assumptions about counseling, such as verbal and emotional expressiveness, the value of insight, cause-and-effect orientations, and the process of communication itself, may differ across cultures. Sue and Sue also addressed the possibility that not only the techniques of counseling but also the goals may not be compatible across cultures. They delineated four conditions that may apply to culturally different clients.

The ideal situation is one in which the therapist uses culturally appropriate treatment processes to help the client achieve culturally appropriate treatment goals. In contrast to this condition are situations in which processes are culturally appropriate but the therapy goals are not, situations in which the goals are culturally appropriate but the processes are not, and, finally, but all too commonly, situations in which neither the goals nor the therapy processes are culturally appropriate.

A somewhat different approach to this issue was proposed by Ibrahim, who emphasized the importance of worldviews in understanding cultural differences in counseling. Ibrahim and Kahn (1987) developed an instrument to assess worldviews in relation to assumptions about human nature, social relationships, nature, time, and activity orientation. Ibrahim suggested that to better match treatment approaches to the client, the first step in counseling should involve understanding the client's worldview and cultural identity.

While the models that have been described here are proposed as general guides to cross-cultural counseling, examples of differences in cultural assumptions and worldviews have also been discussed in relation to specific cultural groups. For example, Heinrich, Corbine, and Thomas (1990) reviewed differences among Native American people and their reactions to counseling. Recognizing that there are more than 300 different nations and equally as many different cultures among Native Americans, these authors explained that many Native Americans who are treated by psychotherapists may experience the therapist's expectations for self-disclosure to be "intrusive and inappropriate." On the other hand, differences in attitudes toward time, a cultural value of silence, and models of health may be misinterpreted by therapists as indications of resistance, defensiveness, or noncompliance.

EXERCISE

In light of the four possible conditions identified by Sue and Sue (1990) and some of the cultural differences just described, select one or two of your preferred therapy models or techniques and consider how these might conflict with the values or traditional practices of people from other cultures. How might the goals you take for granted in therapy conflict with the cultural values of someone from a different background? If possible, after thinking about this for yourself, discuss the matter with someone from a different culture to hear his or her impressions and ideas.

THE CULTURALLY SENSITIVE COUNSELOR

It would be possible to go on to list many potential clashes between therapy assumptions and cultural values for Hispanic clients (Ponterotto & Casas, 1987), African American families (Wilson & Stith, 1991), Asian American clients (Leong, 1986), and many other cultural groups. For examples of specific issues and techniques as applied to 21 different and diverse client groups, see the outstanding text by Lee, *Multicultural Issues in Counseling* (2006).

The question this literature raises is: How can one possibly know everything there is to know to work with people from different cultural backgrounds? What is more, how can helping professionals make therapeutic use of the self as a tool in therapy when the self of the patient has been influenced by so many cultural factors the therapist has not experienced (Greene, Jensen, & Jones, 1996)? As Speight et al. (1991) acknowledged:

> Counselors-in-training have the insurmountable task of memorizing recipes for each of the cultural, racial, and ethnic groups

(including the "exotics"). How many pages would such a cook-book require to address each of these groups? (p. 30)

A related concern was raised by Walker and Staton (2000), who challenged the notion of teaching and testing specific facts as a measure of multicultural competency. Walker and Stanton argued that efforts to define competency based on memorized facts have the potential to give a false sense of competency by equating it with memorized knowledge rather than with developed understanding and skills. What is more, they expressed concerns that this approach risks promoting stereotypes in the attempt to counter the stereotyping process.

Several responses to this issue have been proposed. One approach that is often recommended is to seek a match between client and counselor. According to this approach, counselors would come from the same cultural background as the client and would, presumably, be aware of, and sensitive to, the client's cultural experience. In an empirical study of this model, Wintersteen, Mensinger, and Diamond (2005) reported that matched therapist/patient pairs generally had higher retention rates in adolescent treatment programs as compared to unmatched pairs. Patient ratings of therapeutic alliance were unrelated to racial matching in this study, but therapists in mismatched dyads reported lower ratings of therapeutic alliance.

In contrast to the findings just described, a meta-analytic review of ten different studies of racial-ethnic matching for African American and Caucasian American clients and clinicians showed no significant differences between matched and unmatched dyads (Shin et al., 2005). In a very thorough review of the issue, including the various methodologies and shortcomings in research designs, Karlsson (2005) reported that matching research yielded inconclusive results, with most studies suggesting that matching between therapist and patient does not affect therapeutic outcomes. Karlsson emphasized however, that for certain patients and therapists, matching may indeed be important, but such individual effects could easily be obscured by data gathered from multiple therapists and patients.

Despite the likelihood of benefits for certain individuals, it is seldom possible from a practical perspective to have on staff members of all the various cultures that might be served by a given agency. A second problem, as discussed earlier in this chapter, is that categorizing individuals is neither a simple nor a necessarily desirable process. Speight et al. (1991) pointed out:

> The problem with the matching model . . . is that individuals cannot be categorized so simply. For instance, who would be the best counselor match for a Puerto Rican lesbian, an African American gay man, or a multiracial woman? And what if age, religion, language, physical/mental challenge, acculturation level, generational status, identity development, or socioeconomic status were factored into the matching model? (p. 30)

Ho (1995) made a similar point, cautioning that efforts to focus on group characteristics could make counselors vulnerable to overgeneralizing and stereotyping.

Faced with such complexities, interns and experienced therapists alike may be tempted to throw up their hands and declare that it is not possible to serve everyone. The issues are simply too complex to solve, so let's go on just as we have before and treat everyone alike. Understandable though this reaction might be, therapists can deal more constructively with complex cultural issues and enhance substantially their work with individuals from different cultures (Lee, 2006; Hansen, Pepitone-Arreola-Rockwell, & Greene, 2000; La Roche & Maxie, 2003; Proctor & Davis, 1994; Yutrzenka, 1995).

CULTURALLY SENSITIVE INTERVENTION APPROACHES

Diversity exists not only across cultures but also within cultures. Therefore one should be careful about offering specific recommendations for therapy approaches with members of specific cultures. I have found that a more useful approach is to describe a model for how one might develop and evaluate specific counseling techniques for specific cultures.

CULTURE-SPECIFIC COUNSELING

Despite all that has been written about the differences between and within cultures, attempts to teach students to work with individuals from other cultures have tended to focus on how the predominant counseling and psychotherapy approaches can be adapted to serve people from other backgrounds. While it is probably preferable to adapt therapy to match clients rather than trying to force clients to match the therapy, adapting established methods may still fail. Nwachuku and Ivey (1991) pointed out that the very notion of adapting existing techniques begins with the acceptance of the cultural bias inherent in Western traditional approaches.

As an alternative, Nwachuku and Ivey (1991) described a model for generating "culture-specific" counseling theories and methods. Instead of adapting dominant therapy models to a culture, culture-specific approaches begin by trying to understand the culture's existing ways of helping:

> Culture-specific counseling asks such questions as "How does a particular culture view the helping relationship?" "How do they solve problems traditionally?" "Are there new specific counseling skills and ways of thinking that make better sense in the frame of reference of the culture than typical Euro–North American systems?" (p. 107)

To answer these questions, Nwachuku and Ivey (1991) began by asking individuals from the specific culture to examine their own culture and describe its values and helping styles. Based on this information, they developed training materials to teach counselors about the cultures, cultural values, behaviors, and traditional helping methods. Their research demonstrated that this approach modifies both the thinking and behavior of trainees to bring them more in line with the cultural norms. Nwachuku and Ivey suggested that similar procedures could be used to develop culture-specific training for other cultures.

EXERCISE: EXPLORING CULTURE-SPECIFIC STRATEGIES

To enhance your awareness of culture-specific counseling strategies and the helping models within cultures, select your own culture and, in consultation with others, reflect on its traditional helping models. Try to identify some principles or techniques that would help you advise others about what to consider in working with your culture. Then select a culture with which you are relatively unfamiliar and ask a member of that culture to explore with you that culture's helping models and goals. Again, with the person from that culture, try to identify principles or techniques that would help you advise others about what to consider in working with the other person's culture.

SELF-ASSESSMENT AND A PLAN FOR DEVELOPING COMPETENCIES

Knowing about the importance of multicultural awareness and competencies does not in itself make one aware or competent. Hansen et al. (2006) studied the degree to which the actual activities of practitioners corresponded to the values they reported regarding multicultural psychotherapy. Their results contained both good news and discouraging news. On the positive side, almost all therapists reported that they often or very often engaged in efforts to respect the client's worldview, tried to be aware of their own personal and social biases, sought to establish rapport in "racially/ethnically sensitive ways," and considered the impact of race/ethnicity in diagnoses. On the other hand, 42% of the sample of psychotherapists had not implemented a professional development plan to enhance their competence in multicultural issues, 39% rarely or never sought culture-based case consultations, and 27% said they rarely or never referred clients to providers who were more qualified. More broadly, Hansen et al. reported that for 86% of the items which they identified as being recommended multicultural competencies, their respondents "did not always practice what they believed to be important" (p. 69).

Several key lessons can be drawn from these findings. First, it is not enough to simply study issues in the abstract, one must have a concrete plan for applying what one has studied and one must be diligent in that application. Hansen et al. suggest the use of their research checklist as a means of self-assessment for practitioners to evaluate the degree to which their personal practices correspond to recommended competencies. Roysircar (2004) offers a self-appraisal checklist combined with group and individual activities to enhance awareness of and competence in dealing with cultural issues. An alternative assessment device, the Multicultural Competence Inventory, was described by Green and colleagues (2005).

I encourage you to actively engage in self-assessment activities and to establish specific plans and programs for further enhancing your competencies. I also encourage to put in place a mechanism for ongoing monitoring to periodically evaluate areas in which your own or your organization's clinical activities may fall short of recommended competencies and practice guidelines.

Like all areas of professional development and practice, multicultural competence is not something one simply acquires and then maintains for life. Rather, it is an ongoing process requiring continued study, training, assessment, and supervision. In recent years, numerous books, special issues of journals, and individual articles have been written about working with clients from different populations. In addition, journals are now being published that focus specifically on diverse populations. Examples include the *Journal of Multicultural Counseling and Development, Journal of Black Psychology, International Journal of Intercultural Relations, Journal of Gay and Lesbian Social Services,* and *Journal of Multicultural Social Work.* I strongly encourage you to consult these resources as a regular part of your professional study and to seek out specific opportunities for training workshops and for supervision as part of your internship and your future professional practice.

CULTURAL AND ORGANIZATIONAL CHANGE

The final element of multicultural competence involves working within one's organizational setting and beyond to bring about greater sensitivity to diversity issues. This task is not always easy, and it requires sustained effort. Tori and Ducker (2004) described a multiyear initiative to enhance inclusion of multicultural issues and training in a graduate training program. Elements of this effort included outreach to increase minority representation among all campus groups, specific training for faculty in faculty meetings and through continuing education, and requiring students to take courses and experiential activities to increase their intercultural awareness.

Comparable initiatives were undertaken by Fouad (2006), who identified seven critical elements for a "multiculturally infused curriculum." These elements include making an explicit statement of purpose, actively recruiting and retraining students and faculty from diverse populations, reviewing course content for multicultural infusion, and annual evaluations of student cultural competence. Other authors, such as Resnick (2006), have described efforts to infuse multicultural awareness and skills in counseling centers and other applied settings. All of these authors report that their efforts yielded positive gains, but they also describe a number of challenges and room for further improvements.

Beyond academic and clinical settings, I believe that members of our professions also have a unique role to play in contributing to broader social awareness and change. The issue of political involvement is addressed in more detail in Chapter 10, but for the present let me emphasize that multicultural awareness does not simply involve studying historical issues of discrimination or injustices. Those issues continue to be real and present today, and they continue to impact the lives of our clients as well as our own. Contributing your professional skills and insights, along with your time and effort, can help bring about changes today and for the future.

SUMMARY

Dealing with issues of diversity can be one of the most challenging tasks undertaken by students and interns. There are no simple answers, the issues can strike at the core of who we are, and they will sometimes touch sensitivities or biases that we did not know existed and that may be uncomfortable. In spite of this difficulty, understanding these issues and making that understanding part of our training and our clinical practice is necessary clinically and mandated ethically.

As discussed in this chapter and by numerous other authors, the key starting point is understanding your own background and perspective, including how you may have taken your own cultural identity for granted and how you may have developed certain attitudes or beliefs about others along the way. Then, as you develop your skills as a counselor, I would encourage you to integrate cultural awareness, knowledge, and skills into that development as an essential part of how you think and act, not as an add-on or sidebar to the rest of your training.

Part of this process of integration involves purposeful study of literature in the field with as much commitment as you would give to studying therapy techniques, assessment tools, theories of personality, and other core topics. Beyond academic studies, being open to and seeking out interactions with people of different backgrounds, and really listening to their personal stories, is absolutely essential to translating the intellectual content into visceral, affective understanding.

Finally, keep in mind that the insights you gain through this work will have broader applications to the rest of your life and to society beyond your clinical training and work. It is not just you who must learn more about these issues, it is our society as a whole. The more you understand about yourself and about diversity, the more you will be able to play a constructive role in the broader dialogue.

REFERENCES

Allison, K. W., Echemendia, R. J., Crawford, I., & Robinson, W. L. (1996). Predicting cultural competence: Implications for practice and training. *Professional Psychology: Research and Practice, 27,* 386–393.

Arredondo, P., & Perez, P. (2006). Historical perspectives on the multicultural guidelines and contemporary applications. *Professional Psychology: Research and Practice, 37,* 1–5.

Atkinson, D. R., Morten, G., & Sue, D. W. (Eds.). (1993). *Counseling American minorities* (5th ed.). Dubuque: Brown.

American Psychological Association. (2003). Guidelines on multicultural education, training, research, practice and organizational change for psychologists. *American Psychologist, 58,* 377–402.

Bernal, M. E., & Castro, F. G. (1994). Are clinical psychologists prepared for service and research with ethnic minorities? Report of a decade of progress. *American Psychologist, 49,* 797–805.

Burkard, A.W., & Knox, S. (2004). Effect of therapist color-blindness on empathy and attributions in cross-cultural counseling. *Journal of Counseling Psychology, 51,* 387–397.

Carrillo, D. F., Holzhalb, C. M., & Thyer, B. A. (1993). Assessing social work students' attitudes related to cultural diversity: A review of selected measures. *Journal of Social Work Education, 29,* 263–268.

Coleman, H. L. K. (1997). Conflict in multicultural counseling relationships: Source and resolution. *Journal of Multicultural Counseling and Development, 25,* 195–200.

Comas-Diaz, L. (2000). An ethnopolitical approach to working with people of color. *American Psychologist, 55,* 1319–1325.

Constantine, M. G., (2002). Predictors of satisfaction with counseling: Racial and ethnic minority clients' attitudes toward counseling and ratings of their counselors' general and multicultural counseling competence. *Journal of Counseling Psychology, 49,* 255–263.

Corvin, S., & Wiggins, F. (1989). An antiracism training model for white professionals. *Journal of Multicultural Counseling and Development, 17,* 105–114.

Cross, W. E. (1971). The negro to black conversion experience: Towards a psychology of black liberation. *Black World, 20*(9), 13–27.

Cross, W. E. (1978). The Cross and Thomas models of psychological nigrescence. *Journal of Black Psychology, 5*(1), 13–19.

Deal, K. H., & Hyde, C. A. (2004). Understanding MSW student anxiety and resistance to multicultural learning: A developmental perspective. *Journal of teaching in social work. 24,* 73–86.

Delucia-Waack, J. L. (1996). Multiculturalism is inherent in all group work [Editorial]. *Journal for Specialists in Group Work, 4,* 218–223.

Dobbins, J. E., & Skillings, J. H. (1991). The utility of race labeling in understanding cultural identity: A conceptual tool for the social science practitioner. *Journal of Counseling and Development, 70,* 37–44.

Fouad, N. A. (2006) Multicultural guidelines: Implementation in an urban counseling psychology program. *Professional Psychology: Research and Practice, 37,* 6–13.

Garcia, B., & Bregoli, M. (2000). The use of literary sources in the preparation of clinicians for multicultural practice. *Journal of Teaching in Social Work, 20*(1/2), 77–102.

Green, R. G., Kitson, G., Stern, M. K., Leek. S., Bailey, K., Leisey, M., Chambers, K., Vadas, K., Claridge, R., Walker, K., & Jones, G. (2005). The multicultural counseling inventory: A measure for evaluating social work student and practitioner self perceptions of their multicultural competencies. *Journal of Social Work Education, 41,* 191–207.

Greene, G. J., Jensen, C., & Jones, D. H. (1996). A constructivist perspective on clinical social work practice with ethnically diverse clients. *Social Work, 41,* 2.

Hall, C. C. I. (1997). Cultural malpractice: The growing obsolescence of psychology within the changing U.S. population. *American Psychologist, 52,* 642–651.

Hansen, M. D., Randazzo, K. V., Schwartz, A., Marshall, M., Kalis, D., Frazier, R., Burke, C., Kersher-Rice, K., & Norvig, D. (2006). Do we practice what we preach? An exploratory survey of multicultural psychotherapy competencies. *Professional Psychology:Research and Practice. 37,* 66–74.

Hansen, N. D., Pepitone-Arreola-Rockwell, F., & Greene, A. F. (2000). Multicultural competence: Criteria and case examples. *Professional Psychology: Research and Practice, 31,* 652–660.

Hardiman, R. (1982). White identity development: A process oriented model for describing the racial consciousness of white Americans. *Dissertation Abstracts International, 43,* 104A (University Microfilms No. 82–10330).

Hays, P. A. (2001). *Addressing cultural complexities in practice: A framework for clinicians and counselors,* Washington, DC: American Psychological Association.

Heinrich, R. K., Corbine, J. L., & Thomas, K. R. (1990). Counseling Native Americans. *Journal of Counseling and Development, 69,* 128–133.

Helms, J. E. (1984). Toward a theoretical model of the effects of race on counseling. *Counseling Psychologist, 12,* 153–165.

Helms, J. E. (Ed.). (1990). *Black and white racial identity: Theory, research and practice.* Westport, CT: Greenwood Press.

Helms, J. E., Jernigan, M., & Mascher, J. (2005). The meaning of race in psychology and how to change it. *American Psychologist, 60,* 27–36.

Ho, D. Y. F. (1995). Internalized culture, culturocentrism, and transcendence. *Counseling Psychologist, 23,* 4–24.

Ibrahim, F. A., & Kahn, H. (1987). Assessment of world views. *Psychological Reports, 60,* 163–176.

Johnson, S. D., Jr. (1990). Toward clarifying culture, race, and ethnicity in the context of multicultural counseling. *Journal of Multicultural Counseling and Development, 18,* 41–50.

Karlsson, R. (2005). Ethnic matching between therapist and patient in psychotherapy. An overview of findings, together with methodological and conceptual issues. *Cultural Diversity and Ethnic Minority Psychology, 11,* 113–129.

Kiselica, M. S. (1991). Reflections on a multicultural internship experience. Multiculturalism as a fourth force in counseling [Special issue]. *Journal of Counseling and Development, 70,* 126–130.

Kocarek, C. E., Talbot, D. M., Batka, J.C., & Anderson, M. Z. (2001). Reliability and validity of three measures of multicultural competency. *Journal of Counseling and Development, 79,* 486–496.

La Roche, M. J., & Maxie, A. (2003). Ten considerations in addressing cultural differences in psychotherapy. *Professional Psychology: Research and Practice, 34,* 180–186.

Lee, C. C. (2006). *Multicultural issues in counseling,* (3rd ed.). Washington, D.C.: American Counseling Association.

Leong, F. T. L. (1986). Counseling and psychotherapy with Asian-Americans: Review of the literature. *Journal of Counseling Psychology, 33,* 196–206.

Locke, D. C. (1998). *Increasing multicultural understanding: A comprehensive model* (2nd ed.). Newbury Park, CA: Sage.

Mintz, L. B., Bartels, K. M., & Rideout, C. A. (1995). Training in counseling ethnic minorities and race-based availability of graduate school resources. *Professional Psychology: Research and Practice, 26,* 3.

NASW. (2001). NASW Standards for Cultural Competence in Social Work Practice. (www.socialworkers.org).

Nwachuku, U. T., & Ivey, A. E. (1991). Culture-specific counseling: An alternative training model. *Journal of Counseling and Development, 70,* 106–111.

Parham, T. A. (1989). Cycles of psychological nigrescence. *Counseling Psychologist, 17,* 187–226.

Pedersen, P. B. (1987). Ten frequent assumptions of cultural bias in counseling. *Journal of Multicultural Counseling and Development, 15,* 16–24.

Pedersen, P. B. (1991). Multiculturalism as a generic approach to counseling. *Journal of Counseling and Development, 70,* 6–12.

Ponterotto, J. G., & Casas, J. M. (1987). In search of multicultural competence within counselor education programs. *Journal of Counseling and Development, 65,* 430–434.

Ponterotto, J. G., Rieger, B. P., Barrett, A., & Sparks, R. (1994). Assessing multicultural counseling competence: A review of instrumentation. *Journal of Counseling and Development, 72,* 316–322.

Priest, R. (1991). Racism and prejudice as negative impacts on African American clients in therapy. *Journal of Counseling and Development, 70,* 213–215.

Proctor, E. K., & Davis, L. E. (1994). The challenge of racial difference: Skills for clinical practice. *Social Work, 39,* 314–323.

Resnick, J. L., (2006). Strategies for implementation of the multicultural guidelines in university and college counseling centers. *Professional Psychology: Research and Practice, 37,* 14–20.

Ridley, C. R., Mendoza, D. W., & Kanitz, B. E. (1994). Multicultural training: Reexamination, operationalization, and integration. *Counseling Psychologist, 22,* 227–289.

Rosado, J. W., & Elias, M. J. (1993). Ecological and psychocultural mediators in the delivery of services for urban, culturally diverse Hispanic clients. *Professional Psychology: Research and Practice, 24,* 450–459.

Rowe, W., Bennet, S. K., & Atkinson, D. R. (1994). White racial identity models: A critique and alternative proposal. *Counseling Psychologist, 22,* 129–146.

Roysircar, G. (2004). Cultural self awareness assessment: Practice examples from psychology training. *Professional Psychology: Research and Practice,* (6), 658–666.

Ruiz, A. S. (1990). Ethnic identity: Crisis and resolution. *Journal of Multicultural Counseling and Development, 18,* 29–40.

Smith, T. B., Constantine, M. G., Dunn, T. W., Dinehart, J. M., & Montoya, J. A., (2006). Multicultural education in the mental health professions: A meta-analytic review. *Journal of Counseling Psychology, 53,* 132–145.

Smedley, A., & Smedley, B. D., (2006). Race as biology is fiction, race as social problem is real. *American Psychologist, 60,* 16–26.

Sodowsky, G. R., Taffe, R. C., Gutkin, T. B., & Wise, S. L. (1994). Development of the multicultural counseling inventory: A self-report measure of multicultural competencies. *Journal of Counseling Psychology, 41,* 137–148.

Speight, S. L., Myers, L. J., Cox, C. I., & Highlen, P. S. (1991). A redefinition of multicultural counseling: Multiculturalism as a fourth force in counseling [Special issue]. *Journal of Counseling and Development, 70,* 29–36.

Sternberg, R. J., Grigorenko, E. L., & Kidd, K. K., (2005). Intelligence, race, and genetics. *American Psychologist, 60,* 46–59.

Stoltenberg, C. D. (2005) Developing professional competence through developmental approaches to supervision. *American Psychologist, 60,* 855–864.

Sue, D., Bingham, R., Porch-Burke, L., & Vasquez, M. (1999). The diversification of psychology: A multicultural revolution. *American Psychologist, 54*(12), 1061–1069.

Sue, D. W., Arredondo, P., & McDavis, R. J. (1992). Multicultural counseling competencies and standards: A call to the profession. *Journal of Counseling and Development, 70,* 477–486.

Sue, D. W., & Sue, D. (1990). *Counseling the culturally different: Theory and practice* (2nd ed.). New York: Wiley.

Sue, D. W., & Sue, D. (2003). *Counseling the culturally different: Theory and practice* (3rd ed.). New York: Wiley.

Toporek, R. L., & Reza, J. V. (2001). Context as a critical dimension of multicultural counseling: Articulating personal, professional, and institutional competence. *Journal of Multicultural Counseling and Development, 29,* 13–30.

Vandiver, B. J. (2001). Psychological nigrescence revisited: Introduction and overiew. *Journal of Multicultural Counseling and Development, 29,* 165–173.

Walker, R., & Staton, M. (2000). Multiculturalism in social work ethics. *Journal of Social Work Education, 36*(3), 449–463.

Wilson, L. L., & Stith, S. M. (1991). Culturally sensitive therapy with black clients. *Journal of Counseling and Development, 19,* 32–43.

Wintersteen, M. B., Mensinger, J. L., & Diamond, G. S. (2005). Do gender and racial differences between patient and therapist affect therapeutic alliance and treatment retention in adolescents? *Professional Psychology: Research and Practice, 36,* 400–408.

Yutrzenka, B. A. (1995). Making a case for training in ethnic and cultural diversity in increasing treatment efficacy. *Journal of Consulting and Clinical Psychology, 63,* 197–206.

Zayas, L. H., Torres, L. R., Malcolm, J., & DesRosiers, F. S. (1996). Clinicians definitions of ethnically sensitive therapy. *Professional Psychology: Research and Practice, 27,* 78–82.

CHAPTER 6

CLINICAL WRITING, TREATMENT RECORDS, AND CASE NOTES

The increasing complexity of human lives and situations requires that clinicians be able to clearly express the meaning of their professional judgments so that others can understand and implement them appropriately. Capturing the concrete world by translating observations into narrative is thus a crucial skill for all clinicians.

Alter & Adkins, 2001, p. 496

WRITING SKILLS

Clinical writing is different from other writing you have learned. The purpose, style, subject matter, and format of clinical writing require a new set of skills in which very few students are trained during their undergraduate education. This chapter is designed to help you understand the process and content of clinical writing so you can begin to develop skills that will serve you throughout your academic and professional career.

One way to approach this topic is to assume that students have mastered basic writing skills and need only to focus on the unique aspects of clinical writing. My experience suggests that this assumption is sometimes valid, but more often than not students have trouble with clinical writing because they have yet to develop their general writing skills. Alter and Adkins (2001) reported that an assessment of first-year graduate social work students revealed fully a third who needed writing assistance, but just over half of those students took advantage of a program designed to improve their skills. The same authors (Alter & Adkins, 2006) found comparable results in a more recent study, with a quarter of students in this cohort lacking adequate writing skills. Key areas of deficit included the inability to craft an essay with a persuasive voice and sufficient details.

There is no reason to assume that the results would be more promising for any of the other helping professions. My experience shows that even when students have relative competency

in basic skills, they often need a great deal of assistance in adapting those skills to clinical applications. This is tremendously important because, as Alter and Adkins observed, the lives of clients can be "significantly diminished by social workers' inability to write well, or significantly enhanced by strong writing proficiency" (2001, p. 497).

Based on that experience and the importance of strong writing skills, this chapter offers suggestions both for improving your overall writing skills and for applying those skills to clinical uses. If your writing skills are already well established, you may want to skim the initial portions and spend more time on the later material. Most students will be well advised to read the whole chapter carefully. As Fischer (1994) observed, many of the principles of writing good reports are "commonsensical . . . but not yet commonplace."

WRITING CAN BE LEARNED

It is sometimes said that writing is a gift and cannot be taught. That statement is false. Writing, like any other skill, can be taught and learned by most people. This does not mean we will all win Pulitzer Prizes, but it does mean most students can learn to write reports and notes that are accurate, clear, and in a style consistent with professional standards. If you are fortunate enough to have developed good writing skills already, this chapter will help you adapt those skills to clinical writing. If writing has never been a strong point for you, take heart from the following anecdote.

The summer before my first year of graduate school, I spent two months hiking and climbing in the mountains near my family home in Colorado. Much of that time, I hiked alone, and I often went for several days without speaking, hearing, reading, or writing a word. The experience was therapeutic, but it also posed a problem when graduate school began. Among the requirements for all first-year students was a course in psychological assessment. The course involved learning to administer, score, and interpret the major psychological tests. The course also involved writing two lengthy assessment reports each week.

As an undergraduate, I was an average writer but received no specific training in clinical writing. After spending so much of the summer away from language, I found the task of writing in graduate school extremely difficult. In a time before word processing, I worked days on each report, typing, erasing, retyping, starting over, and finishing at 2:00 or 3:00 A.M. on the morning the report was due. To make erasures easier, I used specially treated erasable paper. To save money on correction fluid, I was tempted to buy a gallon of white interior latex wall paint and use it instead. At one point, when my manual typewriter kept skipping spaces between letters, I literally pitched it out our second-floor window.

Despite my best efforts, on embarrassingly frequent occasions reports were returned with huge red Xs or "NO!" covering the entire first page. With innate clinical skill, I sensed that these messages were a sign of dissatisfaction on the part of my professor. I was right. Indeed, midway through the semester I was told that if my writing did not improve I would have to retake the course or might even be dismissed. Faced with this disheartening news, I asked what I could do to improve my skills. The instructor replied that he did not know. He could teach assessment, but he could not teach writing. I would have to learn to write somewhere else.

The standard resolution to such stories is to conclude: "Looking back on the experience, it was probably very good for me." Without offering that cliché, I can say that as the result of my own difficulties in writing, I may have learned some things that will help readers of this book develop their skills more efficiently. Making these changes in your writing may also enhance your speaking skills. I begin with simple rules that apply to all writing, then proceed to discuss the specifics of clinical records and communications.

FOCUSING READING TO LEARN WRITING

One of the best ways to improve your writing is to change the way you read. Most of the time, when people read, they are interested primarily in the content of what they are reading. They want to know the news of the day, learn what the journal article concludes, or discover how a story turns out. This emphasis on content is a fine way to gather information, but it is not likely to improve your writing. For reading to help improve your writing, you must focus on structure and style, not just on the information. The focus of reading then changes from what the writing is about to how the piece is written.

A useful analogy may be to think about how a person who plays the violin will listen to a violin concerto much differently than a casual spectator with no aspirations of playing the instrument. The casual spectator merely enjoys the melody. The person learning to play attends closely to the technique of the musician.

Similarly, most people who watch movies are interested primarily in the story line, the characters, or perhaps the special effects. Students of film, however, understand the importance of how the movie is made, what camera angles are used, how is the lighting constructed, what are the editing transitions, and for each of these elements, what the director was hoping to achieve.

If you want to learn how to write clinical reports, a good place to begin is by reading reports others have written. When you do this, remember to change your focus. Merely reading the content of other reports will tell you little about how to write about clients you might see yourself. What really matters is the structure and style of the reports. The specific content will change from client to client, but you can use structure and style again and again.

As an exercise to illustrate the distinction between content and style, consider the following sentence pairs. The contents of each pair are essentially the same, but the sentences differ in style and structure. The differences are intentionally subtle, and you are not told which is "better." Your task is to note the differences and give some thought to how they communicate information. You may also want to try rewriting the sentences yourself to see if you can improve them in some way. I will discuss these sentences further in a moment.

EXERCISE

SENTENCE PAIRS

1. A. During the interview, the client said that he had never before been seen in therapy by a therapist.
   B. The client indicated no previous experience in therapy.
2. A. Test results suggest the presence of mild to moderate depression, anxiety, and concerns about family matters.
   B. According to the results of the test, there is evidence of depression in the mild to moderate range, along with anxiety and apparent concerns about issues relating to family.
3. A. William Smith is an affable, energetic, 75-year-old male, who arrived neatly attired in a dark gray suit, spoke openly about his presenting concerns, and expressed a willingness to "do whatever it takes to get going again." Mr. Smith stated that he came to therapy out of concern that his sex life has begun to decline from a frequency of five to three times per week.
   B. William Smith is a 75-year-old male with a presenting problem of decreased sexual performance. At the time of the interview, he was well dressed and groomed and appeared to be well motivated.

PRACTICE AND FEEDBACK

Writing, like any other skill, is learned through practice, but practice alone is not enough. One also needs feedback and constructive criticism. Without feedback, there is a risk of practicing mistakes rather than learning new skills. As an intern, you have access to at least three sources of feedback about your writing. Your peers, supervisor, and course instructor can all offer input about both the style and content of your clinical writing. I encourage you to take advantage of each of these resources, because they will offer different perspectives, and because you may find it easier to work with one person rather than another. In my own experience, when my instructor was unable to help with writing, fellow graduate students were the most valuable source of feedback. Indeed, had it not been for their help, I might not have completed my degree. Later, supervisors at several internship placements offered further assistance. The importance of feedback continues to this day as colleagues, editors, and students offer their comments and criticisms. Indeed, before each new edition of this book, three to five reviewers offer extensive critiques and suggestions. This is not always easy to receive, but it is tremendously helpful, and many of the suggestions have made this edition better than the ones that preceded it.

Just as you must read differently to improve your writing, you must also seek and accept a different kind of feedback. When people ask for comments about what they have written, they often ask with the hope of receiving positive statements. "Looks fine to me," "Very good," "Nice work," and so on, can help us feel good, but such comments do nothing to improve our writing. To make feedback productive, you must be willing to invite and accept blunt criticism and suggestions. Compliments are important, but we learn more by discovering mistakes and correcting them. One student expressed this well when he circulated a draft of his report to several peers with a cover note that said, "Do me a favor and be as critical as you can. Rip this apart. I mean it. I need your honest criticism and suggestions."

Because people are used to asking for and giving only general and positive comments, you may need to take the initiative to ask for more specific and critical suggestions. The most important step is to go beyond global "gradelike" statements and solicit comments about specific parts of what you have written. For example, rather than simply asking people to read your work and tell you what they think of it, ask someone to read each sentence or paragraph and tell you how the writing could be clearer or more succinct. Invite your readers to suggest alternative ways of expressing what you have written. You may even ask them to write the same information in their own words, then compare your work and theirs to see how each might be improved. I often instruct students to exchange their reports and offer one another criticism. With students' permission, I read reports aloud in class anonymously and ask for constructive group feedback about how the writing could be improved. Throughout the feedback process, you must be willing to wrestle with difficult phrases or passages until they come out the way you want. You may also have to throw out some of your favorite passages to make the overall writing work. This process of writing and revising helps develop the skills of the writer and of those who give feedback.

As a way of helping your reader give you the most useful suggestions, you may find the following instructions helpful:

> Please read this as carefully and critically as you can. I am not asking for you to tell me if it is good or bad. I want you to suggest how you think it can be improved. I welcome your comments and will appreciate whatever criticism you have to offer. As you read, please mark any sentences or phrases that are unclear, awkward, poorly worded, ambiguous, uninteresting, or in some other way lacking. If you have suggestions for improving sentences or passages, please feel free to write them. If there are problems with organization, please note them and suggest alternatives. If any information is omitted or is not expressed clearly, please identify what should be added or expressed differently. Finally, if there are any other changes that you think would help, I would welcome your ideas. Thank you in advance for your help. Honest criticism is very hard to find, and I value your assistance.

Instructions such as these facilitate feedback in two ways. First, they give permission for your reader to be critical. Second, they suggest specific areas for the reader to focus on and ways of giving feedback about those areas. The next task is perhaps the most difficult. Having asked for honest criticism, you must be open enough to accept the criticism you receive without getting your feelings hurt or becoming defensive. Another good venue in which to seek and receive such criticism and feedback is a writers' workshop (Drotar, 2000).

REWRITING

Before any of the chapters in this book were ready for publication, they each went through perhaps as many as 20 revisions. This comes as a surprise to some readers, but it merely reflects a basic yet often unappreciated fact about the writing process: Writing skill develops through rewriting (Zinsser, 1998).

There are two ways in which quality writing depends on rewriting. First, to develop your skills as a writer, you must gain practice through revising whatever you write. Writing is like anything else you want to learn. You have to try, make mistakes, try again, make more mistakes, try again in a different way, make more mistakes, and so on, until your skills develop. The process of repeated revision helps you learn more efficient ways of writing and gradually enables you to write better first drafts.

Many students have not had experience rewriting because writing assignments in academic settings seldom require revision. The typical written report is submitted for a grade at the end of a semester, but there may be no requirement or opportunity to receive useful feedback and a chance to rewrite the paper. As a result, students may have some practice in writing first drafts, and they may receive an evaluation of their writing skills, but such assignments do little to teach them how to write. Students do, however, learn the bad habit of expecting to write something once and then be done with it. This experience often creates resistance when students are eventually told they must rewrite a report or paper. It would be much better if every writing assignment in college and graduate school involved at least two drafts and feedback from multiple sources. This would develop the habit of revision and would improve writing skills far more than the predominant single-draft practice (Baird & Anderson, 1990).

Along with improving writing skills, rewriting is important because even the most accomplished authors realize they can always improve their first drafts. No matter how much skill one develops as a writer, rewriting will always be part of the process. Understanding and embracing this reality may be just as important as the development of writing skill itself.

COMMON WRITING PROBLEMS

As an instructor and supervisor, I have read several thousand papers and reports by students. This experience has taught me that most of the problems students have in writing can be grouped into a few categories. These include problems relating to clarity, choice of wording, grammar, transitions between topics, and organization. Students who do not write well produce sentences that lack clear meaning. Their writing often contains words that were chosen carelessly or mean something the student did not intend to say. Poor writers also have difficulty structuring the overall sequence of topics and connecting smoothly from one topic to another. These problems are all remarkably common and can lead to papers that are painfully difficult to read. The good news is that most of the errors can be corrected.

I have found several books to be very useful in helping students learn to write. Three books that address issues common to all writing are *On Writing Well* by William Zinsser (1998), the *Harbrace College Handbook: With 1998 MLA Style Manual Updates, Thirteenth Edition Revised* by Hodges, Horner, Webb, and Miller (1998), and the classic *Elements of Style* by William Strunk, Jr., and E. B. White (2000). Two excellent works geared specifically to clinicians are Norman Tallent's *Psychological Report Writing* (1997) and Constance Fischer's *Individualizing Psychological Assessment* (1994). Tallent has conducted extensive research on clinical reports and writing. Although his title addresses psychologists specifically, the book contains information that is useful to professionals and interns from many disciplines. Fischer's book, in addition to providing one of the clearest descriptions I have found of the assessment and report-writing process, offers extremely valuable writing tips and a host of examples of common student writing errors and how to correct them. One other source that can help beginning clinical writers find suitable wording for reports is *The Clinician's Thesaurus, Fifth Edition: The Guidebook for Writing Psychological Reports* by Edward Zuckerman (2000). There is also a software version available (2000). Faculty seeking to improve their students' writing may want to consult an article by Piercy,

Sprenkle, and McDaniel (1996) that describes three educational approaches to teaching writing to family therapy and physician trainees. Brenner (2003) provides practical suggestions for improving the usefulness and readability of psychological assessments and other clinical reports.

CAUTION: TASTES, SUPERVISORS, AND INSTRUCTORS VARY

The next section reviews the suggestions of the authors previously mentioned as well as insights gained from my own experience as a clinician, supervisor, and instructor. Before I offer those suggestions, a brief caveat is in order. Although I will present examples and explanations of what I consider good and bad writing, other instructors and supervisors may have opinions and preferences that differ from what is said here. If your instructor or supervisor offers alternative expectations or suggestions, there is no need to be frustrated. Instead, try various approaches and examine their differences. As you continue your training, you can develop a style that works best for you.

KEYS TO GOOD WRITING

SIMPLIFY YOUR WRITING BUT NOT YOUR CLIENTS

Strunk and White (2000) instruct the writer to "Use definite, specific, concrete language. Prefer the specific to the general, the definite to the vague, the concrete to the abstract" (p. 15). In a similar vein, "simplicity" is Zinsser's first principle of writing well. As he describes it, "The secret of good writing is to strip every sentence to its cleanest components" (1998, pp. 8–9). I strongly endorse these principles but add that the clinician's task is to simplify writing without simplifying the client. You must strive to write as simply and directly as possible, but you must also communicate accurately about your client.

The following examples demonstrate how simplicity and directness in writing can contribute to improved clinical reports.

EXAMPLE 1

A. At various occasions during the interview Mr. Johnson exhibited signs of nervousness and distress.
B. In response to questions about his family, Mr. Johnson began to shift in his chair, stammered slightly, and appeared to avoid eye contact.

Note how the first example may sound as if it uses clinical language and form, but it actually speaks in very general terms. Words like "various occasions" and "signs of nervousness" do not really tell what the client did or when. By comparison, the second example directly describes Mr. Johnson's behavior and when it occurred. This lets the reader better visualize the client and connects specific behaviors with specific stimuli. Thus, by following the principle of preferring "the definite to the vague, the concrete to the abstract," the sentence is improved both stylistically and clinically.

The second example is one of the sentence pairs presented earlier in this chapter.

EXAMPLE 2

A. William Smith is an affable, energetic, 75-year-old male, who arrived neatly attired in a dark gray suit, spoke openly about his presenting concerns, and expressed a willingness to "do whatever it takes to get going again." Mr. Smith indicated that he came to therapy out of concern that his sex life has begun to decline from a frequency of five to three times per week.

B. William Smith is a 75-year-old male with a presenting problem of decreased sexual performance. At the time of the interview, he was well dressed and groomed and appeared to be well motivated.

Which of the two descriptions, A or B, do you prefer? Why?

This example is more subtle and might be subject to more dispute, but for most situations I would prefer the description offered in A. There are several reasons for this preference. First, although the second example is clearly more succinct, that quality alone does not necessarily mean it is more direct or that better represents the client. Describing a "presenting problem of decreased sexual performance" does not tell the reader what the problem is. For some, decreased sexual performance might mean going from having sex twice a month to once per month. As the alternative version shows, for this man decreased performance has a much different meaning. A second reason I prefer Example A is that it gives the reader a better sense of who the client is as a person, again because the description is more specific. "Neatly attired in a dark gray suit" paints a clearer picture than "well dressed and groomed." Similarly, using the direct quote that the client would "do whatever it takes" brings the reader closer to the client than saying he "appeared to be well motivated."

Fischer (1994) offers advice consistent with this example:

> Early in a report I provide physical descriptions of the client, in part so that the reader can picture the client throughout the written assessment. I try to describe the client in motion rather than statically, so the reader will be attuned to the ways the person moves through and shapes and is shaped by his or her environment. (p. 37)

Please note that although I would prefer the description offered in A for most situations, there are advantages to Example B, and there are instances in which it would be preferable. The main advantage of B is brevity. If time is at a premium and there is little need to convey a sense of the person beyond the clinical data that follow, the description can be shortened. Your task as a clinician and as a writer is first to make a choice about what matters, then determine how best to include that in your report.

OMIT NEEDLESS WORDS

One way to simplify your writing is to leave out words that are not needed. To appreciate this, compare the sentence you just read with the heading that preceded it. The heading, "Omit needless words," was borrowed directly from Strunk and White (2000, p. 17). It conveys the main idea in three words. By comparison, the sentence that followed took seven words (i.e., "leave out words that are not needed") to say the same thing.

Zinsser (1998) observes that "writing improves in direct ratio to the numbers of things we can keep out of it that shouldn't be there" (p. 14). Strunk and White state:

> Vigorous writing is concise. A sentence should contain no unnecessary words, a paragraph no unnecessary sentences. . . . This requires not that the writer make all his sentences short, or that he avoid all detail and treat his subjects only in outline, but that every word tell. (2000, p. 17)

To illustrate this point, let us return again to the examples offered in the discussion of focused reading.

EXAMPLE 3

A. During the interview, the client said that he had never before been seen in therapy by a therapist.

B. The client indicated no previous experience in therapy.

What unnecessary words has the second sentence eliminated? The phrase "During the interview" is removed because it can be assumed that is when the client spoke. The phrase "said that he had never before been seen in therapy," ten words, is replaced by "indicated no previous experience in therapy," six words that mean the same thing. This cutting of words saves time and makes the report shorter but sacrifices no important information about the client. A similar process can be applied to a second example from our earlier discussion. Read the two examples and identify where and how needless words are omitted.

EXAMPLE 4

A. Test results suggest the presence of mild to moderate depression, anxiety, and concerns about family matters.

B. According to the results of the test, there is evidence of depression in the mild to moderate range, along with anxiety and apparent concerns about issues relating to family.

Strunk and White offer similar examples of how everyday expressions contain many needless words. For instance, "This is a subject that . . . ," versus "This subject . . ."; "I was unaware of the fact that . . ." versus "I was unaware that . . ." Common speech also unnecessarily places prepositions after many phrases or uses prepositions when other phrases would work better. Compare "Wake me up at seven" versus "Wake me at seven"; "Find out about . . ." versus "Learn . . ." In the helping professions, clinical verbiage can complicate very simple matters. For example, "The subject was engaged in walking behaviors" versus "He was walking." Or, "He produced little verbal material" versus "He was quiet." or "We said little."

Just as dietary fat clogs your arteries, verbal fat will clog your writing. As shown in the preceding examples, learning to trim unnecessary words or phrases is a key step toward improving your writing. Zinsser puts this very nicely when he says, "Be grateful for everything you can throw away" (1998, p. 18).

As with the earlier recommendation to embrace rewriting, responding to the instruction to shorten your writing will take some adjustment. Students have learned that excess verbiage helps stretch papers to meet the 10-page minimum so often imposed by faculty. Now the message is to shorten those 10-page papers to the fewest pages possible and make every word count. Tallent suggests that one can tell a report is too long if the person who has written it

> is unhappy over the length of time required to write it and experiences difficulty in organizing a multitude of details for presentation. It is too long when it contains content that is not relevant or useful, when the detailing is greater than can be put to good use. (1997, p. 73)

Tallent (1997) offers examples of lengthy reports to illustrate his point. Following one such example he quips, "Just glancing at this report one may wonder if it is too long. On reading it, one may be sure that it is" (p. 139). To avoid such statements about your own work, practice trimming away everything that is unnecessary. You will have much greater impact if you can express the most meaning with the fewest words, rather than the least meaning with the most words.

CHOOSE WORDS CAREFULLY

Along with limiting the number of words you use, be attentive to their meaning. Careful choice of words is essential to all your work as a clinician. In staff meetings, therapy sessions, and your written reports, the words you use will be crucial. As a clinician, you cannot afford to be careless or haphazard about what you say or write. You must be aware of all the subtleties of language and learn to say exactly what you mean. This is especially true of written reports, because once a report is written, others may read it without you being present to explain, clarify, or correct mistakes. Careless use of words can also come back to haunt you if your records or reports are ever used in a legal proceeding.

Zinsser advises: "you will never make your mark as a writer unless you develop a respect for words and a curiosity about their shades of meaning that is almost obsessive" (1998, p. 35). I agree and would expand this statement by substituting the word *clinician* for *writer*. You will never be a fully skilled clinician unless you are acutely aware of words, attend precisely to the words used by others, and think carefully about the words you use.

Tallent (1997) describes a series of studies in which various groups of mental health professionals were asked to indicate what they like and what they dislike in typical psychological reports. Among the factors most often criticized, ambiguous wording was frequently cited as a problem. The use of vaguely defined clinical terms also receives criticism in the literature. Tallent cites a classic study by Grayson and Tolman (1950) in which clinical psychologists and psychiatrists offered definitions for the 20 words most commonly used in psychological reports. Reviewing the list of words and definitions, the authors of the study were struck by how loosely the professionals defined many of the words.

Fifteen years after the original study by Grayson and Tolman, Siskind (1967) replicated the design and found similar results. Although the specific words included in such lists might differ if the study were performed again today, there is no reason to assume the definitional ambiguities would be any less now than they were in 1950 and 1967. For students and interns, ambiguity can be quite challenging because many of the words that sound the most clinical are in fact highly ambiguous. Students may be eager to use technical terms as a way of demonstrating their knowledge to supervisors. The trouble is that a great deal of what passes for clinical wording may sound scientific but often obfuscates rather than elucidates. Harvey (1997) made a similar observation and advises students to shorten sentence lengths, minimize the number of difficult words, and reduce the use of jargon. Fischer recommended to writers: "Say what you mean in concrete terms rather than dressing up the text in professionalese" (1994, p. 125).

Tallent concurs:

> In our view words like *oral, narcissistic, masochistic, immature, compulsive,* and *schizophrenia* are often more concealing than revealing.
>
> Technical words do not cause, but readily lend themselves to, imprecise or incomplete thinking. There is the error of nominalism, wherein we simply name a thing or an occurrence and think we understand something of the real world. (1997, p. 69; italics in the original)

Earlier in this book, I made similar observations about the overuse of the word *inappropriate*. Other words or phrases, such as *manipulative, dependent,* or *just doing it for attention,* are used with similar frequency and with equal ambiguity. As an antidote to such jargon, Fischer asserts:

> Saying what one means, both in speech and in writing, requires one to anchor abstractions in concrete examples. Ask yourself how you would explain what you mean to a 12-year-old. If you can't figure out how to do that then you do not yet know what you mean—what your technical information comes down to in terms of your client's life. (1994, p. 134)

Harvey (1997) takes this advice one step further and actually subjects her student's reports to formal "readability" measures that assess such things as word choice and sentence length. Harvey then uses the measures to calculate a grade and difficulty level and asks students to rewrite their reports so they can be read at grade levels of 13 or below. Harvey explains this approach by pointing out that psychological and other mental health reports are increasingly being reviewed by parents and others who have less formal education than those writing the reports. Thus, making reports more intelligible to these consumers may enhance their usefulness and reduce misunderstandings.

EXERCISE

Read the following three sentences and ask yourself if the differences in wording might communicate subtle yet important differences in meaning.

A. Mr. Smith denied any abuse of alcohol or drugs.
B. Mr. Smith said he does not abuse alcohol or drugs.
C. Mr. Smith does not abuse alcohol or drugs.

In the first sentence of this exercise, we encounter another of the many misused clinical words. The word "denied" in this sentence is very important. In psychological language, "denial" is a form of defense and implies that a person is not being fully honest or is unconsciously repressing information. In this case, it might be that Mr. Smith "denies" alcohol abuse, but we know or suspect that he does in fact abuse. It might also be that Mr. Smith is genuine and does not abuse alcohol or drugs. If that is the case, the second sentence would be better, because it avoids the subtle intimation raised by the word "denies." The third sentence is still more clear about whether or not Mr. Smith abuses, but it may suffer from a different problem. Do we really know the statement is true, or is it just something Mr. Smith has told us? The sentence as written implies that we know it to be fact, but if the source of information is Mr. Smith, we should so indicate.

If this sounds like nitpicking, it is not. To appreciate why, ask yourself what might happen if you gave a report containing these sentences to other professionals who based clinical decisions on a misunderstanding of what you wrote. Do other readers conclude from the first sentence that Mr. Smith really drinks but does not admit it, or do they conclude that Mr. Smith does not drink? Do they conclude from the third sentence that we are sure alcohol and drugs are not a problem, or do they assume that is just what the client has told us? If the scenario of clinical misinterpretation is not convincing, imagine trying to explain the meaning while testifying in your own defense in a liability suit.

One way to reduce ambiguity in reports is to read questionable passages to colleagues and ask them to tell you whether the passage is clear and what they think it means. In some cases, I ask nonclinicians to read my reports and offer feedback. This is particularly helpful if a report might be read by family members or others who are not trained in the profession.

Another, and too often overlooked, tool is the dictionary. I encourage students to use both a standard dictionary and a dictionary of professional terms. Three specialty dictionaries that I highly recommend are the *Counseling Dictionary,* 2nd edition (Gladding, 2006), The *Social Work Dictionary,* 5th edition (Barker, 2003), and the *APA Dictionary of Psychology* (VandenBos, 2006). The standard dictionary can help you understand what words mean and imply in ordinary usage. Be careful, however, not to assume that definitions offered in a normal dictionary carry the same meanings when applied in clinical writing. If a word has specific clinical meanings, the professional dictionary will cite specific meanings within the clinical context. Time after time, students use words they think they know only to discover that the word means or implies something entirely different than they thought. One student used the word *limpid* to describe how a brain-injured patient held his arm. Another spoke of a situation attenuating the client's anxiety when the situation in fact exacerbated the anxiety. I recently heard a colleague repeatedly use the word *duplicitous* when he clearly meant *duplication.*

If you do not know the meaning of any of the words used in the previous paragraph, did you look them up? If not, why? One of my students answered a similar question in class by saying, "I already took the GRE." That student did not get the point, nor did he get a letter of recommendation.

Misuse of clinical terms is also common. Students frequently confuse delusions with hallucinations, obsession with compulsion, schizophrenia with multiple personality, and so on. Certainly one of the most commonly misused terms is *negative reinforcement.* Even if you are sure you know what this means, look it up in a textbook. In one upper-division undergraduate class, out of 20 students who said they were sure they knew the definition, only five were actually right. Again, to appreciate the importance of precise wording, consider that misunderstanding the meaning of negative reinforcement in a report could lead to interventions that are exactly the opposite of what the writer intended.

CLARITY

Choosing words carefully is part of the larger issue of achieving clarity in writing and clinical work. This demand includes both clarity of individual words and clarity in syntax and organization. If the organization of a report is not clear, the reader will have to search to find important information. If the syntax of a sentence is unclear, the meaning may be misinterpreted. For example:

The therapist told the client about his problems.

Whose problems is the therapist talking about—the therapist's or the client's?

Strunk and White (2000) caution: "Muddiness is not merely a disturber of prose, it is also a destroyer of life, of hope" (p. 72). In clinical work, this is not an overstatement. I know of a case in which one therapist told another he had an appointment to see a client "next Friday." As the conversation took place on a Wednesday, the listener assumed the appointment was two days away. The speaker, however, was referring to Friday of the following week. Because the client in question was experiencing a serious crisis, this was a difference of potentially grave consequence.

Although most people would agree that clarity is important in clinical reports, the difficulty lies in recognizing when our own reports are unclear. Because we think we know what we mean when we write something, we assume that what we have written adequately conveys our intention. Thus, we readily overlook passages that may be virtually incomprehensible or, worse, that may appear comprehensible but will be misinterpreted by others.

As suggested earlier, one way to limit misunderstanding is to have someone else read a report before it goes to the intended recipient. If this is not possible, it is often helpful to pretend you know nothing of the case yourself, then read the report out loud. Reading aloud brings out aspects of writing that we do not recognize when we read silently to ourselves. If time permits, another extremely valuable technique is to set a report aside for several days and then read it again with an open mind. Along with helping to identify writing problems, this also allows one to think more about the case before sending the report.

I cannot overemphasize how important clarity is to your writing. Clinicians simply must learn to be extremely careful about their words. You must know and say precisely what you mean. It is not enough to defend with "C'mon, you know what I meant." That may work in everyday discourse, but it is unacceptable in professional work. If the reader does not know exactly what is meant, the responsibility falls on the writer, not the reader. Say what you mean and say it clearly. I feel so strongly about this that I have on occasion told students bluntly, "If you do not want to learn to use words carefully and accurately, you should probably consider another profession."

Know Your Audience

The final recommendation about writing is to know your audience. Some instructors and articles about clinical writing dictate specific and fixed rules for the style and content to be included in clinical reports. I prefer an approach that offers suggestions but at the same time encourages you to choose and adapt your style and content with an awareness of your audience. This principle has also been highlighted by Brenner (2003), who speaks of "consumer-focused" psychological assessment and the importance of making our writing relevant and useful to the people who will be reading it.

Fischer (1994) says repeatedly in her book: "Reports are for readers, not for the author" (p. 115). Tallent stresses this principle as well and cites a report by Hartlage and Merck (1971) that showed that the utility of reports is primarily weakened by, as Tallent (1997) describes it, a "profound . . . lack of reflection by report writers on what might be useful to report to

readers, a simple failure to use common sense" (p. 20). Hartlage and Merck (1971) observed, "Reports can be made more relevant to their prospective users merely by having the psychologists familiarize themselves with the uses to which their reports are to be applied" (p. 460).

A report prepared for a fellow professional in your discipline may differ from a report prepared for an attorney, family members, or others with different backgrounds and needs. Similarly, if you believe certain aspects of a client are being overlooked by others, you may want to emphasize those in your report. The most important thing is for you to write with conscious awareness of how your style and content meet your clinical and professional purpose.

Exercise

As a way of enhancing your awareness of different groups to which your reports might be targeted, read the following list and write some of the concerns that you might keep in mind if preparing a report for each of these people. You might consider such factors as the readers' level of training or knowledge, how much time they have, and the style of reports they are accustomed to reading. How do these and other factors differ for each of the groups listed?

- The client
- Family members of the client
- Insurance companies
- Clinical psychologists
- Counselors
- Social workers
- Psychiatrists
- Nonpsychiatrist MDs
- Schoolteachers
- Students
- Attorneys
- Judges
- Professional journals
- Newspapers
- Others for whom you might write

Reviewing the list should enhance your awareness of general factors to consider in writing, but you must also remember that, regardless of their profession or role, different individuals will have different preferences and needs. One schoolteacher may be well versed in diagnostic categories, but another may know nothing at all about them. One psychiatrist may prefer reports that are as brief as possible and that convey "just the facts." Another may appreciate more detailed reports that convey a sense of the client as a person.

If you know for whom you will be writing before you write a report, it is sometimes a good idea to contact the person and ask about his or her preferences for style and content and any specific requirement for the report. After you write a report, you can follow up by asking the recipient for feedback. Your role as an intern gives you a perfect opportunity to ask for such information, and many people will be glad to offer their suggestions.

THE FUNCTION AND MAINTENANCE OF RECORDS

One of the responsibilities of all health care professions is to maintain accurate records regarding the diagnosis and treatment patients receive. By understanding the function of clinical records and developing a systematic approach to their use and maintenance, you can make record keeping a recognized and accepted element of your clinical training and later practice (Casper, 1987; Kagle, 1993; Van Vort & Mattson, 1989).

Van Vort and Mattson (1989) emphasized that records serve multiple functions. They contribute to the quality of a client's current and future care, satisfy agency requirements, document care for the purpose of third-party reimbursement (i.e., payment for care by insurance companies), and protect against legal actions. The same functions were identified by Reamer (2005) and are in the specified organizational guidelines and codes of ethics of all the major professional associations. Casper (1987) noted that medical hospitals and other health care institutions must maintain adequate records to receive approval from auditing agencies such as the Joint Commission on Accreditation of Hosptials and government agencies in charge of Medicare and Medicaid.

In a brief but highly informative review, Soisson, Vande-Creek, and Knapp (1987) considered the legal importance of records in our litigious society. Based on their review of existing case law, they emphasized that well-kept records can reduce the risk of liability, whereas the lack of good records may in itself be used as evidence that care was substandard. This point was reiterated by Reamer (2005), Harris (1995), and by Bennett, Bryant, VandenBos, and Greenwood (1990), who stated: "In hospital practice it is often said, 'If it isn't written down, it didn't happen' " (p. 77).

For these reasons, an essential part of your responsibility as a professional will be to maintain quality records. To do that, you should understand what goes into records, what stays out, and some of the models for organizing and writing progress notes. Examples of forms for documentation and record keeping can be found in Wiger's (1999) clinical documentation sourcebook.

WHAT GOES INTO RECORDS

EXERCISE

Before reading the following discussion, give some thought to all the information you would like to know about a client. Organize this into categories and create a simple form to use for an initial intake interview. When you have generated your list of key information, compare your ideas with peers to see what their approach is and what issues they have identified that you have overlooked.

When I refer to clinical records in this text, I am speaking of the totality of information pertinent to the client's treatment. The general rule for determining what to put in records is: If something is important, document it and keep a record, but think carefully about what you say and how you say it. Good records should include all present and previous relevant information about a client's history and treatment, current diagnosis, correspondence, releases of information, documentation of consultation, billing information, informed-consent forms, and any other pertinent information. At the same time, however, psychotherapy notes should probably not go in general records because, as mentioned in Chapter 3, HIPAA guidelines protect the confidentiality of psychotherapy notes, but only if those notes are kept separately from the rest of the client's health care records. More will be said about psychotherapy notes later in this chapter.

Different institutions and agencies have different record-keeping technologies. As discussed in Chapter 3, more and more settings are shifting to computerized electronic health or medical records systems (EHRs and EMRs), and these will eventually become the norm. (Bower, 2005; RAND, 2005; Steinfeld et al., 2006). If you have not yet read Chapter 3, now would be a good time to do so, because you will undoubtedly encounter electronic record systems at some point, either in your internship or your later practice. As such, you need to have an understanding of the ethical and legal issues associated with such systems.

In more traditional settings that have yet to adopt an electronic system, typical physical materials involve either manila or metal folders subdivided into sections containing certain types of information. For convenience, subsections are often color-coded and flagged with tabs identifying the contents. To ensure compliance with record-keeping guidelines, most institutions have some form of periodic record review that assesses the content, organization, clarity, and security of records. This has always been good practice but is now mandated under the HIPAA rules.

Whether one is using a traditional paper-based system or an EMR model, any approach is only as effective as the people who use (or in some cases fail to use) it. Kagle (1993), Casper (1987), and Van Vort and Mattson (1989) all described systems for encouraging improved record keeping and greater compliance with agency guidelines. These include simplifying records, reducing redundancy, utilizing established forms to collect information, and using technologies such as computers and dictation systems. Some agencies have also hired time-management consultants to help assess how much time is actually going toward record keeping and how to improve efficiency. With the advent of HIPAA guidelines, most agencies will have procedures and personnel in place specifically to ensure HIPAA compliance regarding electronic records, informed consent, communication of patient information, security and other issues covered under HIPAA.

Perhaps the most concise and informative discussion of how to organize and what to include in records was provided by Piazza and Baruth (1990), who described six categories of material that should go into records. In discussing the utility of their system, Piazza and Baruth noted that it has been used successfully in many treatment settings and that records kept according to the system have consistently passed state and national standards. After reviewing the general categories these authors identified, we will look more closely at progress notes and psychotherapy notes.

Within each of the major categories of record contents, Piazza and Baruth (1990) listed more specific information that should be included. Under the category "Identifying or Intake Information," they suggested that basic personal data such as name, address, home and work phones, date of birth, sex, family members' names, next of kin, and employment status should be recorded. Also indicated here should be information about the date of initial contact, the reason for referral, and the names of other professionals (e.g., physicians, other counselors) who are seeing or have seen the client. Most agencies use standard forms to gather the information in this category. In some instances, the information is completed by the client; in other settings intake specialists or the therapists themselves discuss the information with clients and record the data as the discussion proceeds. Interactive computer programs have also become available to allow clients to enter this information themselves.

Taking this type of information is a straightforward process with most clients, but in some cases clients may not want to be contacted at their home address. For example, I have worked with abused spouses who did not want their partner to know they were seeing a therapist. In these circumstances, you need to flag the record in some way to indicate precisely where and how a client should be contacted and billed. This must be done in such a way that the therapist, secretaries, records departments, or other clerical personnel cannot inadvertently call the client's home to schedule an appointment or send billing information that would reveal the client is seeing a therapist.

The second category described by Piazza and Baruth (1990) contains what they identify as "Assessment Information." This information is typically collected at the outset of treatment for the purpose of developing treatment plans. In some approaches to records, this information might also be included in the initial intake forms alluded to earlier. Within the heading of assessment information, five "domains" are considered by Piazza and Baruth to be essential. The first domain, "Psychological Assessment," addresses the client's "motivation for treatment," emotional status and functioning, cognitive capacity, and history of previous difficulties or treatment. "Social and Family Assessment," the second domain, encompasses the client's early family and developmental history, including parents,

siblings, family dynamics, and any family history of illness. It also includes the client's current family and social status and functioning.

Piazza and Baruth (1990) emphasized the importance of not only considering information about dysfunctional aspects of the client's life but also attending to the client's strengths and resources. Such information is particularly relevant to the third domain, "Vocational/Educational Assessment." Along with information about employment and academic history, this domain takes in avocational interests, as well as leisure and recreational activities. In considering a client's background, it is important to look beyond titles of jobs or education to consider specific skills and accomplishments. Thus, if a woman seeking employment identifies herself as a "homemaker," the counselor should explore the skills, such as money management, planning, organization, and child raising that may have gone into that role. Clients may tend to overlook such skills, but identifying them as resources can be immensely valuable in mobilizing the client's strengths as part of the therapy process.

The fourth and fifth domains are, respectively, "Drug and Alcohol Use" and "Health Assessment." As these titles are self-explanatory, they will not be discussed further here except to emphasize that many helping professionals pay too little attention to the role of physical factors. Physical illness and lifestyle characteristics such as smoking, drinking, sleep patterns, and caffeine use may all be significant causes of, or contributors to, clients' difficulties. I advise interns wherever possible to obtain the requisite information releases and establish close contacts with clients' physicians. I also suggest, as do Piazza and Baruth (1990), that clients who have not had complete physicals within the past year be encouraged to see a physician for a thorough checkup. A number of concerns that present with psychological symptoms may be caused by or related to underlying physical illness. To assess this possibility, you may wish to contact the physician before the client's visit and discuss the physician's findings after the client has been seen. Finally, remember, as discussed in Chapter 3, federal guidelines require that information about treatment for drug or alcohol abuse must be provided special confidentiality protections including special treatment in any record system accessible to others.

In gathering and considering any of the previous data, keep in mind that some patients may be unreliable sources of information. Therefore, with appropriate consent, it is advisable to obtain corroborating information from family or friends. Meeting with family members or friends at intake is virtually an essential for clients who, because of their presenting concerns (e.g., mental disorders, brain injury, certain personality disorders), may not be able or motivated to provide accurate data about themselves. Before making such contacts or conducting such meetings, however, you must be sure to have the client's specific written authorization.

Along with the information described thus far, as part of an initial assessment I strongly recommend that if a client has been or is being seen by other treatment providers or related professionals, you should, with the client's authorization and signed release of information, seek copies of those records. If a client is reluctant to allow you access to such records, that may serve as a red flag for making further inquiries about the client's reasons. You should also be cautious in deciding whether to accept the client for treatment if you cannot obtain past records. From the perspective of managing liability risks, it is not advisable to treat clients without access to information about previous treatment. The reason is that such information can have a significant impact on how you understand the client's present situation and how you provide treatment yourself. If you have not made an effort to gather information about past or other ongoing treatment, and if you do not document that attempt and information in your own records, you could face added problems if legal concerns arise.

With information from the first two categories, clinicians are able to formulate treatment plans. "Treatment Plans" constitute the third category in the record model of Piazza and Baruth (1990). They suggest that the client and the therapist should agree to and sign each treatment plan. At a minimum, the plan should include a statement of the problem, the goal of treatment described in behavioral terms, and the steps that will be taken to achieve the goal. As treatment proceeds, the client and therapist should periodically review the treatment plan to assess progress and adjust the approach or goals as needed.

Managed care and other changes in health care are placing increasing demands on professionals in the mental health field to demonstrate the rationale for, and efficacy of, the work we do with clients (Braun & Cox, 2005; Rupert & Baird, 2004) In some cases, if you have not formulated a sound treatment plan from the outset, and if you do not document through progress notes that your subsequent work with the client has followed your plan, you, the agency you work for, or the client may be denied compensation from the insurer. Thus, along with contributing to the quality of patient care, well-formulated and clearly documented treatment plans can also contribute to your financial well-being and that of your clients.

Ongoing "Case Notes" form the fifth category in Piazza and Baruth's (1990) model. Piazza and Baruth suggested that these notes should include the goals for each session, indications of whether the goals were met, behavioral observations and clinical impressions, and a plan for the next sessions. In light of HIPAA protections for psychotherapy notes that are stored separately, I recommend that therapists simply include in the general record the time and date of the session, whether or not the patient appeared, a brief and very general statement of what occurred in the session, and any relevant follow-up. Notes of the actual content of the session and the therapist's impressions should be kept separately from the general record. At the conclusion of treatment with a client, the therapist should also write a brief synopsis of the case at termination and include it in a termination summary that reviews the origin, course, and result of treatment. If the client will be referred to another professional, the termination summary should include mention of this or of other aftercare plans.

The sixth and final category within records is labeled simply "Other Data." Include here such things as authorization for treatment, releases of information, copies of test results, and communications from other professionals. If you consult with other professionals about a case, make records of the consultation and include them here or in your case notes. Because this portion of records can become quite crowded with miscellaneous material, you may find it useful to organize the material with tabbed inserts.

WHAT STAYS OUT OF RECORDS

PROTECTING CLIENTS

Like all simple rules, there are caveats to the rule of documenting everything that is important. In the case of clinical records, the caveat arises because your case records are not strictly confidential. This reality is clearly recognized in the APA (1993) Record Keeping Guidelines, which state:

> These guidelines assume that no record is free from disclosure all of the time, regardless of the wishes of the client or the psychologist. (p. 985)

Each of the ethical codes also explicitly mentions that information, including information in clnical records, may under certain circumstances be required to be disclosed. Recognizing the possibility that records may be disclosed does not mean that you can afford to be careless or that it is not your responsibility to protect records from disclosure wherever legally required and permitted. It does mean that when you keep any sort of record about clients or their treatment, you should keep in mind the possibility that others might have access to the record.

Institutional settings are an example of where confidentiality of records may be limited. If your treatment records are, or will become part of, a larger record to which other staff have access, it is obvious that your records can be seen by others. Under these circumstances, it would not be in the client's best interests to reveal in such accessible records information that was shared with you in confidence or that might be harmful to the client. This is another reason it is a good idea to keep psychotherapy notes separately.

Another possibility that you should be aware of concerns computerized case notes and outcome data. Wedding, Topolski, and McGaha (1995) provided a comprehensive review of the issues associated with computerized notes, particularly within the context of managed care and cost-containment efforts. Jeffords (1999) reported that the National Research Council found the path of the typical medical record has changed with the proliferation of technology. Twenty-five years ago records were held and used by a personal physician. Today, records may be handled by numerous individuals in more than 17 different organizations. Recognition of this reality is part of the reason the

HIPAA guidelines about electronic data storage, communication, and security are so explicit and, along with specifying what information can and cannot be exchanged, include measures such as passwords and encryption to protect against hackers and other intrusions.

PROTECTING YOURSELF

Just as it is important to protect clients from the possibility that records may be viewed by others, it is also important to protect yourself. No clear-cut rules exist in this area, but interns and clinicians would do well to ask themselves how what they put in records might later sound in a court proceeding. Gutheil (1980) went so far as to suggest that trainees

> deliberately hallucinate upon their right shoulder the image of a hostile prosecuting attorney who might preside at their trial, and that to this visual hallucination they append the auditory impression of the voice most suited to it. (p. 481)

Gutheil (1980) continued, saying:

> Having achieved this goal-directed transient psychotic state, the trainee should then mentally test out in that context the sound of what he or she is about to write. (p. 481)

This does not mean that you should be frightened about everything you write or that you should expect a lawsuit around every corner. At the same time, however, being aware that your records and notes can be exposed and analyzed in litigation serves as a helpful reminder and incentive to keep the quality of your treatment and documentation at the highest levels possible.

Keep in mind, too, that under HIPAA guidelines, clients have access to their own records. Again, psychotherapy notes are protected if kept separately, but in the portion of the record that is accessible to clients upon request, it is advisable to avoid recording your own emotional reactions or opinions about clients if such reactions could be clinically harmful or litigiously consequential when read by a client.

From a liability risk-management perspective, two things to avoid in records are "raising ghosts" and taking blame. By raising ghosts, I mean recording unfounded or unnecessary speculation in your notes. For example, if a client seems a bit down during a session but there is no reason from the client's history, statements, or actions to suspect suicide potential, it would be unwise for a clinician to record "Client was down today but I do not think suicide potential is high." If you mention suicide, you must also assess the potential carefully and document that you did so. If suicide risk is not elevated above normal, do not mention it at all. The same would apply to issues relating to dangerousness to others. Do not simply speculate about something so serious in your notes unless you followed up on that speculation during your session.

A second thing to avoid in records is taking blame. Do not write in your notes that you made a mistake in treatment.

This might feel honest and cathartic, but it could get you into trouble later. If you are tempted to make such an entry, ask yourself what good it serves to write in your own notes that you made an error. You know it yourself, and that is sufficient. Remember the advice your auto insurance company gives you if you are in an accident. If something unfortunate happens and you have to defend an action in court, allow your attorney to advise you but do not put confessions in your records beforehand.

Finally, never falsify records. If your records are demanded for a legal proceeding, you will be asked under oath if your records represent a true and accurate description of your treatment or have been altered in any way since they were originally written. If you alter records and do not so indicate, you may be guilty of perjury. It is far better to be careful in your treatment and in your records to begin with and then to be scrupulously honest if you are ever called to court. If at some point in your work with a client you realize that a previous record was deficient in some way, at the time you notice the deficiency you can make a note that you discovered something that needed to be added or changed in an earlier note. This does not mean you go back and actually change the note. It means you make a separate and later note that indicates the need to adjust, clarify, or correct the earlier note.

For example, suppose that two days after you wrote an entry you are reviewing the notes and reflecting on the earlier session. As you think about the session, you realize that something should be added. At that moment, write the present date and time, then indicate the change or correction. This process demonstrates the value of periodic note review because you must catch such omissions before any trouble develops and legal implications arise. Corrections made after legal action or after an unfortunate event are not likely to carry as much weight in court because they tend to be seen as self-serving.

PROGRESS NOTES AND PSYCHOTHERAPY NOTES

EXERCISE

If you are working in a clinical setting, find out if you can obtain permission to review some of the patient records. Then read the progress notes kept in the records and ask yourself the following questions: Can I detect differences in style or content for different staff members? What notes stand out as useful? What notes are not useful? What matters of style and information account for this difference?

STANDARD FORMATS

In an effort to standardize treatment notes, many agencies have developed or adopted specific guidelines for what should go where in notes. This is very important in medical settings or group-care facilities where many different treatment professionals interact with many different patients and need to have ready access to key information quickly. Without a standard format, it is nearly impossible for different members of a treatment team to find information in a record. Standardized notes also ensure that each member of the team is working consistently on an identified problem or goal for the given patient and that each treatment team member follows a structured procedure in observing the patient's status, recording information about that status, assessing the patient's condition, and basing treatment on the assessment.

It is very likely that your internship placement will have guidelines for keeping records and recording progress notes. If your agency has such guidelines, you must learn them, practice using them, and get feedback to be sure you are writing your notes correctly. As noted earlier, most agencies conduct periodic audits to ensure that record keeping meets agency guidelines. By making sure your records and progress notes are up to standards, you can save yourself and your supervisor problems later. As a check, interns should initiate their own record and progress note review with their supervisors. Supervisors tend to get busy and overlook such details, so it is a sign of responsibility if interns take the initiative to be sure they are keeping acceptable notes.

In your clinical work you are likely to encounter two types of ongoing notes regarding treatment. For convenience, and consistency with laws such as HIPAA, we will refer to these as progress notes and psychotherapy notes. The former describe records that are part of the documentation of patient treatment available to other staff. By comparison, psychotherapy notes are your personal records of the events of specific therapy sessions or related interactions. Understanding the differences between these note types, and learning how to use each effectively, will help you become more efficient and effective in both your treatment and your record keeping.

PROGRESS NOTES

Progress notes are the core of most clinical records. They provide a record of events, are a means of communication among professionals, encourage us to review and assess treatment issues, allow other professionals to review the process of treatment, and are a legal record. Progress notes have also seen increasing use by insurance providers seeking to determine whether a treatment is within the realm of services for which they provide compensation (Kagle, 1993). In writing progress notes, you must keep all these functions in mind.

When I write progress notes, I find it helpful to ask myself several questions. First, as I write, I review the events in order to again assess and better understand what happened. This helps me process and check my treatment. Next, I ask myself: If I read the notes several months or years from now, will they help me remember what happened, what was done, and why?

Because I may not be the only one to read my notes, I consider what would take place if something happened to me and another clinician picked up my clients. Would my notes enable him or her to understand the client and treatment? If I am in a setting where other professionals refer to the same record, I ask whether the notes I write will adequately and accurately communicate to them. I include legibility in this consideration. If my handwriting is so poor that others cannot read it, the notes will not do them or the client much good. Finally, and very importantly, I ask, What would be the implications and impact if these notes were used as a legal document in a court of law?

TYPES OF PROGRESS NOTES

The two most common types of progress notes are problem-oriented and goal-oriented notes. As the names suggest, problem-oriented notes refer to one or more specific problem areas being addressed in treatment (Cameron & Turtle-song, 2001; Weed, 1971), whereas goal-oriented notes focus on specified treatment goals, with each entry relating in some way to a goal. In systems that use problem- or goal-oriented notes, each therapist, or the treatment team as a group, identifies several key areas of focus in the client's treatment. For example, problems might be identified as:

1. Initiates fights with other residents
2. Does not participate in social interactions

    Expressed as goals these might be stated:

1. Reduce incidence of instigating fights
2. Increase socialization

Once a list of the problems or goals is established, progress notes then refer to them by number or name.

The theory behind this approach is that it helps staff target their intervention to meet specific treatment needs or goals. Such notes may also help demonstrate to insurers that the treatment provided is systematic and is related to specific problems or goals for which compensation is being provided.

STYLE OF PROGRESS NOTES

In most progress notes, writing style is not important; clarity, precision, and brevity are. Your goal is to record all the essential information in as little space and time as possible. Because you may be writing and reading notes on many patients each day, you will want to save time by including only the essential details. By keeping your notes succinct, you will also save the time of others who may read them. This is especially important in settings where notes are shared among many professionals, each of whom has contact with many patients. When a clinician must read many notes, every minute saved in reading and writing adds up. As long as the notes are kept accurately and all essential information is provided, the time saved in charting can be better spent in direct clinical contact or other activities.

Using shorthand is one way to shorten progress notes. If you are taking notes primarily for your own use, any system of shorthand will do as long as you can decipher it later. However, if you are writing notes in a record that others share, it is essential that any shorthand be understood by everyone and accepted by your institution. If there is a possibility of misinterpretation, you are better off writing things out in full. You should also be aware that different settings may have different standards for using shorthand or abbreviations, and some may not allow any shorthand at all. If you take notes as part of your internship responsibilities, check to be sure before you write.

STRUCTURED NOTE FORMATS

DART NOTES

Some of the most widely used formats for treatment notes have significant problems, especially when applied to psychological, as opposed to medical, settings. One example is the SOAP format, which is part of the Problem Oriented Medical Records (POMR) system (Cameron & Turtle-song, 2002; Weed, 1971). The SOAP format will be discussed shortly, but first let me offer an alternative that most interns find very helpful as they learn to keep treatment notes.

This system actually evolved out of some joking around about my frustration with the SOAP format, which was at the time required of all notes for my internship placement. The acronym for my alternative system is DART, but it began as DIRT, which shows the humor behind its origin and explains why it would probably never be adopted in hospitals. Humor aside, the letters represent useful concepts that will help guide most progress notes. If your agency does not require adherence to some other standard, the DART format is a good method to follow.

The DART system is most useful when you are writing notes about a specific client or event. The *D* in DART stands for a description of the client and situation. *A* is for assessment of the situation. (This *A* was originally *I,* which stood for the clinician's impression and produced the initial acronym.) *R* is for the response of the clinician and client, and *T* is for treatment implications and plan. One way to think of this system is that when you write progress notes you must tell what happened, what you made of it, how you responded, and what you plan to do, or think should be done, in the future. This sequence of events is not only a useful way to conceptualize progress notes, it is also a useful way to approach a treatment interaction.

DESCRIPTION

The first part of any progress note should describe the basic *W* questions of journalism: when, where, who, and what. In practice, these words are not actually used in the progress notes, but the notes must contain the information the words subsume. Usually, the information of when, where, and who can be conveyed in a single sentence. "When" refers to the date and time the event occurred. Some people prefer to put date and time at the end of a note, but I suggest you start the note with this information for ease of reference later. "Where" indicates the location of the event. If the location is always the same, such as a clinic office, this can be omitted. However, if many locations are possible, as in a school, hospital, or other large setting, it helps to note the exact location. Next you should indicate "who" played a significant role in or observed the event you are noting. Noting who was present can come in handy later if there is a need to get additional information about a specific event or client.

Once you have provided the basic information, you should describe "what" is prompting you to write the note. This may be something routine, such as "Mrs. Smith has shown little change during the past week. She continues to pace the hall and talk to herself." The information may be a significant change in a client's appearance or behavior: "During individual therapy today, Joseph informed me that he has been very depressed and is thinking of killing himself." The more significant the event, the more space will be dedicated to the corresponding progress note. One would certainly want to expand on the second notation.

ASSESSMENT

Having described what you observed, the next step is to record your assessment of what it means. This is the "why" of the event. You do not always have to offer profound insights or explanations, nor do you always have to know what something means. Sometimes the most important notes are about behaviors that stand out precisely because their meaning is not exactly clear. For example, if a client who is normally rather quiet becomes very talkative and energetic, the meaning of the change might not be clear, but one could note it, suggest some possible considerations, or ask others to offer their insights.

To help guide your assessment, think about how the present event or behavior relates to other knowledge you have about the client and treatment. How does the present situation relate to previous behaviors, to recent events, to the treatment plan, to other factors? Remember that most events reflect a combination of both lasting and temporary factors within the individual and within the environment. Thus, you might observe a change in a client's behavior and note that it seems to reflect stresses over recent family conflicts and may also be a reaction to the overall level of tension in the treatment facility. The most important task is to give some thought to what you observed and try to relate it to your overall knowledge and treatment of the client. Again, this is not just good note taking, it is sound clinical practice.

RESPONSE

In good clinical work you must first take in what is happening and what the client is doing and saying. Then you must assess what this means. Your next task is to respond in some way. Your progress notes should reflect this sequence. After describing and assessing a situation, record what you did in response. The description of your response need not be lengthy, but it must accurately note any important details.

Like your clinical response, your record should reflect a well-founded and rational treatment approach. Here it is sometimes helpful to consider how other clinicians might judge your response. It may also be useful to think about the legal implications. As a legal standard, if something is not recorded, it is difficult to prove it was done. Learn to record scrupulously anything you do or do not do that might later be considered important. Be conscientious about noting such things as referring a client to someone else, administering formal tests or other measures, if giving homework assignments or developing contracts, and scheduling future contacts. Also keep notes if you consult with someone about a case. Include both the fact that you consulted and a summary of the consultation and results (Harris, 1995).

To the extent that the severity of a client's concerns or the riskiness of a clinical decision increases, records should be more detailed. Bennett et al. (1990) suggest that records should describe the goal of the chosen intervention, risks and benefits, and the reason for choosing a specific treatment. It is also advisable to indicate any known risks, available alternatives and why they were not chosen, and the steps that were taken to maximize the effectiveness of chosen treatments. In some instances, documenting what you did not do and why you decided not to do it can be just as important as documenting what you did do. As further information, it is often useful to note any information provided to, or discussed with, the client, and the client's response.

In essence, this process is tantamount to "thinking out loud" in the record. Gutheil advised: "As a general rule, the more uncertainty the more one should think out loud in the record" (1980, p. 482). In this process, the clinician is recording not only the action taken but the reasons for taking or not taking an action. If questions arise later, the explanation is already documented. In a legal context, Gutheil stressed that for liability reasons this process is important because it reduces the possibility of a ruling of clinical negligence.

TREATMENT PLAN

Following the description of your immediate response, the final element of a well-written progress note is your plan for future treatment. This may be as simple as a note saying "Schedule for next Monday" or "Continue to monitor condition daily," or it might be more complex, as in "Next session we will explore family issues. Client will bring written description of each family member, and we will complete family diagrams." Notes of this sort allow you to refer back to refresh your memory of what was planned. This might seem unnecessary to you now, but if you have large and complex caseloads, such records will help you keep track of your clients and their treatment.

If you are working in an agency where a daily log is maintained, it is often possible to leave notes there for other staff. For example, you might conclude a note by suggesting that the evening staff keep close watch on a patient. If something is really important, be sure to highlight it in some way in your notes. Use stars, bold writing, or other methods to make the note stand out. If the matter is urgent or life-threatening, do not leave the matter to progress notes alone; speak directly to someone responsible and document the conversation.

DART IN PRACTICE

To demonstrate how the DART notation approach might work in practice, suppose you were working in a school setting and a child came in with severe straplike bruises and welts across his back. You suspect the child may have been abused, so you discuss it with him. He seems to avoid answering but finally says he fell and hurt himself.

The following sample notes illustrate how you might record this using the DART format. In this example, the DART initials are used to help organize the note and for ease of later location of information. As you read the example, identify how and what information is included in each of the main areas. You may find some information following one initial that might also go with a different initial. In contrast to other systems, the DART model is not so concerned with what goes where in the notes. What matters most is that all the important information gets recorded accurately and in a useful manner.

D: 10/18/2004 Monday: After recess at 10 A.M. today, Timothy North was taking his jacket off and in the process his shirt pulled up revealing straplike red welts across his back. At noon break I spoke with him while the other children were out. I said I noticed he had some red marks on his back. He looked away and shrugged without answering. I asked where he got them, and he said he did not know. Then he said he had fallen down over the weekend. I asked if his parents knew, and he said yes. That afternoon I met with the school nurse, Karen Jones, and Tim. The nurse looked at the marks and asked Tim similar questions; he again said he had fallen.

A: The marks do not look like they came from a fall. Karen Jones, school nurse, agrees. We are concerned about possible abuse. This child has come in with questionable bruises before, but none were this severe, and he has always offered plausible explanations. Given the nature of the present marks, we believe the situation warrants notification of Child Protective Services.

R: I notified the school counselor, Alice Black, and we contacted Child Protective Services. The contact person at CPS is William Randolph, MSW. He asked if we thought there was imminent danger of severe harm to the child. We replied that we did not have enough information to know that. He suggested we schedule a meeting for Wednesday,

October 20, at 4 P.M. If further concerns arise before then, we will call and inform him.

T: We will keep watch on Tim and check for further signs of injury. Future action will be determined at Wednesday meeting.

Signed, Joyce Jefferson, MSW, Date, 10/18/2004
cc: Karen Jones, Alice Black, William Randolph

SOAP NOTES

As noted earlier, one of the more common standardized note-taking methods is the SOAP format. So-called SOAP notes are actually part of a broader system known as Problem Oriented Medical Records. Comparable to the structure recommended by Piazza and Baruth (1990), which was discussed earlier in this chapter, the POMR system includes four components, commonly referred to as the clinical assessment, problem list, treatment plan, and progress notes (Shaw, 1997). SOAP notes fall in the progress note portion of this system.

The letters in SOAP stand for subjective, objective, assessment, and plan. "Subjective" refers to information about the client's present situation from the client's subjective position. One way to think of this is as the client's presenting complaint or description of how he or she is doing and what he or she needs or desires. "Objective" information is meant to be the external data that are being observed. In a medical setting, this might be blood pressure, temperature, and the like. Such objective data are often much less clear in psychotherapy interactions than in medical practice, though it is possible to offer descriptions of, for example, the client's affect, appearance, and mannerisms. The "assessment" portion of a note reflects how the therapist integrates and evaluates the meaning of the client's subjective report and the objective externally observable data in light of all the other information known about the client. From this assessment, the plan of treatment action is then recorded.

Although the concepts behind Problem-Oriented Medical Records, from which SOAP developed, are quite valuable, my experience with the SOAP format suggests that the terminology is rather ambiguous for use outside medical settings, and enforcement of the terminology can be paradoxically rigid. This situation can readily lead to needless debate about whether an entry should have been placed in the *S, O,* or *A* section (Cameron & Turtle-song, 2002). I have also found that efforts to conform to rigid SOAP guidelines tend to produce contorted writing that may obscure rather than clarify what happened and what was done about it. Nevertheless, many institutions use the POMR and SOAP system, so you should be familiar with them and develop strategies for following these formats. Cameron and Turtle-song (2002) offered some very useful suggestions for how the SOAP format can be used in mental health settings. If this system is used in your placement, your supervisor will no doubt be very familiar with it and can give you useful suggestions for putting your progress notes in the proper format for that institution. If you are interested in knowing more about SOAP, see the original work by Weed (1971) or the more general review of medical records by Avery and Imdieke (1984). Most settings that use SOAP or any of the other standard note formats will have training material or workshops that can teach you more about writing these notes.

EXERCISE

If you are not already writing clinical notes, you may want to develop your skills by choosing a recent interaction with a friend or client and document it as if you were writing a progress note in a clinical record. If possible, review the note with your supervisor and request feedback about how you could improve the note.

TIME-SEQUENCED NOTES

As noted earlier in this chapter and in the discussion of HIPAA and ethics in Chapter 3, psychotherapy notes are different than progress notes and should not be kept in the patient's general record. In contrast to the DART and SOAP approaches, which are used primarily to record specific events or interactions and are kept in the general record, a therapist's personal case notes from individual sessions typically follow a different format and serve a different purpose. Time-sequenced notes are the most common form of notation for therapy sessions. In time-sequenced notes, the therapy session is described as it progressed, with individual elements described sequentially in the order in which they occurred in the session. Some therapists make these notes during the therapy session. Others wait until the end of a session to record what happened.

The sequential approach is often used for records of therapy sessions because there are simply too many elements to address each separately following a more structured format. Sequential notes also enable the clinician to observe the order of events as they occur within a session. This can provide extremely useful clinical information. For example, it is probably not mere coincidence if a client begins by describing family conflicts, then shifts the topic to problems at work. Sequential notes follow this shift and enable the clinician to notice it in the record even though it might have gone unnoticed during the session. An example of an abbreviated sequentially ordered progress note from a therapy session follows. Note the use of an informal shorthand to save time:

> 2/9/2004 2–3 P.M. JA began session by revu of 1st wks sesn. Said he had thought about it & did not understnd why he had cried about father. We explored this more. JA cried again, rembrd fishing trip and fathr takng his fish away. Felt humiliated. Realized this was typical pattern. Gave recent example of visit during Xmas. His father was critical of JA's job, an argument developed and JA returned home early. We explored pattern of seeking approval and

fearing rejection. JA realized that anger is also there. This comes out in marriage as well. JA is often angry w wife if she disapproves of anything he does. He described two examples, when he cooks and in child care. He is not comfortable with own behavior but is having hard time chnging. Agreed to explore this more nxt sessn.

In a one-hour session, there would obviously be more that could be recorded, but in this example the therapist has chosen to note the events and topics she considered most important. This will vary from therapist to therapist and is also closely tied to theoretical orientation. Analytically trained therapists, for example, would be likely to make much different notes than those recorded by a behavioral therapist.

PROCESS OR PROGRESS NOTES

Process notes are yet another type of note with which you should be familiar. Process notes refer to notes in which the therapist includes personal reflections on not only the observable interactions in treatment but also the therapist's own thoughts and considerations of such things as the unconscious dynamics of a patient or the transference or countertransference issues in therapy. As contrasted with progress notes, which focus more on the externally observable, empirical events of treatment, process notes delve into the psyche of the therapist and patient. Notes of this type can be especially useful in training because they allow interns and their supervisors to review not only what was going on externally during the interaction but what the intern was thinking (Fox & Gutheil, 2000). Professionals trained from a psychodynamic perspective will be quite familiar with process notes and may consider them essential to training and treatment.

Prior to the establishment of the protections now included in HIPAA, many professionals who valued process notes had legitimate concerns that such notes might be sought by insurance companies. Legally, clients also have access to their general medical records, and a client who reads a therapist's private speculations on the client's libidinal attachments, latent desires, or other potentially sensitive matters might not understand the purpose of such notes or the terminology involved. These concerns have largely been addressed by HIPAA protections, but, again, only if psychotherapy notes are kept separately from other records. HIPAA protections notwithstanding, however, be aware that process notes may also be problematic in legal proceedings and, as discussed in Chapter 3, HIPAA does not protect notes against court orders (Harris, 1995).

Given these concerns, many professionals have chosen to reduce substantially or eliminate the introspective and theoretical contemplation that was once standard in process notes. This is unfortunate, because process notes can be tremendously valuable in clinical practice and especially in clinical training. For an excellent review of this topic and suggestions for effective use of process notes, see Fox and Gutheil (2000). Ultimately,

what you choose to put in your notes is up to you and your supervisor, but keep in mind the benefits as well as the risks, and, again, be aware that your notes may be read by other persons.

SIGNING NOTES

The final step in writing progress notes is signing them. As an intern, you should check with your supervisor to be sure you understand exactly how notes or other documents are to be signed and how you are to identify yourself with your signature. Some institutions require interns to sign notes and identify themselves as "Psychology Intern" or "Social Work Student." It may also be necessary for your supervisor to co-sign any work that you write. This might include daily progress notes, or it might apply only to more lengthy reports. Because different agencies or institutions will have different policies, the only sure way to know you are following procedures is to ask from the beginning.

Along with being sure to list your status correctly, you should also consider the legibility of your signature. Mine happens to be almost totally illegible. With experience, secretaries, students, and colleagues all learn more or less how to decipher my scratchings, but those who have less experience and do not know me well are often at a loss. This can present a problem for progress notes, because sometimes there are questions relating to notes, and people need to know who wrote them. If no one knows who you are and they cannot read your signature, it is going to be difficult to find you. My solution is to always print my name above my signature. Because most people will be less familiar with interns than with regular staff, it is especially important for you to be sure people can read your writing and to identify your status clearly.

DICTATION

Whether you write or dictate your progress notes, their content and structure should follow the guidelines offered thus far. This may sound easy, but for most people, dictation takes some getting used to. The typical approach of beginners is to write their notes first, then read them onto the recorder. That is not exactly a model of efficiency. If you work in a setting where dictated notes are an option or requirement, the following suggestions may help.

Dictation is like writing; both take practice to develop. When people begin dictating, it may help to work from a brief written outline. This is not as lengthy or redundant as writing the entire entry beforehand, but it does provide some structure and a reference point. It is also possible to use a general outline, such as the DART format, and then make notes about the specific details for each client or event.

When you are dictating, keep in mind that the people who will transcribe your record have only what they hear on tape as a basis for what they will write. Remember to speak clearly, spell out unfamiliar names or terms, and verbally indicate where punctuation, paragraph breaks, or symbols go. With the advent of digital recording systems, one can now speak quite rapidly, because the person transcribing the note can easily stop or move back or forward to keep up. If a slower, tape-based system is in use, you may need to speak more slowly so the typist can keep up. Whatever system you use, you can save the typist time by using the pause button on the recorder when you stop to think. Also, do not be afraid to make corrections if you realize that you made a mistake or left out a detail earlier in your report. Rather than rewinding and starting over, if you realize you made an error or omission, you can say something like, "I just realized I left out a sentence. Could you go back to just after . . . and insert. . . ." When you have dictated the correction, you can continue from where you left off.

In most large institutions, you may never meet the staff who transcribe your dictated notes. Because I find this structure unfriendly, I make it a point to get to know the people who will be typing my notes. Building relationships with records, secretarial, and other staff is not only rewarding interpersonally, it can also help prevent and more easily resolve a host of problems. Good secretarial work can be extremely valuable, so it is important to respect and support the people you work with. One way to show your respect and build a relationship is to visit with folks when you begin your internship and stop by from time to time later to say hello. It also helps to conclude your records by thanking the person who is doing the typing and acknowledging that person's work.

Future directions for dictation involve voice recognition systems, in which one speaks directly to a computer that then prints the text of what is said. These systems are growing in sophistication and can already manage complex clinical terminology and editing functions. However, such systems require the user to speak clearly and relatively consistently. This may take some getting used to, but with practice one can learn to interact effectively with such systems.

EXERCISE

To gain practice in dictation, think of an interaction that occurred in class or with your peers. Use a tape-recorder and dictate your notes as if they were to be given to a secretary for typing. Then, either type the notes yourself from the tape, or ask a willing friend to try to type from your notes. Your friend can offer feedback about how fast you spoke, whether you misspelled a technical term, whether you were clear about punctuation, and so on. Remember, dictation is a skill that takes time to learn. Do not be embarrassed about hearing your own voice or about how your notes read on the first try. With practice, you will find that dictated notes go much faster and can be just as informative as written notes.

PROGRESS NOTES AND SUPERVISION

I have described the importance of progress notes for meeting agency standards, ethical guidelines, and legal documentation.

In addition, progress notes can also provide useful material for clinical supervision. The general subject of supervision was discussed in Chapter 4, but a few additional comments are warranted in the context of notes.

It is a good practice for interns and supervisors to make reviews of progress notes a regular part of the supervision process. This review serves several functions. As noted earlier, reviewing notes with supervisors helps to ensure that the intern's records are up to agency standards. Because record keeping is an important but often overlooked part of clinical training, supervisors may wish to offer advice about the content or the style of an intern's notes. Reviewing notes also allows interns the opportunity to ask about any issues pertaining to record keeping and note taking. Beyond the clerical aspects of note taking, reviewing notes and records helps supervisors observe what interns consider to be significant about a case or therapy session. Supervisors can monitor the intern's records of the content and process of therapy sessions, and the notes can be referred to as needed to supplement or guide case discussions.

USING YOUR NOTES

Having devoted this chapter primarily to how to keep records and progress notes, it should not be forgotten that the primary purpose of notes is to assist the treatment of your clients. It is surprising how often therapists take notes at the end of sessions but then do not refer to them again before the next session with their clients. This can easily happen as therapists with busy schedules shift from seeing one client to the next with little time in between. Understandable though this may be, the quality of treatment may be lessened as a result.

I confess to having been guilty of this myself on occasion. I recall an instance in which a client said he had given a great deal of thought to what was said last week, and I found myself internally struggling to recall just what it was we had discussed. It has also happened that I "assigned homework" (i.e., suggested that a client do or write something between sessions), which I then forgot to discuss. Clients have called me on this and in some cases have expressed their displeasure over what appears to be a lack of concern or attention.

Beyond a matter of courtesy or simple forgetfulness, many clients may actually consider such oversights unethical. In a survey of 96 adults, some of whom had experience as clients and others of whom had not, Claiborn, Berberoglu, Nerison, and Somberg (1994) found that in a list of statements about 60 possible hypothetical events that might occur in therapy, the statement "Your therapist does not remember what you talked about in the previous session" was ranked fourth highest among events considered to be ethically inappropriate. The mean ranking for this item on a scale of 1 to 5, with 1 being "completely inappropriate," was 1.32. Clearly, at least in this sample, recipients of clinical services placed a high value on therapists being aware of the content of previous sessions.

Given this finding, it certainly behooves the therapist to take the few minutes before a session to review the notes from the last visit. With heavy caseloads and busy schedules, oversights and lapses of memory are almost sure to occur unless clinicians take good notes and then make use of them. On the other hand, clinicians who make efficient use of progress notes will be more aware of the sequence of events across sessions. This will lead to better therapeutic care and will result in higher levels of satisfaction on the part of clients.

OTHER GUIDELINES

This book has emphasized repeatedly that you must know your limits and be open to learning. This applies to records and notes as much as any other aspect of your internship. If you do not know how to write a note, or if you are unsure of the wording to use, ask for help. If you are describing an interaction with a client, do not write notes designed to impress everyone with your skills. While you are an intern, humility is a virtue, and hubris can get you into trouble. Remember simplicity and objectivity.

Another principle of note taking is to be constructive. This is especially important if you are writing notes in a record that is accessible to others. Although part of your task is to assess and try to understand what you observe, your purpose is not to ascribe blame. Your goal is to facilitate treatment, not to be critical of clients or staff. For example, it would not be constructive to write a note such as "Dennis is up to his old tricks again. Found him masturbating in front of the television. Sometimes I think we should cut the thing off." This may sound shockingly callous, but I read precisely this note in staff records. Interns learn by example, but some examples are best not followed. Imagine the impact of such a note if read by an outside professional, a family member, or in a court of law.

For similar reasons, if you are working in an institution where many staff members record notes in the same book, using the record to question or attack the conduct of other staff is not a good idea. Consider, for example, "The night shift is still not following through with last week's treatment plan. How is he supposed to get better if we are not consistent?" This note may stem from legitimate frustration, but a formal progress note may not be the best place to air those feelings. I have read record books that sounded more like a name-calling war between staff than a mutual discussion of treatment. Such notes cannot really be helpful to the clients or the staff. If you have concerns, address them with your supervisor, but keep the progress notes objective.

Finally, from the outset of your career, develop good note-taking and record-keeping habits. Make yourself write notes immediately or as soon after an interaction as possible. Schedule the time you need for note taking and do not sacrifice this to other distractions. Keep your notes as thorough as they need to be, follow any required format, and establish a process of review to ensure that you keep everything up to date.

Faced with the many demands of clinical work, it is all too easy to become careless, or to let other tasks take precedence over note taking (Kagle, 1993). If you need 10 minutes for note taking between therapy sessions, schedule that in and do not allow it to be taken up instead with phone calls or other distractions. Unless they are urgent, save those other matters until you have finished your notes. You will be surprised how much gets forgotten or lost even by the end of the day. The longer you wait to record your notes, the less accurate and less valuable they will be. When it comes to clinical record keeping, a little compulsivity is not a bad quality to develop. Not only will well-kept notes enhance your clinical treatment, they can also make the difference between whether or not an insurance company pays for services. In our litigious society well-kept progress notes may also save you untold legal problems if you are ever called on to produce them in court.

REFERENCES

Alter, C., & Adkins, C. (2001). Improving the writing skills of social work students. *Journal of Social Work Education, 37,* 493–505.

Alter, C., & Adkins, C. (2006). Assessing student writing proficiency in graduate schools of social work. *Journal of Social Work Education, 42,* 337–354.

American Psychological Association: Committee on Professional Standards. (1993). Record keeping guidelines. *American Psychologist, 48,* 984–986.

Avery, M., & Imdieke, B. (1984). *Medical records in ambulatory care.* Rockville, MD: Aspen Systems.

Baird, B., & Anderson, D. (1990). A dual-draft approach to writing. *Teaching Professor, 4*(3), 5–6.

Barker, R. L. (2003) *The Social Work Dictionary* (5th ed.) Washington, DC: National Association of Social Workers.

Bennett, B. E., Bryant, B. K., Vandenbos, G. R., & Greenwood, A. (1990). *Professional liability and risk management.* Washington, DC: American Psychological Association.

Bower, A. G. (2005). *The diffusion and value of healthcare information technology,* RAND (available online at http://www.rand.org/pubs/monographs/2006/RAND_MG272–1.pdf)

Braun, S. A., & Cox, J. A. (2005). Managed mental health care: Intentional misdiagnosis of mental disorders. *Journal of Counseling and Development, 83,* 425–432.

Brenner, E. (2003). Consumer-focused psychological assessment. *Professional Psychology: Research and Practice, 34,* 240–247.

Cameron, S., & Turtle-song, I. (2002) Learning to write case notes using the SOAP format. *Journal of Counseling and Development, 80,* 286–292.

Casper, E. S. (1987). A management system to maximize compliance with standards for medical records. *Hospital and Community Psychiatry, 38,* 1191–1194.

Claiborn, C. D., Berberoglu, L. S., Nerison, R. M., & Somberg, D. R. (1994). The client's perspective: Ethical judgments and perceptions of therapist practices. *Professional Psychology: Research and Practice, 25,* 268–274.

Drotar, D. (2000). Training professional psychologists to write and publish the utility of a writer's workshop seminar. *Professional Psychology: Research and Practice, 31*(4), 453–457.

Fischer, C. (1994). *Individualized psychological assessment.* Monterey, CA: Brooks/Cole.

Fox, R., & Gutheil, I. A. (2000). Process recording: A means for conceptualizing and evaluating practice. *Journal of Teaching in Social Work, 20,* 39–57.

Grayson, H. M., & Tolman, R. S. (1950). A semantic study of concepts of clinical psychologists and psychiatrists. *Journal of Abnormal and Social Psychology, 45,* 216–231.

Gutheil, T. G. (1980). Paranoia and progress notes: A guide to forensically informed psychiatric recordkeeping. *Hospital and Community Psychiatry, 31,* 479–482.

Harris, E. A. (1995). The importance of risk management in a managed care environment. In M. B. Sussman (Ed.), *A perilous calling: The hazards of psychotherapy practice* (pp. 247–258). New York: Wiley.

Hartlage, L. C., & Merck, K. H. (1971). Increasing the relevance of psychological reports. *Journal of Clinical Psychology, 1971, 27*(4), 459–460.

Harvey, V. S. (1997). Improving readability of psychological reports. *Professional Psychology: Research and Practice, 28,* 271–274.

Hodges, J. C., Horner, W. B., Webb, S. S., & Miller, R. K. (1998). *Harbrace college handbook* (13th ed., rev.). New York: Harcourt Brace Jovanovich.

Jeffords, J. (1999). Confidentiality of medical information: Protecting privacy in an electronic age. *Professional Psychology: Research and Practice, 30*(2), 115–116.

Kagle, J. D. (1993). Record keeping: Directions for the 1990s. *Social Work, 38,* 190–196.

Piazza, N. J., & Baruth, N. E. (1990). Client record guidelines. *Journal of Counseling and Development, 68,* 313–316.

Piercy, F. P., Sprenkle, D. H., & McDaniel, S. H. (1996). Teaching professional writing to family therapists: Three approaches. *Journal of Marital and Family Therapy, 22,* 163–179.

RAND Corporation (2005). Health information technology: Can HIT lower costs and improve quality? http://www.rand.org/pubs/research_briefs/RB9136/index1.html

Rupert, P. A., & Baird, K. A., (2004). Managed care and the independent practice of psychology. *Professional Psychology: Research and Practice, 35, 185–193.*

Shaw, M. (1997). *Charting made incredibly easy.* Springhouse, PA: Springhouse.

Siskind, G. (1967). Fifteen years later: A replication of "A semantic study of concepts of clinical psychologists and psychiatrists." *Journal of Psychology, 65,* 3–7.

Soisson, E. L., VandeCreek, L., & Knapp, S. (1987). Thorough record keeping: A good defense in a litigious era. *Professional Psychology: Research and Practice, 18,* 498–502.

Steinfeld, B., Ekorenrud, B., Gillett, C., Quirk, M., & Eytan, T., (2006). EMRs bring all of healthcare together. *Behavioral Healthcare, 26*(1), 12–17.

Strunk, W., Jr., & White, E. B. (2000). *The elements of style* (4th ed.). Boston: Allyn & Bacon.

Tallent, N. (1997). *Psychological report writing* (4th ed.). Englewood Cliffs, NJ: Prentice-Hall.

Van Vort, W., & Mattson, M. R. (1989). A strategy for enhancing the clinical utility of the psychiatric record. *Hospital and Community Psychiatry, 40,* 407–409.

VandenBos, G. R. (Ed.). (2006) *APA Dictionary of Psychology,* Washington, DC: American Psychological Association.

Wedding, D., Topolski, J., & McGaha, A. (1995). Maintaining the confidentiality of computerized mental health outcome data. *Journal of Mental Health Administration, 22,* 237–244.

Weed, L. L. (1971). *Medical records, medical education, and patient care: The problem-oriented record as a basic tool.* Chicago: Year Book.

Wiger, D. (1999). *The clinical documentation sourcebook: A comprehensive collection of mental health practice forms, handouts, and records* (2nd ed.). New York: Wiley.

Zinsser, W. (1998). *On writing well: The classic guide to writing nonfiction.* New York: Harper.

Zuckerman, E. L. (2000). *The clinician's thesaurus: A guidebook for wording psychological reports and other evaluations* (5th ed.). Pittsburgh: Three Wishes Press.

CHAPTER 7
STRESS AND SELF-CARE

When helping professionals tell others about their work, two common responses are: "That must be so difficult, listening to people's problems all day. I don't know how you do it." Or, "Uh oh, I'd better be careful. You're not going to psychoanalyze me, are you?"

Although these comments typically come from people who are not involved in the field, both responses raise legitimate questions and concerns for interns. What does happen to people who work in the helping professions as a result of their work? How do we balance our professional roles with our personal lives away from work? And how can interns manage the demands of internships, school, family, friends, and work without falling apart?

This chapter discusses the stresses that interns and helping professionals experience and the ways those stresses affect our lives and work. The goal of the chapter is to help you understand and recognize the stresses and learn to cope effectively with them.

EXERCISE

Before reading further, take a moment to write down some of your own thoughts about each of the following questions. If you do not have any actual clinical experience yet, answer the questions as you think you might be affected when you are working in a clinical setting.

1. In what ways do you think your work as an intern affects you emotionally now? For example, how do you feel at the end of an internship day? How do you feel on days when you are not at your internship?
2. How does your internship influence your ideas about the clients you work with? About people in general? About people who are close to you? Society?
3. How does your internship affect you physically? What kinds of physical demands or limitations do the activities of your work impose on you? Do you experience any physical responses to working with stressful clients, colleagues, or supervisors?
4. How does your internship affect your close personal or social relationships?

5. Having considered how your internship is affecting you now, how do you think you would be affected if you were a full-time professional in your field?
6. What personal qualities do you think will help you in dealing with the stress of your work? What personal qualities do you think may make it difficult for you to deal with the stress of your work?
7. How will you be able to recognize if you are being affected adversely by your work?
8. How might you cope with a situation in which you come to recognize that you are under excessive stress and your professional effectiveness or personal wellness is being harmed?

However you answered the preceding questions, it is certain that you will be affected by your work. You simply cannot interact with people and not be changed in some way. At the same time, experiences and stresses in your life away from work will influence your performance as a professional (Baker, 2005; Cunningham, 2004; Furr & Carroll, 2003; Kottler, 2003; Norcross, 2005; Mahoney, 1997; Sherman & Thelen, 1998). To make matters still more complicated, you do not always have control or even awareness of just how you will be changed either by your work or by your life away from work. As Guy (1987) observed in his book, *The Personal Life of the Psychotherapist:*

> Since their personality is the "tool" used to conduct this clinical work, who a psychotherapist "is" undergoes constant challenge, review, and transformation. One would certainly hope that the resultant changes are largely positive, improving the therapist's satisfaction with life and relationships. Regrettably . . . it may also be that certain changes have the potential to hinder interpersonal functioning in and outside of work. (p. 105)

Similar observations are offered by Kottler (2003)

> Throughout the process of therapy, the relationship is our main instrument of cure. Although we try to insulate ourselves, and we successfully pretend most of the time, leaks inevitably occur. . . . The more clients talk about subjects that touch on our own

unresolved issues, the more insecure and incompetent we feel about ourselves. (p. 17)

When one realizes that the work of therapy inevitably affects the therapist personally, and when one realizes that the therapist's own awareness and wellness are key elements of the treatment process, it is surprising that many undergraduate and graduate programs pay relatively little attention to this issue (Sowa, May, & Niles, 1994; Sussman, 1995). Fortunately, awareness of this subject appears to be increasing, and a growing body of literature deals with the effects of the helping professions on helping professionals and interns. Perhaps the best news of all is that, overall, in spite of the demands and stresses, most practitioners report generally high levels of satisfaction and reward in their professional lives (Stevanovic & Rupert, 2004). Let us look first at the challenges and stressors, then explore coping strategies and the rewards of the profession.

CLIENT AFTER CLIENT, DAY AFTER DAY

Consider this scenario. You are a beginning professional working in a mental health center. On a Monday morning at 8 o'clock, your first client is a 25-year-old woman who is married to a physically and verbally abusive spouse. The woman has two children and a third on the way, recently suffered the death of her mother, and just found out that she will be laid off from work. The client is basically a caring, hard-working person who finds herself in a terrible situation and feels there are limited ways to get out of, or through, it. You feel very deeply what it must be like for this client and determine to work with her.

Your next client is a 15-year-old boy whose parents are getting a divorce. He has been experimenting with drugs and is afraid he is getting hooked on speed. He has also just been arrested for breaking into a car with some friends and taking a stereo. He has never been in trouble with the law before, and his court date is coming up next week. The boy is seeing you for help in dealing with the drug problem and with the upcoming court date.

The third case of the day is a man ordered by the court to seek therapy following an arrest for drunken driving. He makes it clear that he doesn't really want to be in treatment, has no intention of quitting drinking, and accepts no responsibility for his past actions or for change. He says he will come to meet with you only until the court-ordered time period is up.

It's now just 11 o'clock on Monday. You will see four more clients today, and there are four more days to go until the weekend. Let's throw in as a background issue that your clinic's future is uncertain because federal and local funding for mental health have been reduced and third-party payments from insurers are also being lowered. What is more, there was a recent client suicide, and a series of staff meetings is taking place to review the incident. Finally, several of the staff members do not get along well with each other, so there is a steady state of tension among the staff at the clinic. How are you doing? Oh yes, I forgot to mention that your significant other is upset with you because you are on crisis duty and cannot go away for the weekend.

If this sounds like an atypical scenario, concocted just to present the worst-case picture of professional life, it is not. In fact, in many instances the actual cases and institutional issues are even more challenging than those presented here.

HOW COMMON IS STRESS AMONG HELPING PROFESSIONALS?

Given the kinds of demands just described, it should not be surprising to learn that at one time or another most helping professionals will find themselves working under significant stress. Sherman and Thelen (1998) surveyed practicing psychologists to identify the frequency and degree of impairment caused by life and work events. Their results showed that during the previous year, at least 20% of respondents were dealing with at least one major life stress. Among the more frequently reported stressors were serious illness of a family member, major relationship issues, loans, financial changes, and work-related changes. Stresses at the workplace included such things as working with difficult clients, paperwork, time demands, restrictions imposed by managed-care companies, and office politics. These findings among professionals mirror to some degree the "critical incidents" in the lives of counselor trainees studied by Furr and Carroll (2003).

As a result of such challenges, the clinical performance of therapists is bound to be affected. Indeed, only 38.8% of therapists surveyed by Pope, Tabachnick, and Keith-Spiegel (1987) said they never engaged in clinical work when too distressed to be effective. Of the remaining respondents, 48.5% said they only rarely worked under such conditions, and 10.5% said they sometimes did. This left only 0.6% who indicated they fairly often or very often worked when too distressed to be effective. While it is encouraging to note the small percentage of therapists who acknowledge that they often work when they may be ineffective, this research also suggests that on some occasions more than half of the therapists surveyed worked when their own distress might have impaired their therapeutic effectiveness.

Further evidence of the stresses of clinical work comes from a survey by Ackerley, Burnell, Holder, and Kurdek (1988). In a sample of 562 licensed, doctoral-level psychologists practicing primarily in mental health agencies, results from the Maslach Burnout Inventory (Maslach & Jackson, 1986) showed that nearly 40% of the sample were "experiencing high levels of emotional exhaustion," and just over 34% were experiencing "high levels of depersonalization" (p. 629). Based on a survey that included comparatively greater proportions of clinicians in private practice, Skorupa and Agresti (1993) reported that 25% of respondents scored in the moderate range of emotional exhaustion, and 15% scored in the high range. Skorupa and Agresti also found that the presence of burnout symptoms was positively correlated with the amount of client-contact hours per week. In general, higher numbers of contact hours were associated with higher ratings of physical exhaustion and depersonalization. On a positive note, these results also showed that psychologists who expressed more concern about the risks of burnout tended to demonstrate more knowledge of burnout-prevention techniques and generally lower levels of burnout symptoms.

Most interns are relatively new to the field and full of energy and dedication, so the stress of clinical work may not be an immediate concern. Be aware, however, that the stresses of training and practice can be significant and, in some instances, can contribute to impaired functioning. For example, Boxley, Drew, and Rangle (1986) reported that 66% of the internship sites they surveyed reported having worked with "impaired" interns during the previous five years. The annual rate of trainee impairment was found to be 4.6%. This figure translates into approximately 1 in 20 interns who have difficulties sufficient to meet the definition of "any physical, emotional or educational condition that interferes with the quality of the intern's professional performance" (p. 50). Comparable findings were obtained by Olkin and Gaughen (1991), who surveyed clinically oriented master's programs in a variety of mental health fields. Their results showed that the mean percentage of "problem students" was 4.8%" (p. 283). A problem student was defined as "having problems of such a nature or severity that s/he (a) comes to the attention of the faculty, and (b) requires some response from the faculty" (p. 282). As the definitions used by Boxley and colleagues and by Olkin and Gaughen indicate, not all the cases of impairment identified as "impaired" or "problems" were due solely to stress. Nevertheless, the findings from these studies suggest that preparing interns to deal with stress and personal issues needs greater attention than it has received in clinical training (Bradley & Post, 1991; Lamb et al., 1987; Stadler, Willing, Eberhage, & Ward, 1988).

More recent studies have yielded very similar results to the earlier research. Oliver et al. (2004) surveyed students in graduate clinical psychology programs and asked respondents to estimate the percentages of students they viewed as impaired, describe the types of problems observed, and discuss the adequacy or shortcomings of the training program response. The results of this study were rather qualitative in nature, but overall estimates ranged from 0 to 21% of students considered impaired by their peers, with 12% being described as a typical number of impaired students across programs. The nature of impairments described by students ranged from emotional difficulties, such as depression or severe anxiety, to personality disorders, including narcissistic and antisocial personality traits. Students also identified deficits in basic academic abilities and in clinical skills. Faced with these issues, students reported that they felt frustrated and confused about what to do and expressed concern that impaired peers were in some ways holding back the rest of the class and might also not

be up to the task of becoming professionals. Unfortunately, many of the respondents felt that the training program did not deal well with these issues. Respondents indicated uncertainty about whether training directors even recognized the impaired students as having problems, and if there was recognition, the respondents often reported a tendency to ignore or minimize the problem. One other interesting finding was a report by some students that there needs to also be attention to "impaired training programs"—programs in which the faculty themselves or the inherent structure may be dysfunctional in some way.

Comparable findings were reported in a separate study by Rosenberg, Getzelman, Arcinue and Oren (2005), who note that use of the term "impaired" has come under criticism on conceptual and legal grounds. They suggest "problematic trainees" would be a preferable descriptor. In their research, 85% of the respondents identified at least one problematic peer in their training programs, with the average number of problematic peers identified per program comparable to the numbers reported by Oliver et al. (2004). Also consistent were the kinds of concerns identified, including emotional and personality issues, academic deficiencies, and clinical deficiences. Interestingly, when asked to indicate how they responded to these concerns about peers, expressing concerns to faculty was selected only 23% of the time. It was far more common for students to report talking among themselves or withdrawing from the peer in question. As with the students studied by Oliver et al., reasons for not dealing more directly with the issue ranged from poor relations with and a lack of confidence in faculty, to concerns about the impact on the problematic individual's emotional or professional well-being.

SOURCES OF STRESS

What factors and stressors may be contributing to the reported incidence of impairment among interns and practicing professionals? In a follow-up to the study by Pope et al., Guy, Poelstra, and Stark (1989) sought to identify the sources of stress reported by a sample of 318 practicing psychotherapists. This research revealed that therapists must contend both with stresses directly related to their clinical work and with stresses stemming from issues in their personal lives. When asked to identify sources of personal distress they had experienced in the past three years, 74.3% indicated at least one major source of distress during that time period. Of these, 32.9% identified job stress, 23.2% illness in the family, 20.4% marital problems, 17.9% a death in the family, 15.9% financial problems, 15.7% midlife crisis, 14.7% personal illness, and 10.9% "other." When asked if personal distress resulted in decreased quality of care provided, 36.7% of the respondents said yes, and 4.6% said the distress resulted in inadequate care. The results did not show that any specific source of stress was found to predict either decreased or inadequate treatment care. Older clinicians, however, were more likely to claim that personal distress had no impact on patient care. It was also found that respondents who reported job stress or marital problems were the most likely to maintain that their quality of care had not been reduced due to the stress. In their discussion of these findings, Guy et al. expressed concern that some therapists, particularly those experiencing job and marital stress, may tend to deny the effects of this stress on their clinical effectiveness.

While the studies just described provided data pertaining to experienced and practicing clinicians, other research has included interns and practicum students and has focused in more detail on specific job-related stressors. Following research by Deutsch (1984) and Hellman, Morrison, and Abramowitz (1987), Rodolfa, Kraft, and Reilley (1988) surveyed experienced clinicians, interns, and practicum students working at Veterans' Administration hospitals and counseling centers. Their results identified client behaviors, therapist experiences, and therapist beliefs that were rated as stressful by clinicians, interns, and practicum students.

CLIENT BEHAVIORS

In the findings of Rodolfa et al. (1988), among the most stressful client behaviors were physical assault on the therapist, suicide attempts, and suicidal statements. Compared with more experienced professionals, interns and practicum students were more likely to rate as stressful such client behaviors as blatantly psychotic speech, homosexual and heterosexual flirting, premature termination, and clients' lack of motivation. Similar results were reported by Radeke and Mahoney (2000), who found that suicide attempts, client resistance, and client anger were among the leading stressors reported by therapists.

Fremont and Anderson (1986) looked at client behaviors from a slightly different perspective, asking senior staff members, interns, and practicum students to identify the behaviors of clients that were most likely to make the counselor angry, frustrated, or irritated. Respondents identified a number of incidents, which were then grouped into five categories: client resistance, impositions on the counselor, verbal attacks, the counselor becoming overly involved in client dynamics, and a more general category of other incidents. Specific incidents cited included clients failing to show up for appointments, clients continually blaming others or refusing to work on their own issues, clients asking for special privileges, or unnecessarily calling the therapist at home at odd hours. As in the findings of Rodolfa et al., therapists also expressed concern about verbal attacks or threats of physical harm by clients. Fremont and Anderson noted that for some of the issues, most notably resistance, the experience level of the counselor influenced their reaction, with more experienced counselors reporting less anger in response to resistance.

While certain client behaviors can be stressful to therapists, research has suggested that for certain diagnostic groups therapists may actually be able to cope surprisingly well. For example, Murtaugh and Wollersheim (1997) found, contrary to expectations, that therapists working with depressed clients

did not necessarily show any declines in their own mood. This finding was attributed to the therapists' use of cognitive and emotional coping strategies. More will be said about the use of such strategies later in this chaper in the discussion of self-care.

THERAPIST EXPERIENCES

In addition to exploring client behaviors, Rodolfa et al. (1988) examined therapist experiences and found that the items rated most stressful included an inability to help clients feel better (see also Farber & Heifetz, 1981), receiving criticism from supervisors, professional conflicts, and seeing more clients than usual. As with client behaviors, compared to the professionals, interns and practicum students rated different therapist experiences as more stressful. For example, interns and practicum students assigned higher stress ratings to such experiences as lack of client progress, inability to help clients feel better, criticism from supervisors, and presenting a case in staffing. As these findings indicate, along with the other challenges faced by helping professionals, trainees report the additional stress of supervision and related issues.

THERAPIST COGNITIONS

Stress-producing ideas represent a third area addressed by Rodolfa et al. (1988). Using a version of an instrument originally developed by Deutsch (1984), Rodolfa et al. found that the following beliefs are associated with greater stress among interns: the belief that therapists should always work at peak levels of competence and enthusiasm, the belief that therapists should be able to handle all client emergencies and should help every client, and the belief that lack of client progress is the therapist's fault. Failure to take time off also contributed to reported stress, as did the belief that therapists should be models of mental health themselves.

EXERCISE

You have just read examples of common stress-producing ideas among interns. Take a moment to think about your own beliefs about your internship and clients. Do any of these beliefs unnecessarily add to the stress you experience in your internship or training? If so, how might you change the ideas and your corresponding level of stress? This would be a fruitful topic to discuss with other interns and with your instructor or supervisor. In these discussions, ask your peers or mentors how they have dealt with these issues in their own work.

Rodolfa's findings regarding therapist beliefs and stress are consistent with the results of other research. For example, Hellman, Morrison, and Abramouitz (1987) studied the relationship between therapist flexibility, boundary maintenance, and stress. Of particular interest in this study was the distinction between "fusion" and "boundary maintenance." As they defined this issue, "The boundary dimension reflects attempts to establish highly structured interaction by emphasizing space and time boundaries and adopting clear and explicit roles. The fusion dimension reflects a tendency to blur personal boundaries with the environment" (p. 22).

The issue comes down to one of maintaining a degree of professional distance in which one is able to empathize with clients but not lose, or fear the loss of, one's own identity in the process. Results of the study by Hellman et al. indicated that therapists who were flexible reported less stress overall than therapists who were identified as rigid or dogmatic. With regard to the fusion/boundary questions, therapists who maintained higher personal boundaries reported less stress from such client behaviors as suicidal threats, passive-aggressive behavior, and negative client affect. Based on these findings, Hellman et al. suggested that the stresses created by patient behaviors may be reduced for therapists who can maintain a degree of flexibility and professional distance. They further suggested that for therapists who have greater fusion tendencies or are more rigid in their thinking and approach, working with certain kinds of clients may be unusually stressful.

In thinking about these conclusions, particularly those pertaining to boundaries and fusion, it is important to recognize that the key must be to maintain a therapeutic balance. Although different theoretical approaches place different emphases on the importance of emotional empathy with clients, if one's primary need is to maintain inflexible boundaries, it will be difficult to empathize with a client. Indeed, if carried to an extreme, the clearest way to eliminate therapeutic stress is to create boundaries so strong that one no longer interacts with clients at all. The trick is to find ways that enable you to empathize with, understand, and care about your clients, while still maintaining your role as a professional and your personal identity and life outside the therapy session.

THE EFFECTS OF STRESS

It should be evident from the discussion thus far that there are numerous possible sources of work-related and personal stress in the lives of interns and helping professionals. This raises questions about how such stresses may affect us as individuals and what impact stress has on our work with clients.

PHYSICAL EFFECTS

The mental and emotional toll is probably what comes to mind first when one thinks of the demands on helping professionals, but in many ways the physical costs can be just as high. I have talked to therapists who spend 8 to 10 hours per day seeing clients, one after another, in windowless offices, sometimes taking only 10 minutes for lunch in the middle of the day, then starting right back up again with no other break. This simply cannot be healthy, and it cannot be sustained for long before the effects begin to appear. As one of these therapists said: "Every job has its occupational hazards. For us it's hemorrhoids." He

might have added clogged arteries, atrophied muscles, weight gain, low back pain, and other physical ailments.

Psychotherapy and related activities are not aerobic exercises. In fact, if one watches tapes of therapy, it is startling how little many therapists move during certain sessions. They may spend a great deal of mental energy, but their physical motion is minimal. This lack of motion contributes to what a colleague calls "hypo-kinetic disorders" (i.e., physical illness caused by inactivity).

Commenting on this aspect of therapy, Guy (1987) remarked that other occupations may be relatively sedentary, but:

> Few require that the individual stay riveted to a chair for 50 minutes at a time, without the opportunity to stand up, stretch, or walk around. If a therapist fails to appreciate the need for regular, extended breaks to allow for sufficient physical activity, his or her only exercise is likely to be an occasional brief stroll to the water cooler and restroom between appointments. Day after day of such a sedentary pattern creates a physical fatigue which can negatively impact both the professional and personal functioning of the individual. (p. 82)

This may be part of the reason Radeke and Mahoney (2000) found that one out of five therapists was likely to report some degree of dissatisfaction with his or her weight.

Along with the problems stemming from limited activity, physical problems can also develop from patterns of storing stress through muscle tension. Early in the first month of a summer practicum placement, I developed extreme pains in the area between my left shoulder and neck. The pain tended to subside during the night, then became progressively worse as each day went on. For several weeks I tried warm and cold packs, took an occasional anti-inflammatory, and even tried lying on a tennis ball while rolling it around under my shoulder. All of this was to no avail until one day, while working with a particularly difficult client, I realized that as the client spoke my left shoulder was rising up. Although I was trying to stay relaxed while working with the client, my shoulder was evidently taking the tension. This insight led me to focus on my physical reaction to other clients. I discovered that whenever a session was difficult, my shoulder went up. With that awareness, I was able to self-monitor and relax my shoulder and other muscles as well.

In my case, I stored physical tension in my shoulder. Other interns and colleagues have reported neck pain, aches in their jaws, headaches, tension in their forehead, and pain and tension in other areas. Physical consequences are by no means limited to muscle tension. To the extent that the role of intern creates additional demands, the risk of stress-related illness is increased. It is not uncommon for students to report severe stomach pains and other signs of physical reactions to stress. One colleague even believed he was having a heart attack the night before his dissertation defense. It turned out to be a combination of stress, attitude, and anxiety, but the experience reminded him to be more attentive and take better care of himself physically as well as emotionally.

THE EFFECTS ON SOCIAL RELATIONSHIPS

As mentioned, every helping professional is probably familiar with being introduced to someone who responds with something like, "You're not going to psychoanalyze me, are you?" or, "Uh oh, now I better watch what I say."

In response to those who are concerned that helping professionals are continually evaluating people, the honest answer is probably yes and no. The answer is no because our interactions in social settings and personal relationships tend to be very different from our behavior in a professional role. At the same time, however, all people, helping professionals included, form impressions of one another.

While some people in social settings are worried about casual conversations with therapists, it can also happen that social acquaintances will take the opportunity to seek advice outside the clinical setting. There are many variations to this situation. Sometimes, people will ask your opinion about a general subject because they believe you may have relevant training or education or because they respect your intelligence and want to hear what you have to say on the matter. This is typically a sign of respect for you or your profession, and it is generally benign. The challenge in such cases is to avoid pontificating or speaking as though you have knowledge if you really don't. On the other hand, there are also times when people will begin a statement with something like "You're a therapist . . ." followed by a discussion of their children, spouse, parents, friends, boss, or someone else who is not present at the time.

Although it may be flattering to be consulted for your expertise, you should also realize that social situations in which people seek your "clinical advice" can be fraught with mixed roles, hidden agendas, and incomplete communication. As a general rule, it is wise not to offer any form of clinical advice or interpretation under such circumstances. You are probably hearing only one part of the story, have not been formally contracted to fill the role of therapist, are often in a public setting such as a party, and do not have the environment, time, permission, or pay to do real therapy work. The problem is, how do you refuse to give the desired advice or interpretation without being rude to the person who is asking the question?

When faced with this problem, I try to empathize with the questioner's concern and request for information. Then, having acknowledged their concerns, I indicate that out of concern for the questioner and anyone else who may be involved, I believe it is unwise to give clinical advice outside the clinical setting. I might say something like, "That does sound like a difficult situation, and I can understand you wanting some help in figuring out how to deal with it. But for lots of reasons I generally find it best to avoid giving clinical advice or delving into personal issues too deeply when I'm not actually doing therapy with someone. I hope you can understand."

Many people will let the matter drop at this point, and the conversation can naturally shift to something else. Others will pursue the question further, by asking if you could see them clinically or can recommend someone else who could. You can readily deal with this request through referral to your supervisor or another professional you know.

Another situation that many interns find awkward involves coincidental encounters with clients in nonclinical settings such as the grocery store, movies, or elsewhere. Although this has received relatively little research attention, a study of college therapists found their most common responses to incidental encounters with clients were surprise, uncertainty and, to a lesser degree, discomfort (Sharkin & Birkey, 1992). In comparison, Pulakos (1994) reported that although clients who encountered therapists also mentioned awkwardness among their reactions, they ranked feelings of confidence and surprise higher than feelings of discomfort. For a discussion and exercises relating to therapist reactions to incidental encounters, see Arons and Siegel (1995).

EXERCISE

You may find it informative to think about how you might feel and react to meeting a client in another setting. What do your reactions suggest to you about your role and the therapy process? You might also put yourself in the role of client and think how it would feel to meet your therapist in a public situation. Are there any settings where it would be more or less difficult to encounter clients? What are those situations, and what do the possible difficulties tell you about yourself or your role?

Oddly enough, in encounters outside the office, the awkwardness seems to come because both clinicians and client are worried about being seen "as they really are." This feeling goes both ways, in the sense that just as each person may be afraid the other will see him or her in a different light, there may also be a tendency to not want to see a person as anything other than a client or therapist (Arons & Siegel, 1995).

Along with the issue of revealing different roles outside therapy, awkwardness in coincidental encounters is also created by the confidentiality of therapy and a sense of not knowing whether or how to greet and interact with the other person. This is further complicated if the client or therapist is in the presence of someone else, and introductions seem called for. Given confidentiality concerns, the therapist cannot very well offer the introduction, "This is Eric Johnson; he's a client of mine in therapy."

As a preferred alternative, coincidental interactions with clients can be dealt with much as you would if you met a friend by coincidence in a similar setting. You might briefly ask how things are going, make small talk about the weather, and so on. If others are present and introductions seem called for, names alone are sufficient; one need not provide more information.

In general, it is a good idea to discuss incidental encounters during the next therapy session. Pulakos (1994) noted that 71% of clients in her survey indicated that such encounters were not discussed in the following session. In comparison, results of Sharkin and Birkey (1992) indicated that therapists reported discussing the incident 52% of the time. This apparent discrepancy suggests that perceptions of the importance of such encounters may differ between therapists and patients. I prefer to at least acknowledge such encounters during the subsequent session. If the encounter seems to trouble the client, that may be useful material to address in therapy. If the encounter is unusually difficult for you as a therapist, this might be worth exploring with your supervisor.

A final aspect of your professional role and social relationships is that, whether you like it or not, whenever you interact with other people they may form opinions about both your personal qualities and your presumed qualities as a professional. What is more, based on their interactions with you, some people will form opinions about your profession as a whole. This does not mean that you should always try to present a certain impression in public. (It is okay to go out with paint or mud on your clothes on weekends.) It does not mean that all helping professionals must at all times be models of "perfect mental health." It does, however, mean that you should be aware of the image you create and the effects it might have on others and on your professional role.

For example, if at a party you begin to tell stories about clients, you may preserve confidentiality by not revealing personal data, but the very fact that you are discussing clients publicly may be troubling to others and might be disturbing to the clients themselves if they knew you were doing so. Even if no one could possibly identify the person you are talking about based solely on a story told at a party, merely knowing that clients' lives are talked about publicly could prevent some people from seeking therapy or from being as open as they might need to be in therapy.

Apart from directly discussing clients, if in your life away from therapy you exhibit problems with substance abuse, controlling your anger, or other issues for which people might seek therapy themselves, you may create doubts about your credibility. If these or other behaviors are problems, you may want to consider seeking therapy for yourself to work on them. Self-help workbooks, such as Kottler's *The Therapist's Workbook: Self-Assessment, Self-Care, and Self-Improvement Exercises for Mental Health Professionals* (1999), may also be useful.

THE EFFECTS ON CLOSE RELATIONSHIPS AND FAMILIES

Beyond the social awkwardness that can come with our professions, problems of greater consequence can arise in relationships with spouses, significant others, and family members (Hesse, 2002; MacNab, 1995; Maeder, 1989; O'Conner, 2001). The stresses interns and helping professionals face have contributed to the breakup of many couples, and it is not at all uncommon for therapists to find themselves doing exactly the things they advise their clients not to do. We often work long hours and may not take enough time for recreation or private time with our families or significant others. Tired of "communicating" in our work all day, we may resist talking about our own feelings or those of our partners. We may feel we do not need to hear our partner's problems on top of everything else we have

been dealing with during the day. When concerned partners begin to express feelings about the relationship, we may deny the legitimacy of the concern or become defensive.

Kottler (2003) described the transition from work to home in the following passage:

> We keep a vigilant eye on personal fallout to protect our family and friends from the intensity of our professional life. Yet with all the restraint we must exercise in order to follow the rules regulating our conduct during working hours, it is difficult to not be insensitive, surly, or self-indulgent with our loved ones. All day long we have stifled ourselves, censored our thoughts and statements, and disciplined ourselves to be controlled and intelligent. And then we make an abrupt transition to go home. Much of the pressure that has been building all day long as clients have come in and dumped their troubles finally releases as we walk through the door. If we are not careful, our families will suffer the emotional fallout. (p. 69)

EXERCISE

To help you assess some of the effects of being an intern on your life and relationships, complete the following checklist for yourself and with significant others in your life.

1. How many days each week do you finish the work day feeling drained and lacking in energy or motivation to do much else?_____
2. How many days each week do you finish the work day feeling like you have been successful and have enjoyed your work that day?_____
3. When was the last time you did something with just you and your significant other?_____
4. When was the last time you did something with just yourself and one or more good friends?_____
5. How often in the past month have you not done something with your significant other because of work conflicts or effects?_____
6. How often in the past month have you not done something with friends because of work conflicts or effects?_____
7. Do you feel you listen as well to your significant other or close friends as you would like?_____
8. Do others feel you listen as well to them as they would like?_____
9. What are you doing to take care of your physical health?_____
10. If you were a therapist and had yourself as a client, what would be your advice or exploration regarding self-care?_____
11. What forms of self-care are you not doing and why?_____
12. In a typical week, how often do you find yourself thinking about your internship or clients when you are in other settings?_____

13. How often in your personal life do you experience anger or other feelings to a greater degree or with greater frequency than you would like?_____ Could this be related to stress at work?_____

14. How is your intimate relationship with your significant other?_____ Could work be affecting that?_____

After completing the checklist, I strongly encourage you to review your answers with significant others in your life. If you identify areas of concern, you may want to evaluate together how your internship and personal life are affecting one another. Superb resources for further information about this and other topics of this chapter are Ellen Baker's *Caring for Ourselves: A Therapist's Guide to Personal and Professional Well-Being* (2003) and James Guy's *The Personal Life of the Psychotherapist* (1987). See also Sussman's *A Perilous Calling: The Hazards of Psychotherapy Practice* (1995). More will be said about self-care somewhat later in this chapter.

Should you or a partner feel your relationship is being adversely affected by your work or training, you may want to consider seeing a therapist. One intern I instructed maintained that his clinical training was having only positive influences on his life and relationships. However, when he completed the preceding exercise and discussed it with his partner, he was surprised to discover that from the partner's perspective, the relationship was, in fact, suffering a great deal. As a result, the couple decided to begin therapy together. Sometime later, they confided to me that entering therapy was one of the best decisions they ever made.

SECONDARY TRAUMA

Some of the effects of stress that have been identified thus far are seen in two recognized patterns of reactions that may develop among helping professionals. These patterns are referred to as secondary trauma, also known as vicarious traumatization, and burnout. In essence, secondary trauma means that, as a result of treating patients who have experienced a profound emotional trauma, the therapist is traumatized as well.

For an excellent review of the impact of trauma on patients and the history of interventions to treat trauma, see Gold (2004) and Courtois (2004). With regard to secondary or vicarious traumatization, Cunningham (2004) described vicarious traumatization as the "cumulative effect on the clinician of being exposed to the material presented in clinical sessions by traumatized clients" (p. 306). Pearlman and MacIan (1995) referred to the transformation that occurs within the therapist as a result of empathic engagement with clients' trauma experiences and their sequelae. Brady, Guy, Poelstra, and Brokaw (1999) offered a similar description, suggesting that the impact of vicarious traumatization can be comparable to posttraumatic stress disorder. Hesse (2002) offered a throrough and useful review of this concept and noted that secondary trauma can have an

impact on therapists in a variety of ways, including their sense of self and the world, feelings of trust and safety, relationships with others, and self-confidence as a professional. Cunningham particularly emphasizes the impact of vicarious traumatization on the clinicians' "worldview" and suggests that one's belief system can be challenged as a result, and so too can one's sense of trust, personal safety, and even one's view about human nature.

In recent years an important distinction has been drawn between vicarious traumatization and the concept of burnout, which will be described shortly. This distinction is described well by Tripany, Kress, and Wilcoxon (2004), who note that while burnout may occur in some form in virtually any profession and tends to be gradual in onset, vicarious traumatization results specifically from work with traumatized clients, and the symptoms are directly related to the trauma work. In contrast to burnout, which tends to develop gradually over time, secondary trauma can have an impact on a therapist after a single session with a traumatized patient. Such a sudden onset can be particularly troubling and confusing, especially for beginning therapists or interns who have no frame of reference from which to understand the reaction. Tripany et al. also emphasize that vicarious traumatization is more likely to affect one's worldview and sense of trust. Finally, they and other authors note that vicarious traumatization and burnout are by no means mutually exclusive and, in fact, can and often do occur simultaneously.

Most susceptible to secondary trauma are therapists who are new to trauma work and those with a personal history of trauma (Cunningham, 2004). Thus, interns may be especially vulnerable, both because they are new to the profession and because some percentage of interns will still be dealing with traumas in their own past that they have not yet worked through. While interns may thus be at higher risk, it is important to keep in mind that the risk of such vicarious impacts is likely to be present to some degree for even the most experienced therapists.

Therapists who are experiencing secondary trauma may find themselves reacting with remarkably strong emotions not only to the issues the client is presenting but also to matters within their own lives. If a client describes a particularly horrific incident, the therapist who experiences secondary trauma may have unpleasant dreams and intrusive thoughts and may react with fear, anger, grief, or other strong feelings. The therapist's worldview may also be affected, with the possibility of a lost sense of safety developing or perhaps a cynical view that everyone is corrupt or that no one can be trusted (Trippany et al., 2004). As mentioned earlier, relationships can also suffer, particularly if the secondary trauma in some way triggers an awareness of fears, hurt, or other reactions toward someone in the therapist's own life.

Along with understanding how therapists can be affected personally by secondary trauma, it is also important to recognize the possible impact on the therapy process. For example, because of the challenging nature of the problems presented by traumatized clients, therapy may proceed slowly and with substantial difficulty. This can cause therapists to doubt their ability and may even lead to their trying to rush a patient to a "cure," both so that the therapist can feel competent again and to relieve the therapist of the ongoing trauma of being present as patients work through their painful process. Other possibilities include the therapist's becoming so angry toward the person who perpetrated the trauma as to no longer be effective in treating the victim, let alone the perpetrator.

Hesse (2002) offers particularly valuable insights into the impact of secondary traumatization on therapy, and she emphasizes the importance of the therapist's recognizing and dealing with those impacts effectively so that therapy is not compromised. This can include supervision, personal therapy, limiting the numbers of trauma patients seen at any one time, and finding other outlets for the stress of trauma work. Comparable suggestions are given by Trippany et al. (2004) and by Cunningham (2004), who underscores the importance of both advance preventive measures for students and of dealing responsively and supportively if vicarious traumatization occurs.

To help prevent vicarious traumatization, students can be informed about the concept and can work proactively to identify and anticipate for themselves the kinds of issues or client experiences that might be most likely to trigger a particularly powerful reaction. Cunningham draws from Stress Inoculation Theory (Meichenbaum & Fitzpatrick, 1993) to suggest classroom or supervisory preparatory work using case studies, role-plays, and other mechanisms. Cunningham cautions, however, that, depending on the nature of the trauma and the descriptive material or activities employed, there is a possibility that the preparatory activities themselves could trigger vicarious traumatization on their own. Cunningham offers suggestions for dealing with this possibility and suggests that the manner in which students present or respond to case data may contain clues about how they are dealing with the traumatic events in their clients' lives. Finally, Cunningham emphasizes the importance of providing a supportive, sensitive classroom, group, or supervisory environment to help students who may be experiencing vicarious traumatization resolved.

Many of Cunningham's suggestions are shared by Trippany et al. (2004), who describe the responsibility of agencies that deal with traumatized clients to proactively provide support for therapists who experience a vicarious response. Trippany and colleagues also recommend peer supervision as an added resource and suggest that, insofar as vicarious traumatization can impact one's worldview and sense of trust, spirituality, and a sense of meaning can be important ingredients in how therapists cope effectively with the impact of trauma.

Before leaving this topic to explore the related phenomenon of burnout, it is worth taking a moment to briefly look at three of the more profound experiences that may contribute to vicarious traumatization. The first, suicide, has been an issue in counseling and therapy for years, the second, responses to natural disasters or terrorist events, has gained special attention in response to the events of September 11, 2001 and the aftermath of Hurricane Katrina. Finally, work with soldiers returning from conflicts in Iraq, Afghanistan, and elsewhere can profoundly impact service providers.

PATIENT SUICIDE

Of all the experiences that can confront interns, the loss of a patient through suicide may be the most traumatic. Chapter 3 of this book described what to do if you are working with potentially suicidal clients in order to reduce the risks of suicidal behavior. In spite of your best efforts, however, it may happen at some point in your training or career that you will be confronted with the suicide of a client. Surveys have suggested that as many as one in six psychology interns may experience a patient's suicide during their training (Kleespies, Smith, & Becker, 1990). Nevertheless, training in the assessment and treatment of suicide potential is by no means universal among internships, and systematic support for interns who have lost patients is less frequent still (Ellis & Dickey, 1998).

It is hoped that you will never have to face the loss of a patient to suicide, but the incidence rates are such that you should at least be aware of the possibility should it befall one of your patients or a peer's patient. Many of the emotional impacts that have been described following patient suicide are comparable to those associated with secondary trauma, though likely more acute. These can include intrusive thoughts, disbelief, sadness, fear, doubts about competency, and feelings of guilt and shame (Kleespies et al., 1990). On occasion, the strain of losing a patient can be so great that a trainee will abandon professional training entirely.

To assist trainees in dealing with this experience, Foster and McAdams (1999) recommended that internship sites and supervisors establish procedures to ensure that interns receive follow-up supervision and, if necessary, special help and support. They emphasize the need to review the case to understand what happened and to offer support and coping strategies. The intern's supervisor may also benefit from additional support, as may peers and coworkers who interacted with the patient. Any legal implications should also be addressed, and it is important for interns to have assistance in this regard as most will be quite unprepared to deal with legal matters of this magnitude. Finally, it should be kept in mind that although the acute effects of such profound experiences may diminish in a matter of weeks or months, there may also be lasting impacts that will affect the intern's personal life and work with other clients for a long time thereafter.

NATURAL DISASTERS, TERRORISM, AND WAR

When the concept of vicarious traumatization was first introduced, the predominant focus was on the effects of working with clients and of such issues as suicide, sexual abuse, violence, severe accidents, or illnesses like cancer. Due to events of recent years, the helping professions have been called upon to respond to different traumas on a scale and of a type we have never seen before (Reyes and Elhai, 2004).

In many ways, people across the nation were subject to vicarious traumatization by the events of September 11 and, later, the tsunami in South Asia, then by the images and impact of Hurricane Katrina. On a personal level, my congressional staff and I saw the Pentagon explode from our window in the Longworth House Office Building. We then initiated the evacuation of the building, wondering as we did if a second plane, truck bomb, or other event was imminent and would cause our own deaths. Just a few days later, recognizing the impacts of the experience on my staff and on others, I worked with our employee assistance program to initiate a proactive intervention program to help staff across the Capitol better prepare to assist constituents, some of whom had been in or near the World Trade Center or the Pentagon, others of whom had lost friends or loved ones, and all of whom had been deeply impacted by the event. The additional purpose of the effort was to help the staff themselves who, while responding to the needs of constituents and continuing to perform their other duties, had to also deal with their own losses, with the impacts of vicarious traumatization, and, in this instance, the awareness that, because of where they work, something more could easily happen and they might be in mortal danger themselves at any time.

I share this personal story for several reasons. First, it is possible that you were also impacted by one of these events. It may also happen that in the course of your work or training you will encounter individuals who were affected by these or similar events, and you should be aware that as you seek to assist them you will very possibly be impacted vicariously by their experiences. One of the realizations of my work with congressional staff following September 11 was how important it was to help them deal with their own reactions to the experience in order that they could be more helpful in dealing with the constituents they served. This was particularly important for staff in offices representing congressional districts near the most affected areas of New York City and near the Pentagon. Consistent with the research on vicarious trauma, I was also struck by how the terrorist attacks profoundly shook the worldview of many and created a deeply unsettling sense of uncertainty and vulnerability. Also consistent with the research was my personal observation that one of the most important elements of helping was identifying and strengthening the need for a sense of meaning or purpose to help people get themselves back together and keep serving the public. I am pleased to say that this process proved very helpful for many of the participants, several of whom confided to me later that they had been deeply shaken by the events and were prepared to quit their jobs, but decided to continue on because of the interventions we had offered.

If you do work with people who have experienced these or other, comparable events, be aware that a growing body of literature exists documenting the way such events affected people (Henry, Tolan, & Gorman-Smith, 2004; Meyers, 2006; Silver et al., 2002), the responses of the various professional associations and individuals (APA Policy and Planning Board, 2006; Levant,

2002; Stoesen, 2005), and recommended intervention approaches. (Cook & Schnurr, 2004; Reyes and Elhai, 2004; Weaver, 1995). As a further resource, each of the various professional associations has responded to all of these tragedies with rapid outreach efforts and with online and published information providing useful information to professionals and to the public. Some associations have also established special treatment guidelines and networks of members specifically trained in and ready to respond to disasters (see, for example, the APA Disaster Response Network at http://www.apa.org/practice/drnguide.html). For more information on these efforts, check the various association Web sites. In addition, some graduate programs are now offering areas of specialization in research and treatment approaches relating to natural disasters and terrorism (DeAngelis, 2006).

The final issue to mention here has to do with the impacts of war. When I was beginning my training, veterans of Vietnam were seeking help for the effects of their military service. Many of those veterans and their families are still profoundly affected by that conflict. Today, the fighting in Iraq and Afghanistan has created a new generation of troops, families, and civilians who have been touched, in many cases wounded physically and psychologically by their war experiences. As of this writing, well over a million troops have been sent overseas to the conflict areas since September 11, 2001 (Benjamin, 2005).

To appreciate how working with these veterans and their families may impact you psychologically, let me share just one story told to me by a young marine I met with at Walter Reed Army Hospital. I should advise you in advance that this is an extremely graphic event, but I believe it is worth telling to you because it gives a sense of what some of these individuals have experienced in their lives and how learning about their experiences may, in turn, have an effect on you.

This particular young man was a marine sergeant, former high school baseball star, who had later gone on to become a school athletic coach. Recently married, he was called up to active duty in Iraq, where he and his unit often went on patrols in some of the most dangerous areas of Mosul. On many occasions there had been near misses, and other members of his unit had been severely wounded, with several killed. He described living in constant awareness that "today could be the day."

One afternoon, while driving under an overpass in a humvee, it was his day. The insurgents had planted an improvised explosive device above the roadway so that it would blast down on vehicles passing underneath. The young marine described an instantaneous fireball and deafening explosion. The vehicle flipped over, everywhere there was smoke, searing pain, and confusion. In the initial impact, the sergeant was knocked out, but when he came to he turned to his best friend, who had been driving. As his consciousness returned, he found himself saying, "Hey, we've got to get out of here." Then he realized that his friend, who was sitting in the driver seat right next to him and with whom he had been talking just moments earlier, had been decapitated by shrapnel from the blast. "His head was just gone, not there anymore. Just blood, and flesh and bone." Even as he tried to comprehend what he was seeing, the sergeant realized that the vehicle was on fire and he had to get out himself. That's when he realized that part of one of his own hands was missing, one of his legs was nearly gone, and the rest of his body was peppered with burning shards of metal. Fortunately, other soldiers pulled him from the wreckage, and now, after many months of agonizing surgeries, infections, more surgeries, and physical therapy, he is gradually on the way to recovery. With luck, he may even be able to return home soon, more than a year after he was wounded. He is the first to say, however, that he will never be the same person physically or emotionally as he was when he left for service or the same person he would have been had he never gone.

I am sorry to tell such a tragic and troubling story to you, and I know it may be upsetting. I am even more sorry that such things have to happen at all to human beings. I tell you this here because, given the numbers of people who have served in these conflicts, it is likely that you will at some point work with veterans or their families, and you should have some preparation for what you may encounter. I should also add in this context that one other issue you should be aware of has to do with how your own attitude or that of others about these conflicts may affect your clinical work. Given strong public sentiments on various sides of these conflicts, it is especially important that treatment professionals know and are able to separate their political ideologies from their clinical work with patients.

Finally, I should conclude this section by noting that it is beyond the scope of this chapter or text to describe the recommended treatments for this patient or the thousands more who have been through comparable experiences, disasters, or the attacks of September 11. There are, however, other works (e.g., Bryant & Harvey, 2000; Cook, Schnurr, & Foa, 2004; Creamer & Forbes, 2004; Mangelsdorff, 2006; Reyes & Elhai, 2004) that offer useful insights into these issues. See also the informative Web site eyeofthestorminc.com, which provides many useful tips from John Weaver, a practicing social worker who specializes in disaster response and works closely with organizations like the Red Cross and the Federal Emergency Mangement Agency (FEMA).

BURNOUT

In contrast to secondary traumatization and reactions to acute traumatic events, burnout is a gradual progress in which the cumulative effects of working with difficult patients and in challenging settings slowly wears people down and can sap them of their energy, desire, and ability to function effectively as professionals. The term *burnout* is attributed to Herbert Freudenberger (1974), who introduced it to describe a pattern of responses shown by people who work in committed activities and begin to exhibit declines in personal involvement, effectiveness, or productivity (Farber, 1983b). In addition to psychological changes, burnout has also been shown to have substantial physical impacts, including cardiovascular disease (Melamed et al., 2006). Since its introduction, burnout has been written about and studied in many populations, including schoolteachers, social workers, psychologists, police officers, nurses, physicians, business executives, and others who work in high-stress positions (Farber, 1983a; Golembiewski & Munzenrider, 1988; McKnight & Glass, 1995; Rupert & Morgan, 2005; Söderfeldt, Söderfeldt, & Warg, 1995).

SYMPTOMS OF BURNOUT

In a review of theoretical writing and empirical studies, Farber (1983b) noted that burnout has been defined in several different ways. Some authors and studies emphasize the emotional features; others address physiological symptoms of burnout. The most commonly mentioned symptoms include emotional distancing from clients and staff, decreased empathy, cynicism, decreased self-esteem, physical exhaustion, sleep disturbances, stomach pains, and other stress-related physical complaints. Farber observed that despite differences in emphasis by different authors, "There is general consensus that the symptoms of burnout include attitudinal, emotional and physical components" (p. 3).

Maslach's (1982) description of burnout placed special emphasis on the importance of estrangement from clients and colleagues. Similarly, Pines and Aronson (1988) focused on the withdrawal process that is characteristic of burnout. They noted that professionals who are nearing or in burnout typically seek to withdraw, either physically, emotionally, or mentally. This strategy is perhaps best understood both as a response to the other symptoms of burnout and as a symptom itself.

When therapists begin to experience the unpleasant symptoms of burnout, they seek ways to lessen those symptoms. If other methods are unavailable or fail, physical, emotional, or mental withdrawal provides a way of distancing themselves from clients or work and thereby reducing stress. This is a perfectly understandable response, but it can adversely affect professionals and their clients. Withdrawal can also lead to further frustration and negative feelings as therapists recognize their lessened effectiveness and satisfaction but are unable to find more creative or constructive solutions.

STAGES OF BURNOUT

Many authors who study burnout have emphasized that it is important to view burnout as a process rather than an event. That is, one does not suddenly become burned out in a single day. Rather, a person typically passes through progressive stages on the way to burnout. Kottler (2003) underscored this distinction by suggesting that "rustout" might be a better term than "burnout." Kottler also emphasized that at varying times everyone experiences at least some symptoms of burnout in almost every job. Indeed, Kottler suggested that "The question, then, is not *who* will experience burnout but *how long* the next episode will last." Edelwich and Brodsky (1980) described how people may pass through stages from initial enthusiasm through stagnation, frustration, and, ultimately, apathy. Edelwich and Brodsky emphasized that there is an important difference between frustration and apathy, with burnout associated only with the latter stage. People who are frustrated are still involved, caring, and struggling to make a change. In the frustration stage, there is still a possibility of improving matters and returning to the more positive stage of enthusiasm. When someone becomes apathetic, that person is burned out, and according to Edelwich and Brodsky, this substantially reduces the prospects for positive change.

In the context of the withdrawal process that Pines and Aronson described, apathy may be understood as a result of avoidant learning. Therapists who are burned out have learned that when they try their best to do clinical work, and when they empathize closely with clients, they are often frustrated either by the inherent limitations of the task, the client's lack of change, organizational factors, or other elements that block success or pose excessive demands. This process produces a form of aversive conditioning in which therapists learn that one way to avoid negative consequences is to withdraw from the process. If the empathic sharing of a client's emotional suffering is aversive, the therapist may withdraw emotionally. If efforts to make cognitive sense of client issues or organizational processes do not yield positive results, the therapist may withdraw mentally and just go through the behavioral motions of the job. If the work setting itself becomes associated with unpleasant experiences, the therapist may withdraw physically from the setting. Awareness of this connection is clinically valuable because by identifying a person's pattern of withdrawal, one may gather clues about the key factors contributing to his or her burnout.

MEASURES OF BURNOUT

For both research and clinical purposes, attempts have been made to operationalize the concept of burnout through the development of instruments designed to measure it (Arthur, 1990). Two of the most frequently used instruments are the Maslach Burnout Inventory (MBI) (Maslach & Jackson, 1986) and the Staff Burnout Scale (SBS) (Jones, 1980). Maslach's inventory contains three subscales that address emotional exhaustion, depersonalization, and personal accomplishments. Emotional exhaustion is considered to be the result of the physical and emotional strains of sustained stress. Depersonalization is seen as an attempt to cope with the strain by distancing oneself from clients and peers, and by treating others as objects rather than people. Finally, as a result of the sustained stress and attempts to cope with it, people's personal accomplishments decline. In combination with exhaustion and depersonalization, this can lead to a diminished sense of self-efficacy and possibly depression (Lee & Ashforth, 1990).

The Staff Burnout Scale focuses on many of the same issues as the MBI but emphasizes the physiological and behavioral dimensions. The SBS produces an overall score for burnout, but items can also be grouped into four factors: dissatisfaction with work, psychological and interpersonal tension, physical illness and distress, and unprofessional patient relationships.

Along with their usefulness in helping to identify the symptoms of burnout, these instruments and studies help explain how and why burnout develops. This understanding is especially important to interns and therapists who, because they may be at risk, need to recognize the signs of burnout and cope effectively with its potential causes.

CAUSES OF BURNOUT

Causes of burnout have been attributed to factors within the individual, inherent features of demanding jobs, organizational structure, and managerial approaches (Rupert & Morgan, 2005). Broader social concerns, including worker alienation, have also been identified as contributing to burnout (Farber, 1983b). In addition to these general factors, several authors, including Farber (1983a) and Pines and Aronson (1988) have emphasized that the training and demands of helping professions contribute in unique ways to burnout. In most cases, a combination of these factors leads to burnout. Understanding their relative importance is useful because, as Pines and Aronson pointed out,

> How individuals perceive the cause of their burnout and attribute the "blame" has enormous consequences for action. If they attribute the cause to a characterological weakness or inadequacy in themselves, they will take a certain set of actions: quit the profession, seek psychotherapy and so forth. However, if they see the cause as largely a function of the situation, they will strive to change the situation and make it more tolerable, a totally different set of remedial actions. (p. 5)

Reviewing some of the more commonly identified contributors may help you to recognize whether you or someone you work with is beginning to develop signs of burnout. From that basis you may be able to cope more effectively with the situation. To draw again from Pines and Aronson:

> The first and most important step would be to change the focus from "What's wrong with me?" to "What can I do about the situation?" (1988, p. 5)

INDIVIDUAL FACTORS

Some of the personality characteristics associated with burnout were alluded to earlier in this chapter as part of the discussion of stress and therapist characteristics. Among the characteristics often mentioned are lack of clear boundaries between self and work, extreme degree of empathy, exceptional level of commitment, and a fragile self-concept (Carroll & White, 1982).

Carroll and White also identified poor training as a contributor and noted that training deficits can lead to burnout in two ways. First, inadequate training for a job leaves one feeling unprepared, vulnerable, insecure, and fearing failure. Second, even those who are adequately trained in the skills of their job may not be trained to cope with its stresses. Thus, some people may face burnout because they were not adequately trained for the skills demanded in their job. Others may burn out because they have no training in coping with the emotional demands of the job.

Much as inadequate training can contribute to burnout, in the helping professions the training process itself can pose added risks. Pines and Aronson (1988) described how people who become helping professionals do so out of feelings of concern for others but then encounter problems and suffering that they simply cannot alleviate completely. This can lead to feelings of hopelessness and helplessness that are incompatible with the motives and dedication that first attracted the therapist to the profession. This inherent feature of the helping professional's work is often a key factor in burnout.

Consistent with the previously described results of Rodolfa et al. (1988), Farber (1983a) identified both the challenges of therapy itself and the supervision process as important stressors for trainees. Farber noted that the ambiguity of therapy, the difficulty of learning a complex new skill, and the mixed role of teaching and evaluation in supervision all make the training process highly anxiety provoking for most interns. These are complicated still further by the development of "psychological mindedness" among trainees.

This process is essential to therapy training and can have positive results, but Farber noted that it also has the potential to lead to overidentification with clients. As interns become aware of their own dynamics while simultaneously beginning to fill the role of therapist, they must cope with two sets of issues that are fraught with ambiguity and anxiety. Either alone might be difficult enough, but the combination can be overwhelming.

ORGANIZATIONAL FACTORS

In contrast to approaches that emphasize the individual's characteristics as contributing to burnout, organizational and managerial factors have also been studied. Pines (1982) observed that in studies that compared two different treatment centers, higher levels of burnout were observed in one than the other even though the two were very similar in clients served, location, staffing, and other variables. This difference suggested that organizational factors were involved in contributing to or reducing burnout in the different centers. A similar conclusion was reached by Arches (1991), who surveyed social workers and found that "lack of autonomy and the influence of funding sources are major contributors to burnout" (p. 202).

Pines (1982) identified four broad qualities of work environments that can contribute to burnout: psychological, physical, social, and organizational factors. Pines and Aronson (1988) noted that it is equally important to look for features that help prevent burnout. Such positive features include organizational flexibility, staff autonomy, variety, supportive colleagues, opportunities for breaks in times of stress, limiting the hours of stressful work, and, where necessary, reducing staff-client ratios.

Managerial style has also been identified as a possible cause or preventive element in burnout. Murphy and Pardeck (1986) noted that burnout is probably best prevented by a managerial style that falls somewhere between authoritarian and laissez-faire. They explained that the authoritarian approach does not provide sufficient autonomy or self-direction to staff, does not involve staff in decision-making, and tends to give instructions without explanation. At the opposite extreme, laissez-faire approaches suffer from problems by failing to provide staff with sufficient direction, guidance, or support.

As a final comment on organizational factors and burnout, some authors have drawn a distinction between job satisfaction, job changing, and burnout. This is a useful distinction because the literature suggests it is possible to be satisfied with a job yet still be burned out. This research also helps explain the connection between financial compensation, satisfaction, and burnout.

In a study of how seven job features related to satisfaction among social workers, Jayaratne and Chess (1983) looked at comfort, challenge, financial reward, promotions, role ambiguity, role conflict, and workload. Their results revealed that the facets of challenge, financial rewards, and promotional opportunities were all related to satisfaction, with financial reward being the best predictor of job turnover. Job-related stressors did not appear to affect satisfaction or turnover but might still contribute to burnout. In other words, it is possible for workers to report overall satisfaction with their work and want to stay on the job but still experience the symptoms of burnout. Moreover, workers may change jobs not because they are burned out but primarily for financial reasons. Finally, financial compensation is a useful predictor of whether or not someone is likely to change jobs but does not appear to be strongly related to burnout.

Jayaratne and Chess emphasized that this does not mean that helping professionals do not want or deserve fair financial compensation. Low pay does have direct costs and consequences in worker turnover, but merely adjusting pay is not likely to be a lasting solution to burnout caused by factors other than economic considerations.

THE STATE OF THE WORLD

Along with the stresses relating to clinical activities, field placements and clinical work often bring interns into contact with aspects of life that can be difficult to deal with emotionally and seem intractable or unsolvable. Kurland and Salmon (1992) commented on this and observed that social workers may

> soon fall prey to the perceived hopelessness of the situations and of these monumental social problems unless the teachers, supervisors, and consultants are able to help them go on. (p. 241)

Encounters with deep social ills are often the source of the most profound challenge not only for interns but also for experienced practitioners. How, if we care about others and are drawn to the professions out of a desire to help, can we go on in the face of problems that seem so huge and that do real and lasting harm to so many people? There is no easy answer to this, and when we are unable to cope with the situation, burnout or other symptoms may result.

RECOGNIZING AND UNDERSTANDING YOUR OWN SITUATION AND BURNOUT

The literature on burnout is interesting from a theoretical perspective, but what really matters is how it relates to you personally. There is great variability in the extent to which individual interns and internship settings reflect both the negative and the positive features that have been identified. Some interns are extremely dedicated and sensitive to their clients but are also remarkably fragile and susceptible to burnout. At the opposite extreme, I occasionally encounter interns who seem virtually immune to burnout because they so distance themselves that they do not empathize or connect with their clients. Somewhere in the middle, one finds interns who exhibit a healthy balance of sensitivity to clients and dedication to the field but who are also able to keep a degree of objectivity and detachment that allows them to do good clinical work without excessively carrying the burdens of their clients' difficulties.

Similar variability can be found across internship settings. In the best settings, interns can feel the excitement, caring, staff support, and dedication to the profession and to clients. In other settings, there is a pervasive air of resignation, domination, or hostility.

Interns and their supervisors must be aware of both the individual factors and the situational factors that can lead to burnout. If interns are showing the symptoms described earlier in this section, that is a signal to explore what is happening and what can be done about it. As a relatively simple starting point, and as a way to help prevent burnout by understanding it before it develops, you may find it useful to complete the following exercise.

PERSONAL AND ENVIRONMENTAL BURNOUT PRONENESS OR PREVENTION: SELF-EVALUATION EXERCISE

In light of the material you have just read about burnout, answer each of the following questions.

1. What personal characteristics do you have that could contribute to burnout?
2. What personal characteristics do you think might help you prevent burnout?
3. What features of your current internship setting or possible future settings do you think would contribute most to burnout for you?
4. What internship-setting features could help prevent burnout?

BURNOUT AS A COPING MECHANISM

It is possible to look at burnout from another perspective. In much of the literature and in professional discourse, burnout is viewed as a solely negative situation that should be prevented or avoided. The fundamental problem with this approach is that it overlooks the value and importance of burnout as an opportunity for the individual's learning and growth. If burnout is seen in only negative terms, interns or professionals may tend to deny their feelings lest they acknowledge that they too are vulnerable to something that, because of its negative image, may be stigmatizing. The response may be, "I can't be burned out. Burnout is a sign of weakness or failure, and that just can't be me." Organizations may exhibit similar responses if employees begin to show signs of burnout. "No, our employees aren't burning out. That would mean there is something wrong with our organization, and we know that can't be true." Interns, supervisors, and organizations would benefit from a perspective that views symptoms of burnout as valuable information that something is not working optimally and could be improved. It should also be emphasized that symptoms of burnout do not necessarily mean that the workplace is the only source of the problem. Other factors in the individual's life can also contribute to burnout.

Roberts (1987) suggested that in considering the effects of stress on helping professionals we must take into account the overall quality of relationships and demands in their lives. As Roberts pointed out, all individuals have some limits to the energy, resources, and abilities they can use to manage stress. As one's energy declines, or as normally effective resources fail to cope adequately with stress, the quality of coping responses declines. Thus, symptoms of burnout are a signal that the overall level of stress in a person's life is somehow exceeding his or her coping abilities and resources. From this perspective, burnout is viewed not as a failure but as an effort to cope in a different way.

In a particularly insightful and useful observation, Roberts explained:

> Burnout is perceived as an appropriate coping mechanism under the circumstances given the history of choices, experiences, and resources of the individual. The arena in which this form of coping (burnout) would surface—work, family, or friends—would likely be that one which offers the least resistance or least consequence to the expression of burnout. (p. 116)

In other words, just as the causes of burnout are not limited to the work setting, one can show signs of burnout outside the work setting as well. According to Roberts, burnout is a form of coping, and we are most likely to resort to it where it is safest to do so. This means we must be attentive to burnout not only on the job, but in our relationships, school, and other aspects of our lives. In many cases, burnout may hit relationships well before work because relationships are safer environments. Because it might be safer in some ways to burn out in our relationships rather than our jobs, the relationship and our partners suffer.

If we recognize signs of stress wherever they appear, we can interpret them as a signal that our alternative coping mechanisms are being overwhelmed. From this painful realization, we can begin to explore where the stresses are in our lives and why our other coping mechanisms are not managing them. Thus, instead of viewing burnout and other signs of stress in solely negative terms, we can approach them as signals and opportunities for learning more about ourselves and our situation. How to deal with that awareness is the topic we turn to now.

SELF-CARE

Thus far, this chapter has described some of the stresses of internships and professional activities. Next, we will explore the importance of self-care and suggest strategies for keeping yourself healthy while you strive to assist others. By definition, helping professionals seek to improve the quality of life of the people with whom they work. If you hope to be successful in that endeavor, taking care of yourself is one of the most important, yet sometimes one of the most difficult, tasks you will face as an intern or professional.

Consistent with this text's earlier discussions of evidence-based practice (see Chapter 2), the ideas and recommendations that follow are based on research from a number of authors who have examined the issue of self-care among professionals and interns. For example, Norcross, (2005) conducted an extensive and insightful series of research studies on the use and impacts of personal psychotherapy for educating and training therapists. Osborn (2004) offers research based suggestions for improving what she calls "counselor stamina." Similarly, Stevanovic, and Rupert (2004) describe "career-sustaining" behaviors that help professionals deal with the stresses of their work. Turner et al. (2005) focused specifically on self-care strategies among interns, while Dearing, Maddux, and Tangney (2005) describe study results identifying factors that predict help seeking among clinical and counseling psychology students.

Some may find that the suggestions which follow raise issues that are not often talked about in school or training. Others may resist or possibly even resent suggestions about staying physically healthy or engaging in some form of reflective meditation or prayer. The discussion of financial considerations may also come as a surprise. I am sensitive to such concerns, but I am convinced it is important to address precisely those issues that are normally ignored in academic training but are of critical importance in life and work beyond academia.

I am not suggesting that all interns or professionals must agree with or follow these suggestions, nor do I claim to offer the best or the correct approach to self-care. On the other hand, I cannot emphasize too strongly that the work of helping professionals and the experience of internship training are unique and at times highly demanding. Self-care can be vital not only to your personal health but also to your effectiveness at your internship. Whether you agree with specific ideas or suggestions that are offered, I hope this will stimulate your thinking about how you personally cope with stress and take care of yourself as you attempt to help others care for themselves.

TIME MANAGEMENT

When interns are asked to list the sources of stress in their lives, having too much to do and time management are consistently identified among the primary concerns. This is not at all surprising. In the desire to do a good job on the internship while trying to balance school, work, family, and other demands, it is easy to feel that events control you. The problem is that if you do not manage your time well, you will eventually make inadequate notes, not take the physical and mental breaks you need, take work home, and probably regret it in the long run. If you do not take care of your time, it is symptomatic that you are probably not taking care of yourself in other ways as well. As a colleague of mine says, "If you're too busy to take care of yourself, you're too busy! Something's gotta change." The challenge, of course, is that lack of time is at once a major souce of stress and one of the key obstacles impeding self-care among interns (Dearing, Maddux, & Tangney, 2005).

Interns are not alone in feeling time-related stresses. Many experienced therapists feel overworked, and many professionals do not manage their time well. Especially common are the habits of not allocating sufficient time between sessions and not taking enough breaks from work to stretch or relax.

Some of the best recommendations I have encountered for dealing with these issues come from Osborn (2004), who identifies "selectivity" and "time sensitivity" as two of her seven suggestions for counselor stamina. By selectivity Osborn means "the practice of intentional choice and focus in daily activities and long term endeavors. It means setting limits on what one can and cannot do" (p. 322). Time sensitivity, as described by Osborn, involves being constantly aware of, and thereby in charge of, time and limitations on time. This means everything from terminating therapy sessions on time, to organizing and conducting meetings with fixed agendas, and being cognizant of such things as phone calls, e-mail, and instant messaging, all of which can eat unproductively into your time if not managed well.

As a starting point to help you manage your time better, you may want to explore some of the commercially available time-management systems and training seminars. Companies such as Day-Timer and Franklin Covey produce an array of scheduling and time-management products and offer various training options to help you use these products and manage your time more effectively. Students who have attended such courses generally report very positive results. In my own current work in Congress, I require all my staff to each use either a paper system of this type or a related PDA system and to participate in some form of time-management training. Software such as Microsoft Outlook can also be tremendously helpful in planning, managing, and tracking your time and schedule.

If you use an organized scheduling and time-management system, you may want to incorporate a concept that Fiore (1989) described as "unscheduling." The idea of unscheduling is to begin your scheduling by planning your time to do the things you need for self-care. Once you have set aside the time you need to take care of yourself, you then schedule work and other activities around that. This might sound selfish, but if we do not take care of ourselves, we will eventually be unable to care for others. By scheduling self-care first, we are forced to rethink our priorities.

One reason many professionals have trouble managing their time is that they have not seriously examined how they actually spend their time. When I conducted an informal survey of colleagues in clinical practice, very few had kept precise track of how they spend their time and how long it takes to complete various tasks. In a discussion of fee structure as it relates to professionals' time, Callahan (1994) noted that many therapists in private practice have a false understanding of how much they earn for their efforts because they have not accurately assessed the time they spend outside therapy in tasks such as note taking, correspondence, and phone calls.

EXERCISE: TRACKING WHERE TIME GOES

To help develop your time awareness and management skills, during the next two weeks keep careful track of all the activities you do each day for the full 24 hours. From 12:00 midnight each day to 12:00 midnight the next day, make a note of when you start and stop different activities. This may feel like a nuisance or a waste of time, but in fact it is just the opposite. This is a way for you to begin to understand how not to waste time.

Keeping track of what you do will allow you to get a better sense of where your time goes and how long different activities actually take. For example, if you keep case notes for each session during a week, by recording how long it takes you to write a case note for each client you will become more aware of what that requires. You can then build that time into your schedule. In this process, try to be aware not only of where your time goes now, but also of ways in which you are not spending time that you probably should be. Are you taking time to stretch, to get out of the office, to recover between sessions? If your record reveals that comparatively little time is going to self-care, you may want to "unschedule" more of your time.

Along with budgeting time on a weekly basis for your regular activities, anticipate special time demands, such as preparation for exams, papers, and conferences. As you look toward these events, be sure to allow additional time in your schedule to prepare for them. Avoid the temptation to simply take that added time out of what you have set aside for self-care.

Putting time in our schedule books is actually the easiest part of time management. Sticking to the time you schedule is the hard part. I advise trainees to include in their schedules a certain degree of open time that allows them to deal with unanticipated circumstances. I also advise trainees to make certain time inviolable. Except in extreme circumstances, do not let clients or staff intrude on this protected time. Do not use your note-taking time to instead make phone calls, do not let sessions run longer than they are scheduled, and do not treat time for exercise as a low priority that can easily be sacrificed.

SAYING NO

Keeping certain time for yourself requires the ability to say no. Interns are often overloaded with classes, other jobs, and families. The task of meeting all these demands is exacerbated because many interns, as caring and dedicated people, have difficulty turning down worthy projects. The underlying principle that guides their decisions is to think first of the needs of others, then of their own needs, and almost never of the real limitations of time and the physical demands for rest or sleep. If someone at school needs a hand with a class, an intern offers to help. If volunteers are needed for a community service project, the interns are the first to lend a hand. If extra work needs to be done at the internship, the interns extend their hours.

All these activities are to be commended, and it is admirable that interns are willing to step forward. But it is also important for each of us to learn how to set priorities and make decisions. There is nothing wrong with setting realistic limits and standing by them. There will always be more work to be done than one person can do, and you do not have to feel like you must do it all.

SAYING YES

Learning to say no is an important side of self-care and time management, but learning to say yes to positive activities is just as important. Stevanovic and Rupert (2004) found that among the most common and important career-sustaining behaviors were spending time with partners and families and maintaining balance between professional and personal lives.

When I work with overstressed students or colleagues, the problem is not simply that they have a hard time saying no to extra work. It is also that they have a hard time saying yes to things they enjoy doing. A colleague who was working from 7:00 A.M. to 7:00 P.M. five days a week and half days on Saturday told me that one of his favorite things to do was go sailing. When I asked how long it had been since he had been sailing, he said he had gone once this year and two or three times each of the past two years. If sailing was indeed a favorite pastime, he was certainly not allocating a proportionate amount of time to it.

Rather than agonizing over every opportunity or request to do one more thing, I encourage you to sit down on your own, or perhaps with significant others, and think carefully about how you want to spend your time. It has been pointed out that the amount of time we give to things is one indication of how important we think they are. Yet, when people examine where they are really spending their time and why, they realize that some things are getting far more time than their real importance warrants.

EXERCISE: SETTING PRIORITIES

The previous exercise asked you to examine how you currently spend your time. Now consider where you would like to allocate time in the future. Make a list of things that are important to you, then identify how much time you would like to devote to them. As you do this, do not start with what you are doing and work from there. Instead, first list what is important to you, then compare how you are actually spending your time. You may discover significant discrepancies between what you say matters to you and what you do. Based on this awareness, try to plan a schedule that would allow you to do more of what you have identified as top priorities.

CLOSING SESSIONS

Another common problem regarding time management has to do with keeping enough time for case notes, phone calls, and so on, between appointments with clients. The advice to keep sessions within the scheduled time period is often particularly difficult for interns to follow.

If clients are still talking about an issue when the session is about to end, interns tend to allow or encourage them to keep going. It also happens that some clients do not raise important issues until just before the session ends. This can happen for many reasons. Perhaps the issue is so sensitive that the client spent the entire session trying to gather courage to discuss it. Raising it at the end of the session provides a safety valve of sorts. Another possibility is that a client is testing the therapist; allotting extra time may seem to be a sign that the therapist really cares. Whatever the reason, if sessions run over, that is information the therapist should be aware of and seek to understand. Allowing overruns to occur repeatedly and without examination may mean the therapist is overlooking useful information.

There are several ways to bring sessions to an end constructively. To begin with, as part of the information provided clients at the outset of therapy, one should make clear how long sessions will last. During sessions, the easiest and most direct approach is for the therapist to be aware of the time and, as the end of the session approaches, state, "We need to finish for now." If the client has just raised an important issue, the therapist might observe, "I think what you just spoke of is important and is something we should probably address in the next session. For now, we need to conclude for today." If a client continues talking, the therapist can rise and begin to move toward the door. These methods will be well received and effective in most cases. If a client repeatedly runs sessions overtime, this is something the therapist may need to address. Here again, stating things directly in the form of a process observation can be helpful. "I have noticed that in the last few sessions we seem to raise important issues right near the end and then to run overtime. I want to be sure to give enough time to such things, but it is important to be aware of the conclusion of our sessions. I wonder if there is a way we can address this more effectively?"

In describing these techniques, it must be added that the therapist should, of course, use judgment. There are times when it is essential to run a little over. If a client reveals that he or she is in some danger, if a critical issue absolutely must be resolved, or if some other matter demands immediate attention, the therapist may elect to extend the session. This decision, however, should be made very rarely; if it occurs repeatedly for the same client, the therapist should recognize and address the problem.

It is not only clients who extend sessions past time. It also happens that clients are ready to conclude sessions on time, but the intern, perhaps wanting to feel needed or to "solve the client's problems," overextends the session. This tendency is not only contrary to sound time management, it can also interfere with therapy. The simple reality is that the work of therapy is seldom "finished" by the end of any single session. There will always be more to do, and it is often a very good thing to end a session with work still left to do. Clients are able to continue thinking about things on their own, and therapists need to be able to give them that opportunity. Interns must learn that sessions do not always end as neat or tidy packages, and clients do not, and probably should not, always leave a session feeling that everything has been resolved.

A colleague of mine uses the concept of "holding the question" to help interns understand that not everything is resolved in each session. Holding the question means accepting that some things are best pondered, and one should not expect an immediate answer to every question. Holding the question gives clients time to think about things between sessions. Because life does not always give neatly packaged solutions and we must be able to deal with that fact, developing the ability to hold the question is, in itself, highly therapeutic for clients as well as professionals.

COGNITIVE SELF-CARE

The normal stresses interns experience can often be exacerbated by beliefs interns hold about themselves, their clients, the therapy process, and about broader topics that might best be labeled cognitions about the world. To the extent that these ideas create stress, recognizing and coping effectively with them can be a valuable element of self-care. Turner et al. (2005) refer to this as avoiding wishful thinking and self-blame. Osborn (2004) approaches the matter from a somewhat more philosophical but enlightening perspective, describing it as "inquisitiveness," a term used to indicate the importance of maintaining curiosity and wonder about our work and the people we serve. Osborn also reminds us that it is important to deal effectively with the inherent ambiguities and uncertainties of the helping professions and work with other human beings.

COGNITIONS ABOUT SELF

It is not uncommon for interns to approach their training or placements with unrealistic expectations about their own knowledge, efficacy, or feelings toward clients. For example, interns might believe they must not make any mistakes. Or they might fear that others will recognize their lack of experience. It is also common for interns to want to be liked, perhaps even loved and supported, by all their clients and coworkers.

Deutsch (1984) studied a number of ideas rated by clinicians as stressful and found that the three most stressful ideas all dealt with therapists' needs for perfection. Other stressful ideas included the belief that the therapist is responsible for client change, that therapists must be constantly available to clients, and that therapists should be models of mental health themselves.

For interns, unrealistic expectations about themselves or clients add to the challenges of an already demanding position. At the same time, however, it is quite realistic and to be expected for interns to have some anxiety about their abilities as therapists. Engaging others in a relationship and seeking to help them make difficult changes is indeed a great responsibility. The responsibility is all the more daunting when opinions vary about how to bring about change and there are no clear rules about what is defined as helpful. Interns who do not have some fear about their abilities or about the therapy process are themselves sources of stress and anxiety for their supervisors.

What is required is a healthy balance between anxiety and confidence. Interns who feel they must be perfect at everything will easily become paralyzed and will be afraid to move treatment forward. On the other hand, interns who believe they are already expert are prone to make dangerous mistakes that may, in fact, harm their clients. With this in mind, part of cognitive self-care involves checking one's cognitions about oneself as a person and professional. Interns should ask themselves if they have unrealistically high expectations about what their abilities should be or are. They should also share their ideas with their instructor or supervisor. If your beliefs about what your skills are, or should be, are extreme in either a positive or negative direction, there is a need for personal work.

Self-care also involves keeping a healthy perspective about anxiety itself. Some interns become anxious about being anxious. It is as if they believe that good therapists must be calm and confident at all times, and any hint of anxiety is a sign of weakness or incompetence. Such concerns are understandable, but even the most accomplished professionals will acknowledge that they sometimes wonder whether they really know what is going on with a client or in the therapy process.

Experienced therapists are able to cope with this uncertainty because they have learned to trust the process of treatment even though they are sometimes anxious about it. Skilled therapists also listen to how they are feeling because that information can often provide important insights about what is happening in the session.

In your own training, try to be aware of any beliefs or ideas that place unrealistic expectations on yourself. It may also be helpful to discuss these ideas with your peers, instructor, or supervisor. Do not be ashamed to admit that there are times when you are unsure about what to do. Experienced supervisors will certainly understand this and would much rather an intern talk about such feelings than keep them inside and proceed without seeking assistance. The most important self-care cognition is probably: "I do not have to be perfect, but I do need to get help when I need it."

COGNITIONS ABOUT CLIENTS

Just as unrealistic expectations for oneself can contribute to stress, inaccurate or unrealistic cognitions about clients are also a common source of stress for interns. Fremont and Anderson (1986) suggested that counselors carry a set of assumptions about how clients "should act and how counseling should progress" (p. 68). When these assumptions are not met, counselors may become angry or frustrated. Among the assumptions identified by Fremont and Anderson are:

1. The client is in counseling to get better or to make some changes in behavior. It is part of the client's role to work on personal problems and to follow counselor suggestions.
2. The client should not become too dependent. Some degree of dependency is expected, but it should not interfere with the counselor's private life.
3. The client is expected to appreciate the counselor's expenditure of psychic energy. It is unacceptable for the client to reject this notion, especially with a show of anger or hostility.
4. The client should not successfully manipulate counselor behavior.

Despite, or perhaps because of, the assumptions just described, in the course of your training you will probably find yourself thinking that clients are heroic, lazy, dangerous, suicidal, seductive, distancing, helpless, whiny, crazy, unmotivated, manipulative, passive-aggressive, logical, motivated, creative, suffering, or a host of other things. When you experience such feelings, it may be helpful to keep several ideas in mind.

First, the most stressful of all cognitions about clients is probably the notion that clients should be different than they are. This cognition can take many forms. You may think, "This client should be more open in therapy," or "This client should not be so angry," or "This client should not be so depressed," or "This client should be more appreciative of the service we provide."

However you finish the sentence, believing clients should be different is a good way to create unnecessary and unproductive stress for yourself and your clients. This is not to say that clients would not benefit from change. It is to say that wanting clients to be different, and becoming upset because they are not, is not treatment. Our task is not to identify how clients "should be," then wish that the clients were different than they are. Our task is to help our clients determine what they want to be, then help them achieve that goal for themselves.

A second point to remember is that many interns add to their stress by overgeneralizing beliefs about specific clients to all clients. For example, some interns worry about the possibility of suicide with virtually all their clients. Because suicide is such a serious action, and because it is possible for any person to take his or her own life, this concern is understandable. Most clients, however—even most depressed clients—do not commit suicide. Thus, if you actively worry about suicide for every client, you will do a lot of worrying, and most of that worrying will be unnecessary. A large part of training involves moving from such overgeneralization to more specific applications and more precise understanding. As this happens, you will develop a better sense of when you can relax and when you really do need to be anxious about clients.

COGNITIONS ABOUT THERAPY

Closely tied to the idea that clients should be different are ideas about the therapy process in general. As noted, one such cognition is the belief that clients should not be resistant to change. Interns and beginning therapists often become upset with clients who "obviously need to change" but resist the therapist's best efforts to get them to do something different. In such situations, the problem, and the source of the therapist's stress, is not really the client. Rather, it is the therapist's belief that change is, or should be, easy for people. The reality is that change can be very difficult—sometimes it takes a long time to happen, and people (including interns and therapists) tend to resist change because it is unfamiliar and uncertain. When therapists do not recognize and work with client resistance, they are likely to become frustrated with the client and with themselves. On the other hand, when resistance is understood and recognized as an expected and normal part of the treatment process, a therapist or intern is more able to respond to it effectively.

Another cognition that adds to stress is the belief that the helping professional is responsible for the client's life. Clients come to you or your agency because they want your help in understanding or altering something about themselves or their lives. You charge money for your time, and you have supposedly been trained in ways of helping, so there is at least an implied burden on you to do something useful. At the same time, as just discussed, clients often resist change and do not cooperate in the therapeutic work. This makes it easy to blame clients when progress is not achieved or does not come as rapidly as you or they might hope. Blaming clients for not changing is one way therapists deal with their own frustrations at not feeling successful or validated. But this response is ultimately an attempt to meet the therapist's needs, not the client's.

To deal more effectively with resistance, it helps to think of your role as a catalyst for change but not as the primary agent of change. You cannot, and should not, take full responsibility for solving your clients' problems for them. You must instead recognize that you play an important role in helping clients cope with their situations, discover resources within themselves, and make the changes they need to make for themselves. Ultimately, however, the clients themselves must make those changes; we cannot do it for them.

COGNITIONS ABOUT THE WORLD

Even when interns are away from the internship and clients, experiences in therapy can contribute to cognitions about the world that add to therapist stress. One of the ways this happens is through the development of a rather distorted sense of what constitutes normal. If an intern spends much of the day dealing with people who are experiencing serious problems in their lives, or who are hostile or severely impaired, the experience may cause the intern to begin to believe that most people have such problems. In some instances, this process can actually create or reinforce racial or other stereotypes.

One of our interns, who worked for a semester in a juvenile detention center, said, "I can't believe what those kids are like. I used to think I wanted to have children, but now, if they could turn out like these kids, forget it." By comparison, an intern who worked with abused children found herself "hating those parents and wondering if there are any decent people out there." Another intern worked with patients on the Alzheimer's disease unit of a nursing home. When she had the opportunity to do some intelligence testing with an elderly person who was not demented, she marveled at how intelligent the man was for his age. In fact, he was only in the average range for his age group, but relative to the people she had been working with, he seemed to her to be a genius.

Internship experiences also affect how interns think about systems. For example, an intern who worked in a social service agency became first angered, then frustrated and depressed by the inefficiency of the agency and lack of dedication on the part of many employees. Another intern, also frustrated by systemic flaws, despaired of the helping professions entirely and concluded that she should "change my major, quit trying to help anyone, and just make money."

In each of these cases, experiences with a selected population or system led an intern to hold ideas about the world that were distorted by the internship experience. The potential effect of such ideas was revealed by the intern who said that her experience made her wonder if she really wanted children of her own and by the individual who wanted to leave the field entirely.

Interns should remind themselves that they are dealing with real people, real suffering, and sometimes with real dysfunctional systems. That is part of life, but it is not all of life. If you find yourself getting soured on life or work at your placement, it can be extremely beneficial to seek experiences or information that will present the other side of the picture. Using a sports metaphor, Grosch and Olsen (1995) referred to the value of "cross-training" (i.e., varying jobs and activities to include other perspectives as a way of staying fresh). The interns described here might look for examples of youth who are contributing to their community, parents who are doing a thoughtful, caring job of raising their children, or senior citizens who are mentally alert and involved in programs that keep them healthy. Others might benefit by identifying systems that are successful and are staffed by dedicated, competent people. Such systems do in fact exist, but you may not have the good fortune to find them on your first or second field placement.

Making this effort helps interns come to grips with the reality of human suffering and shortcomings while not losing sight of the equally important reality of human joy, kindness, and health. It is essential for interns to understand that they have the potential to help change dysfunctional systems for the better. If everything already worked perfectly, there would be little need for the human service professions. On the other hand, great strides have been made toward making things better, and in each case these advances have occurred because one or more individuals dedicated themselves to a goal. As a student, and as an intern, you have the opportunity to develop knowledge, experience, and insights that can help you make a real difference in the world. The task will not be easy, and it will probably not be completed in any one person's lifetime, but you can have an effect, and people's lives (including your own) can be more fulfilling thanks to your efforts.

EXERCISE: COGNITIONS REVIEW

Based on what you have read thus far and on your own experiences, review your own beliefs about your role as an intern, the treatment process, clients, or the world as a whole. What beliefs do you hold that may be causing unnecessary stress? What beliefs help you deal constructively with the stresses of your work or training? When you have written your own thoughts, discuss them with your peers and supervisor to get their ideas and feedback. If certain ideas are impacting you adversely, consider developing an active strategy to confront and change those ideas and their effects.

PHYSICAL SELF-CARE

We must all determine for ourselves how we define physical health. In my practice as a medical psychologist, I worked on a daily basis with people who suffered the psychological and physical effects of poor physical self-care. I was also involved in various efforts aimed at preventing illness and promoting better physical wellness. Perhaps because of this background, and because I know firsthand how physically draining internships and clinical work can be, I strongly encourage interns to care for their bodies as well as their minds. Without becoming preachy, I want to help interns develop skills and habits that will serve them throughout their careers. Having seen the physical and emotional toll this line of work can take on people, I feel an obligation to at least raise the issue and perhaps offer some new perspectives.

PHYSICAL EXERCISE

As described earlier, the sedentary nature of clinical work and the tendency to internalize stresses place unusual physical demands on the body. Physical activity can help overcome some of the effects of sedentary work and can help you deal with stress more effectively.

When the subject of physical activity arises, some interns have no problem because exercise is already part of their daily routine. Others indicate that they are interested in exercising but cannot find time. Still others respond as if I have suggested they do something abhorrent.

For those in the first group, one need only encourage continuing what is already in place and jealously guarding the time for daily exercise. For those who would like to exercise but do not find the time, it may be useful to reread the discussion of time management and unscheduling. For individuals who respond negatively to exercise, I can offer a few thoughts based on what has worked with students and with clients wanting to change their physical activity.

First, do not feel you must start a rigorous exercise program right away. Take some time to think about what is or would be healthy for you. As you consider this, do not think in terms of heavy workouts or strict diets when you think of physical self-care. Those terms do not really sound much like care, so it is not surprising that they are aversive. As an appealing and realistic alternative, you are more likely to succeed if you start small and consider your own needs and values. Without launching directly into a full workout regimen, you can find opportunities to incorporate less strenuous forms of exercise throughout the day. You can increase fitness by doing little things such as taking stairs instead of elevators, parking a little farther from the office, or, better still, walking or biking to work. While at work, get in the habit of getting up and stretching between sessions. Similarly, if your work for the day involves long hours of reading, writing, or computer work, you can set a watch or other timer as a reminder to take a break to stretch your body and rest your eyes.

These changes can actually make a noticeable difference in health, but there may also be a need to structure some regular forms of aerobic activity during your week. When you reach this point, you may ask, as do many people, "So how much exercise do I *have* to do?" Specialists in the area of physical wellness suggest that a more successful way to ask the question is, "How little physical activity will let me realize noticeable health improvements?" This reframing removes the sense of obligation, and perhaps, along with it, a degree of resistance. The alternative question also emphasizes that in terms of reducing risk for such illnesses as coronary vascular disease, relatively little exercise can produce significant benefits.

For many people, even those who once thought of exercise as tantamount to self-imposed torture, the break they schedule for exercise soon becomes a highlight of the day, something they look forward to beforehand, enjoy while doing, and appreciate throughout the day. Ideally, exercise should not be something we do "to ourselves." It should be something we do "for ourselves" to release tension and improve our overall well-being.

MASSAGE

For some people, physical exercise may not feel like self-care, but most would agree that therapeutic massage is pretty close to the epitome of self-care. Perhaps the best thing about massage for helping professionals is that it allows you to put yourself quite literally into someone else's hands and let them take care of you for awhile. This is something many of us, particularly in the helping professions, do not do.

An example of the benefit of massage was quite immediate for me as I wrote this chapter for the first edition of this book. In the final stages of preparing the book, I was teaching full-time, doing half-time clinical work, and putting in extraordinarily long days of writing in between. My days often began at 5:00 A.M., and I stayed at it until I could go no further, often continuing until well past midnight. After many months of previous work, this intense effort had gone on with little respite for many weeks, and the effects were beginning to tell. Realizing I needed a break, but under pressure to meet deadlines, the idea of a massage came to me and seemed so appealing I almost called 911-MASSAGE. Fortunately, a massage therapist I knew was able to schedule an appointment for that same day. I explained my situation, lay down on the table, and let her do the work. During the entire massage I only thought about work once, and that was to make a brief mental note to add a word about massage to this chapter. It is not an exaggeration to say that an hour and a half later, I felt like a new person. I still had several long days ahead, but the massage had helped me weather a point of near exhaustion and recharged the batteries to help me get through.

In addition to being a great way to release stress and help one relax, massage is also a good way of monitoring where and how you may be physically internalizing the emotional stresses of your work. Many of us tend to keep the accumulated emotions of our work somewhere in our bodies; headaches, backaches, and other pains may be the result. A skilled massage therapist will locate those places and, while helping to work them out, may give you some clues about where you keep stresses in your body.

MONITORING STRESSES IN THE BODY

Few of us have the time or money to afford a massage every day. Lacking that luxury, we need to learn to deal with physical tensions as they arise during the course of our work.

Another useful suggestion offered by a colleague is to periodically run a "mental body check," noticing any signs of physical tension or other sensations that arise. Perhaps the easiest way to do this is to start at the top of your head and do a quick run-through of your posture, muscle tension, and other internal sensations. It may help to do this as you breathe in and out, thinking of letting go of any tension as you exhale. With practice, this self-check and relaxation can be done in a very short time and in a way that is not noticeable to others. I try to do such checks several times during each therapy session, meeting, class, or other event. This helps to keep physical tensions from building and can reveal clues about how I am reacting to what is happening. When I work with clients, I also observe their physical posture and apparent tension levels. This awareness can provide valuable clues to what is going on clinically.

HEALTHY EATING AND HABITS

Along with a healthy amount of exercise and relaxation, healthy eating is also important. Just as internships can limit the time available for exercise, they often have an adverse influence on how, when, and what interns eat. Many interns are unaware of this until they think about it and realize that, in fact, the internship has affected their eating in several ways.

Some interns find that eating is one of the ways they cope with the stresses of the internship. A common experience is to come home from the internship and feel a need to eat something to help settle down after a demanding day. Interns may also find themselves so rushed at their placements that they seldom take time to relax and enjoy a meal that is really good for them. Instead, "lunch" consists of a bag of chips and a soft drink or coffee (their third cup of five or more per day) from the vending machine or espresso stand.

The issue here is not so much what a person should or should not eat. Rather, the goal is to increase awareness of how you are being affected by, and are attempting to cope with, the challenges of the internship. Poor dietary habits can be intrinsically harmful over the long run, but they can also serve as a signal to help you recognize whether you are taking care of yourself. The same point can and should be made about other habits that are also related to stress and coping.

The use of alcohol, cigarettes, or other drugs is closely tied to stress, and helping professionals are no less vulnerable, perhaps even more so, to abusing these substances. Hughes, De-Witt, Sheehan, Conrad, and Storr (1992) reported that among a large sample of resident physicians surveyed, emergency medicine and psychiatry residents reported higher rates of substance use than residents in other specialties.

In my clinical work and as an instructor and supervisor, I have come in contact with students, supervisors, and colleagues who had significant substance abuse problems. In most cases, these same individuals denied that they had a problem even though virtually everyone who knew them was aware of, and concerned about, the situation. In addition to the damage and difficulties substance abuse causes the individuals themselves, the profession also suffers harm as members of the public look cynically at helping professionals who do not appear able to deal well with problems themselves.

Once again, the goal here is to help interns become aware of signs that may indicate they are not coping well with personal or professional stresses. If you find your own use of legal or controlled substances increasing—if it sometimes feels you just have to have a drink, smoke, pill, or something else to cope with the stress of work—perhaps it is time to examine how work is affecting you or how the habits themselves are affecting your work.

EXERCISE: PERSONAL PHYSICAL HEALTH CARE REVIEW

As a step toward developing physical self-care habits, you may wish to conduct a simple personal physical health care review.

This review involves taking stock of activities relating to exercise, diet, and harmful habits. Write each of these headings on a sheet of paper: Exercise, Diet, Habits. Under these headings, list the things you think are conducive to self-care and the things that might be harmful in some way. Ask yourself how your internship work or other activities relate to what you have written. Finally, give some thought to how changes in your self-care might benefit your internship, school, or other activities, and how changes in those activities could affect your physical care.

EMOTIONAL SELF-CARE

Two brief anecdotes illustrate the need for attending to one's own emotional self-care as an intern or clinician. The first happened to a young intern during his predoctoral internship at a psychiatric hospital. On the last day of work before a holiday, the intern was riding his bike home from an evening group meeting. As he rode, he was thinking about the contrast between the home where he would spend the coming week and the hospital facility where the patients would be. Quite unexpectedly, as the lights of the hospital faded behind him and he turned down a darkened road, he began to cry. In fact, he began sobbing so hard he had to stop his bicycle and sit beneath a streetlight, crying to himself for almost half an hour. He had been working at the hospital for four months and knew some of the patients very well; but until that moment, the full reality of their situation had not really struck him. When the realization hit, all of the emotions stored for months came out at once.

A second incident occurred more recently and demonstrates again how emotional effects of clinical work can sneak up on us. As mentioned earlier, in addition to teaching, I practiced as a psychologist in medical settings. For a variety of reasons, including a difficult course load, challenging cases, seemingly endless and pointless political struggles within the institution, and numerous other factors, I was going through a series of rough weeks at just the time I was teaching the internship class about the topic of self-care. One day in class, I advised the interns to monitor their own emotional status. That same evening, a relatively small dispute with one of my children resulted in my shouting at, and criticizing, the child far more harshly than the situation called for. My wife noticed this and asked if perhaps the stresses at work were a factor in the reaction. Of course, I denied this vehemently (after all, I am writing a book on the subject), but after some reflection I realized she was right. Things at work had piled up, and although I did not think they were affecting me, I was carrying far more emotional tension than I realized.

It is probably not possible or desirable to try to be emotionally unaffected by one's clinical work, but it is vital that we learn to deal with those effects constructively. During a workshop on self-care and managing the stresses of work, several colleagues offered the following useful suggestions.

SELF-CHECKS

Perhaps the most important principle of self-care is to be aware of, and acknowledge, how our work affects us. One counselor said she makes a habit of doing a brief emotional self-check that is comparable to the physical self-checks described earlier. At the end of each session, after the client leaves, she takes a deep breath, closes her eyes, and asks herself how she feels emotionally at that moment and how she felt emotionally during the session. This process helps her to be aware of what she is experiencing, and it can provide new insights into what happened during the session. It also reminds her to relax.

CLEANSING RITUALS

Another colleague, a psychologist who often works with extremely challenging cases, makes use of what he calls "cleansing rituals" to help clear his mind and emotions between sessions. For example, if a session has been very demanding emotionally, he sometimes splashes a bit of cool water on his face afterward. This offers a refreshing break, and it reminds him to be clear before meeting with his next client. He also uses stretching as a way to relieve both physical and emotional tension. After each client, he makes a practice of taking several deep breaths while he stretches his back and legs. With each breath out he imagines letting go of any stresses he might have stored during the session. With each breath in, he reminds himself to be patient and open to the next client's experience. He does not leave the office to invite the next patient in until he feels he has sufficiently processed the interaction with the previous individual.

A different type of cleansing process was described by a social worker specializing in domestic violence. She uses the act of opening the door to her office as a signal to clear her mind for the next client. After finishing her case notes, she puts the client's folder away and says to herself that she will leave the client there until the next visit. This helps to prevent her from "taking her clients home." Using the opening door as a cue helps her meet the next client where that client is, rather than with emotional baggage left over from the previous session. At the end of the day, she uses the closing of her office door behind her as a reminder to leave the work of the day at the office. This allows her to go home to her family without carrying the day's accumulated feelings away from the office. Describing this practice, she noted that if she did not have some way of keeping what she deals with at work separate from her home life, she doubts she would last three months in practice.

MEDITATION AND PRAYER

For therapists with religious backgrounds, prayer can offer another means of coping with the stresses of work. In a discussion of how child welfare workers cope with the effects of secondary trauma, Dane (2000) reported that many of her respondents said their spiritual beliefs helped them find meaning in their very difficult work. Some also offered that they prayed before going on difficult field visits or after working with expecially challenging cases. I have spoken with therapists who have said silent prayers during sessions as both a way of helping deal with the emotional stresses and in an effort to seek guidance for how best to help the client. It is important, however, to keep in mind that while prayer may be helpful to you personally, imposing prayer or religiously based interventions on clients who are not of the same persuasion would not be considered ethical or sound clinical practice.

Meditation has also been helpful to many therapists, and I have found the approach of "mindfulness meditation" to be particularly beneficial in my own work. One of the foremost teachers of this method is a Vietnamese Buddhist, Thich Nhat Hanh. The practice of mindful meditation, which is perhaps best summarized in his book *The Miracle of Mindfulness* (1975), is accessible and easily incorporated into everyday life, and can be of benefit regardless of one's religious beliefs. In essence, mindfulness entails being fully aware of what is happening in the present moment, whether one is walking, eating, or simply sitting quietly and being aware of breathing. Taking a few moments before and after sessions to breathe quietly and mindfully can be remarkably beneficial, as can going for brief, mindful walks outside.

There are, of course, many other possibilities for emotional self-care, and you can probably find ways that work best for you. Whatever approach you develop, it is worth developing some form of reliable practice that you can do between clients, meetings, or other activities and at the end of the day to finish the work and leave it where it belongs.

ORGANIZATIONAL MEASURES AND PEER SUPPORT

Self-care activities can go a long way toward helping clinicians cope with the emotional demands of their work, but proactive organizational activities and the support of other interns or clinicians are also important (Berger, 1995; Guy, 2000; O'Conner, 2001, Turner et al., 2005). If you find yourself feeling overwhelmed by work, or if you are carrying emotions away from your sessions, you may want to spend some time talking with your peers or supervisor about what you are experiencing. This advice, however, is easier to give than to follow. One way to make it easier to follow the advice of self-care is through activities sponsored by the institutions where we work. Another helpful approach involves the development of Colleague Assistance Programs affiliated with state professional associations. Such programs provide peer-to-peer professional support for colleagues facing challenges ranging from personal stresses to ethical dilemmas to significant career changes (Munsey, 2006).

ORGANIZATIONAL FACTORS AND STRUCTURED STRESS MANAGEMENT

In her discussion of the impact of secondary trauma, Hesse (2002) emphasized that agencies in which therapists must deal with victims of psychological trauma or other challenging cases should have organizational mechanisms in place to help therapists deal with the effects of their work. Catheral (1995) recommended an organizational approach that includes identification of staff exposed to secondary trauma, developing a plan for educating staff about the effects of secondary trauma, training in ways of coping with those effects, and, finally, evaluating the success of these efforts and making changes as needed.

Dane (2000) provided an illustrative example of a program designed to help child welfare workers, who must deal on a daily basis with abused children and their abusers. Through focus group discussions, child welfare workers identified the most difficult elements of their work and the impact these have on them emotionally, physically, in their relationships, and in other areas. From that input, a two-day training program was designed to help teach care workers about the stressful impact of the work, signs of burnout, secondary traumatization, and countertransference, and ways of coping with these successfully. Results suggested that this approach was generally well received and helpful, but Dane emphasized the importance of follow-up through monthly discussion meetings, a six-month booster session, and special provisions if highly traumatic events, such as the death of a patient, occur.

LETTING OFF STEAM

The process just described involves structured interactions that occur in private with other peers or colleagues. As helpful as these exchanges with professional peers may be, sometimes it is also incredibly helpful to just let off steam with people who know what the job is like. This is different from talking over one's day with a spouse, and it is different from clinical supervision. The goal is simply to relax and have fun; to do something with your colleagues that has as little to do with work as possible. Even if you are not the social type, it is important to do things with your peers and away from work.

If you do participate in such activities, without taking away the fun, keep three cautions in mind: First, be careful about the locations you choose and issues of confidentiality if the conversation is about clients. Everyone in your group may know about a given client, and there may be interesting or funny stories to share, but if the setting is public and the talk gets too loud, others may easily overhear you. Whether or not they personally know the individuals involved, merely hearing professionals talking, and perhaps even laughing, about clients in public could cast a negative image.

A second concern is that there is a fine line between constructive stress release for staff and destructive derision of clients. It is one thing to say "You'll never believe what so-and-so did today," followed by an anecdote that is funny without being demeaning. It is quite another to say the same opening with a harsh or critical tone, followed by a negative story about how bad the client is in some way. The same principle applies to stories about colleagues. Never forget that clients and colleagues, no matter how frustrating, are people who are doing their best to get by. If it helps for you to laugh, by all means do so. But be sure you are laughing as much at yourself and the wonderful, sad, and confusing thing it is to be human.

Finally, many TGIF activities tend to take place in settings where alcohol is served. This is not necessarily a problem, but keep in mind that alcohol can easily become an external mood controller that one gradually comes to depend on for dealing with stresses. As noted, if this starts becoming a pattern for you or your peers, it is a good idea to explore how well you are coping with stress and what alternatives to alcohol might be more constructive.

EXERCISE: EMOTIONAL COPING

Having read the suggestions about coping with the emotional stresses of your work, this is a good opportunity to do an emotional self-check of your own. As part of this check, identify things you currently do to help care for your own emotional reactions to your work. Also identify things that might be helpful but that you do not currently practice. If you find there are some things you could and perhaps should be doing differently to take care of yourself, develop a plan to implement changes. As a first step in this process, you may want to discuss the issue with a peer and perhaps explore ways of working together to help one another.

MULTIMODAL SELF-CARE

Each of the various categories of self-care activities described above was integrated conceptually by Arnold Lazarus (2000) into what he referred to as "multimodal self-care." Consistent with his multimodal approach to therapy, Lazarus recommended asking yourself the following seven fundamental questions: What fun things can I do? What positive emotions can I generate? What sensory experiences can I enjoy? What empowering and pleasant mental images can I conjure? What positive self-talk can I employ? Which amiable people can I associate with? What specific health-related activities can I engage in?

Coming from a slightly different perspective than Lazarus, but offering a comparably multimodal approach, Norcross (2000) offers a list of self-care strategies that are "clinician recommended, research informed, and practitioner tested." The list begins by recognizing the hazards of clinical practice, then addresses a combination of cognitive, behavioral, and insight-oriented approaches for coping with stress. Norcross also recommends diversification of clinical activities, and, finally, an emphasis on appreciating the rewards as well as the challenges of therapy.

PERSONAL THERAPY

It is often very hard for interns or clinicians to acknowledge that they are having a hard time. The vulnerable moment in which one asks a friend or peer, "Can I talk to you?" can be extraordinarily frightening. Yet that moment can also begin a dialogue that will be of invaluable help. In my own career, there have been a number of times when I recognized that I needed help and had the good sense to ask for it. There have also been occasions when I needed help but was unaware of it or denied the situation. Fortunately, close colleagues who knew me well recognized that things were not right and gently offered an ear. At other times, I have done the same for them. In your own training, try to be aware of when you need support and try to be sensitive to when other interns or professionals could use support from you.

Because all of us are limited in our ability to know ourselves, and because we tend to be so exquisitely creative and effective in defending ourselves from awareness, we need outside information. One way to get such information is through therapy. Many practitioners, including myself, have found that personal psychotherapy is not only beneficial in helping deal with both personal issues and the stresses of practice, but it can also improve your understanding of the therapy process and, thus make you a better therapist (Geller, Norcross & Orlinsky, 2005; Norcross, 2005).

If you choose to see a therapist, you will not be alone in that decision. In a comprehensive review of studies involving a total of 8,000 participantes, Norcross and Guy (2005) found that around 72% of therapists have participated in some form of personal therapy. Mahoney (1997) reported that 87% of respondents attending a continuing education conference indicated that they had been in personal therapy at some point. Based on a review of literature relating to therapy for professionals and trainees, Norcross, Strausser, and Faltus (1988) noted that personal therapy is considered to be a desirable experience by the majority of training programs and practitioners surveyed. What is more, studies of factors contributing to professional development indicate that clinicians rank personal therapy among the three most important contributers, after direct patient contact and formal supervision, to professional development (Orlinsky & Rønnestad, 2005).

The benefits of therapy were demonstrated in research conducted by Andy Carey, Heather Stewart, and myself (1992). Our survey of more than 500 counselors and clinical psychologists demonstrated that the majority of respondents, 79% of the sample, reported they had participated in personal therapy or counseling. Of that group, 93% categorized the experience as from mildly to very positive. Results also showed that on an instrument designed to assess cognitions about clients, the therapy process, and the role of the therapist, 13 out of 38 items yielded statistical significance when therapists with personal experience in therapy were compared with those without such experience (Baird & Carey, 1992; Baird, Carey, & Giakovmis, 1992).

Comparable findings were obtained by Pope and Tabachnick (1994), who reported results from a survey of 800 psychologists. Of those who responded, 84% reported having been in therapy on at least one occasion. The most common reasons identified for seeking therapy included (in descending order of frequency): depression or general unhappiness, marriage or divorce, relationship issues, self-esteem and self-confidence, anxiety, career, work or studies, family of origin, loss, stress, and a variety of less frequently mentioned concerns. Among those who had been in therapy, 85.7% described their therapy experience as having been "very or exceptionally helpful." The chief benefits mentioned were self-awareness or self-understanding, self-esteem or self-confidence, and improved skills as a therapist.

Despite the apparently widespread belief and empirical evidence that therapy is perceived as beneficial for trainees and professionals, this is an admittedly controversial subject. While not recommending that therapy be required for all students or interns in training, the evidence suggests that personal therapy can be a valuable experience for interns and therapists. In addition to helping us become more aware of ourselves, personal therapy also gives us a better awareness of what clients experience when they are in therapy.

Having said that, to be honest I must now add that in the early days of training I might have thrown away any book that recommended therapy for therapists or students. My feeling at the time was that one went into the field because one was pretty well put together to begin with and wanted to use this fortunate status to the benefit of others. That idea seemed at the time to make good sense, and it was certainly very comforting to believe I was so well adjusted as to be able to help others without further work on myself. That this belief was held by someone who was then still in his very early 20s does not seem at all surprising. Indeed, it only served to support a belief that healthy personal adjustment and effective psychotherapy were not necessarily so difficult.

That is how I once felt. As I gained experience, and after a number of challenging events in my personal life, the awareness gradually emerged that even therapists (perhaps especially therapists) have issues that they need to work through. This realization led me to enter a group therapy experience with other professionals. The results were enlightening. Not only did I receive invaluable assistance in recognizing and working through some of my own issues, I also came to know firsthand how therapy can be helpful and how helpful it can be.

EXERCISE

If you have previously experienced therapy or counseling, this might be a good time to reflect on that experience and how it has affected you as an individual and in your work with others. If you have never been in therapy, you may want to consider whether you would be willing to seek therapy at some time. If you find yourself open to the idea, what benefits would you hope to receive? If you are opposed to the idea of entering therapy for yourself, give some thought to the reasons why. You may also want to consider what alternative methods you will establish and practice for coping with how your work affects you personally and how your own issues affect your work.

POSITIVE EFFECTS ON THERAPISTS

Thus far, we have focused primarily on coping with the stresses and potentially negative emotional and physical impacts that face helping professionals and interns. The intent has been to apprise you of some of the personal challenges you may face as an intern or professional. As important as it is to understand the challenges, it should not be forgotten that if stress were the only effect of this work, not many people would go into it. Therefore, it is equally important to recognize and value the positive effects of what you do (Berger, 1995). Kramen-Kahn and Hansen (1998) emphasized that it can be beneficial for stressed clinicians to keep in mind the overlooked rewards and seek out career-sustaining behaviors.

EXERCISE: POSITIVE EFFECTS OF CLINICAL WORK

List the positive emotional effects you derive from your internship training.

List the positive cognitive effects you derive from your internship training.

List any other benefits you derive from the internship.

As you look toward the future, what benefits do you expect to achieve in each of these areas as a professional in the field?

Finally, if you have the opportunity, discuss this question with those who have worked in your profession for some time. Ask them about both the benefits and the stresses, and how they have managed to balance the two.

I have asked numerous interns and experienced therapists about the positive effects they experience from their work. The most frequent response describes a sense of satisfaction in doing something to help others. As one clinician said, "Every now and then you work with a client, and it is just clear that you have been helpful to them. That really feels good to me, to know I made a difference like that." Berger (1995) reported similar statements from senior therapists describing factors that sustain their work. Stevanovic and Rupert (2004) found that therapists identified "promoting growth in clients/helping others" as their highest source of professional satisfaction, followed by intellectual stimulation and other intrinsic rewards.

Other rewards include the opportunity to continue learning, the pleasure of working with colleagues who share similar backgrounds and goals, the intellectual challenges of clinical work, and personal growth (Guy, 1987). Many professionals enjoy the relative autonomy and responsibility of the work, while others emphasize the variety of tasks and clients they deal with. Your own list of benefits may have included those just described or others. Whatever you identified, it is important to recognize the positive elements of your work. If the positive elements begin to decline or are outweighed by the negatives, your motivation, effort, and effectiveness will eventually begin to suffer.

Being aware of the benefits of your training or profession can also influence the quality of your work itself. For example, if one of the benefits for most therapists is the satisfaction that comes when a client makes progress, it is easy for the therapist to become dependent on the client's changing, not for the client's own benefit, but because the client must change in order for the therapist to feel good. Helping professionals must maintain a delicate balance between appreciating the rewards that come from feeling one has helped another person and not becoming dependent on that reward or allowing it to interfere with what one must do to, in fact, be helpful.

FINANCIAL SELF-CARE

The final self-care topic to be addressed here has to do with financial matters. Given the focus of this chapter on managing the stresses that come with internships and clinical work, it must be acknowledged that financial concerns are among the top-ranked sources of stress for people in virtually all lines of work, including the helping professions. I have known more than a few colleagues whose personal lives and clinical work were significantly affected by issues related to financial management. This can become especially important for those in private practice, as clinical and ethical issues regarding termination, referral, and billing can easily become confused with the therapist's personal financial situation at the time. Financial management is also of great importance for interns and recent graduates because debts from student loans can pose special challenges (Winerman, 2006).

Faced with these challenges, many interns and new professionals have received little if any direct instruction or support in learning how to manage their finances. Habben, for example, (2004) observed that "We need to learn early on how to generate revenue, how to market ourselves, how to create a network—all of the things that we psychologists just don't like to do." (p. 54. quoted in DeAngelis, 2005).

In this text, I would not pretend to offer advice on such topics as how you should invest your money, whether mutual funds are superior to money markets, or what the best retirement plan should be. Instead, my goal is to suggest a way of thinking that may help reduce the stresses that so often accompany money matters. Much of what I have to offer in this regard is described well in the book *Your Money or Your Life* (2nd ed.) by Dominguez and Robin (1999). Unlike many books that offer strategies to "get rich quick," Dominguez and Robin set out to help people determine when they "have enough." Their approach is centered around the simple yet profound truth that "Money is something we choose to trade our life for" (p. 54).

From this awareness, it is possible to examine carefully not only the costs of spending money but also the costs of earning it. When one translates dollars earned and spent into life energy sacrificed, three questions naturally follow. Dominguez and Robin (1999, p. 112) suggest we ask:

1. Did I receive fulfillment, satisfaction, and value in proportion to life energy spent?
2. Is this expenditure of life energy in alignment with my values and life purpose?
3. How might this expenditure change if I didn't have to work for a living?

Asking these questions of ourselves, seriously thinking about them in the short term as we go to work and make purchases, and weighing them in the long run as we set goals and plan our lives, can have enormous impact on the way we live. I know colleagues who establish a practice or take a position with an agency, then purchase homes and cars that demand virtually all the income available. These purchases are then followed by luxuries such as sailboats, vacation condominiums, or other "toys" for grownups. To meet these expenses, the individuals increase their practice or take on another position. In the end, they spend so much of their time earning money that they have almost no time to do anything but work to pay for the things they have bought. As Dominguez and Robin (1999) remind us, the monetary cost in dollars is, in fact, paid in life energy. What we take out of life to put into "things" we can never reclaim.

Failure to think carefully about personal values and their relationship to financial matters can easily interfere with all other aspects of self-care. In extreme cases, as noted earlier, financial concerns can also interfere with sound clinical practice. Given this possibility, interns may wish to think seriously about the role of money in relation to their eventual goals and current practices. It can also be valuable to ask yourself what your purpose in life is and how your career and other activities fit within or compete with that purpose. Finally, you may find it enlightening to ask yourself what it means to have "enough" and if you are using your life energy wisely, whether you measure it in time or dollars.

REFERENCES

Ackerley, G. D., Burnell, J., Holder, D. C., & Kurdek, L. A. (1988). Burnout among licensed psychologists. *Professional Psychology: Research and Practice, 19,* 624–631.

American Psychological Association Policy and Planning Board. (2006). APA's response to international and national disasters and crises: Addressing diverse needs. *American Psychologist, 61,* 513–521.

Arches, J. (1991). Social structure, burnout, and job satisfaction. *Social Work, 36,* 202–206.

Arons, G., & Siegel, R. D. (1995). Unexpected encounters: The Wizard of Oz exposed. In M. B. Sussman (Ed.), *A perilous calling: The hazards of psychotherapy practice* (pp. 125–138). New York: Wiley.

Arthur, N. M. (1990). The assessment of burnout: A review of three inventories useful for research and counseling. *Journal of Counseling and Development, 69,* 186–189.

Baird, B. N., & Carey, A. (1992). *The therapist cognition survey: Development, standardization, and uses.* Paper presented at the meeting of the Western Psychological Association, Portland, OR.

Baird, B. N., Carey, A., & Giakovmis, H. (1992). *Personal experience in psychotherapy: Differences in therapists' cognitions.* Paper presented at the meeting of the Western Psychological Association, Portland, OR.

Baker, E. K. (2005). *Caring for ourselves: A therapist's guide to personal and professional wellbeing.* Washington, DC: American Psychological Association.

Berger, M. (1995). Sustaining the professional self: Conversations with senior psychotherapists. In M. B. Sussman (Ed.), *A perilous calling: The hazards of psychotherapy practice* (pp. 302–321). New York: Wiley.

Baker, E. K. (2003). *Caring for ourselves: A therapist's guide to personal and professional well-being.* Washington, DC: American Psychological Association.

Benjamin, M. (2005). How many have gone to war. *Salon.com,* April 12, 2005 http://www.globalsecurity.org/org/news/2005/050412-gone-to-war.htm

Boxley, R., Drew, C., & Rangle, D. (1986). Clinical trainee impairment in APA approved internship programs. *Clinical Psychologist, 39*(2), 49–52.

Bradley, J., & Post, P. (1991). Impaired students: Do we eliminate them from counselor education programs? *Counselor Education and Supervision, 31,* 100–108.

Brady, J., Guy, J., Poelstra, P., & Brokaw, B. (1999). Vicarious traumatization, spirituality, and the treatment of sexual abuse survivors. A national survey of women psychotherapists. *Professional Psychology: Research and Practice, 30*(4), 386–393.

Bryant, R. A., & Harvey, A. G. (2000). *Acute stress disorder: A handbook of theory, assessment and treatment.* Washington, DC: American Psychological Association.

Callahan, T. R. (1994). Being paid for what you do. *Independent Practitioner: Bulletin of the Division of Independent Practice, Division 42 of the APA, 14*(1), 25–26.

Carroll, J. F. X., & White, W. L. (1982). Theory building: Integrating individual environmental factors within an ecological framework. In W. S. Paine (Ed.), *Job stress and burnout: Research, theory, and intervention perspectives* (pp. 41–60). Beverly Hills, CA: Sage.

Catherall, D. R. (1995). Preventing institutional secondary traumatic stress disorder. In C. R. Figley, (Ed.) *Compassion fatigue: Secondary traumatic stress disorder from treating the traumatized.* New York: Bruner/Mazel.

Cook, J. M., Schnurr, P. O., & Foa, E. B., (2004). Bridging the gap between posttraumatic stress disorder research and clinical practice: The example of exposure therapy. *Psychotherapy, Theory, Research, Practice, Training, 41,* 374–387.

Courtois, C. A., (2004). Complex trauma, complex reactions: Assessment and treatment. *Psychotherapy, Theory, Research, Practice, Training, 41,* 412–425.

Creamer, M., & Forbes, D. (2004). Treatment of posttraumatic stress disorder in military and veteran populations. *Psychotherapy, Theory, Research, Practice, Training, 41,* 388–398.

Cunningham, M. (2004). Teaching social worers about trauma: Reducing the risks of vicarious traumatization in the classroom. *Journal of Social Work Eduction, 40,* 305–317.

Dane, B. (2000). Child welfare workers: An innovative approach for interacting with secondary trauma. *Journal of Social Work Education, 36,* 27–38.

DeAngelis, T. (2005). Things I wish I'd learned in grad school. *Monitor on Psychology, 36*(1), 54–57.

DeAngelis, T. (2006). Novel PsyD programs tackle modern ills. *Monitor on Psychology, 37*(5), 33.

Dearing, R. L., Maddux, J. E., & Tangney, J. P. (2005). Predictors of psychological help seeking in clinical and counseling psychology graduate students, *Professional Psychology: Research and Practice, 36,* 323–329.

Deutsch, C. (1984). Self-reported sources of stress among psychotherapists. *Professional Psychology: Research and Practice, 15,* 833–845.

Dominguez, J., & Robin, V. (1999). *Your money or your life* (2nd ed.). New York: Penguin.

Edelwich, J., & Brodsky, A. (1980). *Burnout: Stages of disillusionment in the helping professions.* New York: Human Science Press.

Ellis, T. E., & Dickey, T. O. (1998). Procedures surrounding the suicide of a trainee's patient: A national survey of psychology internships and psychiatry residency programs. *Professional Psychology: Research and Practice, 29,* 492–497.

Farber, B. A. (1983a). Dysfunctional aspects of the psychotherapeutic role. In B. A. Farber (Ed.), *Stress and burnout in the human service professions* (pp. 97–118). New York: Pergamon Press.

Farber, B. A. (1983b). Introduction: A critical perspective on burnout. In B. A. Farber (Ed.), *Stress and burnout in the human service professions* (pp. 1–23). New York: Pergamon Press.

Farber, B. A., & Heifetz, L. (1981). The satisfactions and stresses of psychotherapeutic work: A factor analytic study. *Professional Psychology, 12,* 621–630.

Fiore, N. (1989). *The now habit: A strategic program for overcoming procrastination and enjoying guilt-free play.* New York: St. Martin's Press.

Foster, V. A. & McAdams, Charles R. III (1999). The impact of client suicide in counselor training: Implications for counselor education and supervision. *Counselor Education and Supervision, 39,* 22–33.

Fremont, S., & Anderson, W. (1986). What client behaviors make counselors angry: An exploratory study. *Journal of Counseling and Development, 65,* 67–70.

Freudenberger, H. J. (1974). Staff burn-out. *Journal of Social Issues, 30*(1), 159–165.

Furr, S. R., & Carroll, J. J. (2003). Critical incidents in student counselor development. *Journal of Counseling & Development, 81,* 483–489.

Geller, J. D., Norcross, J. C., & Orlinsky, D. E. (Eds.). (2005). *The psychotherapists' own psychotherapy: Patient and clinical perspectives.* New York: Oxford University Press.

Gold, S. N. (2004). The relevance of trauma to general clinical practice. *Psychotherapy, Theory, Research, Practice, Training, 41,* 363–373.

Golembiewski, R. T., & Munzenrider, R. F. (1988). *Phases of burnout: Developments in concepts and applications.* New York: Praeger.

Grosch, W. N., & Olsen, D. C. (1995). Prevention: Avoiding burnout. In M. B. Sussman (Ed.), *A perilous calling: The hazards of psychotherapy practice* (pp. 275–287). New York: Wiley.

Guy, J. (2000). Holding the holding environment together: Self-psychology and psychotherapist care. *Professional Psychology: Research and Practice, 31*(3), 351–352.

Guy, J. D. (1987). *The personal life of the psychotherapist.* New York: Wiley.

Guy, J. D., Poelstra, P. L., & Stark, M. J. (1989). Personal distress and therapeutic effectiveness: National survey of psychologists practicing psychotherapy. *Professional Psychology: Research and Practice, 20,* 48–50.

Hanh, T. N. (1975). *The miracle of mindfulness: An introduction to the practice of meditation.* Boston: Beacon.

Hellman, I. D., Morrison, T. L., & Abramowitz, S. F. (1987). Therapist flexibility/rigidity and work stress. *Professional Psychology: Research and Practice, 18,* 21–27.

Henry, D. B., Tolan, P. H., & Gorman-Smith, D. (2004). Have there been lasting effects associated with the September 11, 2001 terrorist attacks among inner-city parents and children? *Professional Psychology: Research and Practice, 35,* 542–547.

Hesse, A. R. (2002). Secondary trauma: How working with trauma survivors affects therapists. *Clinical Social Work Journal, 30,* 293–309.

Hughes, P. H., DeWitt, C. B., Jr., Sheehan, D. V., Conrad, S., & Storr, C. L. (1992). Resident physician substance use, by specialty. *American Journal of Psychiatry, 149,* 1348–1354.

Jayaratne, S., & Chess, W. A. (1983). Job satisfaction and burnout in social work. In B. A. Farber (Ed.), *Stress and burnout in the human service professions* (pp. 129–141). New York: Pergamon.

Jones, J. (1980). *The staff burnout scale for health professionals.* Park Ridge, IL: London House.

Kleespies, P. M., Smith, M. R., & Becker, B. R. (1990). Psychology interns as patient suicide survivors: Incidence, impact and recovery. *Professional Psychology: Research and Practice, 21,* 257–263.

Kottler, J. A. (1999). *The therapist's workbook: Self-assessment, self-care, and self-improvement exercises for mental health professionals.* San Francisco: Jossey Bass.

Kottler, J. A. (2003). *On being a therapist.* (3rd ed.). San Francisco: Jossey-Bass.

Kramen-Kahn, B., & Hansen, N. (1998). Rafting the rapids: Occupational hazards, rewards, and coping strategies of psychotherapists. *Professional Psychology: Research and Practice, 29*(2), 130–134.

Kurland, R., & Salmon, R. (1992). When problems seem overwhelming: Emphases in teaching, supervision, and consultation. *Social Work, 37,* 240–244.

Lamb, D. H., Presser, N. R., Pfost, K. S., Baum, M. C., Jackson, V. R., & Jarvis, P. A. (1987). Confronting professional impairment during the internship: Identification, due process, and remediation. *Professional Psychology: Research and Practice, 18,* 597–603.

Lazarus, A. (2000). Multimodal replenishment. *Professional Psychology: Research and Practice, 31*(1), 93–94.

Lee, R. T., & Ashforth, B. E. (1990). On the meaning of Maslach's three dimensions of burnout. *Journal of Applied Psychology, 75,* 743–747.

Levant, R. F. (2002). Psychology responds to terrorism. *Professional Psychology: Research and Practice, 33,* 507–509.

MacNab, S. S. (1995). Listening to your patients, yelling at your kids: The interface between psychotherapy and motherhood. In M. B. Sussman (Ed.), *A perilous calling: The hazards of psychotherapy practice* (pp. 37–44). New York: Wiley.

Maeder, T. (1989). *Children of Psychiatrists and Other Psychotherapists.* New York: Harper & Row.

Mahoney, M. J. (1997). Psychotherapists' personal problems and self-care patterns. *Professional Psychology: Research and Practice, 28,* 14–16.

Mangelsdorff, A. D. (2006). *Psychology in the service of national security.* Washington, DC: American Psychological Association.

Maslach, C. (1982). Understanding burnout: Definitional issues in analyzing a complex phenomenon. In W. S. Paine (Ed.), *Job stress and burnout: Research, theory, and intervention perspectives* (pp. 29–40). Beverly Hills, CA: Sage.

Maslach, C., & Jackson, S. E. (1986). *Maslach burnout inventory manual* (2nd ed.). Palo Alto, CA: Consulting Psychologists Press.

McGlothlin, J. M., Rainey, S., & Kindsvatter, A. (2005). Suicidal clients and supervisees: A model for considering supervisor roles. *Counselor Education and Supervision, 45,* 135–146.

McKnight, J. D., & Glass, D. C. (1995). Perceptions of control, burnout and depressive symptomatology: A replication and extension. *Journal of Consulting and Clinical Psychology, 63,* 490–494.

Meichenbaum, D., & Fitzpatrick, D., (1993). A constructivist narrative perspective on stress and coping: Stress inoculation applications. In L. Goldberger & S. Breznitz (Eds.), *Handbook of stress; Theoretical and clinical aspects* (2nd ed., pp. 706–723). New York: Free Press.

Melamed, S., Shirom, A., Toker, S., Berliner, S., & Shapira, I. (2006). Burnout and risk of cardiovascular disease: Evidence, possible causal paths, and promising research directions. *Psychological Bulletin, 132,* 327–353.

Meyers, L. (2006). Katrina trauma lingers long. *Monitor on Psychology, 37*(5). 46.

Morgan, R. D., Kuther, T. L., & Habben, C. J. (2005). *Life after graduate school in psychology: Insider's aadvice from new psychologists.* New York: Psychology Press.

Munsey, C. (2006). Helping colleagues to help themselves. *Monitor on Psychology, 37*(7), 34–36.

Murphy, J. W., & Pardeck, J. T. (1986). The "burnout syndrome" and management style. *Clinical Supervisor, 4*(4), 35–44.

Murtaugh, M. P., & Wollersheim, J. P. (1997). Effects of clinical practice on psychologists: Treating depressed clients, perceived stress, and ways of coping. *Professional Psychology: Research and Practice, 28,* 361–364.

Norcross, J. C. (2000). Psychotherapist self-care: Practitioner-tested, research-informed strategies. *Professional Psychology: Research and Practice, 31,* 710–713.

Norcross, J. C. (2005). The psychotherapist's own psychotherapy: Education and developing psychologists. *American Psychologist, 60,* 837–851.

Norcross, J. C., Strausser, D. J., & Faltus, F. J. (1988). The therapist's therapist. *American Journal of Psychotherapy, 42,* 53–66.

Norcross, J. C., & Guy, J. D., (2005). The prevalence and parameters of personal therapy in the United States. In J. D. Geller, J. C. Norcross, & D. E. Orlinsky (Eds.), *The psychotherapists' own psychotherapy: Patient and clinician perspectives* (pp. 165–176). New York: Oxford University Press.

O'Conner, M. F. (2001). On the etiology and effecive management of professional distress and impairment among psychologists. *Professional Psychology: Research and Practice, 32,* 345–350.

Oliver, M. N. I, Bernstein, J. H., Anderson, K. G., Blashfield, R. K., & Roberts, M. C. (2004). An exploratory examination of student attitudes toward "impaired" peers in clinical psychology training programs. *Professional Psychology: Research and Practice, 35,* 141–147.

Olkin, R., & Gaughen, S. (1991). Evaluation and dismissal of students in masters level clinical programs: Legal parameters and survey results. *Counselor Education and Supervision, 30,* 276–288.

Orlinsky, D. E., & Rønnestad, M. H. (2005). *How psychotherapists develop: A study of therapeutic work and professional growth.* Washington, DC: American Psychological Association.

Osborne, C. J. (2004), Seven salutary suggestions for counselor stamina. *Journal of Counseling and Developmant, 82,* 319–328.

Pearlman, L., & MacIan, P. (1995). Vicarious traumatization: An empirical study of the effects of trauma work on trauma therapists. *Professional Psychology: Research and Practice, 26*(6), 558–565.

Pines, A. (1982). Changing organizations: Is a work environment without burnout an impossible goal? In W. S. Paine (Ed.), *Job stress and burnout: Research, theory, and intervention perspectives* (pp. 189–212). Beverly Hills, CA: Sage.

Pines, A., & Aronson, E. (1988). *Career burnout: Causes and cures.* New York: Free Press.

Pope, K. S., & Tabachnick, B. G. (1994). Therapists as patients: A national survey of psychologists' experiences, problems, and beliefs. *Professional Psychology: Research and Practice, 25,* 247–258.

Pope, K. S., Tabachnick, B. G., & Keith-Spiegel, P. (1987). Ethics of practice: The beliefs and behaviors of psychologists as therapists. *American Psychologist, 42,* 993–1006.

Pulakos, J. (1994). Incidental encounters between therapists and clients: The client's perspective. *Professional Psychology: Research and Practice, 25,* 300–303.

Radeke, J., & Mahoney, M. (2000). Comparing the personal lives of psychotherapists and research psychologists. *Professional Psychology: Research and Practice, 31*(1), 82–84.

Reamer, F. G. (1992). The impaired social worker. *Social Work, 37,* 165–170.

Reyes, G., & Elhai, J. D., (2004). Psychosocial interventions in the early phases of disasters. *Psychotherapy, Theory, Research, Practice, Training,, 41,* 399–411.

Roberts, J. K. (1987). The life management model: Coping with stress through burnout. *Clinical Supervisor, 5*(2), 107–118.

Rodolfa, E. R., Kraft, W. A., & Reilley, R. R. (1988). Stressors of professionals and trainees at APA-approved counseling and VA medical center internship sites. *Professional Psychology: Research and Practice, 19,* 43–49.

Rosenberg, J. I., Getzelman, M. A., Arcinue, F., & Oren, C. Z., (2005). An exploratory look at students' experiences of problematic peers in academic professional psychology programs. *Professional Psychology: Research and Practice, 36,* 665–673.

Rupert, P. A., & Morgan, D. J. (2005). Work setting and burnout among professional psychologists. *Professional Psychology: Research and Practice, 36,* 544–550.

Sharkin, B. S., & Birkey, I. (1992). Incidental encounters between therapists and their clients. *Professional Psychology: Research and Practice, 23,* 326–328.

Sherman, M. D., & Thelen, M. H. (1998). Distress and professional impairment among psychologists in clinical practice. *Professional Psychology: Research and Practice, 29,* 79–85.

Silver, R. C., Holman, E. A., McIntosh, D. N., Poulin, M., & Gil-Rivas, V. (2002). Nationwide longitudinal study of psychological responses to September 11. *Journal of the American Medical Association, 288,* 1235–1244.

Skorupa, J., & Agresti, A. A. (1993). Ethical beliefs about burnout and continued professional practice. *Professional Psychology: Research and Practice, 24,* 281–285.

Söderfeldt, M., & Söderfeldt, B., & Warg, L. E. (1995). Burnout in social work. *Social Work, 40,* 638–646.

Sowa, C. J., May, K. M., & Niles, S. G. (1994). Occupational stress within the counseling profession: Implications for counselor training. *Counselor Education and Supervision, 34,* 19–29.

Stevanovic, P, & Rupert, P. A. (2004). Career-sustaining behaviors, satisfactions, and stresses of professional psychologists. *Psychotherapy: Theory, Research, Practice, Training, 41,* 301–309.

Stoesen, L. (2005). NASW responds to Katrina's impact, *NASW News, 50*(10). http://www.socialworkers.org/pubs/news/2005/11 /katrina.asp?back=yes

Trippany, R. L., Kress, V. E. W., & Wilcoxon, S. A. (2005). Preventing vicarious trauma: What counselors should know when working with trauma survivors. *Journal of Counseling and Development, 82,* 31–37.

Turner, J. A. Edwards, L. M., Eicken, I. M., Yokoyama, K., Castro, J. R., Tran, A. N. & Haggins, K. L. (2005). Intern self-care: An exploratory study into strategy use and effectiveness. *Professional Psychology: Research and Practice, 36,* 674–680.

Stadler, H. A., Willing, K. L., Eberhage, M. G., & Ward, W. H. (1988). Impairment: Implications for the counseling profession. *Journal of Counseling and Development, 66,* 258–260.

Sussman, M. B. (1995). *A perilous calling: The hazards of psychotherapy practice.* New York: Wiley.

Weaver, J. D. (1995). *Disasters: Mental health interventions.* Sarasota, FL: Professional Resource Press.

Winerman, L., (2006). Postgrad finances 101. *Monitor on Psychology, 37*(7), 62.

CHAPTER 8
ASSAULT AND OTHER RISKS

On the first day of my graduate internship at a Veterans' Administration hospital, the new interns took a tour of the wards, met the staff, and got a chance to talk with some of the patients. As soon as we came through the door on one of the wards, a man with wild, long, gray hair and wide, glaring eyes approached us rapidly. For some reason, perhaps because my appearance resembled his, the patient headed straight toward me, brought his face just a few inches from mine, and shouted some unintelligible words. Not knowing what else to do, I said "Hello." At that he smiled, then turned and walked away, mumbling to himself. That patient was acting very strangely, but he was not dangerous. Indeed, he had been diagnosed with schizophrenia for some 20 years, but he had never assaulted anyone.

Later in the same internship year, I was working with another patient whose behavior was by no means as unusual as the schizophrenic patient I just described. This man was in the hospital for treatment of depression and alcohol abuse. Throughout his stay, he had the habit of leaving the grounds on passes, visiting a nearby tavern, and returning to the ward in a highly intoxicated and belligerent state. After a series of these incidents, the staff decided he would not be allowed any spending money for a period of two weeks. When the patient, who was about six foot four and weighed over 200 pounds, asked for money and a pass so he could go off grounds to purchase a watch, it was expected that he would in fact use the money to buy alcohol. I was given the task of explaining that because of past actions he would not be given any money.

Needless to say, the patient was not happy to learn he could not have his money that week. He argued and tried to bargain, but I insisted that he would have to wait a week. As I turned to go, the patient jumped over the chair, threw his hands toward my throat, and backed me against a wall. He then tried to choke me and smash my head against the wall. I was able to keep his hands away from my throat long enough for help to arrive, but it was a close call to say the least, and it left me bruised and shaken.

The possibility that you will be assaulted during an internship will depend heavily on the setting in which you work and the clients with whom you interact. It will also depend on your own behaviors. Although it may be frightening to think about the possibility of an assault, the intent of this chapter is to help

reduce that possibility by giving you some suggestions for preventing and responding to risks. The message is: Do not be afraid, but do be careful and prepared. I have included this chapter because it is important for interns to have an awareness of the risks involved in clinical work. It is also vital, literally, for supervisors and instructors to help students learn to reduce and cope with those risks. Unfortunately, this subject, as we will see in a moment, is too often neglected by academic programs and training sites.

THE RISKS OF ASSAULT

If the people we worked with were all reasonable, self-controlled individuals, we would probably not encounter them in many of the settings where we work. While most clients, even those with serious mental illness, are not dangerous, behavior can be unpredictable. Those who work with clients committed to psychiatric hospitals should be aware that in most states the criteria for involuntary commitment specify that such individuals must be considered dangerous to themselves or others. Thus, in any setting where clients are involuntarily committed, the possibility of violence must be taken seriously. Further, there are some clients who, in addition to, or as part of, their mental illness, are simply mean and dangerous individuals.

The federal Occupational Safety and Health Administration (OSHA) has produced a series of Guidelines for Preventing Workplace Violence for Health Care & Social Service Workers (OSHA, http://www.osha.gov/Publications/OSHA3148/osha3148.html). Included with these guidelines are statistics from the Department of Justice (DOJ) National Crime Victimization Survey for 1993 to 1999. These data show that

> The average annual rate for non-fatal violent crime for all occupations is 12.6 per 1,000 workers. The average annual rate for physicians is 16.2; for nurses, 21.9; for mental health professionals, 68.2; and for mental health custodial workers, 69.

The OSHA report goes on to note that "As significant as these numbers are, the actual number of incidents is probably much higher." This is due to underreporting, perhaps because assaults are considered "part of the job" in many mental health settings and thus are not reported.

While the OSHA data report on broad categories of assaults within the mental health field, the professional literature provides insights into the frequency of assaults within specific professions. For example, Thackrey and Bobbitt (1990) reported that among participants in a workshop at a VA medical center, 59% of clinical staff and 28% of nonclinical staff participating indicated that they had been attacked at least once. Similar findings were reported from a study in which 116 British psychologists were surveyed (Perkins, 1990, reported by Hillen, 1991). Of this group, 52% said they had been assaulted at least once by a client, and 18% had been assaulted in the year preceding the study. Higher percentages were reported by Tryon (1986), who found that 81% of respondents to a national survey of psychologists had experienced a physical or verbal attack at work. Results such as these have led some authors to conclude that over the course of a career, it is likely that most therapists will have to deal with some form of assault (Whitman, Armao, & Dent, 1976).

The incidence of assault and violent experiences has been studied less frequently among trainees than among established practitioners, but the results are consistent and reveal that the risk of violence is real for trainees and may, in some instances, be even higher. Gately and Stabb (2005) found that among trainees surveyed from counseling psychology graduate programs, 10% of their respondents had been the victims of violence and 26% reported that they had witnessed client violence. This finding is consistent with results of Tully, Kropf, and Price (1993), who also found a 26% rate of respondents who had experienced "some type of violence" at their placement site. Comparable results were also described by Reeser and Wertkin (2001).

Other dangerous and intimidating behaviors have also been studied and are not uncommon in the mental health professions. Purcell, Powell, and Mullen (2005) studied the experience of stalking by clients of psychologists practicing in Australia. Their results revealed a lifetime prevalence of 20% among their respondents, with 8% experiencing stalking within the past 12 months. Romans, Hays, and White (1996) reported a somewhat lower but still troubling frequency, finding that out of a sample of 178 counseling staff members, 5.6% reported they had been stalked, and 10% had a supervisee who had been stalked by current or former clients. Those findings are consistent with the research of Gentile, Asamen, Harmell, and Weathers (2002), who also found an incidence rate of about 10% among their respondents and, interestingly, reported no significant differences in race, gender, or other variables between respondents who had been stalked versus those who had not.

Though less severe than stalking, 64% of the sample studied by Romans, Hays, and White (1996) had experienced some form of harassment by clients. Sexual harassment of female therapists by patients is also not uncommon, as reported by deMayo (1997), who found that more than half of the psychologists responding to

a survey reported having experienced sexual harassment by a patient at some point in their practice.

These findings should not be taken to mean that most patients are dangerous. In fact, most patients do not pose a high risk of assault, harassment, or other threatening behaviors. The frequencies just described and the conclusions of Whitman et al. (1976) derive more from the large number of patients that clinicians encounter during their careers. As a result, even though only a small proportion of patients are likely to be assaultive or threatening, over time there is a good chance that a clinician will encounter numerous patients who are potentially assaultive. Despite the very real risk of assault during one's career, training for dealing with assault is seldom adequate (Thackrey & Bobbitt, 1990; Reeser & Wertkin, 2001).

INADEQUACY OF TRAINING

Notwithstanding, the frequent incidents of violence experienced or witnessed by their respondents, Gately and Stabb (2005) found that trainees rated their preparation to deal with violence as inadequate on every topic presented, including assessment for violence, prevention strategies, safety at the workplace, intervention strategies, and self defense. Spencer and Munch (2003) describe similar gaps in training, noting that prominent social work programs they studied make no mention of safety issues in their curricula or their field placement manuals. Spencer and Munch found this very disappointing in light of prior research showing the relatively high risk of assault and the comparative lack of adequate training. Indeed, more than a decade earlier Gelman (1990) reported that only one out of 95 field learning agreements formally informed students of the potential risks of working in the field setting. Similarly, Tully, Kropf, and Price (1993), found that only 39% of all students surveyed had received any training on the subject from their field instructors. Of the students who had received training in dealing with assault or violence, most perceived it as inadequate. Among field instructors in the same study, 94% identified a need for further training to deal with issues related to physical or verbal assault, but only 8% had actually received such training themselves. Based on these findings, Tully et al. noted that violence in treatment settings seems to be increasing, and, "Without experience and training, students may be unable to manage or contain potentially dangerous situations with clients" (p. 192). To remedy this situation, they recommend that "curriculum materials on violence and safety issues be integrated into the curriculum or included in field placement seminars" (p. 191). Comparable findings and recommendations were offered in a more recent study by Reeser and Wertkin (2001).

Before continuing, one important caveat must be presented. The following discussion is intended to increase your awareness of how you can guard against violent assault by patients or clients. It should not be taken as teaching you how to identify or predict violence. As will be explained shortly, research on the prediction of violence suggests that the accuracy of such predictions tends to be low, even among those who believe they are able to assess violence well. Thus, while you seek to improve your understanding of violence among patients, keep in mind the limitations to your own knowledge and the research within the profession.

COPING WITH AGGRESSION

Coping with the possibility of client aggression involves a combination of knowledge and associated behavioral skills (Tishler, Gordon, & Landry-Meyer, 2000). Underlying all these suggestions is the basic principle that whenever you encounter a situation that is beyond your abilities or poses significant risks, you must inform your supervisor and instructor. This is particularly important in the case of potentially violent clients. If you have reason to believe that a client you work with may be likely to harm him- or herself, or may be dangerous to others, you must let your supervisor know so that staff can take appropriate action to prevent the client and anyone else from being harmed. Do not try to deal with such situations by yourself unless there is absolutely no alternative. If you have no other alternative, even as you deal with a volatile situation yourself, one of your primary goals should be to obtain assistance as soon as possible.

With the awareness that you must contact your supervisor if you think a client or situation may be dangerous, factors to consider in assessing, preventing, and coping with violence include:

1. Understanding that strange and unusual behavior may be distressing but is not necessarily a sign of dangerousness.
2. Understanding developmental differences in clients and recognizing why clients of different ages may act aggressively.
3. Understanding and recognizing motivational factors that may contribute to aggression.
4. Understanding and recognizing situations in which clients may become assaultive.
5. Recognizing individuals who may be more likely to be dangerous.
6. Preventing violence through early establishment of relationships and expectations.
7. Preventing violence that appears imminent.
8. Coping with assault in a way that minimizes harm to yourself and to the client, staff, and setting.
9. Dealing with the emotional aftereffects of an assault.
10. Debriefing to understand why violence occurred and how it can be prevented in the future.

In addition to the discussion that follows, for excellent reviews of strategies for managing violent patients in mental health settings, see Gately and Stabb (2005), Lutzker (2006), Spencer and Munch (2003), Tishler, Gordon, and Landry-Meyer

(2000), and Dunkel, Ageson, and Ralph (2000). For thorough discussions of violence risk assessment, I recommend Douglas and Skeem (2005), Quinsey et al. (2006), and Skeem et al. (2005).

STRANGE BEHAVIOR AND STRANGE PEOPLE ARE NOT NECESSARILY DANGEROUS

People with mental illness are sometimes described as disturbed, but a more accurate description would be to say they are disturbing to others. There is something very troubling about individuals who say and do things that we do not understand and do not fit the norm. When a man on the street corner is talking to voices we cannot hear, when a woman sits staring and snarls at a vision we cannot see, or when someone wears bizarre clothing and dances down the middle of a busy street, most of us become uneasy.

There are probably two reasons for this. First, we are afraid that if people are acting strangely in one way, all their behavior may be unpredictable and possibly dangerous. Second, and equally important, we do not know how to respond to people who act so differently from the way we do.

In your experience as an intern, you will probably encounter individuals who are at least in some ways not like the people you spend time with in your life away from the internship. Depending on how different the clients and setting are from what you are familiar with, you may feel uneasy both about the clients and about yourself. This is normal and is nothing to feel bad or ashamed about. As you gain experience, you will gradually feel more comfortable, and by the end of your internship you will take it for granted that you work in a setting and with people who may have once seemed strange or intimidating.

One of the most important things internships teach us is that people who are different do not necessarily pose a threat to us. The first lesson about dealing with the possibility of violent patients is that most clients are no more violent or dangerous than anyone else. Although clients may display bizarre behavior, they seldom pose a risk in most clinical settings, unless there is a history of violence.

UNDERSTAND DEVELOPMENTAL DIFFERENCES

A 5-year-old throwing a temper tantrum, a 21-year-old starting a fistfight, and a 70-year-old Alzheimer's patient may all engage in assaultive behavior, but the reasons for the assault and the consequences for the individual and the staff members are very different. Although much of the material in this chapter applies to clients of all ages, developmental differences require that we adjust our thinking and behavioral responses to match the age and developmental level of each client.

Take a moment to think about the three clients just mentioned (i.e., the 5-year-old, the 21-year-old, and the 70-year-old). How do the individuals differ, and how do the differences influence what you would think and do about possible aggression? Among the factors to consider are the individual's peer group and peer-group norms regarding violence, the message that violence communicates for each person, the physical and mental capacity of the person to inflict serious harm to people or property, the person's understanding of and attitudes toward the consequences of a violent act, and the person's motivation. Many of these considerations will be addressed in a moment, but exploring them first yourself will deepen your appreciation of the causes of aggression in clients.

UNDERSTAND AND RECOGNIZE MOTIVATIONAL FACTORS

In his book *The Gift of Fear: Survival Signals That Protect Us from Violence,* Gavin DeBecker (1997) uses the acronym JACA to help explain and predict violence. DeBecker, who consults with celebrities, corporations, and others who might face violence, has studied hundreds of violent encounters and individuals. He explains that most people who engage in violence can be understood by considering their justification, alternatives, consequences, and ability. In other words, people who are likely to act violently typically feel their violence would be justified in some way, believe they have few alternatives to violence, can accept or in some cases even desire the consequences that might befall them for their actions, and have the ability to carry out the violent action against their victims. In the following discussion, each of these elements can be seen in the suggestions for assessing violence potential and the recommendations for reducing the risks of violence.

When students are asked why people behave violently, the most common response is that people become violent because they are angry. This is often true, but it does not explain why violence is chosen as a behavior instead of some other response to anger. Focusing on anger as a cause of violence also ignores several other important motivational factors. These include violence as a response to fear, as a response to frustration, and as a way of controlling people. Dubin (1989) emphasized that many patients who become violent are in

> a desperate and panic-stricken struggle to prevent their imagined annihilation, either through the destruction of their physical selves or, even more frightening at times, through the destruction of their self esteem. (p. 1280)

Dubin further observed:

> Paradoxically, clinical staff who are anxious and frightened by a patient whose behavior is escalating toward violence may react

with an authoritarian or counteraggressive response that increases the patient's feelings of helplessness. (p. 1280)

If someone is angry and may become violent, it helps to first try to determine why he or she is angry, then consider why violence is a possible response. Often, you can ask the client directly by saying something like, "I can see that you're upset about something and seem pretty angry. Can you tell me what's going on that has you so upset?" This message, which is not threatening or authoritarian, acknowledges that you recognize the client's present state and are interested in trying to understand it better.

If the client appears likely to become violent, it is probably not advisable to say directly that you are afraid of that possibility. It may, however, be worth asking how the person is feeling at the moment. This may bring the client's feelings out so you can explore what to do with those feelings. If a client responds by shouting at you or making threatening comments, a possible response would be to say calmly, "I understand that you are upset, and I want to listen to what you have to say." This is much more likely to be effective than a response that commands the client to "Calm down," when the client is obviously not interested at the moment in being told what to do or in calming down.

One reason it is important to try to begin a dialogue with an angry client is that we may not understand what he or she is upset about. Some clients become angry because they feel insulted by another client or a staff member. Others may respond with anger to frustrations at work or elsewhere in their lives. For another group of clients, anger is a habitual response to any situation in which they feel insecure. The initial task facing the clinician is to try to understand the client, not to make a judgment about whether or not the anger is an "appropriate" response to a situation. That process may be useful later when the client is in a condition that makes exploration possible, but in a highly agitated emotional state people are not likely to be open to exploring in the abstract whether their anger is justified.

As part of the process of trying to understand why a person may appear angry, it helps to recognize that what appears as anger may not necessarily be a result of anger. As mentioned, violent behavior may be the result of fear, not anger. I have seen clients become violent when they were pressured too strongly to deal with something. A case that comes to mind involved a wheelchair-mobile head-injured patient who struck a staff member who was attempting to transfer the patient to a toilet against the patient's wishes. When the client was asked about the incident later, he revealed that he was not so much angry as frightened that he could fall. When he did not feel anyone was listening or giving him an alternative, he panicked and struck out. Had his therapist recognized his emotional status and acknowledged it, the client might have been able to express his fear verbally and thereby deal with the situation differently.

While most beginning clinicians find violence that grows out of anger or fear understandable, violence displayed for intentional intimidation or manipulation tends to be more difficult to understand and manage. Some clients have learned in their lives that violence is a way to get what they want, and they do not really care if it hurts others or even themselves in the process. For these patients, violence may come as a response to anger or frustration, but it may also be a calculated means of achieving a desired end.

Again, whenever you are confronted by a situation that is beyond your abilities or that appears to pose a risk, you must seek help. If you find yourself faced with a client who threatens violence as a manipulative tool, your best choice as an intern is to seek assistance from someone in the setting who has more training and authority.

SITUATIONAL FACTORS AND VIOLENCE

Along with considering the client's developmental stage and motivations, you should also evaluate immediate situational factors and conditions that might increase the potential for violence. Douglas and Skeem (2005) distinguish between "risk status" and "risk state," with the former being largely static features of the individual's character, and the latter referring to dynamic situational factors within the environment and the individual. Using this approach, Douglas and Skeem advocate moving from violence prediction to violence prevention and reduction through recognition and manipulation of situational contributors to violence. They emphasize that "violence typically has no single cause. Instead, violence is a transactional process that likely reflects multiple causal risk factors and pathways; it is multiply determined" (p. 352).

In recognition of this reality, what are some of the dynamic situational factors that can contribute to or reduce the likelihood of violence? Important situational factors include similarities between the present situation and previous incidents, recent or immediate stress, the presence or absence of certain prescription medications (some of which may decrease assault potential, while others may increase it), alcohol or other drug intoxication, the patient's cognitive functioning, the power differential between the patient and responding staff, and obvious signs, such as gestures or weapons, that reveal violent intentions. Douglass and Skeem (2005) focus particular attention on the internal dynamics of individuals, including variations in such things as negative affect, psychosis, and interpersonal relationships. These elements and others are addressed in the discussion that follows.

SIMILARITIES TO PAST SITUATIONS

A fundamental principle of psychology is that previous behavior is the best predictor of later behavior. If a person has a history of violence that follows certain patterns, you should be attentive to those patterns and any similarities to the present situation. For example, if a patient's history of violence is exclusively confined to assaults on women, the risk factor would be higher for women than for men. While there are no guarantees that men are immune to assaults from such patients, women staff members should obviously use special care in dealing with the patient. Other factors to consider would be patterns in locations of assaults, timing, weapons used, or specific stimuli that appear to have triggered assaults in the past. Recognizing such factors may enable one to control them and thereby prevent or at least anticipate and deal more effectively with the risk of violence.

STRESS

Stress is a situational factor that is often connected with violence. In general, whether or not a person has a history of violence, the level of stress he or she has been experiencing may increase the likelihood of a violent act. Before or during interactions with patients, we should keep in mind what stresses they have been under and how they have coped with stress in the past. If a patient has a history of responding violently when stressed, we should be particularly careful. We should ask what alternatives the patient has other than violence. Is this patient able to deal with difficulties in any other way than through violence? Has he or she had success in the past doing so? To the extent that a patient has a history of violence, lacks alternative behaviors, and is under stress, the potential for violence is likely to increase.

Situational factors also come into play when predicting the potential for violence in the future. A client may seem to be coping relatively well, but if several unfortunate events happen simultaneously, such as a fight with a significant other, getting fired at work, a traffic accident, or some other event, the client might be overwhelmed and act out violently in response.

CONTROLLED SUBSTANCES AND MEDICATIONS

Along with situational factors, certain intoxicating drugs can also increase the likelihood of aggression (Skeem et al., 2005). The so-called war on drugs notwithstanding, alcohol is the most commonly used and abused drug. Alcohol has disinhibiting effects that make some individuals feel invulnerable and that lessen their awareness of fear or pain. Other drugs, such as methamphetamines, tend to produce excitation, feelings of invincibility, and, in some cases, paranoia. This combination of energy, invincibility, and paranoia is extremely volatile. Another drug, PCP, or "angel dust," is well known for its ability to precipitate sudden and lasting psychoses, with violent, almost unrestrainable outbursts typical of the acute phase of intoxication. Trying to reason with someone who is influenced by any of these substances may bring little or no success and has a relatively high potential for violence.

Among the prescription medications that may reduce the potential for violence, antipsychotic, antimanic, and antiseizure medications have long been used to help control violent behavior both in inpatient settings and in the community. For patients who have been prescribed medications to help control their behavior, the risk of assault may be increased if the patient has not been taking his or her medications. For this reason, one of the questions mental health crisis-response teams routinely ask is, "Are you taking your medications?" If a client has not been taking medications as prescribed, the potential for unpredictable behavior goes up.

While correctly prescribed psychotropic medications may help reduce the risk of violence, there is evidence that some medications have the potential to increase the risk in certain patient groups. Haller and Deluty (1990) reported a significant relationship between the prescription of anxiolytics and the severity of patient assaults on staff. They suggested that such medications may produce a disinhibiting effect for some patients. This finding should not be considered conclusive at this point, but it does offer further evidence that clinicians should be aware of medication effects when assessing the potential for violence.

PATIENT MENTAL STATUS

Related to the effects of both prescription drugs and illegal substances is the more general question of the patient's state of consciousness and awareness. Is the patient capable of reasoning effectively and controlling his or her own behavior? Although it is possible to reason with many patients who appear to be at risk for violence, in some patients, conscious awareness is so clouded that reasoning is not possible or practical. For example, some patients with brain injuries, illness, or other neurological impairments may not be in control of their own behaviors or capable of understanding what people say or do to them. These patients may act violently not out of an intention to hurt anyone, but because they are confused and frightened and do not understand their situation or the people who are trying to treat them.

As noted earlier, patients exhibiting certain psychiatric symptoms may also pose a risk of violence that is closely connected to their state of awareness. Patients in an acute phase of mania are not likely to listen well to calm discussion. Paranoid patients may well interpret whatever is said to them as a sign of trickery. The problem each of these conditions poses for treatment staff is that we cannot assume that our normal approaches to talking or reasoning with a patient will have any effect. In some instances, the patient's mental and behavioral functioning may be so severely out of control that only physical or pharmacological measures will be able to prevent them from hurting themselves or others. Failure to recognize or acknowledge such situations may place the helping professional or the patient in jeopardy of being injured.

Some patients, particularly those suffering from certain neurological conditions or drug intoxication, may not be able to control their behavior regardless of the situation or consequences. There are, however, times when patients who seem to be out of control will be able to regain control if they recognize that they will not benefit from violence. To the extent that patients are capable of functioning cognitively and can recognize that they are in a less powerful position, the potential for aggression is likely to go down. Even highly agitated and threatening schizophrenics will often become cooperative without a struggle if enough staff members confront them with an overwhelming physical presence and provide an alternative to violence. It is therefore in the patient's best interest for staff to be aware of the influence of this factor in dealing with potentially or actively violent patients. Approaching a truly dangerous situation with too little power may indirectly encourage a patient to act aggressively. Having insufficient support also tends to increase the likelihood of injuries to staff or clients if an altercation does ensue.

WEAPONS

Finally, regardless of a patient's history or other situational factors, if present behavior suggests that he or she may be dangerous (e.g., the patient is armed with a weapon), we should be careful. This seems obvious, but there is a true account of a patient who entered a clinic carrying a gun and demanding to see a therapist. The therapist was called and was warned that the man had a gun, but he nevertheless came out to talk with the patient. As soon as the therapist entered the waiting room, he was killed by a blast from the gun (Annis & Baker, 1986).

This tragedy may not have been preventable, but it is easy to imagine a similar situation in which a therapist either overestimates his or her ability to manage things or fails to accurately assess the client's intentions. Without blaming the victims in such cases, we need to understand that if a person looks menacing and has the means to cause damage, we must take the risks very seriously. If a patient overtly threatens violence, either by announcing an intent to hurt someone or physical signs such as clenching fists, holding a weapon, or some other sign, exercise extreme caution and summon help. Your task as an intern is to learn, but you should not lay down your life or be injured in the process.

RECOGNIZE POTENTIALLY DANGEROUS INDIVIDUALS

It is extremely difficult to assess dangerousness with any useful accuracy. In part, this is due to the "low-base-rate" phenomenon (Meehl, 1973). In essence, this means that because only a small percentage of individuals engage in violent assault, even a highly accurate test is likely to produce a substantial number of misdiagnoses of dangerousness.

In part because of the low-base-rate problem, some studies suggest that our ability to identify the dangerous personality is not very good, and clinicians' predictions of which patients will or will not exhibit violence are often less accurate than chance guesses would be (Janofsky, Spears, & Neubauer, 1988; Monahan, 1988). More recent studies, however, have countered this conclusion, suggesting that mental health professionals may in fact be able to predict violence more accurately than chance, particularly if they use structured tools to assist in their predictions. McNiel, Gregory, Lam, Binder, and Sullivan (2003) studied the accuracy of three instruments designed to predict violence during acute psychiatric hospitalization. Their results showed that, for purposes of predicting violence in the near term in acute treatment settings, measures of a patient's current clinical profile are more likely to be accurate than historical information. Working within different settings and patient groups, Schaffer, Waters, and Adams (1994) described the use of statistical techniques for predicting violence among hospitalized psychiatric patients and prison inmates. Their results indicated that history, race, personality factors, and vocational stability may be incorporated into predictive equations with useful accuracy. Mossman (1994) utilized quantitative techniques for studying "receiver operating characteristics" and reviewed more than 40 studies of violence prediction. Based on this review, he concluded that although professionals may be able to do better than chance in predicting violence, the best predictor of all appears to be the patient's past behavior:

> Past behavior alone appears to be a better long term predictor of future behavior than clinical judgments and may also be a better indicator than cross-validated actuarial techniques. (p. 783)

The message from this research is that we may be able to do somewhat better than simply guessing, but we should be very cautious about trusting our subjective impressions of who is or is not likely to be dangerous. At the same time, however, we may be able to reduce the uncertainty somewhat by considering a few things that are known about dangerousness. The goal here is not to give you the impression that you are competent to diagnose dangerousness. Rather, it is to provide a framework that will help you structure your thinking about dealing with patients and the issue of dangerousness. With this information you may be able to assess clients and situations more carefully and reduce at least some of the risks.

What do we know, if anything, about predicting dangerousness in individuals? First, as mentioned, previous behavior is the best predictor of future behavior. Thus, a patient who has a history of violent assaults, especially if those assaults are recent, presents a greater risk than someone with no record of assaults (Klassen & O'Connor, 1989; Mossman, 1994). This seems like common sense, and it is, but we often forget to find out about patients' histories before interacting with them. The obvious way of reducing this risk is to include questions about previous violence or criminal acts as part of an intake history. Family members or friends can corroborate this information if they have accompanied the patient to the intake. Wherever possible, it behooves the clinician to review intake notes and case histories before interacting with clients.

If we are aware of past violence, we sometimes fall into a different trap and intentionally disregard or discount the information. In my own experience of being assaulted by a patient, my mistake was to not fully appreciate that the reason the patient in question was not being allowed to have a pass was his belligerent behavior on returning from previous passes. Case notes of the patient described earlier who shot and killed the

psychiatrist showed that the patient had previously made direct threats to kill his doctors.

The potential to ignore or discount past behavior may be due to carelessness, but it may also reflect our need to believe we are somehow more able than others to deal with people. Overestimating our own capacity, we confidently reason that merely because a patient is violent with others does not mean he or she will be violent with us. In some cases, this may be true, but most of the time we base this assumption more on ego than on real data, and it may take us into dangerous situations. In my own clinical and supervisory experience, I have found that this tendency is even more likely when one is dealing with borderline disorder patients, who, paradoxically, may simultaneously be more dangerous and more likely to lead therapists to believe they are immune from risk because they are somehow special.

The tendency to overestimate our own uniqueness or invulnerability was well illustrated by a situation in which a patient who had assaulted several people during the previous two-month period was being transported between wards by a nurse who had been well informed of the case but had never worked with the patient before. Despite the patient's recent actions and the nurse's lack of personal experience with him, she felt that the patient would not harm her because "she had a way with patients." On leaving the locked ward, the nurse, against policy, released restraints that had been holding the patient's hands to a belt around his waist. Seconds after he was released, the patient viciously attacked the nurse. Her life was saved only because of quick intervention by several coworkers who had witnessed the events from a nearby window.

There is a place for compassion, but there is also a place for caution, and the two are by no means mutually exclusive. If excessive self-confidence leads us to do something foolish, we are not acting out of compassion, we are acting of egotistical needs that serve neither our best interests nor those of clients.

If a patient has a history of violence, we should ask what the consequences have been and whether the patient has learned anything from the consequences that would either increase or decrease the likelihood of further violence. For some patients, violence has worked very well as a behavior choice. Although we tend to think of the downside of violence, it can also bring a person power, status, money, self-esteem, protection, momentary release of tension, and a host of other desirable consequences. We forget this at our peril. If someone who has learned from experience that violence works, there is an increased likelihood that this person will resort to it again. There are also patients whose violence may have brought on negative consequences but have failed to learn from experience. This diminished ability to learn from experience is characteristic of the sociopathic or antisocial personality.

Skeem et al. (2005) focused attention on the relationship between psychopathy and violence and the predictive power of certain aspects of the psychopathic profile. Their research suggests the strongest relationship with violence exists for the "antagonism" component of psychopathic personalities. Antagonism was defined in their study as "a highly interpersonal construct that includes such traits as suspiciousness, combativeness, deceptiveness, lack of empathy, and arrogance (p. 461). Based on this finding, Skeem et al. recommend that greater attention be given to personality factors, especially those of antagonism, as part of patient assessments and efforts to predict and reduce violence.

Finally, although there is great variability among patients in different diagnostic groups, certain other diagnoses and symptoms may suggest an increased potential for dangerousness. In considering these groups, it must be emphasized that the majority of patients in each group are not likely to be violent. Although there may be an increased potential for someone with a given diagnosis to act aggressively as compared with someone who has a different diagnosis, just knowing a diagnosis provides little basis for concluding that a patient is dangerous. With the preceding caveats in mind, symptom and diagnostic factors that may increase the risk of assault include patients for whom assault is a presenting problem (Klassen & O'Connor, 1989), patients with personality disorders (Haller & Deluty, 1990), patients exhibiting delusions or hallucinations and patients with manic disorders (Janofsky et al., 1988), and patients exhibiting both self-destructiveness during hospitalization and suicidal behavior before hospitalization (Hillbrand, 1995). For further discussion concerning the assessment and prediction of violence, see Campbell (1995), whose book is part of a series of publications pertaining to interpersonal violence.

EARLY PREVENTION OF VIOLENCE

The best way to deal with violence is to prevent it from happening. The importance of accurately assessing client and situational variables has been discussed. Next we consider how the things we say or do can lessen or increase the potential for violence.

The best prevention of violence is good clinical work. If you are skillful at understanding clients and building therapeutic relationships, you will lessen the likelihood of becoming the target of violence. This does not mean that people who are assaulted are therefore at fault or are, by definition, poor clinicians. Nor does it mean that because you assume you are above average in your clinical abilities (as most of us do), you are protected from harm. It does, however, mean that the way you interact with clients in any given situation will influence their behavior in later situations. It also means that by building positive relationships and a system of interacting that gives clients alternatives to violence, clinicians can reduce clients' potential to resort to violence.

This principle was modeled by a special education teacher who had some of the toughest, most disruptive students in the school together in one classroom. When other teachers heard of the combination of students in the class, they offered their condolences and remarked how awful it must be for the teacher. In fact, her classroom was surprisingly peaceful. This teacher's secret was not in some overpowering discipline technique. Instead, she treated the students in a way that showed she respected and cared for them and that she expected the same treatment in return. She emphasized their accomplishments and got to know each one as an individual. When discipline was needed, she was firm, fair, and consistent. She also made it a point to touch each student in some way and to speak to each one by name every day. As a result, she did not have to deal with dangerous situations because she built a positive atmosphere that prevented such events from developing or escalating.

The setting of your internship or clinical work may not be identical to the classroom just described, but there will be parallels that relate to prevention. Whatever the situation, it is valuable for clinicians to ask themselves if they are paying enough attention to developing the positive side of relationships, setting and modeling expectations of respectful behavior, and setting limits and clear consequences for violent or aggressive behavior.

Prevention also involves being aware of settings and situations that might increase the risk of violence. To some extent, this is common sense, but it is surprising how often people do not stop to think about the risks that might be present. For example, it is generally not advisable for therapists to be alone in rooms with clients who have any history or perceived risk of violence. This also applies in outdoor settings, such as trails or other facilities on or off the institutional grounds.

Automobiles are another potentially high-risk setting, and you should be especially cautious if asked to transport a client somewhere in a vehicle. The risks of something happening in a car are heightened, of course, because if one were assaulted, it would be especially difficult to defend against the assault while trying to maintain control of the vehicle. What is more, it may also happen that a patient would seek to gain control of the vehicle in order to effect some form of escape or for other purposes. Because of these dangers, I recommend that interns use extreme care if asked to drive a client somewhere, and if you are at all concerned about safety, you should either insist on appropriate precautions, such as the presence of other staff or the use of restraints if called for. If such precautions are not available, I encourage you to refuse the request. If someone gets upset with you for that, you can deal with their being upset a whole lot easier than you can deal with being the victim of a violent attack or car wreck.

INSTITUTIONAL RESPONSES TO THREATS OF VIOLENCE

Given the clients and problems addressed in clinical work, it is neither surprising nor uncommon for patients to communicate threats directed either toward specific staff members or at an institution, such as a hospital or mental health center. As noted at the outset, the Occupational Safety and Health Administration has published very detailed and useful guidelines for preventing workplace violence for health care and social service workers (OSHA, 2006). These guidelines note that as part of the Occupational Safety and Health Act of 1970, all employers have a duty to provide a workplace free from recognized hazards. This implies that clinical settings must take proactive measures to reduce the risks posed by violent patients or other hazards.

OSHA guidelines suggest that the basis for efforts to reduce the risk of violence is an explicit written program with clear goals and objectives. Included within this program should be a zero tolerance policy for workplace violence, protections for employees who report violence, a system for prompt reporting, a comprehensive plan for maintaining security, a strategy with individuals specifically responsible for appropriate training and skills, an affirmative management commitment to worker safety, and a comprehensive worksite analysis of risks. Employee responsibilities are also key to making any system work. The OSHA guidelines emphasize that employees must understand and comply with violence-prevention plans, must actively participate in and apply violence prevention and response training, and must report any violence they observe or experience. Other useful elements of the OSHA guidelines include practical suggestions for evaluating and modifying the physical aspects of institutions, such as locks, hazardous material storage, potential weapons, automobiles, security, and so on. Finally, there are also suggestions for what should be included in violence-response training and for establishing proactive programs to help workers who happen to experience an assault or violent act. To help ensure that all these measures are implemented, the OSHA Web site offers a number of useful checklists and self-evaluation instruments.

Recommendations comparable to the OSHA guidelines are also found in the professional literature. For example, Spencer and Munch (2003) provide an excellent review of the risks facing social workers and offer comprehensive, practical suggestions and a self-assessment checklist for agencies to use to reduce the risk of violence. To deal with explicit threats, such as a telephoned or mailed threat of violence, Burgess et al. (1997) refer to the process of threat analysis and suggest considering many of the elements already discussed in this chapter in response to threats. Motive, intent, duration, frequency, delivery style, and level of risk to victims are all considered in their analysis. The importance of taking every threat seriously and conducting careful, step-by-step analysis of severity is given particular emphasis. In addition, Burgess et al. recommend keeping careful records of threats and assigning a team to periodically review threats received, threat management, and outcomes.

Unfortunately, just as many clinical training programs do not have structured training to help interns anticipate and deal with violence, it is also true that many institutions have not implemented the procedures and recommendations just described. One of the things I recommend interns do on their placement site is inquire about what procedures, plans, and policies are in place. I also encourage you to see if any specific training opportunities are available, and if they are, to avail yourself of them. Whether or not such training is provided, the suggestions that follow are based both on research and practical experience and should help you be more prepared to recognize and deal with potentially dangerous situations.

PREVENTION OF IMMINENT VIOLENCE WITH CLIENTS

The first rule of interacting with clients who appear to be agitated is to remain calm and in control. Even if you are afraid a client is about to become violent, showing fear is unlikely to help the situation and may increase the chances that the client will become violent. This is easy to say, but the threat of violence automatically evokes our physiological flight-or-fight response. The rush of adrenaline and other sympathetic nervous system changes may help us to respond physically, but it tends to impede our ability to think clearly and calmly. To help you keep your wits despite fear, practice stepping back physically and mentally to evaluate the situation as objectively as you can and develop a personal safety plan (Tishler et al., 2000).

As you think about a dangerous situation, try to assess quickly what you might do if attacked. Mentally scan the environment, consider your options, assess what help might be available, and, as you speak, move to where you will be the least vulnerable. As you consider safety and protection, try to understand what the client's motivations for violence might be. Running through the earlier discussion of motivation may be helpful and can suggest possible responses to each of the different motivations. In the things you say and do, try to acknowledge the client's distress but do not validate physical aggression as a response. It is important to not ignore threats but to convey that you have noticed and are responding to the client's distress.

For example, if a client is responding out of fear, you can seek to lessen the fear. Giving the client physical space, facing the client from the side instead of directly in front, holding your hands low and relaxed, speaking calmly, and reassuring the client that he or she is safe may all help to lessen fear and the potential for violence. It may also help to say something like, "I can see you are upset, and I would like to help. What can I do?" This statement lets people know you are aware of their condition, and, by asking what they want to do, it offers them a sense of control that may lessen their fear.

In all cases of possible violence, it is important to speak clearly and simply. This is especially important if you determine that the client is confused or disoriented. Short, direct sentences that give specific information are desirable. Sometimes you may need to orient patients to who and where they and you are. For example, to a disoriented patient you might say, "Mr. Smith, you are in a hospital. I am your therapist. Let's sit down and talk." Note how short the sentences are and how they each express only a small bit of information at a time. These sentences also give specific instructions, because in this instance the patient's own thought processes may be so disrupted that he cannot determine what to do on his own.

Along with remembering what you should do in dealing with clients, it is also important to know what not to do. Some suggestions for things to avoid include arguing with a client, making threats that the client knows cannot be carried out, and challenging or daring the client to be violent. You may be able to argue with coworkers and friends without getting in a fight, but this does not always apply to your relationships with clients. Similarly, when not in a clinical setting you might become angry if you are insulted or threatened physically, but you must not respond angrily with violence against a client. While it may be useful to remind clients that there are known and sure consequences for violence, it is probably not a good idea to invent threats that have little probability of being carried out. Empty threats may only serve to remind clients that they can aggress without consequences. For further suggestions about dealing with individuals who are armed and clearly intent on violence, see Burgess, Burgess, and Douglas (1994).

RESPONDING TO ASSAULT

Although the best way to deal with violence is to prevent it from happening, even the best prevention efforts are not perfect. Therefore, you need to give some thought to what might happen if you are assaulted and how you would respond to minimize the harm to yourself, the client, other persons, and property. Among the factors to consider in responding to assault are clothing, office layout, communications, dangerous and protective implements, and assault-response training.

CLOTHING

If you are working in a setting where assault might be a possibility, it is important to dress in such a way that your clothing cannot become an impediment to movement or a weapon that can be used against you. Take a moment to check out your personal attire and ask how it could aid or harm you if you were assaulted. Among the clothing elements that can increase risk are items worn around the neck. Ties, scarves, or strong necklaces all provide tempting and dangerous items for people to grab and possibly strangle you with in a struggle. If something is around your neck it can be extremely difficult, perhaps impossible, to release yourself, and you will have only a very, very short time to get free before losing consciousness.

If ties and scarves present an attractive target to grab, so do large earrings, particularly the loop kind. Regardless of your personal fashion tastes, think of a client grabbing a piece of jewelry or clothing and pulling hard. Then decide if that is really something you want to wear to your work or internship setting. If a dress code requires you to wear a tie or other dangerous items, you may want to discuss the safety implications with your supervisor or the setting director. If all else fails, wear a clip-on bow tie. Who knows, you may start a trend.

While avoiding items of clothing that may harm you if attacked, you should also consider how your clothing might assist or impede your ability to avoid or escape an assault. For example, footwear should be of a sort that enables you to move quickly and have a steady base of support in a struggle. This means that high heels and slick-soled shoes are not recommended. Similarly, tight clothing should generally not be worn, because it may restrict your movement.

Finally, it is important, especially for women, to avoid clothing that might be deemed provocative in some way. While recognizing that in an ideal world people should probably be able to dress however they like, in reality, at your internship, you must recognize the institutional needs and client characteristics and exercise good judgment about your appearance and the impression it creates. If you are assaulted, you do not want to become the target of criticism that you invited the assault by the way you dressed.

OFFICE LAYOUT

Escape routes are the first thing to think about in considering your office layout. If you were attacked or threatened with an attack, how readily could you exit without having to contact the patient? Similarly, could a client who is feeling pressured or cornered escape without having to go through you? The earlier discussion of situational assessment noted that dangerous patients should not be seen alone. If this cannot be avoided, try to find a room with two doors, so that you or the patient can exit easily or help can enter in an emergency. If a room has only one door, be sure that the door cannot easily be locked in a way that would trap you inside and prevent assistance from entering quickly.

Office layout should also take into account the space between client and therapist. When working with potentially dangerous people, leave sufficient space to give you time to react if the client moves to attack you. Although I generally avoid seeing a client "across the desk," the desk can provide an element of protection, and sometimes the space will help a client feel less pressured, thereby further reducing the likelihood of attack. Make sure, however, that the desk cannot easily be turned over, trapping you beneath it.

Visibility is another factor that can increase safety but is often overlooked. If people can see into your office to be sure things are okay, the chance of assault decreases and the opportunities for quick help increase. You should situate yourself in such a way that you can see who is coming and going or who might be about to enter your office. The far wall may seem like a convenient location for your desk, but if it means you must sit with your back to an open door it could leave you very vulnerable. A bit of interior decorating creativity can make for a much safer working environment.

COMMUNICATION

If you were attacked in your office or elsewhere in your workplace, how would people know you needed help? If you are working with someone who might be dangerous, it is vital to have a way of letting others know if you are in trouble. There must also be a way for help to reach you quickly. This means you should establish an unmistakable and unambiguous signal that alerts people when you need help. Some settings provide alarm buzzers on the therapists' desks, others have phone signals, and in some instances a secretary or other staff member checks every few minutes to see how things are going. Leaving your door open may be a viable option, or you might tell the person in the next office to be aware that if sounds of a scuffle emerge, help is needed. If your office is removed from others, it will be especially advisable to have a remote communications device, such as a buzzer or phone.

As you think about how to inform others that you need help, remember that research on bystander assistance indicates that ambiguity may substantially impede the likelihood of help being provided. If you need to send a person to get help, do not simply shout, "Somebody get help!" Chances are, no one will go. Instead, pick a specific person, call that person by name, and tell him or her exactly what to do. "Joe, go to the nurses' station, tell the first staff you can find that there is a fight in room 100, and we need help immediately. Go now and hurry." The importance of being specific applies not only to assault situations, but to any emergency situation you may encounter.

DANGEROUS AND DEFENSIVE IMPLEMENTS

To further enhance your safety, check your office for whatever potentially offensive and defensive implements may be there. Do not keep letter openers, spike-type message spindles, paperweights, and so on, in locations where clients could easily reach them. On the other hand, it is a good idea to have potential shields, such as books, cushions, a wastebasket, and chairs, nearby where you can easily reach them. If you deal with dangerous individuals frequently, you should probably practice grasping a shield, or perhaps even carrying a clipboard, so it becomes a habitual and ready protection that can be used automatically if you ever need it. If you sit behind a desk, as mentioned earlier, the desk should be anchored so that it cannot be tipped over on top of you. It would not be a pleasant experience to have an angry patient overturn your desk and have it land on you, pinning you to the floor. This has actually happened to therapists. Again, the goal is to prevent unpleasantness by preparing for situations before they happen.

ASSAULT-RESPONSE TRAINING

With all the precautions in place, you may still be wondering what to do if you are assaulted. Answering this question is not easy because every situation is unique, and every intern brings different resources to the situation. Recognizing these limitations, some suggestions may prove helpful.

The first suggestion is that you seek some form of specific training in dealing with patient assault (Gately & Stabb; Spencer & Munch, 2003). Many hospitals, mental health centers, and other programs offer such training, which typically involves a discussion of legal and policy issues, assessment of dangerousness, how to prevent assaults, and various means of physically protecting yourself without harming clients. In a study of the effects of such training, Thackrey (1987) found that staff who completed a training course reported significantly increased confidence in their ability to cope with aggression, but they would not be described as overconfident. These gains were maintained at an 18-month follow-up, suggesting that training can have lasting effects.

While such findings are encouraging, it is important to weigh the quality of the training being offered. I am familiar with a widely distributed videotape series that purports to teach therapists how to deal with assaultive or belligerent patients. In my judgment, much of the advice and modeling in this series is extremely naive and may actually be counterproductive.

If you do not have access to a quality program specifically designed around patient assault, some forms of self-defense training may be helpful. Techniques of aikido are particularly adaptable. The nonviolent approach of aikido and the philosophy that accompanies it are useful training for interns and therapists. In addition to their value as training for responding to assaults, I have also found substantial clinical utility to the underlying concepts of aikido (see Tohei, 1966). Other so-called martial arts may also be useful, but for your clinical needs focus on the defensive techniques more than the counterattacking, punching, and kicking skills. Knowing such skills may help boost confidence and could well help you in other situations, but obviously you should not use them to harm or intimidate clients.

If you do not have experience or training in dealing with assaults, your best approach is to use common sense, be creative, do not be heroic, but do resist harm. Common sense suggests that if you are assaulted you need to protect your vital areas, try to escape, and get help. At the same time, creativity can help you defend yourself. The comedian Steve Martin used to say that you could discourage robbery by throwing up on your money. He said it for laughs, but he is not far wrong. Try to rapidly assess the situation, identify options, and seek responses other than what the assailant expects. This may give you an element of surprise, and sometimes it can even stop the attack altogether.

The advice against heroics is meant to give you permission to run away if you must. If someone much larger or stronger poses a threat, you can try to deal with that threat verbally or in other noncombative ways, but if combat appears inevitable, you will probably lose. Under such circumstances, it may help simply to tell the person it is not necessary to fight with you because you will leave.

AFTEREFFECTS

If you do have the misfortune to be assaulted, it is extremely important to deal effectively with the aftereffects. Tully et al.

(1993) noted that some institutions have developed violence plans designed to help victims adjust after an assault. These plans include who to notify, how to handle the assailant, documentation, and steps to help the victim deal with the emotional aftereffects. Gately and Stark (2005) and Spencer and Munch (2003) also emphasized the importance of aftercare for those who have been assaulted.

The first thing to do if you are assaulted is to notify your supervisor so that necessary records can be made. If you are injured, get medical help and be sure that the events are well documented. You may also have to fill out certain incident reporting forms or other paperwork so that you can receive compensation for medical expenses.

If you are not injured, after notifying your supervisor, go somewhere with your supervisor or a colleague and take time to deal with what happened. Immediately after an assault, you will probably experience the physical effects of the crisis. You may find yourself shaking, feel your heart racing, and perhaps feel sick to your stomach. These are normal responses and nothing to be ashamed of or hide. You probably do not want to go right back to what you were doing as if nothing has happened. Give yourself some time to let your body and mind get back to normal.

You will also need to work through the emotions that follow an assault. For example, you might be afraid to go back to the site of the assault. Or you may feel angry; you may want to get back at the client who assaulted you. Depending on the circumstances that led to the assault, you may try to think back to what happened. How did things develop, what might have been done differently, what was done well under the circumstances? All of these questions and feelings may strike at once, and it is not uncommon to find yourself replaying the event again and again in your mind. This process can often take at least several days and as long as a couple of weeks or more to work through.

If the aftereffects of an assault continue and are troubling or interfering with your work, you may want to seek some form of counseling. You and your supervisor should also explore how the experience may affect your work and interactions with clients in the coming days and weeks. If the assault was seen by others, you may feel embarrassed about returning to work. A primary consideration must also be the possibility of the assault recurring. If your supervisor does not raise this concern but it is on your mind, be sure to express it yourself. In order for you to feel safe in returning to your position, you will need to consider this possibility and be assured that steps have been taken to prevent another assault from happening. You will also need to have support to ensure that your clinical work will not be adversely affected by the experience.

You should not be afraid about going to your internship or interacting with clients, but you should be cautious. Knowing your limitations, developing your clinical skills, and seeking assistance when necessary are the keys to safety in your internship and in your future clinical work.

STALKING

Different than a direct assault, but potentially just as dangerous and emotionally difficult, is the possibility of being stalked by a client. As noted earlier, several studies have indicated that being stalked is, unfortunately, not a rare event among practitioners (Gentile, Asamen, Harmell, & Weathers, 2002; Purcell, Powell, & Mullen, 2005; Romans, Hays, & White, 1996). Given this possibility, it is worth taking a few moments to discuss ways of preventing stalking and responding to it effectively if it occurs.

Purcell et al. reported that the most commonly cited reason for clients stalking was resentment, often resulting from a practitioner's offering a professional opinion in a legal matter, such as a child abuse hearing. Other reasons include unsatisfactory termination of clients who did not want treatment to end and infatuation. In 38% of the cases reported, there was some form of threat associated with the stalking. This included threats of physical violence against the professional or family or staff, property damage, and threats of ruining one's reputation or practice in some way.

Most respondents surveyed by Purcell et al. indicated that their training had not adequately prepared them to cope with these situations. In many instances the experience caused substantial emotional stress and resulted in behavior changes, including changes of address, delisting of phone numbers, calls for assistance from police, and consultations with professional colleagues.

Purcell et al. reviewed a number of clinical issues that may be helpful in recognizing and reducing the potential risk of stalking. These include such things as managing transference, dealing effectively with client attraction, maintaining professional boundaries, and careful diagnosis of potential personality disorders. In addition to giving greater attention to such clinical issues, Gentile et al. (2002) found that psychologists who had been stalked took other measures as well, including using an unlisted home address and telephone number, installing an office and/or home alarm system, and carrying mace or pepper spray.

Based on my own experience, I believe that virtually all of the above measures should be standard practice not only for those who have the experience of being stalked but for all practitioners. In addition, there are several measures that these authors did not mention that I would strongly recommend, particularly for interns.

First among these is giving scrupulous attention to not letting personal-contact information become available to clients either intentionally or unintentionally. This means that you simply do not give out a personal phone number or address under any circumstances, period. You may believe a person is completely harmless and think it couldn't hurt to give him or her your address to drop you a line from time to time. But keep in mind that he or she may well pose the greatest risk. That is why it is simply easiest to have an ironclad policy of scrupulously protecting your personal information. If someone wants to write or call, suggest writing to the internship site and let a staff member there pass the letter on to you.

Along with preventing voluntary releases of your personal information, also be careful to avoid theft or other unauthorized access to such information. During one of my internship placements, a client told me up front that he was, in his own words, "a pathological liar." We worked together for much of the year, and when it was time to conclude our treatment at the end of my placement, we had a final session together. For some reason I was called away briefly during that session. As I attended to the other matter I left the client waiting in my office very briefly on his own, then I returned to conclude our interaction. Several hours later I discovered that a very special pen, given to me by my father, had suddenly come up missing. I could not prove that the client took the pen, but no one else had been in the office, and I am quite certain he took it while I was out for just a couple of minutes. The lesson here is that some clients, even after you may have worked with them for a long time, still cannot be trusted. Experienced professionals who have worked with sociopaths would all nod their heads at this story, most likely because they have had something similar happen to them. No matter who the client is, be safe. Do not leave your wallet, purse, credit cards, cellphone, blackberry, or any other item that might have personal information out where someone could either steal it or take a peek at your information. Also, follow suggestions for avoiding identity or credit card theft by shredding critical documents and being sure not to leave credit card receipts, checks, or other items in the trash.

I also advise interns to adopt a heightened state of awareness when they are coming and going from their placements. Taking a second to see if anyone is watching you in an unusual way and looking back in the rearview mirror to see if you are being followed may sound paranoid, but it really is simply a small and prudent precaution to protect your safety. Another helpful suggestion is to tell any roommates, family members, resident advisors or others about the nature of your work, and advise them that if someone calls asking for you whom they don't recognize or who just doesn't seem quite right to them, they should not give out any information but should instead take down the person's contact data and pass it on to you.

This latter suggestion is especially important if you have a spouse and children who could be in jeopardy if someone actually does seek to harm you. Take the time to discuss with your spouse, and the children, if they are old enough to understand, any security procedures you want to follow as a family and any procedures that should be followed if someone unexpected contacts them or something unusual occurs.

Another precaution that I have found very helpful is to build a good relationship with local, neighborhood law enforcement personnel. For students, it is a good idea to let your campus safety officers and police know that you are an intern just so they can keep that in the back of their mind if something happens. The same applies in your community. Find out where the nearest police precinct is and stop by to say hello and get acquainted.

Finally, if you ever become concerned about your personal safety or are being followed, observed, or stalked, make sure you immediately notify your supervisor, your instructor, and, if necessary, law enforcement. I strongly urge you to trust your guts on this, and do not feel embarrassed or ashamed to tell your supervisor that something just doesn't seem right or that you are worried even if you are unsure. It is far better to be safe and take precautions beforehand than to regret later that something was not done.

COMMUNICABLE DISEASES

Just in case the discussion thus far has not been sufficiently disconcerting, there is one final category of risks that go with human services but is seldom addressed by academic institutions or internships. Depending on your placement, it is not at all unlikely that you will come in contact with individuals who have a higher risk of carrying communicable diseases. Institutions where many people live together are prime breeding and transmission sites for colds and flu, and many people who seek human services may practice terrible personal hygiene.

To reduce your risk of contracting a communicable illness, several protective measures should be taken. First, be sure that all of your vaccinations are up to date. I recommend that interns have an annual physical, and the start of an internship provides a good opportunity to review with your health care provider what your vaccination status is for various illnesses. I also encourage all health care workers to get their annual flu shot. This is not only for protection of yourself and the people you live with or around, it is also for protection of patients who could get sick if you come down with the flu. Many institutions will provide vaccinations, especially annual flu shots, free of charge to their treatment staff. Check with your placement to see what is available. You may also want to touch base with your campus health service to see what services of this sort they might provide.

After vaccinations, your next and most important line of defense involves practicing excellent personal hygiene. I have had it happen more than once that a client has sneezed into his hand just before extending it as a greeting for a friendly handshake. It is telling that in most such instances the clients are completely unaware of what they are doing and of the risk of passing on their cold in this way. Less obvious, but perhaps more troubling, is the observation of how many people who use public restrooms do not wash their hands after doing their business there. Given how few people seem to attend to their own personal hygiene, it is all the more important that you attend to yours.

Even though you may not be in a medical setting as part of your internship, make it a habit to follow the "universal precautions" for preventing the spread of illnesses (see the NIH Web site at http://clinicalcenter.nih.gov/ccc/patient_education/pep ubs/infectioncontrol.pdf). These precautions include such measures as handwashing, wearing safety items, and proper disposal of any contaminated material. I encourage you to wash your hands with disinfectant soap after seeing each client. Also, become aware of and avoid touching any part of your face, especially your eyes and mouth. For the protection of your family and friends, make it part of your departing ritual each day when you leave your placement to wash your hands thoroughly one more time.

Finally, as we discussed in the chapter about self-care and dealing with stress, one of the ways you can reduce the likelihood of contracting an illness is by taking care of your overall health. This is not always easy, given the demands of internships, families, dissertations, and work, but try as best you can to find time for sleep, exercise, and a healthy diet. It is worth reiterating that if you do not have time to attend to these things, how much time will you have if you become sick, especially if you contract something serious?

SUMMARY

It would be easier and more pleasant to simply avoid talking about the issues that have been discussed in this chapter. Indeed, that may be precisely why research suggests that so many programs do not give very much attention to either informing their students about these risks or preparing them to cope with them. Unpleasant though it may be, I hope you can understand why I have given these matters so much attention. It is much better to go into your placement informed, aware of, and prepared to cope with any risks rather than pretending they do not exist. I also hope this chapter has conveyed to you that while we can never completely eliminate some of these risks, they are in most cases quite manageable with proper training and sound practice. It is the nature of this work that some level of exposure to danger may always be present, but your actions are the key to keeping the level of risk as low as possible and to coping effectively with any events that arise. Therefore, let me close by urging you to make a specific plan for yourself to implement the precautions recommended in this chapter, get whatever training is needed to enhance your safety, work closely with your supervisor and instructor to address any specific concerns, and scrupulously follow procedures to reduce the risk of violence, illness, or other hazards throughout your training and practice.

REFERENCES

Annis, L. V., & Baker, C. A. (1986). A psychiatrist's murder in a mental hospital. *Hospital and Community Psychiatry, 37,* 505–506.

Burgess, A. W., Burgess, A. G., & Douglas, J. E. (1994). Examining violence in the workplace: A look at work-related fatalities. *Journal of Psychosocial Nursing, 32*(7), 11–18.

Burgess, A. W., Douglas, J. E., Burgess, A. G., Baker, T., Sauve, H., & Gariti, K. (1997). Hospital communication threats and intervention. *Journal of Psychosocial Nursing and Mental Health Services, 35*(8), 9–16.

Campbell, J. C. (Ed.). (1995). *Assessing dangerousness: Violence by sexual offenders, batterers and child abusers.* Thousand Oaks, CA: Sage.

DeBecker, G. (1997). *The gift of fear: Survival signals that protect us from violence.* Boston: Little, Brown.

deMayo, R. A. (1997). Patient sexual behavior and sexual harassment: A national survey of female psychologists. *Professional Psychology: Research and Practice, 28,* 58–62.

Douglas, K. S., & Skeem, J. L. (2005). Violence risk assessment: Getting specific about being dynamic. *Psychology, Public Policy, and Law, 11(3),* 347–383.

Dubin, W. R. (1989). The role of fantasies, countertransference, and psychological defenses in patient violence. *Hospital and Community Psychiatry, 40,* 1280–1283.

Dunkel, J., Ageson, A., & Ralph, C. J. (2000). Encountering violence in field work: A risk reduction model. *Journal of Teaching in Social Work, 20,* 5–18.

Gately, L. A., & Stabb, S. D. (2005). Psychology students' training in the management of potentially violent clients. *Professional Psychology: Research and Practice, 36,* 681–687.

Gelman, S. R. (1990). The crafting of fieldwork training agreements. *Journal of Social Work Education, 26,* 65–75.

Gentile, S. R., Asamen, J. K., Harmell, P. H., & Weathers, R. (2002). The stalking of psychologists by their clients. *Professional Psychology: Research and Practice, 33,* 490–494.

Haller, R. M., & Deluty, R. H. (1990). Characteristics of psychiatric inpatients who assault staff severely. *Journal of Nervous and Mental Disease, 178,* 536–537.

Hillbrand, M. (1995). Aggression against self and aggression against others in violent psychiatric patients. *Journal of Consulting and Clinical Psychology, 63,* 668–671.

Hillen, S. (1991). U.K. study: Half of therapists attacked. *APA Monitor,* 22.

Janofsky, J. S., Spears, S., & Neubauer, D. N. (1988). Psychiatrists' accuracy in predicting violent behavior on an inpatient unit. *Hospital and Community Psychiatry, 39,* 1090–1094.

Klassen, D., & O'Connor, W. A. (1989). Assessing the risk of violence in released mental patients: A cross-validation study. *Psychological Assessment: A Journal of Consulting and Clinical Psychology, 1,* 75–81.

Lutzker, J. R. (Ed.). (2006). *Preventing violence, research and evidence-based intervention strategies.* Washington, DC: American Psychological Association.

McNiel, D. E., Gregory, A. L., Lam, J. N., Binder, R. L., & Sullivan, G. R. (2003). Utility of decision support tools for assessing acute risk of violence. *Journal of Consulting and Clinical Psychology, 71,* 945–953.

Meehl, P. (1973). *Psychodiagnosis: Selected papers.* Minneapolis: University of Minnesota Press.

Monahan, J. (1988). Risk assessment of violence among the mentally disordered: Generating useful knowledge. *International Journal of Law and Psychiatry, 11,* 249–257.

Mossman, D. (1994). Assessing predictions of violence: Being accurate about accuracy. *Journal of Consulting and Clinical Psychology, 62,* 783–792.

Newhill, C. E. (1995). Client violence toward social workers: A practice and policy concern for the 1990s. *Social Work, 40,* 631–636.

OSHA. (2006). *Guidelines for preventing workplace violence for health care & social service workers,* http://www.osha.gov/Publications/OSHA3148/osha3148.html

Purcell, R., Powell, M. B., & Mullen, P. E. (2005). Clients who stalk psychologists: Prevalence, methods and motives. *Professional Psychology: Research and Practice, 36,* 537–543.

Quinsey, V. L., Harris, G. T., Rice, M. E., & Cormier, C. A., (2006). *Violent offenders: Appraising and managing risks* (2nd ed.). Washington, DC: American Psychological Association.

Reeser, L C., & Wertkin, R. A. (2001). Safety training in social work education: A national survey. *Journal of Teaching in Social Work, 21,* 95–114.

Romans, J. S. C., Hays, J. R., & White, T. K. (1996). Stalking and related behaviors experienced by counseling center staff members from current or former clients. *Professional Psychology: Research and Practice, 27,* 595–599.

Schaffer, C. E., Jr., Waters, W. F., & Adams, S. G., Jr. (1994). Dangerousness: Assessing the risk of violent behavior. *Journal of Consulting and Clinical Psychology, 62,* 1064–1068.

Skeem, J. L., Miller, J. D., Mulvey, E., Tiemann, J., & Monahan, J., (2005). Using a five-factor lens to explore the relation between personality traits and violence in psychiatric patients. *Journal of Consulting and Clinical Psychology, 73,* 454–465.

Spence, P. C., & Munch, S. (2003). Client violence toward social workers: The role of management in community mental health programs. *Social Work, 48*(4), 532–545.

Thackrey, M. (1987). Clinician confidence in coping with patient aggression: Assessment and enhancement. *Professional Psychology: Research and Practice, 18,* 57–60.

Thackrey, M., & Bobbitt, R. G. (1990). Patient aggression against clinical and nonclinical staff in a VA medical center. *Hospital and Community Psychiatry, 41,* 195–197.

Tishler, C. L., Gordon, L. B., & Landry-Meyer, L. (2000). Managing the violent patient: A guide for psychologists and other mental health professionals. *Professional Psychology: Research and Practice, 31,* 34–41.

Tohei, K. (1966). *Aikido in daily life.* Tokyo: Rikugei Publishing House.

Tryon, G. (1986). Abuse of therapists by patients: A national survey. *Professional Psychology: Research and Practice, 17,* 357–363.

Tully, C. T., Kropf, N. P., & Price, J. L. (1993). Is field a hard hat area? A study of violence in field placements. *Journal of Social Work Education, 29,* 191–199.

Whitman, R. M., Armao, B. B., & Dent, O. B. (1976). Assault on the therapist. *American Journal of Psychiatry, 133,* 426–429.

CHAPTER 9

CLOSING CASES

By their nature, internships are time limited. Interns should keep this in mind throughout their placement and should plan well in advance for when they will leave the internship (Penn, 1990). This chapter discusses some of the tasks that must be accomplished and issues that arise as one prepares for the completion of an internship. As in other chapters, I recognize that not all interns will be directly responsible for seeing clients or doing therapy. Nevertheless, even if you are primarily in an observational role or working as an aide, you are likely to form close bonds with people and it may be difficult to leave. Understanding the issues involved in leaving and closing cases may help you deal with this process more effectively.

ETHICAL CONSIDERATIONS AND TERMINATION

All of the major professional ethics codes include a discussion of termination, with principles established to ensure, first, that therapy is terminated when the client no longer needs or benefits from it; second, that clients are not "abandoned" (i.e., prematurely terminated without transition or follow-up provisions); and third, that transitions to new therapists are handled in a way that is sensitive to the client's needs and in the client's best interests therapeutically (ACA, 2005; APA, 2002; NASW, 2000).

For interns, the standards regarding termination are especially important because it is common for internship placements to end before treatment of clients has successfully concluded. If adequate provisions and procedures provide for transferring the client to another therapist, this does not constitute abandonment, nor is it an ethical breach. On the other hand, if an intern summarily announces to a client that the internship is ending and the intern will no longer be seeing the client, with no provisions for follow-up or transfer, that would be contrary to ethical standards and to sound clinical practice. As such, it is essential for interns to understand the clinical issues that are associated with termination and transfer, and to make sure that this vital aspect of treatment is handled in a way that is as beneficial to clients as possible.

UNDERSTANDING CLIENT REACTIONS TO EARLY TERMINATION

For interns to deal successfully with termination, it is important to understand how clients and interns are affected by this process. Greenberg (2002) and Penn (1990) point out that clients may experience many thoughts and emotions in response to termination. Clients may become angry over perceived abandonment or a feeling that the therapist has betrayed their trust. Anxiety is also common, as clients wonder if and how they will be able to manage without the assistance of the therapist. Many clients may feel a sense of loss for the therapy relationship and for the therapist.

In responding to these reactions, the therapist should keep in mind that the initial or surface presentation is likely to be only part of the client's overall reaction. Penn (1990) described this well:

> Whatever the initial reaction of a patient to the forced termination, it is likely that his or her reaction is more complex and layered than first seems to be the case. A patient who is in touch with only sadness over the loss of the therapist may find it more difficult to acknowledge anger toward the therapist for causing that loss; one who is in touch with only the rage may be reluctant to feel the tender feelings and the sadness behind the anger. Indifference can alternate with strong feelings of separation anxiety. (p. 381)

Siebold (1992) voiced similar appreciation of the complexity of termination:

> Following the announced ending of treatment, much of what the client raises may relate to termination, but as with many other factors in the client's life, feelings and associations are disguised, denied, or avoided. Time is needed for the person to take in, act out, and master the news. (p. 331)

As part of appreciating the complexity of reactions to termination, therapists should also be aware that the client's reaction to ending the therapy relationship will be closely connected to the client's previous relationship and termination experiences. McRoy, Freeman, and Logan (1986) noted that clients' reactions to the termination process will be influenced by how they worked through earlier separation experiences in their lives and how they have dealt with conflicting feelings, such as dependence and independence, or trust and mistrust.

In other words, although the immediate termination is of the relationship between you and the client, each of you will cope with the termination based in large part on your experience of previous termination experiences in other relationships. Awareness of this fact can be an invaluable aid in helping the therapist make the termination experience part of the overall therapeutic process.

EXERCISE

To further your understanding of client reactions to termination, as described in this section, consider the following questions:

1. How might the client's personality and presenting concerns influence his or her cognitive, emotional, and behavioral reactions to termination? In other words, how will different types of clients cope differently with the termination experience?
2. What kinds of previous termination experiences might influence how a given client will cope with terminating an interaction with you?
3. How will the approach one takes to therapy influence the way clients cope with therapy termination?

UNDERSTANDING INTERN REACTIONS TO TERMINATION

Understanding the client's reactions to termination is only part of the puzzle. For termination to be constructive, interns must also understand their own reactions. As with clients, the effects of termination will vary depending on the intern's personality and the nature of their interactions with specific clients. Siebold (1992) described common therapist reactions to termination and noted that "letting go can be as difficult for the therapist as it is for the client" (p. 331). Curtis (2002) also discussed how termination with certain clients can impact the therapist.

Among the many emotions interns may experience at termination, guilt is especially common. Having encouraged the client to trust, be open, and establish a therapeutic relationship, the therapist is now ending that relationship before the work has been fully accomplished. This may be particularly difficult for interns, who, because they are working with some of their first clients, are likely to establish especially close ties. Being forced to break those ties without realizing the fruits of their joint labor with the client can bring both guilt and frustration.

Closely linked to guilt feelings may be a sense of omnipotence on the part of the therapist or intern. If a therapist feels he or she is the only one who really understands a client, it can be all the more difficult to transfer that client for fear no one else will be able to help. The reverse of omnipotent feelings is seen in an intern's fears that the next therapist the patient sees may in some ways do a better job or will recognize that mistakes have been made. Owing to their relative inexperience, interns may be especially susceptible to concerns of this sort. The evaluation component of internship training is likely to heighten such concerns.

In contrast to feelings of guilt, loss, or concern about the client's well-being, interns also may experience a sense of relief at termination with some clients. As Siebold remarked: "Some clients you'd like to take with you, while others are a pleasure to leave" (1992, p. 330).

Siebold's observation of different therapist reactions to termination with different clients received empirical support from a study by Fair and Bressler (1992). Their results showed that termination planning and emotional reactions differed for patients with *DSM-III-R* Axis I (i.e., in this study, dysthymia, anxiety, or adjustment disorders), as compared to patients with Axis II diagnoses (i.e., for this study, borderline or narcissistic personality disorders). In general, student therapists reported giving less attention to termination planning but having greater emotional reactions to Axis II patients than to Axis I patients. This finding reveals the influence of client type on termination approach and the importance of interns reflecting on their own feelings about clients and the termination process. Whether or not one is glad to terminate a therapy relationship, it is still the therapist's responsibility to try to ensure a productive termination process.

Independent of reactions to specific clients, interns should also be aware of how transitions within their own life and their personal future can influence their management of termination with clients. Gavazzi and Anderson (1987) contrasted the feelings of loss that clients may experience with the elation or relief that interns may feel as they look forward to completing an academic program or going on to other, perhaps more appealing, rotations. Interns who are glad "to be done with" a rotation, or who can hardly wait to start something new, may have a difficult time empathizing with clients who are experiencing loss, anxiety, anger, or other unpleasant reactions to termination.

EXERCISE

Given what has been said about interns understanding their own reactions to termination, the following questions are designed to help you consider your own thoughts about terminating the internship or your relationship with specific clients. These questions might provide valuable material for discussing termination with your supervisor or instructor:

1. What concerns do you have for your clients as you think about concluding your work with them?
2. How are you dealing personally and in therapy with the concerns identified in the first question?
3. Are you giving equal attention to termination for all your clients, or are some receiving more of your energy than others?

4. How might your own thoughts about what lies ahead for you be influencing the way you are interacting with clients or others?

COMMON PROBLEMS IN TERMINATION

One of the reasons for reviewing client and therapist reactions is to help interns anticipate and avoid some of the problems that can contribute to or result from terminations that are not handled well. The key to many such problems is the failure of the therapist to approach the termination process therapeutically. To the extent that the therapist fails to use basic therapy skills, such as understanding the client, monitoring the therapeutic relationship, being aware of process as well as content, and watching for one's own issues, the termination process is likely to be difficult and possibly even counterproductive.

Therapists who fail to understand the possible origins and complexity of client reactions to termination are unlikely to deal with those reactions effectively. Confronted by a client's anger at termination, the therapist may become defensive; confronted by client anxiety, the therapist may be inclined to reassure the client with unrealistic promises. The potential for such responses is increased if therapists are also trying to deal with their own reactions (perhaps including guilt), or their needs to feel needed or competent.

Therapists who are conflicted about termination may also unconsciously pass some of their needs or fears onto the client. For example, Siebold (1992) described how therapists who feel themselves to have been the only one able to help a client might unconsciously communicate this and thereby sabotage attempts to transition the client to another therapist. Therapists may also try to make the client into a "good" client, both to ease the work of the colleague who will take the case and to make it appear that the therapy to that point had been more successful.

In my supervisory experience, I have noted that many interns subtly extract reassurance or perhaps even absolution from their clients. To ease the transition for themselves, interns may create opportunities for clients to tell them how much the therapy has helped or that they are happy for the intern's future opportunities. Such client statements might be perfectly legitimate, but if they are extracted covertly, or to meet the intern's needs rather than the client's, they are less likely to be therapeutic.

Another approach to minimizing the difficulty of transitions is to leave little or no opportunity for clients to express any negative feelings. Some interns wait until the end of a session to tell clients that this will be their last visit. A less blatant approach is to give clients advance warning but then occupy the remaining time or sessions by reviewing only the positive elements of therapy. Such practices may ease the termination process for the therapist, and perhaps for the client as well, but they do not allow clients to work through their full range of feelings about termination.

Throughout therapy, and especially at termination, therapists must remember that their job is to do what is necessary to help the client, not to meet their own personal needs in therapy. If this means learning how to deal with unpleasant and difficult material or interactions, therapists must do so. A therapist who shrinks from that responsibility at termination probably has significant personal work to do in this area and in his or her role as therapist.

TOWARD SUCCESSFUL TERMINATION OR TRANSFER

Although the focus of the discussion thus far, and, for that matter, in much of the literature, has been on the difficulties associated with termination, a properly managed termination has the potential to be an extremely valuable therapeutic experience for clients and interns.

In a discussion of termination in short-term psychotherapy, Quintana (1993) argued that too much has been made of the notion that termination will inevitably be experienced as a crisis by clients. Referring primarily to planned termination (i.e., termination that is mutually agreed on and not imposed by therapist departure), Quintana cited literature indicating that most therapists and clients handle termination well. Indeed, studies reviewed by Quintana show that clients whose therapy was successful describe termination in positive terms, focusing on the progress they have made and on the ending of therapy as a beginning of something new. For clients whose therapy was less successful, termination is less likely to be described in positive terms, with the focus placed instead on disappointment over the limited progress.

Based on his own research and review of the empirical literature, Quintana proposed that instead of focusing solely or primarily on the loss involved in termination, therapists should address termination as an opportunity for development and transformation. Of special importance is the process of helping clients internalize the therapeutic relationship, the gains that have been made, and a new image of themselves as the result of their growth in therapy. Quintana cited a valuable statement by Edelson (1963):

> The problem of termination is not how to get therapy stopped, or when to stop it, but how to terminate so that what has been happening keeps going inside the patient. (p. 23)

What keeps therapy going inside the client, Quintana (1993) asserted, is that clients benefit from recognizing and acknowledging the progress that has been made. Ideas similar to Quintana's were voiced by Siebold (1992) in relation to forced terminations. Like Quintana, Siebold challenged the view that termination is necessarily experienced as a crisis:

> Instead of processes fraught with peril and little benefit, premature endings, although not optimal conditions, are opportunities

for mastery, growth and maturation. The therapist is an active participant who facilitates expression of the full complement of feelings present during this experience, and who believes in the client's ability to survive the loss and to use the process productively. (p. 339)

Greenberg, (2002) offers a number of similar suggestions that can help make for therapeutic termination. Although Greenberg's principles are designed more for the "natural" course of termination that occurs when therapy is completed, several of the principles are still quite useful when an internship concludes and the intern must leave. For example, Greenberg emphasizes working with the client to underscore the client's strengths, review the changes the client has achieved, anticipate future challenges, and underscore that change is an ongoing process with no fixed end-point.

Fundamental to the points made by each of the above authors is the assertion that termination can present an opportunity for further growth if handled properly by the therapist. What are some of the key ingredients to successful termination?

CLIENT SELECTION

In Chapter 2 of this book, it was emphasized that internships are time limited, and this fact must be considered by interns and supervisors throughout their work with clients. Penn (1990) also stressed this point, recommending that patients who have a history of multiple losses should not be assigned to therapists who will likely need to terminate their treatment prematurely.

This point is repeated here for two reasons. First, an intern who has been working with clients for whom termination might be unusually difficult due to past experiences must consider that possibility and address it in the therapy process as termination nears. A second consideration should be careful selection of another therapist to take the case when the intern leaves. As Penn suggested, efforts should be made to avoid referring clients to other therapists or interns with whom the client is likely to experience another forced termination.

WORKING WITH SUPERVISORS TO PREPARE FOR TERMINATION

Before addressing termination in therapy with clients, interns should prepare themselves for the termination process. Self-preparation includes several elements: self-reflection, discussions with instructors and supervisors, and study of termination issues and techniques.

Siebold (1992) advised therapists to explore their own feelings about leaving before raising the issue with clients. In my internship classes, we typically devote at least one or two class periods (or group discussions plus individual sessions) to discussing both general and personal termination issues faced by interns. This process often involves exercises such as those presented earlier in the chapter. We also use the group format of our classes to facilitate discussion about personal termination experiences of interns and about shared reactions to their work in therapy.

In addition to exploring termination in the academic context, interns should raise termination issues with their on-site supervisors. Interns and their supervisor must address two critical issues. First, interns should work closely with supervisors to understand their own reactions and possible approaches to termination with clients. Second, the intern and supervisor must also realize that the intern is simultaneously experiencing a termination with the supervisor.

Several authors have noted that the way supervisors address termination issues with their interns provides a model to help interns learn how to address termination with clients. Gavazzi and Anderson (1987) referred to the "parallel process" that occurs between supervisor and therapist, and between therapist and client. They suggested that supervisors and therapists should engage in a cognitive and affective review of their work together. The cognitive element would address the therapist's strengths and weaknesses, progress made during training, future directions, and so on. The affective review would entail talking about feelings toward one another, the supervisory experience, and termination itself. A similar review on both cognitive and affective levels is recommended as part of the termination work with clients.

One caveat should be mentioned about the supervisor-intern termination process serving as a model for termination with clients. In their study of trainees' impressions of the termination process, Geller and Nash (1987) found that many of the trainees they surveyed were disappointed with how their supervisors handled the termination process with them. Some supervisors were described as offering virtually no help with termination, while others focused solely on the patients' feelings about termination and neglected the reactions of the trainees. Commenting on these results and on their findings, Geller and Nash postulated:

> Supervisors may collude with residents by avoiding discussions about their feelings around termination. If, for example, both supervisor and resident are given to the more distancing style they may in a variety of ways reinforce each other's need to dilute the intense feelings aroused by the anticipated end of their relationship. (p. 23)

This suggests that although the ideal supervisory relationship will address termination issues, it may also happen that supervisors neither help interns deal with client terminations nor effectively address termination of their own relationship with the intern. If supervisors do not introduce the subject of termination, interns may need to raise it themselves. If a supervisor seems uncomfortable dealing with the topic, interns may want to discuss termination with other experienced professionals or with their peers. It may also be possible for interns to observe how other practitioners manage termination. McRoy, Freeman, and Logan (1986) suggested that this observation could occur either directly or via video- or audiotapes of skillful termination sessions.

EXERCISE

Chapter 10 includes a more detailed discussion of termination with supervisors. However, because termination with supervisors is so closely tied to how one terminates with clients, additional reflection on the topic is warranted here. The following questions may help you become more aware of some of the cognitive and affective issues evoked by termination with your supervisors:

1. As you anticipate termination with your supervisor, what kinds of positive experiences during your placement will be easy for you to discuss? What positive experiences may be more difficult or awkward for you to talk about?
2. Having considered positive experiences, what negative experiences or unfulfilled expectations are you aware of? What are your thoughts and feelings as you consider raising these with your supervisor?
3. Does considering the preceding questions enhance your appreciation of what your own clients might be experiencing as they address their own positive and negative feelings about their work and relationship with you?

WHEN AND HOW TO NOTIFY CLIENTS

To allow sufficient time to work through termination, it is essential to notify clients well in advance of the actual termination date. Opinions vary about how much advance time is necessary. Some writers suggest that six weeks is a minimum (Penn, 1990), while others prefer substantially more time (Siebold, 1992). As noted earlier, if interns know from the beginning of therapy that they will be leaving at a specified date, they should probably notify clients of that fact from the outset of treatment.

Penn (1990) advised that therapists and interns need to be careful not to let good intentions about advance notification become lost because of their own anxiety. If one is not comfortable about termination, it can be easy to run out of time in a session, forget to raise the topic, or generate a host of good clinical reasons for delaying the discussion. In part to reduce this possibility, and to allow time in a session for a client's initial responses to the information, Penn suggested raising the topic at the start of a session.

I agree that time must be allowed in the session for patients to respond to the news of termination, but I prefer to first get a sense of how the client is doing that day and what issues seem to be present. To begin a session by announcing that one is leaving, before knowing what is happening with the client, could obscure critical information that may affect how the client will react. My practice is to begin sessions in the usual fashion, checking out what has happened since our last session and what issues the client is interested in addressing during the present session. After listening to these, I then set my mental clock to be sure to raise the issue of termination by at least mid-session. Sometimes this means interrupting the client, and it often means shifting the topic, but I do this to avoid the aforementioned temptation to avoid or delay telling clients.

One reason interns are reluctant to tell clients they are leaving is that the intern is not sure what to say or how to deal with the client's reaction. One intern told me he mentally practiced what to say, much as he had when he broke up with a girlfriend. Another said that she thought about handling terminations in the same way she handled leaving her family at the conclusion of holiday visits. "I just get on the plane and go," she said. "No long good-byes, no tears, I don't like to get emotional, or at least I don't like to show it." These examples reveal both the awkwardness of the subject and how therapy termination tends to evoke previous termination experiences for therapists as well as clients.

I do not have a fixed recommendation for what to say to introduce termination, but I suggest that you think carefully about what your choices may reflect about yourself and may imply for your clients. For example, one intern announced termination to all his clients by saying, "I have some bad news to discuss with you today." This statement assumes both that the intern knows what the client's reactions will be and that the news will necessarily be received as bad. Introducing the subject this way is likely to make it much more difficult to then review the positive gains the client has made or to explore the potential for further growth during the termination process.

My preference is, first, to be sure to address what has happened in the immediate session to that point. I then proceed in a more neutral, open-ended fashion to introduce the news about termination and offer a chance to discuss it. For example, an intern might say: "From what you've said so far today it sounds as though that is something we may need to talk some more about, but today I need to raise another issue, and I want to be sure we have time to talk about it. On (date) I will be finishing this internship, so we need to begin to discuss what that means and what you will want to do from that point. We should also talk about what you feel about the fact that we'll be finishing our work together."

At that point I usually leave some silence, sometimes a rather lengthy silence, to allow the client to think about what has been said. Even though I may have some idea about how a client will react, I do not presume the client's immediate reaction, nor do I impose a plan of my own design. This practice allows clients to respond in whatever way they need, and it encourages clients to be in control of their future. Although I discuss clients' responses and plans with them, I think it important to let those responses and plans be the clients' own, not something I impose on them.

ISSUES TO ADDRESS IN TERMINATION

After taking the preceding preparatory steps and allowing sufficient time, termination should address these key topics: the progress the client has made, future directions for the client either in or out of therapy, and reactions to the termination process. Within these areas, it is important to address cognitive, affective, and behavioral components of the client's reactions and plans.

Quintana (1993) suggested:

> Termination is a particularly critical opportunity for clients and therapists to update or transform their relationship to incorporate clients' growth. For this transformation to occur, clients need to acknowledge the steps they have taken toward more mature functioning. Perhaps most important is for therapists to acknowledge and validate their sense of accomplishment. (p. 430)

Quintana further suggested that techniques for termination should help clients internalize positive images of themselves. Such images, developed from therapy and successful termination, could help clients cope with future crises.

Similar recommendations were offered by Penn (1990), who recommended that therapists "focus with patients on the therapeutic tools that they have grown to use over time and therefore take away with them" (p. 383). Penn suggested that therapists can facilitate this process by citing specific examples in which patients made connections, observed and questioned their own behaviors, or did other work in therapy for themselves. Therapists and clients may also review specific instances in which the client thought, felt, or acted differently than would have been the case prior to therapy. Such concrete examples help strengthen the client's sense that changes have, in fact, occurred and will likely continue after therapy ends.

While recognizing gains is essential, it can be equally necessary to acknowledge any frustrations that may exist over ongoing problems or unrealized goals. This realistic appraisal helps clients and therapists recognize the reality that no treatment can "solve" all of a person's problems and no relationship is without its difficulties.

Acknowledging difficulties becomes especially important if clients will be transferred to other therapists. Gavazzi and Anderson (1987) observed that the outgoing therapist may not want to admit any shortcomings in therapy or identify unmet goals. Similarly, the client may not want to raise these issues, in part so that he or she will not appear disloyal to the therapist. Yet if therapy up to the present is not reviewed openly and honestly, subsequent treatment may be undermined before it begins. Gavazzi and Anderson state the matter directly:

> Quite simply, it is the outgoing therapist's job as translator to address the shortcomings of the past therapeutic effort in order to establish just what has been accomplished and what has not. (p. 152)

The one caveat I would place on this is that therapists must be careful not to blindside clients by suddenly confronting them at the end of treatment with a list of shortcomings. One can imagine the deleterious effect it could have if a client has been encouraged to review his or her accomplishments and progress only to then be confronted by the therapist identifying all the things that have not been accomplished or the areas in which personal improvement is still wanting. Thus, although it can be important and valuable to acknowledge frustrations or shortcomings in therapy, this must be done with discretion and sensitivity.

In addition to evaluating the gains and challenges of therapy, termination work should also address the reactions of therapist and client to ending their relationship. Earlier in this chapter, we explored some of the feelings and thoughts therapists and clients might experience as therapy ends. The closing sessions of treatment are a time to discuss and work through those reactions. Penn (1990) pointed out that patients may be reluctant to discuss their feelings about termination. To help them do so, she recommended asking "what they are feeling" rather than "if they have any feelings." The first question assumes there will be some feelings without presuming what they are. This makes it less risky for the clients to begin to talk about how they are feeling about termination.

While encouraging therapists to provide opportunities for patients to verbalize their reactions, Penn also reminds us that patients may express their emotions indirectly. Apparent changes in attitude toward the therapist, missed or late appointments, sudden appeals for more help, or sudden denials of the need for further assistance, may all be manifestations of underlying reactions to ending the therapy relationship. Therapists need to be alert for such disguised responses and help patients recognize and understand them.

TECHNIQUES FOR TERMINATION

For interesting comparisons of how therapists from different theoretical schools approach termination issues, see Curtis (2002), Wachtel, (2002), Greenberg (2002), and Goldfried (2002). Beyond the usual methods of therapy, several authors have proposed specific techniques to bring out and help deal with issues relating to termination. Gutheil (1993), for example, related therapy termination to other sorts of endings or transitions and noted that rituals are often used to demarcate and aid in such transitions. Common elements of rituals that Gutheil sees as relevant to termination include the sense of specialness, connections to both past and future, dealing with contradiction, coping with emotions, and communication.

Having identified these functions of rituals, Gutheil proceeds to described three termination procedures and how they serve each function. The procedures she identified are evaluation, goal attainment scaling, and the "eco-map."

Gutheil (1993) offered the insight that although evaluation is often viewed as a research or program assessment tool for measuring therapy effectiveness, well-constructed evaluations can also serve to promote useful discussion between therapists and clients. Topics that evaluations raise include where treatment has gone, what has worked and what has not, how each person feels about termination, and what lies ahead. Gutheil noted that the objective nature of a structured evaluation

> can be used as a bridge to the subjective discussion of the loss and the gains. If there are fewer gains than the client hoped for, the objective discussion can give permission to move into the expression of anger or frustration as termination approaches. (p. 171)

To help this bridging come about, several questions are proposed for inclusion in the evaluation process:

- What did it feel like to ask for help?
- What did you like best about our work together?
- What did you like least about our work together?
- What will you miss about our work together?
- What do you look forward to when we stop working together? (p. 171)

These questions promote discussion of many of the key elements of termination addressed in this chapter. They also fit well within the previously mentioned characteristics of rituals as described by Gutheil and with the earlier discussion of client reactions to termination.

Accompanying her endorsement of evaluation and other termination rituals, Gutheil cautioned that the use of rituals should facilitate, not "bind," the expression of emotion. If therapist or client becomes "stuck in the procedure" of the ritual, they may lose sight of its purpose. Gutheil stressed that termination rituals, like all rituals, should be used as means to ends, not ends in themselves. Citing Fox (1993), Gutheil emphasized that it is important to address both the accomplishment of therapeutic tasks and the emotional impact of the ending of the therapy relationship.

EXERCISE

Think of relationships that have ended in your own life and any rituals that might have been part of that process. What functions did such rituals serve for you and the others in the relationship? What similar or different functions would need to be served by rituals to conclude therapy, and what types of activities might best serve those functions?

TRANSFERRING CLIENTS TO OTHER THERAPISTS

Unless the work of therapy is considered to be completed, therapists who must end their work with clients typically make arrangements with other therapists to take the case. Just as problems can arise when therapists terminate their own work with clients, the process of transitioning from one therapist to another also presents a number of therapeutic challenges. Wapner, Klein, Friedlander, and Andrasik (1986) provided an

informative review of the literature regarding transfer. They noted that transferring clients tends to receive insufficient attention in training but often presents a problem for clients. They also suggest that clients who are transferred between therapists tend to terminate prematurely with the second therapist.

Gavazzi and Anderson (1987) listed a number of common pitfalls that can impede effective case transfers. Several of these have already been alluded to. For example, if departing therapists do not deal effectively with their own issues about termination, they may undermine the possibility of the client building a therapeutic relationship with the new therapist. As Gavazzi and Anderson described this process in family therapy, departing therapists may attempt to make themselves "an absent but integral member of the client's system" (p. 148). This may feel comforting to the therapist, and perhaps to the family as well, but it can also block further work with a future therapist.

A second obstacle to effective transition is the tendency for the current therapist to allow too little time for transfer work with the incoming therapist. Just as therapists often allow too little time to work through their own termination with clients, they may allot insufficient time to work with the incoming therapist. I have seen many instances in which outgoing interns attempted to transfer their entire caseload to another person during a one-hour meeting. Such transactions typically involve exchanging case files, offering a few descriptive phrases about each client and their therapy, then moving on to describe the next client in comparably limited terms. Gavazzi and Anderson advise against this practice, noting that unless incoming and departing therapists allow sufficient time for personal interaction, subtle aspects of the therapy process are likely to be lost in the rush.

Another common obstacle to transitions is the failure of the outgoing therapist to ask or discuss with the client how the client feels about switching to a new therapist. Therapists may simply assume that their clients are still in need of treatment without checking with the clients to see how they feel about the matter. Again, this practice may reflect therapists' attempts to assuage their own guilt about leaving. Whatever the therapist's motives, the results are not likely to be positive. At the very least, the client who is transferred without discussion or consent will not feel respected, and this feeling could undo much of the therapy work that has been accomplished up to that point. Further, if a client only reluctantly accedes to seeing another therapist, it is unlikely that interaction will be successful.

TOWARD EFFECTIVE TRANSFERS

Based on cluster analyses of survey results, Robison, Hutchinson, Barrick, and Uhl (1986) identified several common types of reassignment practice in college and university counseling centers. Briefly, their results showed that practices differ in terms of how clients are involved and the practices therapists follow in preparing clients for transfer. Some centers provide almost no preparation and give the client no say in selecting subsequent therapists. Others offer extensive preparation and involve the client working jointly with his or her present thera-pist to select and transition to a new therapist. Robinson et al. drew no firm conclusions about which practice is best, and they recommended further research to determine how different strategies affect client outcome.

Gavazzi and Anderson (1987) suggested that one of the keys to successful transfer is the ability of the current therapist to fill the role of "translator" while helping to build connections and exchange information with the incoming therapist. Four key phases are identified within the transfer process:

> (1) preparing clients for termination and transfer; (2) orienting clients and incoming therapist with one another; (3) bringing clients and incoming therapist together; and (4) facilitating the continuation of the therapeutic process. (p. 145)

The first task in relation to transferring patients is to deter-mine which patients are in need of, and would likely benefit from, continued therapy. It is a mistake to assume that all pa-tients will desire transfer to other therapists. It can also be a mis-take for the therapist to unilaterally determine that a client does not need or want further treatment. If transfer is a viable option at a given placement, one recommendation is for interns or ther-apists to raise the possibility of transfer to all clients as part of the termination process. The option can then be discussed jointly between therapist and client.

Gavazzi and Anderson point out that a client's reactions to working with another therapist are not necessarily indicative of a desire to make further changes. It is possible that a client feels a need for further work, but is daunted by the prospect of starting over with a new therapist. Also, if termination with a current therapist is not handled well, the client may be reluc-tant to risk a relationship with someone new. This latter point highlights that transferring clients to other therapists in no way eliminates the need for the present therapist to deal effectively with termination issues. Indeed, if anything, the prospect of transferring only makes the termination more important, be-cause it will have a direct bearing on how well the subsequent therapy proceeds.

If clients are willing to work with another therapist, or are willing to consider the possibility but are unsure, the outgoing therapist's next task is to help orient the clients to the new ther-apist, and vice versa. The clients, and the incoming therapist will have questions, and the outgoing therapist should help ad-dress these. This part of the process must involve more than a mere exchange of content information and case notes. Gavazzi and Anderson suggest that the departing therapist should antic-ipate and explore client concerns, address these with the clients, and communicate them to the incoming therapist.

The third phase of the transfer process involves the initial meeting between the incoming therapist and the client. Some therapists prefer that the outgoing therapist participate in these initial sessions. Others prefer to allow the new therapist and the client to meet separately. Whichever course is chosen, the outgoing therapist must in this phase begin to relinquish the role of therapist to allow the building of a new relationship.

Also important to this phase is exploring comparisons be-tween therapists as individuals and their therapy styles. Clients will inevitably look for similarities as well as differences be-tween the new and old therapists, and it may be helpful for the two therapists to discuss these differences openly and noncriti-cally. Therapists should remember, and gently remind clients, that the real work of therapy resides with the client. Different therapists will have different ways of aiding this work, but clients can and should continue with the work that has already been initiated even though the therapists have changed. When I am in the role of incoming therapist, I encourage clients to let me know if something I am doing clashes in some way with their expectations or needs. By sincerely offering this opportu-nity, I hope to reassure clients that my aim is to assist their progress, not to compete in some way with their former thera-pist. This also takes some pressure off me, because I do not have to worry that I am going to do something at odds with what has been happening in therapy. Should I in fact do so, clients have the chance to let me know so we can discuss the issue together.

As termination issues are worked through and the client builds a relationship with the new therapist, it eventually be-comes time for the present therapist to say good-bye. This should probably be done with just the outgoing therapist and the client present. An important task of this meeting is to "solidify the fact that the outgoing therapist and client will not see each other again" (Gavazzi & Anderson, 1987, p. 153).

Interns often find it difficult to accept and state that the ending of therapy is indeed the ending of the relationship. Be-cause they may feel guilty about terminating and are concerned about what will happen after they leave, interns sometimes try to reassure clients by promising to visit, write, or in some other way maintain contact. Such promises may be made with the in-tent of helping the clients feel better, but generally the real function is to help interns cope with their own feelings. I recommend that interns avoid such practices.

There are several important problems with offering to stay in contact with clients after termination. First, if continued con-tact in fact occurs, it can inhibit the relationship of the clients with their new therapist. Second, despite their best intentions at the time of termination, the reality is that interns will rarely be able to maintain the kind of contact they may have promised. After an internship or rotation ends, interns move on to other things and cannot find the time to keep in touch with former clients. The result is that interns feel guilty at not keeping up their end of the promise, and clients feel let down.

Ethical problems can also arise if a relationship continues after therapy is terminated. As discussed in Chapter 3, roman-tic, sexual, or other conflicted relationships with former clients are to be avoided, and the therapist's responsibility to act with concern for the client's well-being does not end merely be-cause the therapy relationship has been terminated. Finally, as discussed in Chapter 8, there are also safety and security issues that can be raised in an intern's offer to continue the relationship in some way and exchange personal contact information with clients.

Even though it may be difficult, the best approach is to deal with endings as precisely that: endings. If this is hard, working with peers or supervisors may be helpful, but avoid the temptation to deny the reality of termination by making promises that will not be fulfilled.

Although the focus here has been primarily on situations in which clients will be continuing in therapy, this does not mean that the issue of transfer should be ignored for clients who elect not to work with another therapist at the time. Many clients will, in fact, return later for additional therapy. In anticipation of this possibility, it can be useful to at least introduce them to another therapist and briefly discuss their case with that person. That way, both will be more prepared should the client choose to seek therapy sometime in the future.

REFERENCES

American Counseling Association. (1995). *American Counseling Association code of ethics and standards of practice.* Alexandria, VA: Author. www.counseling.org/resources/ethics.htm

American Psychological Association. (2002). Ethical principles of psychologists and code of conduct. *American Psychologist, 57,* 1060–1073. www.apa.org/ethics/code2002.html

American Psychiatric Association. (1995). *The principles of medical ethics.* Washington, DC: Author.

Curtis, R. (2002). Termination from a psychoanalytic perspective. *Journal of Psychotherapy Integration, 12*(3), 350–357.

Edelson, M. (1963). *The termination of intensive psychotherapy.* Springfield, IL: Thomas.

Fair, S. M., & Bressler, J. M. (1992). Therapist-initiated termination of psychotherapy. *Clinical Supervisor, 10*(1), 171–189.

Gavazzi, S. M., & Anderson, S. A. (1987). The role of "translator" in the case transfer process. *American Journal of Family Therapy, 15,* 145–157.

Geller, J. D., & Nash, V. (1987). *Termination as experienced by therapists-in-training as viewed by psychiatric residents.* Unpublished manuscript, Yale University, Department of Psychology, New Haven, CT.

Goldfried, M. R., (2002). A cognitive-behavioral perspective on termination. *Journal of Psychotherapy Integration, 12*(3), 364–372.

Greenberg, L. S. (2002). Termination of experiential therapy. *Journal of Psychotherapy Integration, 12*(3), 358–363.

Gutheil, I. A. (1993). Rituals and termination procedures. *Smith College Studies in Social Work, 63*(2), 163–176.

McRoy, R. G., Freeman, E. M., & Logan, S. (1986). Strategies for teaching students about termination. *Clinical Supervisor, 4*(4), 45–56.

National Association of Social Workers. (1996, revised 1999). *NASW Code of Ethics.* Silver Spring, MD: Author. www.socialworkers.org/pubs/code/code.asp

Penn, L. S. (1990). When the therapist must leave: Forced termination of psychodynamic therapy. *Professional Psychology: Research and Practice, 21,* 379–384.

Quintana, S. M. (1993). Toward an expanded and updated conceptualization of termination: Implications for short-term, individual psychotherapy. *Professional Psychology: Research and Practice, 24,* 426–432.

Robison, F. F., Hutchinson, R. L., Barrick, A. L., & Uhl, A. N. (1986). Reassigning clients: Practices used by counseling centers. *Journal of Counseling Psychology, 33,* 465–468.

Siebold, C. (1992). Forced termination: Reconsidering theory and technique. *Smith College Studies in Social Work, 63,* 323–341.

Wachtel, P. L., (2002). Termination of therapy: An effort at integration. *Journal of Psychotherapy Integration, 12*(3), 373–383.

Wapner, J. H., Klein, J. G., Friedlander, M. L., & Andrasik, F. J. (1986). Transferring psychotherapy clients: State of the art. *Professional Psychology: Research and Practice, 6,* 492–496.

CHAPTER 10

FINISHING THE INTERNSHIP

The preceding chapter focused primarily on the process of termination with clients. This chapter addresses other important elements of finishing the internship and looking ahead. These include concluding the supervisory relationship, bidding farewell to staff members, expressing your appreciation, requesting letters of recommendation, and considering career options.

Internship opportunities are not easy to come by, and the willingness of an agency or individual to accept interns depends on each intern's doing quality work and leaving a positive impression. Because future interns depend on the good will of a placement site and staff for their opportunities, you must attend carefully to how you conclude your placement.

CONCLUDING THE SUPERVISORY RELATIONSHIP

Several things must be accomplished as part of concluding the supervisory relationship. Without reiterating material from the preceding chapter, there are a few remaining ideas to introduce in the context of termination with supervisors.

ENSURING THERAPEUTIC TERMINATION WITH CLIENTS

Because there are so many things to attend to in the termination process, following some form of structured format can help ensure that termination planning is adequate and addresses critical issues. An instrument that may be very helpful in this regard was developed and tested by Fair and Bressler (1992). The 55-item Termination Scale is designed for use by supervisors and trainees before, during, or after the termination process. The instrument includes two subscales, Termination Planning and Emotional Response to Termination. Items in the Termination Scale are answered on a 6-point Likert-type format with responses ranging from strongly disagree to strongly agree. Sample items from the Termination Planning subscale include:

I understand what this client wants to accomplish before our last session.

My supervisor and I have discussed the pros and cons of transferring this client to another therapist when we terminate.

I have reviewed the other times in this client's life when he or she has ended relationships. (pp. 186–187)

Items from the Emotional Response to Termination subscale include:

I feel more burdened with this client than I have previously.

I feel guilty about terminating with this client.

I have more feelings of love for this client than I used to.

I more often feel an anxious urgency to cure and help this client. (pp. 187–188)

In relation to the topics discussed in the preceding chapter, it should be evident that this instrument addresses many of the key areas and issues of termination. Fair and Bressler suggested that their Termination Scale can serve several functions. Among these are helping to objectify termination despite painful elements, bringing out counter-transference feelings, identifying areas for therapist improvement, and providing a structure to conceptualize termination. Use of the scale also helps supervisors encourage trainees to deal with a process that supervisors know can be challenging emotionally.

EXERCISE

Whether you use Fair and Bressler's instrument or another, it is helpful to follow some format to be sure you cover all the bases and review your own responses to termination. Taking into account what has been said about termination in this and the preceding chapter, generate a checklist for yourself in which you identify key logistical details about termination. For example, your list might include details regarding notification of clients, arrangements for transfer, and so on. Then generate a second checklist that you can use to help monitor your own emotional reactions to termination and how you are coping with those reactions. When you have completed your own scale, you might want to compare it with Fair and Bressler's to see what they have included that you may have overlooked, and vice versa. It would also be helpful to review your ideas with peers, instructors, and supervisors for their feedback.

REVIEWING THE INTERN'S PROGRESS AND AREAS FOR FURTHER GROWTH

Just as it is important at termination to consider the progress the client has made, a comparable process is equally important to the work of concluding supervision. In this process, interns and supervisors should allocate sufficient time to discuss both the development the intern has shown during the placement and any areas in which further growth is needed.

The most common format for reviewing the intern's progress is typically through some type of evaluation procedure. Appendix D presents a form that can be used for evaluations of interns by site supervisors. Although faculty instructors will often ask that such forms be sent directly to them as part of the grading process, the intern and supervisor should first review the evaluation jointly to directly exchange and discuss their ideas and impressions. Alternative evaluation forms have been created by other authors. See, for example, the appendices offered by Falender and Shafranske (2004), who provide examples of separate forms for the evaluation of interns and the evaluation of supervisors.

Perhaps the most difficult part of the evaluation process is being able to give and accept critical feedback constructively. It is natural for interns to hope to hear nothing but praise from supervisors. It is equally understandable that supervisors would want to give all their interns glowing reviews. Praise is important, and one hopes that all supervisors will think carefully about and acknowledge the achievements and efforts of even their most challenging interns. At the same time, however, constructive criticism is essential if interns are to develop beyond their existing levels. While praise helps give one the strength and hope to carry on, constructive criticism helps show directions for further progress. Thus, interns are advised to seek and welcome critical feedback to help identify what they need to work on for the future.

One way to help interns receive criticism constructively is to have them write an evaluation of themselves identifying the things they did well during the placement and areas in which they recognize a need for improvement. Interns can then imagine that their supervisors are not as positive about the intern's strengths and raise a number of additional issues that need work. By anticipating the affective reaction that accompanies negative feedback, the intern is better able to process the feedback cognitively if it comes. This process of self-evaluation also helps set a precedent of personal reflection that should be part of the intern's regular practice throughout his or her career.

EXERCISE

An exercise was just described in which interns are invited to identify their own strengths and weaknesses before meeting with their supervisor to discuss their evaluations. If you do this exercise yourself, be aware of your affective reaction as you imagine as vividly as possible some of the critical things your supervisor might say. Notice any feelings of defensiveness, hurt, or other responses that could interfere with your ability to receive the comments constructively. If you detect such responses, practice relaxing and listening attentively without feeling a need to respond or defend. As part of this exercise, you might also imagine yourself receiving critical feedback yet still thanking the supervisor for giving you his or her impressions. This may not be easy, and it does not necessarily mean you must agree with all the feedback, but it will help you be more open to at least hearing what your supervisor has to say.

FEEDBACK TO SUPERVISORS

As a supervisor, I believe that feedback should be mutual. I encourage interns to tell me what they thought I did well as a supervisor and ways in which I could have done better or can improve in the future. This process helps me become a better supervisor, and it gives the interns an opportunity to practice giving honest feedback. Giving mutual feedback also helps to bring better closure to the relationship. If the communication is only one-directional, interns may be left with a feeling of unfinished business. Talking about their impressions of supervision helps reduce the feeling that something has been left unsaid or is incomplete.

To facilitate the process of giving feedback to supervisors, Appendix I in this text offers a structured format that addresses the key elements of supervision and gives interns a chance to express their appraisal of the supervision on each. If you use this form or have another opportunity to give your impressions to your supervisor, try to keep in mind the principles we have discussed about giving and receiving constructive feedback. Supervisors are human just like anyone else, and they are always glad to receive positive reviews. At the same time, well-intentioned and sensitively communicated criticism can also be welcome.

Because there is an inherent imbalance in the power structure of the relationship between supervisors and interns, interns should think carefully about how they deliver any negative comments to supervisors. If a supervisor invites you to offer your impressions, it is probably a good idea to begin by clarifying what the supervisor is really requesting. You might tactfully inquire about the specific kinds of information the supervisor is interested in. The response to this question can help you determine how best to phrase your comments. Whatever the response, try to present your impressions in a way that the supervisor is most likely to take well.

ENDING THE SUPERVISORY RELATIONSHIP

Even as they attend to all the tasks that have been described here and in the preceding chapter, interns and supervisors are also involved in the process of concluding their personal relationship with one another. Depending on the level and nature of the relationship, this may be a very simple matter, or it could be quite emotional. Whichever is the case, relationship issues should be addressed as part of concluding the supervisory relationship.

Unfortunately, in many cases, neither the supervisor nor the intern raises this issue. The reason is probably that it is not easy to do. Discussing termination issues with clients, ensuring that case notes are in order, and even evaluating the intern's clinical performance are all easier than dealing with how the intern and supervisor feel about one another and about the conclusion of their relationship. Nevertheless, to the extent that the supervisory termination is a model for therapy termination, and if dealing with relationship issues is a necessary part of terminating therapy, those same issues should also be addressed in termination.

The breadth of feelings expressed at termination ranges from bland to profound. I have supervised interns with whom lasting relationships were developed and with whom I still maintain contact. On the other hand, I'm sorry to say that in some cases it seems I have scarcely known interns, and they have known little about me. Talking about these issues at termination helps bring a resolution to the supervision relationship that makes it easier for both intern and supervisor to move on.

As you think about your relationship with your supervisor and about discussing that relationship during termination, you might want to keep in mind a fundamental difference between your experience and that of your supervisor. It sometimes happens that an intern hopes to form an exceptionally close relationship with the supervisor, but is disappointed to discover that the supervisor maintains distance or relates primarily in an objective or didactic, as opposed to a friendly or personal, way. There may be many reasons for this. One of the most common is that although the supervisory experience is unique for the intern, in many instances the supervisor and staff will have worked with numerous interns before and will anticipate more in the future. Thus, an experience that stands out as unique and perhaps profound for the intern may, for the supervisor, be somewhat routine. This does not mean the relationship is unimportant, but it does mean that supervisors may not invest the relationship with the same emotional energy or sense of specialness as interns do.

Because students at internship placements often express frustration at not getting closer to their supervisors, understanding the dynamics just described can help the intern put those feelings into context. This may also help interns appreciate how clients might have different feelings about termination than do interns or therapists. Once again, understanding the supervisory process helps one understand much about the therapy process.

LETTERS OF RECOMMENDATION

Interns who plan to go on to further studies or employment may want to request letters of recommendation from their instructors or supervisors. Even if you do not anticipate applying for anything in the near future, it is a good idea to request a letter now. After several years have passed, it is much more difficult for supervisors or instructors to write the kind of letter that they could compose when your work together is fresh in their mind. If you do not know exactly what you will be doing in the future, you can ask for a general letter of recommendation for either academic studies or work settings. These can then become part of the portfolio that was discussed in Chapter 2.

Because letters of recommendation can be quite important, interns should think carefully about requesting them and should follow certain basic courtesies to make the instructor's or supervisor's task as easy as possible.

REQUESTING LETTERS

The most important thing interns must do if they plan to request a letter is be sure they did the best work possible at the internship. If your work was not of the highest level, you might want to think twice about asking for a recommendation. Just as positive letters can be the key to open doors, negative letters may well lock them shut.

Even though you believe your work merits a positive letter, you should not take this for granted. Whenever you are thinking about asking someone for a recommendation on your behalf, and this applies to all settings, before requesting an actual letter it is a good idea to ask the person directly if he or she can write you a supportive letter. Take care to talk about your specific goals with your supervisor before asking how she or he would feel about writing a letter of recommendation. The reason is that your supervisor might feel very comfortable about recommending you for a certain type of employment or educational program but less comfortable supporting other aspirations.

When you do ask for a letter, be attentive to the supervisor's first reaction. If it is immediately enthusiastic and supportive, you will probably receive a positive letter. If the supervisor thinks a long time, asks if you have thought about seeking letters from others, or otherwise seems reluctant, it is possible he or she has some hesitation about writing a very supportive letter. If you detect such hesitancy, it is acceptable, indeed probably advisable, to ask about your impression in a tactful but forthright way.

Asking if an instructor or supervisor has any doubts or concerns about recommending you might put him or her on the spot, and this can be uncomfortable. On the other hand, if you raise the question, it might be easier for the supervisor to express any reservations. Most supervisors are reluctant to be as blunt as they perhaps should be when they have reservations about a student. As such, they may speak in vaguely positive terms that would result in a rather lukewarm letter. It is better for you to know this in advance so you can make an informed decision and perhaps select an alternative reference.

Apart from trying to solicit positive letters, it can be extremely beneficial for you to hear any concerns your supervisor might have. You might want to take that into consideration in your deliberations about what jobs or positions to apply for. If you respect your supervisors and believe they are caring and honest with you, it is worth listening carefully to their feedback and advice. If a supervisor encourages you to pursue a chosen career or plan of study, that can be a heartening boost to your goals. On the other hand, if a supervisor expresses reservations or suggests alternatives, you may wish to reevaluate your aims.

GUIDELINES FOR SOLICITING LETTERS

If supervisors or instructors are willing to write a letter on your behalf, you can make their job much easier and increase the chances of a good letter by following a few simple steps. Whenever students request a letter from me, I give them the following set of guidelines that help ensure the students do all they can to prepare forms, envelopes, and so on, and give me the information I need to write a strong letter of support.

PROCEDURES FOR THOSE SEEKING LETTERS OF RECOMMENDATION

The following describes my procedures for completing letters of recommendation requested by students:

1. *Advance notice.* As a general rule, I require a minimum of two to three weeks' advance notice between the time a letter is requested and the time the letter must be postmarked. Please plan ahead to allow at least this amount of time and preferably more. As it often happens that many students request letters at the same time, I may not always be able to get a letter out quickly. Therefore, it is advisable wherever possible to give me at least one month's notification.
2. *Preparation of forms.* Many programs request that specific forms be completed by reference sources. If you will be asking me to complete forms, please make my job easier by completing portions of the form that request the following information: my name, my address at the university, the amount of time we have known each other and the nature of our relationship, courses or internship setting in which you were a student or we worked together, my rank, which is _____ in the Department of _____ at _____ College/University. Complete this portion of every recommendation form prior to giving them to me. I suggest you type the information as it will be clearer for others to read. Also, be sure to sign your own name on forms where you are asked. This is mandatory. I will not send forms unsigned by students.
3. *Preparation of envelopes.* For each program for which you will request a letter, please provide a preaddressed and stamped envelope. Be sure you have enough postage for the envelope, the forms, and several pages of my letter. Submit the envelope and the aforementioned forms, paperclipped together such that it is easy for me to locate the form and the corresponding envelope for each program.
4. *Clear instructions.* If you have any special requests or instructions regarding letters or the completion of forms for different programs, clearly indicate those in a cover letter that you give me when you request letters of recommendation.
5. *To help me write the best letter possible in your behalf.* Please provide me with a brief summary of your academic achievements, internships or field experience, research, service, and other personal accomplishments. In this information,

please clearly indicate the nature of our contact. In which classes or activities have we worked together, what did you do in the class or activity that was noteworthy, what other achievements stand out? Also, if there are any special points I should note (e.g., GPA in the major better than overall GPA), please let me know. Finally, if you have written a personal statement for the schools, it might help me to see a copy.
6. *Follow-up.* To ensure that requested letters are actually sent in a timely fashion, please take it upon yourself to contact me several days before the request is actually due to be sure I have completed and mailed the letters. My schedule is often very busy, and I would hate to become so tied up in other things that I fail to send a letter that was requested. You can help me avoid this by following up in a timely fashion.
7. *Notification of results.* Although it is not necessary, I would very much appreciate if students for whom I write a letter would let me know the results of their application process. As faculty, we are very interested in how our students fare, and it is a much-appreciated courtesy when students for whom we have written letters write to us and let us know how their applications went.
8. *Conclusion.* Thank you for your attention to the preceding details. If you have any questions, please feel free to ask me.

CONCLUDING RELATIONSHIPS WITH STAFF

Although interns will interact most closely with their immediate supervisors, they will also come into varying degrees of contact with other staff members. As you prepare to conclude your internship, do not forget to let other staff members know you will be leaving. In most instances, this may simply involve letting people know a few weeks in advance, perhaps by making a brief announcement at a staff meeting, or by posting some form of notice in a lounge. If closer relationships developed, more personal farewells are in order.

If you have been working with a client who is also being treated by a staff member other than your supervisor, you should schedule some time to meet with that person to discuss the case and your work to date. In this process, you must be careful not to violate confidentiality and to consider how information you share might influence the client's future treatment. In most instances, the other staff member will appreciate and make beneficial use of whatever information you provide. There may be occasions, however, when a client might feel betrayed if certain information were divulged to other staff members. If you are unsure about what information to share or how a specific staff member might use that information, consult with your supervisor to discuss the matter beforehand.

LETTERS OF THANKS

Most people who work with interns do so because they care about interns and the profession and want to contribute. Usually, they receive no or minimal compensation for their added responsibilities. Because of this, it is important that as part of concluding your placement, you express your gratitude and appreciation. Unfortunately, writing a thank-you note is a custom that is seldom taught and sometimes seems lost. Even though one has said good-bye in person, taking just a few minutes later on to write a letter of thanks is a simple gesture that will be much appreciated.

As a supervisor and instructor I can personally attest to how it can really make my day to receive a card expressing genuine appreciation for my work. It is not something I necessarily expect, but when I receive a card from a student or intern, the stress, extra hours of work, and time taken from other tasks all feel worthwhile.

I encourage our interns to write several thank-you notes after their internship. The first one should go to their immediate supervisors. These notes need not be lengthy, but at least a few lines acknowledging the supervisor's efforts, time, and what the intern learned as a result would certainly be welcomed. If individuals in addition to the supervisor were particularly helpful to the intern, special notes of thanks to them would also be in order.

Interns sometimes ask if they should write a thank-you even though a supervisor was not "the best." Except in rare instances of extreme conflict, virtually all supervisors should be thanked. Even if supervisors were busier than they had hoped, or other factors somehow diminished the experience, the supervisor still made it possible for the intern to have a real-world learning opportunity. That is valuable and merits an expression of appreciation.

In addition to the note sent to one's immediate supervisor, it is also courteous to drop a note of thanks to the overall agency director. Although an intern may have had no personal contact with the director, the director is ultimately responsible for what happens in the program, and it is through his or her good graces that interns are allowed to train. Recognizing this and acknowledging the work of your immediate supervisor will please both the director and supervisor.

Next, I suggest writing a group thank-you to all the staff the intern worked with at the placement. These notes typically consist of one or two lines and are addressed "To everyone at . . ." This kind of note is often posted on a staff bulletin board for all to see. Again, it is a small gesture, but it helps everyone you worked with feel appreciated and acknowledged.

Another person to whom you may want to send a note is your faculty instructor. Even if the instructor did not have extensive contact with you during the internship, faculty instructors do a great deal of work behind the scenes helping to arrange for placements, keeping in touch with site supervisors, resolving conflicts, and so on. Faculty are like anyone else and would certainly welcome your thanks.

Finally, if someone was especially helpful to you, keep that person in mind down the road as you progress in your training or work. Just as thank-you notes right after an internship are much appreciated, people value learning what happens to their interns over the long run. It is gratifying to receive a letter saying that an intern has gone on in some way and that the efforts of supervisors, instructors, and others contributed to that. Because it is easy to get occupied with other things and let matters like this slip away, you may want to find a strategy to remind yourself in the future to get in touch with the people who helped you in the past. Interns who keep personal schedule books might write a note in a yearly planner. Others might put a memo several months away on a calendar. Other creative possibilities are to leave notes in places you might discover later, such as dictionaries or other reference works. Whether or not and how you leave such notes is up to you, but some kind of follow-up correspondence is a nice gesture. This is especially in order if you have asked someone for a letter of recommendation. They will want to know how things turned out for you, and it can be fun for you to fill them in.

LOOKING AHEAD

So what's next? If you are planning to continue in your studies or go on to work in the field, you might give some thought to what lies ahead for yourself and for the helping professions in general. DeAngelis (2005) has written an interesting article on what recent graduates say they "wish they'd learned" in graduate school. This includes matters such as financial management, salary negotiations, workplace navigation, participating in professional associations, and professional diversification. Plante (1996) offered 10 "principles of success" for trainees embarking on their careers. These include such things as staying on top of new developments, keeping abreast of changes in mental health, keeping in mind why you went into this profession to begin with, and taking pride in your efforts, achievements, contributions, and profession. Expanding on Plante's list by highlighting the importance of being adaptive, Lopez and Prosser (2000) recommend that new professionals diversify their practice, be attentive to paradigm shifts in health care, learn more about the business side of care, strengthen their research and consulting skills, and be willing to break with tradition. I would echo these recommendations and add that perhaps the most important key to success today and in the future is to have lots of keys. The internship experience that you are now completing constitutes one of the more valuable of those keys.

As you look toward a changing employment and service environment, keep in mind that in your academic work and your fieldwork you have developed skills that can transfer from one setting or position to another. In the mental health workplace today and in the future, critical skills include writing well, verbal communication, research, critical thinking, mathematics, and computer skills. In addition to these academic and clinical skills, grant-writing and outcome-evaluation skills are becoming increasingly valuable assets to job applicants in human services employment. Hayes (1997) identified similar skills and asserted that graduates in human service fields tend to possess distinctive knowledge and abilities in these areas. More and more professionals are involved in a combination of activities, including direct services to clients, teaching, consultation, and research. To the extent that you develop different skills, you will be more marketable and have alternatives to pursue if conditions or employment in one area change. For additional job-seeking tips, Plante (1996, 1998) offered helping professionals suggestions for beginning their first employment search.

One final tip about looking ahead is to reach out to former graduates of your institution. Thomas (2005) describes the value of alumni peer-consultation groups for counselors. These groups serve a number of functions, including support and networking, continuing study and education, and practical advice for new graduates. It may be that such groups already exist for your academic institution, and if so, you can learn about them from your department or alumni association. If there is no group affiliated with your school, consider working with your department to start one. Getting started as a professional can be a real challenge, and having a friend or a ready-made group of colleagues to help guide you through can be a tremendous help.

PROFESSIONAL, COMMUNITY, AND POLITICAL INVOLVEMENT

Finally, I encourage you to become actively involved in your community, in your professional association, and in political activities. Although you are probably not aware of it, you are able to study and participate in an internship today because people in the profession before you worked to develop the profession and create the opportunities you now enjoy. So, too, the educational and professional environment of the future is being shaped by the present political and social system and by people who are working very hard and making personal sacrifices to ensure that clients are protected and your opportunities as a professional continue.

Beyond parochial matters of interest to our disciplines, broad social policy has a profound impact on other aspects of our lives and especially on the lives of our clients. As someone involved in human service, you will have a unique interest in the outcome of policy debates, and you also bring a unique and valuable perspective and skill set to those debates. Maton and Bishop-Joseph (2006) discuss ways in which social research has influenced policy-making on such critical matters as *Brown v. Board of Education,* Head Start, and other social issues. These authors then offer recommendations for other areas of policy involvement as well as suggestions for how practitioners and researchers in the social sciences can be more involved and more effective in shaping the debate and resulting policies.

Hamilton and Fauri (2001) point out that social and political involvement is mandated by the NASW code of ethics. Consistent with this principle, their research showed that, in general, social workers tend to be more politically active than the general public. To further enhance this involvement, Hamilton and Fauri discuss ways in which helping professionals can use their theoretical and practical skills to become more involved and successful in political and social advocacy. Putting this principle into practice in social work education, Saulnier (2000) developed and studied the effectiveness of incorporating policy activities into coursework. The results showed that basic training and experience in political activism resulted in increased involvement that was manifested in a variety of ways nearly a year after completion of the course.

For those interested in becoming more involved, practical suggestions for effective policy advocacy at the state level were offered by Hoever (2005). An excellent resource for students interested in understanding more about federal policy in particular is provided by Staller (2004), who offers a primer on how to access and understand information about federal legislation and regulations.

Safarjan (2002) gives more general suggestions for how social and psychological issues can be advanced in the public and political sphere. Included among Safarjan's 12 "principles for advocates" are: the importance of educating policy-makers about your profession and issues, choosing your battles wisely and not spreading yourself too thin, giving credit to others, being generous with time and political contributions to candidates and your association political committees, understanding what is important to policy-makers, and finally, persistence. Real-world, personal examples of political involvement are described well by DeLeon, Loftis, Ball, and Sullivan (2006) and by Abrahamson, Steele, and Abrahamson (2003), who report on the professional and political efforts they and others have put into legislation to establish parity for mental health care.

Protecting and advancing your professional opportunities and interests, and working to ensure that clients receive the services they need, takes tremendous effort, financial resources, and commitment. I encourage you to join your professional organization, contribute through dues and special contributions, and take an active role in the activities. As a student, you may want to become involved in the national student association of your profession. Increasingly, professional associations are including students in their political lobbying efforts and association activities, and this can be a great way to learn more about the process (Chamberlin, 2001).

I also encourage you to learn about and become involved in the political process, if you are not already. Many of the issues you and your clients face are the direct or indirect result of political decisions. At a minimum, your political involvement should include becoming an informed and active voter. This takes more than simply watching TV ads or reading a voters' pamphlet. Citizenship requires a bit of work, but I believe that the rewards of living in a free society and the needs we seek to address through our professional activities make the work worthwhile.

Beyond voting, you may also wish to become actively involved in a political party or other organization dedicated to social change. You needn't be shy or hesitant to take this step, because most political parties and organizations welcome new members and are happy to help you learn about the process as you go along. An excellent way to start is to get in touch with a candidate whom you support and volunteer to work on her or his election campaign. There is no substitute for grassroots activism, and by stuffing envelopes, telephoning voters, driving voters to the polls, waving signs, and the like, you can truly make a difference. In addition to meeting some great people, having fun, and possibly changing the outcome of an election, this involvement will enhance your impact should you later wish to contact that person on behalf of an issue you care about. It is one thing to ask an elected official to do something for you or for an issue you care about. It is much more effective to first show that you support the official, either through your time, your financial contributions, or (preferably) both.

Finally, if you do become involved in political activities, you may at some point want to go beyond working on campaigns or advocating on issues to actually run for office yourself. Miller (2002) described his experiences serving in the Ohio House of Representatives. Other human service professionals, including psychologists, social workers, counselors, and psychiatrists serve in a host of elected offices ranging from city councils to Congress. Speaking personally, from my own experience as a psychologist serving in Congress, I can tell you that elected public service is a tremendously rewarding opportunity. If you chose to pursue it, you will find that your academic and professional training will be helpful in countless ways.

Ultimately, the skills and knowledge you gain in your internship will serve you and others well in many settings, and your opportunities to contribute can and should extend beyond your school or workplace. Our overall goal as professionals, as individuals, as citizens, and as members of our community should be to contribute in whatever ways we can to help improve the lives of others. The sooner you seize that opportunity, accept the responsibility, and engage in the sustained effort to make positive changes, the more impact you will have. I hope you will do so and wish you much success in your endeavors.

REFERENCES

Abrahamson, D. J., Steele, A. P., & Abrahamson, L. S. (2003). Practice, policy, and parity: The politics of persistence. *Professional Psychology: Research and Practice, 34,* 535–539.

Chamberlin, J. (2001). Turning students into advocates. *Monitor on Psychology, 32*(4), 82–85.

DeAngelis, T. (2005). Things I wish I'd learned in grad school. *Monitor on Psychology, 36*(1), 54–57.

DeLeon, P. H., Loftis, C. W., Ball, V., & Sullivan, M. J. (2006). Navigating politics, policy, and procedure: A firsthand perspective of advocacy on behalf of the profession. *Professional Psychology: Research and Practice, 37(2),* 146–153.

Fair, S. M., & Bressler, J. M. (1992). Therapist-initiated termination of psychotherapy. *Clinical Supervisor, 10,* 171–189.

Falender, C. A., & Shafranske, E. P. (2004). *Clinical supervision: A competency based approach,* Washington, DC: American Psychological Association.

Hamilton, D., & Fauri, D. (2001). Social workers' political participation: Strengthening the political confidence of social work students. *Journal of Social Work Education, 37,* 321–332.

Hayes, N. (1997). The distinctive skills of a psychology graduate. *APA Monitor, 28*(7), 33.

Hoever, R. (2005). Altering state policy: Interest group effectiveness among state-level advocacy groups. *Social Work, 50(3),* 219–227.

Lopez, S., & Prosser, E. (2000). Becoming an adaptive new professional: Going beyond Plante's principles. *Professional Psychology: Research and Practice, 31*(4), 461–462.

Maton, K. I., & Bishop-Joseph, S. J. (2006). Psychological research, practice, and social policy: Potential pathways of influence. *Professional Psychology: Research and Practice, 37*(2), 140–145.

Miller, D. (2002). Advancing mental health in political places. *Professional Psychology: Research and Practice, 33*(3), 277–280.

Plante, T. G. (1996). Ten principles of success for psychology trainees embarking on their careers. *Professional Psychology: Research and Practice, 27,* 304–307.

Plante, T. G. (1998). How to find a first job in professional psychology: Ten principles for finding employment for psychology interns and postdoctoral fellows. *Professional Psychology: Research and Practice, 29*(5), 508–511.

Safarjan, W. (2002). A primer for advancing psychology in the public sector. *American Psychologist, 57,* 945–955.

Saulnier, C. F. (2000). Policy practice: Training direct social workers to get involved. *Journal of Teaching in Social Work, 20,* 121–125.

Staller, K. M., (2004). The structure of federal policy: Deciphering the United States Code. *Journal of Teaching in Social Work, 24*(3/4), 47–63.

Thomas, S. R., (2005). The school counselor alumni peer consultation group. *Counselor Education and Supervision, 45(1),* 16–29.

CHAPTER 11
FRUSTRATIONS, LESSONS, DISCOVERIES, AND JOY

At the conclusion of their internship, many interns feel a strong sense of accomplishment and satisfaction. They have enjoyed the opportunity to work with clients, have encountered professionals whom they respect and admire, and are pleased with their own work and what they have learned. This is the ideal. On the other hand, some interns also experience a sense of frustration and disillusionment as they end their internship.

Whatever your experience, this chapter is designed to help put the internship into perspective. The following comments are based on impressions gathered from students, interns, supervisors, instructors, and my own experience spanning more than 23 years of clinical and academic work. I begin by describing certain experiences and lessons that can dim one's enthusiasm for the profession. Then I conclude by offering some more positive thoughts that may help you maintain perspective and keep your spirits up through the hard times that inevitably come in any profession.

LEARNING FROM WHATEVER HAPPENS

Whatever happens at your internship, remember that it is just one experience. Do not make judgments about all settings, staff, clients, or yourself based on a limited sample. Even in the worst settings, with the most difficult clients and most pathological staff members, there are valuable lessons to be learned. You may actually hate a certain setting and want to get out as soon as possible, but this does not mean you should give up or that the experience was a waste of time.

To help you get a handle on what might frustrate or trouble you about your internship, I offer the following list of lessons that eventually occur to us all but are not always pleasant. The point is not to add to whatever woes you may already have discovered on your own but to validate what you may have encountered already or may experience in the future.

EXERCISE

Before reading my ideas, write your own impressions of the negative and positive lessons you have learned during your internship. Try to identify some of the things you have learned about people, systems, the function and outcome of treatment, life in general, and yourself as a person and as a helping professional.

LESSONS WE WISH WERE NOT TRUE

THE PEOPLE IN THE PROFESSION

1. Not everyone in the helping professions is equally able to help others. There are some people who are grossly incompetent. For some clients, tasks, or situations, we must include ourselves in the incompetent category.
2. Very few people who are in fact incompetent are willing to acknowledge that fact. Instead, most are terribly defensive about their skills and their work, and many believe themselves to be outstanding and gifted professionals.
3. Not everyone in the helping professions is really there to help others. Regardless of what they may profess outwardly, some are in the field primarily to satisfy their own needs. In some instances, this means they will act in ways that may be detrimental to clients, their agency, and to you if they stand to benefit as a result.
4. For some people, honesty, openness, caring, and learning are not as important as power, status, appearance, and control. When working with these people, many of the things you assume are the right thing to do may have exactly the opposite effect you intended. Do not let yourself become one of these people.
5. The people described in items 3 and 4 will probably not be interested in changing themselves. Either they do not think of themselves as just described, or they accept the description but do not find anything wrong with their view of the

world. They may also think everyone else is just like them or worse.

6. Not everyone will like or respect you, no matter who you are or what you do. You should be open to feedback, but you do not have to be liked by everyone all the time.

The Systems in Which We Work

1. Ultimately, any system is only as good as the people who operate and use it. No system can succeed if it is run by incompetent or negatively motivated people.

2. Frequently, the people described in items 3, 4, and 5 of the preceding section are in charge of systems.

3. Even well-intentioned programs run by healthy, caring people sometimes do not work efficiently or well. Sometimes the very best efforts of the very best people are thwarted by bad systems or incompetent people running them.

4. Mental illness and a host of other social ills receive very little attention and real support in our society. There is a lot of talk and substantial sums of money are spent, but much of this is symbolic. In relation to where other monies and energy are allocated, what goes to these needs is minuscule. Changing this will require political involvement. Get involved!

5. Many of the problems we deal with as human service workers are rooted in the larger social and economic conditions of our society. Unless the root causes are addressed, systems implemented to deal with the effects are likely to have only limited success.

6. Prevention would work better than most treatments, but money for prevention is very hard to come by, and most people do not want to take personal responsibility for prevention.

7. Coordination between different service systems can be nightmarishly complicated, inconsistent, and inefficient.

8. Sometimes rules and policies seem stupid, but they are based on sound reasons. Sometimes they are just stupid.

9. Much of your professional life, far too much, will be spent in meetings in which little gets accomplished. Learn how to conduct effective meetings yourself so you don't waste other people's time or your own.

10. Much of your professional life will be spent on paperwork. Learn to deal with paperwork efficiently, but do not ignore it or neglect it.

The Clients with Whom We Work

1. Many of your clients will be decent, deserving, and well-motivated people who, for a variety of reasons, you will be unable to help no matter how hard you try.

2. Some clients encounter such incredibly bad luck that it is hard to imagine how they survive. It is also hard to believe that life is in any way fair. Simply put, it isn't. Part of what we are about is trying to make the unfairness livable.

3. Not all clients are motivated to get better.

4. Not all clients are decent and likable people.

5. Some clients are self-serving predators. They will steal from other people, will lie to you, and would probably hurt or even kill you if they thought it would help them.

6. Some clients do not look, dress, act, talk, or even smell very nice.

7. Some clients are well motivated but simply lack the mental or emotional capacity to accomplish what they need to do to help themselves.

The Nature of the Problems

1. The kinds of people and problems we deal with are often overwhelmingly complex. They include psychological, social, economic, physical, spiritual, and genetic factors. This is one of the reasons treatment is so challenging.

2. You will have clients who are in desperate straits because of the social system in which they live. Unemployment, lack of insurance, abusive families, sexism, racism, dangerous neighborhoods, and more all add to whatever other factors the client may present, and few if any of these factors can be dealt with directly by you.

3. Despite what we might wish to believe, everyone may be created equal in rights, but not everyone is created equal in abilities or temperament. Genetics plays a far bigger role than many of us realize in shaping who we are and in causing or contributing to certain illnesses. Some clients are apparently predisposed to become alcoholic, schizophrenic, or bipolar. Others will simply be less able mentally to prosper in this world or to comprehend certain therapy approaches. Still others will be quite well endowed intellectually, but their emotional responsiveness will be minimal.

4. Our understanding of biochemistry and behavior has increased immensely, but it still pales in comparison to what there is left to discover and what we need to know to help our clients. Many of the illnesses clients present have biological bases or will result in biochemical changes, yet our ability to understand and correct the condition is meager at best. On the other hand, many illnesses that are often treated biochemically have their roots in situational factors that, if changed, would largely "cure" the patient's problems.

5. Chance, pure dumb luck, can make everything else irrelevant. A perfectly healthy individual is in a car accident, and his or her life is changed forever. A woman is raped on her way home from work. A client who is unstable but coping loses his job and girlfriend on the same day, and it pushes him over the edge. You can try to reduce some of these things by changing systems and people, but a degree of luck will always be present and can have an impact on us all in profound and sometimes terrible ways.

6. Many of the problems you deal with will be part of repeating cycles that are difficult to interrupt. A father who beats

his children was himself beaten as a child. Children of alcoholic parents become alcoholic themselves. A child who lives in poverty and whose parent is in jail winds up committing crimes himself.

7. Some of the problems we deal with are givens of existence. As such, we must not only help clients deal with those problems, we must deal with the same problems ourselves. Death, relationships, meaninglessness, responsibility, freedom, and uncertainty are part of being alive for client and clinician alike. We, too, are vulnerable.

THE LIMITS TO OUR KNOWLEDGE AND TOOLS

1. In the face of the lessons mentioned thus far, you will often feel you have no idea what the real problem is or how to treat it.
2. There will be times when you have a clear theoretical explanation about the nature of the real problem and its treatment, and you are sure you are right. Some of these times, you will be dead wrong.
3. In the face of the lessons mentioned thus far, you will often feel you know exactly what the real problem is, but it is part of the socioeconomic structure or some other system that you are powerless to influence or to change soon enough for a particular client.
4. Blaming the system rarely helps if that is all you do. You can change the system, but it takes work, commitment, and involvement.
5. Change takes time. In fact, it often takes lots of time. You may never see the long-term effects, good or bad, of what you do for individuals or for the society.
6. Often, no one, not the client, his or her family, his or her friends, you, or anyone else really knows what is going on with a client. Yet, somehow, you are expected to proceed anyway and do the best you can.
7. Many in the public, including perhaps your friends, family, and other professionals, will doubt the validity or value of what you do. This may be due to lack of knowledge, but it may also be due to very good reasons. This can make it hard for you to believe in what you do yourself.

LESSONS ABOUT OURSELVES

1. You will not always live up to your own ideals as a professional or as a person.
2. You will not always be as competent as you would like.
3. There will be times when you do not work as hard as you believe you should. There will be times when you work too hard.
4. You will find yourself doing many of the negative things you believe clients should not do.
5. You will find yourself not doing the positive things you tell your clients to do.

6. There will be times when your own conduct could lead others to wonder about your motives and intentions.
7. There will be many times when you wonder if it is all worth it or if you should be doing something else.

LESSONS ABOUT THE LESSONS

The preceding lessons could easily lead one to abandon the field entirely or to stay with it but become cynical, jaded, and part of the problem instead of the solution. Do not let this happen to you.

The lessons I have described here are only part of the picture. You need to know that part, because it is real and you will have to learn to deal with it. The good news is that you can learn to deal effectively with even the most difficult of these realities. Further, despite the negative aspects of clinical work, there are many positive rewards; on balance, these tend to outweigh the negatives. It is an honor and a privilege to get to do the kind of work we do. Even in the most down times, it is worth remembering that and finding the joy.

DISCOVERIES AND JOY

PEOPLE IN THE PROFESSION

1. There are many fine people in the profession. They are drawn to human services out of genuine concern and caring for others, and they have dedicated their lives and talents toward that end. In many cases, these people could make far more money doing something else, but they have chosen instead to pursue occupations that serve others.
2. People differ in skills and wisdom. By working closely with those more skilled than yourself, and by continually being open to learning, your own skills can rapidly advance. By working patiently with others and sharing your own knowledge, you can help others learn and grow. We can all pass on to others what has been given to us.
3. Perhaps more than any other profession, the human services offer an expectation and opportunity for personal exploration and growth. This is not just about knowledge and technical skills, it is about who we are as people.
4. If you have certain natural abilities, do your best, work hard, listen, and learn, you will probably get along with most folks and will make some wonderful friends along the way. You may also do some excellent work for your clients, and their lives will be better as a result.

THE SYSTEMS IN WHICH WE WORK

1. No system is perfect, but most can be improved by dedicated and competent effort.

2. Some systems really do help people. They may not be perfect, but without them the lives of many would be much worse.

3. It is possible to gradually change the root causes of problems. The process may involve personal change and political action alongside clinical work. The history of civilization is a history of painfully slow advances in how we care for and treat one another, but advances are indeed made, and each of us can contribute to them.

4. Change in systems begins with changes in ourselves.

THE CLIENTS WITH WHOM WE WORK

1. The task of personal understanding and growth is difficult and frightening. Although some clients will not be motivated to change, many will show great courage in the face of incredible obstacles.

2. Some of your clients will be extremely grateful for the help you provide as they struggle to improve their lives.

3. It is a privilege and responsibility to work with people who entrust a portion of their lives to our care. We must respect that responsibility and do our best to honor it.

4. Some of our clients will have lived lives and learned lessons that we have never dreamed of. We may learn more from working with clients than the clients benefit from their work with us.

THE NATURE OF THE PROBLEMS

1. The problems we deal with are extremely complex, but little by little we make strides in understanding them. This is how all knowledge progresses. We may not know everything we would like, but we do know some things and that can be very helpful. Our task is not to know everything already but to apply what we have learned and keep moving forward.

2. Social change is slow, but change does happen thanks to the dedication and sacrifice of a few individuals working for the good of many. You can be part of the change process. To paraphrase Joe Hill, "Don't whine; organize!"

3. Differences in abilities and traits may be genetically influenced, but people are not ruled entirely by genes. Even those with severe limitations in many areas have certain abilities that bring them joy. Nurturing those abilities and strengthening others can make some extraordinarily challenging lives more pleasant. That can be a very rewarding goal.

4. Life is uncertain, and bad things do happen to good people. For some, that is cause for despair; for others, it is the reason we must make the most of every moment. The choice is ours. Watch out for simplistic answers.

THE LIMITS TO OUR KNOWLEDGE AND TOOLS

1. Although our tools are limited, the research evidence shows that overall, the treatment we offer can and does make significant positive differences in people's lives.

2. Differences in theories can be confusing and frustrating. Given the complexity of human existence, we should not expect it to be otherwise. Each theory adds to our understanding and can help us in our work. The trick is to use theories as tools and fit them to our clients rather than fitting clients to our theories.

3. No matter how frustrated you might become with the limits to knowledge or to your techniques, you are not alone. Every job or activity eventually has its limits. The challenge is to learn to deal with them constructively. That, indeed, is the challenge of life itself.

LESSONS ABOUT OURSELVES

1. You do not have to be absolutely perfect in order to help people. Some of your own most difficult struggles can help you find insights that will later serve your clinical work well.

2. You will make mistakes, but for the most part clients are resilient; if you do your best and recognize your limits, things will usually work out.

3. Each of us can make changes, but change takes time. As you work to improve yourself, you will come to understand the task your clients face.

4. There will be times when you wonder if it is all worth it, but there will also be times when it is crystal-clear that something you have done has made a difference. Moments like that are rare enough in any work. When they happen in clinical work, they are especially valuable because people's lives change for the better.

5. You must find joy in your clinical work, but you must also find it elsewhere in your life. Because clinical work is so important, it will bring with it both highs and lows. Therefore, you must be dedicated as a clinician, but do not let that be the only thing that brings you satisfaction. Take care of yourself so you can care for others.

6. Completion of your internship is not an ending, it is a step along the way. Do not expect to ever be done with the process of learning and growth. That is what makes life and learning interesting. Make the most of it. You only get one chance, and it doesn't last that long.

CLOSING COMMENTS

Throughout the book, from the opening chapter to this sentence, I have encouraged interns to be open to new learning and to seek consultation frequently. Now it is my opportunity to put that advice into practice one more time myself. A book of this sort is never really finished. As soon as I write the final words for this page, I will begin to gather information from journals, colleagues, and students for the next edition. This is where I have the chance to learn from you, the reader.

If you found this book helpful, if there are parts that were not useful, if I left things out that should have been included, if you have any suggestions for improvements, or if you care to share any personal anecdotes, I would welcome your input. You can write me at this address:

Brian N. Baird, Ph.D.
P.O. Box 5584
Vancouver, WA 98668

If you include your address, I will try to get back in touch with you.

My goal in writing this book was to contribute to the quality of internship training and thereby enhance the quality of the helping professions. I hope I have met that goal, and I welcome your contributions to making the next edition still more useful.

Thank you for reading this book; I hope it has been helpful. I wish you success in your future studies and work.

APPENDIX A
INTERNSHIP SELECTION CHECKLIST

This checklist is designed to help interns and supervisors select placements that will best meet the intern's educational and training needs.

PREVIOUS FIELD EXPERIENCE

List any previous field experience you have had.

ACADEMIC CLASSES OR SKILLS TRAINING

List any coursework or skills training that would be relevant to an internship (e.g., Human Development, Abnormal Psychology, Theories of Counseling, Assessment).

TIME

Carefully considering the requirements for your program and the various other commitments in your life, how much time can you realistically allocate to this placement each week? Please be specific about days and times you will or will not be available.

TREATMENT SETTING

What treatment settings would best match your abilities and interests at this time?

Indicate any prior course work or experience relating to such settings.

CLIENTS SERVED

What types of clients (e.g., ages, presenting concerns, ethnic or cultural backgrounds) are you most interested in working with at this point in your training?

Indicate any prior courses, training, or experience working with this group.

TREATMENT APPROACH

What theoretical orientation or treatment approach is most interesting to you at present?

Indicate any prior courses, training, or experience working with this approach.

LEARNING OPPORTUNITIES

What sorts of learning opportunities do you hope to have at your internship, and what level of involvement and responsibility would you like? For example, you might want to learn about intake interviews by first observing, then doing part of them with supervision, then doing a complete interview, and then doing a complete interview with a written report. List any opportunities you think would be interesting here. Also note if you already have some experience in an area.

SUPERVISION STYLE AND PERSONALITY

What personal qualities of a supervisor do you think you would work with best?

What personal styles might challenge you but help you learn?

CAREER PLANS

What experiences will be most useful in helping your candidacy for a job or academic admission?

SAFETY AND RISKS

List any concerns you might have about the limits of your abilities or knowledge.

Identify any concerns or questions you have about your personal safety or risks relating to placements.

PEERS

Are there any other interns with whom you would particularly like to be assigned? If so, please indicate who and briefly describe your reasons.

Are there any other interns with whom you would particularly *not* like to be assigned. If so, please indicate who and briefly describe your reasons.

OTHER COMMENTS

Please identify or discuss any issues that you have not had an opportunity to address above.

Appendix B
Placement Information Form

Instructions

This form is designed to provide information about agencies and programs interested in offering placements to interns. Copies of this form will be kept on file for students to review when seeking internships. Please answer all items and feel free to include any additional information that you think important. Thank you for your time and interest in working with us.

Placement name: _____

Placement address: _____

_____

_____

_____

Phone: _____-_____-_____

Contact person: _____

Position title: _____

Phone: _____-_____-_____ ext. _____

Please provide a brief description of the services provided and the clients served by your program or institution:

_____

_____

_____

_____

Please indicate the qualifications you would like interns to have.

Degree level or year in school:

Freshman Sophomore Junior Senior B.A./B.S. M.A./M.S. Ph.D./Psy.D./Ed.D.

Majors acceptable: _____

Prior experience: _____

_____

_____

Other required qualifications: _____

Briefly describe the learning opportunities, responsibilities, and expectations for interns at your placement site:

_____

_____

_____

Please indicate what days and times are available for interns to be at your placement. If you require that interns be present on certain days or times, please indicate those times:

_____

_____

_____

Briefly describe the supervision opportunities available to interns:

Supervisor name: _____

Supervisor position: _____

Frequency of available supervision: _____

Supervisor's theoretical orientation: _____

Other information about supervision: _____

_____

Additional information about your program or the internship:

_____

_____

_____

APPENDIX C
INTERNSHIP LEARNING AGREEMENT RECORD FORM

Date: _____

Intern name: _____   Intern ID# _____

Intern address:

   Street: _____

   City: _____

   Zip: _____

Intern home phone: _____

Intern cellphone: _____

Intern e-mail: _____

Internship site: _____

Internship address: _____

   Street: _____

   City: _____

   Zip: _____

Internship phone: _____

Supervisor name: _____

Supervisor title: _____

Supervisor work phone: _____

Supervisor home phone: _____

Supervisor cellphone: _____

Supervisor pager #: _____

Supervisor e-mail: _____

Description of internship setting:

_____

_____

Intern's schedule:

Day hours

Sun _____ Mon _____ Tue _____ Wed _____ Thu _____ Fri _____ Sat _____

Notes about intern schedule:

_____

_____

Supervision Schedule

Days _____   Times _____

Planned supervisory activities

_____

_____

_____

Theory, Techniques, and Skills to Be Developed

_____

_____

_____

INTERNSHIP GOALS AND LEARNING ACTIVITIES

In the space, below please list your learning goals for the internship and the activities you and your supervisor agree upon to help you achieve those goals. Leave space under "evaluation" to record an evaluation at the end of the internship.

Learning goals	Learning activity	Evaluation
1.		
2.		
3.		
4.		
5.		

Intern signature: _____   Date: _____

Supervisor signature: _____   Date: _____

INTERN EVALUATION: SUPERVISOR FORM

Intern name: _____

Date of evaluation: _____/_____/_____

Supervisor: _____

Internship site: _____

INSTRUCTIONS

This form is designed to help supervisors provide feedback about the performance of interns. I know you are probably busy, but the form usually takes just five or ten minutes to complete, and your answers and comments will be much appreciated. This form will become part of the intern's record for this course and may be considered in assigning grades for the internship. Please answer each item using the scale provided. Space is provided following each category group for specific comments. There is also space at the end of this form for general comments. If you feel it would be helpful to put anything into context from the outset, please feel free to do so below.

Initial Comments: _____

_____

_____

ANSWER CODE FOR EVALUATION ITEMS AND QUESTIONS

NA: Not applicable or not enough information to form a judgment

1. Far below expectations—needs much improvement, a concern
2. Below expectations—needs some improvement to meet standards
3. Acceptable—meets standards at average level for interns
4. Above expectations—performs above average level for interns
5. Far above expectations—a definite strength, performs well beyond average levels for interns

I. BASIC WORK REQUIREMENTS

_____ Arrives on time consistently
_____ Uses time effectively
_____ Informs supervisor and makes arrangements for absences
_____ Reliably completes requested or assigned tasks on time
_____ Completes required total number of hours or days on site
_____ Is responsive to norms about clothing, language, and so on, on site

Comments: _____

_____

Suggested areas for further study: _____

_____

II. ETHICAL AWARENESS AND CONDUCT

_____ Knowledge of general ethical guidelines
_____ Knowledge of ethical guidelines of internship placement
_____ Demonstrates awareness and sensitivity to ethical issues
_____ Personal behavior is consistent with ethical guidelines
_____ Consults with others about ethical issues if necessary

Comments: _____

_____

Suggested areas for further study: _____

_____

III. KNOWLEDGE AND LEARNING

A. Knowledge of Client Population
_____ Knowledge level of client population at beginning of internship
_____ Knowledge level of client population at end of internship

B. Knowledge of Treatment Approaches
_____ Knowledge of treatment approach at beginning of internship
_____ Knowledge of treatment approach at end of internship

C. Knowledge of Treatment Setting
_____ Knowledge of treatment setting at beginning of internship
_____ Knowledge of treatment setting at end of internship

D. Learning
_____ Receptive to learning when new information is offered
_____ Actively seeks new information from staff or supervisor
_____ Ability to learn and understand new information
_____ Understanding of concepts, theories, and information
_____ Ability to apply new information in clinical setting

Comments: _____

_____

Suggested areas for further study: _____

_____

IV. SKILL DEVELOPMENT

(List specific skill areas of focus for this intern during the placement, e.g., assessment, interviewing, diagnosis, individual therapy, group therapy.)

Performance   **Skill Area**

_____   _____

_____   _____

_____   _____

_____   _____

_____   _____

_____   _____

_____   _____

_____   _____

V. RESPONSE TO SUPERVISION

_____ Actively seeks supervision when necessary
_____ Receptive to feedback and suggestions from supervisor
_____ Understands information communicated in supervision
_____ Successfully implements suggestions from supervisor
_____ Aware of areas that need improvement
_____ Willingness to explore personal strengths and weaknesses

Comments: _____

_____

Suggested areas for further study: _____

_____

VI. INTERACTIONS WITH CLIENTS

_____ Appears comfortable interacting with clients
_____ Initiates interactions with clients
_____ Communicates effectively with clients
_____ Builds rapport and respect with clients
_____ Is sensitive and responsive to client's needs
_____ Is sensitive to cultural differences
_____ Is sensitive to issues of gender differences

Comments: _____

_____

Suggested areas for further study: _____

_____

VII. INTERACTIONS WITH COWORKERS

_____ Appears comfortable interacting with other staff members
_____ Initiates interactions with staff
_____ Communicates effectively with staff
_____ Effectively conveys information and expresses own opinions
_____ Effectively receives information and opinions from others

Comments: _____

_____

Suggested areas for further study: _____

_____

VIII. WORK PRODUCTS

_____ Reliably and accurately keeps records
_____ Written or verbal reports are accurate and factually correct
_____ Written or verbal reports are presented in professional manner
_____ Reports are clinically or administratively useful

Comments: _____

_____

Suggested areas for further study: _____

_____

Overall, what would you identify as this intern's strong points? _____

What would you identify as areas in which this intern should improve?

_____

_____

_____

Would you recommend this intern for employment at his or her present level?

Please explain: _____

_____

_____

_____

Would you recommend this intern for continued graduate studies?

Please explain:

_____

_____

_____

Supervisor's signature: _____   Date: _____

Thank you for your time in supervising this intern and in completing this evaluation.

INTERN EVALUATION: INTERN FORM

Intern name: _____

Date of evaluation: _____/_____/_____

Supervisor: _____

Placement site: _____

INSTRUCTIONS

Your supervisor will be asked to complete an evaluation form designed to assess your performance during your internship. This form is provided to help you assess your own performance. It is essentially identical to the one given to your supervisor. The form usually takes just five or ten minutes to complete. It will become part of your record for this course and may be considered in assigning grades for the internship. Please answer each item using the scale provided. Space is provided following each category group for specific comments. There is also space at the end of the form for general comments. If you feel it would be helpful to put anything into context from the outset, please feel free to do so below.

Initial comments: _____

_____

_____

_____

_____

ANSWER CODE FOR EVALUATION ITEMS

NA: Not applicable or not enough information to form a judgment

1. Far below expectations—needs much improvement, a concern
2. Below expectations—needs some improvement to meet standards
3. Acceptable—meets standards at average level for interns
4. Above expectations—performs above average level for interns
5. Far above expectations—a definite strength, performs well beyond average levels for interns

I. BASIC WORK REQUIREMENTS

_____ Arrives on time consistently
_____ Uses time effectively

_____ Informs supervisor and makes arrangements for absences
_____ Reliably completes requested or assigned tasks on time
_____ Completes required total number of hours or days on site
_____ Is responsive to norms about clothing, language, and so on, on site

Comments: _____

_____

Suggested areas for further study: _____

_____

II. ETHICAL AWARENESS AND CONDUCT
_____ Knowledge of general ethical guidelines
_____ Knowledge of ethical guidelines of internship placement
_____ Demonstrates awareness and sensitivity to ethical issues
_____ Personal behavior is consistent with ethical guidelines
_____ Consults with others about ethical issues if necessary

Comments: _____

_____

Suggested areas for further study: _____

_____

III. KNOWLEDGE AND LEARNING

A. Knowledge of Client Population
_____ Knowledge level of client population at beginning of internship
_____ Knowledge level of client population at end of internship

B. Knowledge of Treatment Approaches
_____ Knowledge of treatment approach at beginning of internship
_____ Knowledge of treatment approach at end of internship

C. Knowledge of Treatment Setting
_____ Knowledge of treatment setting at beginning of internship
_____ Knowledge of treatment setting at end of internship

D. Learning
_____ Receptive to learning when new information is offered
_____ Actively seeks new information from staff or supervisor
_____ Ability to learn and understand new information
_____ Understanding of concepts, theories, and information
_____ Ability to apply new information in clinical setting

Comments: _____

_____

Suggested areas for further study: _____

_____

IV. SKILL DEVELOPMENT

(List specific skill areas of focus for this intern during the placement, e.g., assessment, interviewing, diagnosis, individual therapy, group therapy.)

Performance   **Skill Area**

_____   _____

_____   _____

_____   _____

_____   _____

_____   _____

_____   _____

_____   _____

V. RESPONSE TO SUPERVISION

_____ Actively seeks supervision when necessary
_____ Receptive to feedback and suggestions from supervisor
_____ Understands information communicated in supervision
_____ Successfully implements suggestions from supervisor
_____ Aware of areas that need improvement
_____ Willingness to explore personal strengths and weaknesses

Comments: _____

_____

Suggested areas for further study: _____

_____

VI. INTERACTIONS WITH CLIENTS

_____ Appears comfortable interacting with clients
_____ Initiates interactions with clients
_____ Communicates effectively with clients
_____ Builds rapport and respect with clients
_____ Is sensitive and responsive to clients' needs
_____ Is sensitive to cultural differences
_____ Is sensitive to issues of gender differences

Comments: _____

_____

Suggested areas for further study: _____

_____

VII. INTERACTIONS WITH COWORKERS

_____ Appears comfortable interacting with other staff members
_____ Initiates interactions with staff
_____ Communicates effectively with staff
_____ Effectively conveys information and expresses own opinions
_____ Effectively receives information and opinions from others

Comments: _____

_____

Suggested areas for further study: _____

_____

VIII. WORK PRODUCTS
_____ Reliably and accurately keeps records
_____ Written or verbal reports are accurate and factually correct
_____ Written or verbal reports are presented in professional manner
_____ Reports are clinically or administratively useful

Comments: _____

_____

Suggested areas for further study: _____

_____

Overall, what would you identify as your strong points?

_____

_____

What would you identify as areas in which you should improve?

_____

_____

_____

Do you believe you are prepared for employment at your present level?
Please explain:

_____

_____

_____

Do you believe you are ready for continued graduate studies?
Please explain:

_____

_____

_____

Intern's signature: _____ Date: _____

APPENDIX F
EMERGENCY CONTACT AND PROCEDURES INFORMATION

INTERN

Name: _____   Location in placement: _____

Primary work phone: _____-_____-_____ ext _____ Pager #

Secondary work phone: _____-_____-_____ ext _____ Pager #

Primary home phone: _____-_____-_____ ext _____ Pager #

Cellphone: _____-_____-_____ ext _____ Pager #

E-mail:

PLACEMENT SUPERVISOR

Name: _____   Location in placement: _____

Primary work phone: _____-_____-_____ ext _____ Pager #

Secondary work phone: _____-_____-_____ ext _____ Pager #

Primary home phone: _____-_____-_____ ext _____ Pager #

Cellphone: _____-_____-_____ ext _____ Pager #

E-mail:

ALTERNATIVE CONTACT PERSON AT PLACEMENT

Name: _____   Location in placement: _____

Primary work phone: _____-_____-_____ ext _____ Pager #

Secondary work phone: _____-_____-_____ ext _____ Pager #

Primary home phone: _____-_____-_____ ext _____ Pager #

Cellphone: _____-_____-_____ ext _____ Pager #

E-mail:

FACULTY SUPERVISOR

Name: _____   Office location: _____

Primary work phone: _____-_____-_____ ext _____ Pager #

Secondary work phone: _____-_____-_____ ext _____ Pager #

Primary home phone: _____-_____-_____ ext _____ Pager #

Cellphone: _____-_____-_____ ext _____ Pager #

E-mail:

ALTERNATIVE FACULTY CONTACT

Name: _____   Office location: _____

Primary work phone: _____-_____-_____ ext _____ Pager #

Secondary work phone: _____-_____-_____ ext _____ Pager #

Primary home phone: _____-_____-_____ ext _____ Pager #

Cellphone: _____-_____-_____ ext _____ Pager #

E-mail:

Crisis-line number: _____-_____-_____

OTHER RESOURCES

Name: _____   Number: _____-_____-_____

Name: _____   Number: _____-_____-_____

EMERGENCY CONTACT AND PROCEDURES INFORMATION

On this page, list the step-by-step procedures to follow if you have reason to believe that a client is dangerous to self or to others. At the bottom of the page, complete the information for your local mental health agency that handles crises, the closest hospital that accepts mental health crisis referrals, law enforcement agencies, and an attorney you know who specializes in this area and can advise you. If you work in a setting where a crisis with a patient might arise, speak with the individuals listed here to establish a relationship and know their needs and procedures. Complete this form and make the needed contacts at the start of your internship; then keep this form readily available at your work setting.

Step 1:_____

Contact person: _____   Phone number: _____

Step 2:_____

Contact person: _____   Phone number: _____

Step 3:_____

Contact person: _____   Phone number: _____

Step 4:_____

Contact person: _____   Phone number: _____

MENTAL HEALTH CRISIS UNIT

Contact name: _____   Phone number: _____

Contact name: _____   Phone number: _____

LAW ENFORCEMENT

Contact name: _____   Phone number: _____

Contact name: _____   Phone number: _____

HOSPITALS ACCEPTING CRISIS PATIENTS

Hospital name: _____   Unit phone number: _____

Address:_____

Hospital name: _____   Unit phone number: _____

Address:_____

ATTORNEY FOR CONSULTATION

Contact name: _____   Phone number: _____

APPENDIX G

ETHICAL GUIDELINES

Everyone taking part in an internship opportunity is expected to adhere to certain guidelines for ethical, responsible conduct and to adhere to federal and state laws and regulations. This is necessary for your own benefit and protection, as well as for the clients, the placement agency, your instructor, your supervisor, and your academic institution. Certain basic guidelines are described in this appendix, but these are not exhaustive. As an intern you are also expected to learn and adhere to the broader ethical guidelines dictated by their relevant profession (e.g., APA, NASW, ACA), as well as the guidelines specific to their placement agency. In addition, you must familiarize yourself with and follow federal and state laws and regulations (e.g., HIPAA). If you ever have questions about ethics or responsible conduct, contact your instructor or the placement supervisor. At a minimum, interns agree to adhere to the following principles:

1. *Confidentiality.* The identity of clients, or information that would reveal the identity of clients, cannot be revealed without the specific permission of the client and only according to HIPAA guidelines where they apply. The only exceptions are cases in which the client may be dangerous to him- or herself or others and in cases of abuse. In such situations, there may be a legal requirement to inform responsible agencies. There are also certain legal proceedings in which case notes and other records can be ordered to be released by the courts. Interns must familiarize themselves with and adhere to confidentiality procedures of their placements and the laws of the state and federal government. Personal notes pertaining to specific patients and any case material discussed in class must be prepared in such a way that confidentiality is maintained. Any records or communications involving electronic technologies (e.g., computers, e-mail, PDA) must be protected by passwords, encryption, and any other means prescribed by your placement site, academic institution, HIPAA regulations, or other laws. Interns do not discuss cases in public settings outside of class or their internship, nor do they discuss their cases with persons who are not specifically authorized.

2. *Recognition of qualifications and limitations.* Interns must recognize the limitations to their training and abilities and must not exceed these in work with clients. It is incumbent for interns to recognize when clinical situations are beyond their knowledge or ability. When such situations arise, interns will seek assistance from their supervisors and instructor.

3. *Identification as interns.* Interns will explicitly identify themselves as interns to their clients, in reports, and in other professional activities. They will not misrepresent their training, qualifications, or status. Interns who will be at a placement for a limited time will inform clients of that limitation at the outset of therapy and will consider it in their work with clients.

4. *Record keeping.* Interns will accurately and reliably maintain written and other records as required by their placement agency and by state and federal laws.

5. *Dual relationships.* Interns will strictly follow ethical guidelines regarding multiple relationships and will refrain from clinical work with persons with whom the intern is involved in other types of relationships. Such dual relationships may inhibit the effectiveness of the intern's clinical work and may jeopardize both the client and the trainee. For example, it would not be ethical for a trainee to take as a client someone who was a fellow student in class. Similarly, coworkers, friends, and others should not be seen as clients.

6. *Prohibition regarding sexual conduct or harassment.* Under no circumstances shall interns become involved in sexual or romantic relationships of any sort with clients or their family members. Interns will also refrain from sexual harassment and will respect the sensitivity of others regarding sexual matters.

7. *Self-awareness and monitoring.* Interns will monitor their own emotional and physical status and should be aware of any conditions that might adversely impact their ability to serve their clients or placement agencies. If such conditions arise, interns should inform their placement supervisor and instructor.

8. *Ethics discussion with supervisor.* Each intern must discuss the ethical standards of his or her placement with the supervisor before performing any clinical work or patient contact. Space is provided at the bottom of this form to indicate that such discussions have taken place and the intern has been informed of ethical expectations, state and federal laws and regulations, and any other specific guidelines of the agency.

By signing below, the intern agrees to adhere to the guidelines listed above as well as those of the professional discipline, state and federal laws, and the specific placement agency.

Intern signature: _____ Date: _____

Site supervisor: _____ Date: _____

Instructor: _____ Date: _____

APPENDIX H

TREATMENT AGREEMENT AND INFORMED CONSENT

This form is designed for use as an example and template to help you develop a form suited to your own situation. Feel free to use parts of it to draft your own form. Be aware, however, that no claim is made of the legal standing of this model. You must craft your own information with an awareness of the legal and ethical requirements of your position, profession, setting, and state. Be advised that HIPAA guidelines require specific and separate notices. Discuss any document of this kind with your instructor and supervisor before using it with clients.

LETTERHEAD FOR YOUR AGENCY

INTRODUCTION

As a way of introducing myself to clients, I have prepared this brief description of my background, approach, and other information that is important for you to know. Please read this carefully and feel free to ask me any questions about what you have read or any other elements of your treatment. I know this may seem rather formal and that it covers a lot of information, but I believe it is very important for clients to have as much information as possible so they can make informed decisions about their treatment. Again, if you have any questions or concerns at any time please feel free to discuss them with me.

My name is _____ and I am a/an [intern, practicum student, etc.] presently studying at [institutional name] and working toward my [degree]. I have [previous academic qualifications and practical experience].

Throughout my work here, I will be under the supervision of [supervisor name]. His/her qualifications include [list qualifications]. The nature of our supervision will include [describe activities and frequency]. If you have any questions or concerns, please feel free to contact [supervisor name and agency phone number].

Crisis contacts: If for some reason you are unable to contact me or my supervisor, please contact [insert agency contact name and information].

Duration of my work here: My placement at this agency is scheduled to run from [start to stop dates]. On [end date] I will [move on, continue, or other plans]. At that time, clients I am working with will be [transfer or termination plans].

FEES

Fees for services are [describe fees]. All fees will be collected at the time services are provided. Billing procedures will be [describe billing procedures].

In addition to fees for time when I am meeting with you directly, it is also my practice to charge for time required for preparing assessment reports, telephone conversations lasting longer than _____ minutes, consultations, or meetings you have authorized as part of your treatment. I will be pleased to provide you with details of any such costs should they be necessary.

If it happens that you are involved in some way in a lawsuit that requires my participation, you will be responsible for fees associated with my professional time. Because of the demands of preparing for and participating in legal proceedings, my fees for this are _____.

Please be aware that in receiving my services you, not your insurance company, are responsible for full payment of fees. If you want your insurance company to pay for my services, please read your policy carefully to be certain what your coverage provides. If you have any questions, call your insurance provider to be sure. I will be pleased to help in whatever way I can with this process. If conditions of your insurance policy limit the number of sessions your provider will pay for [explain your policy for managing this situation].

Please also be aware that your insurance company may request diagnostic information, a copy of your treatment plan, and case records in order to provide compensation. This information will then become part of their files. Insurance companies are generally quite responsible about keeping this material confidential, but that is something I cannot control or be responsible for. If you wish, I will provide you with copies of any material or correspondence I send to your insurer.

Finally, continuation of treatment depends on timely payment of fees. If you are unable for some reason to pay a bill as requested, please discuss this with me, and we will attempt to make arrangements as needed. However, I reserve the right to discontinue treatment based on nonpayment of fees.

CONFIDENTIALITY AND LIMITATIONS TO CONFIDENTIALITY

I place a high value on the confidentiality of information clients share with me, and I will make every effort to ensure that information about your case will be kept confidential. You should, however, be aware that legal and ethical requirements specify certain conditions in which it may be necessary for me to discuss information about your treatment with other professionals. If you have any questions about these limitations, please ask me about them before we begin treatment or at any time during our treatment. Such situations include [check your state laws before completing this]:

1. If I believe there is a danger that you may harm yourself or others or that you are incapable of caring for yourself.
2. If I become aware of your involvement in abuse of children, elderly, or disabled persons.
3. If I am ordered by a court to release your records. This sometimes happens when clients are plaintiffs in lawsuits and psychological records are subpoenaed as part of that process.
4. If your insurance company requests records in order to verify the services received and determine compensation.
5. [In the case of minors, list any limitations and requirements requiring parental notification and the like.]
6. As part of the supervision process I may discuss your case and share records and other materials [whether note if tapes will be used] with my supervisor [supervisor's name].
7. [Depending on policy and law] I may also discuss information about your case with other personnel within the agency.
8. In the event that I die or become incapacitated I have made arrangements for a colleague to review my records and ensure that patients I am working with receive continued care.

TREATMENT PHILOSOPHY AND FREQUENCY

Briefly, my approach to treatment is best described as [approach used]. In essence, this means [use layperson's terms to describe approach]. This approach to treatment is based on [briefly discuss any relevant research or theoretical literature]. I prefer this treatment approach, but there are other approaches available. If you are interested in learning more about these I would be glad to discuss them with you.

The length of a typical session is [length]. The number and frequency of sessions depends on the client and the nature of his or her concerns. Typically, I see clients for [average number of sessions], but this can vary from as few as [ ] to as many as [ ]. By the [ordinal number of] session, we will discuss how treatment is going and how we expect it to proceed.

CLIENT RESPONSIBILITIES

In order for our work together to be successful, it is essential that clients attend sessions, make a sincere effort to work on the issues we are addressing, and follow through with elements of treatment, such as things to do between sessions, readings, and so on.

If for some reason you cannot attend a scheduled session, please call well in advance and at least 24 hours before your appointment. My schedule tends to be rather full, and if clients do not cancel appointments with sufficient time, that means others who could receive services are unable to.

Repeated failure to attend sessions or to provide adequate rescheduling notice may lead to termination of our work together.

MEDICAL ISSUES

If you have any medical concerns that I should know about, please be certain to inform me of them. I would also like to discuss how you would like communication and information exchanges, if any, between myself and your primary health care provider to be managed.

HANDLING CONCERNS

If any concerns arise at any point during therapy, I encourage you to raise them directly with me so we can work through them. If you feel you cannot deal directly with a concern or issue about your treatment, I will be glad to contact another professional who can help resolve any issues with you.

CONTACTING ME AND CRISIS PROCEDURES

Because of the nature of my work, there will be many times when I am with clients and am not immediately available by telephone. My normal office hours are _____ on _____. If I do not answer the phone, please leave a message and a number so I can return your call. If there is an emergency and I cannot be reached, please contact your physician, the emergency room at your local hospital, or the mental health center crisis line at _____.

CONCLUDING TREATMENT

I believe therapy should continue only until you have reached your goals or are no longer benefiting. If I believe you have achieved your treatment goals or that you are no longer making progress or could benefit more in some other way, I will discuss this with you. If, at any time, you believe it would be best to discontinue treatment you are free to do so, but please discuss this with me directly during a session together. Please also be aware that under unusual circumstances, including but not limited to failure to make timely payements for services, violation of other terms of this agreement, the making of threats or intimidation by clients, I reserve the right to discontinue treatment at my discretion.

ADDITIONAL ISSUES

I appreciate the time you have taken to read this. As I have said before, if you have any questions or concerns now or at any point during your treatment, please feel free to let me know. Please sign below to indicate that you have read this and have had a chance to ask any questions. When we meet, I will give you a copy of this to keep and refer to if you like.

I am looking forward to our work together.

Sincerely,

[Your name]

I have read this document, discussed it with [intern's or professional's name], understand the information contained, and agree to participate in treatment under the conditions described.

Client's name: _____   Date: _____

Appendix I

Supervisor Evaluation Form

This form is designed to give interns the opportunity to provide feedback about the supervision they receive during their internship. This information will be useful in discussions with supervisors and will help your faculty instructor evaluate the learning opportunities at various internship sites.

Each item that follows asks you to indicate the frequency with which activities of supervision occurred, your satisfaction with the activities, or both frequency and satisfaction. Please rate frequency based on a percentage from 0 to 100, with 0 meaning that something never happened, and 100 indicating that the activity happened every time there was an opportunity as described in the item. Please rate satisfaction on a rating scale from 0 to 100, with 0 indicating that you were completely dissatisfied, and 100 signifying that you were completely satisfied. Frequency and satisfaction ratings need not be the same. For example, if you met for fewer than the agreed-upon times for supervision, you might rate the frequency at 75%. Your satisfaction might be anywhere from 0 to 100, depending on what you felt about this issue. Please try to evaluate each item separately from other items. Space is provided at the end for general comments.

PRELIMINARY REMARKS

If you think it will be useful to preface your responses with any introductory comments, please do so here. Additional space is available at the end of the form for general evaluative comments.

_____

_____

_____

_____

_____

_____

_____

_____

_____

_____

_____

SCHEDULE AND AVAILABILITY

1. _____ Frequency   Overall during the internship, approximately how closely did the actual supervision
   _____ Satisfaction   contacts match the agreed-upon plan?

2. _____ Frequency   Apart from scheduled meetings, how available was your supervisor if you
   _____ Satisfaction   requested additional contact?

INTRODUCTION TO SETTING

3. _____ Yes _____ No   Did your supervisor give you a tour or arrange for a tour of the internship site?
   _____ Satisfaction

4. _____ Yes _____ No   Did your supervisor introduce you to other staff when you began the internship?
   _____ Satisfaction

5. _____ Yes _____ No   Did your supervisor discuss procedural matters, agency policy, and the like,
   _____ Satisfaction   when you began the internship?

6. _____ Yes _____ No   Did your supervisor discuss ethical and legal issues when you began the internship?
   _____ Satisfaction

ACTIVITIES AT THE INTERNSHIP

Approximately what percentage of your time at the internship was spent in each of the following activities?

7. _____ Frequency   Observing the milieu of your setting or interacting informally with clients,
   _____ Satisfaction   but not directly observing or participating in treatment or other services

8. _____ Frequency   Interacting informally with staff members
   _____ Satisfaction

9. _____ Frequency   Observing treatment, assessment, or other direct service with clients
   _____ Satisfaction

10. _____ Frequency   Participating in or providing treatment, assessment, or other direct service with clients
    _____ Satisfaction

11. _____ Frequency   Attending meetings other than supervision or informal conversation
    _____ Satisfaction

12. _____ Frequency   Reading records, reports, and the like
    _____ Satisfaction

13. _____ Frequency   Writing case notes, assessments, reports, correspondence, and the like
    _____ Satisfaction

In the space below describe and evaluate any other activities you participated in during your internship.

14. _____ Frequency
    _____ Satisfaction

15. _____ Frequency
    _____ Satisfaction

16. _____ Frequency
    _____ Satisfaction

17. _____ Frequency   Overall, were you able to participate in the activities you had hoped to in the internship?
    _____ Satisfaction

18. What additional activities would have been useful to you during the internship?

_____

_____

_____

ACTIVITIES OF SUPERVISION

Approximately what portion of supervision time was spent in the following activities?

19. _____ Frequency   Using case notes or material to review your interactions with clients
    _____ Satisfaction

20. _____ Frequency   Observing the supervisor providing treatment, assessments, or other services to clients
    _____ Satisfaction

21. _____ Frequency   Providing services yourself under the direct observation of your supervisor
    _____ Satisfaction

22. _____ Frequency   Discussing institutional issues
    _____ Satisfaction

23. _____ Frequency   Didactic instruction in specific topics or skills
    _____ Satisfaction

24. _____ Frequency   Reviewing assessments or other reports you have written
    _____ Satisfaction

25. _____ Frequency   Reviewing case notes or other records you have written
    _____ Satisfaction

26. _____ Frequency   Reviewing assessments or other reports written by your instructor or other professionals
    _____ Satisfaction

27. _____ Frequency   Reviewing case notes or other records written by your instructor or other professionals
    _____ Satisfaction

28. _____ Frequency   Discussing your personal impressions, reactions, and adjustment to the internship
    _____ Satisfaction

29. _____ Frequency   Discussing your relationship with your supervisor
    _____ Satisfaction

In the space below please describe and evaluate any other activities of supervision in which you participated.

30. _____ Frequency
    _____ Satisfaction

31. _____ Frequency
    _____ Satisfaction

32.   What additional activities would have been useful to you in supervision?

_____

_____

_____

INTERPERSONAL ISSUES AND FEEDBACK FROM YOUR SUPERVISOR

The items below refer to how you were given feedback by your supervisor and to the quality of your relationship to one another. Please comment on your supervisor's performance in each of the following areas:

33.   _____ Frequency   Recognizing areas in which your skills or knowledge are relatively strong
      _____ Satisfaction

34.   _____ Frequency   Recognizing areas in which your skills or knowledge need improvement
      _____ Satisfaction

35.   _____ Frequency   Recognizing and complimenting you for accomplishments or things you have
      _____ Satisfaction   done well at your internship

36.   _____ Frequency   Letting you know when your performance has not been good in certain areas
      _____ Satisfaction

37.   _____ Frequency   Providing emotional support
      _____ Satisfaction

38.   _____ Frequency   Dealing with differences between you
      _____ Satisfaction

39.   Based on your experience, briefly describe the ways in which you feel supervision was most helpful to you during your internship.

_____

_____

40.   If there was anything about supervision that was not helpful, please explain.

_____

_____

41.   In what ways do you think supervision could have been more beneficial to you?

_____

_____

APPENDIX J
CLINICAL ACTIVITIES
RECORD SHEET

Date	Total Hours On Site	Milieu Therapy- Observation	Group Therapy	Individual Therapy	Supervision	Testing/ Assessment	Case Management	Staff Meeting	Education	Other

INSTRUCTIONS: For each day you are at your internship site, record the date in the left column, then the total hours for that date, followed by the approximate number of hours spent in each of the activities indicated in the columns to the right. This information will help you, your supervisor, and your instructor monitor the activities and learning opportunities you are involved in. It may also be useful in future application, (e.g., graduate studies, other internships, employment).

This form may be reproduced as needed by the purchaser of this textbook.

PLACEMENT EVALUATION FORM

INSTRUCTIONS

This form is designed to give interns a chance to evaluate the internship site at the conclusion of their internship. The evaluation will be useful to your instructor and to future interns who will be considering where to do an internship. Before answering any individual item, take just a second to review the entire form to see all of the items that will be addressed. Please answer all items and feel free to include any additional information that you think is important.

Placement name: _____

Placement address: _____

Supervisor name: _____

SITE DESCRIPTION

Please describe in your own words the key services provided by this setting.

_____

_____

_____

Please describe the clients served by this setting. Include such things as age ranges, presenting concerns, socioeconomic status, ethnicity, etc.

_____

_____

_____

Please describe the treatment modalities provided. For example, group or individual therapy, family therapy, physical exercises, occupational therapy, etc.

_____

_____

_____

What are the professional backgrounds of the treatment staff on this site. Please list, to the best of your knowledge, the number of professionals by discipline and degree (e.g., 3 MSW Social Workers available at this site).

Numbers	Discipline	Degree Level

Please describe, in your own words, the physical qualities of the setting. Be sure to mention size, age of facilities, level of upkeep, aesthetic qualities, etc.

_____

_____

_____

Please describe the setting of the institution (e.g., rural or urban, neighborhood, etc.).

_____

_____

_____

OPPORTUNITIES FOR LEARNING

Please list the various activities you participated in as part of your internship experience. For each activity, list the modality or instruments used (e.g., the activity might be therapy, the modality might be cognitive/behavioral or group-cognitive therapy; if assessment is the activity, identify the assessment tools used), the weekly frequency of the activity, the total frequency of the activity during the entire internship, the availability of supervision on a 1–5 scale, with 1 being no availability and 5 being maximally available, and the quality of supervision, with 1 being very poor and 5 being outstanding. Please provide any additional comments regarding the activity

Activity: _____   Modality or Instruments Used _____

Weekly Frequency: _____   Total Frequency during Placement _____

Availability of Supervision _____   Quality of Supervision _____

Additional Comments: _____

_____

Activity: _____   Modality or Instruments Used _____

Weekly Frequency: _____   Total Frequency during Placement _____

Availability of Supervision _____   Quality of Supervision _____

Additional Comments: _____

_____

Activity: _____   Modality or Instruments Used _____

Weekly Frequency: _____   Total Frequency during Placement _____

Availability of Supervision _____   Quality of Supervision _____

Additional Comments: _____

_____

Activity: _____   Modality or Instruments Used _____

Weekly Frequency: _____   Total Frequency during Placement _____

Availability of Supervision _____   Quality of Supervision _____

Additional Comments: _____

_____

Activity: _____   Modality or Instruments Used _____

Weekly Frequency: _____   Total Frequency during Placement _____

Availability of Supervision _____   Quality of Supervision _____

Additional Comments: _____

_____

Activity: _____   Modality or Instruments Used _____

Weekly Frequency: _____   Total Frequency during Placement _____

Availability of Supervision _____   Quality of Supervision _____

Additional Comments: _____

_____

OVERALL IMPRESSIONS

Supervisor: Please give a brief description of your experiences with your supervisor. Be sure to mention strengths, areas of concern, and any suggestions for how to improve the supervisory experience.

Staff: Please describe the overall impressions of staff other than your supervisor. Include such things as qualifications, professionalism, relationships with patients, receptiveness to interns, etc.

Clients: Please describe your experience of the clients at this setting. Include the overall client attitudes, motivations, receptivity to working interns, etc., as you observed them.

Treatment or services provided: Please give your overall impressions about the nature and quality of the services provided at this setting. For example, do you think the services are provided well to the clients, are they effective?

Safety or other issues: Please comment about any issues (e.g., safety, hygiene) that you feel are either positive qualities about the placement or areas of concern.

Ethical and professional standards: Please comment briefly about your observations concerning the ethical and professional standards set by the staff at this setting.

FINAL SUMMARY IMPRESSIONS

Finally, please indicate the degree to which you would recommend this placement to other interns (from 1 to 5, with 1 being recommend against, and 5 highly recommend). Please briefly explain the reasons for this recommendation.

INDICES

AUTHOR INDEX

A

Abbott, D., 49, 55
Abeles, N., 27
Abrahamson, D. J., 197
Abrahamson, L. S., 197
Abramowitz, S. F., 142
Abramson, J. S., 79, 82
Ackerley, G. D., 140
Acuff, C., 57
Adams Jr., S. G., 174
Adams, M., 3
Addis, M. E., 27
Adelman, H., 59
Adkins, C., 119
Adolph, J. L., 25
Agate, J., 80
Ageson, A., 170
Agresti, A. A., 140
Aguirre, M. G., 19
Akamatsu, T. J., 85
Albin, D., 3
Alexander Jr., R., 53
Allen, G., 89
Allison, K. W., 107
Alter, C., 119
Alva, L. A., 57
Alvarez, A. R., 38
Anderson, D., 122
Anderson, J. R., 49
Anderson, K. G., 70, 141
Anderson, S. A., 184, 186, 188, 190
Anderson, S. K., 64
Anderson, W., 142, 156
Andrews, A. B., 49
Ankuta, G. Y., 27
Annis, L. V., 173
Antle, B. J., 49, 54
Aponte, H. J., 64, 89
Appelbaum, P. S., 61
Arches, J., 151
Arcinue, F., 70, 88, 141
Arden, I. A., 5, 8, 9, 38
Armao, B. B., 169
Armenian, H., 27
Arons, G., 144
Aronson, E., 149, 150, 151
Arredondo, P., 102, 105
Arthur, N. M., 150
Asamen, J. K., 169, 179
Ashkanazi, G., 43, 49
Ashton, L., 41
Atkinson, D. R., 105, 112
Auerbach, C., 11, 46, 66
Avery, M., 134

B

Baerger, D. R., 54, 55
Bailey, J. S., 86
Baird, B. N., 122, 162
Baird, K. A., 57, 129
Baker, C. A., 173
Baker, D. R., 79, 98

Baker, E. K., 139, 146
Baker, T., 177
Ball, V., 197
Baltimore, M., 69
Barker, R. L., 125
Barnat, M., 80
Barnett, J. E., 48, 63, 68, 69
Barret, B., 49
Barrett, A., 107, 113
Barrick, A. L., 189
Bartell, P. A., 65
Bartels, K. M., 102
Bartle, D., 38
Baruth, N. E., 128, 129, 134
Batka, J. C., 107
Bauer, G. B., 54
Becker, B. R., 147
Becker-Blease, K. A., 68
Behnke, S. H., 41, 50, 58, 70, 71
Beier, E. G., 85
Belter, R. W., 59
Benefield, H., 43, 49
Benjamin, M., 148
Bennet, S. K., 112
Bennett, B. E., 43, 46, 49, 55, 57, 66, 67, 127, 133
Benshoff, J. M., 31
Bent, R., 45
Berberoglu, L. S., 48, 136
Berger, M., 26, 163
Berger, S. E., 56
Berger, S. S., 79
Bergeron, R. L., 49, 53
Berkman, C., 62
Berman, A. L., 54, 55
Berman, E., 90
Bernal, M. E., 102
Bernard, J. M., 68, 80
Bernstein, J. H., 70, 141
Beutler, L. E., 27, 28
Bhati, K. S., 7
Biaggio, M., 64, 65
Binder, J. L., 27
Bingham, R., 104, 105
Birkey, I., 144
Bishop-Joseph, S. J., 197
Blain, M. D., 27
Blakely, E. H., 12
Bloom, J. D., 4, 23
Bobbitt, R. G., 169
Bogo, M., 3, 5, 12, 17, 65, 81, 84
Boisvert, C. B., 27
Bongar, B., 54, 55
Bonner, M., 26
Boonstra, H., 58
Borders, L. D., 31, 32, 80, 97
Boryrs, D. S., 59
Boswell, D. L., 34, 83, 85
Bouhoutsos, J. C., 60, 61
Bovasso, G., 27
Bower, A. G., 51, 127
Bowman, V. E., 64
Boxley, R., 70, 141
Bradley, J., 90, 141
Bradley, L., 82

Bradshaw, J., 47
Brady, J., 146
Braun, S. A., 57, 127
Braun, V., 51, 52
Bregoli, M., 109
Brems, C., 49
Brendel, J., 64, 65
Brenner, E., 122, 126
Bressler, J. M., 184, 192
Bricklin, P. M., 55, 57
Brill, R., 5
Brock, G. W., 49
Brodsky, A., 149
Brossart, D., 68
Brown, H. N., 54
Brown, L. S., 45, 60, 61
Brown, R., 5, 79, 86, 98
Brownlee, K., 32
Brownstein, C., 4
Bryant, B. K., 43, 49, 66, 67, 127, 133
Bryant, R. A., 149
Bubenzer, D. L., 85
Buchholz, E. S., 79
Buckhalt, J. A., 38
Budman, S. H., 68, 69
Burgess, A. G., 176, 177
Burgess, A. W., 176, 177
Burian, B. K., 64, 65
Burkard, A. W., 104
Burkemper, E. M., 46
Burnell, J., 140
Burns, C. I., 89, 90
Busseri, M. A., 10, 12, 43

C

Callahan, T. R., 25, 154
Cameron, S., 131, 132
Campbell, C. D., 10, 12, 63
Campbell, J. C., 175
Carey, A., 162
Carlozzi, A. F., 34, 83, 85
Carney, J. S., 38
Carrillo, D. F., 107
Carroll, J. F.X., 150
Carroll, J. J., 33, 139, 140
Casper, E. S., 127
Castro, F. G., 102
Catanzaro, S., 60, 62
Catherall, D. R., 161
Chamberlin, J., 197
Charny, I. W., 79, 84
Chemtob, C. M., 54
Chen, J., 82
Chenneville, T., 49, 55
Chenoweth, M. S., 64, 65
Chess, W. A., 151
Chien, D., 58
Cho, M. E., 5, 8, 9, 38
Christian, W. P., 11
Claiborn, C. D., 48, 136
Clark, D., 54
Clark, J. J., 62
Clarkin, J., 82
Claus, R. E., 44

241

SUBJECT INDEX